Affairs of State

Affairs of State

The Untold History of Presidential Love, Sex, and Scandal, 1789–1900

Robert P. Watson

ROWMAN & LITTLEFIELD PUBLISHERS, INC.
Lanham • Boulder • New York • Toronto • Plymouth, UK

Published by Rowman & Littlefield Publishers, Inc.
A wholly owned subsidiary of The Rowman & Littlefield Publishing Group, Inc.
4501 Forbes Boulevard, Suite 200, Lanham, Maryland 20706
www.rowman.com

10 Thornbury Road, Plymouth PL6 7PP, United Kingdom

British Library Cataloguing in Publication Information Available

Library of Congress Cataloging-in-Publication Data
Watson, Robert P., 1962–
    Affairs of state : the untold history of presidential love, sex, and scandal, 1789–1900 / Robert P. Watson.
        p. cm.
    Includes bibliographical references and index.
    ISBN 978-1-4422-1834-5 (cloth : alk. paper) — ISBN 978-1-4422-1836-9 (electronic)
    1. Presidents—Sexual behavior—United States—History. 2. Presidents—United States—Biography. 3. Presidents' spouses—United States—Biography. 4. Adultery—United States—History. 5. Scandals—United States—History. I. Title.
    E176.4.W38 2012
    973.09'9—dc23
    [B]

                                                                    2012020637

∞™ The paper used in this publication meets the minimum requirements of American National Standard for Information Sciences—Permanence of Paper for Printed Library Materials, ANSI/NISO Z39.48-1992.

Printed in the United States of America

Contents

Preface

Every American schoolkid grows up learning about the great and heroic deeds of the presidents. While this is altogether right and proper, it tells only part of the story of leadership. The presidents, first ladies, and their aides were, after all, people. As such, they fell in love, made mistakes in both their personal and professional lives, and brought all this baggage into the White House. But because most scholars of the presidency, authors of textbooks, and our schoolteachers were not trained in matters of the heart or hearth, intimate stories of love, sex, and scandal in the White House are rarely—if ever—told.

This book, however, tells the "other side" of presidential history. The pages in the book also reveal that, although sex scandals among politicians frequently appear in the headlines today, such affairs of state are not new. There is a long history of mistresses, romances, and scandals in the nation's highest office. Indeed, even a cursory look beyond the military victories and political battles exposes a number of embarrassing scandals and stories of personal weaknesses.

I love history. But more than lists of dates and places, I especially enjoy reading about the personal side of the individuals who shaped history. Therefore, one of the goals of this book was to use love, sex, and scandal to breathe life into our early presidents. It is precisely such intimate moments, as much as stories of wars and elections, that offer us important lessons in presidential character. I hope you enjoy them as much as I do.

I wish to acknowledge the patience of my family—Claudia, Alessandro, and Isabella—during the time it took to research and write this book. My friend, Steve West, was helpful in reading an early draft and offering constructive feedback. Thank you also to Carrie Broadwell-Tkach, history editor; Janice Braunstein, assistant managing editor; Karie Simpson, assistant editor; Lillia Gajewski, proofreader; and the rest of the staff at Rowman & Littlefield for publishing this book. Lastly, the fun and uninhibited discussions that arose during my lecture series on the history of presidential scandals for Florida Atlantic University's Lifelong Learning Society and aboard Celebrity cruise lines helped to shape the direction of this book. So, I extend my thanks to those spirited audiences.

Stay tuned for the companion book, which will examine presidential love, sex, and scandal in the twentieth century.

They Don't Teach
This Stuff in School

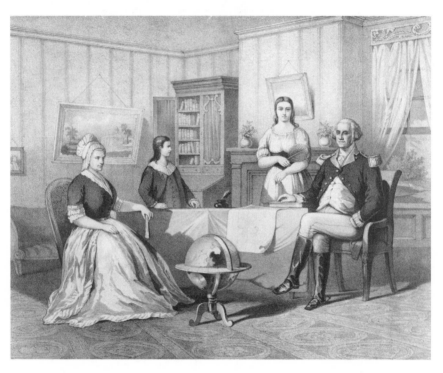

This lithograph of George Washington and his family served as an idealized image of the American family. Library of Congress Prints and Photographs Division, LC-USZ62-117747.

⚔ 1 ⚔

Say It Isn't So!

The world has no business to know the object of my love.

—George Washington

FOR THE LOVE OF A LADY

If there had not been a George Washington, there might never have been a United States of America. Without Washington, there was no soldier capable of commanding the ragtag band of poorly trained, ill-equipped farmers, blacksmiths, and shop owners who, against all odds, defeated the world's most powerful army in the Revolutionary War. Without Washington, there was no leader whose sheer presence could keep the tempers, egos, and parochial state interests that simmered throughout the Constitutional Convention focused on the larger prize of a unified nation. Without Washington, there was no politician possessing the elusive combination of inspiration and restraint necessary to shape the vaguely defined office of president of the new republic. And without Washington, there was no universally respected statesman to lend legitimacy both at home and abroad to the fledgling, debt-ridden experiment in popular democracy called the United States of America.

Historians agree that perhaps no other man alive in the late eighteenth century could have led a volunteer militia against the world's greatest military force and won, yet alone presided over the Constitutional Convention, served as the new government's first president, and come to symbolize the nation. This bold assertion takes into account the other founding fathers, who were a particularly impressive lot themselves. Their names rightfully ring out across time as America's most revered patriarchs: Gouverneur Morris, Thomas Jefferson, James Madison, John Adams, John Hancock, and Charles Pinckney, to name a few. Cerebral, schooled in the classics, and visionary as they might have been, most of Washington's fellow revolutionaries lacked his combination of stoic discipline, military experience, and familiarity with the backwoods terrain of the land. It is almost certain that even the likes of John Adams, Thomas Jefferson, or Benjamin Franklin would have failed in military matters where Washington succeeded.

Paradoxically, an integral part of what made Washington *Washington* came courtesy of what he did *not* share with the other founders. Washington was tempered by a less privileged upbringing and a severely limited education that occasioned in the young man such contradictory passions as a boundless ambition yet a humble awareness of his own shortcomings. Much of Washington's education and experiences were practical in nature. They came courtesy of his early careers as a surveyor and soldier rather than from an aristocratic father's library or the halls of an elite academic institution. While Adams practiced law, Jefferson played the violin and collected fine wines, and Madison read the classics, Washington worked with his hands and fought Indians in the western edge of the colonies.

Still more of what defined Washington was the stuff of legend. He possessed that special "something" that cannot be taught or learned. His signature traits—enormous personal magnetism and a natural ability to inspire and lead men—were what elevated him above others, then and now. In short, Washington had the character and the bearing of a leader: he was a leader among leaders.

Yet, had it not been for three women in Washington's life, it is doubtful that Washington would have become the man he did or that history would remember his name. All three of these women were, to various degrees, romantic interests. Washington's mother, Mary Ball Washington, and his sister, Betty Washington Lewis, played little role in shaping the man who could have been America's first king. Therefore, absent the love and influence of three ladies, the drama of liberty and democracy imagined in Philadelphia and fought for in the long and bitter revolution might never have been staged.

The Hand That Was Dealt

As a young man, George Washington found himself in the impractical predicament of having an unquenchable thirst for fame and material comfort while possessing but modest means and a meager education. The reality of Washington's state of affairs was such that it was unlikely he would achieve his dual dreams of serving as a British officer and becoming a gentleman planter. The same might confidently be said of any man sharing his humble station in life.

Young George had a somewhat difficult family life. He was the firstborn son of Augustine Washington's second marriage to Mary Ball, who wed Augustine three years after his first wife died. George Washington thus suffered the misfortune of being a "middle child" born of a irreparably strained second marriage. Moreover, it would be an understatement to say that Mary Ball Washington was a source of irritation for her husband as well as for her oldest son. Those who knew her found her to be mercurial and temperamental at best.

Born in 1709, George's mother lost her father when she was the tender age of three. She was then orphaned at twelve. Under that unfortunate circumstance, in accordance with her late mother's will, Mary was placed in the care of the noted attorney George Eskridge. But the scars from her early life never healed. As an adult, Mary Washington would complain to anyone unlucky enough to encounter her that she was treated poorly by friends and family and that she was destitute, which was untrue.

Mary's relationship with her son was repeatedly put to the test by her constant public accusations against him that he neglected her needs, which was also untrue. Even though George would send his mother money throughout her lifetime, she repeatedly asked him for more and just as frequently announced that he had ignored her pleas for help. On one such occasion, in 1755, while George was suffering the hardships of a frontier campaign during the French and Indian War, his mother wrote requesting more money, butter, and a new servant for her home. Indeed, Mary Washington challenged the patience and love of her famous son until her death from cancer shortly after he assumed the presidency in 1789. Not only did she persistently beleaguer him for funds, but it seems that she died a Tory, unwilling to side with the fledgling nation her son was leading.

Many great men of history were "made" by strong, loving, ambitious mothers. George was not one of them. Mary Ball Washington was not one of the three women who molded the raw but eager young man. Equally problematic for George was the fact that his father, Augustine, treated the offspring from his preferred first marriage more favorably than those from the difficult second marriage. Accordingly, young George never received the schooling, attention, opportunity for travel, or inheritance enjoyed by his older half-brothers Lawrence and Augustine (who was known as "Austin").

George was only eleven years old when his father died suddenly in 1743. Augustine died with means and had built himself a large estate. But the bulk of it was willed to George's older half-brothers, leaving Mary's family a relatively small portion of the wealth. Therefore, after his father's death, George and his siblings from that second marriage found themselves significantly diminished financially and socially. It was during this critical time in his adolescence that George looked to his older half-brother, Lawrence, fourteen years his senior, for inspiration. Lawrence had served under Admiral Edward Vernon in the British navy and regaled his young, impressionable half-brother with adventurous stories of the high seas. Thus, George grew up wanting more than the quiet life of a small-town farmer he seemed destined to live. He tried to convey to his mother the virtues of serving in the British navy like Lawrence, but she would hear nothing of it.

History is not sure why Mrs. Washington kept her tall son confined to her humble cottage. Perhaps she did not have or want to spend the money. Perhaps she wanted the dependable young man around to help her manage the household. Perhaps because of her own losses and hardships as a child, Mrs. Washington rejected her son's requests to travel and to and be educated in England. Thus, George received but a meager education in colonial Virginia, likely from tutors—although the details of his education remain uncertain. He did, however, learn to read, write, and perform basic mathematical tasks.

Although Washington later served in the colonial militia, his numerous requests to become an officer in the regular British command were repeatedly and flatly rejected. In the middle of the eighteenth century, there was an ocean of difference between the status of an officer in a *colonial* regiment and one in the *king's* army, something that was not lost on the ambitious young man. A surveyor's apprentice clinging to a middle rung on the social ladder was simply not the type of man the Crown elevated to its own elite officer corps.

With the deck stacked against him, it was obvious that a comfortable life, a quality formal education, and the prospect of material wealth were not in Washington's future. It would seem that young George's boyhood dreams would remain just that—dreams. But he had a plan to marry above his station and began pursuing the company of older, wealthier women.

"Ye Ladye Was in Ye Mood"

One strategy the future president pursued during his adolescence to improve his station in life was to attempt to woo the wealthy debutantes of Tidewater society, the very class to which he sought membership. Unfortunately for Washington, however, the aristocratic fathers of the well-bred young ladies of the Potomac failed to see any potential in the strapping but ungainly teenager who showed up at their doorsteps awkwardly hoping to court their daughters. The belles themselves, who were often a bit older than Washington, also expected more promising and lucrative prospects than he offered. Still, Washington was persistent.

Even though Washington seems to have been a mite awkward around women as a teenager, his irrepressible optimism that he would somehow marry above his station was at once admirable and audacious. His setbacks included embarrassing moments such as during the summer of 1751 when two young girls stole the teenaged Washington's clothing while he was skinny-dipping in the Rappahannock River near his mother's house. One of the girls, Mary McDaniel, was caught and accused of "robbing the clothes of Mr. George Washington when he was washing in the river." Her penalty from the authorities was fifteen lashes to the back.

Unfortunately, neither Washington's audacity nor his buoyancy in rejection did him any good. He was playing way out of his league. As was the case with his desire to receive a royal military commission, in matters of courtship young George Washington was rejected—coldly and completely. Unlucky at love, a youthful Washington poured his frustrated passion into copying poetry he read. He also composed his own lines, including the zinger, "Poor restless heart, wounded by Cupid's dart." Another effort, which Washington appears to have composed but never sent, came after being rejected by the wealthy and beautiful Frances Alexander. It shows Washington to be a budding poet and a lad of considerable sensitivity but obvious disappointment:

> From your bright sparkling eyes, I was undone;
> Rays, you have more transparent than the sun,
> Amidst its glory in the rising day,
> None can you equal in your bright array;
> Constant in your calm and unspotted mind;
> Equal to all, but will to none prove kind,
> So knowing, seldom one so young, you'll find
> Ah! Woe's me, that I should love and conceal,
> Long have I wish'd, but never dare reveal,
> Even though severly Loves Pains I feel.

Another of Washington's early interests was a young girl named Grimes. Washington referred to Miss Grimes as his "Low Land Beauty," a reference to the lowlands of Tidewater, Virginia, a term he used for other belles in the region. Grimes later married Henry Lee, and their son would become the famous General Henry Lee, known as Light Horse Henry and, ironically, one of Washington's favorite officers during the Revolution. Undeterred, young Washington continued to try to court women far above his station in life, including fifteen-year-old Betsey Fauntleroy, the daughter of a wealthy planter from Richmond, who captured George's heart in 1752. However, Betsey's father believed Washington to be too poor to earn his daughter's hand, and she instead married a wealthy planter's son. This scenario—interest in a wealthier girl, rejection from her and her father, and her marriage into money—became familiar math to Washington.

While in New York in 1756, Washington met Mary Elizabeth Philipse. He was instantly smitten and nicknamed her "The Agreeable Miss Polly." Miss Polly enjoyed many important social connections and was a statuesquely tall, sophisticated, and wealthy woman. But she too rejected Washington's ham-fisted, physical overture. Washington's explanation for the reason he was dumped was "not waiting until ye ladye was in ye mood." Miss Polly eventually married Captain Roger Morris, who served with Washington in General Braddock's army in Britain's war against the French and, as fate would have it, was the only officer besides Washington to survive the disastrous western campaign that ended Braddock's life. Later, Polly and her husband ended up remaining loyal to Britain during the Revolution. In another interesting twist of fate, Washington commandeered their home for his headquarters during the war. It was rumored at the time that Washington occupied the Morris home because Mrs. Morris had rejected him, but it was also rumored that, while at the Morris home, Washington had a sexual affair with Polly.

A Chance Meeting

It took a good number of years for Washington's amorous luck to change. In the winter of his twenty-sixth year—by eighteenth-century standards a considerably ripe age to be unmarried—and holding the rank of colonel in the colonial regiment, Washington was traveling from his military headquarters on what is now the western edge of Pennsylvania to the city of Williamsburg on the eastern shore of his native Virginia. Eager to arrive in the colonial capital well in advance of a scheduled meeting with the king's governor, Washington and his favorite manservant were traveling light and fast on horseback. Historical accounts suggest the date of the trip to be sometime in February or March 1758.

En route, the two riders passed the Chamberlayne estate, owned by a wealthy attorney and politician. Richard Chamberlayne and his wife were neighbors and acquaintances of the Washington family, hailing from the eastern Tidewater region of Virginia. That very evening, the couple happened to be hosting at their home the colony's wealthiest widow, Martha Dandridge Custis.

Unfortunately, there is no surviving eyewitness account of the first encounter between George Washington and the distinguished dinner guest, the woman who would quite soon become Mrs. George Washington. If letters were written describing both guests' impressions of the other or retelling what was said, such documents are lost to history. However, one reliable source for that meeting has survived the centuries. Many years after George Washington stopped at the Chamberlayne estate, Martha Washington's grandson penned the account of his famous grandparents' meeting that winter day. The book, *Recollections and Private Memoirs of Washington*, was written by George Washington Parke Custis in midlife—and long after his grandparents' passing. It was published posthumously by his daughter, the wife of Civil War general Robert E. Lee. In the book, Martha's grandson remembered a touchingly romantic bedtime story his grandmother had told him during his childhood. According to Custis, it went like this: Colonel Washington initially declined Richard Chamberlayne's offer to join him for dinner, citing the urgency of getting to Williamsburg for his meeting with Governor Robert Dinwiddie the next morning. Washington's intention appears to have been to stop at Chamberlayne's only long enough to water and rest his horse and to pay a courtesy call on his affluent neighbor and then move on. Washington was known for being notoriously punctual and a man of habit and routine. However, on hearing that Chamberlayne's dinner guest was none other than Martha Custis, the colonel changed his mind. And change his mind he did. Washington ended up staying for dinner, lodged for the night, and joined the widow again for breakfast the next morning. This chance meeting would prove to be a turning point in Washington's life, one that would ultimately help to shape American history. It introduced George Washington to one of the three women who would influence the great leader.

History does not record exactly when or how Washington asked Martha to marry him. But we do know through the memoirs of Martha's grandson as well as from other family accounts that a proposal was made very soon after that meeting. Only days after meeting Ms. Custis, the impatient suitor paid a visit to her, most likely at her mansion in Williamsburg (known as "The Six-Chimney Home") and most likely immediately after he concluded his business with Governor Dinwiddie. The petite but plump recent widow must have made quite an impression on the muscularly tall and ambitious colonel, or perhaps it was her wealth and social position that impressed. Either way, Washington spontaneously altered his travel plans at the Chamberlayne home just to meet her.

According to Washington's account ledger, he visited Martha at least two more times in March of that year and appears to have proposed either during that third visit or, more likely, on a subsequent visit days later in early April. A clue exists as to the probable timing of the engagement in a letter that Washington wrote on April 5, 1758. In the letter, Washington makes a request of the London merchant, Robert Cary and Company, to send him clothing for a special occasion. Wrote Washington, "By the first Ship bound to any part of Virginia . . . [send] as much of the best superfine Blue Cotton Velvet as will make a coat, waistcoat and breeches for a tall man." At the very same time, Martha was writing her own letters concerning a forthcoming special occasion. She requested to have her favorite nightgown dyed a "fashionable color" and ordered a seamstress to make "one Genteel suite of cloths for myself," presumably in preparation for the big day.

Washington's courtship of the widow likely began the moment he met her, and the engagement occurred with much haste. Marital plans were made between the colonel and the widow with an urgency rarely seen in the mid-eighteenth century, even among widows who tended to remarry as soon as opportunity presented itself. People lived shorter lives then, and mortality rates during childbirth were of a frequency that we in modern times could scarcely comprehend. Clearly, there were practical reasons to expedite second marriages. Yet, after a rushed courtship, curiously, the marriage date would not arrive until an otherwise normal and unhurried nine months had passed.

Could it be that Washington's "love at first sight" gave way to convention and prudence? Or was passion but one among other factors guiding the Washington–Custis union? It seems almost certain that Washington sought to secure the hand of the wealthy, older widow before the golden opportunity passed to one of what must have been a bevy of other, more affluent suitors. He could then afford to wait the conventional period before marrying. For her part, it is possible that Martha was only too anxious to accept the hand of the statuesque, never-married officer so close to her own age. Her first husband had been much older, meek, and chronically ill. At the same time, because she had inherited so much money and landholdings, Martha did not need to consider her suitor's wealth. Besides, Martha had two infant children to think of, and she needed assistance in managing her vast estate.

When George and Martha were married on January 6, 1759, it was at her first husband's family home in Virginia's New Kent County. Coincidentally, the residence was named "The White House." The groom wore gold knee buckles and the "blue cotton velvet" coat made from the "best superfine" material he had ordered the previous spring from his London merchant. It was now trimmed opulently in red and silver. After the ceremony, the couple "honeymooned" for a few days at Martha's home. Presumably, and to the satisfaction of George, the bride wore her "favorite nightgown," which she had dyed a fashionable color for effect after their whirlwind engagement.

A More Perfect Union

Martha Dandridge Custis was perhaps the wealthiest widow in the entire Virginia Colony when George Washington met and wed her. With the passing of her first husband, Daniel Parke Custis, after just a few years of marriage, Martha inherited plantations in five counties, 15,000 acres of fertile farmland, roughly 200 slaves, and a fortune of cash, stocks, and notes in a London bank account. From an economic and practical perspective, Martha was a darn good catch. She was one of the most eligible women of her time and surely must have attracted a number of promising would-be suitors. It would also have been a boost to Washington's ego to win the hand and heart of the type of woman he had dreamed of marrying since his teenage days.

Whether it was true love and happiness or the prospects of great wealth and status that motivated Washington will never be known for sure. The answer is not clear but is certainly worth contemplating (and is explored in chapter 4 of this book). Either way, Washington finally did find the older, wealthy woman of his youthful dreams and failed romances (Martha was a year older than George). What is certain is that Washington moved with considerable speed to court and secure a nuptial commitment from the widow Custis. In taking on this responsibility, Washington also gained more than a wife. He became a stepfather for Martha's two young children from her first marriage. This would ultimately prove to be fortuitous, given Washington's apparent infertility—he never had children of his own. But Washington gained even more than material wealth and a wife and family; he secured for himself status. The marriage brought with it the kind of social and economic clout that opened doors, instantly placing Washington within the privileged class to which he had always aspired.

Had George not married the widow Custis, there might not have been a General Washington or a President Washington much less the Washington revered by all as "The Father of His Country." Had Washington not married Martha, it is doubtful that the sparingly educated surveyor and colonial militia officer would have been in a position even to be invited to Philadelphia along with the future fathers of the nation to discuss the "British problem." Undoubtedly, marriage positioned Washington for the greatness that he longed to achieve and offered him an opportunity to demonstrate his considerable talent.

History speaks volumes of the glorious "self-made man." We have deified such men whose lives started in relative obscurity and amidst great challenge but who rose to lofty heights by the sweat of their brow and sheer force of their irrepressible talent. But scholars have largely ignored the "other side" of the story behind so many men who left indelible marks on history. Washington was indeed a great man, arguably the nation's finest leader and foremost citizen. Of that there is little doubt. But, more to the point, Washington was also a "wife-made man." It would then seem fitting that we recognize Martha Washington—the woman whom Washington loved or married for money—as "The Mother of Her Country" and one of the three women who "made" Washington.

"ALL MANNER OF DEBAUCHERY"

Other women affected Washington's growing reputation. During Washington's early military career and again in the revolutionary struggle, there were allegations that his soldiers committed "all manner of debauchery, vice and idleness." Even Washington's "hometown" newspaper, the *Virginia Gazette*, leveled charges against his troops and, by proxy, against him. Soldiers will be soldiers, and such stories are not unique to the history of warfare, but the claims did threaten the commander's reputation.

One such allegation was that Washington's soldiers had their way with Indian women, and it has even been suggested that Washington joined in the sexual debauchery, favoring an Indian woman named Bright Lightning, the daughter of the Delaware chief White Thunder. Such rumors were not helped when General Charles Lee was accused of smuggling young girls into the winter camp at Valley Forge.

Another embarrassing scandal was dubbed the "Washerwoman Kate Affair." During the Revolution, Washington's friend, a congressman named Harrison, was charged with procuring inappropriate supplies in Philadelphia for the general and his army. Harrison sent a letter to Washington that was intercepted. The letter became fodder for Washington's critics and the press because Harrison was said to have tried to obtain a young girl for his commander, writing foolishly,

> As I was in the pleasing task of writing to you a little noise occasioned to turn my head around, and who should appear but pretty little Kate, the washerwoman's daughter, over the way, clean, trim, and rosy as the morning.
>
> I snatched the golden glorious opportunity, and but for that cursed antidote to love, Sukey [his wife], I had fitted her for my general against his return.
>
> We were obliged to part, but not till we had contrived to meet again. . . .
>
> I give you now and then some of these adventures to amuse you and unbend your mind from the cares of war.

Because Harrison and Washington were on reasonably close terms, it can safely be assumed that Harrison was familiar with Washington's status as a married man. On the other hand, Harrison also should have known that, even if the account is accurate, the image-conscious Washington would have frowned on creating even the appearance of such impropriety. There is no record that Harrison ever did bring women to camp, and the stories about Washington's soldiers running amok with young women are questionable and must be weighed against Washington's known record as a disciplinarian who tolerated no dishonorable behavior. The matter remains unresolved by historians.

Washington was, however, a slave owner, and it was said by his enemies that Washington partook of the practice of "night walking"—slave owners having sex with their female slaves. To slander his reputation, the British spread such rumors during the war. The famous British historian Arnold Toynbee even claimed that Washington died of a cold on a chilly December evening, contracted while in the company of female slaves. The claim is suspect, however. A surviving letter written at the time of Washington's death and cited by Toynbee and other critics incorrectly listed "PM" instead of "AM" as the time that Washington rode to inspect his farms and slaves. Moreover, Washington was known to disapprove of night walking and discourage excessive sexual behavior of his employees and slaves, not only for moral reasons but also because of economics—it made overseers and slaves too tired, or "unfit" in Washington's words, for a full day's labor the next morning.

Washington Slept Here

Generations of schoolchildren have been fed the myth while visiting countless homes and historic sites dating to revolutionary America that "Washington slept here." It is true that the general, because of the necessities of war and the realities of working as a young land surveyor, was widely traveled. But, while it is good for tourism, many of the claims are doubtful. But the question of with "whom" Washington slept might very well be asked along with "where" the "Father of His Country" slept.

Marvin Kitman, author of the book *The Making of the President, 1789*, claims that Washington slept with many women and spent little time with his wife, Martha. Indeed, during the War for Independence, the general was away from his wife for years, giving him ample opportunity to stray. But opportunity does not imply guilt. The Washingtons joined one another in winter encampments as often as possible and despite the hardships of travel for Mrs. Washington. Kitman even offers a list of Washington's lady "companions." It is, of course, difficult to prove or disprove any of the alleged affairs, as there is some (but not much) circumstantial evidence for all of them but zero conclusive proof for any of them. Kitman's list includes the following: several wives of Washington's generals, such as Kitty Greene, Lucy Flicker Knox, Clement Biddle, and Elizabeth Gates; socialites, such as Lady Kitty Alexander Duer, Mrs. William Bingham, and Mary Gibbons; the hosts of taverns and boardinghouses where he stayed, such as Phoebe Fraunces, daughter of a tavern keeper, and the daughters of a Mrs. Watkins, whose boardinghouse Washington enjoyed in Paramus, New Jersey; political acquaintances, such as Aaron Burr's wife (Theodosia Provost Burr), Ben Franklin's goddaughter (Mrs. Bache), with whom Washington frequently danced at parties, and Eliza Powel (wife of Philadelphia's mayor); and even the iconic Betsy Ross, seamstress of the revolutionary flag.

In the case of Kitty Greene, the twenty-two-year-old beauty and flirtatious wife of General Greene, she all but admits to affairs in her letters, including a fling with Washington's young French aide, the Marquis de Lafayette, and several of his officers. Surely a woman with Mrs. Greene's apparent morals and track record would have jumped at the chance to bed the leader of the war effort, but this does not mean it happened. What is known is that, at one of the gala balls in Washington's honor, the general danced with Mrs. Greene for much of the night. Nevertheless, Washington often danced with his female guests. Many women regarded Washington as a highly capable and enthusiastic dancer, and it was not uncommon for Washington during his generalship and presidency to dance late into the evening with the leading ladies in attendance. As to whether Washington consummated these flings, we will likely never know, but it is likely that at least some of the allegations are true.

The historical record clearly indicates that Washington enjoyed the attention and company of women. For example, during his presidency, he toured much of the South. During his travels, he meticulously recorded how young ladies came out to show their respect when he passed by, and he even bothered to count and vainly record the exact number of well-wishers. He also frequently noted details about the women he encountered, such as their hair, clothing, and so on. A French officer in Washington's headquarters at Morristown, New Jersey, further noted that the general "admires pretty women . . . notices their gowns and how their hair is dressed. He does it quite openly, and before his wife, who does not seem to mind at all."

Given his unhappy childhood and bitter disappointment with continual rejections by women during his youth, Washington probably derived pleasure from knowing that many women greatly admired him. The women who waited in line to meet, curtsey toward, or dance with the president were, after all, of the same class that captured his attention as a young man. Whether these accusations are true is unknown, but the possibility of such is intriguing.

In a larger sense, questions about both the sexual affairs and loving marriages of Washington and other presidents have not yet been adequately explored—until now.

THE STATE OF DENIAL

It appears that George Washington's wife was not the only woman who shared and shaped his remarkable life and career. There were two other women, one of whom was quite possibly the love of Washington's life. Whereas Martha Washington's role in her husband's life was, initially, that of enabler—she provided the financial means, the material comforts, and admission to high society that would allow his talents and exceptional character to take hold—two other women would serve in the fashion of mentor, motivator, and muse. Their names were Eliza Willing Powel and Sally Cary Fairfax.

The details of these relationships, however, are not always welcomed by Washington scholars and therefore are largely unknown to the public. Professor Nathaniel Wright Stevenson, for instance, writing in a leading scholarly journal in the early twentieth century, utterly dismissed what he called "the Sally Fairfax myth." Speaking as the voice of professional historians, Stevenson scoffed at colleagues who failed to, as he saw it, stick to the cold, hard facts when examining historic figures such as Washington.

What was it that occasioned Stevenson's wrath and the rift among scholars? A few historians dared suggest that Washington may have loved a woman other than his wife. "Impossible," rallied Washington scholars. It was, after all, "the Father of His Country" about whom they were speaking. Thus, many academicians and Americans deemed it irreverent and unthinkable—indeed unpatriotic—to even suggest that the infallible Washington was capable of such an impropriety. To ponder, much less argue, such a possibility was to risk unraveling the founding myths and American creeds that have nurtured generations of American schoolchildren.

From surviving letters and documents, however, it is clear that George Washington was, at the least, very close friends with Eliza Powel and Sally Fairfax. Washington shared a deep affection for and occasional flirtation with these women—the enchanting Sally Fairfax during his late teenage years and through the French and Indian War and the sassy Eliza Powel during his presidency. Evidence suggests that it is far more accurate to say that Washington was under their spell. From the moment the teenage Washington met the alluring Sarah "Sally" Cary Fairfax, the eighteen-year-old bride of his neighbor, George William Fairfax, he was taken by her natural grace, her easy charm, her effortless wit, and, of course, her rare beauty. Washington, it would seem, was utterly bewitched from the start. As one descendant of Sally Fairfax put it, Washington "bowed at her shrine." Likewise, Washington deferred to Mrs. Powel to a degree unseen among other friends, and he extended to her extraordinary courtesies to flirt, criticize, motivate, and advise him.

The "Other Woman"

George Washington had a relatively humble start in life while Sally Fairfax resided at the very pinnacle of the high society that Washington aspired to join. Virginia, more so than any other colony, had a strong and rigid caste system, reflecting British social customs and conventions. The colony's noblesse maintained strict codes of behavior and interaction whereby only the gentry were seated in the court of Governor Dinwiddie and Lord Botetourt or were in attendance at the levees and balls of leading families. It was the lineal descendants of old and powerful families who controlled the landed estates and the reins of power in the Old Dominion State.

This was the world only glimpsed by a young George Washington, a world to which he had no access as a boy or teen. No bloodline more reflected this elite class than the Cary–Fairfax family, to which Sally was the eldest and most favored daughter. Sally was politically astute, socially adept, and particularly well educated for a woman of the day. As is clear from Washington's letters, he sought her advice on matters both personal and professional. Fortunately for Washington and for history, Sally was only too happy to offer it to him. Both were aware of his inadequate education and limited exposure to the larger world, so it was she who introduced Washington to literature, music, and the important art of social conversation. Even Washington's writing improved markedly after meeting Sally. It is not by coincidence that the most carefully crafted, tenderly playful, and personally revealing letters surviving from his life are those written to her. Indeed, there is a reason for this.

It was Sally Fairfax who was perhaps the first to see the enormous potential in the young Washington. It was she who took him under her wing. It was she who sat him at her feet in the court of Virginia aristocracy, exposing him to the social graces and the people he would need to know to advance economically and politically. Sally inspired her adoring young neighbor to become more than he was, to focus his ambition, and to rise to greatness. During the crucial formative years of Washington's life, Sally Fairfax functioned as his informal tutor and his inspiration. In return, it was Sally for whom Washington displayed courage on the battlefield. Quite possibly, it was Washington's beguiling neighbor who, although she was forbidden fruit, forever captured his heart.

The Romantics?

Professor Stevenson and other leading scholars labeled those historians "irresponsible" enough to express an interest in Washington's relationship with other women "the romantics." In so doing, Stevenson and others dismissed any discussion of a romantic relationship as inappropriate and lacking in scholarly rigor. Or, one might say, such scholarship was viewed by the academic establishment as rather "soft and squishy." Such soft research is in stark contrast to the supposed cold and calculating manner used by those who write the history we read. Yet it seems far more certain that it was Stevenson and status quo scholars who were the naive romantics. Why? For them to think that an ambitious, adolescent Washington was incapable of falling under the spell of a beautiful, intelligent, and wealthy woman two years his senior or an elegant, witty widow late in life is nothing shy of "soft and squishy" research itself or, to borrow their own term, "romantic."

Washington was truly among the greatest of men, but he was still a man. The historical record suggests that he was mad about Sally Fairfax and closer to Eliza Powel than just about anyone else. It is therefore a disservice to history and to the truth if the full nature of the George–Sally and George–Eliza relationships were not examined (as they are in chapter 3). After all, as one observer noted of Sally Fairfax, "She it was who filled his soul with high aspirations and incited him to brave deeds of arms, urging him to a nobler career than that which satisfied the great majority of the gentry about him, and from her he drew his ideals of a hero's wife."

Does all this somehow detract from or lessen Washington's accomplishments?

Not at all. On the contrary, it humanizes a man who is too often viewed as a mythical figure and remembered more by monuments than in the flesh and blood. Washington, perhaps more than any other president or any of the founders, is an enigma who seems almost unknowable. Yet it is through his relationships with Sally and Eliza as well as his marriage to Martha that we witness another side of the hero. Through them, we are introduced to a teenager almost foolishly giddy with lust and ambition, a young man who is an astute student and appreciative of his female mentor, a soldier inspired in battle by a beautiful woman yet one wise enough to make the best of a golden opportunity, a father who adopts children not of his blood, a husband who cherishes his wife's devotion, and a president who seeks the counsel and intimate companionship of a worldly widow.

It is possible to trace Washington's emotional maturation and the development of his social temperament through his relationship with these women, especially Sally. Here again, we are treated to a Washington uncertain about whether to follow his conscience or his heart. In a day and age where class status was fixed, that such a woman as Sally Fairfax—older, married, wealthy, and far beyond young George's rung in life—was the object of Washington's affections, suggests there was something special about this unrefined, fatherless teenager. At the same time, that someone of Sally's status made the effort to expand and nurture her young, uneducated neighbor reinforces that notion.

Yes, Washington was capable of love and even lust but also of restraint. Moreover, that Washington the revolutionary leader was inspired by two beautiful, flirtatious women does not preclude him from also being motivated by honor and liberty, qualities that history has rightly affixed to him. It would appear that both sets are true. It is not uncommon to overly romanticize our past heroes and leaders, imbuing them with only the most admirable and noble of attributes and intentions while ignoring their very human frailties. Everyone does it, from professional historians and journalists to politicians and patriotic citizens and even parents telling bedtime stories to their children.

Until the highly public foibles of recent political leaders were made public, generations turned a blind eye to the possibility that Washington and other presidents were capable of loving women other than their wives or engaging in inappropriate sexual behavior. Those who write our history have often been unwilling to even imagine immoral behavior among our leaders. But the reality has been quite different. Our political heroes and leaders have been human, and some of them all too human. Yet few scholars are themselves trained in matters of the heart or hearth, so it is perhaps obvious that the love interests and sexual shenanigans of presidents have been overlooked by the historical record.

The fact of the matter is that there is a long history of sexual impropriety, marital peccadilloes, and lapses of judgment and integrity associated with leaders both in the United States and around the world. At the same time, there are happy and healthy marriages as well as genuinely sappy love affairs that flourished in the White House. Both types of stories fill the pages of this book. In fact, so widespread in our political past are such stories of love and lust, of sex and scandal, that they could fill many volumes of books. To be sure, political spouses and mistresses, through their loving marriages or purely sexual relationships, have played a role in shaping the events and leaders that, in turn, made history. While George and Martha Washington may have had a solid marriage and George may or may not have sexually consummated his relationship with Sally Fairfax or Eliza Powel, the impact of these two women on Washington's life and career nonetheless warrants careful study. And Washington was not the only one of our presidents or political leaders shaped by women.

The Other Side of History

Together, this reality fairly constitutes what can be described as "the other side of history." What we do know, in a larger sense, is that the fingerprints of women are all over the history of the United States. Perhaps nowhere in American society has this been more the case than in the nation's highest office. The hand of a woman—often that of a mother, frequently that of a wife, and sometimes even that of a mistress—has helped shape the lives and fortunes as well as the misfortunes and ruin of our commanders in chief beginning with Washington. Indeed, the general is not alone among presidents and leading political figures on the national stage whose story is incomplete without considering the central roles played by wives and mistresses, love and lust, marital bliss and infidelity, and passionate romance and salacious sexual scandal.

For whatever reasons, history has rarely recorded these affairs of state.

Marilyn Monroe singing a sultry version of "Happy Birthday, Mr. President" to John Kennedy in front of thousands at his forty-fifth birthday party in Madison Square Garden. Courtesy of Antique Art Salon.

❦ 2 ❧

Presidential Peccadilloes

I stick by my principles, and one of my principles is flexibility.

—Senator Everett Dirkson

There are scandals, and then there are *political* scandals, but the granddaddy of all scandal is a White House scandal. Presidents have lied, covered up secret operations, ignored the Constitution, personally benefited from public office in inappropriate ways, and succumbed to those most human of emotions: power, jealousy, paranoia, and sexual urges. So too has scandal touched nearly every president. The sins run the gamut from unfortunate mistakes of *omission* to thuggish crimes of *commission*.

An example of the former occurred when Ulysses S. Grant failed to keep his staff, who participated in the Credit Mobilier and Union Pacific Railroad scandal, on a short leash. This brouhaha occurred when a sham corporation was established to overbill the railroad, then overbill the government, and pocket the difference. While Grant himself was not behind the illegal or inappropriate activities, omission or not, the responsibility of his staffers ended up squarely on the desk of Grant. As Harry Truman was fond of saying, "The buck stops here."

An example of the latter, a crime of commission, is Richard Nixon's complicity in the botched burglary attempt on the Democratic Party headquarters at the Watergate Hotel, subsequent cover-up, and the shocking audiotapes that recorded the president sounding both devious and bigoted. Unlike Grant, Nixon was the source of much of the wrongdoing that occurred in his administration, which highlights the point that not all presidential misbehavior is equal. Some scandals are worse than others.

Arguably one of the worst public scandals to rock the White House was uncovered shortly after the death of President Warren G. Harding. The president, who died halfway into his presidential term in 1923, was thus spared the embarrassment of facing his accusers. Still, the Teapot Dome scandal implicated Harding's senior presidential aides and cabinet officers in an illegal deal to benefit personally and financially from the leasing of federal petroleum reserves at a site for which the scandal was named. And Teapot Dome was only the tip of the iceberg as far as Harding's misdeeds were concerned. Harding was, at best, incompetent and, at worst, complicit in the illegalities. Yet, despite the gravity and extensiveness of Harding's scandals, it would seem that most every administration has failed to learn the lessons about scandal from its predecessors.

In the 1980s, the public's trust, already weakened by Watergate and the Vietnam War, was dealt another blow by Ronald Reagan's Iran-Contra affair. In a complicated web of intrigue that reads like a spy novel, the White House funneled aid to the "Contra" rebels, who were attempting to oust the leftist government of Nicaragua. At the same time, Reagan's aides set up an elaborate chain of backroom deals with shadowy figures in Iran and the international arms dealing community that involved providing missiles to terrorist groups, all in order to free American hostages in Lebanon. The two incidents, separated by half a world, were connected in a financial scheme of unreported offshore accounts that would independently pay for the two "policies." The White House was violating both American law and its own stated policy by negotiating with and arming terrorists and by maneuvering around the Boland Amendment that made it illegal to fund war in Central America.

Reagan's national security team of Admiral John Poindexter and Robert "Bud" McFarlane faced legal charges for their role in planning the affair, and Secretary of State George Shultz and Secretary of Defense Caspar Weinberger had their reputations tarnished while attempting to exonerate themselves of wrongdoing. However, as is so often the case with high crimes and misdemeanors in and around the White House, those involved were not held accountable for their deeds. CIA director William Casey died of a brain hemorrhage during the ordeal and became something of a scapegoat for the administration after he took his secrets to the grave. The zealous marine, Lieutenant Colonel Oliver North, who carried out the various illegal deals, pleaded "the Fifth" during his subpoenaed appearance before Congress. North ended up parlaying his moment in the spotlight into a lot of money, working as a motivational speaker and as a commentator for Fox News. After the scandal, the disgraced marine also nearly won a seat in the U.S. Senate, running as a Republican in the state of Virginia.

President Reagan's second term in office was hampered by the scandal to the extent that Reagan was forced to go on television and address the nation about the charges that he traded arms for hostages, negotiated with terrorists, and illegally diverted funds for a covert war. Yet, even as Reagan accepted responsibility (sort of), he tried to have it both ways by defending his earlier actions with the following line: "My heart and my best intentions still tell me that's true, but the facts and the evidence tell me it is not." Still, Reagan left office in 1989 with high public approval and remains one of the nation's most beloved former presidents despite the scandals.

Other culprits not only escaped virtually unscathed from the scandal but prospered as well. Reagan's vice president, George H. W. Bush, claimed to have been "out of the loop" despite compelling evidence that he was in the planning meetings for the covert deals. He was elected president following the end of Reagan's second term in office, at which point he issued pardons for other Iran-Contra scandal coconspirators during the Christmas season, a time when Americans are at their most forgiving (and distracted).

A century of scandal closed with one of the most bitter, partisan, and highly public controversies in White House history. It involved President Bill Clinton, who, after failing to learn from countless earlier extramarital escapades, was nearly removed from office by impeachment because he lied repeatedly about a foolish sexual liaison with a young intern. Clinton's Republican opponents essentially shut down government with a costly two-year-long investigation of the affair and suffered the political blowback from a country tired of the partisan rancor. It did not help the Republican Party that Congressman Henry Hyde, Congressman Bob Barr, and other lead Republican prosecutors of Clinton in Congress, including even Speaker of the House Newt Gingrich, themselves were having or had enjoyed sexual affairs while they were casting moral condemnation on the president.

The new century dashed any hope the public held out for a new era of good government and ethics. The presidency of George W. Bush only further eroded public trust in the office, dragging the presidency through abuses of power and a modus operandi of secrecy. Bush's reign produced an unnecessary war on false pretense, mismanagement of that war to a degree of incompetence nearly unimaginable, identity leaks of a CIA agent as part of a petty political vendetta, and billions of dollars unaccounted for in suspect, no-bid defense contracts.

At the least, it is obvious that there is a long history of scandal associated with the presidency.

SIBLING RIVALRY

Presidents even suffered through embarrassing scandals caused by their siblings. Two recent examples were especially ridiculous. One of them involved Bill Clinton's younger half-brother, Roger, who was born in 1956 and named for his alcoholic, abusive father. Roger was something of the anti-Bill; he certainly became a lifelong ne'er-do-well.

In 1984, when Bill Clinton was governor of Arkansas, Roger was arrested for cocaine possession. Unlike many politicians who use their influence to intervene with the courts however, the elder Clinton allowed Roger to be sentenced. Roger Clinton served one year in federal prison. One would think that a stint behind bars would be just what a troubled sibling needed to realize the error of his ways. However, failing to learn from his mistakes or demonstrate even an inkling of respect or sensitivity toward his half-brother's high office, Roger continued to be an embarrassment and a scandal waiting to happen. Over the course of his brother's governorship and presidency, Roger continually provided fodder for the tabloid press and the president's critics because of his drug use, partying, shameful attempts to "cash in" on his brother's fame by becoming a rock star (critics rightly panned his work), and getting arrested for brawling while attending a sporting event.

As Bill Clinton departed the White House, like most presidents, he pardoned a lot of people. Some of the pardons were appropriate, but several showed very poor presidential judgment. One of his controversial pardons, made on the final full day of his presidency, was for his brother Roger. But, given this chance to start anew, Roger acted as he always had: he was arrested and charged with two counts of drunkenness and one count of disturbing the peace less than one month after his pardon. The former drug addict and alcoholic pursued yet another career—one of the few occupations suited for him—acting in low-budget horror and campy juvenile comedies, perhaps using his personal story as inspiration for his "art."

Bill Clinton was not alone. Jimmy Carter suffered through the scandals of his brother, Billy. The younger Carter, born in 1937, used his "fifteen minutes of fame" to play the "country bumpkin." To the delight of the tabloid media, Billy Carter held "country court," mouthing off about the issues of the day, all the while guzzling beer at garages, atop rusted automobiles, and in other colorful locations. In 1977, during Jimmy Carter's first year in the White House, Billy endorsed a gimmicky product named "Billy Beer." He also once emptied his beer-filled bladder in a very public display that captured headlines and reddened the presidential face.

Often dressed like a character out of the hit television shows *The Beverly Hillbillies* or *Hee Haw*, the college dropout seemed to delight in embarrassing his older brother during his presidency. But what started simply as foolishness turned real when Billy Carter irresponsibly began commenting on U.S. policy in the Middle East. Even though he was an uneducated drunk with few job skills, the president's brother was offered—and accepted—three trips to Libya in 1978 and 1979, paid for by the rogue Libyan leader Muammar Qaddafi. Billy Carter later registered as a foreign agent of the Libyan government, receiving a loan in excess of $200,000 and served as a consultant.

The president's embarrassing brother went so far as to attempt to serve as a business associate for the terror-sponsoring government and to broker various nebulous deals for them. The timing could not have been worse. Back home, the president was engaged in a historic peace accord between the Israelis and Palestinians and, later, struggled through a 444-day hostage crisis in Iran.

The fun and games stopped for Billy Carter. Billy Beer went under, he was forced to sell his home and owed the IRS back taxes, and Congress held hearings into Billy's influence peddling with the Libyans. All the while, Jimmy Carter, who had perhaps fewer scandals than any other president, suffered through what became known as "Billy-gate."

THE PRESIDENT'S BETTER HALF

Living in the White House is like living in a fishbowl where the intimate details of private lives are lived out in a highly public arena. As such, presidential wives have found themselves embroiled in scandal. One such example of a scandal involving a president's spouse surfaced because of Nancy Reagan's taste in expensive clothing. Some of Mrs. Reagan's critics pointed to the hypocrisy surrounding the First Lady's desire to be the most lavishly attired spouse in history while her husband made draconian cuts in social programs for the poor. The president even callously waved off concerns about reductions in children's health and nutrition by claiming that poor children have access to nutritious food because "ketchup is a vegetable."

Mrs. Reagan, meanwhile, was hosting white-tie galas and ran afoul of procedures governing whether presidents (and presumably their wives) could accept expensive gifts while in office. Ignoring the moral and legal reasons to refrain, Mrs. Reagan accepted a near limitless supply of gowns and jewelry from top fashion houses, even "shaking down" designers by actually "requesting" gifts from them. Moreover, instead of returning the items or donating them to charity as good sense would dictate, she added insult to injury by keeping several items.

Ironically, Mrs. Reagan's predecessor, Rosalynn Carter, was criticized for just the opposite. Mrs. Carter wore the same gown to the White House inaugural festivities that she wore some years before to her husband's gubernatorial inauguration in Georgia. She repeatedly tried to "dress down" in order to save taxpayer dollars by holding less formal events at the White House. But she was criticized for both, giving validation to the old expression that "you are damned if you do and damned if you don't."

Regrettably, sometimes the criticism has been completely misguided and directed at the most noble of deeds. Both Lou Hoover and Eleanor

Roosevelt hosted black guests in the White House, and both were summarily condemned throughout the South for "defiling" the president's home. Newspapers from Alabama to Tennessee criticized the first ladies, and state legislatures from Texas to Georgia passed resolutions of condemnation and censure. Angry members of the Georgia House of Representatives passed a resolution expressing "regret over recent occurrences in the official and social life of the national capitol, which have a tendency to revive and intensify racial discord." *The Mobile Press*, in an article titled "The White House Tea," complained that Mrs. Hoover "offered to the South and to the nation an arrogant insult." Similarly, *The Commercial Appeal*, a Memphis-based newspaper, suggested on June 17, 1929, that the nation should, accordingly, "drop the 'White' from the White House." These trailblazing first ladies endured scandal when they should have been celebrated for their truly enlightened and bold actions.

Another First Lady who found herself knee deep in controversy for a seemingly noble gesture was Betty Ford. Most presidents and first ladies like appearing on popular television shows because of the positive exposure it generates and the softball questions generally asked by the hosts. But why the Ford administration ever agreed to allow Mrs. Ford to appear on *60 Minutes* is a case of astoundingly poor political judgment. The show, after all, gained fame for its muckraking, confrontational style of journalism. Mrs. Ford, who had a penchant and reputation for, refreshingly, speaking her mind and not demanding to see the questions ahead of time, walked into an ambush when she appeared on the set. The First Lady's interview on *60 Minutes* ended up raising eyebrows and causing political problems for the Fords. It might have even contributed to Gerald Ford's razor-thin defeat in the election of 1976.

On the show, Mrs. Ford was asked her thoughts about the possibility that her teenage daughter may have used drugs or engaged in premarital sex and what she would do if she found out. Her answer, given with innocence and honesty, was that she hoped it would not happen. But she also stated realistically that teenagers in the 1970s were known to be promiscuous and to experiment. Either way, Mrs. Ford emphasized, she would always love her children and stand by them. To most people, this would seem to have been the correct answer to an inappropriate question rather than the other way around. But it brought harsh criticism that Mrs. Ford was too outspoken. Religiously conservative Americans felt it inappropriate to discuss such matters in public regardless of the fact that the question should not have been asked and the First Lady was simply expressing a parent's support for her children. Preachers throughout the South wrote nasty letters to Mrs. Ford and took to calling her "No Lady" rather than the "First Lady."

Another unfortunate attack against the First Lady occurred when she talked openly about her bout with breast cancer in 1974. Mrs. Ford had the good sense to encourage women to be screened for the disease. As later letters that would pour into the White House indicated, the lives of numerous women were likely saved because they took Mrs. Ford's sage advice to visit their physicians for screenings. However, because the issue of breast cancer (and the word "breast") was not one that was discussed in public in earlier times, Mrs. Ford's comments about the disease were roundly criticized. Happily, Betty Ford lived long enough to see history judge her words and deeds on behalf of raising teenagers, breast cancer awareness, and treatment for substance addiction as heroic. She almost single-handedly destigmatized breast cancer and mammograms simply by talking openly and publicly about them.

Unlike most first ladies, Betty Ford continued to speak her mind on sensitive issues such as abortion rights and the Equal Rights Amendment (ERA), even if her position ran contrary to that of her husband. When women's rights was still a controversial political issue, Betty Ford joined First Lady Rosalynn Carter onstage at the 1977 International Women's Year Conference in Houston and encouraged members of Congress to support passage of the ERA. When criticized for her strong public support of the ERA, the First Lady defended herself, in typical Betty Ford fashion, maintaining, "Being ladylike does not require silence."

MUCH ADO ABOUT NOTHING

Fortunately, some potentially scandalous incidents involving members of the first family have been ignored or excused. For instance, both Betty Ford and Florence Harding were divorcees when they married the men that would one day become president, and Florence had a child from her first marriage. Neither divorce became a serious news story even though a failed marriage was a sensitive matter for politicians in earlier times. But other scandals involving members of the first family seem to be little more than rumormongering and nitpicking by political opponents and were rooted in political opportunism rather than in fact.

A case in point was the scandal involving Margaret Taylor, the wife of President Zachary Taylor. In the 1848 election, Mrs. Taylor was depicted by political satirists and opponents of her husband's Whig Party as an illiterate hick. She was caricatured in newspapers and pamphlets smoking a corncob pipe. There is no evidence that Mrs. Taylor ever did smoke a pipe, but she did endure a tough life on the rugged frontier. There was—and remains—more attention paid to her pipe than to the fact that she raised six children—two of whom died in infancy in the same year—largely on her own and on her husband's meager military salary.

Julia Grant, a warm, competent, and vivacious hostess, was teased by some of her husband's critics for having a crossed eye. So sensitive was the First Lady about the hurtful remarks that she even contemplated corrective surgery despite the fact that such an operation was both extremely rare in the 1860s and potentially fatal. To her husband's credit, U. S. Grant would hear nothing of the medical procedure, noting that he loved his wife just as she was. Similarly appalling was the criticism directed at Ida McKinley because of her epilepsy. Critics claimed that the First Lady was also a spy.

In the late 1890s, little was known about the affliction to the extent that some guests to the McKinley White House were uncomfortable around the First Lady. Custom dictated that individuals with epilepsy were to be shielded from public life. But President William McKinley, ever doting on his wife, chose not only to have the First Lady join him at state functions but also to break with convention that called for presidents and first ladies to sit across from one another. The president sat his wife at his side so that, in the event Mrs. McKinley suffered an attack at dinner, the president would throw a white napkin over her head and excuse himself in order to attend to his wife's condition.

Another example of the absurd involved Lucy Hayes, wife of President Rutherford B. Hayes. She was impolitely nicknamed "Lemonade Lucy" for her opposition to alcohol. When the First Lady refrained from serving liquor at White House events, she came under criticism from both sides of the issue. The women's temperance movement was upset that the First Lady would not fully endorse or join their teetotaling ways, yet the social crowd in the nation's capital city, accustomed to more robust presidential parties, also voiced their displeasure with her alcohol-free events. In spite of her public image, the truth of the matter was that Mrs. Hayes did, on a rare occasion, serve alcohol.

The First Lady tried to please both sides and ended up pleasing neither one. Similarly, the nineteenth president's wife encountered criticism on the question of women's suffrage. Mrs. Hayes was the very first presidential spouse to graduate from college—completing her studies at Ohio Wesleyan in 1850 and even writing a class paper in support of the rights of women. She was also a progressive thinker for the times. While in the White House, however, Mrs. Hayes declined requests to speak out in favor of a woman's right to vote. Once again, Mrs. Hayes received criticism from both sides of the debate that she was too progressive and not progressive enough.

Another challenge facing the first family was that, for much of the early history of the presidency, the White House and its grounds were completely open to the public. This severely limited the first families' privacy, as it was common to find people milling about the property, picnicking on the lawn, or even knocking on the door of the executive mansion. In fact, a few early presidents were rudely surprised to encounter strangers roaming the hallways of the private residence or sleeping on a White House couch while recovering from a night of hard drinking. So, First Lady Frances Cleveland, who had young children during her husband's second term in the 1890s, wisely decided to have a gate erected in order to restrict public access to the grounds. Even though the action was necessary in order to protect her children from large crowds of strangers and even though she continued to offer the public generous hours for and terms of visitation, Mrs. Cleveland was nevertheless roundly criticized.

Similarly, the White House used to be open to the public every New Year's Day for a large, free reception. It was not until 1933 that the annual New Year's Day reception was ended. The custom was stopped by President Herbert Hoover and his wife, Lou. Bitter from the loss to Franklin D. Roosevelt in the November elections of 1932 and with the nation suffering from the Great Depression, the Hoovers decided to close the people's house and cancel the traditional event. Not surprisingly, they were criticized for the decision.

The charming Dolley Madison, still the standard to which first ladies are held when it comes to hostessing, attracted more than her share of detractors. This incorrigible lady gave her critics a full quiver of arrows to shoot back at her—she drank, wore too much makeup, appeared in scandalously low-cut dresses, and chewed snuff. Sporting a purple "Queen Dolley" turban, often adorned with colorful peacock plumes and attended by a court of debutants, Mrs. Madison was an imposing figure. Something of a cross between Princess Diana and Mae West, Mrs. Madison was loved by much of the public despite the minor scandals—or perhaps because of them. Indeed, the gossip associated with her served only to further enhance her stature and the public's interest. Everyone wanted an invitation to one of Mrs. Madison's parties, which were so crowded that people referred to the gala affairs as the "squeeze" or "crush."

Although these examples of scandal might seem to be much ado about nothing, first ladies and first family members paid a high price for living in the building. Indeed, the range of criticism and scandal concerning the occupants of the White House covers nearly every imaginable deed as well as those deeds only imagined by critics. Scandal comes with the office, as even the wives of George Washington and Abraham Lincoln were criticized (for having too many regal horses pull their carriages and for spending too lavishly during a war). The White House is not for the squeamish. As Rosalynn Carter stated,

> I had learned when Jimmy was in the state Senate that you're going to be criticized no matter what you do. If you stay in the White House and pour tea, you'll be criticized because you don't get out. If you get out a lot, you are trying to do too much. I had learned even before I got to the White House to do what I thought was important, because the criticism is going to come.

FINDING MARITAL BLISS IN A FISHBOWL

It is challenging enough to keep a marriage together and to raise well-adjusted children, but trying to do so amid the glare of the world's press would seem an impossible task. And this has often been the case in the White House. While presidents pursue election to high office with relentless zeal, the same cannot always be said of their wives and children. Thus, the utter loss of privacy and the many demands of the office have often been quite taxing on members of the first family. This is especially true during times of family strife.

One such example involved the eldest child of John Quincy and Louisa Adams, George Washington Adams, who suffered a number of difficult setbacks in his life. Born in 1800 in what is now Germany while his father was serving in a diplomatic capacity for the young republic, Adams was a graduate of Harvard and a brilliant attorney who even studied law in the offices of Daniel Webster. Like his father and grandfather before him, Adams entered public life, gaining election to the Massachusetts legislature in 1826.

However, though gifted, Adams was also a troubled young man who was unstable emotionally and appears to have suffered a then misunderstood psychological impairment (he suffered from hallucinations and paranoia). He let his law practice collapse, amassed high debts, and impregnated a woman out of wedlock, creating a string of salacious scandals. In 1829, Adams's mental state was such that, while aboard a ship en route to New York, he confronted fellow passengers with wild accusations in a state of panic and disillusionment. It remains uncertain as to whether he committed suicide by jumping overboard or whether he simply fell to his death accidentally.

His mother, Louisa Catherine Adams, the only First Lady born outside the United States (she was born in England), blamed her son's mental condition and death on his father. Louisa resented the long hours that John Quincy Adams worked and accused him of neglecting his family and being too demanding of their eldest son.

Roughly two and a half decades later, president-elect Franklin Pierce and his wife, Jane Means Appleton Pierce, suffered a similar tragedy. The Pierces were the odd couple, causing ample strain in their marriage. Jane was dowdy, ultrareligious, and something of a wallflower; Frank was outgoing and had a passion for politics. The couple suffered through the loss of two (Franklin and Robert) of their three children in infancy. They therefore clung emotionally to their sole surviving child, Benjamin, born in 1841.

Pierce enjoyed a very successful political career, serving in the New Hampshire legislature, where he rose to the rank of speaker of the state house. He was later a popular member of the U.S. House of Representatives and U.S. Senate, one whose name was often tossed about as a candidate for the presidency. Pierce, who when first elected was the youngest member of the Senate, shocked the political establishment when he resigned his seat in 1842. He did so for several reasons, including his health and the desire to make more money in private law practice. Perhaps the main reason for his early retirement, however, was his wife's repeated insistence that he leave politics. To Jane Pierce's puritanical mind, politics was the work of the devil, and a part of her always blamed her husband and his career for the deaths of her two infant children.

Pierce did return to private law practice in Concord, but he kept his political options open, becoming the Democratic Party chairman of the state and helping to elect James K. Polk president. Unbeknownst to his wife Jane, Pierce also agreed to throw his hat into the ring in 1852 as a "dark horse" candidate. He ended up winning. Of course, Mrs. Pierce was less than happy with the decision and dreaded the prospect of going to the White House. She also worried about her son's safety.

On January 6, 1853, before Pierce's inauguration, the family traveled by train to Andover, Massachusetts, then back again to Concord. Shortly after departing for the return trip, the train derailed, and the passenger car carrying the Pierce family rolled down an embankment. The only fatality in the wreck was young Benjamin Pierce, age twelve. Pierce and his wife witnessed their son being crushed. The emotional impact of this bizarre accident on the parents was severe. Franklin Pierce, already prone to alcoholism and depression, succumbed to these old nemeses, while Jane Pierce went into seclusion, carrying locks of her dead sons' hair and reading Scripture from sunrise to sunset.

Consequently, Pierce attended his inauguration on March 4 without his wife, who blamed her husband's political ambition for the death of their last child. Needing assistance with the social affairs of the ceremony, Pierce asked the outgoing First Lady, Abigail Fillmore, to preside at the official inaugural functions in place of his own absent wife. Mrs. Fillmore, though reluctant, accepted because of the terrible tragedy just weeks prior. In a cruel twist, Mrs. Fillmore caught pneumonia while standing in for Mrs. Pierce during the long, cold outdoor activities. She never recovered, and just three weeks later, Abigail Fillmore was dead. The next year, the Fillmore's youngest daughter, Mary Abigail, age twenty-two, died suddenly of cholera.

Mrs. Pierce, already emotionally vulnerable, deeply depressed, and prone to religious interpretation, read into the fact that her substitute had died and concluded that God was punishing the family for Franklin Pierce's political ambitions. She stayed away from the White House and arrived only reluctantly and much later on the invitation of her husband's close friend and secretary of war, the infamous Jefferson Davis, and his wife Varina, who had invited Mrs. Pierce to help care for the Davises' new child. Mrs. Pierce missed her boys and sought to heal through the care of the Davis child. But the infant died soon after Jane Pierce arrived at the White House. She never recovered from any of these tragedies, living as a recluse and earning the nickname "The Shadow" because of the paucity of her public appearances.

Presidential families have found it extraordinarily taxing to live in the White House, not only because of the many demands of the office but also because of the bewildering array of scandals that have touched nearly every presidency and nearly every member of the presidential family. And then there is the matter of sexual affairs in the White House.

SEX IN THE WHITE HOUSE

What *Not* to Do When Your Wife Has Cancer

John Edwards, a handsome, youthful-looking senator from North Carolina, was the golden boy of the 2004 presidential race. Fresh faced and charismatic, he impressed most observers and even occasioned comparisons between himself and John F. Kennedy. Even though Edwards had been in the U.S. Senate only a single term, he gave the vastly more experienced John Kerry a run for his money in the Democratic primary. As such, when Kerry secured his party's nomination for president, he selected Edwards as his vice-presidential running mate. Although the ticket lost a tight race to George W. Bush and Dick Cheney, Edwards was positioned to be the front-runner for the 2008 campaign.

Part of Edwards's charm was his family life. He and wife Elizabeth had been college sweethearts and seemed to have a fairy-tale marriage. Elizabeth endeared herself to voters with her combination of lawyerly wit and soccer-mom-next-door image. Moreover, the couple's three children looked as if they were straight out of a *Town and Country* magazine ad. Yet the family had grit, enduring the tragic death of a teenage son a few years before and dealing stoically and candidly with Elizabeth's announcement at the end of the campaign that she had cancer. From 2004 through the lead-up to the 2008 campaign, the public followed with interest and deep concern Elizabeth's very public battle with cancer. Accordingly, there was some debate about whether Edwards would run for president given his wife's condition. The public and prognosticators were split over whether Edwards should decline to run in 2008 in order to spend more time with his ailing wife and spare her the grueling schedule of a presidential campaign. However, Mrs. Edwards signaled her blessing for the campaign and even agreed to campaign as much as her health would permit. It was an inspiring story of courage and civic duty.

However, as Edwards was struggling to keep up with his party's front-runners, Senators Barack Obama of Illinois and Hillary Clinton of New York, his campaign was confronted with a sensational tabloid rumor. The *National Enquirer* claimed that the charismatic Edwards was having an affair. Because the source was a tabloid rag, most pundits and the mainstream press dismissed the story, and Edwards waved off the questions as absurd and inaccurate. His denial of the affair was accepted—for the moment. However, very early one spring morning in Los Angeles, the tabloid magazine's photographers captured Edwards leaving a hotel room registered to a woman named Rielle Hunter. Hunter was working for the Edwards campaign as a consultant hired to film short vignettes about the candidate. It was later revealed that she was hired personally by the candidate.

Hunter was a complicated woman who had changed her name and lived a tough and transient life. She had apparently waited after hours at campaign events for the opportunity to meet Edwards, and when the opportunity presented itself, she introduced herself by telling the candidate how "hot" he was. Edwards's ego took the bait, and the two began their reckless sexual affair. The added baggage for the candidate was that he was having an affair while his wife was dealing with cancer and raising young children. Not surprisingly, Edwards's career in politics took an irreparable hit. After repeatedly denying the story, on August 7, 2008, Edwards admitted to ABC News that he had the affair.

As the story unfolded, things became only messier. It turned out that Hunter was paid an inexplicably large amount of money for the poor-quality fluff she tried to pass off as a campaign documentary. It was then revealed that Hunter had given birth to a child during the campaign. The media obtained the birth certificate of Hunter's baby girl and discovered that the information identifying the father on the certificate was blank. The former golden boy of the party was now reduced to answering questions about whether he would submit to a paternity test. And then another strange wrinkle was added to the soap opera: a loyal and longtime aide to the former senator seemed to defuse the story momentarily when it was suggested that he had fathered the child. But, days later, the married aide decided that he did not want to fall on the sword for Edwards and switched his position. It turned out that his job for the campaign included "babysitting" Rielle Hunter during her pregnancy, hiding her from the press, and finding places for her to live. As the story gained momentum, the once-loyal aide announced that he was preparing to write a kiss-and-tell book about the affair and that campaign money was spent on Hunter and her child.

During the media frenzy that followed, even the candidate's best asset—his wife—became another problem for Edwards. Mrs. Edwards answered questions frankly, saying that she did not know if her husband had fathered Hunter's child. In numerous appearances on popular television talk shows, Elizabeth Edwards appeared understandably angry with her husband and soon after the campaign ended released a book that cut her philandering spouse no slack. When it rains, it pours, and so it was for Edwards. Around the time of his wife's book tour, it was confirmed that Edwards had fathered Hunter's child. The book sold well, and the couple separated. Two years later, Elizabeth Edwards succumbed to her disease, and John Edwards was relegated to political obscurity, save for the brunt of an occasional late-night comedy joke and a trial over misuse of campaign funds.

The timing of the story, which broke only weeks before Election Day in 2008, was such that, had Edwards managed to defeat Obama and secure the party's nomination for president or had he been selected as the Democratic vice-presidential candidate, the bombshell revelation would surely have changed the outcome of a presidential election. John Edwards certainly was not the first presidential candidate whose campaign was derailed by a sexual affair. In fact, he was the second major presidential candidate in as many decades to crash and burn because of an intriguing sex scandal.

No Excuses

One of the most notorious sex scandals in modern times involved Gary Hart. The Democratic senator from Colorado had perhaps the most highly publicized affair until President Clinton was nearly impeached in 1998 for his dalliance with the intern Monica Lewinsky. Unlike Bill Clinton and a few others who had affairs before running for the presidency but still managed to win the election, knowledge of Hart's affair and the ensuing media coverage of it affected the outcome of a presidential campaign.

Born Gary Hartpence in 1936, the aspiring politician legally changed his last name in 1961. Even from an early age, Hart was considered by many to be presidential timber. A graduate of Yale Law School and Yale's Divinity School, Hart had also attended religious schools and was considered a bright, honest, and clean-cut politician with an impressive grasp of the issues, a commendable record in the U.S. Senate, and an unblemished family life. Even though he lost his bid for the Democratic nomination in 1984 to Walter Mondale, Hart impressed many Democrats to the extent that he entered the 1988 campaign as the likely nominee.

Throughout the early portion of the campaign in 1987, rumors circulated that Hart was having an affair. However, Hart's marriage appeared to be solid, and no firm evidence ever emerged to give any credibility to the whispers. The candidate himself emphatically denied the rumors. Then, on May

3, 1987, a story appeared in the *New York Times* about Hart's alleged womanizing. To reporters' questions about possible affairs, Hart responded in a testy manner and denied the validity of the rumors. But he then proceeded to issue a bold challenge to the press, daring them, "Follow me around. I don't care. I'm serious. If anybody wants to put a tail on me, go ahead. They'll be very bored." Rarely has a more foolhardy response to a question been uttered by a politician. Hart was inviting trouble, and the *Miami Herald* took the candidate up on his challenge. While staking out Hart's Washington residence, reporters observed a young woman named Donna Rice entering and leaving the senator's townhouse.

Donna Rice had met the presidential candidate earlier that year at a fund-raiser in Miami. Born in 1958, Rice had modeled since the age of thirteen and graduated from the University of South Carolina, where she was an honors student, cheerleader, and beauty pageant contestant. The former Miss South Carolina World had moved to New York City to pursue a career in modeling and acting but eventually settled for minor television roles in Miami. The damning evidence of the Gary Hart–Donna Rice affair came in the form of a photograph of the front-running presidential candidate with the twenty-nine-year-old beauty sitting on his lap. The photo, published by the tabloid paper *The National Enquirer*, showed the tanned couple smiling and enjoying a getaway in Bimini. The real nail in the coffin of Hart's campaign, however, was that the two lovers were aboard a pleasure yacht named, appropriately enough, the *Monkey Business*. In the photo, a smiling Hart was wearing a T-shirt identifying him as a "crew" member of the *Monkey Business*. Indeed.

Hart, like so many other candidates on the campaign stump, had become so drunk with the sexual opportunities available to a powerful politician that he had thrown all caution and morals to the wind. The candidate once callously checked into an exclusive hotel with a stewardess from his incoming flight in tow and was seen in the company of a mistress by senior members of his own political party and prospective fund-raisers for his campaign. Over the course of the campaign, Hart went from being a policy wonk and happily married man to having a latent adolescence, falling prey to the bevy of beautiful, young women whom powerful men attract. Hart was also a victim of believing his own positive press. Like other politicians, Hart started living like the rules did not apply to him. In May 1987, only five days after the story was published, the Hart presidential campaign folded its tent. Despite constant hounding by the press, a stoic Mrs. Lee Hart announced that she would remain with her husband, deciding that life with Gary was preferable to life without him.

In December 1987, Hart made a token effort at returning to the campaign, but it went nowhere, and he bowed out for good after falling far behind in the early primaries. The affair ended his political career and a likely presidency. The Donna Rice incident aside, Gary Hart's career remained one of distinction, suggesting that it might be possible to separate a politician's personal and professional lives. Hart emerged as one of the earliest voices warning about the threat of terrorism and the nation's poor state of homeland security. In fact, as one of the cochairs of the 1998 Bipartisan Commission on Terrorism, appointed by President Bill Clinton, Hart nearly foreshadowed the 9/11 tragedy in his report on terror readiness. The former senator was also ahead of the curve in warning the country about global environmental degradation and, after leaving politics, also served as a distinguished professor at the University of Colorado.

As for life after her moment of fame, Donna Rice received many lucrative offers for jobs and appearances and turned down a request to pose for *Playboy* magazine. She did, however, serve as the spokesmodel for the new, aptly named product "No Excuses Jeans." In 1994, Rice moved on with her life and married Jack Hughes. She also had a religious awakening and embarked on a new career as, of all things, an antipornography crusader. In 1999, the Republican leadership in the U.S. Senate pulled out all the punches when they appointed Donna Rice Hughes to a congressional panel charged with protecting children from child porn and sexual indecency.

Hellcats

For whatever reason, unlike the previous two examples, some presidential sex scandals never became sensational news stories. Consider the real story of Ronald Reagan's sex life in contrast to his idealized image. Reagan, a popular and ruggedly handsome actor in his prepresidential years and a father figure while in the White House, played the field with numerous Hollywood starlets and models, such as Doris Lilly, Betty Powers, and June Travis, with whom he starred in *Love Is on the Air*. Other Reagan conquests included the voluptuous Lana Turner, the star of *They Won't Forget*, and Ila Rhodes, the beauty who appeared with him in the action films *Secret Service of the Air* and *Hell's Kitchen*.

In 1940, Reagan married the glamorous actress and divorcee Jane Wyman, his costar in the film *Brother Rat*. Prolific in both dating and acting, the star's career peaked around the time of his marriage. After 1943, however, Reagan received fewer and fewer choice roles and resorted to making B movies. The actor's marriage, like his movie career, went into decline. Shortly after, it was revealed that Reagan's wife had been having an affair with the actor Lew Ayres. She filed for divorce in 1948.

Single again, Reagan resumed his penchant for dating younger actresses. Just shy of four years after his divorce from Jane Wyman, Reagan started dating another actress, Nancy Davis, after meeting her on the set of the film *Hellcats of the Navy*. Reagan's relationship with his latest actress was far from monogamous, and she had her own reputation as having been with a number of actors. The book *The Peter Lawford Story*, which the late actor had started to prepare just before his death, was completed by Lawford's fourth wife, Patricia, to whom he was married at the time of his death in 1984. The autobiography makes some shocking claims about the future wife of Ronald Reagan. Lawford himself was quite the playboy and admitted to preferring sex with multiple young actresses. As such, Lawford came to know such starlets as Lana Turner, Judy Garland, and even Nancy Davis through his affairs. He claimed that before she was Nancy Reagan, Nancy Davis came to Hollywood from Broadway looking for a career and "to have a good time." Lawford and his wife claim in the autobiography that "[Nancy] was rather wild, the delight of a number of men and the lover of the alcoholic actor Robert Walker." Walker would die tragically in his early thirties.

When preparing the book, Lawford's wife, Patricia interviewed her late husband's Hollywood friends who recalled the story when "three or four of us walked into Bob Walker's house and saw a naked Nancy Davis standing there looking shocked at being caught like that. She grabbed a towel and ran into the bathroom." Lawford and his wife also claim that Nancy was known less for her acting skills than for something else. In the book, they state that "when she was single, Nancy Davis was known for giving the best head in Hollywood." Peter Lawford would know. He told the story of traveling with Nancy and her actor-boyfriend Bob Walker to visit her mother and stepfather. During the long car drive, Nancy "entertained them orally on those trips, apparently playing with whichever man was not driving at the moment."

The days of serial dating for Reagan and Nancy Davis came to an end, however. For his part, Reagan was quoted as having an epiphany during his bachelor days: "I woke up one morning and I couldn't remember the name of the gal I was in bed with. I said, 'Hey, I gotta get a grip here.'" Nancy had the dashing actor and former head of the Screen Actors Guild in her sights and was determined to become Mrs. Ronald Reagan. In 1951, Nancy found herself pregnant and informed Reagan, who did the honorable thing. The couple married in March 1952. Two months later, it was announced that Nancy Reagan was pregnant. Roughly five months after the announcement (and seven months after the wedding), the Reagans' daughter Patti was born. Yet there are allegations and evidence that Reagan was not yet ready for married life or to live by the standards set by his earlier epiphany or later beliefs as president. Ronald Reagan was not present at his daughter Patti's birth. It has been suggested that he might have instead been with his mistress, Christine Larson, at the time. Reagan ended this affair with Larson but was motivated to do so only after arriving at her apartment to find her with another man.

Hellcats would be Nancy Reagan's eleventh and final film. From that moment on, she devoted herself full-time to being a dutiful wife and to pushing her husband's career. The couple ended up having a very warm, close, and faithful marriage. Still, Peter Lawford's wife remembered him laughing when Ronald Reagan was elected president in 1980 and then cursing the couple for the hypocrisy of their now conservative, moral image. Lawford remembered the Reagans from their wild sexual days in Hollywood. Of course, the Hollywood studios, much like the Republican Party, downplayed Reagan's divorce from Jane Wyman and claimed that, as a struggling actress, Nancy Davis had been too busy with her career to date. Apparently, such fantasies really are possible in Hollywood and the White House.

THE EXECUTIVE (PLAYBOY) MANSION

The sexual behavior of most presidential candidates and presidents remains relatively unknown. Little has been written about such private, intimate aspects of a president's life, and it is still uncertain as to whether the public has a right to know about such information or whether such scandals affect presidential performance. What seems certain is that sexual indiscretions and affairs have always been a part of the presidency. The presidency has experienced interracial affairs, same-sex affairs, affairs with married women and girls young enough to be presidential daughters, flings with prostitutes and spies, and children born out of wedlock.

For instance, Martin Van Buren's vice president, Richard Johnson, was said to have a black lover—quite a scandal in the mid-nineteenth century. Andrew Jackson and George W. Bush were notoriously wild and mischievous during their teenage and early adult years. Even the scholarly Thomas Jefferson was accused of having an affair with a married woman while serving in a diplomatic capacity in France and was alleged to have had a liaison with Dolley Madison, the wife of his good friend, secretary of state, and future president. Even if Jefferson's relationship with his successor's wife was greatly exaggerated, Jefferson did have an ongoing affair with a biracial slave mistress with whom he fathered several children.

If it is possible sexually, it likely happened in the White House. The presidential historian Paul F. Boller, pondering the existence of sex scandals in the White House, suggested that "it would be easy to write a lengthy book about the sexual shenanigans of the American presidents." But he then qualified his statement by adding, "not really," because the majority of the presidents behaved. Is Boller correct? Yes and no. Some did, and some did not.

Of the forty-three (Grover Cleveland served two nonconsecutive terms as the twenty-second and twenty-fourth president) commanders in chief (through Barack Obama), twenty-six of them appear to have passed historical scrutiny without a sexual affair that could be labeled scandalous—that is, an affair while in the White House, an affair while married, or a premarital affair of a salacious nature. That leaves another seventeen in question. At least twelve of the seventeen philandering presidents had noteworthy affairs prior to their years in the White House. At least seven presidents had sexual affairs both before and during their presidencies. This includes Thomas Jefferson, Woodrow Wilson, Warren G. Harding, Franklin D. Roosevelt, John F. Kennedy, Lyndon B. Johnson, and Bill Clinton. Moreover, each of these men had multiple affairs, including some that were quite reckless and shocking. And those are the ones we know of. It is possible—and highly probable—that the bedroom behavior of some other former presidents as well as soon-to-be presidents is equally scandalous but has thus far remained unknown to historians and the press.

Whether presidents who had affairs before but apparently not during their White House years should be included in the history of White House affairs is certainly a point open to debate. The same can be said of those presidents who appear not to have had affairs but still had intriguing sex lives and marriages. For instance, we have no reason to believe that John Quincy Adams ever strayed from his marital vows, but he had a rotten and, at times, scandalous marriage. His wife blamed him for the apparent suicide of their son and even used her husband as the inspiration for a character in an unpublished tract she wrote. The plot: an ambitious politician ignores his suffering wife and cares little for his family.

Several arguments exist for including all these incidents in this book. One obvious reason for considering these as affairs of state is that the future president was married when the indiscretion occurred. Moreover, many of the affairs happened while the future presidents were serving in a lower public office, busy advancing their careers toward the pinnacle of electoral politics—the White House. Some of the prepresidential affairs are worth a closer look because of the sensational details of the story. More often than not, the impact of such outrageous scandals and sexual affairs by politicians has been harmful to both the public and the health of democratic government. Quite simply, there are also some shocking, pornographic, and "what-were-they-thinking" affairs. More practically, such flings may offer insights into the president's personality. As was the case with George Washington, the impact of women and affairs ultimately shaped the lives and political careers of presidents.

The prevalence of scandal in American politics and the White House may also give us a somewhat altered and more realistic view of the history of the presidency compared to the idealized version taught in school. Taking a serious look at love, sex, and scandal in the White House offers an interesting, important, and heretofore unused tool for learning about the character and personality of our leaders. In the presidency, after all, character is king.

The difference between, say, James Buchanan and Abraham Lincoln, who served back-to-back as our fifteenth and sixteenth presidents, respectively, has less to do with education, experience, oratory, or luck than it does with Lincoln's remarkable character and Buchanan's less-than-impressive moral fiber. This glaring difference in presidential character is apparent when Buchanan barely lifted a finger as the Republic dissolved into civil war in contrast to Lincoln's herculean effort to preserve and ultimately strengthen the Union. The differences between Herbert Hoover and Franklin D. Roosevelt, our thirty-first and thirty-second presidents, or Theodore Roosevelt and William Howard Taft, our twenty-sixth and twenty-seventh presidents, is equally a lesson in character. In each case, one man governed ruinously; the other brilliantly. Each of these sets of presidents faced similar challenges at similar times in history, yet the way they responded to the challenges of their time could not have been more different.

Historians have long examined the great and failed decisions of presidents to learn more about the men who served in the White House. The extraordinary handling of the Cuban missile crisis reveals as much as about John Kennedy as does his mishandling of the Bay of Pigs. At the same time, Franklin Roosevelt's Lend-Lease and Thomas Jefferson's Louisiana Purchase offer us insights into the men who undertook these momentous initiatives, as do Richard Nixon's Watergate scandal and Warren Harding's Teapot Dome scandal.

Historians also study the traits of leaders in order to construct profiles of them. Were they decisive or timid? Honest or corrupt? Inquisitive or intellectually disinterested? Inspiring orators or ineffective communicators? But a president's experiences with love, sex, and scandal provide equally useful tools for understanding their character and personality. A closer look at affairs, relationships, and scandals provides an interesting lens for understanding presidential temperament, judgment, and values. These discoveries also help to breathe life into the private person behind the public figure.

It should come as no surprise, then, that the sex lives of presidents have, at times, been an issue considered worthy of media attention. At other times, they were not. Sex scandals have been a part of campaign strategies—both by those campaigns seeking to dodge a bullet about past sexual indiscretions and by those slinging mud about their promiscuous opponents. These scandals have also been a part of the decision-making process of the voters.

Although sexual misbehavior among presidents is neither new nor any more prevalent today, it would appear that both voters and the media are more informed and therefore more concerned with sex scandals today than in an earlier day and age. For instance, when rumors arose in the 1880 presidential election that the Republican nominee, James A. Garfield, had engaged in extramarital affairs, it marked perhaps the very first time that the public had reliable evidence of such behavior in a candidate. However, Garfield's affairs were largely a nonissue during the campaign, and Garfield was elected president. In the subsequent presidential race, Democrat Grover Cleveland also had a sexual scandal. The charge was that the candidate had, some years earlier, fathered a child out of wedlock. Cleveland's critics and opponents—and a few newspapers—armed with sordid tales of Cleveland's alleged sex-capades, went on the attack. But, as was the case with Garfield, Cleveland was elected in 1884 over the strong evidence of guilt. In fact, all the way back to Thomas Jefferson's first term in office (1801–1805), allegations emerged in print that the president had a long-term affair with a slave named Sally Hemings. It was even reported in newspapers that the affair produced several illegitimate, biracial children. Nonetheless, Jefferson was resoundingly elected to a second term in 1804.

IF MEN WERE ANGELS

The story is not all doom and gloom. There have been presidents who were unquestioningly loyal and faithful to their wives. Such was the case with Teddy Roosevelt, William Howard Taft, and Calvin Coolidge. Likewise, some first couples had good marriages that endured even the trials and tribulations of the White House. Among the strongest marriages both before and during the White House years were those of John and Abigail Adams, James and Sarah Polk, Ulysses and Julia Grant, Herbert and Lou Hoover, Harry and Bess Truman, and Jimmy and Rosalynn Carter.

Along the way, there have also been touching stories of love and devotion that, like the scandals and infidelity, merit a closer look for what they tell us about the president's character and role of the First Lady and first family in both shaping the president's temperament and governing.

President Truman gives history a glimpse into the depth of his commitment to his wife, Bess Wallace Truman. One of the many moments that affirmed his love for and devotion to Mrs. Truman occurred during the famous Potsdam meeting at the close of World War II. While there for talks among the "big three"—Truman, Winston Churchill, and Joseph Stalin—in July 1945, a young army officer assigned to Truman made the mistake of assuming that the former senator, like so many other politicians and leaders, would be interested in the company (and services) of an attractive young woman. Arriving in Potsdam, the president was offered by his assigned aide "anything, you know, like women." Presumably, a menu of redheads, blondes, and brunettes was to be offered to the commander in chief. But Truman cut the young officer off in midsentence, growling, "Listen, son, I married my sweetheart! She doesn't run around on me, and I don't run around on her. I want that understood. Don't ever mention that kind of stuff to me again!"

The previously mentioned incident tells us something about Truman's character. This was a president, after all, who met his future wife when they were children, never loved another woman, and patiently waited years before she finally agreed to marry him. Even late in his life, Truman was still writing gushy, romantic letters to his wife, expressing his love for her often in a way that embarrassed the glum and retiring Mrs. Truman. In fact, late in life, Truman caught his beloved Bess going through a box of their love letters. To his shock and dismay, Truman, who was quite the historian and pack rat, observed his wife throwing the juiciest ones into the fireplace. With the prospect of losing the letters, a distraught Truman cried out for his wife to "think of history!" Still casting the steamy notes to the flames, she replied, "I am!"

True-blue husbands like Truman aside, as the subsequent chapters of this book point out, the nature and extent of presidential and political sexual scandals are far beyond what is learned in school in terms of their audacity, complexity, frequency, and consequence. These sexual shockers in the history of the White House provide a unique lens by which to view the presidents. Indeed, it would seem that political leaders today have failed to learn the lessons of their predecessors' scandals. It would also seem that the American public has yet to learn its lesson and hold political leaders accountable for their dirty deeds.

Scandal has been an ever-present part of America's political past and scandals have played an important role in American political life. Along the way, we have found these foibles, follies, and fairy tales to be irresistible. As such, the story of love, sex, and scandal in the White House is, in part, a story about us. It is possible that James Madison would agree with all these points. The founding father and fourth president once famously quipped that "if men were angels, no government would be necessary." Well, if the presidents were angels, this book would not be necessary. But they were not, and it is.

Ten Stories of Presidential Love, Sex, and Scandal

The full-length portrait of George Washington was painted in 1797 and is the most famous painting in the White House. Painted by G. Stuart, engraved by H. S. Sadd. Library of Congress Prints and Photographs Division, LC-USZ62-7585 DLC.

⋛ 3 ⋚

"I Profess Myself a Votary to Love"

I have always considered marriage as the most interesting
event in one's life, the foundation of happiness or misery.

—George Washington

A LETTER FROM HISTORY

To most Americans, George Washington is arguably the least accessible of
the founding generation. He remains more myth than man and is remembered more as a monument than in the flesh and blood. And that is precisely
the way Washington wanted it.

Part of his extraordinary legacy as the first among his countrymen is to
be expected, given the fact that he was the commander who, against all odds,
defeated the British and brought independence to the colonies. Likewise, as
the first president of the fledgling nation, Washington secured the future of
the new experiment in popular democracy and in so doing assured his place
at the pinnacle of fame. An adoring and appreciative nation wholeheartedly
bestowed on their father the larger-than-life status as demigod. Indeed, part
of the image of Washington that remains is by design.

Washington was excessively image conscious and took great pains to
craft himself in the likeness of the great Cincinnatus and the other heroes
of his impressionable adolescence. Lacking an advanced education, a position among Virginia's gentry, or either the oratorical or the written skills of
other leaders, a young George Washington willed himself to attain the stature later associated with him. Washington saw himself as Cincinnatus, the
duty-bound citizen-soldier who put down the plowshare to save the Republic,

then, having served his countrymen, humbly returned to his farm. It was an example unlike any other from history, and the example was not lost on Washington. Washington longed to achieve fame and throughout his public career privately reveled in his growing reputation. The image that Washington wished for and so calculatingly designed remains, and history remembers about as much of him as he wanted remembered.

"On the other hand, the world knows nothing of the beautiful and talented woman who had no little share in shaping the destiny of one of its foremost men," suggested Wilson Miles Cary, a descendant of the previously mentioned woman. Washington received a little help from his wealthy neighbor, Sally Fairfax, in casting his heroic image. As one historian flatly argued, "Sally Fairfax's influence on George Washington cannot be overstated."

The Sally Fairfax Myth

Wilson Miles Cary was a descendant of three of colonial Virginia's most important families: the Carrs and the Randolphs, who were part of Thomas Jefferson's extended family, and the Cary family, of which Sally was a part. As such, Cary was both the great-great-grandnephew of the author of the Declaration of Independence and a blood relation to George Washington's Sally Fairfax, sharing Sally's maternal family name.

Born near Baltimore, Maryland, in 1838, Cary was educated at "Thomas Jefferson's College"—the University of Virginia, nicknamed for the founder and designer—and became an attorney. True to his Virginia roots, Cary fought for the Confederacy during the Civil War. The eccentrically aristocratic Cary never married, was even said to have a strong likeness to Jefferson, and shared his famous relative's taste for literature, wine, architecture, and music; in short, Cary was a "Renaissance man" just like Jefferson.

Cary also had a passion for his family's history. During his life, he collected the letters and remembrances of the Cary family and conducted extensive genealogical research as part of a planned book project on Sally's relationship with Washington. He even lived near to where his distant relatives resided, in Fauquier County, Virginia, and named his home after Sally Fairfax's estate, "Belvoir."

But Cary died in 1914 before he could finish the book on Mrs. Fairfax. Wilson Cary's manuscript, however, was edited and completed by Dr. Lyon G. Tyler, noted Virginia historian and son of former occupants of the White House, President and Mrs. John Tyler. Dr. Tyler was named for the former First Lady's wealthy and powerful father and became the president of the College of William & Mary, which was the alma mater of both Thomas Jefferson and John Tyler.

In the book, both authors—Cary and Dr. Tyler—paint a clear picture of a George Washington who was smitten by Sally from the time he met her to the day of his death. Cary family history remembers that Washington and Mrs. Fairfax carried on a lifelong flirtation, even while Washington was planning to marry Martha Dandridge Custis. This bond continued after Washington's marriage. When the book was published in 1916, the implications of its bombshell revelation were many. The most important and controversial passages were those devoted to the argument that it was Sally's hand that helped groom and mold the young Washington into the man history remembers.

But the book also shed light on Washington's famously formal and impenetrable persona. Washington is widely regarded as a man of moderation, discipline, and prudence. This much is true. Yet he was filled with near uncontrollable passions for Sally Fairfax. Many professional historians, however, were unmoved by the Cary–Tyler book, labeling any possibility of a loving relationship between Washington and Sally as the "Sally Fairfax myth." Historians who were tempted to pursue the leads offered by the book—then and in subsequent years—were discouraged from doing so through criticism from their peers. Likewise, a stone wall of resistance by the community of Washington scholars maintained that historians must stick to the cold, hard facts and not be misled by such preposterously "romantic" notions that Washington could have loved a woman other than his wife or that Washington was not a "self-made" man.

Nevertheless, through the twentieth century, some scholars were taking notice of the existence of clues pointing to an unusually close relationship between Washington and the woman described as "beautiful and brilliant."

An Unknown Letter

The interest in the Washington–Fairfax relationship was initially prompted when a collection of historic letters owned by the well-regarded Bangs and Company were auctioned off on March 31, 1877. Among the cache of letters auctioned were the writings of Washington, including a particularly interesting letter he wrote to Sally Fairfax. The tone of this and other letters exchanged between the two from the 1750s until Sally's departure for England in 1773 was unmistakable. In the letters, George and Sally discussed a number of issues, including the French and Indian War, family matters, and their friends. The letters are unmistakably warm, engaging, and playful in tone, in sharp contrast to the stiffly formal manner with which George wrote to others. The mythical, monumental Washington, it appeared, was a human being after all.

In one particular letter, written by Washington on September 12, 1758, he admits to an inquiring Sally that he was a devotee to love. Washington uses the word "votary," which has the meaning of a religious vow or fervent devotion, much as a monk would have to his faith. At the time of its auction, eighty years had passed since the letter was written, and now history was presented with a dilemma. What did Washington mean in the passage? Was he admitting his love for Martha or Sally? Some scholars thought that the letter was a forgery, while others maintained that it was written in jest and simply could not mean what it said.

The controversy arose because the letter was written by Washington while he was engaged to Martha Dandridge Custis. The controversy stemmed from the following passage to Sally: "Tis true, I profess myself a Votary to Love . . . I feel the force of her amiable Beauties in the recollection of a thousand tender passages that I wish to Obliterate, till I am bid to revive them—but experience alas! Sadly reminds Me how Impossible this is."

The words are passionate, and the meaning is as it appears to be. However, there is a less tantalizing explanation. It appears that the letter was misunderstood. The letter is real, and it was produced by Washington's pen. It is also true that, in this and other letters, there was no mistaking that Washington was enamored with Sally. However, the previously mentioned passage appears to be Washington's response to Sally's letters asking about his engagement and his feelings for his fiancée. Washington, writing from the battlefield at Fort Cumberland, admits in a cryptic manner to Sally his devotion to love, and the object of his affectionate words could be either Martha Custis or Sally.

It appears that Sally was one of the few with whom Washington discussed his engagement and one of the very few—possibly the only one—with whom Washington confided his intimate feelings about the engagement. Yet, at the same time, Washington's vague and confusing wording to his mentor and good friend might have been a last-ditch effort before getting married to let Sally know his true feelings for her. As a case in point, in another letter to Sally that Washington wrote from his encampment at Raystown, he ponders the following: "Do we misunderstand the true meaning of each other's Letters? I think it must appear so, tho' I would feign hope the contrary, as I Cannot speak plainer without—but I'll say no more and leave you to guess the rest."

The letters exchanged between Washington and Sally often hinted playfully of a deeper, unspoken nature to the relationship, as is apparent in these lines. It seems probable that Washington was discreet enough never to raise the subject that could not be raised, but that in so many words he expressed his feelings for Sally in the only way possible. He hinted but never broached the subject of Sally's marriage and the almost inescapable reality that Sally could not divorce her husband and remarry her younger admirer. Had Washington pursued such a blunt line of questioning, it is likely that Sally would have ended or at least cooled their friendship. Surely, Washington understood such a risk. Similarly, why else would Washington state in the letter that he has been unsuccessful in attempting to "obliterate" his "recollection of a thousand tender passages"?

There are two explanations. One is that Washington was pining away for Martha while forced to remain in camp during the war. The other is that he wondered whether the forthcoming marriage would heal his broken heart over Sally. The "thousand tender passages" that Washington referred to might be the letters and romantic whispers he exchanged with Martha. But this is doubtful, as the couple had courted only very briefly and Washington had even less time to visit his fiancée because of the war, whereas Washington and Sally had exchanged warm and personal letters for years, during which time the close neighbors saw one another frequently. From Washington's surviving letters, we know that Sally wrote him back thirteen days later answering the news of his engagement, but, sadly, her response did not survive history.

The context within which the letter was written sheds some light on the possibility of the latter interpretation. In the summer of 1758, shortly before the letter was written, Washington again returned from the battlefield, this time not just homesick or heartsick but physically exhausted and in poor health. Several months after his engagement with Martha Custis, it was Sally Fairfax who nursed Washington back to health, providing teas and home cures for him while he convalesced at Mount Vernon. The social strictures of the time would have frowned on Martha being alone with George in such an intimate setting prior to their marriage, and Martha did have two young children in her care. But Martha had slaves in her employ to help with child rearing, and it was not as if she was a teenage girl living with her parents. Martha was a wealthy widow.

Washington's letters to Sally around this time are especially suggestive and warm. Just days after the cryptic "Votary to Love" letter and weeks after he was nursed back to health by Sally, Washington again wrote to her on September 25, 1758, from his camp with a thinly veiled and romantic innuendo: "I should think our time more agreeably spent, believe me, in playing a Part in Cato with the company you mention, and myself doubly happy in being the Iuba to such a Marcia as you must take."

Sally had exposed Washington to literature and theater, among other learned passions, and it was clear that she continued her tutelage for many years. In the previously mentioned passage from Washington, he eludes to Cato's character Marcia, who "towers above her sex" as the fairest, most charming, most sophisticated of all women. Iuba is, not surprisingly, in love with Marcia, but he is also inspired by her to bravery in battle. Sally, who also happened to "tower above her sex," inspired Washington throughout his early military career and quite possibly later during the Revolutionary War. Washington, the astute student, was using his lesson on Cato, as it mirrored his and Sally's lives. Much as Iuba would have, Washington also wrote Sally after a particularly difficult battle where his army suffered many losses. But the soldier's thoughts were on glory and heroism: "Thus it is the lives of the brave are often disposed of: but who is there that does not rather envy than regret a death that gives birth to honour and glorious memory?"

The illness, combined with the stress of battle and his fatigue, most likely left Washington both dependent on Sally and emotionally vulnerable during his convalescence. At the time Washington was in Sally's care, her husband was away in England. There is no evidence whatsoever that exists to verify whether the two close friends ever consummated their relationship sexually. However, during Washington's military leave, the ingredients were there to the extent that, if they ever acted on their feelings, this would seem to have been the perfect moment. Individuals often develop strong emotional attachments to those ministering to them in time of need and weakness. Perhaps this happened during Washington's recuperation and explains the vague meaning of the letter and his admission to being a "Votary to Love."

There is much that we do not know about the Washington–Fairfax relationship. For instance, because nearly all of Washington's letters to Martha are lost to history, we do not know whether he wrote to Martha in the same warm tone he used when writing to Sally.

Some scholars who read the auctioned letter of 1758 believed that Washington might have been professing his devotion to Martha. In Appleton's *New American Cyclopedia*, for example, the editor, a Mr. Everett, mistakenly believed that the September 25, 1758, letter was written to Washington's fiancée, Martha Custis, because the tone of the letter unmasked Washington's love. As to the contents of the letter, Wilson Miles Cary concluded, "We can scarcely believe this to be the Washington of history, but it is the Washington of nature!" In fact, the young Washington's letters were so boldly suggestive that Sally eventually had to slow down the colonel's passions in a manner befitting her status as a married woman.

RULES OF CIVILITY

George Washington was born at 10:00 on the morning of February 22, 1732, in Virginia's Westmoreland County. Some sources list the date of Washington's birth as February 2. Part of the discrepancy can be explained by a change in the official calendar used during his lifetime. The old Julian calendar ran slightly longer than an exact year and had to be adjusted. The new Gregorian calendar, which was originally established in 1582 and named for Pope Gregory, did just that and was ultimately adopted by Britain and its colonies in 1752. Thereafter, Washington's birth (like everyone else's) was adjusted.

The Washingtons had emigrated from England around 1657 or 1658. George's father, Augustine Washington, was the grandson of the first Washingtons to cross the Atlantic. Augustine had lost his first wife and remarried. George happened to be the firstborn of that second marriage to Mary Ball. George also had a younger sister and three younger brothers, along with two older half-brothers.

As a young boy, George lacked the opportunity to travel and receive a quality formal education like his two older half-brothers. The education he received was therefore rudimentary and consisted of a few years of tutors offering instruction in astronomy, geography, and mathematics. George never attended college, and his father stressed proper writing, grammar, and strict adherence to the codes of etiquette. But Washington had an insatiable appetite to improve himself. Too poor to purchase the popular book *110 Rules of Civility*, the teen copied the entire book by hand. Later in life, Washington purchased a few historical biographies and military books.

Through the repetitious exercise of copying the book over and over, Washington not only improved his writing ability but also learned how a true gentleman was expected to act. Washington put the rules to memory and then to heart: do not spit around others; don't talk with your mouth full; keep your clothing on in the presence of others; don't pick food from your teeth in public; your recreations should be manly, not sinful; follow your conscience; and so on. And so, with the aide of this book and Sally Fairfax, Washington was maturing into a proper young gentleman.

Starting a War

Few indicators from his youth would have foreshadowed the greatness that Washington would one day attain. Unlike the other founding fathers, Washington's ambition, interest, and experience were neither classical nor intellectual in nature. Rather, they were practical and honed on surveying missions and the battlefields of the frontier. Washington studied the practical vocation of surveying and also became a self-trained expert in agricultural sciences and economics.

As a twenty-one-year-old officer in the colonial units of the British army, Washington boasted about a successful skirmish with the French in 1754, even suggesting, "I heard the bullets whistle and, believe me, there is something charming in the sound." Even King George II, after reading of the absurdly naive remark, dismissed Washington, saying, "He would not think so if he had been used to hearing many." A more mature, war-weary Washington recognized the ridiculousness of his youthful boasting. Years later, when asked about the embarrassing description, Washington noted flatly, "If I said so, it was when I was young."

In 1753, the British governor of Virginia, Robert Dinwiddie, deployed troops on a diplomatic mission. They included a young officer named George Washington. Washington was to attempt to encourage the French to abandon the Ohio River valley and to dissuade the chiefs of the Six Nations from aligning with the French. As Washington set off on his first real mission, conflict was on the horizon, and tensions ran high in the colonies. The French were constructing fortifications from Lake Erie to the Ohio River and making alliances with Indian nations in the region, all of which rightly worried Governor Dinwiddie.

What followed was a less-than-exemplary start to Washington's military career. Indeed, the blunders made in Washington's first command, in what is called the "Jumonville affair," were a major reason for the start of the Seven Years' War with the French. Ironically, the taxes that the British imposed on the colonies after this war (started by Washington) provided the spark that ignited the American Revolution, which was led by Washington.

In late May 1754, a very green Major Washington was leading his unit through southwestern Pennsylvania. While camped in a natural clearing called Great Meadows, Washington received a report that the French were nearby. On the stormy, moonless night of May 27, 1754, Washington led forty soldiers through the thick of the surrounding forest to find the French. At dawn, they encountered a small detachment of roughly three dozen French regulars and Indians camped in a ravine. With no sentries posted by the French, Washington, forgetting that it was a diplomatic mission, was able to easily encircle the enemy.

A shot was fired, but who fired first remains debated. It is likely that either Washington gave the order to open fire or a nervous, young soldier, after a long, difficult night traveling through dense woods, pulled the trigger. After fifteen minutes of fighting, thirteen French soldiers and their Indian allies were killed, as was their commanding officer, Joseph Coulon de Jumonville. Surprised, trapped, outnumbered, and without their commander, the French surrendered, and Washington took twenty-one prisoners. One man escaped and made it back to the main French fort to warn of the attack.

At age twenty-one, Washington had won his first battle. But the sweetness of victory turned sour when the French press reported that the party that Washington attacked was also on a diplomatic mission. This explained why so few soldiers accompanied de Jumonville. But Washington maintained that a diplomatic party would not be camped in a ravine off the established road. The ensuing outrage over the fight contributed to the start of a long war and set in motion a series of events that would forever change America. Or, as Horace Walpole noted, "a shot fired by a young Virginian in the backwoods of America set the world on fire."

Fortunately for Washington, Governor Dinwiddie and his fellow countrymen treated the returning major as a hero. The governor and most Virginians dismissed the French claim about the diplomatic mission. In fact, Dinwiddie had wanted to alert both the Crown back in England and the leaders of the Virginia Colony of the imminent French threat. Thus, he shamelessly used the incident to beat the drums for war. The governor had Washington's battlefield diary published in London in 1754 as *The Journal of Major George Washington*. This raised awareness about the need to fight the French while also raising Washington's stature. The Virginia House of Burgesses expressed formal appreciation for Washington's victory and awarded him with a "bonus" of fifty pounds. Washington was at the center of much larger events and, despite his blunder, landed on his feet.

After the publication of *The Journal of Major George Washington* caught the attention of leaders on both sides of the Atlantic, Dinwiddie was authorized to call up a volunteer militia to fight the French. Anyone enlisting in the new regiment was rewarded with the promise of land in the new territories to the west. Washington was again called by Dinwiddie to share the leadership of the campaign with two more experienced officers. Fate and opportunity intervened again, as the two senior officers died unexpectedly, leaving Washington as the de facto commander. As the commanding officer, Washington was promoted to colonel and entitled to 10 percent of the land shares, which he would personally later survey, claiming the best parcels for himself. This second command brought fame and fortune but also near ruin. Washington made another grand blunder that should have ended his burgeoning career.

The colonel led his troops back to Pennsylvania to engage the French. Anticipating French aggression, Washington devoted most of June to erecting what he described as a "small palisaded fort" near present-day Farmington, Pennsylvania, which he named Fort Necessity. On June 9, additional troops with supplies and nine small cannons arrived to reinforce Fort Necessity, which was now defended by 293 officers and soldiers. A few days later, 100 British regulars arrived, and an emboldened Washington prepared for victory. But, unfortunately for Washington, the French soldier who escaped Washington's earlier attack on de Jumonville managed to lead a sizable French force from Fort Duquesne back to the site of Washington's ambush.

On July 3, roughly 600 French soldiers and 100 Indian allies encircled Washington's small fort. To make matters worse, not only was Washington trapped and outmanned, but he had ignored the advice of Indians and his officers and unwisely selected a boggy hollow for the site of his fort. The French had the high ground and cover of the thick woods, while Washington's men were immobilized by heavy rains that turned the fort into a swamp. A brief skirmish ensued, resembling more shooting fish in a barrel than a battle. Washington lost one-third of his soldiers and was forced to surrender.

In the negotiations, Washington's troops were allowed to remain free and return to Virginia—which they did unceremoniously on July 4, 1754— but the terms of surrender forced the colonel to admit to the "assassination" of de Jumonville, aiding the French propaganda.

The Making of Greatness

Washington's war record was mixed, but even though it contained some inexcusable bungles, he won the respect of his countrymen. More important, he attracted for himself considerable fame and most likely gained confidence in his ability to command men. Still, Washington never really put to bed the insecurities of his upbringing. Years later, as the hero of the Revolution, a mature Washington was back home at Mount Vernon receiving a steady stream of well-wishers and outpouring of gratitude from the newly independent nation. Yet one of his priorities was gathering his youthful writings and correcting them for grammatical mistakes and misspellings before allowing them to be released to the public and copied for history. Even while serving as the nation's beloved first president, Washington, according to Thomas Jefferson, was "extremely affected by the attacks made and kept up on him in the public papers. I think he feels those things more than any person I ever met with."

It was the image-conscious Washington who, when traveling from town to town by carriage, often mounted his steed and checked the neatness of his uniform before presenting himself to the awaiting citizens. It was the image-conscious Washington who practiced the art of the proper bow, greeted the public from atop a raised dais, and even stared at himself in the mirror, all in an effort to present himself as he wanted others to know him.

At the Second Continental Congress in 1775, Washington was the only delegate to show up in full military regalia, yet claimed not to desire the command of the revolutionary army. Washington wore his French and Indian War uniform, which he had personally designed and which caused his fellow delegate, John Adams, to quip that Washington had so much gold embroidery affixed to his uniform that he doubted there would be enough in all of England to attire the British officers.

But Adams missed the point. The former colonel stood out among those gathered as one of the few who saw combat and stood a head taller than most. But Washington also wore his image with valor and not swagger. Washington's posture, his clothing, his firm jaw, and his fixed stare were all a part of his creation. The famous portraitist Gilbert Stuart, who painted Washington in strategic pose, noticed in his subject raw passions masked by a crafted image. Commented Stuart of Washington's juxtaposition of primal forces, "All his features were indicative of the most ungovernable passions, and had he been born in the forests . . . he would have been the fiercest man among the savage tribes."

Always a bit insecure about his intellect and inadequate education, Washington was a man of few words and not prone to eloquent oratory. One of the items of advice he passed on to his nephew was to "avoid becoming a babbler." Washington practiced what he preached. In 1758, at the end of his colonial military career, Washington was summoned to the Virginia House of Burgesses. The members were in the midst of a debate about the difficult question of how to defend the frontier and, related, wanted to thank Washington for his service in that matter. Speaker John Robinson asked the colonel to rise. Embarrassed, Washington simply stood before the burgesses without uttering a word, even though he had political aspirations, sufficient ego, and ample reason to launch into an "acceptance" speech. After what must have been an awkward moment of silence, Robinson mused, "Sit down, Mr. Washington, your modesty equals your valor."

But such examples are not meant to suggest that Washington was not bright or capable of decisiveness. Rather, Washington led by actions, not by words, contrasting him to his more cerebral and verbose peers who gathered at Philadelphia. Or, as he explained in his own words, "With me it has always been a maxim . . . rather to let my designs appear from my works than by my expressions." To Washington, reputation was everything. Eventually conquering enough of his insecurities, as general and later as president,

Washington was able to both request and act on the advice of his officers. A far less secure man would have felt threatened to solicit, much less welcome, such advice.

Throughout his life, Washington was a hard worker. He personally oversaw his farms even when he had hired others to do so and shared the difficult living conditions of his troops during the war. Moreover, through his suffering from an array of maladies—dysentery, fever, smallpox, violent headaches, rheumatism, and the loss of his aching teeth—he developed an inner strength and resolve while outwardly revealing few signs of discomfort. The general preferred stoicism to medicine. Of each physical ailment, military setback, or political challenge, Washington would characteristically remark, "Let it go as it came."

The awkward, insecure lad had willed himself to greatness. As his wartime friend, the Marquis de Lafayette, said of Washington, "Had he been a common soldier, he would have been the bravest in all the ranks; had he been an obscure citizen, all his neighbors would have respected him."

Lafayette, like many other men of the time, later named his son for Washington. At six feet two inches in height, with size thirteen shoes, broad shoulders, powerful hands, and an enormous head, Washington was a giant of a man. A big man even in the early twenty-first century, he literally towered over his peers in the eighteenth century. Washington was also the best horseman of his times, an avid foxhunter, and a rugged outdoorsman. Even when well advanced in age, Washington could easily match the physical abilities of men in their prime. He was the picture of strength and determination. With auburn hair, steel gray-blue eyes, and a prominent Roman nose, Washington looked the part.

The man who once ordered busts of Alexander the Great, Julius Caesar, the Duke of Marlborough, Frederick II of Prussia, and other noted leaders to adorn his home would equal the exploits of the lot of them. Washington would, most assuredly, approve of the famous painting by E. Leutze of him crossing the Delaware River standing in Napoleonic pose at the front of the lead boat, as surely would Sally Fairfax, who helped craft Washington's image and inspire his achievements.

Surveying a Future

After the passing of his father, the eleven-year-old Washington looked to his half-brother Lawrence as a father figure. Lawrence often shared stories of his travels and military campaigns as a member of the British navy with his younger sibling. The stories had a profound impact on Washington, who was growing increasingly ambitious and restless in his teenage years.

Frequently, George would visit Lawrence at his midsized home built by their father on the banks of the Potomac River. Lawrence had named the home and surrounding farm after his former commanding officer, Admiral Edward Vernon. As an adult, the home would pass to George's ownership, and he would improve the property through a series of enlargements and architectural enhancements. The Mount Vernon of his youth also provided Washington a glimpse into the lives of the colony's aristocracy, many of whom lived nearby, including the Fairfax family.

Washington, who had been working on his manners and longing for opportunity and excitement, was invited to join Lawrence and the Fairfaxes at parties at Mount Vernon and the Fairfax estate, Belvoir. Lawrence married very well, wedding Colonel William Fairfax's daughter, Anne. Another member of the powerful Fairfax family, Hannah Fairfax, married George's cousin, Warner Washington. Through marriage, new possibilities arose for the teenager, who now came into contact with the upper echelon of Virginia society. This was a whole new world for the strapping teen and one to which he hungered to belong. Around this time, George too decided that he would "marry up" socially.

At sixteen, George was invited to join the Fairfax family on missions to survey the surrounding frontier lands. As a boy, George had studied surveying and gained some experience measuring Lawrence's turnip field. The party traveled on horseback and camped under the stars in uncharted regions for many days, during which time they mapped out vast tracts of new territory. Fairfax's surveying trips were high adventure for young Washington. The teen also met Indians and, in addition to getting a kick out of watching their dances, learned much from them about the outdoors. These lessons would one day serve him well when fighting the British.

From that moment on, an unlikely relationship emerged between the portly English nobleman and the naive younger teenager. It was during this time that the sixteen-year-old Washington first met Fairfax's new wife, Sally.

A year later, in 1748, probably encouraged by Sally Fairfax, Washington started his own surveying business while continuing to work with the Fairfaxes in the Shenandoah Valley. Young Washington enjoyed some success and was known for his hard work, eagerness, and honesty. He was well liked by those employing his services.

A year later, at the age of eighteen, Washington was appointed surveyor of Culpeper County and started acquiring land. The following year, in 1750, tragedy struck when Lawrence became very ill. He died in 1752, and George was appointed by Governor Dinwiddie to fill his late half-brother's post at the rank of major with a salary of 100 pounds and command of the colony's southern district. Eventually, George would also inherit Lawrence's home, Mount Vernon.

Out of His League

After first meeting Sally Fairfax in December of his sixteenth year, Washington mustered the courage to knock on the door of Colonel Wilson Cary and request permission to court one of Sally's sisters. As such, the young, uneducated, and poor teenager found himself in the impossible position of aspiring to join the ranks of the Fairfax and Cary families. When Washington arrived at the Cary home, Sally's father is said to have glared at the wistful interloper with a mixture of disbelief and scorn before answering Washington: "If that is your mission here, sir, you may as well order your horse. My daughter has been accustomed to her coach and six." Colonel Cary's reference was to the six matching horses that pulled his daughter's carriage, not the broken-down farm animal owned by Washington. The door was slammed shut in the young man's face.

Sally was two years Washington's senior and had recently married George William Fairfax, Washington's surveying employer. The Cary family historian and descendant, Wilson Miles Cary, describes Washington as being vulnerable to the fairer sex: "In youth his heart seems to have been peculiarly susceptible to female influence." Cary believes Washington even tried to pursue Sally's sister, Mary, and quite possibly Sally too, along with other belles of Tidewater aristocracy. But the girls' father, Colonel Cary, summed up the impossible situation to his lovelorn, teenage neighbor, advising Washington that his daughter was "a princess out of thy star; this must not be."

Washington admitted that he had "fallen into a sadness" after the rejection. Such rejections seem to have helped to inspire his desire to achieve greatness. One story, the veracity of which remains in question, has Washington riding triumphantly through the streets of Williamsburg, Virginia, many years later at the head of his victorious revolutionary army. While doing so, the general noticed a lady watching him with great admiration but also turmoil because it turned out that she was one of the women who rejected his youthful advances. Washington saluted her with his sword, and she is said to have fainted at the gesture.

It has been suggested that the lady in question was Sally's sister, Mary. But this is doubtful because Washington's gallant parade through Williamsburg did not take place until after Lord Cornwallis and the British surrendered in October 1781. Sally's sister, Mary Cary Ambler, died a few months earlier in May of the same year. On the other hand, it is possible that the event happened but that either the city or the lady in question differed.

Sally's husband, George William Fairfax, was George Washington's Tidewater neighbor. Fairfax looked kindly on Washington. He was wealthy, older, sophisticated, and apparently unthreatened by his young neighbor's adulation of his wife. Lawrence Washington married Anne Fairfax and enjoyed a close relationship with her family, and Lawrence's home, Mount Vernon, was conveniently located near the Fairfax estate, Belvoir.

For a few happy years, Lawrence Washington and his wife resided at Mount Vernon, located on a hill overlooking the Potomac River. After Lawrence's death in the summer of 1752, the home passed to his widow and their young daughter. But when the daughter died and the widow quickly remarried and moved away from Mount Vernon in 1754, the home belonged to George.

THE FAIRFAXES OF VIRGINIA

Sarah "Sally" Cary Fairfax was a member of two of Virginia's wealthiest families. A number of accounts of Sally by her contemporaries spoke of her as the epitome of grace and beauty, a sophisticated yet playful and very popular woman. The historian Professor Stevenson offered a particularly flamboyant description of her: "Mrs. Fairfax was a charming young person with beautiful eyes and an ironical mouth—her portrait being the evidence—so sure of herself that she could flirt with the Evil One and with no depressing results—except perhaps to His Satanic Majesty."

The Cary family was described as "allied by blood to well-nigh every historic family in the State." Records of the family dating to the sixteenth century show the Carys to enjoy a prominent status even then and to hail from the Devonshire region of England. The first of Sally's direct bloodline to come to America was her great-grandfather, Colonel Miles Cary (1620–1667), of Warwick, England, who arrived in Virginia in the mid-seventeenth century and acquired land and prospered.

The Cary family estate, Ceelys on the James River, was one of the largest in the colony. It was at Ceelys where Sally was born in 1730. Sally's father, Colonel Wilson Cary (1703–1772), was the grandson of that first Cary to come to the colony. Sally's father inherited Ceelys and was one of the region's leading men and a member of the House of Burgesses. Because of a fire in 1826 that destroyed the family home and records, not much is known about Sally's mother, Sarah Pate, except that she was an elegant and respected woman from a prominent family.

Colonel and Mrs. Cary had four daughters, the eldest of them being Sally. Beautiful, intelligent, witty, lively, and well regarded throughout the region, Sally appeared to be exceptionally well educated both under her father's guidance and most likely by the best tutors in the area. She was fluent in French and well read by the standards of women of her day or any day. Sally was also the toast of Tidewater aristocracy and, apparently, of a number of would-be suitors. Not surprisingly, she was courted "far and wide" by the sons of prominent families. Cary family history records numerous examples of Sally's popularity and beauty.

One of the stories notes that Sally was so well known that, while riding in a carriage to attend a social function at military headquarters, she encountered an armed sentry guarding the camp. The soldier stopped her and asked her for the password she needed to be admitted to headquarters. When Sally replied that she did not know the password, she was asked her name. When the sentry discovered the identity of the beautiful visitor, he immediately allowed her to pass through the line because the officers had selected her name as the password.

Eighteen-year-old Sally married George William Fairfax, heir to a title and vast estate. On December 17, 1748, the *Virginia Gazette* newspaper posted the announcement as follows: "Married, on the 17th inst., George William Fairfax of His Majesty's Council, to Sarah, eldest daughter of Colonel Wilson Cary of Ceelys." George Fairfax's father was one of the most powerful men of his time. A widower, the elder Fairfax had raised his son in England, remained in the good graces of British society, and was known for hosting the grandest of balls in Alexandria and Williamsburg. Curiously, an unsubstantiated smear on Colonel Fairfax's good name was that he kept a black mistress and that his son, George, was the child of that illicit union.

George Fairfax and his wife Sally lived at Belvoir, a handsome and expansive estate built in the seventeenth century. The marriage was somewhat arranged, bringing together the two prominent families. But, if not passionate, it was nonetheless a solid marriage. One of Sally's children, named for his grandfather Wilson, would one day marry Jean Carr, daughter of Dabney and Martha Carr. By marriage, this union aligned the Cary and Fairfax families with Thomas Jefferson's family. Jean Carr was Thomas Jefferson's niece by way of his sister Martha.

In the Tidewater region, courtship season coincided with the high social season, which occurred in the winter. Formal receptions were held at the governor's palace in Williamsburg, and leading families hosted teas, parties, and dances. The four Cary daughters took their place at the forefront of these events. Like Sally, her sisters, as they say, also "married well." Sister Mary married the heir to Jamestown Island, Edward Ambler; sister Anne married Robert Carter Nicholas, the colony's treasurer; and the youngest Cary daughter, Elizabeth, married another Fairfax brother, Bryan Fairfax.

Belvoir

Some of the happiest moments of George Washington's life and his fondest memories involved Belvoir. As a naive sixteen-year-old, Washington was quite smitten not only by Sally but also by the place she called home. Belvoir was a mansion featuring many guest rooms and probably the most elegant furnishings and dining room that the young Washington had ever seen. The 2,000-acre estate included stables, farms, an orchard, and slave and servant quarters. At Belvoir, the Fairfaxes raised tobacco, corn, and other profitable agricultural products. Sally also maintained a large garden on the grounds that featured her favorite flowers, such as posies and daffodils.

During the social season, Sally would "grace and charm the social circle that centered at Belvoir." Belvoir provided George Washington with his first taste of the lifestyle that he only dreamed of and afforded him exposure to the leading citizens of the region who would soon change his life. As he wrote in 1748 shortly after meeting Sally, during one of the first of his many visits to Belvoir, "I might, was my heart disengaged, pass my time very pleasantly as there's a very agreeable young lady lives in the same house."

Indeed, young Washington wrote to a friend of the great desire he felt while in the company of Sally and her sister Mary at Belvoir. But the impossibility of acquiring the hand of one of the Cary women also revived in Washington memories of the many disappointments he experienced while attempting to court above his social station in life. One girl from the lowlands of the Virginia coast caught Washington's eye:

> Only adding fuel to the fire, it makes me the more uneasy for, by often and unavoidably being in the company with her, revives my former passion for your Low Land Beauty, whereas was I to live more retired from young women, I might in some measure alleviate my sorrows by burying that chaste and troublesome passion in the grave of oblivion or eternal forgetfulness.

Even after his marriage to Martha Custis, George Washington and Sally Fairfax remained in one another's company. The couples frequently dined, played cards, and danced together; went for carriage rides; and visited the same homes during the social season. Presumably, George and Sally danced together, as it is well documented that Mrs. Washington did not dance but that her husband did. Washington's enjoyment of dancing was matched only by his skill and the number of willing partners who lined up for the privilege of his attention.

The letters exchanged by George and Sally were long and warm and signaled the unmistakable closeness and trust the two shared. Washington signed his letters to Sally, "Y[ou]r. most obedient most obliged H[um]ble. Serv[ant]" or "I am most unalterably Your most obed[ien]t. and Obl[i]g[e]d." Both waited in anticipation for the next letter or visit from the other, which was evident in the passionate tone of their writings when they were separated. For instance, in response to Sally "apologizing" for the excessive length and warmth of one of her letters, Washington wrote the following:

> One thing more and then [I] have done. You ask if I am not tired at the length of your letter. No, Madam, I am not, nor never can be while the lines are an Inch asunder to bring you in haste to the end of the paper. You may be tired of mine by this.

The Braddock Affair

Washington had sought glory on the battlefield since his youth when he reveled in stories that his older half-brother, Lawrence, told him about serving in the navy. In 1753 and 1754, Washington received a commission as a major—later a lieutenant colonel—in the Virginia colonial militia. These first years in uniform coincide with the critical time of Sally Fairfax's most profound influence on Washington, and it was she who inspired him to bravery and glory, emboldened his confidence, and honed his ambition.

After the mixed record of his command in the Jumonville affair and the Fort Necessity embarrassment, Washington was fortunate to be assigned as a senior aide-de-camp to the dashing British general Edward Braddock. Although he would not know it, Washington was headed for a third disastrous battle. After the colonial governors appealed to the Crown to address the growing threat from the French, Major General Braddock was dispatched to defeat the French in the Ohio Valley, something that Washington had been trying unsuccessfully to accomplish.

Two infantry regiments arrived with Braddock. The general, a career soldier with forty-five years of military service behind him, assumed the role of commander of all British and colonial forces in North America. By 1755, the conflict had become a difficult and protracted campaign throughout the frontier borders of the colonies. But fighting slowed during the winter social season, and the toast of Williamsburg's season that year was the charming British general, who was much admired by the ladies in attendance.

Both Sally and Washington were in attendance at the winter socials in the colonial capital in 1755. It is probable that Braddock, who was known for his appetite for attractive women, had his eyes on Sally. It also appears that Sally at least felt complimented by the general's attention.

Even though Sally was married, it was not uncommon for innocent flirtations to spark at dances and simmer throughout the social galas, where noncouples danced and dined together. However, at one point during a gala, Braddock's attentions were otherwise engaged by a Mrs. Wardrope, bruising Sally's ego, as she was not used to rejections. In a letter to Washington that no longer exists, Sally must have pondered the keys to Braddock's heart and his reasons for falling for Mrs. Wardrope because Washington wrote her back from the battlefield with an answer. With a lightheartedness rarely seen in letters written by Washington, he explained Braddock's choice in a way that was surely designed to make Sally feel better:

> I have at last with great pains and difficulty discovered the reason why Mrs. Wardrope is a greater favorite of Genl. Braddock than Mrs. F[airfa]x, and met with more respect at the review in Alexandria. The cause I shall communicate, after having rallied you upon neglecting the means which produced the effect. And what do you think they were? Why, nothing less, I assure you, than a present of delicious cake and potted wood-cocks! which so affected the palate as to leave a deep impression upon the hearts of all who tasted them. How, then, could the General do otherwise than admire, not only the charms, but the politeness, of this lady!

According to the love-struck Washington, the way to a man's heart was through the stomach, even in the case of the lustful Braddock. We do not know Sally's response after receiving the letter, but surely she appreciated Washington's affectionate and teasing tone.

In the spring, the social season winded down, and Braddock's army set out to engage the French at Fort Duquesne. Washington had written to Sally within one day of departing on his mission. Shortly thereafter, on May 30, he was sent by Braddock back to Williamsburg to procure additional supplies for the army. Washington used the occasion to visit with Sally. During the brief interlude at Belvoir, Washington's passion for Sally was apparently in full display, causing both of them to worry that perhaps he was being too forward and obvious in his feelings for her. Innocent flirtations during the gaiety of a social ball were one thing, but Washington was visiting a married woman and friend while on a military mission of the highest order.

From surviving letters, it seems that Sally tried to defuse any appearance of impropriety by having Washington start sending news of his military exploits to her family and friends rather than directly to her. Although her request is understandable, Washington nevertheless fretted over its meaning. In a letter written on June 7, 1755, one week after his visit, Washington worried about their visit and friendship:

When I had the happiness to see you last you express'd an inclination to be inform'd of my safe arrival in Camp with the Charge that was entrusted to my care, But at the same time desir'd it might be communicated in a Letter to somebody of your acquaintance. This I took as a gentle rebuke and a polite manner of forbidding my corresponding with you: and [I] conceive this opinion is not ill founded when I reflect that I have hitherto found it impracticable to engage one moment of your attention. If I am right in this, I hope you will excuse the present presumption and lay the imputation to elateness at my successful arrival. If, on the contrary, these are fearful apprehensions only, how easy is it to remove my suspicions, enliven my spirits, and make me happier than the day is long, by honouring me with a correspondence which you did once partly promise to do.

Back in the field that summer, Washington was part of a force of 2,400 British infantry, colonial volunteers, and Indians under Braddock's command. Braddock called for a simultaneous attack against French forts in the Ohio Valley and decided that he would personally lead the expedition against Fort Duquesne. Ironically, the army followed the same trail through the wooded mountains that Washington had hacked out of the wilderness a year earlier during the Jumonville affair to attack the very same fort whose men had crushed Washington's command at Fort Necessity.

The problem was that the trail was narrow and uneven. Braddock ordered his army to widen the path to twelve feet in order to accommodate wagons and cannons. This slowed progress to a snail's pace and occasioned a great expense of time and energy. It also gave the enemy time to prepare. Braddock further weakened his position by dividing his army into two commands—Braddock in the lead with most of the men and a few cannons and a second force under the command of Colonel Dunbar following a few days behind.

By early July, Braddock's army had finally reached the forks of the Ohio River, crossed the Monongahela River, and closed in on Fort Duquesne in southwestern Pennsylvania. Unfortunately for his army, General Braddock's graces did not extend to military strategy. His skill fell far short of the length of his service. A number of fateful decisions left Braddock's army vulnerable. On July 13, 1755, after crossing the river, the long line of Braddock's forces was attacked on both sides. Volleys of musket fire poured out from the cover of the forest, unseen except for the pillows of smoke that covered the narrow trail. From the cover of the forest, French troops and their Indian allies sprang on the officers at the front of the column, killing many. As Braddock's front lines attempted to fall back, their retreat was blocked by the mass of the remainder of the 1,400-man army.

With Braddock shot and six of his eight officers dead or dying at the head of the army, panic seized the troops. Soldiers began to flee but were blocked from doing so by the large number of men on the narrow trail. The massacre lasted three hours, and the British sustained 900 casualties before managing to retreat. An army that was said to be invincible was, in short order, decimated. The British might have been aided by the native tribes in the area, but after General Braddock dismissed an offer of alliance by the powerful Delaware chief Shingas, the warriors joined the French.

All might have been lost on the trail to Fort Duquesne if not for the quick thinking and courage of Colonel Washington, one of two officers not killed in the initial strike. Washington managed to orchestrate a reasonably organized retreat. While riding bravely among the men and between them and the French attackers, all the while shouting out orders, Washington had two horses shot out from under him. Bullets ripped through his coat but did not harm him. Indians who witnessed the fighting spoke of Washington as a spirit who could not be killed. The Reverend Samuel Davies, an influential Presbyterian minister, preached that providence had saved Washington "for some important service to his country." The Davies sermon would later be reprinted in a newspaper in Philadelphia, further contributing to Washington's growing fame.

It was Washington who saved the army from total annihilation that day. A far more humbled Washington than just one year before, when he boasted of the "charming" sound of bullets during his first battle, recorded his feelings after the fight: "The shocking scenes which presented themselves in this Nights march are not to be described. The dead, the dying, the groans, lamentations, and crys . . . of the wounded for help were enough to pierce a heart of adamant." The straggling remnants of the army, carrying their dying general, beat a hasty retreat to reunite with Colonel Dunbar's forces. Ironically, they made camp just one mile from Great Meadows, where Washington had built Fort Necessity the previous year. That evening, General Braddock died. It was said by the attending physician that his death was a result of anxiety rather than his battlefield wounds. Washington presided at the burial the next morning. Then, as the army headed back east away from the site of the ambush, Washington ordered the men to march over the site of Braddock's grave, thereby erasing any sign of its location lest the French and Indians discover it. Washington later recorded his thoughts about Braddock: "Thus died a man, whose good and bad qualities were intimately blended. He was brave even to a fault and in regular Service would have done honour to his profession. His attachments were warm, his enmities were strong, and having no disguise about him, both appeared in full force."

Whether or not Washington believed in the adulation he received or the providence attributed to him, his bravery during the ambush was but one instance of his courage under fire. Later, in a nighttime conflict when his men began accidentally firing against one another, Washington stepped in front of the volleys and, with his sword, knocked the aim of the muskets up in the air and stopped the firing.

After the disastrous Braddock campaign, the next few years were challenging for Washington. The French and their Indian allies had capitalized on their victory over Braddock by terrorizing settlers on the western edge of the colonies. Panic descended on the Crown's subjects, many of them fleeing back east as the war spread. As a colonel with slightly more than 300 men and too few supplies in his command, Washington was impossibly charged with defending the Shenandoah Valley and western frontier of Virginia during this time. His requests for more supplies and men, like his repeated requests for a regular commission in the Royal Army, were flatly denied.

Washington, however, emerged from the Braddock defeat a hero. Tempered by battle, his character was hardening. Yet command in a colonial regiment bore no resemblance to command in the British army. Even a colonel in the colonials was, technically, under the command of a new lieutenant commissioned from the Crown. The reality of his stagnant military situation festered. Growing increasingly frustrated and discouraged with his station, Washington attempted in both 1755 and 1757 to gain a seat in the Virginia House of Burgesses. He lost both elections. Washington frequently turned to Sally, who consoled him and offered him advice.

Letters from the Front

Sally Fairfax saw Washington off when the twenty-three-year-old lieutenant colonel joined Braddock's army prior to the doomed siege of Fort Duquesne. She was both a source of inspiration for Washington during the battle and a trusted confidante with whom Washington could discuss his true feelings about the war. For instance, after the crushing defeat by the French, Washington was both outraged by the incompetence of the campaign and worried about any possible detrimental effects to his own reputation because of his association with it. He confided in Sally in a way that he did with no other, admitting that "so miserably has this expedition been managed" that he assumed that everyone associated with it would be "condemned" by history. His continued frustration with his military career was underscored by his longing to impress Sally by achieving a higher rank.

Washington was on good terms with the Fairfax family and had written to them about his well-being during his military campaigns. However, he showed bad form by indiscreetly imposing on Sally's family members with repeated requests to have them ask her to write to him. Sally maintained an active correspondence with Washington during the war but was limiting the frequency of her letters so as to not cross the line of their innocent relationship and to gently give the same hint to Washington. He could not get enough of her letters and seemed unaware of his indiscretions. In so doing, he crossed the line of propriety.

Sally's brother-in-law, Bryan Fairfax, and possibly other family members expressed concern about the nature of Sally's friendship with Washington. Bryan noticed and was scandalized by the closeness of the two. Writing to Washington, Bryan encouraged Washington to focus on fighting the enemy, which was, after all, "a nobler prospect" than "reflections of hours" on Sally. About Washington's possible intentions, Bryan suggested that the young officer should "banish them from your thoughts." Bryan Fairfax apparently also rebuked Sally for how flirtatious and forward she was with the young colonel, and it seems that Sally's relationship with her husband's brother soured as a result of the incident.

Bryan Fairfax was the third son of Colonel William Fairfax and younger brother of George William Fairfax, Sally's husband. Bryan married Sally's younger sister, Elizabeth Cary, and lived near them in the town of Alexandria. Like his older brother and sister-in-law, Bryan was loyal to the Crown, but unlike them, he did not return to England during the upcoming revolutionary conflict.

So well regarded was the third Fairfax brother that he and his immediate family were not harassed by patriotic colonials during the Revolution, unlike the fate that befell other Tories remaining in the former colonies during the fighting. But the Fairfax family suffered the fate of two wars. Not only did the Revolutionary War separate the family and uproot them from their Virginia homes, but the ongoing conflict with the French killed two of Colonel William Fairfax's sons while in service of the Crown. In 1746, one son died in the Indian Ocean during an engagement with a French warship, the other in 1759 during the siege of Quebec.

Despite their political differences and the tension over his relationship with Sally, Washington retained his closeness to Bryan Fairfax, writing him periodically. Or it is possible that Washington simply continued niceties with Sally's brother-in-law out of a longing to see Sally. During the Revolutionary War, a letter written from Valley Forge on March 1, 1778, to Bryan stated,

> The friendship which I ever professed and felt for you met with no diminution from the difference in our political sentiments. I know the rectitude of my own intentions, and, believing in the sincerity of yours, lamented, though I did not condemn, your renunciation of the creed I had adored.

While fighting the French, Washington was often "homesick" during the time from 1753 to 1759 when he was away from his Tidewater home and friends. The letters he received from Sally remained foremost in his thoughts. When Washington initially resigned from his command in the Virginia militia in late 1754, it appears that he did so partly because of Sally. Washington biographer Rupert Hughes claims that the then-major was depressed and pining away for Sally. Scholars believe that Washington resigned largely for three reasons: Washington had a number of disagreements with Governor Dinwiddie, he had inherited Mount Vernon in December of 1754 and was very eager to finally be the master of such a home and to "fix it up," and he longed to again be near Sally.

She lifted his spirits sufficiently that, after the social season of February and March of 1755, Washington had reenlisted as a volunteer aide to General Braddock. In fact, Professor Hughes wondered if Washington did not join the Braddock campaign because Braddock was so popular during the social season. Washington wanted to be Braddock, a dashing, popular, and powerful general. By joining Braddock's officer corps, Washington might also impress Sally.

After surviving the fateful Braddock campaign of 1755, one of the first things Washington did was write to the Fairfax family with news of the battle for Sally. He then departed for home. Just days after the battle, the Fairfax patriarch, William Fairfax, wrote expressing to Washington his pleasure that he had returned safe and sound. Attached to the letter was a note from his daughter-in-law, Sally, that read,

> After thanking Heaven for your safe return, I must accuse you of great unkindness in refusing us the pleasure of seeing you this night. I do assure you nothing but being satisfied that our company would be disagreeable should prevent us from trying if our Legs would not carry us to Mount Virnon this Night; but if you will not come to us tomorrow morning, very early, we shall be at Mount Virnon.

The lighthearted admonishment from Sally for not stopping to see her immediately points to Sally's obvious feelings for Washington. Washington paid his respects to the Fairfax family, visiting them the very next day.

THE OTHER "OTHER WOMAN"

"Tributes of Affection"

Washington served much of his two terms as president in Philadelphia. The nation's capital city—which would one day bear his name—was still being built. In Philadelphia, Washington enjoyed an unusually close, trusting relationship with Elizabeth Willing Powel, wife of the city's leading merchant and mayor. Their friendship predated the Revolutionary War and involved much letter writing.

On the completion of his second term in office in March 1797, Washington departed the city and, six days later, arrived home at Mount Vernon. To lighten his load, Washington gave away and sold at public auction some of the furnishings and belongings from his presidency. A few days after arriving at Mount Vernon, he received a letter from Mrs. Powel informing him that she had discovered something in his large, rolltop desk, hidden in one of the many small drawers. She described her find as "a large bundle" of Washington's "love letters to a lady." She wrote to Washington, "Yet I will with the Generosity of my Sex relieve you, by telling you that upon opening one of the Drawers of your writing Desk I found a large Bundle of Letters from Mrs. Washington bound up and leveled with your usual Accuracy." The letters were inadvertently left behind by Washington and might have proven embarrassing for such a public man. According to Mrs. Powel, "Tho' curiosity is supposed to be a prominent Feature of the female Mind," she assured him that she did not open the letters and sealed them three times over with a personal seal. Despite her claim, we do not know if Mrs. Powel opened and read the letters, but it would seem that, even though Washington organized his letters methodically, she would have had to read them in order to know their contents. What is obvious is that she absolutely delighted in the discovery. Indeed, she relished in the irony that such a careful, image-conscious man would be so careless, and she chided him—as almost no one else dared to do—that she never knew him to make such "blunders."

In possession of highly personal letters, Mrs. Powel wished to discharge herself of the responsibility. So she wrote to Washington's trusted aide, Tobias Lear, who was still in Philadelphia, and asked him to personally deliver the "large bundle" to Washington. As she put it, "Mr. Lear was present, I immediately desired him to take Charge of the Package,—which he declined doing, alleging that he thought it safer in my Hands." It is surprising—and potentially insightful—that Lear refused. Lear had also helped Mr. and Mrs. Washington with their public and private correspondence and was a member of their household who would later marry into the family. Mrs. Powel stated that she even repeatedly "urged Lear but he was inflexible." Why would the ever-loyal Lear so uncharacteristically fail to comply with a request from such a prominent woman and close friend of Washington? We will likely never know the answer, but it suggests that something else was involved in the correspondence or that the letters were not those from Washington's wife.

Lear, like Washington and Powel, appears to have recognized the sensitivity of the letters.

Mrs. Powel sealed the letters and sent the package directly to Washington, writing to her close friend on March 11, 1797, two days after his departure from Philadelphia,

> My very dear Sir Like a true Woman (as you will think) in the Moment of Exultation, and on the first Impulse (for you know we are never supposed to act Systematically or from attentive Consideration), I take up my Pen to address you, as you have given me a complete Triumph on the Subject of all others on which you have I suppose thought me most deficient, and most opposite to yourself; and what is still more charming—Your Candor shall preside as Judge,—nay you shall pass Sentence on yourself, and I will not appeal from your Decision. Suppose I should prove incontestably—that you have without Design put into my Possession the Love Letters of a lady addressed to you under the most solemn Sanction; & a large Packet too.

Mrs. Powel closed her letter by expressing some concern about Mrs. Washington worrying about the content of the letters. She thanks Washington for his "Tribute of Affection"—meaning his desk and an apparent gift of lamps—but says that only from him would she accept such an item without paying. Not only does Mrs. Powel's letter reveal her delight in making Washington uneasy about the letters, but it also drips with innuendo, such as when she states that she did not want the letter to cause him to think of her. Many of her letters to Washington were similarly playful and flirtatious.

George Washington answered Mrs. Powel's letter shortly after receiving it. Writing to her on March 26, 1797, he goes to great lengths to downplay the whole matter either out of embarrassment or out of jest. Washington described the letters as belonging to his wife and being anything but "love" letters. Echoing Mrs. Powel's cryptic and teasing tone, Washington answered,

> Had it not been for one circumstance, which bye the bye is a pretty material one . . . that I had no love letters to lose . . . your letter would have caused a serious alarm; and might have tried how far my nerves were able to sustain the shock of having betrayed the confidence of a lady. But although I had nothing to apprehend on that score, I am not less surprised at my having left those of Mrs. Washington' in my writing desk; when, as I supposed I had emptied all the drawers; mistaken in this however. I have to thank you for the delicacy with which they have been treated. But admitting that they had fallen into more inquisitive hands, the correspondence would, I am persuaded, have been found to be more fraught with

expressions of friendship, than of *enamoured* love, and, consequently, if the ideas of the possessor of them, with respect to the latter passion, should have been of the *Romantic* order to have given them the warmth, which was not inherent, they might have been consigned to the flames.

The "Saucy" Mrs. Powel

It is fortunate for Washington—and perhaps also ironic—that it was Mrs. Powel who discovered the letters. Who was Elizabeth Willing Powel? "Eliza" was Philadelphia's most famous socialite and capable hostess. John Adams, one of many prominent guests she entertained, spoke fondly of Eliza's extravagant galas with their "sinful dinners." Another admirer described her as being "a saucy, interesting, attractive, intelligent, flirtatious woman . . . the epitome of confidence, determination, and class."

Surviving portraits show an attractive woman with a long, slender neck; light-blue eyes; smooth complexion with soft features; and an elegant bearing. Born in 1743 to Charles Willing and Ann Shippen, Eliza both came from money and married into even more money when, in 1769, she wed Samuel Powel. The Powels first came to the colonies from England in 1685 and established themselves through both industry and opportune marriages as one of Philadelphia's foremost families. After dropping the second "l" in his last name, Samuel Powel became the city's leading merchant and earned the nickname "The Patriotic Mayor" while serving as Philadelphia's last colonial mayor before the Revolution and first after the Revolution.

Eliza was one of Washington's closest intimates—and more. Eliza shared many traits with Sally Cary Fairfax, Washington's beautiful, older neighbor and mentor. Not surprisingly, Washington relished Eliza's company, and Eliza Powel was so moved by her friend that she composed verses in honor of him, such as on the occasion of the president's sixtieth birthday. The Washingtons were frequently guests of the Powels and dined and lodged at the Powel home, even celebrating their twentieth wedding anniversary there. The Powel estate also inspiring some of the famous improvements Washington made to his home, Mount Vernon. On occasion, the general even attended Mrs. Powel's parties and galas without his wife, and thus the two danced the night away together.

As was mentioned earlier, Washington was noted for his dancing. Benjamin Franklin's daughter once attended a social event where she observed the general in action. Writing to her famous father, she described Washington dancing for three straight hours on the second-floor ballroom of the Powel mansion. This was not uncharacteristic. One admiring woman wrote to a friend that "General Washington throws off the hero and takes on the chatty, agreeable companion, he can be down right imprudent sometimes—such imprudence . . . as you and I like."

Every summer, Philadelphians of means would escape the summer heat and diseases that plagued the times. Thus, during the yellow fever panic in August of 1793, Washington repeatedly invited—even begged—the Powels to stay at Mount Vernon. When it was clear that the couple refused to abandon their city, Washington also chose to remain in Philadelphia with the Powels and against the advice of his friends and aides. Sadly, Samuel Powel was one of the many victims of that epidemic, and Eliza's relationship with Washington grew closer after the mayor's passing.

Washington greatly valued the independent-minded Eliza's counsel, and she freely gave it. Eliza Powel loved politics and was keenly perceptive of people. While Washington was grappling with questions about his presidency, she cautioned, "Be assured that a great deal of the well-earned popularity that you are now in possession of will be torn from you by the envious and malignant should you follow your inclinitions." When Washington was considering retirement after a single term in the presidency, Eliza joined others in urging him to remain in office. The country was not yet on firm footing. It needed him, she advised.

Eliza's pleas to Washington seem to have resonated with him far more than those of others both because she was a close friend and because she knew so well Washington's personality and desire for fame. Washington was famously guarded when it came to his feelings, and he kept an emotional distance from those around him. Yet it is clear that the general opened up his personal life to Eliza, like he did with Sally Fairfax, letting out his frustrations about his lack of a formal education and unhappy childhood. She was one of the very few people—along with Sally Fairfax and his wife, Martha (and possibly Mrs. Robert Liston, the wife of a Scottish diplomat)—to be truly privy to the inner Washington. Eliza understood Washington's dual nature of being filled with insecurities yet boldly longing for fame. In a way, they were kindred spirits who shared a dark susceptibility to self-doubt but exuded public confidence. Because she understood him, she could both motivate and flatter him. Such was the case when she wrote with a plea for Washington to remain in office for a second term because he was

> the only man in America that dares to do right on all public occasions. . . .
> You have shown that you are not to be intoxicated by power or misled by
> flattery. You have a feeling heart and the long necessity of behaving with
> circumspection must have tempered that native benevolence which might
> otherwise make you too compliant. . . . For God's sake, do not yield that
> empire to a love of ease. . . . You love philosophical retirement; convince

the world, then, that you are a practical philosopher and that your native philanthropy has induced you to relinquish an object so essential to your happiness.

Eliza understood Washington well enough to know that, while he longed to return to Mount Vernon, he needed to secure the nation and his legacy. She even goaded him when he affirmed his interest in retirement by asking him, "Have you not often experienced that your judgment was fallible with respect to your happiness?" The noted historian Richard Norton Smith concluded, "Few had ever used such unvarnished language in addressing Great Washington, but Mrs. Powel was rarely shy about deploying her strongest weapons, beginning with Washington's famous sensitivity to public opinion." Washington was eager to retire to Mount Vernon. Despite this fact, a few months after leaving Philadelphia, he returned for a five-week stay in early autumn. For some reason, Washington did not promote his visit, nor did he arrange it as a triumphant return that one might expect for someone with Washington's sense of image and accomplishments. In fact, city elders barely had time enough to plan a suitable welcome for the former president. Crowds did gather at the spur of the moment to catch a glimpse of the hero of the Revolution. Washington also came without his wife and stayed at Mrs. White's boardinghouse on Eighth Street. During his long visit, he spent a lot of time with his friend, the widow Eliza Powel, who canceled all social commitments to have breakfasts, lunches, dinners, walks, and carriage rides with her dear friend. The unstated purpose of Washington's trip seems to have been to visit Eliza.

It is not possible to determine whether Washington's special relationship with Mrs. Powel—like that of his relationship with Sally Fairfax—ever became physical. But both women brought out a warmer, more personal, and playful side of the serious Washington. Washington's relationship with Sally and Eliza was such that both women felt free to express themselves in ways that were flirtatious, forceful, and highly personal; at the same time, the general, who opened up to nearly no one, opened up to them.

After Washington's death, Martha Washington fulfilled a request by Eliza Powel and sent her a lock of the general's hair. Eliza cherished it until her death, and the memento can now be seen on display at the preserved Powel home on Third Street in Philadelphia.

"THE HAPPIEST IN MY LIFE"

The rising tensions through the early 1770s between the colonists and the Crown suggested the possibility of war. The Fairfax family, loyal to the

Crown and worried about their vast fortune, decided to move back to mother England in 1773. Their good friend and neighbor George Washington was put in charge of renting the Belvoir estate in their absence. Eventually, when it was obvious that the Fairfaxes would not be returning anytime soon, Washington had the heart-wrenching task of auctioning the home in 1774.

This he did. But of all the items in the Fairfax estate, the only one Washington purchased for himself at the auction was Sally's silk bedroom pillow, which remained in his possession until his own death. One can only imagine the memories and feelings it evoked during the ensuing years that forged a nation.

Although the family intended to return to Virginia after the British squelched the revolutionary fervor of the upstart colonists, the return never happened. George Washington never again saw the object of his affection. The Fairfaxes never crossed the Atlantic again. George William Fairfax would lose much of his vast holdings and wealth in Virginia. He died in Bath, England, on April 3, 1787, at age sixty-three without ever attaining the family title. His death occurred just days before Washington would depart for Philadelphia to preside over the Constitutional Convention.

After winning the Revolution and setting the new nation on its path as the inaugural president, in 1796 Washington's attentions again returned to Belvoir. He attempted to sell the entire estate to Sir John Sinclair. Washington's surviving letters show his honesty and attachment to Belvoir, as he admitted the pain of seeing the property fall into disrepair. Sinclair never bought the property, the land remained idle for several years, and eventually the buildings were lost to fire.

What Might Have Been

After leaving the presidency in 1797, Washington returned to Mount Vernon. There, he retired on the edge of the Potomac River, living another two years before his death on December 14, 1799. In retirement, Washington's thoughts returned not only to Belvoir but also to the estate's mistress who occupied a special place in his heart. In surviving letters, Washington twice admits to spending the happiest moments of his life at Belvoir with Sally Fairfax. One of the two letters was written by Washington just one year after his presidency. It bears the passion of the restless, young bachelor who was so long ago bewitched by his beautiful, older neighbor. But the words were written in the autumn of Washington's life and after nearly four decades of marriage to his wife, Martha.

In a way, the letter is a fitting close to the relationship, for it began with Washington's audacious ambition and awkward admiration of Sally. And it concluded in a letter written from the vantage point of a man who had attained reverence and glory beyond his wildest dreams. The "Father of His Nation" had returned to where it all started and was introspective, perhaps pondering what might have been.

Sally Fairfax was a sixty-eight-year-old widow when she received the letter. Slipping the ocean of distance between them, Washington penned one of the most touching and loving verses of his life, revealing that Sally was never far from his thoughts. One May 16, 1798, from his home at Mount Vernon, the former tongue-tied admirer wrote,

> Five and twenty years have nearly passed away since I have considered myself as the permanent resident at this place, or have been in a situation to indulge myself in a familiar intercourse with my friends by letter or otherwise. During this period so many important events have occurred and such changes in men and things have taken place as the compass of a letter would give you but an inadequate idea of. None of which events, however, nor all of them together, have been able to eradicate from my mind the recollection of those happy moments, the happiest in my life, which I have enjoyed in your company.
>
> Worn out in a manner by the toils of my past labour, I am again seated under my vine and fig tree, and I wish I could add that there were none to make us afraid; but those whom we have been accustomed to call our good friends and allies, are endeavouring if not to make us afraid, yet to despoil us of our property, and are provoking us to acts of self defence which may lead to war. What will be the result of such measure, time, that faithful expositor of all things, must disclose. My wish is to spend the remainder of my days, which cannot be many, in rural amusements, free from the cares from which public responsibility is never exempt. Before the war, and even while it existed, although I was eight years from home at one stretch (except the en passant visits made to it on my marches to and from the siege of Yorktown), I made considerable additions to my dwelling houses and alterations in my offices and gardens; but the dilapidation occasioned by time and those neglects which are co-extensive with the absence of proprietors, have occupied as much of my time within the last twelve months in repairing them, as at any former period in the same space: and it is a matter of sore regret, when I cast my eyes towards Belvoir, which I often do, to reflect, the former inhabitants of it with whom we lived in such harmony and friendship no longer reside there and that the ruins can only be viewed as the memento of former pleasures. Permit me to add that I have wondered often, your nearest relations being in this country, that you should not prefer spending the evening of your life among them, rather than close the sublunary scene in a foreign country, numerous as your acquaintances may be and sincere as the friendships you may have formed.

The historian and descendant of Sally, Wilson Cary, concluded that Washington could not erase Sally from his mind or heart. All Washington's battles, his sturdy marriage, the accolades of political triumph, and the long separation of distance and time together, suggested Cary, "failed to obliterate the traces of that passion which still slumbered in his heart till almost the day of his death for the woman who had first stirred his soul to its depths."

Advice of the Heart

Were the elder Washington's feelings for Sally reciprocated? There are ample indicators throughout the course of their relationship that Sally felt deeply for Washington. Late in life, it also appears that Sally may have regretted what might have been. Wilson Cary recalled family tradition that, in her last years, Sally was thinking of Washington: "She survived him many years, and family papers supplement the tradition that she truly lamented the choice of her heart."

In 1788, with Washington preparing to assume the new nation's inaugural presidency, Sally was alone in Bath, upset at the loss of the Fairfax family fortune and still grieving the loss of two children and a niece. She penned an emotional letter to her sister-in-law. At issue was a family wedding, apparently opposed by many—including the recipient of the letter—because the sister-in-law's daughter was marrying a man from a lower social class. Sally speaks up for the bride-to-be and for true love while perhaps recalling her own choices:

> There was a time of my life when I should not have been well pleased to hear of the union between a daughter of yours and Mr. ——; but thank God, I have outlived those prejudices of education, and know now that the worthy man is to be preferred to the high-born who has not merit to recommend him. In this country we every day see the daughters of noblemen give their hands to nabobs just returned from India with great wealth ill-gotten. When we enquire into the family of these mighty men we find them the very lowest of people.

Sally Fairfax saved much of George Washington's correspondence, but, tragically, all her letters to him are lost but one, and it is simply a postscript attached to a letter that gently chides Washington for not immediately coming to see her after his return from the battlefield. It is tantalizing to contemplate what these lost letters might have told us. Yet from the surviving letters, we are offered a very intimate lens by which to view a far more human side of Washington than that passed down by the writers of textbooks. As one historian noted, "Many passages of George Washington's letters are cryptic, written as if he knew they might be discovered." In no other surviving letters does Washington write with such blatant warmth and hints of playfulness than those meant for Sally.

Life can be cruel. Sally Fairfax was expatriated from her beloved Virginia for forty years, twenty-five of them alone as a widow and childless. She still had relatives back in Virginia with whom she corresponded but never again set foot in America. She spent her final years in Bath, where she remained vigorous and interested in politics. For instance, in 1794, she took the shocking position of criticizing the British government for meddling in French affairs.

Sally died alone in 1811 in her mansion in Lansdowne Crescent, near Bath, where England's aristocratic class would go to play and recuperate.

Martha Washington sat for the noted portraitist Gilbert Stuart, but she was often a reluctant subject. Published by L. Prang. Library of Congress Prints and Photographs Division, LC-USZ62-3833 DLC.

❦ 4 ❧

"Domestic Felicity"

It is as if I was a very great somebody.

—Martha Washington

WORTHY PARTNERS

The day had come: December 14, 1799. News of George Washington's death spread throughout the land. Far and wide, to every farm and outpost and even across the Atlantic Ocean, the word had traveled. To many, his passing marked the end of an era: a single generation of revolutionary giants whose vision and actions cast off the yoke of monarchy and the tradition of government of, by, and for a few. To historians, the era stood at the crossroads of history. The Old World would slowly begin giving way to the New World, and the central figure in the revolutionary drama that unfolded in the late eighteenth century was none other than Washington. Neither the might of the kings of Europe nor the revolutionary pens of Thomas Jefferson or Thomas Paine nor the genius of James Madison or John Adams would stand as a monument to the age and its event. Rather, it would be the stoic character of Washington.

For the people, the death of the great Washington was met by a deep sadness and near religious transcendence befitting none other than a deity. But also, with the father gone, a nervous hesitation gripped the country as the realization set in that they were on their own. To the citizens of the new republic, a future without their general must have seemed inconceivable, so central a player had he been during the momentous three decades that closed the century and gave birth to a nation. To his wife, the general's passing would have marked an equally dramatic and even more personally challenging time.

Their partnership had spanned four long turbulent decades, and she was the quiet and dependable woman behind the man. But history has not remembered how Martha Washington endured her husband's death, nor has the story of her role in his life or their lives together been fully told. The great general was gone, but his widow lived.

Snow, Hail, and . . . Fire

Washington voluntarily relinquished the reign of power as the new nation's inaugural president in 1797. In so doing after two terms in office, he established the precedent of limiting future presidential terms, as codified many years later in the Twenty-Second Amendment to the U.S. Constitution.

Washington would enjoy another two years with his wife at his beloved Mount Vernon. In retirement, he still rode on his horse to each of his farms to oversee the planting and harvest, and he worked hard to reinvigorate the farms that had been neglected during his seven years as general and eight years as president.

Washington's death came unexpectedly and rather suddenly. Although the hero of the Revolution had suffered periodic bouts of illness throughout his sixty-seven years, he generally enjoyed decent health. He was a large and robust man. The approach of winter in 1799 found Washington quite fit, contentedly enjoying his home, farms, family, and the steady flow of visitors he received since leaving the presidency. Approaching his sixty-eighth birthday, Washington was, however, quite old for a man living at the time.

The circuit that the general rode around his farms that December was a long one, covering a considerable distance across his landholdings. Washington was accustomed, however, to such lengthy and vigorous rides, having visited his farms on a nearly daily basis over the course of his adult life whenever he was home. Washington was also an accomplished rider, noted for his vigor and comfort in the saddle. Yet that morning, a sudden snow and hailstorm blew coldly across eastern Virginia, catching Washington while on his rounds. After returning home at his usual time in midday for dinner, Washington complained of a sore throat, and his wife noticed that his neck and upper back were soaking wet. That night, he awoke in a chilled sweat with an inflamed throat and pneumonia. Mrs. Washington was nervous and wanted her husband's physician summoned immediately. Washington dismissed her worries.

By morning, Washington was gravely ill. Doctors were rushed to his bedside, where they treated him with, among other remedies, bloodletting, which surely only exacerbated the situation. Remaining in bed the next day, he posted what would be the final entry in his daily diary. Washington recognized the futility of the situation and resigned himself to the inevitable, saying to his doctors, "I feel myself going. I thank you for your attention. You had better not take any more trouble with me, but let me go off quietly; I cannot last long."

Then, turning to his family's longtime trusted aide, Tobias Lear, Washington whispered instructions for his own burial: "I am just going. Have me decently buried and do not let my body be put into the vault in less than two days after I am dead." After Lear replied, "Yes, sir," Washington muttered, "'Tis well." His final action was to take his own failing pulse.

The "Father of His Country" was dead on December 14, 1799, aged sixty-seven years, 295 days. The cause of his death was pneumonia.

Love and Letters

Washington is well remembered and the subject of countless biographies and enduring admiration. But there is a major facet of his life that has gone largely unexamined: his marriage. Of his family life, marriage, and wife, little is known. Did he love his wife? Was he faithful to her? Was theirs a solid marriage or a difficult one? Did Washington consult his wife in matters of politics, and did she have an impact on his political decisions?

Because Martha Washington spent so many years at her husband's side and survived him, she is an excellent source for discovering the gaps in our understanding of Washington's home life as well as his personal nature. To that end, her recollection and remembrances as well as their correspondence yield invaluable bits of information. But the road to discovery is a difficult one. Few historians have paid attention to Mrs. Washington, and most of the couple's letters have been lost to history. There have been numerous cases of hoaxes, forged letters, and mistakes in unveiling the letters exchanged by the Washingtons. One of the more famous ones was thought to be a love letter from the general to his wife that even made it into several published biographies and works of Washington's papers. One of the early Washington historians, Benson J. Lossing, claimed to have seen one heretofore unknown love letter when visiting the home of Martha's grandson, George Washington Parke Custis, in 1860.

However, this letter and many others have been dismissed by historians as forgeries. The dean of Washington historians, Douglas Southall Freeman, identified several errors in these forgeries. In some of the hoaxes, the dates and locations listed in the letters are not factual; in others, the salutation that Washington always used when writing women was absent, or key words were spelled differently than the way the Washingtons spelled. For instance, in one letter, the word "opportunity" is spelled correctly. Yet both Washingtons always misspelled the word.

It is also possible that Martha, seeking to recover a degree of privacy that eluded her in marriage, destroyed the letters at some point during the two years and 159 days she survived her husband. It was not uncommon for couples in the eighteenth century to burn their love letters. For instance, the Washington relative Lund Washington instructed his wife to destroy their correspondence after his death. One bit of evidence that Mrs. Washington consigned their letters to the flames comes from the journal of Jared Sparks. On February 26, 1828, twenty-six years after Martha's death, Sparks visited the Washington granddaughter and recorded the following: "My principal objective was to ascertain what became of General Washington's letters to his wife. Mrs. Peters assured me that, shortly after General Washington's death, Mrs. Washington burnt all these letters except two which seemed to escape by accident."

Even though most of the letters exchanged between the Washington couple seem to have been lost, history owes a debt of gratitude to Martha's grandson and his daughter, Mrs. Robert E. Lee. Their efforts helped to preserve and organize what letters of Martha Washington do exist. Although the letters tell us much about her life, regrettably nothing written in her hand from the first twenty-six years of her life survives. Equally regrettable is the fact that so few of the letters exchanged by the Washingtons survive.

But there are letters written by Mrs. Washington from the period from 1757 until her death that are known to exist. Thankfully, the largest portion of Mrs. Washington's correspondence dates from the years of her husband's presidency (1789–1797). It is through this correspondence that we have the clearest picture of the life and marriage of the Washingtons.

One of Martha's favorite pen pals was her niece, Frances Bassett Washington, known as "Fanny." Beautiful and feminine, Fanny was the daughter of Martha's sister, Ann Maria Dandridge Bassett, who married Burwell Bassett. Fanny's mother died unexpectedly in 1777, and in 1784 the fifteen-year-old Fanny came to live with Mrs. Washington at Mount Vernon. At the same time, George Washington's twenty-one-year-old nephew, Major George Augustine Washington—named for his famous uncle and his famous uncle's father—who had served as an aide to General Lafayette during the Revolutionary War, moved to Mount Vernon to help manage the prosperous farms.

With the help of Mrs. Washington, who played matchmaker, the two young residents of Mount Vernon fell in love and married. Fanny then acted as hostess and head of the household when Martha was in New York and Philadelphia during her husband's presidency.

Fanny and Martha wrote frequently to one another during this time, and of the mountains of letters they probably exchanged, approximately forty still survive. The two women discussed a rich array of topics, including the health of Martha's grandchildren and Fanny's children, friends, relatives, and life at Mount Vernon.

Tragically, Major George Augustine Washington contracted tuberculosis, which George and Martha Washington nicknamed "the family disease," and died in April 1793. A widow with three young children, Fanny Bassett Washington remained at Mount Vernon. In 1795, Franny married another resident of Mount Vernon, Tobias Lear, the Harvard-educated tutor of Martha's children and grandchildren and personal aide to George Washington. This long and tender relationship suffered "the family disease" when Fanny, already ill at the time of her marriage, succumbed in March 1796.

After the death of Fanny Bassett Washington Lear, Martha developed a close relationship with another niece, although no one would ever replace Martha's cherished Fanny. Frances Henley was the daughter of Martha's youngest sister, Elizabeth Dandridge Henley, and was also nicknamed "Fanny." The "Second Fanny" was a regular visitor to and sometimes lived at Mount Vernon during the final years of the lives of George and Martha Washington. She too exchanged many letters with Martha.

A year after Martha's death, the Second Fanny, just like her cousin before her, became enamored of Tobias Lear. The two married in June 1803. It was but one of many marriages that occurred among Mount Vernon's residents. Martha would have approved. Tobias Lear kept his correspondence with General Washington and both his wives' correspondence with Mrs. Washington in a large trunk. After Lear's suicide in 1816, his widow, Fanny Henley Lear, had the foresight to preserve the papers. In an effort to protect the letters, later in her life the Second Fanny gave a "trunk full" of papers to George Washington Storer, her late husband's nephew. The year was 1854. And so Martha Washington's letters were preserved over time.

The letters show that Martha struggled with grammar and spelling. Her letters frequently neglected to use punctuation and show that she was a phonetic speller. She seems to have been painfully aware of these deficiencies and, early on, had her husband write some of her letters. From the letters, it is possible to piece together a sense of the Washington marriage. It is also evident that Martha was a regular woman who struggled with the problems of everyday life as it was in the eighteenth century. But the letters also reveal an extraordinary side of Martha's personality and a strong, if passionless, marriage.

THE WIFE OF WASHINGTON

Martha Dandridge Custis Washington is known only as the wife of the great Washington. It is this simple and one-dimensional image of her as a quiet, dutiful wife standing in the considerable shadow of the nation's father by which she is remembered. In a way, it is not surprising that this is the picture that remains of Mrs. Washington. After all, she lived at a time before women enjoyed basic political or human rights.

The year 1999 marked the bicentennial of Washington's death, and the nation was treated to a yearlong celebration of his life. The event featured traveling museum exhibits, a renovation of the 555-foot-tall Washington Monument, and new scholarship on the general and president. However, what was noticeably absent from the fanfare was any serious attention given to his wife or acknowledgment of the vital role she played in his life.

In 1993, a wreath-laying ceremony at her tomb at Mount Vernon honored the 262nd anniversary of Martha's birth. Two years later, in March 1995, Colonial Williamsburg hosted a five-day forum on women in history titled "Beside the Great Man: Martha Washington in Williamsburg." A postage stamp issued several decades before and an earlier commemorative coin bore Mrs. Washington's likeness. In 1997, when PBS aired a series about the American Revolution titled *Liberty*, an impressive production with costumed actors, they decided not to depict Washington on-screen with an actor. The general was but a voice, a presence befitting his stature as disembodied spirit of the nation. But the series neglected to fully explore Mrs. Washington or the marriage, missing the fact that they were two ordinary people who, together, were caught up in extraordinary times and rose to extraordinary heights to both forge and define their age.

More Than Meets the Eye

One way to humanize the mythical Washington is to explore his marriage. George had been married to Martha for sixteen years when he was selected to participate in the revolutionary political events unfolding in the colonies. The Washingtons were celebrating their twenty-fourth year as husband and wife when he signed the peace treaty with the British that ended the War for Independence. And at the time Washington took the oath of office and accepted the awesome challenge of serving as the new nation's first president, Martha had been his wife for more than three decades. Mrs. Washington thus had a front-row seat to history in the making. In the words of Joseph Fields, who edited her surviving correspondence, "Martha Washington directly helped shape the future of the young nation."

Martha had a high forehead, a prominent nose, a small mouth, and a thickly proportioned jaw within her oval face. With brown hair and hazel eyes, she possessed average looks and was described neither as attractive nor unattractive by those who knew her. Of normal height for a woman of the time, next to the enormous Washington she was nonetheless a petite five feet tall. Martha's frame filled out with the passing of years to the familiar plumpness that she carried as Mrs. George Washington. As a mature woman, her features also softened under gray hair and a grandmotherly countenance. It has probably not helped her reputation as an inconsequential homemaker that the ever-humble Martha once quaintly described herself as "an old-fashioned Virginia house-keeper, steady as a clock, busy as a bee, and cheerful as a cricket." This she was. Like the caricature of the kindly grandmother, Martha preferred an organized home and busy kitchen and really did spoil her little boys rotten.

Martha's fate has also been sealed by a few portraits for which she sat late in life. Every time a likeness for Martha has been required, a portrait of a plump grandmother wearing both her signature white, matronly bonnet and a blank, disinterested stare is reproduced. In each of these paintings, Martha looks completely bored as if forced to sit for the portrait against her will.

Martha allowed herself to be painted with her grandchildren, and this further shaped her image as a grandmother. After all, the public—then as is the case now—was eager for images of their beloved first family. Although reluctant, fortunately Martha did sit for original portraits, many of which appear to be accurate likenesses. The noted artist Charles Willson Peale, after having painted a full-length Washington at the Battle of Princeton, wanted to paint the general's wife, whom he saw as the symbol of the Revolution. Peale was impressed both with Martha and with his painting of her, stating, "I had the favor of Mrs. Washington to set as she passed through the city, and the likeness is much approved of, and I have her promise for the last sitting as she returns this spring."

Martha did oblige Peale again in Philadelphia on her way from Washington's winter headquarters in Morristown, New Jersey, back to her Virginia home. Unfortunately, at least one of the Peale portraits of Mrs. Washington that we know of has been lost. Remarkably, there are a total of sixty surviving portraits drawn, painted, or reproduced of Mrs. Washington. Late in life, after the general's passing, Martha sat for one final portrait in 1801. She did so at the request of her grandchildren and wanted it to capture her "every day face" so that they would remember her as she was.

A Picture and a Thousand Words

One of the earliest portraits shows Martha as more than the matron in her white bonnet depicted in most books. Dating to 1757, two years before marrying George, Martha was painted by the famous English portrait artist John Wollaston. The attractive twenty-five-year-old subject is wearing fine silk and lace and projects an elegant and vivacious demeanor. The pose is standing while holding a flower in an outstretched arm, a common symbol at the time used to denote the aristocratic class. Her eyes, somewhat almond shaped, appear mysterious and far from the dull, listless gaze found in later portraits.

This portrait suggests a somewhat different image of Martha than history remembers. Dandridge family history also suggests that, as a young woman, Martha was feisty and liked to ride horses. Indeed, a man on horseback once approached the Dandridge home and announced his interest in courting the young girl. However, the would-be suitor did not offer Martha the courtesy of dismounting to make his inquiry. It is said that the teen not only declined the offer but also reached up and slapped the man across the face.

Martha Washington was routinely described as "amiable" and in other, similar and positive terms. Despite living the most public of lives, she seems to have been remarkably without enemies and able to endear herself to nearly everyone she met. About Martha, the astute and often critical judge of character Abigail Adams concluded, "I [was] much more deeply impressed than I ever [was] before their Majesties of Britain." Tobias Lear, who knew the Washington family better than anyone, said of Mrs. Washington,

> She is one of those superior beings who are sent down to bless good men. . . . She is everything that is benevolent and good. I honor her as a second mother and receive from her all those attentions which I should look for from her who bore me.

Even common soldiers in Washington's often-suffering army hailed her as their beloved "Lady Washington." Dr. James Thacher, who dined with the Washingtons at the general's winter camp, recorded in his diary one of the most prescient assessments of her:

> Mrs. Washington combines in an uncommon degree great dignity of manner with the most pleasing affability, but possesses no striking marks of beauty. I learn from the Virginia officers that Mrs. Washington has ever been honored as a lady of distinguished goodness, possessing all the virtues which adorn her sex, amiable in her temper and deportment, full of benignity, benevolence, and charity, seeking for objects of affection and poverty, that she may extend the sufferer the hand of kindness and relief. These, surely are the attributes which reveal a heart replete with those virtues which are appropriate and estimable in the female character.

Martha Washington was not simply domestic; she was one of the most gracious, celebrated, and capable hostesses in all of Virginia. She was not simply a grandmother but also someone who somehow persevered through the tragically untimely deaths of nearly everyone she loved. She was not simply a loyal wife but also a patriot who abandoned her desire for privacy for her sense of duty to her husband and country.

Christmas Surprise

The wife of Washington never wanted her husband to lead the colonial army. Quiet and private, she preferred the tranquillity of plantation life to the dangers of war and the disruptions of public life. But, like her husband, Martha had a strong sense of duty. She supported him and his service to the cause. But she did much more—Martha became a symbol of the Revolution and an idealized image of motherhood. Against her wishes, she emerged as an iconic figure in her lifetime.

On June 15, 1775, the Continental Congress appointed George Washington commander in chief. The task must have seemed to Washington hopeless and probably to Martha as well. Three weeks later, the general took command of 16,000 poorly trained and equipped men and proceeded to suffer several devastating losses, sagging morale, and an unresponsive Congress.

But the colonial army made it through the year. The signing of the Declaration of Independence on July 4, 1776, provided a symbolic and inspirational albeit temporary victory for the cause. But its promise seemed to ring as empty as a cracked liberty bell and was accompanied by an unfulfilled request for additional supplies and munitions. Within weeks, the army was dealt serious setbacks. For example, on August 27, 1776, at the Battle of Long Island, the colonials were forced to retreat by a superior British force. On October 28, the dispirited colonial militia endured another defeat at the Battle of White Plains.

The glory of the Declaration was now months past, replaced by the chill of winter and the bitter taste of defeat. The outlook for Washington's army was bleak. They had been beaten and chased from New Jersey across the Delaware River to Pennsylvania. December 1776 found the troops facing a long, cold winter encampment while lacking sufficient food, warm clothing, boots, guns, and ammunition. The terms of enlistment were up for many of Washington's men, and only a few contemplated "reupping" for duty. Funds were depleted, Congress was uncooperative and ineffectual, and there was growing discontent with the general's leadership by political leaders as well as by his own officer corps. Washington faced the very real prospect that the war effort would not survive the long winter. A risky and most unconventional action, however, might save the cause. Thus, Washington gambled and had to do so before the new year.

Some of the most feared warriors of the Revolution were the Hessians. Brutal and disciplined German mercenaries paid by the British to terrorize the colonials, a force of more than 1,000 Hessians camped within marching distance on the New Jersey side of the Delaware River from the Americans. General Washington planned a daring surprise attack in the predawn hours the day after Christmas.

Using the cover of night on December 25, Washington packed cannons and men into small boats and ordered his weary, sick troops across the icy river. After pulling off the difficult logistical crossing, the army still needed to march a considerable distance to meet a force that many of them viewed as unbeatable. Undetected by the Hessians, who were groggy from a full night of food, drink, and celebration, and in no shape for combat, Washington managed to array his men in position within the enemy compound. The surprise worked. Rustled from bed by the sound of gunfire, the Hessian force quickly surrendered. The Hessian losses were considerable, including their commanding officer, and Washington took hundreds of prisoners and secured both his first convincing victory of the war and ample supplies from the Hessian stores. He lost not a single man and managed to slip back across the Delaware River to the safety of Pennsylvania, in part because a large British force thought to be in the vicinity never appeared. It turned out that their commander had marched his army north in order to see his American mistress!

The remarkable victory staved off further defections in camp and political unrest in Congress. Washington and his army would make it through winter, their spirits briefly lifted. Another tough winter would come, and Washington came to rely on something else to make it through the harsh weather.

A Savior in Winter

The year 1777 brought more defeats for the colonials. The British had control of the seas and ports, leaving the eastern seaboard defenseless. The British landed 17,000 of their finest soldiers at Chesapeake Bay under the command of General Sir William Howe with the intention of taking Philadelphia. Washington's ragtag band of 12,000 fought surprisingly well but eventually succumbed to Howe. One of the most important cities fell into British hands. Thus, by fall, it appeared that the fight for independence was exactly where it was one year prior: doomed.

After draining losses that fall—Brandywine Creek on September 11, 1777, and Germantown on October 4, 1777—the army faced another long, cold winter with inadequate food and supplies. It was to be a winter that would test but ultimately save the army. It happened at Valley Forge.

The British were warmly and safely hunkered down in Philadelphia, Pennsylvania. On December 19, 1777, Washington's men set camp a few miles outside the city at Valley Forge. The contrast in conditions between the two armies could scarcely be more severe. As the troops set about building some 2,000 small huts, miles of trenches, and a few artillery redoubts, their general wrote home to his wife that he would be unable to come home to Mount Vernon. But Washington sent for Martha right away after she initially suggested the idea. A little-known fact is that the great Washington was prone to fits of melancholy and sagging confidence, and such was his state when he made camp that winter.

After a long and dangerous wilderness trek in the dead of winter across muddy, unpaved trails beginning on January 16, 1778, Mrs. Washington arrived at Valley Forge that February to be reunited with her husband. Martha was troubled to find George "much worn with fatigue and anxiety," saying, "I never knew him to be so anxious as now." It was difficult enough on her to have had to abandon her home and surviving child, but she dutifully shared the spartan conditions of military life and her husband's small cabin. Smallpox, influenza, typhus, and dysentery plagued the camp, claiming even more lives than starvation, the weather, or the Redcoats. In fact, Mrs. Washington endured the hardships of camp each and every winter of the long war. She also very reluctantly agreed to her husband's request that she be vaccinated for smallpox in order to come to camp.

Mrs. Washington's bravery and actions would serve the war effort in a vital way. In camp, the beloved wife of the General Washington proved to be tireless, cooking for the officers, mending uniforms for enlisted men, nursing the sick, hosting dinners and religious services, organizing theatrical and singing performances, and, perhaps most important, calming her husband's frayed nerves and sagging spirits. In one of her many letters to her friend, Mercy Otis Warren, written from camp, Martha described "British cruelties" and the difficult but "tolerable" condition of the headquarters and their "hutts." In these letters, Mrs. Washington unwittingly revealed that her husband must have discussed details of the war with her. She appears to have been privy to much of the camp life, functioning as her husband's assistant as he organized and answered his war correspondence and a source of comfort and inspiration to the entire camp.

At one of the most critical hours of the war, a plump grandmother carved out a much-needed sense of normalcy and home life at camp and "mothered" the army. "God bless Lady Washington" became the motto of the appreciative soldiers. Most assuredly, George Washington felt the same way. Indeed, it is difficult to overstate the valuable role her presence had on the general and his troops.

Martha also enjoyed the company of the wives of some of the officers while in camp, including Mrs. Knox, Mrs. Clement Biddle, Lady Stirling, and a few others. A Mrs. Westlake, who visited the camp, commented that she never encountered anyone so industrious and dedicated to the troops:

> I never in my life knew a woman so busy from early morning until latest night as was lady Washington, providing comforts for the sick soldiers. Every day, excepting Sunday, the wives of officers in camp, and sometimes other women, were invited to Mr. Pott's to assist her in knitting socks, patching garments, and making shirts for the poor soldiers, when materials could be provided. Every fair day she might be seen, with basket in hand, and with a single attendant, going among the huts seeking the keenest and most needy sufferer, and giving all the comforts to them in her power. . . .
>
> On one occasion she went to the hut of a dying sergeant, whose young wife was with him. His case seemed to particularly touch the heart of the good lady, and after she had given him some wholesome food she had prepared with her own hands, she knelt down by his straw pallet and prayed earnestly for him and his wife with her sweet and solemn voice. I shall never forget the scene.

In February, the Prussian officer Friedrich Wilhelm Augustus von Steuben arrived in camp. It was Baron von Steuben, despite his lack of English, who relentlessly drilled and eventually whipped the militia into a professional army. But it was Lady Washington who provided an example of calm and confidence for not only her husband but the entire army. The Continental army not only survived that winter but also emerged ready to fight. After Martha bid fond farewell to the troops, the army routed the Redcoats on June 28, 1778, at Monmouth and, by mid-August, had driven the British out of New Jersey.

Just One of the Soldiers

The following winter of 1778–1779, Mrs. Washington arrived at her husband's Middlebrook, New Jersey, headquarters and stayed until June 4. When she arrived, she found the soldiers busy setting up tents and building log cabins, but she dismissed any special attention that would be paid on her lodging and comfort. Two carpenters were assigned to build a room for Mrs. Washington, who said to one of them that she wanted nothing regal, only practical. Her only request: "Now, young man, I care for nothing but comfort here, and should like you to fit me up a closet on one side of the room and some shelves and places for hanging clothes on the other." The carpenter, like others in camp, liked the general's wife but noted her common demeanor, describing her as "a portly-looking, agreeable woman of forty-five."

When Lady Washington arrived to stay at the home of Ephraim Berry during one winter of the war, Mrs. Berry did not realize the identity of her famous guest. Because of Martha's plain dress and unassuming demeanor, on meeting her Mrs. Berry assumed that she was being introduced to Mrs. Washington's domestic attendant. Similarly, her common appearance was noted by a few of the officers' wives who were already in camp when Mrs. Washington arrived at Morristown in January 1780. They gathered to greet the great woman but recorded being quite surprised that she arrived in a simple carriage and wore common clothing, a bonnet, and no jewelry.

Martha was utterly unassuming in her ways. One woman visitor to camp described her meeting with Mrs. Washington as follows:

> Yesterday, with several others, I visited Lady Washington at headquarters. We expected to find the wealthy wife of the great general elegantly dressed, for the time of our visit had been fixed; but, instead, she was neatly attired in a brown habit. Her gracious and cheerful manners delighted us all, but we felt rebuked by the plainness of her apparel and her example of persistent industry, while we were extravagantly dressed idlers, a name not very creditable in these perilous times. She seems very wise in experience, kind-hearted and winning in her ways. She talked much of the sufferings of the poor soldiers, especially of the sick ones. Her heart seemed to be full of compassion for them.

Thus became Martha's routine in camp, repeated each winter of the war. She arrived anywhere from mid-December until February and stayed until May or June. When threats to her safety because of the knowledge of her annual journeys to camp became obvious, Mrs. Washington was escorted by a small detachment of roughly ten members of the dragoon unit.

From the beginning of the conflict, George Washington worried about his wife's safety. In fact, a rumor in 1775 raised the possibility that Lord Dunmore and the British were planning to burn Mount Vernon and capture Mrs. Washington. Once, at the start of hostilities, a British ship was sighted off the coast not far from the Potomac River by the Washington home. Fearing for Mrs. Washington's safety, George Mason was dispatched to remove his general's wife from harm's way. Only after much complaining—and then very reluctantly—did Martha agree to abandon her home. But only temporarily.

Martha returned home the next day and, from then on, dismissed any fuss over her safely. But the entire war experience and winter encampments were not easy on her. During the 1779–1780 winter headquarters at Morristown in New Jersey, General Washington described the conditions as "the severest trial" of the war. Food and supplies ran short, and payments owed to the army were not forthcoming. Desertions reached crisis levels, and in

May shots were fired when the army nearly disbanded during a mutinous rebellion. The general posted a "lifeguard" composed of loyal troops around his headquarters to ensure his safety both from a surprise British attack and from his own frustrated men. Martha was reminded every day of the threats to both her own life and her husband's. Still, Mrs. Washington endured freezing temperatures and a thick snowfall that brought travel to a standstill at Morristown.

BY THE SWEAT OF THEIR BROWS
AND WITH PLENTY OF LUCK

The wife of Washington was from English stock. The Dandridge side of Martha's family traced their lineage to Oxfordshire, England, and the nearby villages of Appleford, Blewbury, Dorchester-on-Thames, and Drayton St. Leonard. Their family story is one of struggle but success and included many painters and working-class farmers who occupied a rung on the social ladder somewhere between the wretched poverty of the masses and comfort of the aristocracy. Many of them prospered and learned to read and write despite their occupations. Along the way, the family survived both the famous plague of 1665, which killed an estimated 100,000 people, and the "Great Fire" of London in 1666, which killed thousands more and destroyed as many homes.

One of the earliest records of Martha's ancestry places her great-great-grandfather, Bartholomew Dandridge, in the town of Drayton St. Leonard in the late sixteenth century. Bartholomew, who was a farmer, married Agnes Wilder in 1604, and the couple had eight children before his death in 1638. Their children included William, born in 1613, and Francis, born six years later. Both brothers appear to have fought on the side of the Royalists in the civil wars that ravaged the country during their lifetimes. After surviving the wars, the brothers enjoyed modest prosperity. William Dandridge had three sons—William, Francis, and John. William's younger brother, Francis, and his wife, Ann, had three daughters and two sons—also (unimaginatively) named Francis and John (common names in the Dandridge family for generations).

Both Dandridge boys sent their oldest sons (and namesakes) to be formally educated by Sir John Fettiplace, who ran a school in Dorchester-on-Thames. As was common among most families lacking the economic means to educate all their sons, the fate of second- and third-born boys was to be apprenticed in the trades. This was the case for the younger Dandridge boys. William, for example, sent his third son, John, to London to apprentice for a master painter, and the boy eventually became a successful house painter, stainer, and designer of coats of arms.

Young John Dandridge, son of William, enjoyed considerable success as a painter and chose a bride named Bridget Dugdale. However, Bridget died while still a young woman after giving birth to a son, also named John, about whom little is known except that he died in 1695.

With the status of "master painter-stainer" while still a relatively young man, John Dandridge remarried. His second wife's name was Anne, and they had thirteen children, seven of whom survived to adulthood. Two of the seven children—William, born in 1689, and John, who was born in either 1700 or 1701 (one credible account gives July 14, 1700, as the date)—ultimately carried the family's hopes and legacy to the New World. The two Dandridge boys, aged twenty-six and fifteen, traveled to the Virginia Colony in 1715. After crossing the Atlantic, the brothers settled in Elizabeth City County, where they prospered as merchants, accumulating a respectable degree of wealth and land. The older brother, William, was officially named as surveyor of new lands in Virginia and North Carolina, and in 1727 he was appointed as a commissioner. A year later, he was commissioned at the rank of colonel in the colony's militia, ultimately finishing his military career as an officer in the Royal Navy.

William built a home, named Elsing Green, on the bank of the Pamunkey River in King William County, Virginia, where he lived until his death in 1743. Younger brother John also succeeded in acquiring land and gaining appointment to a minor public office.

John purchased tracts of land in Hampton and Hanover counties in Virginia that made him money. In 1730, he acquired a 500-acre parcel on the bank of the Pamunkey in nearby New Kent County, where he built his home. It was on this property in 1730—the year he bought the land and built the home—that John Dandridge, the fourth-generation descendant of the English farmer Bartholomew Dandridge, married Frances Jones. Frances, whose father emigrated from England, came from a line of well-educated and respected preachers.

The Jones family arrived in the colonies earlier than did the Dandridges, and they seem to have had a less challenging ordeal. The record of the Jones family dates to shortly after the dawn of the seventeenth century, to one Rowland Jones, who was educated at Christ Church, Oxford. Rowland held office as a clerk and rector of several churches in and around Buckinghamshire, England. His son, named for him, was educated at Oxford's Merton College and also became a preacher in Buckinghamshire. In the mid-seventeenth century, it was he who first crossed the Atlantic Ocean.

Arriving in Virginia, Rowland Jones helped establish the Bruton Church in Virginia, where he served as rector until his death in 1688. Reverend Jones lived in Williamsburg and was a prominent citizen in the colony's most important town. The reverend had a son named Orlando, who was born in 1681 and attended the College of William & Mary in 1698. Orlando Jones endeared himself to many of the colony's leading citizens and became a member of the House of Burgesses in 1714, representing King William County.

Around the turn of the century, Orlando married Martha Macon, one of four children of Gideon Macon. Mr. Macon, born in 1650, was a wealthy planter, attorney, and elder in several churches and also served in the Virginia House of Burgesses in the 1690s and until his death in 1703. The Macon family hailed from the Auvergne region of France before immigrating to York County in the Virginia Colony. They later moved to James City County, then resettled in New Kent County in 1682.

After a few years of marriage, Orlando Jones and Martha Macon celebrated the birth of a daughter, Frances, on August 6, 1710. Frances lost her father, Orlando, in 1719 and had a difficult childhood. Frances Macon Jones, the third-generation descendant of Reverend Rowland Jones of England, eventually married John Dandridge on July 22, 1730. The marriage was below her family's social standing, but her new husband showed great promise and had done reasonably well for himself.

One year later, a daughter was born at their new home, Chestnut Grove. Keeping the custom of both sides of the family, they decided to pass along the family name: they named their baby Martha.

"Patsy"

Very little is known about Martha's youth, as none of her letters from this period of her life survives. However, a few documents chronicling the Dandridge family history do remain.

Martha was the firstborn child of John and Frances Dandridge of New Kent County, Virginia. The Dandridge family Bible records the date of birth as shortly after the noon hour on June 2, 1731. Some accounts list her birth as June 13 of the same year, and a rare source or two list other dates. The confusion over the date results, in part, from changes made in the old calendar to a more accurate calendar during her lifetime.

Martha, who was called "Patsy" by friends and family, was the first of five Dandridge children. Discrepancies also exist regarding the number of children born to John and Frances Dandridge. Some sources claim five children, while others list up to eight children in the household. The historical contradictions, however, have a rather straightforward explanation. Martha's parents had five children prior to John Dandridge's death in 1756. The widow, who survived her late husband by almost thirty years, remarried.

With her second husband, John Flournoy, a watchmaker, Frances had three additional children. The children included five girls and three boys. Martha's younger brothers, John, William, and Bart, were, for instance, only one, three, and four years her junior, respectively. The youngest of her stepsiblings, however, was born when Martha was twenty-five years old and already a mother of four young children.

Martha's father, John, was a county clerk and owner of a 500-acre plantation on the edge of the Pamunkey River in eastern Tidewater Virginia. The family owned a few slaves, enabling them to grow tobacco commercially. The family home at Chestnut Grove was a comfortable, two-story building with two chimneys, one on either end of the home. The home contained a separate kitchen area apart from the main dwelling, as was the norm at the time in order to prevent the house from catching fire.

Williamsburg, which was only twenty-two miles from the Dandridge home, functioned as the social, economic, and political center of the entire colony and, especially, for the Tidewater region. Its proximity allowed the Dandridges to mix with some of the colony's leading citizens and offered not only social opportunities for the family but also economic benefits for John Dandridge's agricultural enterprise. Accordingly, the Dandridges were, in the words of leading Washington biographer Douglas Southall Freeman, members of Virginia's "second-tier" gentry. Fine farms, wealthy neighbors, and prosperous villages could be found in the vicinity of their home.

The plantation defined the lifestyles of wealthier citizens, most of whom were loyal British subjects, as most likely were the Dandridges. Tidewater plantations produced tobacco and other agricultural products, much of which was sold back to England. In return, the colonists of the area bought supplies and products from London merchants. Beyond this economic attachment to mother England, Virginia's aristocracy—and even the "lesser" aristocracy, to which the Dandridges belonged—along with much of the middle class were very British in their customs, beliefs, and political allegiances. The area was also quite conscious of class standing and status, more so than perhaps any other region in the colonies.

Aside from what is known about plantation life in general, about all that is known about Martha's childhood is that it appears to have been a normal and happy one. With such a large family living on a large plantation, Martha, as eldest daughter, would surely have helped cook, clean, make clothing, and host the Dandridge guests. She probably also helped raise her younger siblings. The fact that Martha grew up to be such a capable homemaker and celebrated cook and hostess likely resulted from her early experiences. We know that the Dandridges also enjoyed numerous visits from relatives living nearby, including a paternal uncle, William Dandridge; Martha's maternal grandfather, who was a popular cleric; and a well-known colonel and his wife, who lived just across the Pamunkey River. This latter couple brought with them to Martha's childhood home their four girls and two boys, likely play pals for young Martha.

One of Martha's loves as a child was horses, and it appears the young girl was a competent rider. As an adult, she denied herself this joy, possibly because of social mores that frowned on such physical activities for ladies or, more practically, because of the weight she gained on a short frame. However, throughout her life, she enjoyed carriage rides.

Details of Martha's education are sketchy. However, even the wealthiest of colonial families did not formally educate their daughters. Most Tidewater families of the Dandridge family's status supplemented a daughter's education with a small library of books in the home and the employment of traveling tutors from time to time. Because Martha's ancestors on her mother's side of the family included several preachers and well-educated men, the family would have had ample books and tutors for the young girl. As an adult, Martha's grammar and taste in literature show her to be marginally educated. Like most girls, Martha's education was practical in nature and feminine in function and was designed to both assist the family and prepare her for spousehood and motherhood. Growing up in the 1730s and 1740s, especially as the eldest daughter of a large family, she would have been taught to cook, clean, knit, sew, embroider, wash clothing, administer herbal medicines, and raise children. She appears to have also been versed in gardening, basic health care, art, and music (she played the spinet, a small harpsichord popular at the time). The family also attended church regularly, further exposing her to reading and lessons in morality. Religion would end up offering Martha some comfort later in life during the many tragic losses she endured.

As the county clerk, John Dandridge held a minor political position, and both the Dandridge family and the Jones family were somewhat connected politically in the region. As a result, Martha likely attended parties and balls in Williamsburg during the winter social season, and her exposure to political life might also have come at an early age while helping to host leading citizens in the family home.

At age fifteen, Martha Dandridge was a Virginia belle, and the historical record shows that she attended at least one grand ball at the governor's palace in Williamsburg as a debutante during the administration of Governor William Gooch. It is not certain, however, how many suitors she attracted. A reasonable guess would be an average amount, meaning a handful. The teenage Martha was neither wealthy nor poor, neither well educated nor uneducated, and considered neither attractive nor unattractive.

A Marriage Proposal

The teenage Martha did attract one very noteworthy suitor named Daniel Parke Custis, one of the colony's wealthiest and most eligible bachelors. Daniel was born in 1711, making him twenty years Martha's senior. However, Daniel's family was as scandalous as they were wealthy. One relative, for whom he was named, moved from Virginia to assume the governorship of a Caribbean colony. However, he had a mistress in England and affairs with married women in the Caribbean and fathered children out of wedlock. His behavior and an angry mob in Antigua eventually did him in. Governor Daniel Parke was murdered in 1710.

The Custis family traced their arrival in the Virginia Colony to around 1610. John Custis and his wife, Joanne Powell, had been innkeepers in Rotterdam. They had six sons and one daughter, three of whom—John II, William, and Joseph—settled in Virginia. All the Custis boys did well for themselves. One of their descendants, Anne Custis, married Colonel Argall Yeardley, the son of Sir George Yeardley, the royal governor of Virginia. The eldest son, John II, became the sheriff of Northampton County and an elected council member. He married Elizabeth Robinson, and they had one son, John III. This son served in politics as a council member and married Margaret Michael. Margaret and John III's eldest son, John IV, inherited great wealth and property and was the father of Daniel Parke Custis.

Daniel's father, John, married Frances Parke, the daughter of Virginia's colonial governor and, it turns out, a political enemy of the Custis and Yeardley families. Not surprisingly, the marriage would be a disaster and the source of much gossip among neighbors.

There is some evidence that Martha knew Daniel since her early childhood. They lived in the same county, and, because the two attended St. Peter's Church near Martha's home, they likely met in church. Martha's father served as a deacon and Daniel Parke Custis as a warden in the church. Both families also attended parties and balls in the Williamsburg area. However, because of the considerable age difference, it is doubtful that the two had much interaction. The problem for Martha, Daniel, and most everyone else was Daniel's father, John Custis. The elder Custis, who lived from 1678 to 1749 and was one of the king's councilors for Virginia, was well known as one of the most foul-tempered and difficult citizens of the colony. Scholars describe John Custis as "eccentric and domineering," and his bad marriage and passing of time only made him more ornery.

The elder Custis wanted his son to marry Evelyn Byrd, daughter of Colonel William Byrd of Westover and a young maiden famous for her beauty and accomplished manner. It also helped the conniving and money-obsessed John Custis that a union with the Byrd family would enhance the Custis family's status. Master Custis expected the marriage to occur, and both fathers began discussing the details of the wedding. Although Colonel Byrd was somewhat guarded on account of Custis's displeasing personality, he ultimately wrote to both Daniel and John with his approval of the marriage, doing so in a manner suggesting that Evelyn Byrd had several other suitors.

After considerable effort to arrange the marriage, it was an infuriating blow to John Custis when his son's affections were directed not at the Byrd daughter but to the far less aristocratic, less attractive, and less wealthy Dandridge daughter. Daniel Custis had been linked romantically to a number of prominent women but remained unmarried at the shockingly advanced age of thirty-seven. It is unknown why Daniel did not marry earlier. He was the only son and heir to one of the wealthiest and most prominent families in Virginia. It appears, however, that Daniel's temperamental father refused to give his blessings to most of Daniel's loves, and Daniel was too meek to stand up to his father. John Custis was suspicious of any family seeking to marry into his money and refused to recognize Daniel's courtship of young Martha.

Although advanced in years (he was seventy) and eager to see his only son marry and continue the family line, John Custis had been in such an unusually unpleasant marriage that it seems to have jaded his view of marriage. As a young man, John Custis had been deeply in love with his fiancée, writing just months prior to the planned marriage, "May angels guard my dearest Fidelia and deliver her safe to my arms, at our next meeting; and sure they won't refuse their protection to a creature so pure and charming, that it would be easy for them to mistake her for one of themselves." Against the advice of his friends but apparently to please his family, John Custis ended up backing out of the marriage at the last moment to marry another woman, Frances Parke, daughter of powerful politicians. Frances moved her husband not to poetry, as Fidelia did, but to anger. Custis never forgave himself for not marrying his true love. At the same time, from Frances's perspective, marriage to John Custis would have been no walk in the park. Frances had to endure his volatile disposition, pining away for Fidelia, and his constant philandering with young slave girls, which he hardly seemed to try and hide from his wife or neighbors.

The elder Custis would take his anger about his marriage to the grave— literally. Frances Parke passed before John Custis. But he never forgave her for a bad marriage. In his own last will and testament, John directed his son, Daniel, under strict penalty of disinheritance, to have engraved on his tombstone, along with his name, titles, and age, the words "and yet lived but seven years, which were the space of time he kept a bachelor's home at Arlington, on the Eastern Shore of Virginia." So bad was the marriage that John did not consider the nine years he was married or even the thirty-four years he lived as a widower without remarrying as "living." Even in his eternal slumber, he only wanted to remember the time from his adolescence at age thirteen until his marriage at age twenty.

Young Martha Dandridge had likely never traveled beyond Williamsburg, and her family lacked the standing and wealth of the Custis family. But by age seventeen, "little Patsy" had blossomed into a poised, young woman and did win the heart of Daniel Custis. History does not record what it was that piqued Daniel's passion for the teenage girl. It is likely that he watched her grow from infancy to adolescence to near womanhood. Two years removed from entrance into society at the governor's palace in Williamsburg, she remained unspoken for but was of the age to begin making plans.

It would seem to be by some miracle that the stubborn John Custis changed his mind and agreed to his son's marriage to Martha Dandridge. Even in his late thirties, Daniel was weak and, confronted with the reality of disinheritance, hesitated to stand up to his father. But others intervened on his behalf. Two of Daniel's friends, John Blair and Thomas Lee, interceded with the old man, but they were also unable to dislodge the ornery Custis's opposition to the marriage. So Daniel then turned to James Power, a well-known lawyer, member of the House of Burgesses from New Kent County, and family friend. By this time, John Custis was refusing to speak to his son because of the marriage.

Change of Heart

John Custis's objection to Martha's lower social standing and insufficient dowry was such that he threatened to leave the entire family fortune to a slave and disinherit his only son. The slave in question was a mulatto boy named Jack, who was like a son to John Custis and was most likely his biological son. Jack was about ten or eleven years old at the time of Daniel's wedding to Martha, and his mother was, in John Custis's words, the "Negro Wench Young Alice," one of the slaves that Master Custis visited during his regular "night walks" to the slave quarters at his plantation.

John Custis had made plans so that the boy, Jack, was well taken care of after the master's death. In 1744, a few years before Daniel's engagement to Martha, Jack had been ill, and John Custis worried terribly about the boy's health. During the ordeal, the sixty-six-year-old Custis petitioned Virginia's colonial governor to grant the boy his freedom. John Custis said that it would break his heart if his "dear black boy Jack" died without being free. Ultimately, in 1748, fearing his own mortality, John Custis freed Jack, then deeded him 250 acres of land, cattle, hogs, sheep, and other items. Care was also given to provide Jack's mother and four other slave boys the same age—all likely sired by master Custis—with fancy clothing, money, and other necessities.

With his health failing, in 1749 John Custis purchased another sixteen acres next to Queen Mary's Port and set it aside for Jack. Distrusting his own son, Daniel, to see to Jack's best interests, the elder Custis hired a man named Matthew Moody of Williamsburg to handle the Custis estate when he died. In November 1749, the old man even ordered the executor of his will to have a nice home built for the boy, giving detailed instructions in it on how to do so. The will also stipulated that Jack live with Daniel Custis until adulthood.

Thus, when John Custis threatened to give everything to "dear black boy Jack," it was understood by his son and everyone else that he meant it. It was with this threat hanging over the engagement that Daniel asked James Power to bring his considerable reputation and eminence to the task of changing the elder Custis's views on Martha. Power discussed the prospective marriage with John Custis and had some success where others had failed. A compromise was brokered and probably arranged by Power to have the seventy-year-old tyrant at least meet the seventeen-year-old girl in Williamsburg before making his final decision. One can only imagine Martha's emotions and nervousness at the prospect of the meeting. John Custis had already derailed at least one other attempt by his son to marry and likely numerous others.

With the marriage hanging in the balance, Martha met with John Custis. What Martha could have said or done to sway the unswayable Custis may never be known, but the young girl must have charmed the harshness out of her future father-in-law. After the meeting, he agreed to the marriage. In fact, John Custis found himself "as much enamoured of [Martha's] character" as was Daniel. Noting the change of heart, Power wrote in haste, advising Daniel to marry before John Custis changed his mind. Of the old man's change of heart, Power said to his friend, Daniel,

> This comes at last to bring you the news that I believe will be most agreeable to you of any you have ever heard. That you may not be long in suspense, I shall tell you at once. I am empowered by your father to let you know that he heartily and willingly consents to your marriage with Miss Dandridge—that he has so good a character of her that he had rather you should have her than any lady in Virginia—nay, if possible, he is as much enamored with her as you are with her person, and this is owing chiefly to a prudent speech of her own. Hurry down immediately, for fear he should change the strong inclination he has to your marrying directly. I staid with him all night, and presented Jack (the slave boy) with my little jack's horse, bridle and saddle, in your name, which was taken as a singular favor. I shall say no more, as I expect to see you soon to-morrow.

Sometime soon after this meeting, John Custis finally wrote, "I give my free consent to the union of my son with Miss Martha Dandridge." With Martha as his inspiration, Daniel moved quickly to marry his young bride. Both Custis men made a wise choice, and John quickly came to be pleased with his new daughter-in-law.

John Custis did not have long to enjoy his new daughter-in-law's company. Nor did he live long enough to know that four grandchildren would be born. The elder Custis died on November 14, 1749, soon after the marriage and only eight days after deciding to make Daniel the sole executor of his will. The generous provisions in the will and the medical attention that John Custis sought for his beloved black son, Jack, were futile. Less than two years after his own death, the slave boy died on September 9, 1751. He was either twelve or thirteen.

The "White House"

In 1749, Daniel Parke Custis and Martha Dandridge married in the Custis family home, known ironically enough as the White House. The White House was but one of several properties throughout the colony owned by the family. Other properties were located in Hanover, James City, King and Queen, King William, and York counties. The Custis holdings also included Custis Square, one of the largest mansions in the capital city of Williamsburg (known informally as the "six-chimney home"), a large workforce of slaves, and accounts in London banks. The White House, a thriving plantation estate spanning some 17,000 acres located in New Kent County near the Pamunkey River, was not far from the Dandridge home.

The bride was eighteen, the groom thirty-eight. When Daniel's father died, the couple moved into the White House plantation. As a gentleman planter, Daniel did not himself farm. In fact, he was too frail to even supervise the business. Rather, he employed overseers, including two men named Epaphroditus Howle and John Roan, to manage the plantation's day-to-day operations.

Wealthy women like Martha had a "kitchen garden" that provided a source of fresh vegetables, fruits, herbs, and flowers in warmer seasons. Martha's gardens were located near the home, and she always enjoyed gardening and had a small staff to assist her in the garden, kitchen, and home. Like other women, Martha spent her days making home necessities like soaps, clothing, and candles. Martha treasured a cookbook and a general health book containing homeopathic cures and remedies that had been her mother-in-law's. From surviving accounts of when she was the wife of George Washington, we know that she was a skilled maker of clothing, spending a lot of time weaving, sewing, knitting, and spinning. A few slaves assisted her in these enterprises.

The Custis family lived comfortably, and Martha was treated well by Daniel. By all accounts, it seems to have been a happy marriage. Daniel ordered for his wife the finest and latest clothing from England, expensive furniture from London merchants, and anything Martha desired. They traveled to Williamsburg often, staying at their six-chimney mansion on Francis Street near Nassau Street. There they enjoyed the winter social season full of parties, theatrical performances, and dining with friends.

Daniel and Martha had four children over the first six years of their marriage, each carrying the maternal family name, suggesting that he was much closer to his mother than his difficult father. The children were Daniel Parke II, born in 1751; Frances Parke, born in 1753; John Parke, born the following year; and Martha Parke, born one year later. The firstborn carried his father's name; the youngest was named for her mother. As was common for families of social standing and economic means, the Custis family had portraits painted of the entire family. One of them, by John Wollaston, the noted English portraitist, was painted around 1757 and is probably the last painting of Daniel before his untimely death. Wollaston also painted Daniel in full length and the whole family together with Martha elegantly attired.

Tragedy Strikes

The happy marriage did not last long. Martha lost her first two children in infancy. The boy, Daniel, died in 1754 just three years after his birth; Frances passed in 1757 at age four. During the time of these two deaths, there would have been little time for grieving. Martha was taking care of infant children and gave birth near the time of the loss of her firstborn. One can only imagine the crushing sadness Martha must have experienced and the resolve she needed to pull through the losses.

The years 1756 and 1757 were especially trying times for the young mother. On August 21, 1756, Martha's father, John Dandridge, died at the age of fifty-six while visiting relatives in Fredericksburg. The record is not completely reliable, but accounts suggest that he died of a cerebral hemorrhage.

Over the next year, Martha gave birth to her fourth child, witnessed the death of her second child, and lost her husband to a heart attack. Daniel had been ill during much of their marriage, and, at the time of his passing in the summer of 1757 at age forty-five, the couple's infant son was gravely ill.

After her husband's death, Martha commissioned a seamstress named Elizabeth Vaughn, who lived near the White House plantation, to make a mourning dress for her. Another painful reminder of the loss came by way of the full-length portrait of Daniel painted by John Wollaston. The finished product was delivered in October, just three months after Daniel's passing. It was meant to celebrate what would have been Daniel's forty-sixth birthday. Martha graciously accepted and paid for the portrait. She also organized Daniel's funeral and ordered a tombstone from the family's English merchant, Robert Cary and Company. It read, "Here lies the body of Daniel Parke Custis, esquire who was born the 15th day of October, 1711 and departed this life the 8th day of July, 1757. Aged 45 years."

Widowhood was a harsh experience in the eighteenth century. Women had limited legal rights, an inability to earn a living on their own, and strict social mores about how they lived their lives and how they remarried. The Custis family was very affluent, but Martha could hold the wealth and land for her children only until such a time that a male relative or her oldest son would inherit it. Prevailing custom was such that fatherless children were often raised by a guardian, even if the mother survived. Guardians were usually married male relatives, such as the mother's father or father-in-law or perhaps a brother with the means to provide for the children. Martha might have faced this dilemma, but her husband's family members were deceased, as was her own father.

Martha thus assumed full guardianship of her two young children, the Custis farms and homes, stock in the Bank of England, and other assets. By September 1757, Martha had complete power of attorney over the children and Custis fortune, making her the matriarch of the powerful family and perhaps the wealthiest woman in the colony. After only eight years of marriage and at age twenty-six, Martha had already buried two children, her father, her father-in-law, and a husband. Martha grew to be a hypochondriac but for good reason. Shorter life expectancies and high infant mortality rates were an ever-present reminder of the fragility of life in the eighteenth century. Each fever or cough, every accident or infection, could prove fatal, and Martha always worried herself sick over her children and relatives. The Martha that history remembers as the wife of Washington was a much different—more somber, private, and matronly—woman than the spry and lively wife of Custis. Such a change in her demeanor seems perfectly understandable in light of the tragedies.

Surviving a Ruinous Scandal

The young widow was raising infant children, managing one of the largest plantation businesses in the colony, and adjusting to life without her husband. On top of that, she had to contend with a potentially ruinous legal affair. The details of the lawsuit are vague, but the matter stemmed from a dispute over proper ownership of land held by Daniel Custis's maternal grandfather, the late colonial governor Daniel Parke.

Shockingly, even though he was very wealthy and quite ill, Daniel Custis died without providing a will, suggesting a sudden death rather than succumbing to a protracted illness, something that the historical record indicates. Because there was no male heir to the Custis tobacco fortune, Martha had the daunting task of trying to mitigate the long-running lawsuit against the plantation and properties. Believing that they had the upper hand on an emotionally vulnerable widow, the plaintiffs were emboldened and aggressively pursued the lawsuit.

To her credit, Martha hired powerful attorneys to remedy the matter. They included John Mercer, Benjamin Eggleston, John Blair Jr., John Prentis, Peter Scott, and Benjamin Waller, a member of the House of Burgessses, judge, and treasurer of Virginia. Judge Waller wrote to Martha, also recommending that she add to her legal team John Robinson, the noted speaker of the Virginia House of Burgesses, and John Randolph, a member of the House of Burgesses and attorney general for the Crown. Martha's legal team seems to have been the eighteenth-century version of the "dream team," pointing to the extraordinary wealth of the Custis family and the sensitivity of the lawsuit.

Martha had the good sense to surround herself with the right people and the lawsuit was settled in her favor. One of her attorneys, Robert Carter Nicholas, in a letter written on August 7, 1757, offered the widow his full support and services as her counselor. Nicholas also stated that he was impressed with Martha's remarkable resiliency in the face of tragedy and her steady handling of the legal matter. Judge Waller also wrote to Martha, suggesting that she hire Joseph Valentine, a highly capable manager, to oversee her plantations. The plantation prospered under Martha's control. She obtained a good price from London merchants for her tobacco crop that fall and also requested that money owed to her from the Bank of London be sent at once. She also discontinued her business dealings with unreliable merchants.

It is clear that Martha involved herself in the business, investments, and landholdings. In one letter to a merchant (John Hanbury and Company), written on August 20, 1757, Martha informed him of the death of her husband but assured him that business would continue as usual:

> I take this Oppertunity to inform you of the great misfortune I have met with in the loss of my late Husband. . . . As I now have the Administration of his Estate and the management of his Affairs of all sorts I shall be glad to continue the correspondence which Mr. Custis carried on with you.

Similarly, writing to Robert Cary, with whom the Custis family had traded tobacco and purchased goods, Martha informed him of her husband's death but stated her interest in continuing his services. In particular, she wanted his help in distributing the present crop of tobacco in London. Writing on that same day in August, she stated,

> Without Will and left but two Children his Estate will be kept together some time and I think it will be proper to continue this Account with you in the same manner as if he was living, as most of the goods I shall send for will be for the use of the Family. . . . I shall yearly ship a considerable part of Tobacco I make to you which I shall take care to have as good as possible and hope you will do your endeavor to get me a good price.

She did, and he did. These two letters are among the earliest surviving letters written by Martha. Martha wrote many other letters to these men and other merchants and managed the business in such a way that the plantation's profits increased under her stewardship beyond that enjoyed by either John or Daniel Custis. By employing such talented and powerful men to assist her with the family lawsuit and the operation of the plantation, Martha showed herself to be judicious and politically savvy. She also kept a rational head during an emotionally wrenching time. Behind the appearance of a reserved, matronly housekeeper was a strong, shrewd woman.

SECOND LOVE

Widows tended to remarry quickly in the eighteenth century. And so it was for Martha Dandridge Custis, one of the wealthiest widows in the colony. As was mentioned in the opening chapter, we are not exactly sure how and when George Washington and Martha Dandridge Custis met, but we do know that their chance encounter at the home of a Mr. Chamberlayne in the spring of 1758 resulted in George's immediate and vigorous courtship of the wealthy widow. Whether the dinner at the Chamberlayne home marked the first time the two had met is uncertain, but it seems likely that they would have at least made one another's acquaintance in Williamsburg. The Washingtons and the Dandridges were from similar classes (until George's father died), both families visited the same places, both had connections to Williamsburg, and Tidewater society was a closely knit one.

Martha's fortuitous marriage would have made her a name among Williamsburg's elites, and Washington's growing military reputation had spread among Williamsburg's citizens. It is also probable that Colonel Washington was not the only prospective suitor for the wealthy widow, and this might have factored into the expediency with which Washington courted Martha. The couple wasted little time, marrying on January 6, 1759, at the White

House, the home that the bride inherited from her first marriage. Forty guests were in attendance for the 1:00 p.m. ceremony.

The union was, if not a romantically passionate one, a mutually agreeable arrangement. Under the laws governing marriage and property, Washington secured for himself not only a bride but also a vast fortune and extensive landholdings. The marriage put him on the social and financial map in Virginia society. But the strapping military officer also offered the promise of a fatherly role model for Martha's young children and a steady partner eager to help run the prosperous plantation.

"Agreeable Consort"

Later in life, George Washington wrote to a friend and offered a sense of his life with Martha: "I am now I believe fixed at this seat with an agreeable consort for life and hope to find more happiness in retirement than I ever experienced amidst the wide and bustling world." Washington's choice of words suggests contentedness and comfort in the marriage. Historians echo this sentiment, believing that George and Martha had a solid and faithful marriage although not one of great passion. They shared temperaments and tastes. Both were free of the vices of alcohol, gambling, sexual affairs, and idleness that governed the ruling aristocracy of the time. Rather, they were both active churchgoers who enjoyed dinners at home, entertaining guests, carriage rides, and the theater. They also loved family life at Mount Vernon. Both were early-to-bed, early-to-rise hard workers who were dependable and valued their privacy, social appearances, and reputations. In short, although the Washington marriage was perhaps not the marriage that George had hoped for or Martha's first, they were partners in many ways.

The marriage did have its strains, foremost among them the fact that the couple never had children of their own. Some scholars feel that Washington was unable to father a child, perhaps a result of contracting measles as a young man on his only trip abroad—to Barbados—leaving him infertile. Both husband and wife were frustrated by their inability to have children, but Martha's two surviving children—John Parke, nicknamed "Jacky," and Martha Parke, nicknamed "Patsy"—were raised as if they were Washington's children.

Around the time of the marriage, Washington's widowed sister-in-law passed away, and he inherited her home—Mount Vernon. The couple moved to Mount Vernon shortly after the wedding and, with Martha's money, continued to renovate and refurbish the home throughout their lives. Mount Vernon became the centerpiece of their lives together for four decades, even when Washington was away in the service of the new nation. The home reflected their temperaments and tastes, both practically and architecturally, and the couple considered their best years those when they were home together. For fifteen years before his service to the American Revolution, Washington enjoyed life at Mount Vernon as a gentleman planter. He ordered for the home busts of Alexander the Great, Julius Caesar, and other noted leaders and warriors, perhaps foreshadowing the coming end of domestic tranquillity at Mount Vernon. It was also at Mount Vernon where Martha entertained a nearly nonstop parade of guests, well-wishers, and dignitaries who enjoyed Mrs. Washington's famous "great cake," a monstrous delicacy made with forty eggs and lots of fresh fruit, such as cherries and apples or raisins and citrus. The cake reflected the hostess's notorious sweet tooth.

The Marquis de Lafayette, France's hero of the American Revolution and Washington's good friend, visited Mount Vernon in the summer of 1784. Lafayette developed a fondness for Mrs. Washington that she reciprocated but did try her patience at one point. George Washington loved dogs, which he used when engaged in one of his favorite recreations—foxhunting. The general had an entire pack of French hounds—large, loud, and aggressive dogs barely tolerated by the lady of the house. During Lafayette's visit, he gave Washington more dogs as a gift, but one of the hounds, named Vulcan, managed to get loose. The dog stole one of Martha's prized Virginia hams from her kitchen, and this did not sit well with the hostess, who took great pride in her cooking and in her hams.

When Lafayette arrived back in France, well intentioned, he nonetheless unwisely sent Washington more French hounds as a gift. According to her grandson, George Parke Custis, Mrs. Washington eventually made her husband get rid of the dogs. Washington even stopped hunting foxes. Both decisions would have been difficult ones for Washington. Even so, the Washington marriage was a firm and reliable one, a partnership that helped to forge a new nation.

"My Dearest"

Shortly after Mrs. Washington's death, her granddaughters Eleanor, who was nicknamed "Nelly" and to whom Martha was very close, and Martha Parke Custis Peter stumbled by chance onto a small cache of their late grandmother's letters. These few letters—likely the only ones to survive history—were discovered in a desk in the small room on the third floor of Mount Vernon, the room Martha chose to occupy after the death of her husband. The letters provide insights as to the Washingtons' feelings for one another—and much more. The good news is that more than 150 of Martha's letters survive. Even though the letters exchanged between the Washingtons are lost, three of them managed to survive history, and we have evidence of the contents of a fourth letter. This latter letter has subsequently been lost, but it did survive the initial destruction of the Washington correspondence. It was the only one of the four remaining letters between husband and wife written by Martha. The other three surviving letters were written by George.

Writing on March 30, 1767, Martha shared with her husband, who was in Williamsburg, information on the weather conditions at Mount Vernon. Martha missed her husband, stating, "My Dearest, I am sorry you will not be at home soon. . . . Your most Affectionate, Martha Washington." The tone is simple and warm and reveals Martha's devotion to George. However, it clearly lacks the passion and playful innuendo of Washington's correspondence with Sally Fairfax or Eliza Powel. Whether this is because of the natural tempering that comes after eight years and two months of marriage we cannot be sure. The 1767 letter also reflects George Washington's almost obsessive interest in recording details about the weather and business of his farms. We know, for example, that when he was not home to take his daily recording of the weather conditions at Mount Vernon, he employed Martha in the task.

One of the letters that survives was written by George to Martha on October 1, 1782, and it simply extends an introduction to her of a friend whom she would soon be meeting. It is also matter-of-fact in its tone and, unfortunately, offers us little in terms of insights into the Washington marriage other than a lack of heated passion. Washington wrote to "My dearest":

> If this letter should ever reach your hands, it will be presented by Mr Brown,—son to a Gentleman of that name in Rhode Island, from whom I have received civilities, & to whom, or his connections I could wish to make returns.—As he has thoughts of going into Virginia I recommend him to your notice & Attention

But the other two surviving letters are of consequence. One, dated June 18, 1775, was written from Philadelphia when Washington received news of his appointment as commander in chief of the Continental army. The usually stoic Washington offered a glimpse behind his public persona when he expressed reservation about his appointment. In a husbandly manner, he also both worries about Martha's well-being and reassures her of his affection for her. Washington wrote to his wife,

> I am now set down to write you on a subject which fills me with inexpressible concern and this concern is greatly aggravated and increased, when I reflect upon the uneasiness I know it will cause you. It has been determined in Congress, that the whole army raised for the defence of the

American cause shall be put under my care, and that it is necessary for me to proceed immediately to Boston to take upon me the command of it.

You may believe me, my dear Patsy, when I assure you, in the most solemn manner that, so far from seeking this appointment, I have used every endeavor in my power to avoid it, not only from my unwillingness to part with you and the family, but from a consciousness of its being a trust too great for my capacity, and that I should enjoy more real happiness in one month with you at home, than I have the most distant prospect of finding abroad, if my stay were to be seven times seven years. But as it has been a kind of destiny, that has thrown me upon this service, I shall hope that my undertaking it is designed to answer some good purpose, You might, and I suppose did perceive, from the tenor of my letters, that I was apprehensive I could not avoid this appointment, without exposing my character to such censures, as would have reflected dishonor upon myself, and have given pain to my friends. This, I am sure, could not, and ought not, to be pleasing to you, and must have lessened me considerably in my own esteem. I shall rely, therefore, confidently on that Providence, which has heretofore preserved and been bountiful to me, not doubting but that I shall return safe to you in the fall. I shall feel no pain from the toil of the danger of the campaign; my unhappiness will flow from the uneasiness I know you will feel from being left alone. I therefore beg that you will summon your whole fortitude, and pass your time as agreeably as possible. Nothing will give me so much sincere satisfaction as to hear this, and to hear it from your own pen.

Washington goes on to discuss the fact that he had drafted a will and prepared plans in the event of his death. After excusing himself because he had but little time and many letters to write, the general promised Martha that he would write again and signed his letter, "My dear Patcy, Yr affecte Go Washington."

The letter is revealing for two reasons. First, it depicts a close relationship and Washington's concern for his wife's emotional well-being. It must be remembered that Martha suffered the loss of several family members. She must have opposed his departure for Philadelphia and the prospect of his being selected to lead the war because Washington tries hard to both soothe her and reassure her that he did not desire the command, and this is, of course, baloney. Washington was the only man in attendance at the famous gathering in Philadelphia who was, from head to toe, attired in full military uniform. He lusted for the opportunity.

Second, Washington worried about whether he was up to such an awesome challenge. He admits that the command is "a trust too great for my capacity." It seems that once Washington achieved his goal, the realization settled in that he might be in over his head. Part of his expressed concern might also have been because of the hopeless prospects of leading a ragtag band of poorly equipped farmers against the world's most powerful military. The new general even states to his wife that he would rather be at home with her. It is uncertain, however, how much of this confession is truthful and how much of the statement is due to nervousness or the gravity of the situation or whether it was simply to further calm a wife who disapproved of his absence and worried herself sick about his safety. During the war, Washington also thoughtfully had relatives and friends visit Martha in an effort to lift her spirits. Either way, Washington is hesitant and reveals some self-doubt when it comes to his abilities, reflecting what many scholars have suggested about the complex personality of the private Washington. And in so doing, Washington shares his intimate concerns with his wife and possibly also drew strength from her, much as he had from Sally Fairfax.

The other surviving letter exchanged between the Washingtons is also of consequence. It too hints at a caring marriage. Written on June 23, 1775— five days after the previously mentioned letters—the general provides his wife with an update as he departs for headquarters at Cambridge, Massachusetts, writing to his "dearest,"

> As I am within a few minutes of leaving this City, I could not think of departing from it without dropping you a line; especially as I do not know whether it may be in my power to write again till I get to the camp in Boston—I go fully trusting in that Providence, which has been more bountiful to me than I deserve and in full confidence of a happy meeting with you sometime in the Fall—I have not time to add more as I am surrounded with Company to take leave of me—I retain an unalterable affection for you, which neither time or distance can change. My best love to Jack & Nelly, and regard for the rest of the Family concludes me with the utmost truth & sincerity.

On Marriage

Fortunately, Washington left behind his thoughts on marriage, women, and love. Washington had been raised to put "judgment" over "passion," something he practiced and counseled throughout his life, and was challenged to do because of Sally Fairfax, his wealthy neighbor and object of his passion. This too was the case in marriage, where he placed tranquillity above excitement. The contrast could not be more stark than when Washington wrote comparing and contrasting youth's "giddy round of promiscuous pleasure" with the "domestic felicity" of marriage. More darkly, Washington's opinion of marriage included the blunt assessment that "the madness ceases and all is quiet again. Why? Not because there is any diminution in the charms of the lady, but because there is an end of hope."

Washington once advised his stepdaughter on the topic of marriage, offering the following sober words:

> Do not then in your contemplation of the marriage state look for perfect felicity before you consent to wed. Nor conceived, from the fine tales the poets and lovers of old have told us of the transports of mutual love, that it has taken its abode on earth. Nor do not deceive yourself in supposing that the only means by which these are to be obtained is to drink deep of the cup and revel in an ocean of love. Love is a mighty pretty thing, but, like all other delicious things, it is cloying; and when the first transports of the passion begin to subside, which it assuredly will do, and yield, oftentimes too late, to more sober reflections, it serves to evince that love is too dainty a food to live on alone.

Once again, the practical overruled the passionate. According to Washington, the key to marital bliss is "good sense, a good disposition, and the means of supporting you in the way you have been brought up." Furthermore, he advised, "In my estimation, more permanent and genuine happiness is to be found in the sequestered walks of connubial life than in the giddy rounds of promiscuous pleasure."

Despite marrying late, Washington had always placed the utmost importance on marriage, noting, "I have always considered marriage as the most interesting event in one's life, the foundation of happiness or misery." And Washington did find happiness—at least comfort and tranquillity—in marriage. Washington once took the time to hand-copy a verse titled "True Happiness," which offered the following advice:

> These are things which once possessed
> Will make a life that's truly blessed;
> A good estate on healthy soil
> Not got by vice, nor yet by toil;
> Round a warm fire, a pleasant joke,
> With chimney ever free from smoke;
> A strength entire, a sparkling bowl,
> A quiet wife, a quiet soul.

It is difficult to find a verse that more fully reflects Washington's values and life than these lines. After an unhappy childhood and early adulthood marked by frustration and turmoil, it was through marriage to the widow Custis that Washington finally attained everything his life had been missing—everything, that is, except his true love. It is impossible to read

Washington's thoughts on marriage and not think of his long-held affection for Sally Fairfax and possible thoughts of what might have been.

Washington ultimately accepted the reality that he could never have Sally as his wife. Sally was married, and both their mutual honor and the strict social conventions of their neighbors forbade it. At the same time, he could not ever close his heart. Rather, Washington carried his feelings for Sally for the rest of his life. Even after marriage, the two neighbors—with their spouses—frequently picnicked and socialized together. Whether Mrs. Washington knew of her husband's history with or feelings for their beautiful neighbor, she did not record such. But it seems most likely that the perceptive Martha would have known, and even a man as stoic as Washington would have trouble hiding his true feelings.

Washington informed Sally Fairfax of his intention to marry Martha, and it seems that Sally was one of the first to know about the plans. But Sally wrote to Washington inquiring about his future bride and wishing him good luck with marriage. On his engagement to Martha, Washington wrote to Sally on September 12, 1758, from Fort Cumberland,

> Yesterday I was honour'd with your short but very agreeable favour of the first inst. How joyfully I catch at the happy occasion of renewing a cor-rispondance which I fear'd was disrelish'd on your part, I leave to time, that never failing Expositor of all things, and to a Monitor equally as faithful in my own Breast to Testifie. In silence I now express my Joy. Silence, which in some cases—I wish the present—speaks more intelligibly than the sweetest Eloquence.
>
> If you allow that an honour can be deriv'd from my opposition to our present System of management, you destroy the merit of it entirely in me by attributing my anxiety to the animating prospect of possessing Mrs. Custis, when—I need not name it, guess yourself—should not my own Honour and Country's welfare be the excitement? 'Tis true I profess my-self a votary to Love. I acknowledge that a Lady is in the case; and, further, I confess that this Lady is known to you. Yes, madam, as well as she is to one who is too sensible of her Charms to deny the Power whose influence he feels and must ever submit to. I feel the force of her amiable beauties in the recollection of a thousand tender passages that I could wish to obliter-ate till I am bid to revive them; but Experience alas! sadly reminds me how impossible this is, and evinces an Opinion, which I have long entertained that there is a Destiny which has the sovereign control of our actions, not to be resisted by the strongest efforts of Human Nature.
>
> You have drawn me, my dear Madam, or rather have I drawn myself, into an honest confession of a Simple Fact. Misconstrue not my mean-ing, 'tis obvious; doubt it not, nor expose it. The world has no business to know the object of my love, declared in this manner to—you, when I want

to conceal it. One thing, above all things, in the World I wish to know, and only one person of your acquaintance can solve me that, or guess my meaning—but adieu to this till happier times, if ever I shall see them; the hours at present are melancholy dull—neither the rugged toils of War, nor the gentler conflicts of A⸺ B⸺s is in my choice. [The historian, Worthington Chauncey Ford, suggests that A and B stand for Assembly Balls.] I dare believe you are as happy as you say. I wish I was happy also. Mirth, good Humour, ease of Mind, and—what else? cannot fail to render you so, and consummate your Wishes.

If one agreeable lady cou'd almost wish herself a fine Gentleman for the sake of another, I apprehend that many fine Gentlemen will wish themselves finer e'er Mrs. Spotswood is possessed. She has already become a reigning toast in this Camp, and many there are in it who intend, fortune favouring, to make honourable scars speak the fullness of the Merit and be a messenger of their Love to her.

I cannot easily forgive the unseasonable haste of my last Express if he depriv'd me thereby of a single word you intended to add. The time of the present messenger is, as the last might have been, entirely at your disposal. I can't expect to hear from my Friend more than this once, before the Fate of the Expedition will somehow or other be determin'd. I, therefore, beg to know when you set out for Hampton & when you expect to return to Belvoir again, and should be glad to hear also of your speedy departure, as I shall thereby hope for your return before I get down; the disappointment of [not] seeing your family wou'd give me much concern. From anything I can yet see 'tis hardly possible to say when we shall finish. I don't think there is a probability of it till the middle of November.

A Letter unlike Any Other

Unique among Washington's surviving letters, the previously mentioned one is rambling, secretive, and filled with innuendo about double meaning. The letter was written in response to Sally's questions about his engagement. It is almost impossible, knowing what we do about Washington's feelings for Sally, not to arrive at the conclusion that the letter is actually cryptically and desperately telling her that she is his true love. Curiously, Washington's engagement to Martha comes at the same time Sally had cooled the temperature of their friendship and frequency of their correspondence.

At the least, Washington is being romantically playful with Sally and vague about his feelings. It is not possible to tell if his thoughts are directed at his fiancée or Sally, and it would seem that this was precisely Washington's intention. In her letter, Sally wondered whether Washington's engagement was causing him so much anxiety, but he refutes this conclusion in a way that suggests that the source of his anxiety was that he was resigned to marry a woman other than Sally.

Washington curiously mentions Martha's last name in the letter but then says that the object of his love is known to Sally. Why say this after first mentioning Martha's name unless the intention is to hint that the true love is none other than Sally? Washington goes on to ask Sally not to mention his love to anyone else, which is also curious, as is his statement that only one person, who happens to be known to Sally, can truly help him at this time. The unnamed person was, of course, Sally herself. Moreover, the letter drips with uncharacteristically sappy references to the difficulties of destiny and resisting passions when it would be expected to be filled with platitudes for his soon-to-be bride.

Three months after penning this letter to Sally, Washington married the widow Custis. The marriage was described by the noted historian Richard Norton Smith:

> Neither partner entertained illusions. For him, the plump, amiable widow was a sensible alternative to Sally Fairfax, the worldly, alluring wife of Washington's best friend and Potomac neighbor. For her, the dashing veteran of British campaigns in the Ohio River Valley promised to be a good manager of her estate and an attentive guardian to her children.

Because they appear lost to history, we may never know the nature of Washington's other letters to his wife. Yet the surviving letters to Martha are far less playful and far more pedestrian than those exchanged with Sally. Even through marriage, it would not be his "good and happy wife" and his "agreeable Consort for Life" but rather Sally who was Washington's inspiration.

Interrupted

The domestic tranquillity that Martha so enjoyed was shattered. The revolutionary political events of her lifetime and her husband's central role in them interrupted life at Mount Vernon, as did the death of her two remaining children. Her daughter, Patsy, had long suffered from epilepsy, and the couple had unsuccessfully sought cures far and wide for the affliction. They even tried an iron collar that was recommended to them as a possible cure. In 1773, while seated at the dinner table, Patsy suffered another seizure and died. She was only seventeen.

Washington described Patsy's death and his wife's reaction to it in a matter-of-fact somberness, writing in his account book that "this sudden and unexpected blow has almost reduced my poor wife to the lowest ebb of Misery." Martha was so devastated that, even one year later, she was still in mourning and unable to gather herself emotionally to attend the wedding of her only surviving child, son "Jacky," to Eleanor "Nelly" Calvert of Maryland in February 1774.

When the War for Independence broke out, the matter of Jacky's participation in it created tension in the home. Not only was it upsetting to the disciplined Washington that Jacky was somewhat irresponsible and thriftless; it was an embarrassment for the general that his own stepson was not in the fight. But Martha refused to allow Jacky to enlist, having already lost three of her four children. Finally, as the tide of the war had turned to favor the colonials, Martha reluctantly agreed to permit Jacky to serve but only as an aide-de-camp in Washington's own headquarters during the Battle of Yorktown. However, when he reported to duty, Jacky contracted camp fever. Hearing the alarming news, Martha and Jacky's wife, Nelly, rushed to be at his bedside. But it was too late. The death of her sole surviving child in 1781 dealt Martha Washington a devastating blow.

Jacky and his wife had four children at the time of his death: Elizabeth, nicknamed "Eliza," who was born in 1774; Martha, nicknamed "Patty," who was born in 1777; Eleanor, nicknamed "Nelly," born in 1779; and George Washington, nicknamed "Wash," born in 1781. It was only the presence of her grandchildren that helped to console Martha. As was often customary, Martha adopted the two youngest children of her daughter-in-law and late son. She raised Nelly, who was a toddler at the time of Jacky's death, and Wash, who was born around the time of his father's passing. The two older siblings lived with their mother, but the family often visited Mount Vernon, as did other relatives. Martha was able to continue to enjoy a household full of children. However, the firstborn grandchild, Eliza, died in childhood, but the other three children would enjoy long lives.

Heroine

George and Martha Washington spent four decades together as husband and wife during the most momentous of times, making theirs a shared legacy. The plump grandmother and homemaker turned out to be a gifted hostess, co-manager of a thriving plantation, and a source of strength for the foremost man of his times. Indeed, even though Martha Washington always longed for a quiet family life, she ended up living a life befitting a Shakespearean play—complete with war, death, personal strife, and public service, all the while helping to change history.

Hers was a difficult and tragic life. She endured the death of so many family members and loved ones and had her husband called away from her by duty. George Washington was away from his wife during both the First and Second Continental Congresses in 1774 and 1775; then, as leader of the colonial forces, he was away from Mount Vernon for more than seven difficult years until he resigned his commission on December 23, 1783. Martha also faced the prospect that her husband would be killed in the line of duty.

An extremely private woman, Martha nonetheless brushed aside her privacy to lead a very public life and emerge as one of the symbols of the American Revolution. In fact, Martha took to wearing only homespun garments rather than those made in England as a sign of her support for the cause. Every winter Martha trekked the long, cold distances by wagon or carriage to join her husband in his winter headquarters—Cambridge, Valley Forge, Morristown, Newburgh, and Annapolis. Accordingly, it is probable Martha had the distinction of seeing more of the country than any other woman at the time. Nearly everywhere she went, she was met by adoring crowds eager to greet the great Lady Washington.

While in camp, she shared the hardships, tending to the wounded soldiers, cooking, praying, cleaning, and assisting her husband. A mother to the army, Mrs. Washington soothed the frayed nerves and sagging spirit of both the camp and her husband. Yet, through it all, Martha retained a sense of perspective and her trademark humility. As wife of the president, Martha traveled to New York City, the temporary seat of the new government. Along the way, she was greeted by cannonade salutes, gawking crowds, and parades in cities such as Philadelphia. Of the experience, Martha shrugged it off as "great pomp as if I had been a very great somebody." The wife of the foremost man of his times even referred to the social events held in honor of the new president and his wife as "empty ceremonies of etiquette." Preferring the quiet life to the splendor of the presidency, Martha spoke of the "burden" of her "lost days" in service to her husband's career and the nation. However, like her husband, Martha had a strong sense of duty. She put her personal preferences, family life, and safety aside to serve the nation.

During the inaugural presidency, Martha was once again called on to sacrifice and serve. She did so by forging the roles and duties of the president's wife. While little was known about what the president should do, even fewer guidelines existed for what the first president's wife should do. Mrs. Washington managed to find the perfect blend of royalty and domestic simplicity befitting the new democratic nation. She presided over socials and "levees" held on Tuesdays and Fridays, returned endless social calls, hosted dignitaries, and offered her husband a source of strength and support.

Martha Washington was tireless in her work. Writing to her family and friends of the new presidential office, the First Lady stated, "I have not had one half hour to myself since the day of my arrival." After George Washington's service in the war and again after his presidency, Martha opened her home to a steady stream of visitors, guests, and dignitaries. Mount Vernon was as much a boarding home and restaurant as it was a private home. In fact, in retirement, George Washington once noted, "Unless someone pops in unexpectedly, Mrs. Washington and I will do what has not been [done] by us in nearly twenty years—that is set down to dinner by ourselves."

That she was an ordinary person who lived an extraordinary life is only partially true. In the remembrance of one family slave, "The General was only a man, but Mrs. Washington was perfect."

Martha lived two and a half years beyond her husband. Her pain at losing him was such that she never again stepped foot into the bedroom they shared at Mount Vernon. Even with her husband gone, she was denied the privacy she longed for. Yet Martha stoically and dutifully met the crowds of well-wishers who paid respects to the fallen leader and his widow. One such account of Mrs. Washington's state after her husband's passing comes from John Marshall, chief justice of the Supreme Court and a friend of the late president. After visiting the widow to offer condolences, the chief justice wrote to his wife that while Martha appeared pleasant and accommodating, she did not have "the sort of cheerfulness as formerly."

Martha Washington died on May 22, 1802, of "severe fever." She is interred beside her husband, where her sarcophagus reads, "Martha, consort of Washington." An obituary at the time of her death provides a better description, calling her a "worthy partner" for the most worthy of all men.

Gilbert Stuart captured the "Sage of Monticello" at work in his study.
Library of Congress Prints and Photographs Division, LC-USZ62-117117 DLC.

⊰ 5 ⊱

Slave Owner and Slave Lover

[This is] the most extraordinary collection of talent . . . that
has ever been gathered together at the White House—with
the exception of when Thomas Jefferson dined alone.

—John F. Kennedy welcoming a group of
Nobel laureates to the White House

IT'S IN THE DNA

As the author of the Declaration of Independence, the third president of
the United States, governor of the Old Dominion State, and founder of the
University of Virginia, among other accomplishments, Thomas Jefferson's
position in history has been more than assured. Part of Virginia's founding
dynasty, his political career as a member of the House of Burgesses and Continental Congress placed him at the center of revolutionary events and allowed
him to play a key role in the establishment of the United States of America.

Likewise, Jefferson's presidency is considered one of the greatest and
most important in American history by scholars, as he paid off the revolutionary debts and expanded the country with the inclusion of the expansive Louisiana Purchase. The population soared from 5 million to 8 million people
during his presidency from 1801 to 1809. His political philosophy, which
embraced the notion "that government is best which governs least," remains
a defining part of the American civic creed. Jefferson also embodied for the
world the best of what America offered—inventor, philosopher, and human-
ist; Jefferson was the "Universal Man." Jefferson's book *Notes on the State of
Virginia* remains one of the most important sources for understanding social
and political life in the period surrounding the nation's founding.

Even Jefferson's peers on the committee assigned in Philadelphia to draft
a declaration declaring the colonies' independence—all great and learned men
themselves: John Adams, Benjamin Franklin, Robert Livingston, and Roger

Sherman—were so duly impressed with his literary, philosophic, and intellectual abilities that they wisely chose him to author the founding document. Indeed, Jefferson alone has the standing as the epitome of American ideals more so than perhaps any other person, including George Washington and Abraham Lincoln. Thus said historian James Parton in 1874 that "if Jefferson was wrong, America is wrong. If America is right, Jefferson was right."

Therefore, it is not surprising that Jefferson has been the subject of countless books and scholarly works, while the Thomas Jefferson Foundation, Monticello Foundation, and others have worked tirelessly to preserve his home and his memory. Much is known about Jefferson because scholars have preserved, edited, and published his writings—quite an undertaking considering the fact that the great founder wrote some 18,000 letters in his lifetime. But Jefferson's legacy is multifaceted and not without controversy. He was an immensely complex individual who evoked a wide array of emotions from his contemporaries, including jealousy, anger, and admiration. Even such figures as George Washington, John Adams, James Madison, and Alexander Hamilton—all of whom worked closely with Jefferson on the founding of the Republic—believed him to be a rather intriguing and complicated individual.

So too was Jefferson very reluctant to share personal revelations with his contemporaries and future readers of his letters. It is difficult to "read his mind," as he often wrote cryptically and with an eye to his historical reputation. During his attempts at courtship as a college student, for example, Jefferson worried that his letters might fall into the hands of others, so he devised a system of coded communication with his friend John Page. It was a variety of shorthand mixing Greek and Latin. He later created a numerical cipher for his letters with James Madison and James Monroe.

As such, there are stories of Jefferson still waiting to be discovered and told. And so it was in 1998 when Jefferson, dead for more than a century and a half, commanded the front page of the *New York Times*, the front cover of the magazine *U.S. News & World Report*, and a special episode of the popular television show *Oprah*. The cause of all the commotion was the publication in the British journal *Nature* of the findings of a team of geneticists, led by Dr. Eugene A. Foster, who examined DNA evidence for possible paternity of the children of Jefferson's slave Sally Hemings. The tests fingered Jefferson.

The Debate

The study tested the Y-chromosomal haplotypes for four groups of men to see if their male descendants shared DNA with the male descendants of Sally Hemings. The four were Sally's son Eston Hemings; Jefferson's grandfather Field Jefferson; John Carr, who was the grandfather of the Jefferson's nephews; the Carr boys (Samuel and Peter, who frequently visited Monticello and were known to "enjoy" the company of slave girls); and Thomas Woodson, a slave at Monticello. The study's authors proclaimed that Jefferson appeared to have fathered Sally's last child.

The publication prompted Oprah Winfrey to host family reunions in 1998 for both the black and the white descendants of Jefferson, many of whom had never met. Some of Sally Hemings's descendants also attended the annual Monticello Association gathering of Jefferson descendants. The topic was also discussed at a national conference in 1999, held at "Mr. Jefferson's School"—the University of Virginia—and National Public Radio hosted Sally's descendants on the air. Likewise, *Ebony* magazine, with one of the nation's largest black readerships, has followed the Sally Hemings story for years, and a made-for-television miniseries named for the slave mistress was made.

But controversy ensued with some pretty heated responses from the community of Jefferson historians. For example, the original November 5, 1998, article was rebutted in the same journal on January 7, 1999, and the *Wall Street Journal* published an editorial on Independence Day of 2001 refuting the study. Several conservative publications joined them, and both conservative scholars and organizations dug their heels in, with the Monticello Association voting in May 2002 not to admit descendants of Sally Hemings to the organization. Some noted historians, such as Paul Boller, had long dismissed the possibility of an affair and attributed the public interest in it as stemming solely from the 1974 publication of Fawn Brodie's *Thomas Jefferson: An Intimate Life*, which went so far as to claim that Jefferson and Sally spent thirty-eight happy years together. Another of the early books to discuss the subject was Winthrop Jordan's *White over Black*, published in 1968 but with little notice.

The Pulitzer Prize winner and dean of Jefferson scholars, Dumas Malone of the University of Virginia, denied any possibility of an affair with Sally and attempted to discredit Brodie. Professor Malone even tried to stop a televised movie about Jefferson and the affair from airing. Joseph Ellis, noted historian and author of the otherwise excellent biography of Jefferson *American Sphinx*, claimed that Jefferson's most sensual statements were aimed at "beautiful buildings" rather than beautiful women. It is undeniable that Jefferson was passionate about architecture and art. For instance, while in France, Jefferson wrote a letter to Mme. de Tess in Paris, admitting,

> Here I am, madam, gazing whole hours at the Maison square, like a lover at his mistress. . . . This is the second time I have been in love since I left Paris. The first was with a Diana at the Chateau de Laye Epinaye in the Beaujolois, a delicious morsel of sculpture, by Michaelangelo Slodtz. This, you will say, was in rule, to fall in love with a fine woman: but with a house! It is out of all precedent!

However, this does not preclude him from also being passionate about women, which was clearly the case and is evident in his love letters to Maria Cosway and other belles. One of the early Jefferson scholars, James Parton, in *Thomas Jefferson: A Life*, was even less veiled in his defense of Jefferson's sanctity, saying, "Jefferson had no more acquaintance with Sally Hemings than the most repulsive of his slaves." However, as is discussed later in this chapter, such actions and statements are simply naked (and racist) attempts to preserve Jefferson's reputation. The truth of the matter is that Jefferson's letters dripped with sexual innuendo and passion for the fairer sex. Indeed, the *William and Mary Quarterly* (published at Jefferson's alma mater) published an article in 2000 supporting the possible paternity, and a number of writers, including Jefferson biographer Fawn Brodie, and historians such as the Thomas Jefferson Memorial Association's Annette Gordon-Reed, accept the strong likelihood of the affair.

In January 2000, the Thomas Jefferson Foundation—the operator of Monticello—released the report of its own commission on the "controversy," stating, "Although paternity cannot be established with absolute certainty, our evaluation of the best evidence available suggests the strong likelihood that Thomas Jefferson and Sally Hemings had a relationship over time that led to the birth of one, and perhaps all, of the known children of Sally Hemings." But the Jefferson Foundation's report drove an even deeper wedge between Jefferson enthusiasts who had long been bitterly divided over the controversy. On the heels of the report, the new Thomas Jefferson Heritage Society split from the foundation over the issue and organized the "Jefferson-Hemings Scholars Commission" to study the paternity question. On April 12, 2001, the new commission released a 565-page report that concluded, to no one's surprise, "The Jefferson-Hemings allegation is by no means proven."

The Jefferson Heritage Society suggested that Jefferson's younger brother, Randolph, who was in his forties and fifties when Sally's children were born, might have been the father and claimed that Sally was but a "minor figure" in Jefferson's life. Two members of the commission, Robert Turner and David Mayer, added a new wrinkle to the controversy when they suggested that the original study was rushed to publication in order to benefit President Bill Clinton, who, in 1998, was facing charges that he had an affair with a young intern. To their minds, the announcement of Jefferson's affair might link the embattled Clinton to the great Jefferson and thereby help the president avoid impeachment.

Whether or not Jefferson had an affair with a slave, one thing that is not open for debate is that the "controversy" has been soiled by racist overtones. One of those claiming that the affair occurred is Byron Woodson, author of a book on his family history and an eighth-generation descendant of what he describes as "Thomas Jefferson's second family." Although most scholars deny Woodson's claims, including those who believe that Jefferson did father children with Sally, nor did it help Woodson's case that he refused to submit blood samples to the team of geneticists who performed the controversial DNA paternity test, Woodson does make a valid and touching point. He describes the two centuries of "racial codification" that his family has endured, including during their efforts to uncover the truth behind the Jefferson and Hemings children.

Indeed, the story of a Jefferson affair had been rumored since his presidency. The rumor has been kept alive all this time by occasional publications on the topic, such as the 1848 poem titled "Jefferson's Daughter" and the subsequent novel on the topic titled *Clotel, or the President's Daughter* in 1853 by former slave William Wells Brown.

There were twenty-five male Jefferson relatives when Sally lived, complicating the matter of determining paternity, and many historians have opposed the idea that Jefferson fathered Sally's children. However, the balance is changing. Where once scholars did not even deem the allegation to be worth mentioning, there is now a growing consensus that Jefferson likely had a long-term affair with his slave. In February 2003, however, the Jefferson Foundation revised its statement, adding,

> Although the relationship between Thomas Jefferson and Sally Hemings has been for many years, and will surely continue to be, a subject of intense interest to historians and the public, the evidence is not definitive, and the complete story may never be known. The Foundation encourages our visitors and patrons, based on what evidence does exist, to make up their own minds as to the true nature of the relationship.

Perhaps the magazine *Science* put it best when, on January 8, 1999, it suggested of the controversy that both sides were being misleading. The debate continues.

JEFFERSON'S "UNKNOWN WIFE"

John Wayles was the fourth of five children from a family of modest means. It appears as though he was not well educated but that he compensated for it with great energy and charisma. Wayles has been described as "unusual" in his abilities, filled with "gusto," and a "generous host." Jefferson offered the following words about his future father-in-law: "a lawyer of much practice, to which he was introduced more by his great industry, punctuality and practical readiness, than to eminence in the science of his professor. He was a most agreeable companion, full of pleasantry and good humor, and welcomed in every society."

Wayles emigrated from England with little but by his thirties was wealthy beyond his imagination, becoming one of Virginia's leading planters, slave traders, and attorneys. Along the way, he accumulated 135 slaves and several plantations totaling 11,000 acres. But he was less fortunate in marriage. He married his first wife, Martha Eppes, in 1746, but she died in 1748, one week after a daughter was born. Some accounts suggest that she had twins—one that was stillborn; the other died hours later—before giving birth again in 1748. The daughter who was born in 1748, named for her mother, would grow up to become Mrs. Thomas Jefferson.

Wayles married a second wife, Mary Cocke, and the union produced four daughters—Sarah, who died young; Elizabeth; Tabitha; and Anne—and then the second Mrs. Wayles died. He then married a third wife, Elizabeth Lomax Skelton, in January 1760. The third Mrs. Wayles died on May 28, 1763. It appears that Wayles then vowed never to marry again. He never did. Instead, Wayles purchased a slave named Elizabeth (nicknamed "Betty") from a shipping captain named Hemings. Elizabeth Hemings would become his mistress. Accounts vary, but the slave mistress, Elizabeth, and her new master had between five and seven children together at the Wayles plantation. She may also have had up to seven children with another slave.

The future Mrs. Jefferson was born on October 19, 1748, in Charles City County, Virginia, at her father's plantation. The family home, known as "The Forest," was not far from Williamsburg. It appears that Martha spent her entire youth on the family plantation, with occasional visits to Williamsburg and the homes of prominent neighbors. Her upbringing, about which very little exists, was likely one of privilege and comfort. She did, however lose a mother, two stepmothers, and at least one half-sister.

Martha appears to have attended—and would have been expected to have done so given her father's wealth and their close proximity to the colonial capital—social events in Williamsburg. It is also probable, given her father's reputation as a generous and gregarious host, that social events were held at The Forest, with Martha, as the eldest daughter, helping to host them. Area planters and dignitaries would surely have been invited to dine at the Wayles home, and, conversely, the Wayles family would have received its share of social invitations. Because her father buried three wives and lived for some years as a widower, it is probable that Martha's domestic education came at an accelerated pace. She was thrust into the role of homemaker, hostess, and surrogate mother to her younger sisters at a tender age. Martha knew how to make soap, candles, butter, and other household staples of the eighteenth century; she could cook, sew, and treat illnesses with homemade remedies. Later, as Jefferson's wife, Martha demonstrated skill in managing a household and a thriving plantation with estates, farms, a large slave population, attendant overseers, frequent visitors, and so on. Martha also helped Jefferson organize family finances and order supplies.

Befitting the wife of Jefferson, Martha was not only literate but also well read for a woman of her time. She enjoyed poetry and fiction. Families of comfortable means often employed tutors to educate their daughters (who did not attend school), and this was likely the case for Martha. Her education focused on literature, music, dancing, Bible study, and French. She also sang and played the harpsichord very well, suggesting that she had lessons as a child.

On November 20, 1766, Martha married a man four years her senior named Bathurst Skelton. She had celebrated her eighteenth birthday just one month prior. In 1767, a son, John, was born to Martha and Bathurst. But before the couple had a chance to celebrate their second wedding anniversary, Bathurst Skelton died on September 30, 1768. In 1771, the child died, leaving Martha both childless and a widow. The following year, she married Thomas Jefferson. But this is about all that history remembers of the wife of Thomas Jefferson. Marriage is one of the few facts of Jefferson's life that has not been sufficiently examined. To be sure, Martha Wayles Skelton Jefferson remains an enigma and is perhaps the least known of all the spouses of American presidents. Very little of their lives together has been recorded or saved. It appears that the primary reason for this is that Jefferson destroyed all their correspondence and every one of the portraits of his wife, most likely by burning them in the days after her premature death on September 6, 1782. Evidence that Jefferson was capable of such an emotional act comes from the man himself, who admitted in letters shortly after Martha's death that he was in a "stupor of mind" for some time. Relatives and friends described Jefferson as "inconsolable" after his wife's passing, and Jefferson's oldest daughter, Martha Jefferson Randolph, remembered her father suffering "violent bursts of grief" lasting several weeks.

The widower confined himself to his room for three weeks after the tragedy and was at his lowest state after losing his wife. Although we cannot be sure of the details surrounding this great loss to history, many scholars believe that Jefferson erased every physical connection to his wife out of profound grief over her passing. Indeed, she is the only wife of an American president (even though she died several years before her husband's presidency) for whom we don't know how she looked.

Absence of evidence, however, is not evidence of absence. It is probable that Martha sat for a number of portraits, even though some scholars suggest that she may never have done so. This is unlikely given her social status. It was, after all, common for plantation owners in the Virginia Colony to commission portraits—family, individual, and locket-size paintings. These portraits were often completed by traveling artists plying their trade among the plantation aristocracy—to which both Jefferson and Martha's father belonged.

The mystery of Martha Jefferson is also in part due to the fact that Jefferson rarely mentioned his wife in his voluminous writings. For instance, he only hints at the love for his wife and their happy marriage in his autobiography. Reading his memoirs from a modern perspective, one might be tempted to conclude incorrectly that their marriage was but a minor event in his life. In fairness to Mrs. Jefferson, the autobiography of that period was less a personal story than a public defense of the author's political record. In Jefferson's time, it was considered disrespectful to discuss a lady's life in such public documents. For instance, Jefferson's dear friend and political disciple James Monroe omitted any viable mention of his wife in his writings despite the fact that they enjoyed a long and harmonious union. So too was Jefferson an intensely private individual, one averse to sharing the personal in public. Dumas Malone, the noted Jefferson biographer, for example, suggested that Jefferson's failure to discuss his late wife in his writings was because of the pain it caused him to even utter her name. As another historian observed, "Because of this impenetrable silence on his part, probably we shall never know much about Martha Wayles Jefferson and her life with him."

Indeed, Jefferson's relationship with his other lovers and mistresses has generated more interest among scholars than his marriage to Martha. History has recorded and remembered little of the wife of the author of the Declaration of Independence, but there are clues about the importance of both marriage and mistresses to Jefferson's life, happiness, and political career.

Bachelor Jefferson

Thomas Jefferson was born on April 13, 1743, in the family home, Shadwell. His father, Peter, was a large and powerful man who owned a 10,000-acre estate in Virginia; his mother, Jane Randolph, was the daughter of the adjutant general of Virginia, Isham Randolph, and was descended from a large and prominent family. John Marshall, the first chief justice of the U.S. Supreme Court, was but one of the many influential members of the Randolph clan. Jefferson himself had six sisters and one younger brother, Randolph.

Jefferson was educated in the local schools by the Anglican clergy until the age of seventeen, when he attended the College of William & Mary, where he studied law. Young Jefferson was a regular guest at the residence of Governor Francis Fauquier, a pupil of the famous Edinburgh professor Dr. William

Small, and something of an apprentice to the noted attorney George Wythe. As such, Jefferson received the finest education available in colonial times.

Tragically, however, Jefferson's father died in 1757 when Thomas was fourteen, and the youngster had a strained relationship with his mother, one that he seems never to have fully put behind him. A number of accounts of Jefferson as a young man describe him as reasoned, fastidious, and solemn yet passionate, intellectual, and artistic. All these features are seen in Jefferson's romantic life—along with another, more complicated side of the man. Jefferson would end up having a number of love interests and court some of the most beautiful and accomplished women of both America and Europe, but it was not always so. As a youth, he was quite shy and socially awkward around women despite his enormous intellect and potential. One biographer described the young Jefferson as follows:

> At this time he could not have been described as a handsome lad. He was tall, thin, rawboned. His hair was red, his face freckled, and his features pointed. But he possessed charm because of the unusual intelligence shining in his face, the benevolence of his expression, the fluency of his conversation, and the humor and pleasantry that brightened it. If his angular height made him a bit awkward, he was none the less a favorite with the girls.

Jefferson loved to dance and flirt and was a regular at the social season in Williamsburg, where he pursued a number of charming belles. Around the age of twenty (some reports give nineteen, others twenty-one), Jefferson tried to court Rebecca Burwell. Miss Burwell, age sixteen and seventeen during the time Jefferson pursued her, was from a prominent family in York County in the Tidewater region of Virginia, but she had been orphaned. She was described very positively in all accounts, including being "pretty and charming, graceful and elegant, with rosy cheeks, bright blue eyes, and golden hair, and with a proper social background." It seems likely that Rebecca was the object of Jefferson's desire during his college years.

The two met at a dance in the Apollo Room of a Raleigh tavern, and the young suitor was tongue-tied. He admitted to his friends that he "expected to have performed in a tolerably creditable manner . . . but, good God!" This nervousness around Rebecca continued. For instance, he again approached her and "planned to say a great deal," but his words were but "a few broken sentences, uttered in great disorder, and interrupted with pauses of uncommon length."

Jefferson carried a watch with her portrait in it, not only demonstrating his affection but also suggesting that she reciprocated by giving him the miniature. Unfortunately for the lovelorn lad, the watch leaked, and rain ruined the image. Jefferson was upset but undeterred, saying, "Although it may be defaced, there is so lovely an image imprinted on my mind that I shall think of her too often, I fear, for my peace of mind."

Scholars are split as to whether Rebecca was Jefferson's primary love interest. However, even though he courted other belles, such as Sukey Porter and Alice Corbin, his letters about Rebecca give him away. While Jefferson revealed his infatuation with these other women, he considered a marriage proposal for Rebecca. Jefferson frequently discussed Miss Burwell with his friends Will Fleming and John Page (who would later become governor of Virginia). Writing to his friend Will, Jefferson sought advice on both Rebecca and marriage but also revealed his interest in playing the field. Fleming told Jefferson to marry but to do so with someone other than Rebecca. The future president responded boastfully,

> No, thank ye; I will consider of it first. Many and great are the comforts of a single state, and neither of the reasons you urge can have any influence with an inhabitant and a young inhabitant of Williamsburg. For St. Paul only said it is better to be married than to burn. Now I presume that if that apostle had known that providence would at an after day be so kind to any particular set of people as to furnish them with other means of extinguishing their fire than those of matrimony, he would have earnestly recommended them to their practice.

However, both Rebecca and Jefferson had mixed feelings about the courtship, and she eventually turned him down. He contemplated confronting her again about her feelings but experienced cold feet such that he even wanted his friend John to intercede on his behalf. Jefferson continued to hold out hope that she would experience a change of heart, describing himself as "mortified" by her rejection. Jefferson wrote to John, this time on Christmas Day of 1762, upset that he was unable to win Rebecca's heart, saying, "Remember me affectionately to all the young ladies of my acquaintance, particularly the Miss Burwells, and Miss Potters, and tell them that though that heavy earthly part of me, my body, is absent, the better half of me, my soul, is ever with them." He would have similar feelings when other young Williamsburg belles rejected him. Clearly, Jefferson was bothered by the failed courtship. He tried to move beyond it by joking with his friends that all of them should go to Europe to get over their broken hearts and that he would build a boat and name it *Rebecca*, which would occupy a few years of his time. If he was not over her by then, suggested Jefferson, the "devil was in the romance." More than a year after being dumped, Jefferson was still thinking about Rebecca, who later married a prominent gentleman named Ambler. Interestingly, many years later, Jefferson did sail to Europe for the purpose of mending a broken heart.

Jefferson Courts a Widow

Most of Jefferson's male friends married early, but he waited until the age of twenty-six to court the widow Martha Wayles Skelton. The woman Jefferson was courting was described as genteel, charming, and a good mother. But, perhaps more than anything else, nearly everyone who encountered her saw fit to mention Martha's physical beauty. Martha's great-granddaughter Sarah Randolph described her as having lovely hazel eyes and auburn hair:

> A little above middle height, with a lithe and exquisitely formed figure, she was a model of graceful and queenlike carriage. Nature, so lavish with her charms for her, to great personal attractions, added a mind of no ordinary caliber. She was well educated for her day, and a constant reader; she inherited from her father his method and industry, as the accounts, kept in her clear handwriting, and still in the hands of her descendents, testify. Her well-cultivated talent for music served to enhance her charms not a little in the eyes of such musical devote as Jefferson.

Granddaughter Ellen Randolph Coolidge remembered her grandmother as follows:

> My grandmother Jefferson had a vivacity of temper which might sometimes border on tartness, but which, in her intercourse with her husband, was completely subdued by her exceeding affection for him. This little asperity however sometimes showed itself to her children, and of course more to my mother, her oldest child, than to others who were much younger . . . it would be doing an injustice to my grandmother, having spoken of her small defects, not to say that they were entirely redeemed by her good qualities. All the family traditions were greatly in her favour. She had been a favorite with her husband's sister, with his family generally, and with her neighbors. She was a very attractive person and my grandfather was tenderly attached to her. She commanded his respect by her good sense—and domestic virtues, and his admiration and love by her wit, her vivacity, and her agreeable person and manners. She was not only an excellent housekeeper and notable mistress of a family, but a graceful, ladylike and accomplished woman, with considerable powers of conversation, some skill in music, all the habits of good society, and the art of welcoming her husband's friends to perfection. She was greatly liked by them all. She made my grandfather's home comfortable, cheerful, pleasant, just what a good man's home should be. . . . Her loss was the bitterest grief my grandfather ever knew, and no second wife was ever called to take her place.

Jefferson's biographers also noted the many flattering descriptions of his wife. Joseph Ellis, for example, called her "attractive and delicate," while

Claude Bowers acknowledged her defining trait as being "beautiful," and Willard Sterne Randall described her as "a little above medium height, slightly but exquisitely formed. Her complexion was brilliant—her large expressive eyes of the richest shades of hazel—her luxuriant hair the finest tinge of auburn." E. M. Halliday concurred: "There is a fair amount of indirect evidence suggesting that she was extremely beautiful and vivacious, bright and accomplished—as indeed would be expected by anyone familiar with Jefferson's tastes."

Only a few weeks after turning eighteen, Martha married Bathurst Skelton, born in June 1744, on November 20, 1766, at the Wayles family home. We are not sure how or where Martha met Skelton, but a clue comes from the fact that Skelton's older brother, Reuben, had been married to Elizabeth Lomax. After Reuben Skelton's death, Elizabeth became wife number three for Martha's father, John Wayles. Thus, the families would have known one another and probably dined together. Bathurst probably attended his older brother's widow's marriage, the wedding that brought the two families together.

Bathurst Skelton was, by all accounts, reasonably prosperous. Unfortunately, little is known about the marriage or their lives together except that a son, John, was born on November 7, 1767. Bathurst did not live to see his son's first birthday, though, dying on September 30, 1768, less than two years after marrying Martha. After losing her husband, Martha moved back to The Forest to live with her father. Wealthy, beautiful, and accomplished, Martha was an attractive catch. Once the proper mourning period had passed, the young widow had many suitors, including Jefferson.

As with so many facets of Martha's life, the facts surrounding her meeting of and courting by Jefferson are frustratingly few. We do not know where, when, or how they first met, but they started courting in 1770. Coincidentally, both Jefferson and Bathurst Skelton were at the College of William & Mary together, so Jefferson was most likely aware of his schoolmate's marriage. Another reasonable guess is that they met in Williamsburg, the political, commercial, and social center of the colony in which both lived.

Martha was barely at the tail end of the proper mourning period, but Jefferson was determined, writing to John Page, "I am an advocate for the passion: for I too am *coelo tactus*" (which means "touched by Heaven"). Indeed, Jefferson visited Williamsburg and Martha often in 1770 with his servant Jupiter. Red haired and a bit shy, Jefferson was nevertheless a robust six feet two inches in height with large hands and feet. He had aged very well and was considered to be handsome (he even had great teeth for the time). He therefore cut a dashing figure in the colonial capital. Jefferson was five and a half years older than Martha, close enough in age to have crossed paths as children yet far enough apart that, had they done so as teenagers, Miss Wayles might have been too young for Jefferson to have noticed her. And, in fact, Jefferson does not mention it in his letters.

The social anxiety that Jefferson felt about earlier romances was again present. In a few letters, he worried about whether his feelings for Martha were mutual. In a response to one such letter, a Mrs. Drummond dismisses Jefferson's worries: "Let me recollect your description, which bars all the romantical, poetical ones I ever read. . . . Thou wonderful man, indeed I shall think spirits of a higher order inhabit your airy mountains—or rather mountain, which I may contemplate but can never aspire to." Mrs. Drummond reminds Jefferson that the widow Skelton has "good sense, and good nature," and she offers words of encouragement that Martha will not refuse her suitor's love. Jefferson's neighbor closes her letter by saying that she suspects that Martha's heart may already be "engaged."

Jefferson and Martha would make a good team. Not only did they share tastes in literature, theater, and music, but they were intellectual companions. The couple shared a music teacher, the Italian maestro Francis Alberti, and often performed together with Martha on the harpsichord and Jefferson on violin. Both sang, although Martha had the far better voice and Jefferson sang only in private. Family lore suggests one touching story of their musical courtship. Other suitors had come to The Forest to court Martha but, waiting outside, overheard Jefferson and Martha playing a duet. The music was so lovely that the rival suitors, dejected, are said to have departed without interrupting the lovers, giving up hope of winning her hand.

This closeness allowed the couple to comfort one another later in life during the periods of grief that would plague both of them throughout their lives. For instance, Jefferson's sister Elizabeth, who was three years his senior, was mentally retarded and died at age twenty-eight. It was Martha who Jefferson turned to during his mourning. Jefferson loved children and was more playful with them than most men of the time. As a mother, Martha likely noticed this trait. Indeed, Jefferson cared for Martha's infant son during the time they were courting.

During the courtship, Martha's sister, Tabitha "Tibby" Skipworth, served as the couples' chaperone. Both Tibby and her husband, Robert, supported the marriage and said in a letter to Jefferson that they were eager to "be neighbors to a couple so well calculated and disposed to communicate knowledge and pleasure." During their courtship, Jefferson frequently met Martha near a "spring" where they would sit and delight in one another's company. He described it as "the scene of every evening's joy." He wrote to the Skipworths about his courtship of Martha, saying that the two would

talk over the lessons of the day or lose them in music, chess, or the merri-
ments of our family companions . . . the heart thus lightened, our pillows
would be soft . . . come, then, and bring out dear Tibby with you, the first
in your affections, and second in mine. Offer prayers for me, too, at that
shrine to which, tho' absent, I pay continual devotion. In every scheme
of [my] happiness, she is placed in the foreground of the picture, as the
principal figure. Take that away, and there is no picture for me.

Jefferson was impatient to make Martha his wife. He made several visits
to The Forest during the courtship, with at least three of them coming in 1770.
According to his account book, Jefferson spent more money than usual on
clothing during the courtship and ordered that a family coat of arms be made.
In June 1770, he also purchased gifts from a London merchant named Thomas
Adams for his bride-to-be, including what he described as "a forte-piano"
custom-made "of fine mahogany, solid, not veneered," and "a large umbrella
with brass ribs covered with green silk." The instrument was originally to be a
clavichord, but Jefferson changed his mind and purchased a newer fortepiano.
Jefferson's instructions were for the "finest possible" presents, "worthy of the
acceptance of a lady for whom I intended it." Ironically, the gifts violated the
colonial Non-Importation Act, suggesting the depth of Jefferson's feelings for
Martha. Jefferson justified the order and patriotic predicament by saying that
he intended to store the instrument until the order was overturned.

The couple planned to marry in the summer of 1771, but three factors
intervened to delay the wedding. The first was the death of Martha's infant
son, John, on June 10, 1771. The boy was not yet four years old. The death
of her first child, coming only a few years after her first husband's passing,
dealt a severe blow to Martha. The untimely death delayed by six months the
planned wedding.

Jefferson also wanted the renovations to his home to be completed by the
wedding, but the progress was slow, and Monticello would remain unfinished
when the couple eventually married (Jefferson changed the name of his home
from The Hermitage to Monticello, Italian for "little mountain," around
1767). While courting Martha, Jefferson began the expansion of his palatial
estate. Jefferson not only rushed the construction but also frequently talked
with her of his grand plans for the architecture, landscaping, and gardens.
However, the Jefferson family home, Shadwell, in Goochland County (now
Albemarle), was lost in a fire on February 1, 1770, and this both depressed
Jefferson and further set back his construction schedule. Moreover, his impressive collection of books and personal mementos were lost. He shared his
frustration with Martha, who encouraged him to restock his library.

In fact, Jefferson became somewhat obsessed with the home. An out-
building known as the South Pavilion was completed in the summer of 1770.

In November, Jefferson moved into a small living area. In February 1771, he wrote to his fiancée,

> I have lately removed to the mountain from whence this is dated, and with which you are not unacquainted. I have her but one room, which like the cobbler's, serves me for parlor for kitchen and hall. I may add for bed-chamber and study too. . . . I have hopes however of getting more elbow room this summer.

However, a third obstacle to an expedited wedding may have been Martha's father. Even though Martha had been married before and was an adult, the social strictures of the time still required the support of her father, John Wayles, and Jefferson worried about whether his would-be father-in-law would stand in the way. There is some evidence to suggest that he did just that. For instance, in February 1771, Jefferson fired off a letter to a friend named James Ogilvie angry over "the unfeeling temper of a parent who delays, perhaps refuses to approve his daughter's choice." We are not certain why—perhaps because Martha was his eldest daughter or (initially) because a child was involved—but Martha's father was not forthcoming with his blessings. Some scholars have suggested that it may have been that Wayles was concerned that Jefferson was not sufficiently well born to marry Martha, which is interesting given Wayles's own modest origins. As such, a more likely answer may have to do with Wayles's concerns about his own fortune and Jefferson's mismanagement of money.

As a result, when Jefferson married Martha, he did so quickly, and they married in the middle of winter, something that was rare in colonial times. Moreover, rather than continue the wedding celebration, the newlyweds departed immediately for the long ride to Jefferson's home despite a driving snowstorm. Another clue about the couples' fallout with Martha's father comes from a letter that John Wayles wrote on October 20, 1772, fully ten months after the wedding, complaining that "I have heard nothing about dear Patsy since you left this place." Likewise, Martha was pregnant within weeks of marriage, and it appears that she may not have notified her father that he was about to again become a grandfather. John Wayles died just months after writing his complaint, a little over a year after Martha's wedding date, and it is uncertain as to whether he ever saw his daughter or son-in-law again after the wedding.

Wedding Day

When, by what manner, and to what degree John Wayles ultimately gave in to the wedding is unknown, but Jefferson moved quickly. Few weddings were held in winter, but, in the company of his servant Jupiter, Jefferson departed on December 23, 1771, for The Forest. First, he signed a "wedding bond" and purchased, on December 30, a marriage license in Williamsburg for the sum of forty shillings.

The couple was married on January 1 at the Wayles home, The Forest, with two clergy presiding, a fiddler for entertainment, and a house full of guests. A large, rich black cake—a family favorite—was served (the recipe called for twenty eggs, two pounds of powdered sugar, two pounds of butter, two and a half pounds of white flour, five pounds of fruit, one-half pint of wine, one-quarter ounce of mace, an ounce of nutmeg, and a hint of brandy). After the wedding, there was a grand party thrown by Martha's father, but Jefferson described the wedding matter-of-factly in his memoir: "On the first of January 1771 I was married to Martha Skelton, widow of Bathurst Skelton, and daughter of John Wayles, then 23 years old."

Jefferson biographer Joseph Ellis believes that Jefferson completed his developing self-image as an aspiring "paterfamilias" by marrying Martha. Indeed, her dowry more than doubled his holdings in land and slaves. Like several other future presidents, most notably George Washington (and everyone profiled in the coming chapters), Jefferson married well and married above himself socially. With Martha's inheritance and Jefferson's own profitable law practice, the couple enjoyed a growing fortune. Not long after the wedding, Jefferson commented on his wealth as a result of his marriage and the passing of John Wayles, saying, "The portion which came on that event to Mrs. Jefferson after the debts should be paid, which were very considerable, was about equal to my own patrimony, and consequently doubled the ease of our circumstances."

Despite a snowstorm, the couple set off immediately after the wedding party for Monticello. Traveling by carriage, the newlyweds visited sites such as Jefferson's boyhood home but had to detour because of the storm. Jefferson and others describe two to three feet of snow that day, so much that they had to abandon their carriage (known as a "phaeton") and leave it at Blenheim Plantation, the home of one of their mutual friends, Colonel Edward Carter. In his own words, Jefferson deemed it "the deepest snow we have ever seen." After a brief respite from the weather, the couple covered the last eight miles to Monticello on horseback. Even though Martha had grown up on and around horses, she was frail, and the long ride west through a blustery winter snowstorm and across hills and ruggedly rural terrain would have been a challenge. They were determined to get away from her father and start the honeymoon.

The exact details of their honeymoon at Monticello are not recorded, but it appears that the bride and groom finally arrived at Monticello late in the evening to a quiet home, with the slaves asleep and fireplaces cold. They must have been exhausted and chilled. Without waking the slaves, Jefferson found a good bottle of wine and lit a fireplace, and the couple slept under a blanket in a small building at the end of the home's South Wing. As a result, this room has come to be known today as the "Honeymoon Cottage," although during his lifetime it served as Jefferson's office.

Life at Monticello

Life at Monticello would have been both familiar and unfamiliar to Martha. She lived her entire life on plantations and was an accomplished hostess and household manager, but the region around Monticello was sparsely populated. Indeed, it was more the frontier than anything she had experienced before. But Monticello was more than a home. It was a bustling plantation with a large slave labor force that produced a number of crops and tended to livestock and dairy cows, a popular destination for the leading citizens of the colony, and an estate with serene gardens, stables, orchards, smokehouses, and some of the most impressive architecture in the colonies; it even boasted acres of woodland stocked with deer. Perhaps more so than any other home in the colonies, Monticello was defined by elegance and prosperity, and its owner placed an emphasis on leisure activities, something quite uncommon for the times. Poetry was read, music was performed, parties were thrown with fine foods, wines were showcased, and books were collected. Jefferson even took care that his chefs—a slave named Ursula and her son, Isaac, who were brought to Monticello around 1773—were well trained in the culinary arts and even prepared French food.

This is the home that Mrs. Jefferson enjoyed but also managed. Long after her passing, Monticello's slaves remembered in an interview how Martha came into the kitchen regularly "with a cookery book in her hand and read out of it to Isaac's mother how to make cakes, tarts, and so on." She also supervised and partook in the sewing, soap making, washing, and even the brewing of beer. Jefferson was an overly generous host. A steady stream of visitors, overnight guests, and dignitaries were found at Monticello, all of which further occupied Mrs. Jefferson's attentions. After the death of Jefferson's dear friend and brother-in-law Dabney Carr, Carr's widow and six children came to live at Monticello.

Another part-time resident was Philip Mazzei, a native of Florence, Italy, who visited Monticello in the fall of 1773 and purchased land near Jefferson to build a home and vineyard. Mazzei brought workers from Italy to construct his home and work his vineyards and was often at Monticello until he moved back to Italy in 1779. As a side note, although Mazzei and

Jefferson became close friends, this appears not to have been the case for the wives. Jefferson once referred to Mrs. Mazzei as suffering "traces of vanity and pride" and, after hearing more troubling reports of her behavior, said bluntly, "She is really a great bitch."

Martha not only was busy but also would have needed to be precise in her duties, as Jefferson was notoriously particular about his food, drink, and every detail of his home. For the next ten years, Monticello would be her home. She did travel occasionally to Williamsburg and visited friends such as the Carters at their plantation, and in early 1776 and again in the summer of 1779, Mrs. Jefferson and her daughters enjoyed extended stays with her sisters at The Forest. It seems that she was disinterested, however, in attending the winter social season and political events in Williamsburg and Philadelphia because of her poor health and numerous pregnancies. Martha, after all, bore six children over the ten years that she was married to Jefferson.

During the Revolutionary War, there was an added burden, as social events at the home took on a political tone, and it was not uncommon for Jefferson to host fifty guests, all of whom were served the latest French foods and expensive wines. Despite her pregnancies and illnesses, Martha assisted in both planning and hosting many of these affairs, although she, at times, had to excuse herself from making an appearance. An example of the latter comes from Jefferson's governorship. Because of the war and her poor health, Martha did not officially serve as the First Lady of Virginia.

Still, numerous letters from Monticello's guests offer praise for their hostess. A Mr. Phillips wrote in 1781, "I embrace this opportunity of assuring you that I retain a particular remembrance of the Civilities I received when in Virginia from you, Sir, and Mrs. Jefferson to whom I request my Compliments."

Likewise, another guest thanked Jefferson for the hospitality and wrote that his wife, Lucy, "unites in most sublime Compliments to Lady & family." And a soldier visiting Monticello wrote of Mrs. Jefferson, "In all respects a very agreeable, sensible & accomplished Lady." One of her good friends and visitors was the wife of Major General Friedrich von Riedesel, a former commander of the Hessian troops captured at Saratoga during the war. The Riedesels had three daughters near in age to Martha's young daughters, and the Baroness von Riedesel was a talented singer who performed at Monticello with and to the delight of her hostess. In a letter to Jefferson, Riedesel wrote, "Madame de Riedesel, who never can forget the esteem and friendship she has so justly consecrated to Mrs. Jefferson, desires me to insert her sincerest compliments both to her and your Excellency." These magical nights with the Riedesels often included other German officers and an abundance of food, wine, and music. Another German, the Baron de Geismer, joined Jefferson on violin at these dinners/nights of music. The Italian virtuoso Francis Alberti also visited Monticello and both performed and offered musical lessons to the Jeffersons.

While Martha was gracious toward the home's many visitors, one cannot help but get the feeling that, at times, she only tolerated all of Jefferson's political and intellectual guests and that many of the guests reserved their warmest regards for Mister, not Missus, Jefferson. Martha's health and numerous pregnancies also functioned to cool her vivacious personality. One of Monticello's frequent guests and a valued friend of Jefferson was the French nobleman Maquis de Chastellux, who observed Martha's delicate health and described her in understated terms as "mild and amiable."

Tragedy Strikes—Again and Again

Martha lost her son, John, from her first marriage. Young John Skelton, born in 1767, died in 1771 at the time that Thomas Jefferson was courting Martha. Her first child with Jefferson was born on September 27, 1772, a few days shy of nine months after their wedding day. The child, weak and small like many of Martha's children, would, however, end up being the only offspring to live a long life. Jefferson named his daughter after his wife and nicknamed her "Patsy." Jefferson called his wife "Patty."

In succession, Martha had five more children. Another daughter, Jane, was born in 1774 but died the next year. A son, named for Jefferson's father, Peter, was born on May 28, 1777, but died only three weeks later. A third Jefferson daughter was born in 1778 and named Mary. Nicknamed "Maria" and "Polly," she is the only other Jefferson child to live until adulthood. But Maria died while in her mid-twenties, passing in 1804. In 1780, Martha had another daughter, named Lucy Elizabeth, but the child died less than five months later. One year after that, in 1782, she had yet another daughter named for the couple's recently deceased girl. But the second Lucy lived only three years.

Childbirth would ultimately prove to be Martha's undoing, which was the same tragic fate suffered by her own mother. Frail and frequently both ill and pregnant, Martha's pregnancies were challenging physical and emotional ordeals for her. Similarly, she was slow to recover from each birth. In each instance, Jefferson remained as close as possible to his wife, helping to nurse her through the pregnancies. Indeed, Jefferson disliked being away from his wife, especially during her illnesses. In a letter to a friend written in 1781, Jefferson wrote, "The day is so very bad. . . . Mrs. Jefferson is in a situation in which I would not wish to leave her."

The call to arms and the call to public service, however, necessitated sacrifice on his part and on the part of his wife and family. But Mrs. Jefferson appears to have taken her husband's career-related absences poorly. There is a possibility that she suffered from depression as well as from numerous illnesses. In her account books, for example, there are long periods where she simply appeared to stop writing and either did not record or failed even to purchase household items. During these times, she ceased acting as Monticello's hostess, remaining in bed and excusing herself not only from the home's guests but from her family as well. Occasionally, such as in 1776 during the meeting of the New Assembly, Jefferson's wife and eldest daughter accompanied him to Williamsburg, where, at least during one such instance, they stayed at the home of Jefferson's good friend and mentor George Wythe. But often she remained home and failed even to respond to her husband's frequent letters.

In an effort to find balance between his public and his private life, Jefferson still accepted political assignments but always tried to minimize his time away from home. But public service came between the Jeffersons, something that distressed him. During the 1775 session of the Continental Congress in Philadelphia, Jefferson's wife was ill and unable to accompany him. During the meeting, Jefferson expressed both concern and displeasure with the infrequency of letters he received from the home front and the tone of the few that did arrive. For instance, in October, Jefferson wrote to his friend John Page, "I have set apart nearly one day in every week, since I came here, to write letters. Notwithstanding this, I have never received the scrip of a pen from any mortal breathing." Martha failed to write to her husband, who decided to return to Monticello early.

It is well known that Jefferson declined a commission to France offered by the president of the Continental Congress and did so in part because of his wife. Indeed, Jefferson frequently appealed to his political colleagues to excuse his absences, leading some of them to even joke about his early departures from meetings while others complained about it. As such, most colonial leaders were privy to Jefferson's concern for his wife's fragile health. Thomas Nelson, for one, urged Jefferson not to miss the famous session in Philadelphia, suggesting that he should bring Mrs. Jefferson to stay at the Nelson home where "Mrs. Nelson shall nurse her and take all possible care of her." Likewise, Horatio Gates invited Jefferson to bring his wife to the Gates estate and to visit the therapeutic warm springs nearby. Edmund Pendleton wrote to Jefferson, begging him to remain longer in Philadelphia during the historic 1776 meeting, and later pleaded with his friend to remain in public life, saying, "Having the Pleasure of Mrs. Jefferson's Company, I hope you'll get cured of your wish to retire so early in life from the memory of man, and exercise your talents for the nurture of Our new Constitution."

The pleading did little. Immediately after completing his work on the triumphal Declaration of Independence, Jefferson's account ledger reveals that he went shopping and bought his wife seven pairs of gloves. Eleven days after the document was adopted, Jefferson wrote to his friend and relative Francis Eppes, "I wish I could be better satisfied on the point of Patty's recovery . . . I had not heard from her at all for the two posts before, and no letter from herself now." Martha was again ill, and given her silence, it appears that she was again upset with her husband's absence. The author of the Declaration of Independence resigned before the Continental Congress concluded the very session that would change history in order to be at his wife's side.

The war with Britain presented the Jeffersons with further challenges to domestic tranquillity. During his governorship, there were warnings—some of them real—that the "British are coming!" General Charles Cornwallis and Benedict Arnold, for example, repeatedly threatened Virginia, and there were rumors of a planned capture of Jefferson himself. All this required the governor to evacuate his family. During the war, Jefferson's family moved between the governor's palace in Williamsburg, Monticello, other locations around Charlottesville, and back to the Wayles family estate in Charles City. They were even sent to stay at the Coles Plantation while Jefferson stayed in Williamsburg, and in the spring of 1780, with the British advancing toward Williamsburg, they evacuated to Richmond. Of the threats, Jefferson wrote to his wife in November 1775 dismissing "the alarms of Lord Dunmore." But the threat from the British was imminent enough to prompt Jefferson's friend James Monroe to write, "I hope . . . that neither yourself nor Mrs. Jefferson have sustained injury from the obtrusion of the enemy." Monroe also later proclaimed his pleasure on learning of the Jeffersons' "safe retreat from Richmd. to Charlottesville." There, the family was reunited.

In addition to threats of capture and the presence of war, there were threats to Monticello. British troops, under the command of Captain Kenneth McLeod, did in fact arrive on the grounds of Monticello shortly after New Year's Day in 1781. It appears Jefferson was warned of the pending attack at the eleventh hour by a rider on horseback and was able to safely remove his family. Fortunately for Jefferson and history, all the Brits did was help themselves to the home's famous wine collection before leaving.

Martha Jefferson's health worsened through the war and with each pregnancy. The loss of so many children at such a young age also took a toll on her mental health. By 1782, she was pregnant for the seventh time—and the sixth time in ten years. Already weak and emotionally drained from the deaths of four children, the most recent the year prior, this final pregnancy was even more precarious than the others. Mrs. Jefferson gained far too much weight and was weaker than ever. Too ill to receive guests, perform any household duties, or even sit comfortably, Mrs. Jefferson remained bedridden and turned over the management of Monticello to her slaves. Jefferson declined all public duties and offices offered him at this time in an effort to remain at his wife's side. We do not know her exact illness, but Martha remained in a weakened state throughout the pregnancy, causing her husband and his friends to worry for her life.

On May 8, 1782, another daughter was born, named after their child, Lucy Elizabeth, who died the year prior. In spite of the mother's grave condition, the baby was healthy. Family history tells that the baby weighed an astonishing sixteen pounds at birth, hastening Mrs. Jefferson's decline. As her condition worsened, Jefferson wrote to James Monroe twelve days after the birth, saying, "Mrs. Jefferson has added another daughter to our family. She has ever since and still continues very dangerously ill." Martha never recovered.

Death of Mrs. Jefferson

Weakened from a difficult birth of her seventh child in spring, Martha remained in a precarious state throughout the summer. Years later, their daughter Martha Jefferson Randolph, as a girl of ten, remembered watching her father at her mother's bedside throughout her final pregnancy and the agonizing days leading to her death:

> He nursed my poor mother in turn with Aunt Carr [Jefferson's sister] and her own sister—sitting up with her and administering her medicines and drink to the last. For four months that she lingered he was never out of calling. When not at her bedside, he was writing in a small room which opened immediately at the head of her bed.

On September 6, 1782, Jefferson wrote in his diary, "My dear wife died this day at 11:45 a.m." Jefferson's daughter described her grieving father as needing to be led from the deathbed to his library by his sister "almost in a state of insensibility." She then noted, "He then fainted." She remembered her father keeping to himself for three weeks, locking himself in his room, pacing constantly, and sobbing throughout the ordeal. It was during this time of vulnerability that he likely destroyed all his wife's letters and portraits in an effort to erase all evidence of her. Not surprisingly, Jefferson's family and friends worried about his emotional swings. As daughter Martha noted, "My aunts remained constantly with him for some weeks." She added,

> When at last he left his room he rode out and from that time he was incessantly on horseback rambling about the mountain in the least frequented roads and just as often through the woods; in those melancholy rambles I was his constant companion, a solitary witness to many violent bursts of grief.

Even years later, when recollecting her mother's death, Patsy remembered the pain it caused her father, admitting, "The violence of his emotion to this day I dare not describe to myself."

It took Jefferson until late September to come out of his deep withdrawal, and when he did, he rode his horse through the surrounding woods like a man possessed by a demon. Around this time, notes began appearing again in his account book. He also started to compose letters. These surviving letters are very intimate and revealing. For instance, he finally answered his friend the Chevalier de Chastellux, apologizing for the delay in writing, which he attributed to "the state of dreadful suspence in which I had been kept all summer and the catastrophe which closed it." Jefferson added that his friend's letter "found me a little emerging from that stupor of mind which had rendered me as dead to the world as she was whose loss occasioned it. Your letter recalled to my memory, that there [are] three persons still living of much value to me."

He also wrote to his Italian friend Mazzei, who, on learning of Mrs. Jefferson's death, wrote to Jefferson that "the memory of [your] saintly late wife saddened me, and the solitude rendered my sorrow even more profound." One of the first letters Jefferson wrote after his wife's death was to Martha's sister, then living at The Forest, reassuring his sister-in-law that the children were

> in perfect health and as happy as if they had no part in the unmeasurable loss we have sustained. Patsy rides with me 5 or 6 miles a day and presses for permission to accompany me on horseback to Elkhill whenever I shall go there. When that may be however I cannot tell; finding myself absolutely unable to attend to any thing like business. This miserable kind of existence is really too burdensome to be borne, and were it not for the infidelity of deserting the sacred charge left me, I could not wish it's continuance a moment. For what could it be wished? All my plans of comfort and happiness reversed by a single event and nothing answering in prospect before me but a gloom unbrightened with one cheerful expectation. The care and instruction of our children indeed affords some temporary abstractions from wretchedness and nourishes a soothing reflection that if there be beyond the grave any concern for the things of this world there is one angel at least who views these attentions with pleasure and wishes continuance of them while she must pity the miseries to which they confine me.

Jefferson remained, according to his daughter, "inconsolable" for months. He continued to sob every night and broke down whenever he appeared in public or tried to talk about his deceased wife. News of his wife's death and his deep depression traveled quickly throughout the colony. Letters reveal that friends, family members, and political leaders all worried about his sanity and vulnerability. Edmund Randolph, a friend and relative, provides an example of this when he wrote, "I ever thought him to rank domestic happiness in the first class of the chief good but scarcely supposed that his grief would be so violent as to justify the circulating report of his swooning away whenever he sees his children."

A touching story remains of Martha's final moments. Edmund Bacon, the longtime overseer at Monticello, described Mrs. Jefferson's deathbed scene as follows:

> The house servants were Betty Brown, Sally, Critta, and Betty Hemings, Nance, and Ursula. . . . They were in the room when Mrs. Jefferson died. . . . They have often told my wife, that when Mrs. Jefferson died, they stood around the bed. Mr. Jefferson sat by her, and she gave him directions about a good many things that she wanted done. When she came to the children, she wept, and could not speak for some time. Finally she held up her hand, and spreading out her four fingers, she told him she could not die happy if she thought her four children were ever to have a stepmother brought in over them. Holding her other hand in his, Mr. Jefferson promised her solemnly that he would never marry again.

The authenticity of this account has been questioned by some scholars and accepted by others. Critics point out that it was told many years after Bacon's service with Jefferson, and Bacon mistakenly stated that there were four children when there were only three Jefferson children alive at the time. However, the other details check out, and Bacon—as well as anyone else in Jefferson's employ—would not have forgotten Mrs. Jefferson's death or such a powerful scene as the one he described.

As suggested, it is possible that Mrs. Jefferson made a request of her husband never to remarry. Martha lost a mother she never knew and endured two stepmothers. A poor relationship with them may explain her concerns about a stepmother raising her daughters, as might the fact that she had so painfully lost four of her seven children in infancy. The scene at Mrs. Jefferson's bedside becomes all the more emotional because of a discovery made many years later. After the death of the Jefferson daughter, Martha Jefferson Randolph in 1836, a folded sheet of paper was found containing a lock of her mother's hair and a note. An inscription on the note identified the author as Jefferson's daughter. It read, "A Lock of my Dear Mama's Hair inclosed in a verse which she wrote." What it contained is nothing less than remarkable and heart wrenching.

It appears that, from her deathbed, Mrs. Jefferson and her husband recited their favorite love verse together and then copied it in a note. The verse comes from the popular book *Tristram Shandy* by Laurence Sterne, published in the middle part of the eighteenth century. In a noticeably frail hand, Mrs.

Jefferson began the verse with weak strokes of the quill: "Time wastes too fast: Every letter I trace tells me with what rapidity life follows my pen. The days and hours of it are flying over our heads like clouds of a windy day never to return more—everything presses on."

The verse continues, but it is written in Jefferson's distinctive handwriting and with darker, firmer strokes, as it appears that he either took the instrument from his dying wife or placed his hand around hers to finish their special verse: "and every time I kiss thy hand to bid adieu, every absence which follows it, are preludes to that eternal separation which we are shortly to make." This deathbed exchange constitutes the only writing between them known to exist.

Jefferson was only thirty-nine at the time of his wife's death. He was wealthy, famous, and the father of three daughters. Throughout his life, he retained a deep passion for the fairer sex, and it was very common for widows and widowers to remarry shortly after losing a spouse. Yet Jefferson would never remarry. Why? The only obvious answer is the alleged deathbed vow to his wife never to do so. Noted Jefferson biographer Joseph Ellis described Martha's death as "the most traumatic experience of [Jefferson's] entire life." Jefferson, who kept locks of his deceased wife's hair, was certainly in a condition to have made such a vow never to remarry.

Jefferson's love for his wife, along with the impact of illnesses and displeasure with his public career, affected his political service. In so doing, it may have altered the course of history during those momentous years. During their marriage, Jefferson served in a number of offices and fulfilled many political functions—Virginia House of Burgesses (1772–1775), Virginia Provincial Convention (1774 and 1775), Albermarle County Officer (1775), delegate to the Second Continental Congress (1775–1776), Virginia Assembly (1776 and 1781), committee revising Virginia's laws (1776), chairman of the Albermarle County Committee of Safety (1776), governor of Virginia (1779–1781), and Congress (1781)—yet his heart was always conflicted and his mind often distracted by the home front. At times, Jefferson was wracked by the guilt of leaving her.

Sadly, only one Jefferson child, Martha, would grow old. Daughter Mary was said to resemble her mother—both were beautiful but frail. Mary died in her twenties of childbirth, just like both her mother and her grandmother. Martha Jefferson was buried at Monticello near her children, close relative Dabney Carr, and her husband's sister, Jane. Jefferson erected a marble tombstone to mark her grave. It contains an inscription saying that she had been "torn from him by death." The engraving also contains the first two lines from the *Iliad* and is written in Greek. The translation says, "If in the house of Hades men forget their dead, Yet will I ever there remember you, dear companion."

A RETURN TO PUBLIC LIFE—AND LOVE

Jefferson turned down political offers to serve his country abroad, not wanting to leave his wife. As he explained during the war, "But such was the state of my family that I could not leave it, nor could I expose it to the dangers of the sea, and of capture by the British ships." Even after his wife had passed, the grieving Jefferson was still declining offers to serve his country. On November 13, 1782, for example, Jefferson was reluctant to accept a request from Congress, writing, "I had two months before lost the cherished companion of my life, in whose affections, unabated on both sides, I had lived the last ten years in unchequered happiness."

However, Jefferson ultimately decided to return to public life, largely in order to escape the memories of his wife. Jefferson was feeling her presence everywhere and in everything he did at Monticello. As such, in 1785 he accepted a diplomatic mission to France. Initially, he was to assist John Adams and Benjamin Franklin in their trade negotiations, but he then served as the U.S. minister. The assignment proved to be the medicine that his broken heart needed. He purchased an expensive home on the Champs-Élysées and filled it with servants and fine furnishings. Jefferson's five years in Europe were spent in the court of King Louis XVI, traveling, collecting French art, and enjoying the architecture and wine of France. It was also in France that he met Maria Cosway.

The Charms of a Lady

It was John Trumbull, the famous artist who was also friends with Jefferson and, for a time, Jefferson's house guest, who introduced the grieving widower to Richard Cosway and his wife, Maria. It happened when Trumbull, well known for both his partying and his artistic talent, invited Jefferson to view the domed Halle aux Bleds in August 1786. It was there that Jefferson met the Cosways.

Richard Cosway was a celebrated English artist and miniaturist who had painted London's aristocracy as well as the Prince of Wales and one of the prince's mistresses. Short, round, and seventeen years his wife's senior, Cosway was a "vain, undignified little man, who flirted openly and was the butt of jokes." Cosway's unsavory reputation was a result not only of his ego but also of his sexual scandals, which included flings with some of the male models he painted. He was also known for having a young, beautiful wife.

Maria Louisa Catherine Cecilia Hadfield Cosway was in her twenties. Worldly and sophisticated, Maria was born in Florence to English parents and was herself a talented artist and musician. The young woman painted and sketched and, just like Jefferson's late wife, had a lovely voice and was skilled with the harpsichord. One account described her as "the embodiment of the eighteenth-century ideal of grace and beauty—slim, graceful figure, fashionably, almost extremely dressed." Her voice, it was said, was "musical and soft—her speech an appealing mélange of five or six languages which she spoke fluently but somewhat imperfectly."

She was also stunningly beautiful, a "golden-haired, languishing Anglo-Italian, graceful to affection, and highly accomplished." Maria shared traits with Jefferson—she was artistic, smart, well read, and bold. Her remarkable "deep blue" eyes could also be teasing, flirtatious, and "pouting." Surviving full-length portraits of her reveal her beauty. In one portrait she looks delicate and in another lively and confident. Not surprisingly, Jefferson fell hard for her, and the jinx was immediate. After attending the party where he met Maria, Jefferson was scheduled to attend a dinner with the prominent, elderly duchesse d'Enville and the duchesse de la Rochefoucauld. He canceled, making up a diplomatic excuse in order to stay with Maria. That evening, the two stayed late to watch a fireworks display.

Like a puppy dog, Jefferson could not leave Maria's side. With Richard Cosway otherwise preoccupied or traveling, Jefferson became Maria's constant companion. For instance, six weeks after Jefferson met Maria, Richard Cosway traveled back to London in mid-September, leaving Maria alone in Paris—with Jefferson. Together, the two attended parties, were guests at the court of Louis XVI and Marie Antoinette, and took in plays, such as *Les Deux Billets*, a comedy about love and an unlikely suitor (coincidentally enough). Arm in arm, they traveled to see the sites of France and picnicked in the French countryside. During this period when Richard Cosway was in England, Jefferson fell for Maria in another way. It seems that the lovers were on a picnic in the countryside when Jefferson, showing off for his young mistress, tried to jump over a fence (one account of the story suggests that he was jumping over a creek), caught his heel, and fell. Landing hard and at a bad angle, Jefferson broke his wrist.

Evidence for the story comes from a Mr. Le Veillard, who, on September 20, 1786, wrote that the "day before yesterday Mr. Jefferson dislocated his right wrist when attempting to jump over a fence in the 'Petit cours.'" Writing to William Stephens Smith in late October, Jefferson described the incident as follows: "How the right hand became disabled would be a long story for the left to tell. It was by one of those follies from which good cannot come, but ill may." To Maria, Jefferson wrote two weeks after the incident, saying, "I have passed the night in so much pain that I have not closed my eyes." Maria responded with an apology "for having been the Cause of your pains in the [night]." The wrist gave him problems for the remainder of his life, and the break was, unfortunately, to his writing hand.

Maria Cosway was unlike any woman Jefferson had ever met, especially the demure women from Virginia. Some historians suggest that Jefferson never loved any woman—even his wife—the way he loved Maria Cosway. One scholar described the affair as a "generous spasm of the heart," while another spoke of Jefferson being "head over heels in love." The writer Shelley Ross believes that Jefferson "came out of his emotional shell" because of Maria. Indeed, Jefferson's writings suggest as much. The hills, rainbows, and fields now seemed more beautiful to Jefferson, and life again had meaning. Jefferson admitted to Maria that he was happy again for the first time since his wife died.

Jefferson was forty-three when they met; Maria was twenty-seven. Jefferson, who watched what he ate and exercised, had aged very well and was youthful in his forties. He was a statuesque six feet two inches, with a ruddy complexion, cerebral disposition, and passion for music. Jefferson's tastes were much more to Maria's preference than those of her husband. They seemed a perfect match. Not even Maria's marriage cooled their emotions. The marriage was a loveless and peculiar one. In fact, Jefferson joined the Cosways on outings to the Louvre and Versailles. Maria did not love her husband and most likely knew about the affairs he had with the nude models he painted—male and female. Cosway married his wife because she was young and beautiful and attracted attention wherever she went.

For her part, Maria was pushed into marrying Cosway. As a child, Maria survived a murder rampage by a deranged nursemaid. Four of her siblings were killed by the maid; Maria was the sole survivor. The traumatized young girl was sent to be raised in a convent, which is where she developed her considerable musical and artistic skills. At the age of only nineteen, Maria was even an elected member of the Florence Academy of Fine Arts. At the convent, she also developed a passion for the church and was considering taking the vows of a nun, but her ambitious mother removed her from the convent and took her to London in an effort to marry the beautiful young girl to money and fame. It worked. Cosway, for all his faults, was famous and wealthy. Although unhappy in marriage, the union did allow Maria to travel among fellow artists and to experience the cultural sites of Europe she so loved. As such, Maria met and associated with some of the leading figures in the intellectual, political, and artistic worlds of France, Italy, and England. She enjoyed traveling and spending time away from her husband, preferring France and Italy to damp England. More important, with her husband either away or engaged in extramarital affairs, it provided her the freedom to paint, compose music, and write poetry.

"My Head and My Heart"

Jefferson's pen provides evidence of his love for Maria. His poetic letters to her are likely the most sentimental and intimate he ever wrote and therefore are among the most revealing. Jefferson destroyed all the letters he exchanged with his wife, so history does not know if he wrote to her in such a sweet and romantic tone. But Jefferson saved all of Maria's letters for the rest of his life—and, happily, his writings to her have also been preserved. When they were apart, he pined away for her and begged her either to not leave him or to be sure to visit him often. In one such letter, Jefferson tried to prevent Maria from leaving by pleading,

> When you come again, I will employ myself solely in finding or fancying that you have some faults, and I will draw a veil over all your good qualities, if I can find one large enough. I think I shall succeed in this. For, trying myself to-day, by way of exercise, I recollected immediately one fault in your composition. It is that you give all your attention to your friends, caring nothing about yourself.

Arguably, the most remarkable letter Jefferson ever wrote was a twelve-page muse he composed on October 12, 1786, when Maria was leaving France—and Jefferson—for good. Richard came back to France for his wife, and their departure to England was delayed, only enhancing Jefferson's pain. The letter is Jefferson's tender good-bye. With his right wrist still healing from the fall incurred while trying to impress Maria, the letter—the longest of Jefferson's life—was composed with his left hand and is sometimes referred to as his "my head and my heart" letter. Jefferson gave the letter to his trusted friend, the artist John Trumbull, to deliver to Maria. The letter passionately recalled their time together, the places they visited, and the sites, art, and plays they experienced. But it opens with memories of his emotion when Maria departed for England: "Having performed the last sad office of handing you into your carriage at the Pavillon de St. Denis, and seen the wheels get actually in motion, I turned on my heel and walked more dead than alive, to the opposite door, where my own was awaiting me." The letter, however, uses the analogy of a wrestling match between the head and heart. Jefferson explains, "Seated by my fire side, solitary and sad, the following dialogue took place between my Head and my Heart."

HEAD: Well, friend, you seem to be in a pretty trim.

HEART: I am indeed the most wretched of all earthly beings. Overwhelmed with grief, every fibre of my frame distended beyond its natural powers to bear, I would willingly meet whatever catastrophe should leave me no more to feel or to fear. . . .

HEAD: These are the eternal consequences of your warmth and precipitation. This is one of the scrapes into which you are ever leading us. You confess your follies indeed: but still you hug and cherish them, and no reformation can be hoped, where there is no repentance. . . .

HEART: Oh my friend! This is no moment to upbraid my foibles. I am rent into fragments by the force of my grief! If you have any balm, pour it into my wounds: if none, do not harrow them by new torments.

HEAD: . . . I often told you during its course that you were imprudently engaging your affections under circumstances that must cost you a great deal of pain . . . that the lady had moreover qualities and accomplishments, belonging to her sex, which might form a chapter apart for her: such as music, modesty, beauty, and that softness of disposition which is the ornament of her sex and charm of ours. But that all these considerations would increase the pang of separation.

Jefferson worried that he would never see Maria again and longed to turn back time. He also spoke of Monticello in an effort to entice her to visit. Although many scholars see the struggle between Jefferson's head and heart ending in a draw, it was ultimately won by the head—Jefferson did not follow Maria to England, the two never tried to marry, and Jefferson eventually returned to Virginia. Perhaps the head obeyed a deathbed vow never to remarry, or perhaps Jefferson's thoughts of a daughter needing his attention motivated him. There is some evidence to suggest that Jefferson's eldest daughter may also have been jealous and disapproving of Maria.

However, the longest passages in the letter were written by the heart, and Jefferson admitted that his heart caused him much pain and many sleepless nights. Jefferson was still grieving his late wife and did not want to open himself to further emotional pain, but his heart admits, "I should love her forever." Moreover, Jefferson wanted Maria to write and hoped that they would remain in contact, saying, "If your letters are as long as the Bible, they will appear short to me. Only let them be brim full of affection." Not only did he want her to write, but Jefferson asked his lover to write passionately about her true feelings for him. Such words, he admits, would be "food for my soul." At one point, Jefferson even wrote that he wished to be a bird so that he could fly to be at her side.

Jefferson's letters to Maria closed with such warm wishes as "Sentiments of sincere affection and esteem." The letter in question bids her a romantic farewell:

When wafting on the bosom of the ocean I shall pray it to be calm and smooth as yours to me. . . . Adieu, my dear friend. Be our affections unchangeable, and if our little history is to last beyond the grave, be the longest chapter in it that which shall record their purity, warmth and duration.

It was signed, "Je vous aimerai toujourns" ("I will always love you"). After Maria's departure, Jefferson was barely able to hold himself together. In the carriage awaiting Jefferson was the sixty-seven-year-old French scholar Pierre d'Hancarville (Jefferson spelled it "Danquerville" in a letter to Maria). D'Hancarville, who was recently released from debtors' prison and had previously been expelled from Italy, was a close friend of Richard Cosway. He wrote and studied exotic history and was known for his explicit and illicit illustrations and views. In fact, his work was considered pornographic in much of Europe. Richard Cosway shared d'Hancarville's love of the perverse. After Maria's departure, Jefferson collapsed into the carriage next to d'Hancarville.

Maria seemed somewhat baffled by the letter, and her reply to it was vague. On October 30, 1786, she responded, first in English, then in Italian. She also wrote again on November 17 and November 27. The two continued to exchange letters, and Maria frequently asked for news about Jefferson. On November 19, Jefferson wrote to Maria, saying that it was she who deserved to be the first to receive a letter written from his newly mended right hand. He admitted that the wrist still hurt while writing and apologized for having to keep the letter to a short one page. He also did not sign the letter, probably because of concerns about his reputation should such love letters to a married woman become public. Jefferson also took care to secure reliable individuals to deliver his letters to her. Although he did not sign letters, he ended them with loving phrases in Italian and French.

When Maria did not hear from Jefferson, she expressed concern about his well-being. He often requested her company, hoping that she would agree to travel to America, but dreaded being rejected by her, admitting, "I had rather be deceived, than live without hope. It is so sweet!" Jefferson promised to show Maria America's natural beauty: "I shall meet you there, and visit with you all those grand scenes."

Of course, some scholars, including Dumas Malone and Bernard Mayo, have tried to dismiss the head-and-heart letter to Maria. Malone suggests that it was, at best, full of "vexing qualifications" and was less emotional than some of the letters Jefferson wrote to Abigail Adams. Mayo described it as only "affectionate" and but a letter of "friendship." Although history rightly preserves Jefferson's reputation and the integrity of his marriage, the words in this and other letters are undeniable proof of his deep but conflicted love for Maria Cosway.

A Proposition

One of the most famous and consequential political feuds in American history was between Thomas Jefferson and Alexander Hamilton. The two men were opposites, and in their case opposites did not attract. Hamilton was born illegitimately in the Caribbean. Scrappy, outspoken, and confrontational, he envisioned an active, centralized government led by a strong executive. Jefferson, sophisticated and philosophical, resided near the top of Virginia aristocracy and favored an inactive, decentralized government led by the House of Representatives. The two men were among the primary architects of these two competing visions that formed the conceptual foundations for the American system of government. And they did not like one another.

Their feud carried over into the inaugural administration of the new nation. So frustrated was Jefferson with President George Washington's preference for Hamilton, who served as the secretary of the treasury, that he resigned his position as secretary of state in protest. In addition to their disagreements over political philosophy, the role of government, and policies of the Washington administration, they were rivals for a mistress.

Jefferson's Maria Cosway was a friend of Angelica Schuyler Church, who happened to be Hamilton's sister-in-law. Miss Church appears to have been the object of both men's sexual desire.

Both before his marriage to Martha Wayles and after her death, Jefferson seemed incapable of "sustained intimacy" with women, including nonsexual relationships and even his relationships with his mother and daughters. Jefferson could be "wooden" and professorial in his tone to his daughters, but his letters to the youthful Rebecca Burwell, Maria Cosway, and Angelica Church reveal a flirtatious and sentimental side of Jefferson. The noted historian Joseph Ellis describes such moments as "playfully intimate."

Angelica Schuyler Church was known on both sides of the Atlantic for her family's wealth and for her beauty and charm. Her husband, John Barker Church, was a member of the British Parliament, and she thus divided her time among New York, London, and Paris. Long the object of a lustful Hamilton, who likely had a long-term affair with his wife's beautiful sister, Angelica also caught the eye of Jefferson while he was in Paris. Angelica traveled to Paris with her husband and Jefferson's close friend, the artist John Trumbull. As such, the two shared the same social circle in Paris, and they often attended, with Trumbull and Maria Cosway, the same parties. Interestingly, Maria was aware of Jefferson's desire for Angelica and vice versa. In more than one instance, Maria became jealous of Jefferson's affection for her friend and accused Jefferson of ignoring her in favor of Angelica. In March 1788, Maria began a letter to Jefferson as follows: "I have waited some time to trie if I could recover my usual peace with you, but I find it is impossible yet, therefore Must address Myself to you still angry. Your long silence is impardonable."

Three months later, Maria ended a letter to Jefferson, saying, "Tho' you neglect me, I force myself to your recollection." Jefferson responded that he had been traveling through Holland and the Rhineland. He then added that the first item of business on his return was to write Maria. The two women vied for Jefferson's attention and letters, although they seem to have remained friends throughout. For example, Maria once wrote to Jefferson of her friendship with Angelica and the question of Jefferson's passions, saying,

> She Colls' me her Sister. I coll' her My dearest Sister. If I did not love her so Much I would fear her rivalship. But, no, I give you free permission to love her with all your heart and I shall be happy if you keep me in a little corner of it, when you admit her even to reigning Queen.

In the late summer of 1788, Angelica and Maria were enjoying one another's company in England. Angelica wrote Jefferson of the matter, informing him that the two "sisters" were "enjoying the quiet of the country" together. Maria, she said, regularly "plays and sings" and thinks of Jefferson and that "we very often wish that Mr. Jefferson was here, supposing that he would be indulgent to the exertions of two little women to please him."

But, while Jefferson was emotionally crushed when Maria departed Paris, he seems more flirtatious and sexually suggestive with Angelica. Even though the two spent time together in Paris during the few months that Angelica visited, they were hardly inseparable, as was the case with Maria. Jefferson's passion for Angelica was less the deep emotion he felt for Maria than it was sexual lust. The two were also drawn together in a far more innocent way—Angelica's daughter Catherine (nicknamed "Kitty") became good friends with Jefferson's second daughter, Maria. The children wrote, and both families exchanged gifts for the girls.

Jefferson was upset when Angelica, like Maria before her, made plans to leave Paris. In fact, Jefferson wrote to Angelica after she departed from Paris, using virtually the same language that he employed in a letter to Maria: "When you come again I will employ myself solely in finding or fancying that you have some faults, and I will draw a veil over all your good qualities, if I can find one large enough."

At one point, Jefferson invited Angelica to travel with him by ship back to America. In a letter discussing the travel plans, Jefferson offered a "negotiation" regarding the terms of their rooming arrangement while crossing the Atlantic. He writes, "You shall find in me all the spirit of accommodation with which Yoric began his with the fair Piedmontese." This is a reference to the work of Laurence Sterne, who wrote a sexually charged passage about a character named Yoric, who shared a "wet and tempestuous night" with the beautiful Piedmontese while the two were traveling together. Their negotiated sleeping arrangement was that their beds, placed side by side, would be separated by a thin curtain. However, Yuric proposed to have a small whole cut in the curtain near their waists, saying it would be "no more than an ejacu-lation." However, Piedmontese worried that it would constitute "an entire infraction of the treaty." Angelica would have been familiar with the writings of Sterne, just as was Jefferson's wife.

Curtain and strategically cut holes aside, Angelica declined Jefferson's travel offer. But the unusual love triangle involving Jefferson, his political rival, and his rival's sister-in-law continued.

Lascivious Behavior?

Maria Cosway seemed to not only enjoy but also need Jefferson's admiration, and it is clear that he offered it in abundance. Jefferson loved the works of Sterne and quoted him often in his letters to Maria. Maria was also familiar with Sterne, and both enjoyed his popular book *Tristram Shandy*, which brimmed with sexual innuendos. Sterne's own life mirrored his novels in that he had sexual affairs. In fact, his critics often gossiped about his "lascivious behavior." But the book sold well.

Jefferson frequently toyed with sexual innuendos, á la Sterne, in his let-ters to Maria. For instance, while writing about his travels, he tells her, "I could think of nothing but the promontory of noses." Jefferson then went on to comment about the noses of others. This is an unmistakable sexual reference used by Sterne in *Tristram Shandy* and elsewhere for another male anatomical feature. Even though Maria was familiar with Sterne, she failed to comment on it in her replies to Jefferson's sexually charged hints. Jefferson conjured other romantic scenes and phrases for Maria in his letters. Before she returned to Paris, he wrote, "Come then, my dear madam, and we will breakfast every day . . . dine under the bowers of Marly, and forget that we are ever to part again." They both flirted openly and teased one another, such as when Maria pouted, "Do you not deserve a longer letter, my dear friend? No, certainly not, and to avoid temptation, I have a small sheet of paper." Jefferson responded in a note to John Trumbull, who was on his way to visit with Maria, "My love to Mrs. Cosway. Tell her I will send her a supply of larger paper." Touché.

Gentlemen of the time often wrote overly sentimental letters to females and were overtly flirtatious despite the prudish underpinnings of society. Infidelity occurred and was not unusual and was likely more common than history suggests, especially in Europe. Maria clearly did not let her husband or her marriage interfere with the time she spent with Jefferson. Indeed, she was freer than most married women to do as she pleased and was even linked romantically in rumor with the Prince of Wales before she met Jefferson. Af-ter nine years of marriage and only months after returning to England from her time in France with Jefferson, Maria gave birth to a girl. The possibilities of paternity are, of course, delicious but uncertain.

After his love returned to England, Jefferson was distraught. But Maria returned to Paris in the fall of 1787 for a four-month visit, and her husband did not accompany her. She had returned to see the gala opening of the Grand Salon of the Louvre but also made sure that she had time to see Jefferson. Interestingly, however, the spark between Jefferson and Maria never again burned as bright as it did before her departure. Their letters suggest that they did not spend as much time together as one might expect. Rather, Maria spent most of her time in the company of other artists. Jefferson tried to see her more often but was unable to do so. He once wrote to John Trumbull, saying that he had called on Maria "numerous times" but she was not home.

Curiously, when Maria departed for London on December 8, 1787, she was a no-show for a planned farewell breakfast with Jefferson. A letter to her from Jefferson does not, as far as is known, appear until mid-January. Their future correspondence remained warm but never again captured the passion during their affair in 1786. It is hard to say why. Perhaps they resigned themselves to the reality of the situation, or perhaps Jefferson's pledge to his late wife continued to pain his conscience. Maria seems always to have needed Jefferson's attention and affection, and she demonstrated anxiety about him and their relationship in her letters.

In an effort to mend his broken heart (and wrist), after Maria departed, Jefferson went on a three-and-a-half-month journey through France and Italy, using spa treatments and other therapies. Nothing worked for either malady. Maria and her marriage also suffered, likely because of the affair with Jefferson. After her daughter was born, in 1790 Maria abandoned both the three-month-old child and her husband and moved to Italy. There, she ran away with an Italian opera singer named Luigi Marchesi. Maria's decision to leave her husband occurred around the time Jefferson finally departed Paris and returned to Virginia. It is likely that her passionate affair with Jefferson aroused in her the desire and will to leave her husband, and it is not difficult to imagine Maria leaving her husband for Jefferson—if he had asked.

Tragically, Maria's daughter died at age six. Later in life, Maria established a girls' school in collaboration with the church. After Marchesi's death, she returned to where she began, retiring to a convent where she remained until her death on January 5, 1838. After they departed from France, Jefferson and Maria would never again see one another. It is interesting to consider what might have happened had Jefferson offered Maria the opportunity to leave her husband, which she ultimately did after her affair with Jefferson ended and she ran away with an Italian opera singer. Conversely, had he married Maria, Jefferson would not have been elected president.

THE "AFRICAN VENUS"

Back in Virginia, Jefferson's last-born daughter, Lucy, whose difficult birth had likely hastened Mrs. Jefferson's death, suffered a bad bout of whooping cough. In October 1784, the child succumbed to the affliction, only two years after her mother's untimely death. Jefferson was in Paris during his daughter's ordeal. He learned of little Lucy's passing from the Marquis de Lafayette on his return trip from Virginia to visit George Washington.

None other than Abigail Adams, wife of Jefferson's rival John Adams, chided him for not having his family together with him in Paris. Jefferson's second daughter, Maria, was also still living back in Virginia. Only his first-born, Martha, had accompanied Jefferson to France. Back in America, Mrs. Adams wrote to Jefferson after the passing of his youngest daughter, Lucy,

> Had you been no other than the private inhabitant of Monticello, I should, ere this time, have addressed you with that sympathy which a recent event has awakened in my bosom; but reasons of various kinds withheld my pen, until the powerful feelings of my heart burst through the restraint, and called upon me to shed the tear of sorrow over the departed remains of your beloved and deserving daughter—which I most sincerely mourn.

Abigail penned the letter even though Jefferson and her husband were on the outs. Arguably, one of the most complex political relationships in American history was the one shared by Jefferson and John Adams. Few others played more central roles in the nation's founding than Jefferson and Adams. Both men served in Washington's inaugural administration and as secretary of state and vice president, respectively, and during Adams's presidency, Jefferson was vice president. The two men also emerged in the wake of Washington's death as the figureheads of the young republic's new political parties—the Federalists (Adams) and Anti-Federalists (Jefferson)—and their rivalry was such that Jefferson challenged Adams during his reelection effort in 1800.

The division occasioned by the election—and Jefferson's subsequent victory—destroyed the already strained relationship. So hurt was Adams by Jefferson's challenge and his public defeat that, under cover of darkness in the wee hours of the morning, the president snuck out of the capital city the day of Jefferson's inauguration in March 4, 1801. Back home in Massachusetts, Adams stopped communicating with Jefferson, with the exception of a letter demanding that his foe stop writing to Mrs. Adams, who had always been somewhat smitten with Jefferson.

It was Abigail who, when Jefferson's two surviving daughters were in France, helped arrange for their care. Maria Jefferson's death thus hit Abigail hard, and although both men were at an impasse, Abigail remembered in a letter to Jefferson the "attachment which I formed for her when you committed her to my care upon her arrival in a foreign land." It was also Abigail who initiated the thawing in the Adams–Jefferson standoff, and because of her, the two old statesmen resumed their friendship. Even though Abigail died on October 28, 1818, the two founders continued to exchange warm letters. Thanks to their letters, the rich memories of the momentous events these two men shaped remain today as an invaluable resource for history.

Back in Paris, even though Jefferson had traveled to France with his eldest daughter, he was not spending much time with her, and she seems likely to have been lonely. That changed when Jefferson discovered that his daughter was contemplating joining a monastery in France. Enraged, Jefferson promptly enrolled the young girl in a secular school. Jefferson also took the advice of Mrs. Adams and sent word back to Virginia requesting to have his other daughter, Maria, travel to France to join what remained of his family. He vowed to spend more time with his two remaining daughters.

While eldest daughter Martha grew tall and stately like her father, even inheriting his physical appearance and intellect, Maria was said to resemble her beautiful mother. Like her mother, Maria was frail and, two decades later, died on April 17, 1804, of complications from childbirth. The tragic date also marked the midpoint of Jefferson's two terms as president. Although Jefferson loved his daughters, they always reminded him of his late wife, and his grief remained. After Maria's death, Jefferson wrote, "Others may lose of their abundance, but I of my want, have lost even the half of all I had. . . . [I] now hang on the slender thread of a single life."

Sally

One of those gathered at the bedside of Mrs. Jefferson when she died in 1782 was a nine-year-old slave girl. Two years later, when Jefferson's last-born daughter, Lucy, died, and Abigail Adams encouraged Jefferson to bring his other daughter, nine-year-old Maria, to live with him in Paris, this same slave girl accompanied the second Jefferson daughter. Her name was Sarah "Sally" Hemings. Fate was such that Jefferson had requested that another slave at Monticello named Isabel travel with his daughter, but eleven-year-old Sally was sent in her place, likely because Isabel was pregnant. Of the young slave girl, Abigail Adams again offered sage advice, writing to Jefferson that Sally was but a child herself and that his daughter needed the assistance of an older, more experienced maid.

Had Jefferson heeded her advice, history would have been different. Sally's son, Madison Hemings, recorded his memoir, *Life among the Lowly*, first published on March 13, 1873, in the Ohio newspaper *Pike County Republican*, that when Sally returned with Jefferson from France in 1789, she was pregnant with Jefferson's child. There is, however, no account of Sally giving birth in 1790 in Jefferson's "Farm Book," where he meticulously kept track of everything happening to his slaves and at his estate. Scholars, such as the noted Jefferson biographer Dumas Malone, are skeptical of Madison Hemings's claim and suggest that his memoir may have been altered by those with political motives. After all, some of the prose used in the memoir, they argue, was too sophisticated for an uneducated slave. But this assumes that Madison did not receive any assistance in publishing the memoir. Another criticism of the claim of paternity is that Madison was sixty-eight when he recorded his recollections with the Ohio newspaper, although such intimate family events would not fade from memory. S. F. Wetmore, one of those who assisted in the publication, later testified that the memoir was factual.

Either way, there is no account of Sally giving birth until 1795. According to some alleging to be the slave descendants of Jefferson, the child in question, born when Sally arrived back in Virginia, was Thomas C. Woodson, who lived from 1790 to 1879. However, Sally's own son, Madison, says that the newborn child died immediately. Most scholars discount the Woodson family claim and are, at best, mixed on the allegation of paternity by Madison Hemings.

Sally was documented as having six children, two of whom died in infancy, including a daughter born in 1799. The four who survived were Harriet (1795–1797), Beverly (1798–1822), Madison (1805–1877), and Eston (1808–1856). It is probable that Jefferson fathered all these children, and Madison Hemings maintains as much, saying that "we were the only children of his by a slave woman." Jefferson was sixty-two when Madison Hemings was born at Monticello and named for Dolley Madison, wife of Jefferson's secretary of state (and the next president), who was visiting at the time of birth on January 19, 1805. The only slaves freed by Jefferson were the children of Sally. Of them, son Beverly moved to the nation's capital city and lived as a white man, marrying a white woman. Daughter Harriet also moved to Washington and married a white man. Eston married a black woman in Virginia, then later moved to Ohio and Wisconsin and had three children. Madison also married a white woman and worked as a carpenter and bricklayer. He had nine children, one of whom, Thomas Eston Hemings, fought for the Union during the Civil War but died in the infamous Confederate prison at Andersonville, Georgia, in 1863.

According to Madison Hemings, his grandmother, Elizabeth, lived until 1808. Accounts vary, with some suggesting that she had twelve children and others fourteen children, with six of them fathered by a white man (Mrs.

Jefferson's father, John Wayles) and the others presumably fathered by a black slave. All the children, remembered Madison in his memoir, lived in Jefferson's "great house." Madison's mother, Sally Hemings, was born into slavery in 1773, the daughter of John Wayles—the father of Jefferson's wife—and his slave mistress, Elizabeth Hemings. She lived but a short time at the Wayles plantation in Cumberland County, Virginia. John Wayles died the next year, and the infant girl became property of Wayles's eldest child, Martha Wayles Jefferson, and was sent in 1774 with her mother and siblings to live at Monticello, where she eventually became a maid for Jefferson's daughters.

In his memoir, Madison Hemings says that his great-grandfather was a white man named Hemings, an Englishman who captained a trading ship that did business in Virginia. One of his customers was Martha Wayles Jefferson's father. Madison's great-grandmother was an African slave who was the mistress of Captain Hemings when he was in port in Williamsburg. The historical record is unclear, but perhaps the slave woman was owned by John Wayles. A daughter, named Elizabeth Hemings, was born, and Captain Hemings attempted to purchase her from Wayles. However, according to Madison Hemings, Wayles rejected the "extraordinarily large price" offered by the captain. Madison suggests that Wayles kept the child at his plantation not because he was moral and did not want to separate a mother and child but because of his curiosity about biracial children—curious indeed, as later this child would become Wayles's mistress. After burying three wives, Wayles took the now-mature Elizabeth as his mistress, and she would have six children with Wayles—three sons and three daughters: Robert, James, Peter, Critty (or "Critta"), Thena, and the youngest, Sally Hemings.

Other accounts suggest that Elizabeth Hemings was Captain Hemings's property and that Wayles purchased her or that she was exchanged in lieu of the money owed to Wayles by the captain. There is even some evidence that the captain attempted unsuccessfully to kidnap the slave girl from Wayles's plantation, but Wayles foiled his plan by keeping the mother and baby in his home rather than outside at the slave quarters. Either way, Elizabeth Betty Hemings and her children, including one-year-old Sally, went to live at Monticello after their master, John Wayles, died.

In his memoir, Madison Hemings also claims that, when Jefferson was in Paris, Sally "was just budding into womanhood" and became Jefferson's "concubine." She was about fourteen years of age when apparently a sexual relationship emerged with Jefferson. While in Paris, Jefferson purchased fashionable clothing for Sally and possibly taught her to read and write as well as to speak French. At the close of Jefferson's diplomatic service, "when he was called back home," Madison said his mother "was *enceinte* by him" (meaning pregnant). According to the memoir, Sally Hemings enjoyed

France and did not want to return to Virginia and be "re-enslaved," even stating that she "refused to return with [Jefferson]." In order to entice Sally to return with him, Jefferson is then said to have "promised her extraordinary privileges and made a solemn pledge that her children should be freed at the age of twenty-one years."

"Night Walking" and Slavery

Thomas and Martha Jefferson considered their slaves to be an extension of their own family and encouraged their slaves to learn various industrial arts, such as cabinetmaking and spinning. Of course, such a fact does not excuse them of owning other human beings. Likewise, the acquisition of trades by their slaves also directly benefited the Jeffersons. Unlike most slave owners, Jefferson did not purchase slaves. His plantation was worked by slaves he inherited or the children of his slaves.

As an intellectual, Jefferson recognized the irony in the author of the Declaration of Independence owning slaves and readily acknowledged the inhumanity of the institution of slavery. Yet he kept his slaves. As a man of science, Jefferson was also curious about the similarities and differences he noted between himself and his slaves and "the real distinctions which nature has made." Among the distinctions Jefferson claimed to observe were all sorts of beliefs that are downright ridiculous from today's perspective, including that blacks need less sleep, that blacks are equal to whites in memory but "much inferior" in reason and "dull" in imagination, that "in music they are more generally gifted than whites with accurate ears for tune and time," and that the black skin secretes a "disagreeable odour" that "renders them more tolerant of the heat." He did find that blacks were at least as brave and more adventuresome but because "a want of forethought . . . prevents their seeing a danger till it is present."

Jefferson also believed that blacks were more emotional and gave examples, including that "after a hard labour through the day, [he] will be induced by the slightest amusements to sit up till midnight, or later, though knowing he must be out with the first dawn of morning." The other example had to do with sex, where he felt that blacks were "more ardent after their female" than whites and that they enjoyed much more "commerce between the two sexes almost without restraint." However, love to blacks seemed to be "more an eager desire, than a tender delicate mixture of sentiment and sensation."

Jefferson pondered the complicated question of freeing slaves. On the one hand, he recognized that slavery was wrong and understood the "deep rooted prejudices entertained by the whites." Jefferson wrote about "the ten thousand recollections, by the blacks, of the injuries they have sustained." On the other hand, he excused southern slave owners by saying that the Romans had treated their slaves far worse. He observed, "As far as I can judge from the experiments . . . made, to give liberty to, or rather, to abandon persons whose habits have been formed in slavery, is like abandoning children." Although well intentioned, this perspective is utterly damning from today's perspective. Jefferson failed to do the right thing regarding slavery, believing that the problem "will probably never end but in the extermination of the one or the other race."

Prior to the Civil War, the myth of the innocent southern belle is frequently offered as a defense of the acceptance of slavery—and the associated evils of "night walking" by southern plantation owners. Of course, it is laughable to suggest that the wives and daughters of slave owners did not recognize the horrors of buying and selling or whipping slaves, the inhumane living conditions of slave quarters, or the sexual affairs that white owners had with their slaves. White women living on plantations spent more time around African slaves than they did around other white families. Surely, Martha Jefferson would have recognized her father's affair with the slave mistress Elizabeth Hemings just as Martha Jefferson Randolph observed Sally Hemings having children who resembled her own father and not the male slaves at her home. Still, some historians excuse southern women as innocent and ignorant when it came to slavery, just as some scholars suggest that Martha Wayles Jefferson knew nothing of her father's long affair with Elizabeth Hemings. Of course, both positions are absurd.

Evidence exists both for and against Jefferson's affair with Sally Hemings. Perhaps the strongest case against the existence of the affair comes from Jefferson's descendants. Jefferson's grandson, Thomas Jefferson Randolph, told biographer Henry Randall just prior to the Civil War that the Carr boys admitted to having sex with slaves. Randolph therefore fingered Jefferson's nephew, Peter Carr, as the guilty party because he often visited and lived for some time at Monticello and was just three years Sally's senior. Jefferson's account books do show the Carr boys being at Monticello around the time that Sally would have become pregnant. In fact, Randolph claimed that Peter Carr cried about fathering Sally's children, saying to his younger brother, Samuel, "Aren't you and I a couple of ———— pretty fellows to bring this disgrace on poor old uncle who has always fed us! We ought to be ————." The expletives were deleted by history, but the meaning of the claim is clear, although it is odd that Randolph puts the blame on Peter but then said that both Peter and Samuel ("we") were misbehaving with Sally.

Other descendants of Jefferson also pointed blame at the Carr boys. Jefferson's granddaughter, Ellen Randolph, placed paternity with the younger Carr brother, Samuel. For instance, in a letter she wrote on October 24, 1858, discussing the "yellow children" of Monticello, Ellen claimed that the Carr boys even laughed and joked about "old grandfather had to bear the blame" for their "misdeeds." It is hard to imagine Jefferson's "favorite" nephews boasting and joking about such a scandal, and the accounts of both grandchildren, who were but babies during the time the incidents occurred, contradict one another, with one blaming Peter and the other blaming Samuel and one claiming that both boys cried about it while the other claimed that both laughed about it.

One thing seems certain: Martha Jefferson Randolph, Jefferson's daughter, discussed the sensitive matter of Sally's biracial children with her own children before her death in 1836 and suggested that it was the Carr boys who fathered the slaves. This is the likely genesis of the Jefferson grandchildren's beliefs about the "yellow slaves" at Monticello.

If paternity was not with the Carr boys, why would Jefferson's daughter not name a visitor to Monticello or someone other than a close relative as the father? But, if the Carr boys were the fathers of Sally's children, the Jefferson family was still disgraced by the incidents. A Reverend Hamilton W. Pierson, president of Cumberland College of Kentucky, interviewed the overseer of Jefferson's farms, Edmund Bacon, in 1862. On the topic of Jefferson's light-skinned slaves, Bacon recollected that Jefferson

> freed one girl some years ago before he died, and there was a great deal of talk about it. She was nearly white as anybody, and very beautiful. People said he freed her because she was his own daughter. She was not his daughter, she was ———'s daughter. I know that. I have seen him come out of her mother's room many a morning when I went up to Monticello very early.

The identity of the man Bacon described is uncertain because it was removed at some point by a reader or owner of the letter.

However, there are also arguments that the affair between Jefferson and Sally Hemings did occur and that Jefferson fathered Sally's children. Although Jefferson's grandson was said to claim that Sally "was treated and dressed just like the rest [of the slaves]," there is evidence to the contrary. Sally enjoyed a preferential status at Monticello. The light-skinned Sally Hemings was a "house" slave, meaning that she worked in the home as a maid to Jefferson's daughters rather than toiling in the fields as a farmworker. Her siblings also held similar "house" positions at Monticello. It seems unusual that the Carr boys (and Peter was Jefferson's favorite relative) would risk their famous and powerful uncle's reputation and wrath by seeking pleasures with his preferred slave. Although it is morally troubling to contemplate, it would seem far easier for the Carr boys to have visited the young slave girls living in the nearby slave quarters than to have tried to bed Sally in Monticello. Sally's special status at Monticello might have been because of her relationship with Jefferson or her own mother's status at the Wayles plantation as a mistress of John Wayles. Another reason may have been that Martha Wayles Jefferson and Sally Hemings were half-sisters, both having the same father.

Sally's bloodline included an impressive and charismatic father and a beautiful biracial mother, and she probably shared a strong resemblance to her stepsister Martha Wayles Jefferson, who was routinely described as very attractive. It would not be difficult then to imagine Jefferson being drawn to a younger and more exotic version of his beloved late wife. Many accounts also exist that describe Sally's own children having a strong resemblance to Jefferson.

The matter of Sally's children also speaks to Jefferson's views on and reputation regarding slavery. In a way, of course, he is damned if he did and damned if he did not father Sally's children. He was, after all, a slave owner. If Jefferson fathered the children, his relationship with Sally could hardly have been completely consensual from her perspective—he owned her, and she would have been but a teen when the affair may have started. But if the two developed a strong fondness or love for one another, we see a different side of Jefferson, although it may well have been that Sally was simply an outlet for his sexual gratification—and a very attractive one at that. Even if Jefferson were not the father, the fact that one of his preferred "house" slaves was bearing a white man's children suggests that the Sage of Monticello permitted the unforgivable practice of night walking in his own home. Jefferson, like most whites in America at the time, considered Africans to be morally and intellectually inferior to whites, but it is hard to imagine him condoning such behavior among his relatives and white guests. As such, Jefferson likely experienced great guilt in sleeping with Sally Hemings.

The Callender Incident

Sally spent over two years in France with Jefferson, returning to Virginia with him in 1789. Whether she returned pregnant is uncertain, but it is possible that she bore Jefferson several biracial children back at Monticello who were described as resembling their master in many ways. This occurrence would not have been lost on other slaves at Monticello, Jefferson's friends and relatives, and his political opponents. Indeed, rumors emerged during Jefferson's presidency of his slave mistress. The story broke during Jefferson's second year as president when, in September 1802, the Scottish journalist James Thomson Callender published his scandalous version of the rumor.

Callender, who fancied himself a "muckraker" but wallowed in the mud of tabloid reporting, had worn out his welcome in Scotland because of the political battles he picked and the aggressive attacks he launched against prominent leaders. Disgraced, he emigrated to America in 1793 and picked up right where he left off. Callender was actually a former ally of Jefferson's who helped Jefferson and his supporters, including James Monroe, by authoring friendly stories about them and sensationalized, critical articles about their Federalist opponents.

For instance, Callender had defended Jefferson in 1800 against Federalist charges that the great founder was "debauched" and "anti-Christian"; however, Callender's motivation had less to do with political ideology than it did with being a drunk whose hand was always open to the highest bidder—which was usually Jefferson. The scandalmonger went so far as to label George Washington a "revolutionary profiteer," John Adams "a British spy," and John Jay a "traitor." It was even Callender who released the story of Alexander Hamilton's controversial affair with Maria Reynolds.

But Callender's welcome wore out on this side of the Atlantic. He was jailed for nine months and fined $200 for violating the Alien and Sedition Acts under President John Adams. When Jefferson was elected in 1800, Callender shamelessly contacted his former benefactor to request money and help in getting out of prison. Callender also wanted to room at Monticello and demanded the job of postmaster of Richmond. In 1801, Jefferson came to Callender's defense under the auspices of free speech and used the powers of the presidency to remove the judge who had earlier jailed him. Jefferson also "pardoned" Callender. However, the president did not permit Callender to move into Monticello. Because Jefferson only offered Callender $50 and no job, his former ally turned his pen against Jefferson. He even represented Jefferson's gift of $50 as "hush money" designed to buy his silence.

As such, on September 1, 1802, a shocking story about Jefferson and written by Callender appeared in the *Richmond Recorder*:

> It is well known that the man, whom it delighteth the people to honor, keeps, and for many years past has kept, as his concubine, one of his own slaves. Her name is SALLY. The name of her eldest son is TOM. His features are said to bear a striking although sable resemblance to those of the president himself. The boy is ten or twelve years of age. His mother went to France in the same vessel with Mr. Jefferson and his two daughters. The delicacy of this arrangement must strike every person of common Sensibility. What a sublime pattern for an American ambassador to place before the eyes of two young ladies!

Callender said that there had been a few rumors prior to the article in the Richmond paper. For example, a few years earlier, *Rind's Federalist* newspaper suggested that Jefferson had an affair. Had the story gained more traction, guessed Callender, Jefferson would have been denied the presidency. Callender went on, claiming, "By this wench, Sally, our president has had several children," whom he called "Yellow Toms," and maintained that all Jefferson's neighbors were aware of the affair and children. Playing to racial fears, the article pointed out that the author of the Declaration of Independence chose "African stock" to "engraft his own descendants" and was somehow functioning as a "ring leader" for slaves while maintaining a "Congo harem" in the presidential mansion. In another article, Callender claimed that Jefferson's slave mistress "is said to officiate, as housekeeper at Monticello."

A follow-up article in the *Richmond Recorder* appeared on October 20, 1802. In it, Callender admits to and corrects some mistakes made in the first article. For instance, Callender claimed that Sally accompanied both of Jefferson's daughters to France when only Maria was aboard the ship. However, the whole family—Sally included—returned together. Callender expressed surprise and disappointment that other newspapers were still denying the allegations. He even suggested that Jefferson's affair with Maria Cosway fizzled because of the affair with Sally Hemings, whom he called "the AFRICAN VENUS." But the stories did have legs. Jefferson's Federalist critics latched on to them, and a minor scandal erupted. Newspapers spoke of "Black Sal," "Dusky Sally," and the "mahogany-coloured charmer." Poems and songs were composed to embarrass the president. For instance, Joseph Dennie, the editor of *Port Folio*, a Philadelphia publication, composed a poem in honor of the question of the paternity of the Hemings slaves:

> Of all the damsels on the green;
> On mountain or in valley;
> A lass so luscious ne'er was seen;
> As Monticellian Sally;
> And, 'Yankee Doodle,' whose the noodle?
> What wife were half so handy?
> To breed a flock of slaves to stock;
> A blackamoors the dandy.

Callender's drinking caught up with him. In 1803, the year after breaking the story of Jefferson's slave mistress, his body was found floating in the James River near Richmond. Although Callender had many enemies and it was tempting to conclude that foul play was involved, it appears that he simply died of alcoholism.

"The Betsy Walker Affair"

It was James Callender who also reported on another scandal associated with Jefferson—the "Betsy Walker affair." Betsy was the wife of John Walker, one of Jefferson's Albemarle neighbors and a close friend from Jefferson's youth when both attended the James Maury School and the College of William & Mary. Jefferson was even an usher in Walker's wedding and was named by Walker as the executor of his will. Prior to the affair, Walker may even have asked Jefferson to take care of his family in the event of his death. The closeness of the two men makes the affair even more damning.

Some sources say that the affair began in 1768, but most place the date of the affair in 1769. There are two versions of the story. At twenty-five, Jefferson fell for Betsy Walker. It appears that Jefferson tried to entice her into having sex. One account suggests that John Walker was away working on an Indian treaty when Jefferson tried to enter Mrs. Walker's bedroom. The other version has Jefferson visiting a friend's home with the Walkers. When Mrs. Walker excused herself to prepare for bed, Jefferson followed her to the bedroom and propositioned her. Mrs. Walker had to fight Jefferson off with scissors. Either way, the story is rather racy for the early nineteenth century.

On April 5, 1805—during Jefferson's second term as president and two and a half years after the Sally Hemings story hit the papers—the *New York Evening Post* published a story about Jefferson and Betsy. The newspaper claimed that Jefferson "stole to the chamber" of his absent friend late at night and tried to "violate his bed." In the article, a letter from John Walker was printed, saying,

> We [Walker and his wife] went on a visit to Col. Coles a mutual acquaintance and a distant neighbor. Mr. Jefferson was there. On the ladys retiring to bed he pretended to be sick, complained of a headache & left the gentlemen among whom I was. Instead of going to bed as his sickness authorized a belief he stole into my room where my wife was undressing or in bed.

Walker was retelling the story in 1805, many years after the incident, and scholars suggest that the letter's motivation may have been political rather than factual. Walker had not only a personal falling-out with Jefferson but also a political one because of Jefferson. Walker had lost a Senate race to Jefferson's close ally and future president, James Monroe. Moreover, Jefferson's Federalist opponents kept the story in the public fore, accusing him of "adultery." Conversely, in later years, both America's critics and northern abolitionists seeking to discredit slavery kept the Hemings and Walker affairs alive. Thus, politics may have factored into the accusation.

For his part, Jefferson typically refused to discuss scandalous matters. However, when the story broke, Jefferson wrote to his secretary of the navy, Robert Smith, saying, "You will perceive that I plead guilty to one of their charges, that when young and single I offered love to a handsome lady. I acknowledge its incorrectness. It is the only one founded on truth among all their allegations against me." Although Jefferson admitted to the affair with Mrs. Walker, he indirectly denied the "other" allegations against him—meaning the affair with Sally Hemings.

Thirty-five years after the incident, Jefferson admitted to poor judgment in the Walker affair. However, he never discussed the matter of Sally Hemings. In a statement to George Logan, Jefferson declined to comment on Sally but stated, "As to federal slanders, I never wished them to be answered, but by the tenor of my life. . . . The man who fears no truths has nothing to fear from lies."

THE WOMEN IN JEFFERSON'S LIFE

Jefferson vowed he would never "expose his soul to such pain again" after his wife's death. He would rather be "lonely and vulnerable." It is all but certain that Jefferson's marriage was, in the words of one historian, "singularly happy." According to another historian, the couple "loved each other greatly." Beyond loving his wife, Jefferson put great stock in marriage, and his "marriage seemed to steady him." Jefferson never did remarry, and it is possible that a pledge to his dying wife on her deathbed was the reason. But he did turn his formidable pen toward matters of the heart and did fall in love and in lust with several women, and it is hard to imagine that he did not consummate his love with at least some of these women.

Jefferson tended to pursue married women as if their marital status provided some assurance against falling in love and remarrying. All these women were impressive, beautiful women who shared his artistic and intellectual tastes. But he seemed wracked with guilt and anxiety, even while pursuing them with romantic verses and sexual innuendoes. Maria Cosway recognized Jefferson's need to pull back from the relationships, writing to him in February 1787, "Are you to be painted in future ages sitting solitary and sad, on the beautiful Monticello, tormented by the shadow of a woman?"

Jefferson's view of women was conventional and defined by the times, but his preference for accomplished women suggests complexity in his beliefs about women. He valued domestic service and did not see roles beyond childbearing and a husband's happiness. He once wrote to Angelica Schuyler Church that "the tender breasts of young ladies were not formed for political convulsion." As a single parent, he raised two daughters and emphasized their domestic responsibilities to sew, cook, and learn to "make a pudding yet, to cut out a beefsteak, to sow spinach, or to set a hen." But this was expected of all women. To his eldest daughter, he offered advice on marriage and happiness:

Sweetness of temper, affection to a husband and attention to his interests, constitute the duties of a wife and form the basis of domestic felicity. The charms of beauty, and the brilliance of wit, though they captivate in the mistress will not long delight in the wife; they will shorten even their own transitory reign if as I have often seen they shine more for the attraction of everybody else than their husbands.

To his other daughter, Maria, he gave similar marital advice, noting that "nothing can preserve affections uninterrupted but a firm resolution never to differ in will." Indeed, he admitted as much, saying, "A modest wife shall do her part tending home and children dear, piling high the sacred hearth with seasoned firewood against the coming of her weary husband." This view of women is nowhere more apparent than in a letter Jefferson sent to a young man from Virginia named John Banister Jr., son of a close friend. Banister Jr., who was also a student of Jefferson's colleague George Wythe, wrote Jefferson, asking for advice during his upcoming visit to France. Jefferson responded with a warning:

He is led by the strongest of all the human passions into a spirit for female intrigue destructive of his own and others happiness, or a passion for whores destructive of his health, and in both cases learns to consider fidelity to the marriage bed as an ungentlemanly practice inconsistent with happiness: he recollects the voluptuary dress and arts of the European woman and pities and despises the chaste affections of those of his own country; he retains thro' life a fond recollection and a hankering after those places which were the scenes of his first pleasures and of his first connections.

Jefferson contrasted the domestic Virginia housewife with the liberated Parisian women, saying that the latter were less domestic and more sexual. With their "voluptuary dress," these women were "inappropriate and tempting." Of Parisian and Virginia women, his preference for Virginia women was obvious as a "comparison of Amazons to angels." Of the liberated French women, Jefferson said,

The domestic bonds here are absolutely done away. And where can their compensation be found? Perhaps they may catch some moments of transport above the level of ordinary tranquil joy we experience, but [these] are separated by long intervals during which all the passions are at sea without rudder or compass.

One can see Jefferson's own decisions in his advice to his daughters, marrying a domestic woman but lusting after free-willed and adventurous women. These free-willed women brought out the passion in the reasoned, intelligent, and fastidious Jefferson, who appreciated their zest for life.

POSTSCRIPT

Sally Hemings's children were the only slaves Jefferson freed. Virginia law at the time required all freed slaves to leave the state within one year of being freed, and Sally's children moved away and married. Sally remained with Thomas Jefferson for the remainder of his life, functioning as a chambermaid and living in Monticello in a room accessible to Jefferson's living quarters by a covered passageway. After his death, she remained to take care of the family of Jefferson's daughter, Martha. She eventually moved to nearby Charlottesville but also spent time at Monticello helping his daughter and her family until her death in 1835 at age sixty-two. Jefferson made but a few references to Sally in his account book and correspondence but no words of her own pen or any likeness of her remains.

Jefferson's wife, Martha, died nineteen years prior to his presidency, so it is difficult to say for certain what type of First Lady she might have been. However, it seems likely that she would have done little because of her poor health and preference for private life. It is also possible that, had she lived, Jefferson would have turned down additional offers of public office. Jefferson wrestled unsuccessfully to balance the demands of public and private life during their decade-long marriage, and the loss of so many children and his wife's failing health caused him to contemplate retirement from public life. In a revealing letter to James Madison, Jefferson complained, "I think public service and private misery inseparably are linked together." After all, he accepted the diplomatic post in France only after his wife's death—and two years after at that.

For instance, Jefferson wrote of his temptation to retire to private life at Monticello, but he also wrote cryptically with an eye to the future and his own enduring reputation. Thus, it is difficult to take at face value such comments by Jefferson. In a letter to David Jameson, Jefferson admitted, "The day is so very bad . . . Mrs. Jefferson is in a situation in which I would not wish to leave her." He then begged out of attending a political event, as he often did. For example, he once did so, explaining, "The situation of my domestic affairs renders it indispensably necessary that I should solicit the substitution of some other person here . . . [the] delicacy of the house will not require me to enter minutely into the private causes which render this necessary."

Another time, Jefferson was perhaps even more forceful, begging Richard Henry Lee to replace him as a delegate in Philadelphia: "For god's sake, for your country's sake, and for my sake . . . I am under a sacred obligation to go home." Jefferson stayed in Philadelphia only because his presence was needed to achieve quorum. It is ironic that the hero of that famous convention was a reluctant participant. In fact, in September 1776, when his replacement arrived, Jefferson was so impatient to return home that he departed immediately and even drove the carriage horses himself to quicken the journey.

Indeed, the happiest times in Jefferson's life, according to his letters, were between public positions when he was at home with his wife and family, such as before and after his governorship. Jefferson states that he was "never happier than when at Monticello with the wife to whom he was devoted and the small children he adored." Writing to his friend, the Chevalier de Chastellux, about Martha's death, Jefferson revealed that

> before that event, my scheme of life had been determined. I had folded myself in the arms of retirement, and rested all prospect of future happiness on domestic and literary objects. A single event wiped away all my plans and left me a blank which I had not the spirit to fill up.

These thoughts are echoed in a letter to his trusted friend James Monroe where Jefferson complains about the difficulties of balancing public life and family:

> Before I ventured to declare to my countrymen my determination to retire from public employment I examined well my heart to know whether it were thoroughly cured of every principle of political ambition, whether no lurking particle remained which might leave me uneasy when reduced with the limits of mere private life. I became satisfied that every fibre of that passion was thoroughly eradicated. I examined also in other views my right to withdraw. I considered that I had been thirteen years engaged in public service, that during that time I had so totally abandoned all attention to my private affairs as to permit them to run into great disorder and ruin, that I had now a family advanced to years which require my attention and instruction . . . that by constant sacrifice of time, labour, loss, parental and friendly duties, I had been so far from gaining the affection of my countrymen which was the only reward I ever asked or could have felt, that I had even lost the small estimation I before possessed.

It is possible that Jefferson was simply wracked with guilt over being away while his wife's health deteriorated and three children died in infancy. However, Jefferson shared thoughts of retirement with his closest friends. Therefore, had Mrs. Jefferson lived, Jefferson may never have accepted the secretary of state position in the Washington administration or even sought the presidency.

Thomas Jefferson died a much poorer man than the man who penned the Declaration of Independence. His depleted finances were the result of his lavish entertaining, experimentation with new agricultural and architectural techniques, a fondness for books, expensive tastes and hobbies, establishing the University of Virginia, and helping fill the shelves of the new Library of Congress. Jefferson also tended to ignore his finances and mismanage his business interests while the massive debts he inherited from his wife's father took their toll. Jefferson also died a less happy man than the one who married Martha Wayles, and, ironically, the day came on July 4, 1826, which happened to be the fiftieth anniversary of the signing of the Declaration of Independence and the same day that his old friend and former rival John Adams died. In fact, the two had grown so fond of one another in old age, exchanging correspondence on a regular basis, that Adams's last words were "Jefferson lives." But the Sage of Monticello had died two hours earlier at his beloved home.

Despite the tragedy of losing so many siblings at such a young age, Jefferson's eldest daughter lived a long life like her father. Eleven of her twelve children reached adulthood, and Jefferson, in his last days, delighted in having a full household of children. He was, to the end, a doting grandfather. The descendants of Martha Jefferson Randolph married blood relatives, British aristocrats, relatives of Paul Revere (whose heroic ride during the war warned colonists of British attack), relations to Presidents James Madison and Andrew Jackson, and even the descendants of Pocahontas. The descendants of the tragic union of Thomas Jefferson and Martha Wayles turned out to be, like Jefferson himself, an impressive lot and include diplomats, politicians, military leaders, financiers, and intellectuals, all reflecting the extraordinary talents of Jefferson himself.

Andrew Jackson's imposing presence is apparent in this painting. Painted by D. M. Carter, engraved by A. H. Ritchie. Library of Congress Prints and Photographs Division, LC-USZ62-5099 DLC.

⚕ 6 ⚕

"A Petticoat Affair"

Female virtue is like a tender and delicate flower, let but the
breath of suspicion rest upon it, and it withers and perhaps
perishes forever.

—Andrew Jackson defending the reputation of
a sexually promiscuous woman

INDIAN ATTACK

Andrew Jackson and his wife, Rachel, enjoyed one of the better marriages in
the history of the American presidency. However, Mrs. Jackson became one
of the most famous—or infamous—women in the country in the early 1800s
because of a marital scandal. It was a scandal that would affect the outcome of
at least one presidential election and the future of the national political parties.

Rachel Donelson was born on June 15, 1767, in Pittsylvania, Virginia,
the ninth of eleven children to Rachel Stockley and John Donelson II. Both
sides of the family were well off, and Rachel's father enjoyed a lot of success as
a planter, surveyor, land speculator, and iron maker. Donelson also served in
the military, achieving the rank of colonel, and was a member of the Virginia
House of Burgesses from 1769 to 1774. Colonel Donelson made money buying land in the western frontier and investing in settlements. As such, when
Rachel was twelve, the colonel led a group of 120 settlers from rural western
Virginia to the wilds of Tennessee. The group departed from Virginia on December 22, 1779, and, along the way, suffered from a smallpox outbreak and
attacks from Cherokee Indians. They did not arrive in Tennessee until April
24, 1780, and set about the difficult task of establishing small settlements in
Cumberland and Nashville. Young Rachel, a gifted horseback rider with dark
hair and dark eyes, survived the long and arduous journey to become the belle
of these new lands.

Although Colonel Donelson had negotiated treaties and land deals with Indian nations in the region, an attack shortly after the settlers arrived in Tennessee forced several of the families to leave. Donelson was undeterred, returning to Nashville in 1785 to rebuild the settlement. However, once again, within months another attack occurred, and Donelson, some of his sons, and several others were killed. Rachel and her mother, along with other families, remained in Tennessee despite the threat. It must have been an unimaginably harrowing time for the young girl and her widowed mother.

On March 1, 1785, at the age of seventeen and against her mother's wishes, Rachel married Captain Lewis Robards, who was ten years her senior. The couple moved back to Virginia and lived in a home with Robards's mother. Even though it was a failed marriage, Rachel stayed with Robards. It was, after all, highly unusual for a wife to leave her husband in 1785. Evidence suggests that Robards was abusive and may have cheated on Rachel even though, when drunk and jealous, it was he who accused her of the very same sin. By 1788, she could stand no more and ran away from the marriage, although one historical account suggests that he threw her out of the home.

Adulteress

Rachel moved back home with her widowed mother to escape her abusive husband. At one point, she returned to Robards to give the marriage another chance, but the situation continued to deteriorate. For a second time, Rachel fled to Nashville, riding the very horse that was a part of her wedding dowry. It was around this time, in 1788, that Rachel met Andrew Jackson. Rachel's mother opened the family home to boarders, and one of the guests was the tall, dashing lawyer, who happened to be a bachelor. The two developed an instant and very deep connection, with the blessing of Rachel's mother.

It was Jackson who encouraged Rachel not to go back to Robards because of her safety and happiness. Because women lacked the right to legally initiate a divorce, Jackson counseled Rachel on how to request a divorce through her estranged husband. When Robards threatened to come to Nashville to take Rachel with him to Kentucky, it was Jackson who protected Rachel by taking her (and even her mother) to Natchez, Mississippi, which was then part of the territory of Spanish Florida. There they remained until enough time had passed for Robards's fit of anger to pass. Jackson monitored the delicate situation, and his sense of chivalry was such that he pledged to defend Rachel, which he most certainly would have done had it become necessary.

Rachel eventually decided to stay in Nashville for good and asked her husband for a divorce in 1790. The difficulties of divorcing were many at the time. Many southern states forbade it prior to the Revolution, but most offered some form of legal divorce after the war, although the laws were vague. Robards requested a divorce from the Kentucky legislature, which appears to have granted him the right to petition in court but did not grant the divorce outright. Nor did Robards conclude the matter. As such, Rachel incorrectly assumed that she was divorced.

Thus, when Rachel married Jackson in August 1791 in Natchez, she was technically married to two men at the same time. Rachel was unaware of this quandary and would not discover the shocking truth until 1793. It was that same year that Robards learned that his wife married Jackson. When he did, he tried to sue, alleging adultery and claiming that Jackson had knowingly eloped with his wife. However, Jackson wrote to Robards, threatening to cut off both of his ears (and perhaps other parts) with a sword if divorce was not immediately offered. A showdown was averted—Robards must have understood that when Andrew Jackson made a threat, he meant it. Word arrived to Rachel that Robards finally acted. Her divorce came on September 27, 1793. It was one of the first legal divorces in Kentucky, and Robards likely saved his own life in offering the divorce.

Mrs. Donelson expressed relief that Jackson still wanted to marry her daughter, asking her son-in-law, "Would you sacrifice your life to save my child's good name?" Jackson replied, "Ten thousand lives, madam, if I had them!" Thus, on January 17, 1794, Jackson married his wife for a second time in a quiet, civil ceremony. Both were twenty-four and were deeply in love.

However, the divorce did nothing to stop the budding adultery scandal that was spreading around the state. The damage had already been done. Rachel had been labeled a "bigamist" and was named by Robards in the divorce proceeding as an "adulteress." It did not help things that both Rachel and Andrew were terribly thin skinned. Even though Rachel was somewhat ignorant of the full extensiveness of the gossip against her, over the course of her life the scandal ate away at her happiness. Because Rachel's father had been a founding father of the communities in the region, she was well known to many, and the fame put the scandal in the public spotlight. Worse yet, Jackson's growing political career made him—and his wife—targets, and the salacious nature of their scandal made for a large target.

Jackson's legal and political careers also required him to be away from home quite often. Rachel complained that he slept away from home more often in a given year than he slept in his own bed. This claim was probably true, as Jackson's career took off around this time. The year the couple married for the first time, Jackson became attorney general for the Tennessee Territory and five years later, in 1796, was elected to Congress. He served for one term. In 1798, he was elected to the U.S. Senate but resigned during his first year in office, frustrated with the administration of President John Adams and wanting to spend more time in Tennessee near Rachel. Jackson returned home but was elected soon thereafter at the age of thirty-one as judge on the Tennessee Superior Court. He served for six years on the bench, stepping down in 1804. The position put more money in Jackson's pocket and also afforded him more lucrative political and economic contacts. Rachel was not happy about the demands of that office either, but her husband was no longer gone for months at a time—at least for the time being.

Rachel grew to resent Jackson's absences. Arguably, with the exception of the first year of their marriage—before they discovered the truth about Rachel's divorce—the happiest time of their marriage was from 1821 until 1823, when Jackson was out of public office. During this time, he enjoyed the life of a gentleman farmer. Marriage in general agreed with Jackson. Orphaned as a child, the extended Donelson clan became Jackson's family, and Rachel was known to soothe Jackson's notoriously wild side—in many ways. Indeed, as one biographer noted, marrying Rachel "was perhaps the happiest event of his life for the union proved an enduring success." However, in 1823, he again departed for Washington to serve a second stint in the U.S. Senate and, one year later, was a candidate for president of the United States.

Scandals and Duels

The sordid details of Rachel Jackson's marriage, divorce, and second marriage became one of the most famous scandals in the early nineteenth century. The details were often exaggerated for political purposes by Jackson's enemies—it was even said that Rachel smoked a pipe—and the scandal even became a key issue in Jackson's presidential campaigns.

Next to Aaron Burr and Alexander Hamilton, Andrew Jackson is remembered as perhaps the country's most famous duelist. Jackson, however, dueled more often than the two political rivals who so infamously fought in New Jersey in 1804. Jackson had an exaggerated sense of chivalry and need to defend his wife's honor to the point where he was willing to kill a man at the slightest comment. He was also easily provoked and tended to personalize disagreements to the point where he saw nearly every political disagreement as a personal attack and private vendetta. Moreover, dueling was, at the time, considered an acceptable way for gentlemen to settle disagreements. If slandered or maligned, a man might seek redress or satisfaction not through the courts but on the "field of honor." As such, Jackson was something of an avid practitioner of the duel, although at times he did not adhere to the customs governing the confrontation. Truth be told, Jackson was more the hotheaded brawler than the gentleman duelist.

One such example was Jackson's long-standing feud with John Sevier. Sevier was a dangerous opponent and one of the most powerful men in the region. He served multiple terms as the governor of Tennessee and went on to be a judge on the Tennessee Superior Court. He was also a Revolutionary War hero. The bickering nearly ended up killing both men. One of the many points of contention between the two political rivals was a suspect land deal between speculators in North Carolina and Tennessee in which Sevier was front and center in the scandal. Jackson pressed to extradite the guilty parties from North Carolina, but Sevier blocked the effort, in part to protect himself from incrimination.

The rivalry lasted for many years and appears to have started when Sevier blocked Jackson's bid for promotion to the rank of major general on February 5, 1802. Sevier found himself term limited from the governorship and wanted the job Jackson had been pursuing—commander of the Tennessee militia. An election was held that ended in a seventeen-to-seventeen tie. The new governor, an ally of Jackson's, broke the tie and awarded the command to his good friend. Even though Jackson had bested Sevier in the contest to become Tennessee's military commander, Sevier used his ample contacts in the state legislature to have a bill passed that split the command into two separate commands, with Sevier as the other commander. The following year, Sevier again ran for governor, and Jackson released damning evidence of Sevier's misconduct. The disagreements became personal and escalated to the point where both men were slandering one another in the press. The story ran in newspapers such as the *Knoxville Gazette* on July 27, 1803: "Know ye that I, Andrew Jackson, do pronounce, public, and declare to the world, that his Excellency John Sevier . . . is a base coward and poltroon. He will basely insult, but has not the courage to repair." Sevier countered by publicly calling Jackson a "petty forging lawyer."

And so it was that tensions were raised to the point where, when Jackson ran into Sevier in public in the town of Knoxville in October 1803, a confrontation occurred. Sevier started by loudly belittling Jackson as an insignificant man who lacked the proper public and military service. Jackson defended himself by citing his record. However, Sevier bellowed in mockery, "Service? I know of no great service you have rendered the country, except taking a trip to Natchez with another man's wife." Sevier crossed the line, and Jackson, who was always highly volatile and overly sensitive to criticism of his wife, exploded: "Great God! Do you mention her name?"

Sevier challenged Jackson on the spot: "Draw!" Both men pulled pistols and shot wildly. The bullets missed their mark, but one scraped a bystander. A scuffle ensued, the men had to be separated, and a ranting Jackson challenged Sevier to an official duel. The details are foggy, but it appears that Sevier refused to duel on Tennessee's "sacred soil" because he deemed Jackson an unworthy foe. But both men continued their highly public campaign to discredit one another in the papers and by personal correspondence, with

Jackson writing, "Did you take the name of a lady into your polluted lips? Did you challenge me to draw, when you were armed with a cutlass and I with a cane, and now sir . . . you shall atone for it or I will publish you as a coward and a poltroon."

Sevier countered, "Your conduct . . . shows you to be a pitiful poltroon . . . I shall not receive another letter from you, as I deem you a coward." A duel was arranged in Indian Territory that bordered Tennessee, and the two men rode to demand honor. En route, Jackson saw two riders approaching, leapt off his horse, and drew two pistols. With both men screaming profanities, Sevier also dismounted. Not waiting for the "proper" duel, the governor drew his sword. In the melee, Sevier's horse was spooked and ran off, taking the saddlebag containing his pistols with it. Violating the protocols governing such challenges, Jackson drew his pistol and aimed it at his unarmed opponent, and Sevier turned and ran for cover behind a tree. Sevier's "second" and a growing crowd of onlookers rushed in to stop Jackson from firing. The two men never dueled again, and they never reconciled. But they lived, which is more than can be said of other rivals of Andrew Jackson.

Jackson's motive for dueling and brawling was, more often than not, his wife's reputation rather than high political principle or the heated policy issues of the day. When men commented on Rachel Jackson or her marriage— even when it was true—Jackson sought satisfaction in pistols, swords, or fists. Perhaps the most famous incident was Jackson's duel with fellow Tennessee attorney Charles Dickinson.

Dickinson was well known throughout the state as a powerful, popular, and witty figure. He also happened to be something of a trick-shot artist. It was alleged that he once shot through a string at twenty-four feet. He carried the broken string as a reminder of his skill and as warning to would-be opponents. In fact, brandying the string, Dickinson boasted, "If General Jackson comes along this road, show him that!"

Dickinson and Jackson had a horse-racing debt to settle that, allegedly, also involved Dickinson speaking ill of Mrs. Jackson, labeling her an "adulteress." He also labeled Jackson a coward, and the general, blood boiling, demanded that the insults be settled immediately on the dueling fields. The two met in 1806 in Logan County, Kentucky, just across the border with Tennessee. Normally, duels involved the participants standing at ten paces or twenty-four feet, determining who had the benefit of having the first shot, and then taking turns shooting. At that distance, it is still possible to see the whites of an opponent's eyes, so it was an incredibly risky and unnerving "game." In the case of the Jackson–Dickinson duel, however, the rules were for a quick-draw duel. Accordingly, Jackson was at a competitive disadvantage in either type of duel because of Dickinson's expert marksmanship.

Jackson calculated that he was less likely to be able to hit his opponent in a quick draw. Jackson knew of Dickinson's skill, so the general opted to let Dickinson draw and shoot first while he stoically stood his ground and took the shot. Jackson's plan was that, if he lived, he would then have the "luxury" of taking his time, aiming, and being sure of hitting Dickinson. It was a bold and foolish strategy—but it worked.

When the duel began, Dickinson, as expected, drew with lightning speed and fired. Jackson did not fire and remained standing, leading the marksman to blurt out in disbelief, "Great God! Have I missed him?" In fact, he had not. The bullet hit Jackson squarely in his chest and lodged precariously close to his heart, so close that it could never be removed surgically. Jackson ended up carrying the painful reminder of this duel with him the rest of his life. The blood welled up around Jackson's chest, but he did not fall. Teeth clenched with pain, Jackson carefully began to take aim. Dickinson lost control and was overcome with panic, babbling on about Jackson not dying. He had to be calmed down by the officiator of the duel. Jackson again raised the pistol and took aim, but the hammer stuck. After what must have seemed an eternity, Jackson aimed again, fired, and hit Dickinson.

Dickinson bled to death. Before leaving the duel, Jackson, still bleeding and grimacing through the searing pain, snarled, "I'd have hit him if he had shot me through the brain." The large audience that gathered to observe the spectacle got their money's worth. Jackson's notoriety rose as a result of the duel.

One of the least honorable feuds and duels that Jackson engaged in involved the Benton brothers, Thomas Hart Benton, a colonel in Jackson's command, and his brother Jesse. It occurred seven years after the famous Dickinson duel and began when an officer in Jackson's command named William Carroll asked the general to stand in as his "second" in a duel with Jesse Benton. Jackson, forty-six at the time, replied, "Why, Captain Carroll, I am not the man for such an affair. I am too old. The time has been when I should have gone out with pleasure; but, at my time of life, it would be extremely injudicious. You must get a man nearer to your own age." But Carroll asked again, this time begging, so Jackson reluctantly agreed. During the duel between Benton and Carroll that occurred in the summer of 1813, Benton apparently ducked down and spun around in a circle to fire. During the acrobatics, Benton was hit in the buttocks by Carroll's bullet. Jackson, who years before had stood straight and stoic as Tennessee's finest marksman shot at him, criticized Benton for cowardice. When Benton's brother, Thomas, heard of the slur, he vowed revenge and even insulted Jackson as being too old to duel. Surprised by the threat and insult from someone in his command, Jackson wrote Thomas Benton to ask if the threat was true.

Benton responded that Jackson should have acted to stop what was an un-necessary duel, which was true. Benton added,

> I have not threatened to challenge you. On the contrary I have said that I would not do so; and I say so still. At the same time, the terror of your pistols is not to seal my lips. What I believe to be true, I shall speak; and if for this I am called in account, it must ever be so.

But the tensions rose as both Benton brothers bad-mouthed Jackson. As expected, Jackson swore to horsewhip the brothers when he next saw them. Shortly thereafter, when Jackson went to the Nashville post office to pick up his mail, the adversaries ran into one another. Jackson deliberately walked up to Thomas Benton to provoke him, then pulled out a whip and yelled, "Now, you damned rascal, I am going to punish you. Defend yourself!"

When Benton reached for what was likely his pistol, Jackson pulled a gun on the brothers, who wisely turned and fled to a nearby lodge. However, Jesse Benton turned and fired a shot at Jackson, hitting him in the shoulder and shattering the joint. As Jackson fell to the ground, he shot at Thomas Benton but missed. Jackson's good friend John Coffee, who was walking with Jackson, bent down to aid his friend and observed a growing pool of blood on the ground. Coffee also squeezed off a shot at the Bentons but, like Jackson, missed. Meanwhile, Jackson's nephew, Stockley Hays, who was carrying a sword cane, pursued and attacked Jesse Benton. Hays struck a severe blow across Benton's chest, breaking the cane in two and knocking Benton to the ground. Hays then dove on his uncle's foe and pulled out a short dagger that he used to repeatedly stab Benton in the arm and body. The crowd that had gathered to watch the brawl pulled Benton and Hays apart, and Jackson was carried to the Nashville Inn for medical attention. A physician was sum-moned and, seeing the extent of the damage to Jackson's shoulder, contem-plated amputation. But Jackson growled, "I'll keep my arm," and offered a thinly veiled threat of what might happen if he awoke from unconsciousness with only one arm.

After the incident, Thomas Benton picked up both Jackson's sword and his nephew's broken cane and paraded them about as evidence of victory. Jackson was furious and called the Bentons failed assassins. Thomas Ben-ton realized the danger in angering Jackson, writing, "My life is in danger." Later, when both men were elected to the U.S. Senate the same year, Benton worked to gain Jackson's friendship and became one of his supporters.

One of the most heroic of Jackson's numerous confrontations and du-els occurred, ironically enough, while serving as a judge. Judge Jackson was holding court in a rural village when a case came before him involving Rus-sell Bean, a giant of a man accused of horrifically cutting off the ears of a child during one of his frequent drunken rampages. During the proceedings, which were going against the accused, Bean simply stood and walked out of the courthouse.

The sheriff and startled onlookers were too intimidated to stop him, so Jackson ordered, "Sheriff, arrest that man for contempt of court." When the sheriff still refused to do so, Jackson told him to "summon a posse, then, and bring him before me." Even then, the sheriff and posse returned empty handed to the courthouse. When they confronted Bean, he threatened to kill them all. The sheriff and posse had backed down.

Jackson had enough and decided on the spot to resolve the matter himself. Storming out of his courtroom, the judge grabbed two pistols and met the hulking Bean in the middle of town. Bean stood menacingly in the street, wielding guns, while curious onlookers watched the showdown from the shadows. Undeterred, Jackson walked right up to the man-mountain and demanded, "Surrender, you infernal villain, this very instant, or I'll blow you through!" To the delight (and relief) of the town, Bean gave up and went without further incident to court. He would later say that he saw "shoot" in Jackson's eyes. Bean admitted, "Says I, Hoss, it's about time to sing small, and so I did." The bullet wounds to the shoulder and chest from Jackson's duels stayed with him the remainder of his life and contributed to Jackson's ongoing health problems and chronic pain.

Even though Jackson's reputation suffered because of his hair-trigger temper and frequent disagreements and duels, in other ways his reputation as a tough guy was growing. Even when not dueling, Jackson repeatedly displayed the kind of bravado and bravery associated with heroic legends from antiquity and Hollywood action films of today. Some people loved him and some hated him, but on the frontier and even "back East," people were hearing the name Andrew Jackson.

A WHORE IN THE PRESIDENT'S MANSION

Rachel Jackson had aged poorly. By 1820, Mrs. Jackson had gained an unhealthy amount of weight and was far from being the spunky young woman Jackson had met so long ago. She handled the scandal over her marriage very badly, allowing the stress to rack her nerves and diminish her health both physically and emotionally. She was frequently ill, and the scandal had changed her in other unappealing ways. Rachel became judgmental, religiously intolerant, and angry. Even though the couple seems to have come closer together because of the attacks against Rachel's reputation, there was continued strain in the union over Jackson's career as well as his frequent and long absences from their home. Another problem in the marriage was that the couple had no children. Jackson loved and wanted his own children, so they adopted as godparents some of Rachel's nieces and nephews, including Andrew Jackson Jr., son of Rachel's brother, Severn.

Rachel thus wanted nothing more than for Jackson to retire from public life. This, she hoped and prayed, would also put an end to the very public brouhaha over her marriage. However, Jackson finished the 1824 Senate session with a growing reputation. He was increasingly seen by the people of Tennessee and elsewhere (especially on the frontier) as presidential. But, once again, with Jackson's reputation growing, so did public talk of Rachel's scandalous marriage.

When Jackson began campaigning for the presidency, the sordid details of Rachel's first marriage became a prominent part of both the 1824 and the 1828 races. Jackson's many enemies, along with some newspapers, made an issue of the scandal, calling Mrs. Jackson an "adulteress" and "bigamist." One newspaper editorial asked, "Ought a convicted adulteress and her paramour husband to be placed in the highest offices of this free and Christian land?" A campaign pamphlet produced by Jackson's opponents stated, "Anyone approving of Andrew Jackson must therefore declare in favor of the philosophy that any man wanting anyone else's pretty wife has nothing to do but take his pistol in one hand and a horsewhip in another and possess her."

The criticism was such that a nerve-racked Rachel opposed her husband's presidential aspirations, saying to her niece,

> I do hope they will leave Mr. Jackson alone . . . he has done his share for his country. How little time has he had to himself or his own interests in the thirty years of our wedded life. In all that time he has not spent one fourth of his days under his own roof.

But, in 1824, Jackson, along with four others—Henry Clay, John C. Calhoun, John Quincy Adams, and William H. Crawford—emerged as the favorites among the people and, to a lesser degree, party leaders. In the days of "King Caucus," party leaders gathered the year of a presidential election and nominated their candidate. Moreover, the old political party system of the Federalists versus the Democratic-Republicans was collapsing, meaning that there was uncertainty about the role of the parties. All five of the frontrunners for the presidency were men in the mold of Democratic-Republicans like Thomas Jefferson and James Madison. They therefore agreed on most issues, and this meant that personal differences among the candidates were brought to the fore and would decide the election.

Jackson frightened party leaders. Some of them attempted to discredit Jackson by claiming that he would arrive in the president's mansion "with a scalping knife in one hand and a tomahawk in the other, always ready to knock down, and scalp any and every person who differed." But even this did not dampen Jackson's prospects. Where the other candidates had connections to the established order and enjoyed only regional bases of appeal—Adams in the North, Crawford in the South, and Clay in the West—Jackson was the spoiler with a broad, national following.

As such, there was much uncertainty on February 14, 1824, when party leaders gathered. The problems were compounded when only sixty-eight of the 261 invited delegates showed up, and fully forty-eight of those in attendance were from just four states: Georgia, New York, North Carolina, and Virginia. The balloting ended with William H. Crawford receiving sixty-four votes, John Quincy Adams only two votes, and Jackson and Nathaniel Macon one vote each. Albert Gallatin was the vice-presidential nominee. This meeting only highlighted the elitist caucus system. It also contributed to the growing public resentment of the system embodied by King Caucus. This public backlash benefited Jackson because of his status as an outsider. Jackson captured the popular mood well in a letter to his friend, John Coffee, the day after the caucus when he fumed,

> Everything is carried by intrigue and management. . . . It is now a contest between a few demagogues and the people; and it is to be seen whether a minority less than one fourth of the whole members of Congress, can coerce the people to follow them; or whether the people will assume their constitutional rights and put down these demagogues.

An Election like No Other

On March 4, 1824, a monkey wrench was thrown into the process when Calhoun withdrew as a presidential contender but threw his hat in the ring for vice president. Crawford had suffered a stroke the year prior, and his recovery was not what many had hoped for. With Crawford's support waning, only three candidates seemed viable. In the fall election, Jackson won the popular vote with 152,901 to John Quincy Adams with 114,023 votes. Clay and Crawford each had around 47,000. Jackson also carried the Electoral College vote by a margin of ninety-nine to eighty-four (for Adams), with Clay and Crawford splitting the remaining seventy-eight votes. Fully eleven of the twenty-four states went to Jackson.

Calhoun's plan worked, as he secured the vice presidency. However, a problem arose in that a candidate needed to win a majority of the Electoral College to claim the presidency, and Jackson, while having the most votes, had only a plurality of the vote. Still, Jackson assumed that he won, though he needed to get to 131 votes for a majority. In the event that no president won a majority, a system was in place to select a president. The Twelfth Amendment to the Constitution—added in 1804 after the misfired 1800 election between Jefferson and Adams, which needed thirty-seven votes to resolve the tie—required the U.S. House of Representatives to pick among the top three vote getters, which were Jackson, Adams, and Clay. Each state would get one vote.

Clay had always viewed Jackson as a rival for the presidency and, as such, threw his support behind Adams. As the Speaker of the House, Clay was influential in swinging a lot of votes. Clay also traveled to Massachusetts to meet with Adams, giving the impression of a deal in the works. Jackson, who was back in the capital city on December 24 for the end of the legislative session, observed the bitter political infighting surrounding the election controversy. He commented to a friend, "Rumors say that deep intrigue is on foot . . . that Mr. Clay is trying to wield his influence. . . . Others say the plan is to prevent an election all together. This last I do not believe."

Indeed, the bickering in the House lasted into 1825. Unfortunately for Jackson, he suffered both a bad fall and illness that winter and thus was not able to be visible during the critical weeks of the electoral negotiations in the House. According to the Twelfth Amendment, each state was given one vote, and this final vote came at noon on February 9, 1825. Adams was pronounced the winner over Jackson—thirteen states to seven states. One of the first orders of business by Adams was the selection of Calhoun as his vice president, something that seemed to affirm rumors of a "corrupt bargain" to defeat Jackson.

Said Jackson of the process and outcome, "I weep for the liberty of my country." He summed up the vote by the House as a deal by the caucus, which he described as "the great whore of Babylon." Indeed, the outcome smacked of cronyism and of insider deal making, and voices across the country expressed displeasure with the vote and process. Jackson's position that the president should be elected only "by the free suffrage of the people" was shared by many. As to Clay, Jackson cited Scripture, saying, "So you see, the Judas of the West [Clay] has closed the contract and will receive the thirty pieces of silver. . . . His end will be the same. Was there ever such a bare faced corruption in any country before?"

Rematch

During the entirety of Adams's term in office, Jackson's supporters worked to keep their leader's name in the forefront of public opinion, setting up a rematch for 1828. It would be a classic showdown and one of contrasts even though both men were born in 1767 and had similar views on many issues. But Adams was the Harvard-educated son of a president and Jackson the orphaned son of the frontier. For the legions of Jackson supporters throughout the country, Adams was "King John the Second," who lived in "kingly pomp and splendor" in his "presidential palace," whereas Adams's supporters saw Jackson as a commoner from the frontier whose supporters, it was said, carried hickory brooms and sticks as gimmicks.

President Adams stayed above the fray, focusing on governing rather than his increasingly popular opponent. However, the same could not be said for friends of the administration. The attacks against Jackson and his wife were among the nastiest yet seen in American politics and ultimately contributed to 1828 being one of the most negative campaigns in American history.

For example, during the campaign, a newspaper editor in Philadelphia printed what was known as the "coffin handbill," named for the six black coffins depicted on the cover and widely circulated with the damning headline "Some Account of the Bloody Deeds of General Jackson." The pamphlet claimed Jackson executed six soldiers for no reason in 1813 during the Creek Indian War. The wording used in the handbill was "shot dead." The story also personalized the incident, stating that all the soldiers were patriotic volunteers and that one of the men, John Harris, had been a "preacher of the gospel." The tract claimed that the soldiers had served honorably and simply wanted to go home. Jackson countered that the men had been guilty of desertion and that Harris was a mutineer who stole supplies and attempted to incite other soldiers to desert. The general said that all were tried in a fair manner and found guilty.

But what incited the public were the stories about Jackson's mother and wife. Newspapers called Jackson's mother a "common prostitute," his wife a "bigamist," and the candidate himself a man guilty of "wife theft." Jackson, already known for a hair-trigger temper, went into a fit of rage each time the scandal made the papers. While Jackson responded with anger, Rachel suffered great shame, and her emotional state declined throughout 1828. She wrote to one friend in July 1828, saying,

> The enemies of the General have dipped their arrows in wormwood and gall and sped them at me. Almighty God was there ever any thing to equal it . . . to think that thirty years had passed in happy social friendship with society, knowing or thinking no ill to no one—as my judge will know—how many prayers have I offered up for their repentance.

To make matters worse, Mrs. Jackson's adopted son, Lyncoya, died on June 1, 1828, after a protracted illness. Rachel had been nursing him through illness and took his loss poorly. Lyncoya, who was a Creek Indian, had come to live with the Jacksons after becoming orphaned when the general defeated his nation at the Battle of Horseshoe Bend in 1814.

The election of 1828 went to Jackson, who carried the popular vote by roughly 140,000 votes—or 56 percent of the total. He also won the Electoral College comfortably over Adams, 178 to 83. When Rachel received news of Jackson's victory, she commented, "For Mr. Jackson's sake, I am glad. For my own part, I never wished it." Indeed, Rachel Jackson never wanted to be the First Lady. As she said, "I had rather be a doorkeeper in the house of my Lord than to live in that palace in Washington."

That December, Mrs. Jackson went shopping in Nashville to prepare for her move to Washington. While in town, she overheard people gossiping about her scandalous marriage. She also noticed stares from strangers. In a fit of anxiety, Rachel fled into the offices of a newspaper owned by one of her relatives, where, to her dismay, she read yet another story about her marriage in that very newspaper. Rachel's realization of the extensiveness of the scandal—something Jackson had tried to shield from her—was a severe emotional blow. From that day on, Rachel began sobbing incessantly. She also delayed the anticipated departure date of their trip to Washington to December 23 and even began threatening not to leave The Hermitage. She summed up her anxieties about the scandal in a letter to her niece:

> Listening to them, it seemed as if a veil lifted and I saw myself, whom you have all guarded from outside criticism and surrounded with flattering delusions, as others see me, a poor old woman. I will not go to Washington, but stay here as often before in Mr. Jackson's absences.

Rachel should have heeded the old warning to be careful what you wish for. After wishing and hoping that she would not have to move to the White House, on December 18 she became very ill, complaining of pain in her chest and arm and of shortness of breath. Her screaming and weeping built to a chorus of agony. Two days later, it appears that Rachel had a heart attack. Jackson remained at his wife's side, even sleeping on a couch near her bed. But, as Rachel was preparing for bed on the evening of December 22, Jackson stepped momentarily out of the room. At that very moment, Rachel collapsed and died.

On Christmas Eve of 1828, over 10,000 people gathered for Rachel Jackson's funeral. She was buried at The Hermitage in the very dress she had purchased to wear to her husband's inauguration. For Jackson, part of his life ended, and the election was bittersweet. "A loss so great . . . can be compensated by no earthly gift," he admitted.

OLD HICKORY

Andrew Jackson was born on March 15, 1767, in Waxhaw, South Carolina, near the North Carolina border. He was the youngest of three sons. Because the state border was redrawn multiple times, there is some dispute in the Carolinas as to which state can claim the seventh president as a favorite son. Most historians side with South Carolina.

Jackson's father, Andrew, was a farmer and recent immigrant from Ireland. Andrew Sr. and his wife, Elizabeth "Betty" Hutchinson, along with their two young boys, departed Ireland for America in 1765. It appears that they arrived in Pennsylvania but traveled to the Waxhaw region of the Carolinas to live among the Scotch–Irish farming communities there. Andrew Sr. suffered a severe injury while trying to move a large log and died just a few days prior to his third son's birth.

Betty Jackson named the son for her recently deceased husband and passed along to the young boy her red hair, bright blue eyes, and indomitable disposition. The widow raised her three young sons but was assisted in doing so by relatives. She later moved to Lancaster County, South Carolina, to live with her sister, Mrs. Jane Crawford. It has been suggested that Betty Jackson gave birth to Andrew at her sister's home, but it is also possible that she had the child while stopping at the home of another sister, Mrs. Margaret McCamie, who lived just across the border in North Carolina. Jackson claimed that he was from the Waxhaws in South Carolina.

Andrew's mother recognized her son's intelligence and dreamed of her boy becoming a Presbyterian minister. Even though the family was poor, Mrs. Jackson prioritized her son's education above that of her older boys. From age eight until thirteen, Jackson was sent to study under Dr. William Humphries and the Reverend James White Stephenson. However, Jackson proved to be a poor student and even less inclined toward the cloth. He would always be a poor speller and naturally rebellious.

"The Brave Boy of the Waxhaws"

After his oldest brother, Hugh, joined the Patriots against the British, Andrew and the middle brother, Robert, ran away to fight in the Revolutionary War. At thirteen, Andrew was too young to enlist, so he lied about his age and joined the "irregulars" in fighting a guerilla insurgency against the Redcoats. In April 1781, after participating in ambushes and skirmishes in the woods of the Carolinas, Andrew and Robert were captured and imprisoned by the British. The boys and their comrades were marched forty miles in the heat and with no water. Already severely weakened, the boys contracted smallpox in the dirty conditions of the prison. The oldest brother, Hugh, had died of a heatstroke during the Battle of Stone Ferry in 1779, so Mrs. Jackson, determined not to lose her other sons, went to the prison to beg for her boys' release.

While imprisoned, Robert Jackson was struck hard on the head by a British officer. He was knocked down and appears to have suffered a serious injury. Tall, skinny, and full of fire, young Andrew nearly died at the hands of the same British officer who insisted that Jackson shine his boots. When Andrew refused, the officer struck the boy with his sword, but Jackson blocked the full brunt of the blow with his left arm, suffering only minor injuries to his arm and a cut on the head. The incident would be retold, earning Jackson the nickname the "Brave Boy of the Waxhaws." Later, as a successful military commander and politician, Jackson's strength and resolve was rewarded with the widely known nickname "Old Hickory."

The British released the two young boys to the care of their mother, but the entire family contracted camp inflictions and struggled to travel back to their home. The two boys were shoeless, but Robert was so ill that he had to be transported on horseback. Andrew walked the whole way. Sadly, Robert died of smallpox only two days after his release, and Andrew nearly followed him to the grave. Back home, Andrew's mother, Elizabeth, departed for Charleston to nurse other boys suffering in British prisons and hospitals. Sadly, in the service of others, Mrs. Jackson contracted another common camp disease and died in the fall of 1781. Jackson was only fourteen and was an orphan. His mother's departing advice was not to quarrel or rely on the courts but to "settle them cases yourself." Jackson never learned the first lesson but would live and nearly die by the second.

Jackson spent the next few years traveling and squandered what little there was of his inheritance. He taught school for one year but never liked it and was too undisciplined and lazy to organize his lesson plans. Jackson studied law and was admitted to the North Carolina bar in 1787 but just barely so. He preferred gambling, drinking, chasing women, and brawling. His late mother would also have been disappointed that Jackson skipped his share of Sunday services and developed a salty tongue and passion for prostitutes, cockfighting, cards, and horse racing. It was widely agreed on by the townsfolk where Jackson lived that the wild youth would soon get himself killed. Once, for kicks, the mischievous teen sent invitations to the town's formal Christmas gala to two prostitutes. Jackson and the mother–daughter prostitute duo were thrown out of the party. Because of this incident and others, Jackson wore out his welcome in Salisbury, North Carolina.

Despite this—or perhaps because of it—Jackson was popular with the ladies. By eighteen, he was tall with steel-blue eyes and a funny, engaging demeanor. His first love was likely his cousin Mary Crawford. They may have courted when he was seventeen and living in the Waxhaws. Later, in Salisbury, North Carolina, where he was living temporarily while studying law, Jackson had several romances. One was with Nancy Jarret, who acknowledged Jackson's way with the town's women, saying, "There was something about him I cannot describe except to say that it was a presence." Jackson also had a nineteen-year-old slave mistress.

After leaving Salisbury, Jackson was invited to be a prosecutor for some of the new, frontier communities west of the Appalachians near Nashville. The area was desperate for attorneys, and, through hard work and charisma, Jackson prospered in the sparsely populated frontier. He bought and traded land, horses, and slaves and made some money. One of Jackson's friends and business partners was William Blount, who, in 1790, became governor of the Tennessee Territory. Jackson now had the connections to match his growing reputation in the region.

Hero of New Orleans

What put Jackson on the national political map and completed his growing reputation as a "tough guy" was his remarkable victory in the War of 1812. In June 1812, after Britain had repeatedly raided U.S. merchant vessels, the United States declared war on Great Britain, and Jackson offered his services, only to be rebuffed. However, Tennessee was later ordered to form a militia. Governor Blount put his friend Andrew Jackson in charge of the force. With 2,000 volunteers, Jackson was ordered to the Gulf Coast to prepare for a possible British invasion. En route, however, the War Department sent word that the Tennessee boys would not be needed. Jackson, furious at being denied a chance to fight, spent the summer of 1813 awaiting new orders.

That September, new orders arrived. Jackson was to punish the Creek Indians for alleged massacres of white settlers in the frontier regions of Alabama. Jackson attacked the Creeks in several battles throughout northern Alabama, the most famous of which was at Horseshoe Bend in March 1814. It was there that the Creeks were decimated. Pressing his advantage, Jackson proved to be vicious or strong—depending on one's perspective—in the terms of the Creek surrender and assumption of their lands, which further contributed to his growing reputation.

The hero of the Creek campaign was then given command of the southern frontier in May 1814. Jackson immediately began dealing with the British invasion and enjoyed success, winning the Battle of Mobile Bay and defeating British units at Pensacola. But by November 1814, word arrived that a huge invasion force of 14,000 battle-tested soldiers was headed for New Orleans.

Jackson arrived in New Orleans to save the town from what appeared to be imminent destruction. Jackson had been ill during the journey to the city, and when he arrived on December 1, 1814, many residents were less than impressed with the size of his army—perhaps 2,700 raw volunteers—and the fact that an uneducated, sick heathen was in command. A near panic ensued. Jackson's forces would be greatly outnumbered, and the city had only 700 men available for defense, with many ill and others planning to evacuate. But Jackson, forty-seven at the time, with wavy iron-gray hair and exuding confidence, impressed enough of the city elders that they stayed and dug in for the coming fight. Of Jackson, one lady remarked to a critic, "Is this your back woods-man? Why, madam, he is a prince?"

Jackson proceeded to organize one of the more motley forces in the history of warfare. To supplement his army, he enlisted Cajuns from nearby swamps, Indians, freed blacks and slaves, and the city's Spanish and French residents, who bickered throughout the ordeal. To complete the city's defenses, Jackson joined forces with the notorious Haitian-born pirate Jean Lafitte and his brothers-in-arms Dominique and Pierre. Lafitte and his crew of bootleggers and cutthroats had previously offered their services to the British, but the admiralty declined because of Lafitte's unsavory reputation and many demands. Jackson, however, though offended by the pirates, was pragmatic. He needed Lafitte and recognized the benefit of enlisting such skilled sailors and tough fighters. Lafitte also spoke the many languages of Jackson's new ragtag army.

The city's leaders were not pleased with Jackson's unusual alliance, but it would prove to be a wise one. Likewise, Jackson upset many by declaring martial law in the city, dissolving the legislature, and executing any deserters. He firmly established himself as in charge of New Orleans.

As expected, the British armada, some sixty ships strong, arrived in the Gulf of Mexico on December 13, 1814, and made landfall near New Orleans. Five American gunboats attempted to defend Lake Borgne but were overwhelmed. However, in the exchange, the British suffered greater casualties than the small American navy, perhaps foreshadowing the disaster that would soon befall the invaders. Jackson also succeeded in temporarily blocking the British advance during numerous skirmishes when both sides fought to a draw. This and a foolish decision by the British command delayed the main invasion, giving Jackson additional time to add men to his 3,500-man force and fortify his defenses by erecting a large, mounded earthworks around the city.

The legendary general Sir Edward Michael Parkenham arrived to take charge of the British invasion and ordered a full frontal assault on Jackson's entrenched forces on January 8, 1815. Jackson always claimed that the luck of the Scotch–Irish was on his side, and this appeared to be the case because everything that could have gone wrong for the British did go wrong. This included the weather, as a fog as thick as soup blanketed the battlefield and disoriented the British. British warships intended to provide cover for their ground forces by sailing up a canal and laying down heavy cannon fire. But a levy broke, draining water from a canal and grounding the huge ships. Shockingly, the British officers neglected to bring ladders that would be needed to climb Jackson's earthworks. As a result, the invasion became a massacre, as the British suffered in excess of 2,000 casualties, with many of their officers, including General Parkenham, killed. Jackson lost only thirteen men, with another fifty-eight missing.

Ironically, the decisive battle had no bearing on the war. Unbeknownst to either the British or the Americans, negotiators had successfully concluded a peace treaty on Christmas Eve in Ghent, Belgium. Given the primitive systems of travel and communication at the time, the forces at New Orleans did not learn of the end of the war until days after their battle.

The War of 1812 was an unnecessary and unpopular war, but Jackson emerged as one of the very few bright spots and the hero of New Orleans (the famous square today bears his name and statue). He was now known throughout the country. Jackson was not a talented strategist, and he lacked both patience and military training, but he was decisive and commanded the respect of his men. He also always wanted to avenge the death of his two brothers and his mother during the American Revolution and even the score with the British. As he once wrote to his wife before the battle, "I owe to Britain a debt of retaliatory vengeance . . . should our forces meet I trust I shall pay the debt." The victory at New Orleans was deeply satisfying for the new national hero.

The Widower President

Jackson was a complicated man. While he inspired reverence and loyalty among many and claimed to be utterly disinterested in public accolades and tributes, in truth he enjoyed such praise. Indeed, Jackson presented himself as modest and humble but was neither. He was a hellion in early life, his conversation was frequently littered with profanities, and he enjoyed many mistresses, prostitutes, and concubines. Likewise, his cultural tastes tended toward raunchy theater and horse racing, but he belatedly became a very religious man. For a man who lived so recklessly for much of his early life, this conversion was ironic.

The general was a faithful husband and a patient father to his godchildren and adopted children and was also generous toward orphans and widows of soldiers lost in battle, seeing to their education and care. But he showed little concern for others. His relationship with women, except for that of his wife, could be purely physical, yet he had an exaggerated sense of chivalry and flew into rage over the slightest insult of a woman committed by others. Many of his duels and feuds were a result of degrading remarks directed at his wife.

Although he was a poor writer, he was an inspired orator who trusted few people but wisely enlisted others—including Martin Van Buren, Justice

Roger Taney, and nephew Andrew Jackson Jr.—to draft his correspondence and public comments. But he also devoted time to reworking earlier papers in order to position himself favorably in history. Consequently, his papers were always concise and well organized. Disinterested in intellectual pursuits and unquestioning when it came to divine providence, Jackson was nonetheless a quick study. He also demanded that others respect his privacy and was quick to fly off the handle when his privacy was violated, yet he saw no harm in looking into the private lives of others and even read the private mail of those who worked for him.

All this simply exacerbated his response to the political scandals during the 1824 and 1828 elections and the attacks directed toward his wife and himself. Jackson entered the presidency a widower, with the pain of his wife's passing still fresh. Believing that Rachel had died from a broken heart because of the public criticism of her marriages, the new president growled, "May God Almighty forgive her murderers, as I know she forgave them. I never can." And he never did. In memory of her, Jackson wore a black armband to his inauguration and brought into the presidency bitter resentment toward his enemies and his wife's critics. In fact, when Jackson took the oath of office on March 4, 1829, from the East Portico, John Quincy Adams was not present. Jackson did not invite him.

Jackson entered the presidency as a political outsider, the first to do so. A common man from the frontier lacking formal education, Jackson was in poor health from a chronic cough and digestive problems, chest pains and headaches, and a lifetime of duels and combat. He was also sixty-two, making him the oldest man yet to serve in the nation's highest office. But his fame among common folks continued to grow while serving. One such incident that helped reinforce the tough frontiersman image from his dueling days was when Robert Randolph, a would-be assassin, approached Jackson on the steps of the Capitol in May 1833. The deranged man pulled two guns, but, miraculously, one after the other, both failed to fire. Jackson pulled his cane and set about beating the man and had to be pulled off his attacker. However, so too did the incident affirm Jackson's paranoia, as he believed that his political enemies were behind the attack.

Minus Rachel's soothing hand, Jackson's infamous temper and ornery side took center stage, and the wild, frontier brawler reemerged during his presidency. And he would have benefited from his wife's presence, as the scandals that he and his wife encountered prior to and during the elections were nothing compared to what he would face as president. To be sure, the fearmongering during the campaign that a whore would reside in the White House proved true. Jackson's next scandal was the perfect storm.

ANOTHER "WHORE" IN THE PRESIDENT'S MANSION

Jackson referred to her as "Little Friend Peg" or simply "Little Peg." The general first met Peg in 1823 when she was a young girl, and he showed her much favor. As a U.S. senator, Jackson, like so many other members of Congress who were bachelors or whose wives did not make the trip to the capital during legislative sessions, stayed at the boardinghouse that Peg's father operated in the capital city. The Franklin House, located on I Street in Washington, was more than a boardinghouse; it was a tavern of mixed repute. In spite of this or perhaps because of it, Franklin House was a very popular drinking hole with Washington's elected officials. And part of the reason for its popularity was Peg.

William O'Neale, Peg's father, was an immigrant from Ireland and a friend to Jackson, who referred to the O'Neales as an "agreeable and worthy family." Peg had been born at Franklin House in 1799, the oldest of six children. Whatever good nature was exchanged between Jackson and Mr. O'Neale was nothing compared to the new senator's feelings toward Little Peg. Jackson called Peg "the smartest little woman in America" and was completely smitten with her in a fatherly way and seems to have viewed her as the daughter he never had. Later, however, as Peg grew into a ravishingly beautiful and scandalously flirtatious woman, Jackson's relationship with her was more complicated.

Peg's mother was very devout and organized performances on the Christian Sabbath, something that seems rather ironic given Peg's eventual charms. She even played the piano and sang for Dolley Madison, the beloved wife of the framer, secretary of state, and fourth president. Jackson wrote quite innocently to his wife about Little Peg, who sang and performed on Sundays at Franklin House for the many politicians who ate, drank, and boarded there, that "every Sunday evening [Peg] entertains her pious mother with sacred music to which we are invited." Mrs. Jackson, who by then had become quite judgmental and intolerant, also seemed impressed with Peg. No doubt, had she lived, Mrs. Jackson would have been less approving of the type of performances that Peg offered in her teenage years.

Peg grew into an enticingly beautiful and flirtatious young woman. Her sharp green eyes and thick mane of black hair only enhanced her natural charisma. One admirer described her as a "well-rounded, voluptuous figure, peach-pink complexion . . . large, active dark eyes, . . . full sensuous lips, ready to break into an engaging smile." She was also very confident around powerful, older men and knew how to charm them. Peg was known to speak her mind and to enjoy politics and the raunchy jokes told by the guests at Franklin House at a time when women were expected to be demure. Not surprisingly, Peg's sultry charms were much in demand by the politicians who visited Franklin House. Many of them bought her gifts and sought her attention. As she would later remember, "I was always a pet" to them.

"The Politician's Pet"

The problem was that Peg was accused of adultery and developed a reputation as a sexually loose woman. Jackson, who always defended Peg, even in the face of damning evidence, seems to have equated Peg's ordeal with his own wife's ordeal, whose reputation also suffered. The stories about Peg were many, and she was romantically linked with countless politicians and military officers. Among her love interests was the noted political leader Albert Gallatin. At fifteen, she tried to elope with Major Francis Smith Belton, an aide to General Winfield Scott, but, while sneaking out her bedroom window, happened to knock over a flowerpot put there by her father expressly for that purpose. Hearing the crash, William O'Neale awoke just in time to drag his lovelorn daughter back into the house. One story suggested that she rejected a suitor who was so enamored with her that he swallowed poison rather than live without her.

On more than one occasion, Peg tried to run away with her lovers. When Peg's parents suspected their daughter of planning to elope with one of two military officers courting her, they sent her away to a finishing school across town. This was but one instance of many when the O'Neales frequently tried, to no avail, to calm their promiscuous daughter. Peg disliked the strict school and wrote home promising not to elope if she could return to Franklin House: "Dear Father: for the Lord's sake come and take me home; and if you will do so I will promise to be the best girl you ever saw, and I assure you that under no circumstance shall either Root or Branch take me away from you." However, back at the tavern, she simply incorporated the refinements that she learned at school into her already formidable arsenal, making herself more desirable by speaking some French and displaying her improved talents for music, singing, and dance.

In 1816, Peg married John Bowie Timberlake. The bride was seventeen and the groom thirty-nine. Timberlake had watched Peg through her open window (and it would not be surprising if Peg knew as much and was "performing" in view of Timberlake) and told her that it was "love at first sight." He proposed that very night. The couple married on July 18, 1816, and moved into a home that William O'Neale owned across the street from the tavern. Unfortunately, Timberlake proved incapable of holding a job and managing his finances.

The couple had three children together. A son, named for Peg's father, died only weeks after being born, and Peg suffered miscarriages. Deeper into debt and after several attempts at various endeavors, including opening a small store, Timberlake decided to go to sea, resuming an earlier career in the navy. However, Timberlake died in April 1828 off the coast of Europe while serving aboard the USS *Constitution*. The cause of death was listed as "pulmonary disease," but rumors circulated that Timberlake was drunk or perhaps even committed suicide to avoid his creditors or because of the shame over his wife's alleged affairs, including the possibility that their children were fathered by other men. It was known that Timberlake suffered from depression, and one source of the rumors was that Peg had three children and more than one miscarriage, yet Timberlake was often at sea, including four years of duty on the *Constitution*. One of Peg's daughters, Margaret Rose, was even born around the time that Timberlake returned for shore leave in 1825.

Jackson was furious at Timberlake's inability to earn a living and his cowardice, and this suggests that Jackson believed that Peg's husband killed himself, for he worried that Peg's reputation would be harmed (it already had been). Peg had financial difficulties during her marriage and especially now that her husband was dead. Thus, it was Jackson who not only defended Peg from charges of adultery and promiscuity but also helped cover her debts. Jackson was aided in these pursuits by his good friend and fellow Tennessean senator John Eaton. The two senators from Tennessee dipped frequently into their own finances to help the Timberlakes and, later, to care for the widow. Before his death, Timberlake had written to his wife that, if anything happened to him, she could trust John Eaton. It appears that Senator Eaton was funneling money to Timberlake. Incredibly, Jackson and Eaton even tried unsuccessfully to have the Senate reimburse Peg for her late husband's losses while at sea.

Eaton was nine years Peggy's senior, a rich widower and popular politician. Eaton met Peg in 1818 and, like Jackson, had met her when he lodged and drank at Franklin House. In fact, it was Eaton who recommended the boardinghouse and tavern to Jackson. Eaton, although younger than Jackson, had been the general's political mentor and tireless advocate. Eaton was a principal promoter of Jackson's military feats during the War of 1812 and helped make Jackson a national hero.

After her husband's death, Peg had moved back to Franklin House with her daughter, Mary Virginia. There, she renewed her role at the tavern, discussing politics while serving and entertaining the guests. As before, Peg was good for business. Soon after Timberlake's death, Senator Eaton began escorting Peg around town. And so the gossip started. The 1828 campaign was already awash in cutting attacks regarding the reputation of Jackson's wife, and now they were joined by rumormongering about the reputation of Jackson's supporter and his mistress. And Peg proved to be fertile ground for scandal—there were charges that her husband was in debt and killed himself, that Peg eloped multiple times, that Peg had sexual affairs and children outside her marriage, that duels had been fought over her, and so on. Jackson saw these attacks as he saw those against his wife, and his response was the same.

"The Petticoat Affair"

Andrew Jackson had a long-standing feud with John C. Calhoun, the powerful South Carolinian and former Speaker of the House. The two were rivals and Calhoun, who was serving as vice president under John Quincy Adams, viewed Jackson as his main competition for the presidency. Moreover, during Jackson's leadership in the campaigns against the Creek, Chickasaw, Choctaw, Cherokee, and Seminole nations, he had made mistakes that Calhoun attempted to use against him. For instance, Jackson was known to be brutal in implementing "Indian removal" treaties. Also, while attempting to subdue the Seminoles in 1818 and 1819, Jackson invaded Spanish Florida, and an international crisis followed. Jackson maintained that he was acting on orders from Calhoun, then the secretary of war under President James Monroe. However, both Monroe and Calhoun denied ever authorizing such orders, and Calhoun used this incident and others to repeatedly attack Jackson.

In the election, Jackson reluctantly agreed to retain Calhoun as his vice president. This selection and Jackson's cabinet appointments were well received by politicians and the Washington establishment. However, a firestorm ensued when Jackson named his friend John Eaton as his secretary of war. The reason was that Eaton had, days before, married Peg on January 1, 1829, at the O'Neale residence, only eight months after the death of Peg's husband, just seven short weeks after Jackson's election, and eleven weeks prior to his inauguration.

Eaton had long wanted to marry Peg but worried about the appearance of marrying her so soon after the passing of John Timberlake and the fallout of her illicit reputation. Jackson advised his friend to ignore the gossipers, writing, "If you love Margaret Timberlake go and marry her at once and shut their mouths!" Peg had become perhaps the most scandalous woman in Washington and a constant source of gossip among the city's newspapers, social crowd, and, most important, the wives of Congress and Jackson's new cabinet. Louis McLane of Maryland, who served as Jackson's secretary of the treasury and later his secretary of state, quipped that Eaton had "just married his mistress— and the mistress of 11-dozen others!" Ignoring the scandal, Jackson stood by Eaton and named him as his secretary of war despite the political threat it posed. He also naively hoped that Eaton's high position in government would erase the scandal and enhance Peg's reputation. Coming on the heels of such a hard-fought and bitter campaign, however, the supporters of John Quincy Adams were in no mood for reconciliation. Jackson's enemies pounced, and the city, already muddied from perhaps the nastiest campaign in history, was torn apart by the scandal. The scandal also fractured Jackson's cabinet.

Being a widower without a daughter of his own, Jackson needed a hostess to preside over social affairs for the inaugural and at the executive mansion. Shockingly, he compounded his political problems by asking the newly wedded Peg, only twenty-nine at the time, to assist in such important functions. All the ugly campaigning that a whore—Jackson's wife—would reside in the president's home proved prophetic in a roundabout way. Little Peg was running the home. As a result, many Washington wives boycotted Jackson's inaugural, and the cabinet wives refused to attend the planned cabinet dinner. It was custom at the time in high society for wives to pay visits on one another and to leave calling cards that would be returned. However, the cabinet wives refused to repay visits to Peg Eaton and were led in their rejection of Peg by Floride Calhoun, the wife of Jackson's vice president and political enemy.

Jackson supported the Eatons in public, arguing that their marriage was "right & proper." At one point, Jackson exploded while defending Peg, insisting that "she is as chaste as a Virgin!" The comment, in support of a promiscuous mistress and mother of three, became a joke in the capital city, leading Jackson's foe from the 1824 election, Henry Clay, to remark snidely of Peg that "age can not wither her nor custom stale her infinite virginity." Eaton was so outraged that he wanted a duel. The result? In the words of Margaret Bayard Smith, a Washington society woman and wife of the president of Bank of the United States, Peg's reputation was "totally destroyed."

All the while, the cabinet was unable to meet for the customary cabinet dinner, so, with Vice President Calhoun back home in South Carolina, Jackson summoned the cabinet to meet on September 10, 1829, also inviting his former ally the Reverend Ezra Stiles Ely and the Reverend John N. Campbell to represent the city's clergy, who had been especially critical of Peg.

At the special meeting, Jackson awkwardly tried to defend Peg to the assembled guests, suggesting that "female virtue is like a tender and delicate flower, let but the breath of suspicion rest upon it, and it withers and perhaps perishes forever." He even insisted that he had taken affidavits from individuals who knew Peg and had considered the case for and against her. Like the judge he had been, Jackson stated that he was ruling that there was nothing to the scandal. The problem was that Peg occasioned far more than a "breath" of suspicion, and the cabinet and Jackson's old friend the Reverend Ely were not moved by the president's arguments. Rather, they were insulted by the ploy. The meeting was a failure, and the political stalemate over the scandal continued to affect Jackson's presidency and the nation.

It is clear that Jackson viewed the snub from the cabinet wives and Washington society as plots against him, believing himself to be a victim of "one of the most base and wicked conspiracies." Accordingly, he dug his heels in and made the "Petticoat Affair" a personal matter. When his supporters, for instance, tried to talk him into removing Eaton from the cabinet, Jackson refused defiantly, saying, "When I am mature in my course I am immovable." He also lashed out at anyone opposing Peg, labeling them "malcontents," and was so blinded by the affair that when his beloved niece Emily Donelson, who served as presidential hostess, said of Peg that she was "society too disagreeable to be endured," Jackson made Emily and her husband, who was Jackson's personal secretary, pick sides. When they sided against Peg, Jackson sent both packing back to Tennessee. Even when Secretary Eaton tried to reason with his boss, Jackson roared, "Do you suppose that I have been sent here by the people to consult the ladies of Washington as to the proper persons to compose my cabinet?"

Peg also suffered from the attacks. When she complained of her treatment to the president, Jackson offered what comfort he could, saying, "I tell you, Margaret, I had rather have live vermin on my back than the tongue of one of these Washington women on my reputation."

Ultimately, Jackson's planned cabinet dinner ended up being delayed by nine months because of the scandal. When it finally occurred in November 1829, it was an uncomfortable event lacking any conversation. Jackson sat Secretary Eaton and Peg beside himself as his honored guests. The cabinet officers and their wives rushed through their meals and departed. Future affairs were again boycotted by the cabinet wives, and the brouhaha led to a popular toast in the capital city. Guests raised their glasses to "Here is to the next Cabinet—may they all be bachelors—or leave their wives at home!"

The "Little Magician"

Jackson's entire agenda was affected, and the federal government was gridlocked by the Petticoat Affair. Newspapers spoke of the "collapse of government" that Peg helped bring about and likened Jackson's administration to the "reign of Louis XV when Ministers were appointed and dismissed at a woman's nod, and the interests of the nation were tied to her apron string." Of the matter, the politician and intellectual Daniel Webster noted in January 1830, "It is odd enough, that the consequences of this dispute in the social . . . world, is producing great political effects, and may very probably determine who shall be successor to the present chief magistrate." Indeed, it did.

In April 1831, Secretary of State Martin Van Buren announced his willingness to resign from the cabinet, thus allowing Jackson an excuse to reorganize the body and bring loyalists into the administration. Thus, in the power struggle that emerged over Peg, Jackson's entire cabinet was dumped or reshuffled. In the process, Jackson tried to appoint Van Buren as the U.S. minister to Great Britain. But Calhoun used his influence in the Senate to kill the appointment, gloating that Van Buren's career would thus be ruined: "It will kill him, sir, kill him dead!"

Calhoun and Van Buren had emerged as rivals not only within the cabinet but also for the presidency, and Calhoun wrongly assumed that he had dealt a severe blow to both Jackson and Van Buren. The rivalry between the two men was of personal interest to Jackson for another reason. Calhoun had been a ringleader in the anti-Peg faction in Washington, whereas one of the few cabinet members to embrace Peg was Van Buren, who referred to the affair as "Eaton malaria." Van Buren was joined by a handful of allies, including William T. Barry, the postmaster general, who defended Peg. It was Peggy Eaton who had nursed Barry's sick child back to health during a severe illness. Amusingly, one of the reasons for Van Buren's acceptance of Peg was that he was a widower and therefore did not have a wife to worry about Peg's promiscuous reputation.

The rift between Jackson and Calhoun reached new lows. The two also nearly came to blows over South Carolina's attempt at nullification, which Jackson took as not only a prelude to disunion and war but also a personal attack. The president thus issued his famous threat to personally go to the Palmetto State and "hang the first person" he encountered to the first available tree. Jackson also invited Calhoun and other rabble-rousers to a dinner in April 1830 where he eyeballed Calhoun while toasting, "To our federal union: it must be preserved."

Calhoun reasoned that Jackson and those who supported him like Van Buren would be disgraced by the Petticoat Affair. Thus, it was best to distance himself from the president, something that Calhoun did by resigning the vice presidency and moving back to South Carolina. After Calhoun resigned the vice presidency and Van Buren's ambassadorial appointment was defeated, Jackson picked Van Buren as his new number two. Calhoun had misjudged Jackson's resiliency and popularity among the public. Jackson remained popular and personally backed Van Buren in the 1836 election. Because of his support of Little Peg, Martin Van Buren, dismissed by many as the "Little Magician," received a strong endorsement from Old Hickory and was elected president.

POSTSCRIPT

The 1824 and 1828 elections affected the political order beyond the selection of a president. Jackson and his supporters viewed Adams as "His Fraudulency," and Old Hickory refused to be a part of the established party. As it was, the old party structure was falling apart going into 1824, and Jackson's victory in 1828 ended the party system that existed from the presidency of the first Adams through the presidency of the second Adams. Jackson then created the new Democratic Party and ushered in "coonskin democracy," a grassroots shift in political power to the common man. The election was good for democracy, as some 800,000 more people voted in 1828 than in the previous election, making this the first time in the young republic's history that a significant percentage of the people were involved in the political process.

In both elections, Jackson's enemies attacked him for being uneducated and uncouth, and this only played into his image as a man of the people. The 1828 election also marked a sea change in the presidency insofar as the country electing a new kind of president. After six elite men of great privilege (Washington had a modest upbringing but enjoyed great wealth at the time of his presidency) in the office, the country was about to have its first frontier president. While elites bemoaned the results, the people were enthralled. Jackson-mania swept through the country. The aristocrats were out, common folk were in, and coonskin caps replaced powdered wigs. One party leader sneered, "It was the howl of raving democracy."

In one way, the fears surrounding Jackson's presidency came true. At his 1829 inauguration, crowds of frontiersmen showed up, many in buckskin and carrying hickory sticks to symbolize their hero. The inaugural party devolved into a drunken melee, with Jackson's frontier supporters helping themselves to the executive mansion's furniture, wallpaper, and knickknacks. Blocks of cheese were knocked to the floor and ground into carpeting under boots, and drunken revelers discharged pistols. Jackson was even forced to flee from the president's home for his own safety. Eventually, large bowls of punch and booze were placed outside the mansion to entice the partiers out of the house so that order could be restored.

As for John and Peg Eaton, Jackson sent his friend to serve as the governor of the Florida Territory during the second term of the Jackson administration. Two years later, he named Eaton U.S. minister to Spain. Even though her scandals followed them across the Atlantic, these were among Peg's happiest years. She loved Madrid. Shockingly, Eaton and Jackson had a falling-out, leading Van Buren to recall Eaton from his ministership. Eaton even supported Van Buren's Whig Party opponents, including William Henry Harrison, in the 1840 election. Jackson remained loyal to Van Buren but stopped speaking to Eaton for nearly four years. Fortunately, the old friends reconciled shortly before the general's death on June 8, 1845, after a prolonged illness.

Jackson was buried next to his wife at his home, The Hermitage, in Tennessee, near a garden that Rachel had planted. His last words were, "I hope to meet you all in Heaven—yes, all in Heaven, white and black." As testimony to the scandals she endured, Jackson had engraved on Rachel's tombstone the words, "A being so gentle and so virtuous slander might wound, but could not dishonor."

Rachel Jackson remains something of an enigma to most Americans. Tragically, a fire on October 13, 1834, during Jackson's second term as president destroyed The Hermitage. In it, many of Rachel's personal letters and memorabilia were lost to history. But Andrew Jackson became one of the mythic heroes of the American story and was the dominant political figure on the national landscape in the long decades between Thomas Jefferson's presidency and the election of Abraham Lincoln in 1860.

Jackson's good friend John Eaton died in 1865, the same year as Lincoln's assassination, leaving a small fortune to his widow. Peg's two daughters survived to adulthood, and both married well in the nation's capital city. At fifty-nine, the wealthy widow met a nineteen-year-old Italian dance teacher and womanizer named Antonio Buchignani. The Italian was giving dance lessons to Peg's young granddaughter, Emily. Peg again proved that even in her advanced years, she was the most scandalous woman in Washington—she married Buchignani, forty years her junior. However, not long after, Buchignani disappeared, robbing Peg of all her money and valuables and running off with her granddaughter Emily. Emily and Buchignani stayed together for several years and had two children, but he never married her, even though an outraged and embarrassed Peg had divorced him. Ultimately, Buchignani would leave Emily and run off with another woman.

Destitute, Peg moved in with her grandson, John, and later lived at Lochiel House, a home for impoverished women. It was there that she died at the advanced age of eighty on November 9, 1879. Peggy O'Neale Timberlake Eaton Buchignani was buried next to her husband, Senator Eaton, in one of the city's most exclusive cemeteries—the Oak Hill Cemetery. In reference to the cemetery and the criticisms she endured at the hands of Washington's elite, the *New York Times* wrote of Peg's death that "doubtless among the dead populating the terraces [of the cemetery] are some of her assailants and cordially as they may have hated her, they are now her neighbors." Forever.

John Tyler was painted late in life during the Civil War and while married to his young second wife. Brady-Handy Collection, Library of Congress Prints and Photographs Division, LC-USZ62-13010 DLC.

⊰ 7 ⊱

A Near Miss

Sex at age 90 is like trying to shoot pool with a rope.

—Camille Paglia

UNLIKELY EVENTS

The Peacemaker

By all accounts, February 28, 1844, was a beautiful day. There was little wind and no chop on the Potomac River, complementing the festive occasion of the large warship's ceremonial voyage. Aboard the USS *Princeton*, the navy's most advanced warship and the first steamer in the fleet featuring a screw propeller, was a collection of Washington's leading dignitaries, including President John Tyler and members of his cabinet. The *Princeton* had been designed by the noted Swedish naval architect John Ericsson, who would later build the USS *Monitor*, which gained fame during the Civil War as the Union's most celebrated warship. Also aboard the *Princeton* was the "Peacemaker," the U.S. Navy's newest and largest cannon.

Some 400 guests and their families boarded the *Princeton* that day near Alexandria for a luxurious cruise on the Potomac, replete with a dinner party and musical entertainment. The ship was commanded by President Tyler's good friend Captain Robert Stockton and adorned with flags from around the world. To the delight of the passengers, the captain demonstrated the ship's high speed and technological innovations. There was nothing like it afloat.

The day's itinerary called for the president's party to cruise past George Washington's former home, Mount Vernon, on the banks of the Potomac and then return to the capital city. Sailing back up the river, the ship slowed when passing Mount Vernon in order to salute the nation's first president by having the band play "Hail to Columbia." Captain Stockton also ordered the massive, new cannon to fire three times. The guests had just finished the last course of dinner, and some were mingling on deck, enjoying the music and preparing for the firing of the cannon. Some guests, however, remained belowdecks, still finishing their dinners. One of those was the recently widowed president, who was obviously smitten by the company of the young, beautiful Julia Gardiner. He had followed her that day as a puppy dog follows its owner. She remained belowdecks, so he did too, offering toasts in her honor. The report of two massive shots bellowed through the bowels of the ship, and the passengers applauded the spectacle, enticed by the power of the huge weapon. Guests continued funneling up the ladders from belowdecks as the captain ordered the crew to prepare the third shot.

The president was encouraged to come on deck for the firing but remained momentarily to offer a final toast to his guests and the ravishingly attractive Miss Gardiner, whom he had been attempting to court. As Tyler, with Miss Gardiner at his side, prepared to ascend for the third firing of the Peacemaker, the cannon exploded. The sound was described by those on board as sickening and deafening. Heavy pieces of shrapnel flew across the deck, striking and killing five, knocking others off their feet. Those killed were two members of Tyler's cabinet—Secretary of the Navy Thomas Gilmer and Secretary of State Abel P. Upshur, Commodore Beverly Kennon, a diplomat named Virgil Maxcy, and the father of young Miss Gardiner, David Gardiner. David Gardiner, a former state senator from New York and one of the state's wealthiest citizens, had been invited that day as Tyler's personal guest. Gardiner brought his daughter Julia, with whom the president was enamored, and her sister Margaret aboard for the cruise.

Several members of the crew lay wounded and bleeding on the deck along with the president's black servant, who later died from his injuries. Captain Stockton, who was standing near the cannon at the time of the explosion, and Senator Thomas Hart Benton, who took the place of Tyler beside the captain to preside over the ceremonial salute to Washington, were knocked flat to the deck, shell-shocked and temporarily unable to hear. Had Tyler not been belowdecks with Julia, he would have been standing beside Captain Stockton when the cannon exploded. It is possible that Tyler would have been seriously wounded or killed. In the 1840s, the chain of presidential succession was not yet clear and had been contested when Tyler himself ascended to the presidency on the death of his predecessor. Thus, had Tyler—who was serving without a vice president—been killed in the mishap, the nation would have been left without a president or obvious successor.

After the explosion, Julia Gardiner learned that her father had been killed, and she collapsed. Tyler personally carried the young woman off the ship and took her to the White House to recover. He insisted that her family members stay with him and that she take time to convalesce under his direct supervision and care. Days later, a funeral procession over one mile long was held in honor of the dignitaries lost in the freakish accident. Afterward, the bodies were placed in state in the White House on Tyler's orders. Both of the fallen cabinet members had been close to Tyler, and the nation was shocked by the event. They would soon be shocked by another presidential action. Shortly after recovering, Julia agreed to a secret engagement with the president.

Tyler

John Tyler remains one of the least known of American presidents and has the dubious distinction of being the first "accidental" president. Born on March 29, 1790, at Greenway, the family plantation located between Richmond and Williamsburg in the Old Dominion State, Tyler was the son of a prominent family with English ancestry. Henry Tyler (1604–1672) was John's great-grandfather and the first Tyler to come to America. He did so in 1653, leaving Shropshire, England, for Williamsburg, Virginia.

John's father fought in the Revolutionary War and was a popular politician who rose to be Virginia's governor from 1809 to 1811 and also sat on the state circuit court. John lost his mother when he was only seven and, subsequently, became very close to his father. As a boy, Tyler grew up listening attentively to his father's tales of battle and politics. His father, a disciple of Thomas Jefferson and an opponent of the U.S. Constitution, also imparted his political views on young John, who would grow up as a believer in states' rights and an opponent to most federal policies and programs.

Little is known about Tyler's childhood in Charles City County other than that he frequently suffered from digestive problems, and the ailment bothered him his entire life. Family lore holds that, as a child, John seemed fascinated with the stars and even tried to reach up as if to touch them. This prompted his mother to proclaim, "This child is destined to be a president of the United States, his wishes fly so high." It is also known that Tyler was fond of animals and had many pets, including his beloved canary he named Johnny Ty. But he was also a headstrong and rebellious child who once organized his peers to rebel against an overly stern teacher named William McMurdo.

Tyler was enrolled in the preparatory school of the College of William & Mary when he was twelve. He graduated in the year 1807 at age seventeen after studying English literature, the classics, history, and economics. Because he was a good student, his father arranged for him to study law with his cousin, Chancellor Samuel Tyler, and the famed attorney Edmund Randolph, who had served as the country's first attorney general.

After finishing his legal training, Tyler practiced law and showed himself to be a capable defense attorney and a gifted orator. Enjoying much success in law, Tyler turned his attention to politics, which, as was the case with his father, turned out to be his true passion. At twenty-one years of age, Tyler was already serving in public office; he had been elected to the Virginia legislature in 1811. Standing slightly over six feet in height and with steely blue eyes, Tyler was a dashing, popular figure who was establishing himself as a political force in Virginia. That continued when, in 1816, he was elected to the U.S. House of Representatives.

But Tyler also had a stubborn streak and a demeanor that ultimately limited his political accomplishments and that, with time, seems to have grown worse. Tyler frequently found himself in the minority on the issues and was often unwilling to compromise with colleagues or opponents. He voted against the Missouri Compromise, for instance, but did so believing that it might delegitimize the institution of slavery. He also had a falling-out with President Andrew Jackson and his supporters because of Jackson's criticism of South Carolina over the state's nullification threats, and afterward he emerged as a vocal critic of Jackson and his own Democratic Party. Similarly, when Congress passed the Force Act, which allowed the federal government to use force to enforce laws, Tyler was the only member of Congress to vote against it.

Accordingly, Tyler often ran afoul of his own party and ended up switching his allegiance to the Whigs. His decision was made easier by many leaders in the Democratic Party who were planning to throw Tyler out of the party. Tyler's prickly disposition and stubborn personality seemed to worsen with every political battle and was the reason he resigned his House seat in 1821. But Tyler was elected two years later to the Virginia legislature and in 1825 became governor of the state. Two years after that, he was elected to the U.S. Senate and arrived in Washington in March 1827. Even though his wife was too ill to travel with him and he left behind a house full of children, Tyler spent nine of the happiest years of his life in the Senate, and this says something about his first marriage and capacity as a father. Nevertheless, his wife, Letitia, did manage to join him for a winter social season in the nation's capital city, which delighted Tyler. Many of his letters from this time survive and show that he missed his children. But family matters were offset by the fact that Tyler's reputation was growing within the new Whig Party and beyond Virginia.

Tyler was a complex man. He was simultaneously stubborn and principled. Raised an Episcopalian, Tyler became more of a deist as he aged and was tolerant of all faiths. He detested religious hypocrisy and individuals who rejected any views outside their own religious beliefs, whom he saw as zealots. As a result, Tyler always championed the Jeffersonian notion of a separation of church and state affairs. In some ways, Tyler was a natural when it came to politics; in other ways, not so much. George Wythe Munford, the clerk of Virginia's House of Delegates, commented about Tyler that

> everybody could approach him without the least restraint, and he transacted business with such promptness that it was a pleasure to have official intercourse with him. He was so frank and generous, so social and cordial, so genial and kind, and withal so manly and high-toned, and so familiar with the duties of his station that you were ready to give him your hand and heart in return for his, which he seemed ever ready to proffer.

At the same time, Tyler was often difficult, unyielding, and judgmental. Sometimes, his response to a situation seemed to depend on and differ by the day, hour, or minute. Theodore Roosevelt would, many years later, declare that "Tyler has been called a mediocre man, but this is unwarranted flattery. He was a politician of monumental littleness." He also became the first president to be abandoned by his political party and threatened with impeachment.

Even though he enjoyed serving in the Senate, Tyler also resigned this seat. He did so in 1836, again in protest to certain policies. That same year, he threw his hat in the ring for the Whig Party vice presidency but was unsuccessful. However, he was again elected to the Virginia legislature for a third time. By this time, Tyler had become a strict constructionist, meaning that he read the Constitution literally and without interpretation, implied powers, or flexibility. Tyler therefore opposed most federal initiatives and programs and had thoroughly split from his former Jacksonian loyalties. In addition to his stubbornness, Tyler was becoming increasingly prudish. He was a stickler for codes and rules with his children, would not allow his daughter to answer a letter from a first cousin because of how it might look, and even opposed many dances, including the waltz, because he thought it obscene. Tyler, who was not home with his family for the Christmas holiday, wrote in disgust to his daughter on December 26, 1827, after seeing the waltz performed at a holiday party that it is "a dance which you have never seen, and which I do not desire to see you dance. It is rather vulgar I think." Tyler ended up being hypocritical and judgmental, the traits he always professed to detest.

An Impossibly Long Courtship

Letitia Christian was born on November 12, 1790, at Cedar Grove in New Kent County, Virginia, about eighteen miles from Richmond. She was the third of eight daughters and one of twelve Christian children. Her father, Robert Christian, was a prominent planter who was active in politics. Letitia's mother, Mary Browne, also came from a wealthy family. Unfortunately, none of the letters of her youth survived history, and we thus know little about her childhood. Therefore, we know her from only a few references to her in her husband's letters and those of children. Surviving portraits of Letitia show a pensive and slender woman with large, dark eyes and a pale complexion. Her unsmiling image in the portraits lacks emotion or even a hint of an intrigue. She was described as fragile, something that is apparent in the portraits, but she was also said to have been attractive in her youth and refined in her actions and interactions with others.

As an adult, Letitia liked knitting and gardening and was both religiously devout and introverted. Her temperament aside, her good looks and family's prosperity ensured that she had many suitors as a young woman, most of whom were far wealthier than John Tyler. Letitia met Tyler at a party in 1808, and they began courting. It appears that Letitia's parents opposed her marriage to Tyler, in part because of politics. The Christians were Federalists, while the Tylers were Jeffersonians and supporters of the Democratic-Republican Party. As a result, John and Letitia's courtship was one of the slowest and longest of any presidential couple. Over the course of nearly five years, Tyler pursued Letitia in a lukewarm manner, but we are not certain as to the full nature of their romance. The few surviving accounts of their long courtship are mixed. They may have been in love, but there may have been issues other than the Christian family's political objections. Tyler did, however, write sonnets to Letitia and later described their marriage as an "ideally happy union."

Another possible reason for the slow courtship may have been Tyler's finances. The Tylers were by no means poor—his father served as governor—but they were "land rich but cash poor," and Letitia's family was far wealthier. Tyler wrote to his bride-to-be shortly before their wedding about the topic of money:

> You express some degree of astonishment, my Letitia, at an observation I once made to you, "that I would not have been willingly wealthy at the time I addressed you." Suffer me to repeat it. If I had been wealthy, the idea of your being actuated by prudential considerations in accepting my suit, would have eternally tortured me. But I exposed to you frankly and unblushingly my situation in life—my hopes and fears, my prospects and

my dependencies—and you nobly responded. To ensure to you, happiness is now my only object, and whether I float or sink in the stream of fortune, you may be assured of this, that I shall never cease to love you.

Only one of Tyler's love letters to Letitia from their courtship survived history. Although the answer may never be known, it is likely that he seldom wrote to her. The letter in question was written on December 5, 1812, and is affectionate and warm in tone but lacks the depth of passion that one might expect of two young lovers preparing to marry. Rather, the letter is more philosophical and reads like the correspondence of a couple married for several years. Their passion may have also been cooled by distance. Because they did not live in the same town, the couple probably saw one another only rarely. They would have courted during winter social seasons in Richmond and Williamsburg and while Tyler was serving in the state legislature, which was not far from the Christian home.

As the wedding date approached, one historian noted that "Tyler even approached marriage without experiencing the fears and thrills that are generally incident to the acceptance of a new responsibility." Indeed, Tyler admits to his brother-in-law six days prior to his wedding,

> On the 29th instant I lead my Letitia to the alter. I had really calculated on experiencing a tremor on the near approach of the day, but I believe I am so much of the old man already as to feel less dismay at a change of situation than the greater part of those of my age.

The dispassionate tone of the relationship was likely also the result of both Letitia and John possessing prudish tendencies. In other letters, Tyler suggests that he had never even hugged Letitia prior to marriage and that their first and only kiss during their long engagement was on her hand and occurred only three weeks before the wedding. And this was after nearly five years of courtship. Not surprising, one Tyler biographer stated, "Tyler's love-making must have been conducted strictly in accordance with the conventional rules laid down by the planter aristocracy of the day." Tyler offers history a clue when he praises his wife as "perfectly reserved and modest."

In a letter to his eldest daughter in 1830, Tyler offered the following advice:

> I could not hold up to you a better pattern for your imitation than is constantly presented to you by your dear mother. You never see her course marked with precipitation; but on the contrary everything is brought before the tribunal of her judgment, and her actions are all founded in prudence.

The couple finally married at Cedar Grove on March 29, 1813, the day of Tyler's twenty-third birthday. Tyler's law practice was doing well, and he planned to continue his political career. Tyler benefited immeasurably by marriage; it greatly enhanced his landholdings. Letitia's parents died soon after the wedding, and much of their land and money went to the newlyweds.

The newlyweds moved to "Mons Sacer," a plantation next to Greenway, Tyler's childhood home. The plantation was nicknamed "Woodburn," and the Tylers lived there for six years before purchasing Tyler's childhood home in 1821. Letitia had helped to manage her father's plantation, so she was experienced at housekeeping, cooking, entertaining, raising children, and the myriad tasks necessary for such an enterprise. This is fortunate because the burden of raising so many children and maintaining the plantation fell to her. Tyler was often away from home because of his career. Other factors intervened. Just four months after the wedding, Tyler departed to fight in the War of 1812 as a captain of the "Charles City Rifles." However, his unit, which was assigned to protect Richmond, never saw combat.

Seven of Letitia's children survived infancy—four daughters and three sons—the first of which, Mary, was born in 1814. A daughter, Anne Contesse, died at three months, and a ninth child may have been stillborn. Although she was a doting and good mother, the birth of so many children took a toll on her health. John and Letitia always struggled to live within their means and were frequently short of cash. The rapid succession of nine Tyler children also drained the family finances along with the eventual task of marrying off so many daughters. Already frail, Letitia struggled to remain involved in her maternal responsibilities and in helping to run the household. The fact that her husband was away more than he was at home did not help. Her health and the responsibility of so many children (and so many pregnancies) also precluded Letitia from being involved in Tyler's career. Nor did she express much interest in politics. She did not travel with him to the sessions of Congress or the state legislature, to political events, or to other ceremonies. Only once did she travel to Washington for the winter social season of 1828–1829, and she was limited in her role as Virginia's First Lady during his governorship.

Letitia was always religious. A devout reader of the Bible, she taught her children using Scripture, kept the book on her nightstand, and drew comfort from it as her health declined. Two years before Tyler became president, Letitia suffered a stroke and never fully recovered. By the time she became First Lady, she was described as an "invalid" and was incapable of attending most presidential events, much less hosting them. In fact, she is documented as attending only two events, one of them the wedding of her daughter, Elizabeth, in January 1842. During her brief time in the presidential mansion, Letitia generally remained in seclusion.

AND TYLER TOO

William Henry Harrison had led a full and difficult life of military service, commanding small garrisons and fighting in some of the most remote of American territories. His career included serving as an aide-de-camp to General "Mad" Anthony Wayne, one of America's best-regarded military leaders. This propelled the otherwise mediocre Harrison's career, and he gained some distinction as a fair-minded and successful Indian fighter in the "West." Although Harrison eventually rose to the rank of general, it was, in many ways, an inglorious career. A high-profile command eluded him, even though he was the son of a signer of the Declaration of Independence.

Harrison was born in 1773 at his family home, Berkeley Plantation, in Virginia. He attended Hampden-Sydney College, and his family connections allowed him the privilege of studying medicine under Dr. Benjamin Rush, the most celebrated physician of the day. A medical or political career beckoned, but Harrison enlisted in the military in 1791.

Harrison's military career was also mixed when it came to the pressing matter of the "Indian question." At one point, Harrison was ordered to acquire land from Indians, but he was reluctant to do so out of concern for the "first Americans." His reputation as a champion of the native people was furthered when he requested that smallpox inoculations be available to them and banned the sale of liquor to Indian nations. However, Harrison was still very much a man of his times, for he negotiated a treaty in 1809 that transferred a whopping 2.9 million acres of Indian land to the U.S. government, resulting in the heightening of tensions.

Fighting ultimately broke out, and when it did, Harrison led U.S. forces against the native population. His opponent was the famed Shawnee chief Tecumseh, who believed that, because all Indians were brothers, their land could not be negotiated away without the consent of *all* Indian nations. This was not politically possible, and the U.S. government had little interest in Tecumseh's ideas. Thus, on November 7, 1811, Harrison led an army of roughly 1,000 men against the Indian nations of northwestern Indiana. The enemies met near the Tippecanoe and Wabash rivers, where Tecumseh's 650 braves initiated a surprise attack in the early morning hours. They caught most of Harrison's force asleep and unprepared.

After two hours of ferocious fighting that resulted in roughly 400 casualties, Harrison managed to defeat his opponent. He also proceeded to punish a nearby Indian village by burning it to the ground. Historians have questioned whether this village was even involved in the earlier battle. They have also criticized Harrison for not being ready for the surprise attack. Harrison's troops suffered more casualties during the engagement than they should have. Either way, Harrison's victory at the Battle of Tippecanoe ended the main Indian uprising, and the general's supporters began a campaign to promote him as an American hero.

Harrison's military service was interrupted by a variety of political posts. For instance, he was appointed by President John Adams as secretary of the Northwest Territory in 1798. He served for two years, and his family needed the money the position paid, but Harrison's politics put him at odds with the anti-Federalist governor of the territory, Arthur St. Clair. Harrison was elected by a close vote of eleven to ten over Governor St. Clair's son to be the first delegate to represent the territory in 1799 when they sent a nonvoting representative to Congress and later served as the governor of Indiana Territory from 1800 to 1812. During his service to the territory, he was instrumental in promoting land and homesteading acts that opened the Northwest Territory to waves of settlers. Governor Harrison avoided political conflicts and was thus able to be appointed by presidents of both political persuasions, and he also delivered several Indian treaties that furthered white settlement in Indiana and Illinois.

Harrison also served as a congressman from Indiana from 1816 until 1821 and as a senator from Ohio from 1825 to 1828. In 1828, he was appointed as the U.S. minister to Colombia but was unsuccessful in that post and was recalled by President Andrew Jackson. Truth be told, Harrison served without distinction in every office and struggled with various commercial enterprises, losing money in each one, but was aided throughout his career by the imagined and wholly undeserved reputation affixed to him as the "Washington of the West."

After the 1836 election, which saw Andrew Jackson's handpicked successor, Martin Van Buren, win, the new Whig Party, eager to defeat Van Buren for reelection, began looking for a presidential candidate for 1840. The Whigs gained the support of those elites who had been removed from office by Jackson and his supporters and needed someone with Jackson's heroic image who could defeat his Democratic Party and "coonskin democracy" movement for the common man. However, the lesson of Jackson was clear—the Whigs did not want another powerful president who was beyond the control of his supporters and the political establishment. Harrison was the perfect choice. He was, at best, compliant if not completely disinterested in governing, and the public loved his image as a rugged frontiersman and military hero.

Thus, Harrison became the Whig presidential nominee in 1840, and the branding process began, manufacturing an image complete with a cute "ditty" referencing his alleged military victory over Tecumseh's warriors and the name of his vice president: "Tippecanoe and Tyler Too!" The nickname "Old Tippecanoe" even hearkened to Jackson's moniker, "Old Hickory," and it was said that this obscure and mediocre son of privilege was a hard cider–drinking man born in a log cabin, content to sit in retirement waxing philosophical about the issues of the day. Old Tippecanoe was made out to be part George Washington and part Andrew Jackson, both powerful and, at six feet two inches, statuesque leaders. Few people knew anything else about Harrison or his position on the issues, but none of that mattered. They loved the image. Old Tippecanoe won the election.

His advanced age and poor health became minor issues, so Harrison traveled from Ohio to the East Coast so that the public could have a look at him. But what the public discovered was that Washington and Jackson he was not. Critics observed that Harrison was "an old broken-down feeble man." Another described Harrison as "a small and rather sallow-looking man, who does not exactly meet the associations that connect themselves with the general." Even Harrison's wife wanted her husband to stay in retirement and worried about his age and health.

To prove his critics wrong, Harrison delivered a long and eloquent Inaugural Address on March 4, 1841, which ran to nearly two hours in length. Because he neglected to wear a winter coat and gloves for the long ceremony, attempting to demonstrate his tough frontier image, he succumbed to the cold and rain. After the inauguration, Harrison came down with pneumonia. The pressures of meeting with so many people and staffing his administration were too burdensome for the sick, weak president, who was the oldest president yet to serve at the time. He was bedridden for days. The new president even deferred his entire legislative program to the whims and wishes of Congress and his party, including the politics surrounding the "Caroline Affair," an abortive plan to initiate a revolution in Canada in 1837, something that angered the British.

As Harrison was recovering, he took a morning walk to purchase vegetables and produce but caught another cold. Days later, on April 4, the president was dead, only one month into his presidency. He was sixty-eight, the oldest president elected until Ronald Reagan in the 1980s. Harrison's body was sent back to Ohio to his wife, who never even traveled to Washington.

Harrison's last words were said to have been uttered to Tyler: "Sir—I wish you to understand the true principles of Government. I wish them carried out. I ask nothing more." But this is baloney. Tyler was not in the capital city at the time of Harrison's death.

Until Harrison's death, few people or politicians had given much thought to the vice president. But now that "Tyler Too" was the president, debate began in earnest. Should the vice president call for a special election, or should he govern? The office had, heretofore, received little attention and less consideration. John Adams, the country's first vice president, viewed the office as the least significant one imaginable. Years later, Franklin Roosevelt's first vice president, John Nance Garner, quipped that the office was not worth a "warm bucket of spit." His actual choice of wording was another four-letter word that rhymed with "spit" but was censored by the press.

It was Fletcher Webster, son of the famed secretary of state Daniel Webster, who was sent to inform Tyler that the president had died. Tyler had no idea that Harrison was even that ill when Webster arrived by horse at his home on Sunday, April 5, with the tragic news. In fact, Tyler did not even know Harrison. It was a political marriage of convenience and image designed by Whig leaders. A little over one week later, Tyler moved to the executive mansion.

Another Tragedy in the White House

Rightly or wrongly, Tyler would go down as one of the most controversial presidents in history. Even though he was chided by his critics as "His Accidency," it was Tyler who helped establish the precedent—and subsequent protocol and eventual constitutional amendment—for presidential succession that when a president dies in office or is removed because of incapacity or impeachment, the vice president becomes the legitimate president. Many political leaders were suggesting after President Harrison's death that the vice president serve only as a caretaker president and call for another election. The Constitution was not clear, and specificity was not added to the language by either amendment or statue until after World War II and again in the 1960s with the Twenty-Fifth Amendment. But Tyler was, if little else, stubborn. He refused to step aside or call for an election, seeing himself as the legitimate president.

The new president encountered opposition from the outset both from within his party and by his Democratic rivals. He also struggled with his wife's deteriorating health. Letitia Tyler never recovered from the stroke she suffered in 1839, which left her partially paralyzed and "confined to her chamber for two years." When Tyler learned that he was the president, there was even speculation as to whether Letitia would—or could—travel to Washington. In fact, she had been too ill even to attend her son Robert's wedding to Priscilla Cooper in 1839.

As a result of the First Lady's health, Tyler's daughter-in-law, Priscilla, served as the mansion's hostess. At twenty-four, she was young and beautiful and had been a talented actress. Priscilla's father, Thomas Cooper, was a famous actor who was acclaimed for his role as Othello, while Priscilla once played Desdemona. Tyler's son, Robert, caught her performance in the role and, like many other men, was instantly entranced.

Priscilla loved serving for the president at social events and working with the capital city's political elite. She hosted the likes of Charles Dickens and Washington Irving at the White House. Her social calendar included two parties per week and regular dinners during the city's winter social season, and she was a natural, serving with enthusiasm and grace. Priscilla even caught the attention of the great Dolley Madison, who offered her advice on matters of hosting. One of the grandest events in the Tyler White House was the wedding of daughter Elizabeth Tyler to William Waller on January 31, 1842. The guest list included numerous dignitaries and was in the capable hands of Priscilla Cooper Tyler. For the first time as First Lady, Letitia managed to make it downstairs for Elizabeth's wedding. Letitia did, however, always maintain an interest in the goings-on of the household and offered advice from her bed.

Priscilla offers an insight into Letitia's life and condition during the presidential years when she described her mother-in-law as follows:

[She] must have been very beautiful in her youth, for she is still beautiful now in her declining years and wretched health . . . she is gentle and graceful in her movements, with a most peculiar air of native refinement about everything she says and does. She is the most entirely unselfish person you can imagine. I do not believe she ever thinks of herself. Her whole thought and affections are wrapped up in her husband and children. . . . The room in the main dwelling furtherest removed and most retired is "the chamber," as the bedroom of the mistress of the house is always called in Virginia . . . here mother with a smile of welcome on her sweet, calm face, is . . . always ready to sympathize with me in any little homesickness which may disturb me . . . notwithstanding her very delicate health, mother attends to and regulates all the household affairs, and all so quietly that you cant tell when she does it. All the clothes for the children, and for the servants, are cut out under her immediate eye, and all the sewing is personally superintendented by her. All the cakes, jellies, custards, and we indulge largely in them, emanate from her, yet you see no confusion, hear no bustle, but only meet the agreeable result.

Letitia suffered a second stroke in 1842, and her health further deteriorated over the summer months. That September, Priscilla departed for New York to visit her family. Knowing that the end was near, the First Lady had sent her son to quickly get Priscilla and bring her back to the White House so that she might see her daughter-in-law one last time. Robert and Priscilla arrived too late. The First Lady, who had watched her bedroom door in hopes that her beloved son and daughter-in-law would arrive, was dead after a four-year illness. Letitia Tyler had held roses—her favorite flower—in each hand during her final moments, her head still facing the door. She was the first presidential wife to die during her husband's presidency.

Tyler had been on the receiving end of some very harsh attacks in the press, but this ceased momentarily out of respect for the late First Lady. The funeral was held in the East Room of the White House on September 12 with the Reverend Dr. Hawley from St. John's Episcopal Church presiding over the service. *The National Intelligencer* newspaper said in Letitia's obituary,

> This most estimable lady was, in life, more truly than we can represent her in words, a Wife, a Mother, and a Christian—loving and confiding to her husband—gentle and affectionate to her children—kind and charitable to the needy and the afflicted. Deeply impressed in her early life by her highly respected and pious parents, with the truthful and heavenly doctrines of the meek Jesus, in all her actions, with whatever sphere in life connected, self was forgotten by her and the good alone of others remembered, which won for her wherever she was known the love and esteem of all.

A SECOND MRS. TYLER

With the White House in mourning, the already limited social calendar was stopped, and meetings were curtailed. Priscilla Cooper Tyler continued to serve as the official hostess from time to time, that is, for the few events that were held. However, her husband, Robert, who was an employee in the federal lands department, took a job in Philadelphia, so they were unable to assist the newly widowed president. Tyler's daughter, Elizabeth, had married the year before and moved away, and his daughter, Alice, was too young to serve. Fortunately, Tyler's second daughter, named for her mother and married to a naval purser named Robert Semple, assisted with the running of the White House.

But it did not help. Tyler's presidency was in ruin, and he struggled to come to grips with the loss of his wife. He had stubbornly opposed his old political party, the Democrats, and was now opposing his new political party, the Whigs. But, because he had earlier abandoned the Democrats to become a Whig, Tyler found himself afoul of both parties and even his own cabinet. The president continued to advocate states' rights and the cause of slavery while opposing nearly all federal projects, including "internal improvements" (infrastructure). Just about the only successes he enjoyed were the annexation of Texas in 1845 and the admission of Florida to the Union that same year. But the highlight of his otherwise failed presidency would soon arrive in the form of a new First Lady.

The "Rose of Long Island"

Julia Gardiner was born on May 4, 1820, on Gardiner's Island, a scenic region of New York named for her family. It was Julia's noted grandfather, Lion Gardiner, who purchased the 3,300-acre tract on the eastern tip of Long Island. Julia's father, David Gardiner, was descended from the English Gardiner family, who came to the colonies in 1635 and settled in Connecticut. David Gardiner was a graduate of Yale and was one of New York's most prosperous landowners. He worked as a successful attorney in New York City and served for a time as a state senator. In a letter to her mother, Julia said of her father, "Papa was the only handsome man (except the President) I have ever seen."

Julia enjoyed a most privileged and comfortable upbringing and made her much-anticipated debut as a debutante at age fifteen. She attended the finest finishing schools and was educated at an elite New York City boarding school—Madam N. D. Chagray's Institute—in 1835, where she studied math, history, English composition, French and English literature, and music. As such, she was very well educated for a woman of the early nineteenth century. She was the third of four Gardiner children and first daughter. Her mother, Juliana McLachlan, also came from great wealth and affluence, the daughter of a brewing magnate. Mrs. Gardiner was an opinionated, strong woman known for her willingness to pick an argument and for dominating her husband, family, and anyone she encountered. She was also not shy about informing her children of their family's financial and social superiority.

Julia inherited a bit of her mother's headstrong and haughty ways, and Mrs. Gardiner had trouble controlling her eldest daughter. Short, plump, with large dark eyes, black hair, and a flirty, talkative, and overly confident demeanor, Julia was considered to be attractive by most men and had an abundance of romances. But Julia was also considered improper and a bit forward for a girl of the times. For instance, much controversy came from an advertisement featuring her likeness.

Society girls were not supposed to appear in ads. President Theodore Roosevelt's wife, Edith, once advised that the name of a true lady ought to appear in newspapers but three times—birth announcement, wedding announcement, and obituary. But Julia posed for the Bogert & Mecamly Dry Goods and Clothing Store in 1839. A lithograph of the ad ran that year and the following year in the newspaper *Brooklyn Daily News* and caused such a stir in New York society that Mrs. Gardiner removed her daughter from social events for most of 1840—until tongues stopped wagging. It also piqued the interest of many admiring men, including a judge who was so moved by Julia's beauty that he wrote a poem about her titled "Julia—Rose of Long Island." The sonnet, which included the sappy line, "I grieve my love a belle should be," was printed in the paper on May 11, 1840, and signed with the pen name "Romeo Ringdove." Other men followed suit in writing about Julia, and the poem earned Julia the nickname, from that moment on, the "Rose of Long Island."

The Gardiners also sent their daughter to Europe in September 1840 both for the cultural tour expected of daughters from the most prominent families and to wait out the gossip over her advertisement. Julia enjoyed England and France and attracted more than a fair share of suitors before returning home in September of 1841. It was while in Europe that the Gardiners learned that President William Henry Harrison had died and that Vice President Tyler was the new president.

That December, David Gardiner took daughters Julia and Margaret to the nation's capital city for the popular social season, where the Rose of Long Island was pursued by many of the leading politicians, including Congressman Francis W. Pickens of South Carolina, Congressman Richard D. Davis of New York, U.S. Supreme Court Justice John McLean of Ohio, and even the legendary Henry Clay. Several of her suitors remembered her from her debut a few years earlier at Saratoga Springs, and there were so many social invitations and such an abundance of gentleman callers that Mr. Gardiner decided to extend their stay and rented a larger home on Pennsylvania Avenue in the city. Julia relished the attention and quickly developed a passion for politics and politicians. She emerged as one of the most visible figures at the city's many events, where she was frequently escorted by a young naval officer named Richard Waldron.

David Gardiner also secured for his daughters an invitation to the White House, where she met the recently widowed president. Although the White House was still officially in mourning, President Tyler made an occasional appearance at events. When he met Julia, he was instantly smitten and spent the duration of the party in her company. Tyler invited Julia and her family back for dinner at the White House on Christmas Day.

Throughout the remaining social season in January and February 1843, the Gardiners were frequent guests of the president, and the rumor arose that the older widower was courting the young debutante. Julia, however, had become practiced at putting off her suitors while not shutting the door to future prospects, and she managed to gently but flirtatiously keep Tyler at bay. In doing so, she also avoided a very public scandal over the courtship. But at a grand ball held on February 22 in honor of George Washington's birthday, Tyler could stand it no longer and proposed marriage to his attractive young guest. She declined the first offer, which was customary, citing her surprise and concern that the romance was moving too quickly. The First Lady had been gone only three months when Tyler met Julia, and the president's proposal came only five months after his wife's death. The proposal, ironically enough, occurred one year—nearly to the day—before the fateful explosion aboard the warship *Princeton* that would kill Julia's father.

The romance blossomed. Even Julia's meddling mother approved, but it is not hard to imagine such an image-conscious socialite like Juliana Gardiner jumping at the opportunity to marry her daughter to the sitting president of the United States. But both Julia's mother and her father tried to slow the courtship for obvious reasons. Julia was already the gossip in Washington and was being far too forward and flirtatious with the widowed president. Young Miss Gardiner also heaped praise on Tyler to both the president and others at his social events. Even after their wedding, Julia shocked the public by always kissing Tyler and making obvious shows of affection with him in public. Such things simply were not done at the time.

Julia recalled the moment when she met the president:

> I remember my first visit to the white house, where we went a few evenings after our arrival in Washington with a congressional party . . . the president's break with the whigs had been the occasion of unprecedented political excitement, and his name was on all lips. When I look back on this day and see him as he stood in the "Green Room," the room between the "East" and the "Blue" at the moment of our introduction, it appears to me no marvel, acquainted as I am with his high-toned nature, that the wild phrensy of political misrepresentation left no impression of bitterness, either upon his countenance or his voice or demeanor. He welcomed us with an urbanity which made the deepest impression upon my father, and we could not help commenting, as we left the room, upon the silvery sweetness of his voice, that seemed in just attune with the incomparable grace of his bearing and the elegant case of his conversation.

Tyler did not let Julia's rejection of his proposal slow his courtship. He invited the Gardiners back for tea at the White House three days later and took Julia to a musical performance that evening. The concert marked the president's first social event outside the White House since his wife's passing, and this occasion was not missed by the city's newspapers or Washington's social crowd. Julia's parents knew that another proposal was forthcoming, so they extended their planned stay in Washington beyond the close of the social season in early March. Sure enough, Tyler proposed again.

The third time often proves lucky, and it was for Tyler. Julia accepted the president's third marriage proposal on March 27, 1843. However, Tyler wanted an early fall wedding, but Mrs. Gardiner, mindful of the importance of ensuring that the proper mourning period had passed, insisted that the wedding day be delayed. As such, John Tyler and Julia Gardiner were engaged, but the Gardiners departed for New York with no firm wedding date set but plans to return early to Washington for the following winter's social season.

An Unlikely Marriage

The Gardiners returned for the winter social season of 1843–1844, this time with their eldest daughter already engaged to the president. The tragic death of Julia's father during the explosion on the warship *Princeton* that February had the effect of hastening the wedding of John and Julia. After the incident, Tyler insisted that Julia recuperate in the White House under his supervision. After two months, Julia's emotional state had improved, and Tyler wrote to her mother on April 20 asking for Julia's hand in marriage. The widow granted her permission but did express some concern about Tyler's finances. Juliana Gardiner held the president in high regard but knew that her daughter was used to great wealth, far beyond Tyler's means. Mrs. Gardiner also urged her younger daughter, Margaret, to live in the White House with Julia and keep an eye on the headstrong new First Lady. However, Julia wrote back to her mother, saying, "I very well known every eye is upon me, my dear mother, and I will behave accordingly."

Julia's older brother, Alexander, handled the details of the wedding. In the company of his son, John, and good friend, Captain Stockton, the president departed Washington in late June 1844 to marry young Miss Gardiner. The wedding was on June 26 and held at the Church of the Ascension on Fifth Avenue in New York City. Alexander served as best man and Julia's sister, Margaret, as a bridesmaid. The bride was twenty-four years old and the groom three decades her senior. The wedding was a quiet affair, with only a few close friends and family members in attendance. Tyler had managed to keep the date and details of the wedding a secret, so many of their friends along with members of the press and public did not learn of the wedding until after it occurred.

Many letters exchanged by the Tylers survived history, but they are from the period after the Tylers married. Nothing exchanged between them during their courtship exists, but history still affords a glimpse into their courtship and union. From the evidence, it is clear that the Tylers enjoyed a very strong and affectionate marriage despite their vast age difference. So too were they surprisingly compatible. Both loved animals, and their home at Sherwood Forest was filled with pets. They also enjoyed music—Tyler was a talented violinist and Julia an accomplished guitarist. Indeed, the couple was in love, and the union seems to have rejuvenated Tyler, who described his bride as "the most lovely of her sex."

Tyler was not shy about offering his praise to his new wife, proclaiming her to be "the most beautiful woman of the age and at the same time the most accomplished." He gushed that "she is all that I wish her to be," and Julia echoed his sentiment, claiming that "nothing appears to delight the President more than . . . to hear people sing my praises." The admiration was mutual. Years later on the occasion of Tyler's sixty-second birthday, Julia composed a poem for him that read, "What e'er changes time may bring, I'll love thee as thou art!"

However, there was strain in the marriage. For instance, Julia's relatives in New York were abolitionists and disagreed with Tyler's stance in support of slavery. Julia adopted her husband's views on slavery and later supported southern secession and war, greatly frustrating her family. Julia even picked up many of the mannerisms of southern culture and soon passed herself off as a belle of Dixie.

There was also strain from Tyler's family. Tyler had children older than Julia, and he was nine years older than Julia's mother. His four daughters disapproved of their new stepmother, who was near to them in age, seeing her as pretentious and vane. Daughters Letitia and Elizabeth were shocked by the wedding and did not care for Julia. Neither daughter accepted Julia as their new stepmother and later, in the postpresidential years, challenged her authority in running Sherwood Forest. Daughter-in-law Priscilla, who had been serving as hostess for the president, had moved to Philadelphia, so the management of social affairs in the White House had fallen to Letitia. However, neither Letitia nor Priscilla ever warmed up to Julia, and Letitia was unhappy about Julia assuming responsibility for the White House. Daughter Alice, who was seventeen at the time of the wedding, is the only daughter who eventually warmed up to her new stepmother. The Tyler boys, however, were fond of Julia, but John Jr.'s wild drinking and partying embarrassed the family and became a source of tension in the household.

Additionally, although the marriage was strong, Tyler was prone to fits of jealousy. Even though Julia never seemed interested in younger men—she was always attracted to older, powerful men—she was a helpless flirt and continued to be so throughout their marriage, even in the White House.

After the wedding, the couple enjoyed breakfast with the Gardiners at the family home, then toured New York's harbor by ferry, and visited New Jersey. The couple then departed for their honeymoon, visiting Philadelphia and Washington, D.C., and spending a few quiet days at Tyler's estate, Sherwood Forest, as well as one month at Tyler's summer home, a four-room cottage in Hampton, Virginia.

After their honeymoon, the newlyweds returned to the White House and opened the building to the public. For the first time since Dolley Madison reigned, the White House and capital city hosted lavish events and, courtesy of the new First Lady, enjoyed a full social calendar. With both Jackson and Van Buren being widowers, the death of Harrison, and the passing of Tyler's first wife, the White House had not seen such events in years. Not everyone was pleased, however. Tyler's daughter-in-law, Priscilla Cooper Tyler, regretted having to abandon her hosting duties, and it did not help that the new First Lady was her replacement. Priscilla shared her concerns, writing to Julia just prior to the wedding,

> I find that my spirits sink lower and lower at the idea of leaving Father [Tyler]. I am, in fact, as devotedly attached to him as though he were my own dear parent. . . . During nearly five years that I have lived with him his lips have never opened but to speak words of love to me and mine . . . and every action of his life towards me has been dictated by affection and kindness. You will not wonder, then, that I mourn to heave him.

The new First Lady dazzled Washington society, and huge crowds gathered for all her events. Julia immediately demonstrated her skill as an accomplished hostess. She organized her social events as if presiding at court in Europe, borrowing customs she observed while touring England and France. Her sister Margaret, cousins Mary and Phoebe Gardiner, and young Alice Tyler functioned as her court, musicians greeted guests with regal compositions, and the White House staff and coachmen were attired in fancy livery. These attendants escorted her in a regal coach pulled by four horses. (It was said that the new First Lady used more horses and finer ones than the Russian ambassador and other visiting dignitaries.) Likewise, in an effort to boost her husband's sagging political stock, Julia ordered a band to play "Hail to the Chief" whenever Tyler was introduced to his guests. The custom stuck and remains popular today. Eager to please her guests and delighted with her new role, Julia's beauty, youth, vivaciousness, and happy demeanor endeared her to the capital city's political elite.

Amidst the extravagant balls and galas, where the First Lady donned opulent gowns, exotic feathers in her hair, and, in the fashion of queens, jewels on her forehead, the public quickly overcame its surprise at the wedding and shock of the age difference between the president and First Lady. Her beauty was on everyone's lips, as noted by Jessie Benton Fremont, wife of the politician John Fremont, who commented, "Miss Gardiner was very handsome and has retained great health and youthfulness of appearance." Even James Buchanan, the future president, noticed that Tyler's glum mood had lightened, commenting that the "old sourpuss" had himself "a belle and a fortune."

The criticism that she did receive was largely because of a social calendar that was perhaps a bit too full with parties that were "over the top." Because of the large crowds that showed up for her events, the First Lady was forced to limit the guest lists but in so doing made the functions only even more exclusive and upset those unable to attend. Julia could also be snotty and self-absorbed and went too far in having a raised platform with a queenly chair arranged for her to use when greeting "her" guests. Trunks of gowns, diamonds, and jewels were purchased along with an exotic Italian greyhound as a pet. But, mindful of the legacy of Letitia Tyler, Julia typically wore the colors white (satin) and black (lace), suitable for periods of mourning. She failed, however, to tone down her public displays of affection for her new husband.

After years of neglect, the presidential mansion was redecorated with expensive French furniture. Julia even used part of her fortune to do so. Ironically, she is credited with introducing the polka and waltz at her social events—the very dances that her husband had earlier condemned as immoral. A New York composer arranged a piece dubbed "Julia Waltzes" in her honor, popularizing the dance in America, and the press began referring to her as "Lady Presidentress." Indeed, she was the first presidential spouse to sit for a daguerreotype, a predecessor to photography, and she had the foresight to hire professionals to assist her with her social functions and with the press, becoming the first person in the White House to set up regular interviews with reporters and use what amounted to press releases. Recognizing that she was a poor speller and writer, Julia enlisted the support of her sister, Margaret, who functioned as the First Lady's private secretary.

Julia loved politics and supported her husband's decision to annex Texas. In fact, to build support for annexation, she lobbied Congress, distributed copies of the resolution to key individuals in the capital city and important friends of her family in New York City, and sat in the visitor's gallery during congressional debate on the issue. Tyler even attributed the passage of the annexation measure to Julia's efforts, giving her the gold pen he used to sign the proclamation annexing Texas. She made it into a necklace and wore it in public, including at a party she hosted in honor of the signing. One political cartoon showed the country's newspapers standing at a fork in the road, one way to reelection and the other path to defeat. But on the path was Texas with an image of Julia walking down that path.

Julia's most famous moment as First Lady, however, was a grand New Year's Day reception held in 1845. She had invited 2,000 guests, but 3,000 turned out for a party where wine was served by the barrel and dozens of bottles of the most expensive champagne complemented a veritable feast of fine foods. The party was applauded as the grandest event held in Washington since Dolley Madison was First Lady. Julia also billed the event as Tyler's "farewell" celebration, and the unpopular president even quipped, "Yes, they cannot say now that I am a president without a party!" While Tyler was threatened with impeachment and is remembered by historians as a failed president, Julia's experience in the White House was quite different. Although she spent only eight months as the First Lady, Julia Tyler established herself as one of the most celebrated hosts in the history of the White House.

First Widow of the Confederacy

The president and the First Lady departed the capital city after the inauguration of the new president, James K. Polk, on March 3, 1845, and stayed in a nearby hotel before traveling to the Tyler home, Sherwood Forest. Back in Virginia, Tyler's neighbors, much like his daughters, failed to warm to Julia, also finding her to be too haughty. In Julia's defense, part of the cool treatment was because she hailed from the North, and communities across Virginia and the South rarely opened their arms to Yankees in the three decades leading up to (and after) the Civil War. In their "retirement" at Sherwood Forest, Julia eventually won over most of her neighbors through a combination of her willing acceptance of all things southern and her indefatigable personality.

Five of Julia's seven children were born in the Old Dominion State, and she busied herself serving as mistress of a large, thriving plantation with her children—David "Gardie" (born in 1846), John Alexander (born in 1848), Julia (born in 1849), Lachlan (born in 1851), Lyon (born in 1853), Robert (born in 1856), and Pearl (born in 1860). The couple encountered financial problems, and Tyler went back to his prepresidential legal practice to supplement their income. But the marriage remained strong, and Julia always referred to her husband as "The President."

As the fever of disunion swept the country, the Tylers were front and center in the debate. Julia became a leading defender of slavery and the southern cause, writing scathing letters to abolitionists and publishing articles in newspapers. After the *Southern Literary Messenger* published one of Julia's opinions in February 1853, a series of letters were exchanged between the former First Lady and prominent women in Britain. Such notable women as the countess of Carlisle, the duchess of Sutherland, the countess of Derby, Viscountess Palmerston, and Lady John Russell replied to the 1853 publication with an open letter from the women of Britain criticizing slavery and calling for abolition. But Julia responded aggressively, telling the women that Britain had no right to tell Americans what to do and that they should tend to their own problems, pointing to numerous social challenges in the British Isles. She also reminded them that slavery started when America was a British colony, and she denied the harsh image of slavery presented in the famous book *Uncle Tom's Cabin*, maintaining incorrectly that the book was misleading.

When secession occurred in 1861, Tyler was elected to the Confederate Congress. The two prepared for war, standing staunchly behind the South. Julia had the foresight to collect her husband's political papers at the beginning of the war and store them in a bank vault in Richmond. Tragically, however, the bank was destroyed during the fighting. Julia's two oldest sons dropped out of Washington College to join the Confederate army. Both survived the war and prospered in the postwar years, with David serving as a successful attorney, Virginia state senator, and member of the U.S. House of Representatives and John Alexander serving as a military officer and, later, mining engineer.

Their father, however, fared less well. Tyler suffered a stroke shortly after his election to the Confederate Congress. Nonetheless, he was not deterred and departed for Richmond in January 1862 to assume his duties. With her husband gone, Julia had a terrible dream on the evening of January 9 that John Tyler was dying. So the next day she traveled to Richmond, where, to her relief, she found her husband in good health. But on January 12, Tyler became seriously ill and passed out. His physician, Dr. William Peachy, diagnosed the malady as a "bilious attack of bronchitis." Severely weakened, Tyler returned home with his wife, but the trip took its toll, and Tyler died on January 18 at the age of seventy-two. A failed president, his legacy was further tarnished by his firm support for slavery. A part of his legacy would, however, survive in that he was the most prolific of presidents, fathering sixteen children, fourteen of whom survived to maturity, including his last child born when Tyler was seventy years old.

Julia suffered greatly with her husband gone and never fully moved beyond his passing. The family also suffered from the war. Although she had been given a vast fortune when she married, her husband had accumulated sizable debts, and Julia spent wildly on luxurious clothing and jewelry, lavish furnishings, the finest carriages, and expensive trips to spas such as White Sulphur Springs and Point Comfort. When Commodore Beverly Kennon presented the Tylers with the yacht *Pocahontas* as a gift, Julia had the crew dressed in the finest livery and the craft redecorated. As such, during the outbreak of hostilities, Julia was forced to sell off her properties at a lower value to cover her debts. With her children ill, she was forced to flee to New York for their safety, sneaking through a northern blockade. Four of Julia's children were sent to live with relatives while she and her youngest visited her mother in Gardiner's Island. However, Julia continued to support the Confederacy and write letters against the Union, even trying to spy for the South. On more than one occasion, she was almost arrested.

As the war was coming to a close, Julia's mother died in October 1864. Although Mrs. Gardiner never accepted her daughter's southern sympathies, she changed her will on her deathbed in order to leave most of her fortune to Julia. Julia's brother, David Lyon Gardiner, challenged the new will in court, claiming that his mother was angry with her daughter, but Julia manipulated with "undue influence" their dying mother. The case dragged on in court for three years until a New York court ruled in 1867 that the revised will was void. However, the following year, the New York Supreme Court divided the Gardiner estate in order to grant Julia her fair share.

By the middle of the war, Julia was destitute, having lost everything in the fighting. During the three years that the family will remained in court, Julia struggled mightily. Returning home to Virginia, she found Sherwood Forest damaged and looted and was forced to sell it at great loss to the government. Julia proceeded to fight for a pension, taking up the issue repeatedly with Congress. However, she was denied because of her close ties to the Confederacy. In 1870, however, Mary Todd Lincoln was voted a special pension by Congress, so Julia again pursued the cause. Finally, after years of requests, she was granted $1,200 in 1880. It was Julia's lobbying, along with the assassination of President James Garfield in 1881, that convinced Congress to take care of presidential widows. Beginning in 1882, Julia and other widows received an annual pension of $5,000.

Throughout her life, Julia worked diligently to keep her husband's memory alive and enjoyed the successes of her children, especially her oldest, David, who was her favorite child. Julia's visitors were forced to endure a proud mother bragging endlessly about her children. Her son, Lyon, went on to become the president of the College of William & Mary, his father's alma mater. Julia sent her two eldest sons to Germany to be educated and was forced to send her daughter and namesake to a convent in Canada because of the sexual flirtatiousness the young girl apparently inherited from her mother. It did not work, and as a teenager, Julia married a debt-riddled farmer named William Spencer. Sadly, Julia died in childbirth in 1871 at the tender age of twenty-one, and this took a toll on her mother's mental health.

The widow was plagued later in life from rumors that she participated in supernatural ceremonies and believed in the occult. It is hard to determine the basis for the rumors and whether they were true. Julia moved to Georgetown and had joined her husband's Episcopalian church. She became increasingly religious and then converted to Catholicism. She also often discussed her dream only days before her husband's death that foreshadowed his passing. Late in life, she returned to Richmond, but her health declined throughout the 1880s. Julia passed away on July 10, 1889, while staying in the same hotel in Richmond where her husband had stayed only days before his death. She was buried next to her husband.

James Buchanan was fussy and fastidious, including when he was painted, such as in this painting from the end of his presidency. Engraved by permission from the original by J. C. Buttre. Library of Congress Prints and Photographs Division, LC-USZ62-96357 DLC.

⇥ 8 ⇤

"The Siamese Twins"

I'm too shy to express my sexual needs except over the phone
and to people I don't know.

—Comedian Gary Shandling

A WEDDING TRAGEDY

By 1815, James Buchanan was an up-and-coming attorney in Lancaster, located in the rolling farmlands of southeastern Pennsylvania. A few years before, at the age of twenty-three, he had been elected to the Pennsylvania statehouse, making him the youngest member of the legislature. The political exposure helped his law practice, as is evident from the fact that he raised his rates considerably at this time and took on powerful clients. In 1816, Buchanan joined a successful law practice and quickly emerging as the leader of a Masonic Lodge, one of Lancaster's foremost citizens, and perhaps the town's most eligible bachelor despite the fact that he did not actively court women.

The irony was that this most eligible bachelor was uncomfortable in the company of young women. But he was also awkward around young men, seemed to have anxieties about his sexuality, and tended to overcompensate by being unnaturally loud and wild, even dancing on tabletops at taverns. Such was the case during his regular boozing sessions with pals like Molton C. Rogers, the son of Delaware's governor.

Buchanan relished the attention he received by Lancaster's leading families, many of whom made it known to him that their daughters were available and interested. Still, Buchanan remained a bachelor and showed little interest in women other than when their attention bolstered his vanity. All that changed when his pal Molton Rogers introduced Buchanan to Anne Caroline Coleman. It was in 1818, while Rogers was courting Eliza Jacobs, daughter of a wealthy family living in Lancaster, that he introduced the two. Anne was Eliza's cousin, and Rogers arranged for Buchanan to escort Anne when the couples attended social events.

Anne was quite the catch for the ambitious Buchanan. Although not considered to be beautiful, with black hair, slight features, and dark, alluring oval eyes, Anne was thought to be somewhat attractive. She also happened to be the daughter of one of the wealthiest men in the country. Both Buchanan and Anne were beyond the marrying age of the time—Anne either twenty-two or twenty-three (accounts vary) and Buchanan already twenty-nine. This was considered very old for an unmarried man, especially one who had never courted much less ever been engaged.

The two were introduced in 1818 at a grand ball held at the White Swan Inn in town, and through the coming months their relationship grew. Buchanan joined Anne on sleigh rides, at lavish parties and dinners thrown by Lancaster's leading families, and at mansions owned by Anne's father. Although he was intensely ambitious and, at six feet tall and with blond hair, considered attractive as a young man, Buchanan felt that he might be courting above himself. And Anne's finances convinced his apprehensions.

Anne was still unmarried, perhaps because of her complex personality that included mood swings ranging from "proud and self-willed, tender and affectionate, quiet and introspective, or giddy and wilde." She also had a father who tended to be overly protective and suspicious of any of her suitors. Robert Coleman had migrated from Ireland in 1764 at the age of sixteen with little more than the clothing on his back. Industrious but hot tempered and vindictive, Coleman had prospered beyond his wildest imagination. He had a reputation for being very difficult and had driven away all four of his daughters' previous suitors. Perhaps he recognized their ulterior motives and financial intentions, for Coleman himself had married well. His wife Margaret came from money and a powerful political family. In 1809, Coleman moved his wife and nine children to Lancaster and set up iron factories in the area. He also served as a trustee at Dickinson College, Buchanan's alma mater. As such, Coleman would have been familiar with Buchanan's mixed record while at the school, yet another reason to oppose the union with his daughter.

By the end of the summer of 1819, Buchanan and Anne Coleman were engaged, as were their friends Molton Rogers and Eliza Jacobs. Both couples planned elaborate weddings, although Anne's seventy-one-year-old father and mother remained unconvinced about the intentions of their future son-in-law. The problem began when Buchanan traveled to visit his family in Mercersburg to inform them of the engagement. He then traveled to Bedford Springs, a scenic vacation spot with lakes and luxury hotels.

Eventually arriving back in Lancaster, he claimed not to have time for Anne because of pressing business matters, although he did have time to travel and vacation.

At that time, Buchanan was representing the Columbia Bridge Company, which was involved in an expensive lawsuit. Given the financial panic of 1819 that swept the country, Buchanan threw himself into the case in order to win a lucrative settlement. The case took him back to Philadelphia, resulting in Buchanan not seeing his fiancée through the fall of that year.

Not surprisingly, Anne and her parents were worried, and the town began to gossip. One scholar speculates that Buchanan may have had cold feet, citing Buchanan's "negligent treatment" of Anne as a source of strain in the relationship, concluding that he "seemed more interested in his legal and political career than he was in her." A neighbor of the couple recalled the reason for Anne's hesitancy being "that Mr. Buchanan did not treat her with that affection that she expected from the man she would marry, and in consequence of his coolness she wrote him a note telling him that she thought it was not regard for her that was his object, but her riches."

Suicide?

Buchanan again departed on business, and the town's gossip suggested that he may even have been seeing another woman. Although this is highly doubtful, Anne had heard the same rumors. Various letters that survive from that time provide a clue as to the source of the problem—Mrs. William Jenkins. One letter, written by the niece of Mrs. Jenkins, describes the incident:

> Some time after the engagement had been announced, Mr. Buchanan was obliged to go out of town on a business trip. He returned in a few days and casually dropped in to see . . . Mrs. William Jenkins, with whose husband he was on terms of intimate friendship. With her was staying her sister, miss grace hubley, . . . a pretty and charming lady. From this innocent call the whole trouble arose. A young lady told Miss Coleman of it and thereby excited her jealousy. She was indignant that he should visit anyone before coming to her. On the spur of the moment she penned an angry note and released him from his engagement. The note was handed to him while he was in the courthouse. Persons who saw him receive it remarked afterward that they noticed him turn pale when he read it. Mr. Buchanan was a proud man. The large fortune of his lady was to him only another barrier to his trying to persuade her to reconsider her rejection of himself.

Anne ended the engagement and was depressed for days afterward. It appears that her mother suggested she travel to Philadelphia with her younger sister, Sarah, in order to take her mind off the difficult situation. In Philadelphia, the girls would visit their older sister, Margaret, and take in the cultural sites of the city. Anne agreed, setting off for Philadelphia on December 4. But Buchanan was too busy to see her or try to dissuade her, eventually succeeding with a sizable settlement in the Columbia Bridge Company case two days after Anne's trip. Unbeknownst to him, Anne had died in Philadelphia shortly after arriving. Their mutual friend Judge Thomas Kittera described the tragedy in his home city of Philadelphia, writing in his diary,

> At noon yesterday, I met this young lady on the street, in the vigour of health, and but a few hours after her friends were mourning her death. She had been engaged to be married, and some unpleasant misunderstanding occurring, the match was broken off. This circumstance was preying on her mind. In the afternoon she was laboring under a fit of hysterics; in the evening she was so little indisposed that her sister revisited the theatre. After night she was attacked with strong hysterical convulsions, which induced the family to send for physicians, who thought this would soon go off, as it did; but her pulse gradually weakened until midnight, when she died. Dr. Chapman, . . . says it is the first instance he ever knew of hysteria producing death. To affectionate parents sixty miles off what dreadful intelligence—to a younger sister whose evening was spent in mirth and folly, what a lesson of wisdom does it teach. Beloved and admired by all who knew her, in the prime of life, with all the advantages of education, beauty, and wealth, in a moment she has been cut off.

On December 9, a messenger arrived from Philadelphia with the awful news of Anne's death at her sister's home, suddenly and around midnight. Word of the death spread through Lancaster like wildfire, and a variety of explanations were given, including illness or heartbreak, accidental overdose of laudanum or chloral hydrate, and suicide. The general consensus was summed up by one neighbor's gossipy letter: "Mr. Buchanan did not treat her with that affection that she expected from the man she would marry." Indeed, even Buchanan's pals thought that he was only after Anne's money, and the town blamed Buchanan for Anne's death.

Like many of those in town, one woman wrote of the former couple, "I believe that her friends now look upon him as the murderer." The Coleman family concurred—for good reason: Anne was only twenty-three and had been in good health, and she was in the company of her family and a physician when she died. However, the medical diagnosis of her "hysterical convulsions" and other evidence allows for the very real possibility that she took her own life. It is worth noting that Anne's younger sister would later commit suicide after her father broke off her engagement.

Anne's obituary in the *Lancaster Intelligencer & Weekly Advertiser* appeared on December 11, 1819, and stated, "Departed this life, on Tuesday morning last, in the 23rd year of her age, whilst on a visit to her friends in the city of Philadelphia, Miss Anne C. Coleman, daughter of Robert Coleman, Esquire, of this city." The death notice in the *Lancaster Journal* the day prior read that she had died "very suddenly, on Wednesday night last, whilst on a visit to Philadelphia in the 22nd year of her age, Miss Ann Coleman, daughter of Robert Coleman, Esq., of this city." It appears that Anne died of a laudanum overdose around midnight on the evening of December 8, 1819.

Anne's body was brought back to Lancaster on December 11 and buried at the St. James Episcopal Church the next day. Many people attended the service. One of them, however, was not Buchanan. Anne's father refused to allow Buchanan to attend the funeral or be a part of the procession afterward. Buchanan was hurt, but it was more his pride and public image than love that caused him pain. He seems not to have even tried to comfort Anne or repair the damaged relationship. Nor did Buchanan ever offer an explanation for his behavior or an apology. His feelings around this time have more to do with his own injured sensitivities.

Aware of the anger directed at him in town, Buchanan was unable to face anyone in public, especially Mr. Coleman. Instead, he fled to Judge Walter Franklin's home, where he tried to compose a tribute to Anne. Some accounts suggest that the judge ended up writing it for Buchanan. Others state that a printer who was visiting the judge helped write the tribute because Buchanan was "so disturbed by grief that he was unable to write the notice." Either way, a tribute was published in the *Lancaster Journal* and other papers. Buchanan composed a letter for Anne's father. It appears that either Buchanan never mailed the letter or that Mr. Coleman, still blaming Buchanan, never opened the letter and returned it to the sender. It was addressed to "My dearest sir" and read,

> You have lost a child, a dear dear child. I have lost the only earthly object of my affections without whom life now presents to me a dreary blank. My prospects are all cut off & I feel that my happiness will be buried with her in the grave. It is now no time for explanation but the time will come when you will discover that she as well as I have been much abused. God forgive the authors of it. My feelings of resentment against them whoever they may be are buried in the dust.
>
> I have now one request to make & for the love of god & of your dear departed daughter whom I loved infinitely more than any human being could love, deny me not. Afford me the melancholy pleasure of seeing her body before its interment. I would not for her would be denied this request. I might make another but from the misrepresentations which must have

been made to you I am almost afraid. I would like to follow her remains to the grave as a mourner. I would like to convince the world & I hope yet to convince you that she was infinitely dearer to me than life. I may sustain the shock of her death but I feel that happiness has fled from me forever. The prayer which I make to god without ceasing is that I yet may be able to show my veneration for the memory of my dear departed saint by my love respect & attachment for her surviving friends.

May Heavan bless you & enable you to bear the shock with the fortitude of a Christian.

Many years later as an old man, Buchanan gave orders to the executors of his will to burn all letters with Anne. All were destroyed except the one written to Anne's father on December 10, 1819, regarding Anne's death. Questions remain as to why it was not sent by Buchanan, whether it was sent, and, if so, why it was unopened and returned by Mr. Coleman and why it was never burned by the executors of the Buchanan will. We still do not know the answers.

A few days after the funeral, during the early dawn hours, Buchanan slipped out of town on a stagecoach and headed west to Mercersburg to see his family. He was described as being "numb" and "confused" at the time. Buchanan also understood that he could not possibly remain in Lancaster over the holiday season. One resident of the town wrote of the situation, "After Mr. Buchanan was denied his requests, he secluded himself for a few days and than sallied forth as bold as ever. It is now thought that this affair will lessen his consequence in Lancaster as he is the whole conversation of the town." Indeed, Buchanan did regain his composure and returned to the town, busying himself in 1820 with his work. Ironically, the scandal further raised his profile, and his reputation as someone who preferred work over love actually served to help his business.

Although his pride and vanity were hurt, his heart seems not to have suffered. His character did harden after Anne's death, and he became a more serious individual. Buchanan started writing darkly and matter-of-factly from then on, seeing hardship as inevitable in the world. For instance, he was fond of saying that "it is better to bear the ills we have than to fly to others we know not of."

A Closeted President?

Questions beyond whether Anne committed suicide remain. While Buchanan was struck by Anne's death, it always seemed that his vanity rather than his heart suffered. As best as we can tell, Buchanan was not one to visit Anne's grave or try to repair his relationship with her family and friends.

Nor did he hang Anne's portrait in his home or keep a locket containing her likeness. Visitors today to Buchanan's home, Wheatland, see a lovely portrait of Anne, painted by the artist Thomas Sully. But this was displayed by the home's staff long after Buchanan's death and less for historical accuracy than for tourism. Neither Buchanan's political career nor his ambition was derailed by Anne's death.

Few questions were ever raised about the circumstances of Anne's death outside of those living in Lancaster. Buchanan never married—the only president never to do so. Indeed, he never seriously courted women or showed any emotional or physical interest in them. It is doubtful that Anne's death was the reason for Buchanan's lifelong status as a bachelor. Rather, her death, in a cruel way, deflected questions about his sexuality and his disinterest in women. Instead, Buchanan's heart-wrenching remarks that Anne was "the only earthly object of my affection" and "my love is in the ground" served as romanticized reasons or excuses for never again courting and remaining single. Accordingly, Buchanan was largely able to avoid questions about his bachelorhood.

All of this raises the question of Buchanan's sexuality. While there is no direct evidence one way or another about Buchanan's sexuality, there are ample indicators that Buchanan may have been homosexual or perhaps celibate. He neither displayed nor seems to have enjoyed physical or emotional intimacy during his life, and he was described as "eunuch-like" with "endomorphic features" of both the body and face, "characteristic of asexual men with low testosterone." Buchanan's critics commonly joked or attacked him for his sexuality, noting, among other attributes, his "shrill, feminine voice, and wholly beardless cheeks." Indeed, Buchanan's "baby face" was such that he never had to shave.

Buchanan biographer Jean Baker sums up Buchanan's lack of affection and attention toward his fiancée and the fact that he never married: "His reasons may have involved sexual preference, for there has long been suspicion that our only bachelor president was a homosexual." Historian Shelley Ross echoed these suspicions, while the noted historian Paul Boller Jr. agreed that Buchanan was effeminate and something of a wimp. But Boller suggests that the fifteenth president may not have been homosexual and probably did not have sex with men. Rather, Buchanan simply showed homosexual inclinations and may have been asexual.

So too has the popular press largely ignored this facet of Buchanan's life. A study of the history of homosexuality by Neil Miller titled *Out of the Past* does allege that the first openly gay person in the United States to run for political office (the San Francisco Board of Supervisors) occurred in 1961, but Buchanan may have been the country's first gay president. However, the issue has been largely ignored by historians and forgotten by history. As to why, Buchanan's biographer offers a reason: "Overall, given the importance of his administration, James Buchanan has not attracted much historical interest, mostly because his successor's story is so compelling and his so dismal." But it is a story to tell, and some of the evidence regarding Buchanan's probable homosexuality is compelling.

OLD BUCK

Buchanan's father, James, was an orphan who emigrated from Ireland at age twenty-two in 1783. He married Elizabeth Speer, a Scotch–Irish Presbyterian and neighbor of his brother. Mrs. Buchanan was a refined woman who was well read for a woman of the times, while her husband owned a small store and invested in land, eventually doing rather well for himself. Their son, James, was born in 1791 at a frontier outpost near Cove Gap in Pennsylvania and was the second child but oldest surviving child of eleven Buchanan children. In 1794, the family moved to Mercersburg, where Buchanan spent his formative years.

While both parents emphasized reading and a solid education for their son and instilled in him their high hopes for his future success, they were overly indulgent of him even through his teenage years. Consequently, James was somewhat spoiled, soft, and sheltered and would later have a sense of self-entitlement. Mrs. Buchanan was also very religious and emphasized morality in the upbringing of her children; one of her sons even became a preacher. Interestingly, even though James decided against a career serving God, he was always attracted to older male role models, including preachers. One of the earliest influences in his life was John King, a charismatic and popular Presbyterian minister in Lancaster. Later, in college, he sought out the mentoring of James McCormick, his professor at Dickinson College.

Getting Schooled

Buchanan was an intelligent young man and an excellent student. In 1807, at the age of sixteen, he enrolled at Dickinson in nearby Carlisle. The town and campus were known more for the drunk revelers who prowled the streets than for anything else, and Dickinson was then a struggling backwater college with very few students. Some of the new buildings on campus were lost to a fire, and the entire campus was in a period of turmoil when Buchanan began his studies there. Only forty-two students showed up on campus that fall, discovering that few dormitory rooms were ready for them.

The school employed only three professors. In fact, the situation was so dire that Jeremiah Atwater, Dickinson's new president, would curse the campus, saying, "I hope that as god has visited other states, he will yet visit Pennsylvania." Buchanan echoed his campus president, complaining that the college "was in wretched condition."

Professor McCormick was Buchanan's favorite teacher. A math professor and friend of the students, McCormick allowed several of the students lacking accommodations to stay at his home, where his wife cooked for them. Despite the conditions of the campus, Buchanan commenced his studies with high hopes but was soon distracted by the social scene and regular visits to taverns. The irresponsible youth, who was always uncomfortable around his male peers, resorted to acting out—he drank wildly, began smoking cigars, destroyed property, and even threw food like a child in the school cafeteria. He noted that "to be a sober, plodding, industrious youth was to incur ridicule of the mass of the students." Buchanan's self-described major became "mischief."

Buchanan received a shock the summer before his senior year at Dickinson when his father informed him of a letter from the campus president saying that James had been expelled for bad behavior. The Dickinson Board of Trustees backed the expulsion. Buchanan's no-nonsense and overly protective father was rightly angry with his son and sent young Buchanan to talk to Dr. King, his minister, and Professor McCormick. Both men seem to have offered the wayward lad "a gentle lecture." Fortunately for Buchanan, the Reverend King intervened on the student's behalf but made him pledge on his honor to behave. In truth, Dickinson was so strapped for cash and students that the trustees were quick to readmit him.

Buchanan returned to school that winter, more serious and intent on graduating. Despite his misbehavior, Buchanan was so bright (and the student body so poor) that he was at the head of his class. But the fact that things came easily for him and that he managed to avoid responsibility for his actions only exaggerated his confidence, arrogance, and sense of privilege. He graduated on September 25, 1809. But graduation was not enough. So conceited was Buchanan that he demanded to receive at the graduation ceremony both the school's honors—the literary award sponsored by the Union Philosophical Society and the Belles-Lectures Society award.

The faculty was outraged by his arrogance and felt that Buchanan's unruly behavior disqualified him. Buchanan had been the unanimous choice for the first award, but the faculty withdrew his name, as he refused to accept responsibility for his actions and dismissed the faculty's judgment. Instead, he resorted to lobbying for himself and threatening to lead a student boycott of the ceremony if he did not win the second award too. The entire campus was whipped into controversy by the scandal until Buchanan's father intervened and counseled his son to accept defeat with grace. A compromise was reached: Buchanan would call off the protest, joint award winners would be announced, and Buchanan would be able to speak at graduation along with the other award winner. Even though Buchanan ultimately backed down, he immaturely used the opportunity to speak at commencement to make fun of the college, president, and faculty. Later in life, Buchanan dismissed his youthful indiscretions as being under the influence of popular but rowdy boys at school and claimed that he was but "a clever and spirited youth."

Vanity and Arrogance

It is difficult to understand James Buchanan's rise in politics when one considers his numerous personality flaws, chief among them his vanity and arrogance. For instance, when he traveled back home to Mercersburg to bury his father and, as the eldest son, take care of family affairs, he became angry when he discovered that there was no will and that he was expected to assume guardianship for some of his less fortunate nieces and nephews. Buchanan did not want the responsibility and seemed never to show empathy, compassion, or love, even in the case of family affairs and even when he had the means to provide for his relatives. Rather, he was selfish and self-centered. This characteristic reflects his own father's belief and paternal advice that "the more you know of mankind the more you will distrust him." Indeed, like his father, Buchanan would become a pessimist.

Growing up, James had few close friends. This would remain true later in life. Even the rowdy gang of boys with which he associated in college was more for show and seems to have been but a way to push back against authority and overcompensate for his lack of masculinity. He was a loner and intellectual but one who was often uncomfortable in the company of fellow politicians and intellectuals. As such, he exhibited the dangerous trait of wanting to surround himself with individuals who did not challenge him, something that would later hurt his presidency. He also wrestled with questions of morality, thinking often about religion and wanting to be a Christian, but he only gave lip service to such concerns and never considered himself to be a believer. All this is consistent with Buchanan's struggle with his own identity.

As a loner, Buchanan was never given a nickname by friends or peers—although late in his political career, he was referred to as "Old Buck" or, less popularly, "Old Public Functionary." Neither name was meant as a compliment. In the nation's capital city, Buchanan also gained a name among the city's political elite, "Aunt Nancy," a common slang term in the nineteenth century for someone who was gay.

Physically, Buchanan was tall and slightly heavyset and had a ruddy complexion. He was considered handsome. His white hair was always worn in a particular fashion—short, neat, and jutting up and outward on top—and he could be excessively particular about his appearance and downright fussy about clothing, food, and furnishings. Indeed, he was an impeccable dresser and was known for his cultured manners. Buchanan always wore the exact same style of white shirts and black suits and preferred that his collar be meticulously starched and turned up. Only the latest and best fashions were used, including his fixation with silk stockings and handkerchiefs as well as fine liquors and cigars. So particular was Buchanan that he regularly returned items that were not of his taste or brand and even let it be known which brands and styles were to his satisfaction. This fussy and vain streak in him is something that anyone who encountered Buchanan immediately noticed.

Buchanan's prickly and prissy demeanor comes through in his letters, such as the letters he wrote in 1847 spreading rumors about Pennsylvania's governor. In a letter to Jesse Miller, a former congressman from Pennsylvania and the state's secretary of state, Buchanan complains about his rivalry with the governor. After bad-mouthing his opponent and grumbling that the governor appointed someone Buchanan did not like, Buchanan claimed that the disagreements would not affect any of his friendships and that he would act honorably. Yet Buchanan cannot help himself. He continues his whining, saying, "It is true I thought [the governor] had gone a little too far in formally proclaiming his neutrality between that 'blathering' dastard Frazer and myself. He might have felt neutral: but I should rather he had not expressed his feelings. But no matter. Enough of this." Buchanan concludes the letter by getting snippy with Miller's wife, saying, "Tell Mrs. Miller I feel greatly indebted to her for her invitation; but would have been much more gratified, had it arrived in time to enable me to accept it."

Not surprisingly, Buchanan has been described in a number of ways that are anything but flattering, including excessively formal, very fastidious, prissy, aloof, fastidious, haughty, distant, reserved, pessimistic, and weak. Some of his letters, including his memoir, were even written in third person. Buchanan grew to be overly sensitive to criticism and was emotionally fragile and incapable of revealing his feelings, even to those who knew him the best.

One possible explanation for his aloof demeanor was that he was very conscious of his one eye, which had a habit of wandering. He was also nearsighted in one eye and farsighted in the other. Because of his condition, which is known as exodeviation, Buchanan always cocked his head to one side.

Buchanan had few firm views on politics or religion and was not an ideologue. Rather, he was practical but struggled with making decisions.

Despite his long and successful career in politics, he was not adroit politically, held only vague beliefs and views on political issues, and was often plagued by confusion and indecision. Of course, the flip side to these traits was that Buchanan was capable of approaching issues and decisions in a very lawyerly manner and did not let passion govern his actions. He was also dull. While others might enjoy hiking, studying nature, or fishing, one of Old Buck's favorite pastimes was simply to sit alone in his bedroom and look out the window at a nearby stream. He was a dull man utterly lacking in hobbies, friends, and convictions.

One particularly interesting example of Buchanan's famous indecisiveness and pettiness occurred between Buchanan and Andrew Jackson. Although Jackson was from Tennessee, the two men were aligned politically to the extent that the *Kentucky Gazette* even suggested Buchanan as Jackson's vice president in the 1832 election. Jackson ultimately offered Buchanan the U.S. ministership to St. Petersburg, Russia. The message was delivered in late May 1831 by Jackson's good friend Secretary of War John H. Eaton.

Buchanan had much to consider, including how the post positioned him for a run at the presidency and the practical matter of having to leave William Rufus King, his partner of many years. But he was incapable of making a decision and offered numerous excuses and delays. For instance, Buchanan wrote back to Secretary Eaton on June 4 worrying that he did not know French (the language of diplomacy) well enough and complaining of his many other pressing responsibilities. Of course, Andrew Jackson never responded well to disagreement and had Secretary Eaton immediately dispatch another letter on June 7 saying that Buchanan's alleged responsibilities and concerns "can no doubt be remedied."

But then Buchanan shifted his focus and expressed worry that it was too late in the season to travel to St. Petersburg. The exchanges continued ad nauseum, with Eaton informing Buchanan that he should depart in spring when the ice breaks. Jackson eventually lost his temper with Buchanan's hesitancy and whining, instructing his aide to tell Buchanan to prepare to depart "unless something more than is now expected arises when the President will rely on Mr. Buchanan's patriotism to proceed!" Shockingly, Buchanan continued to whine, writing back again on June 12 and resigning himself that "I can no longer hesitate to accept the Russian mission." Yet he goes on to worry about his language skills and the gossip directed at him regarding the appointment. Finally, on June 15, Eaton informed Buchanan that Jackson fired off a "hasty note" that "is quite like himself, candid & frank." The president demanded in a terse tone that his hesitant appointee "go on & make his preparations, & let the newspapers make any comments that they may think proper, & mind them not."

While Buchanan wisely stopped writing back to the president and Secretary Eaton, he did continue to complain about the appointment and worry about the gossip to other politicians. His complaining continued nonstop while in St. Petersburg. However, the complaints had some validity. Conditions for the American minister were spartan, and he was even unable to get American newspapers. Also, Buchanan's mother had hoped that her son would not go to Russia, and she ended up dying in the summer of 1833 with her son overseas and unable to visit her. It is also likely that Buchanan missed his partner King. At one point, a dejected Buchanan reported to the president in his usual complaining tone that he was "nearly fagged out." Of course, the term held a different meaning at the time.

THE WOMEN IN BUCHANAN'S LIFE

At times, Buchanan seems to be asexual. In his voluminous collection of papers and letters, he does not discuss love or lust, women, or physical attractions. There were, however, a few rumors that were associated with Buchanan. For instance, as president, Old Buck was touring the country. Secretary of the Interior Jacob Thompson, describing the tour, noted that Buchanan "kissed hundreds of pretty girls which made his mouth water." One rumor was that Buchanan was having an affair with the widow of President James K. Polk—Sarah Childress Polk. However, Mrs. Polk emphatically denied the charge, remained loyal to her husband and his memory, and, in fact, never really thought highly of Buchanan. The rumor is baseless.

In an exchange with Mrs. Francis Preston Blair in 1837, Buchanan wrote a curious letter in response to her invitation to a social event, saying, "I would gladly join your party to the Hermitage next year . . . but long ere that time I expect to be married and have the cares of a family resting upon my shoulders." The reply is puzzling because we know of no love interest of Buchanan's or even any serious interest in ever marrying, and he did not mention it elsewhere. The likely explanation is that Buchanan was simply saying what would be socially expected of him.

There are really only two women other than Anne Coleman with whom Buchanan was ever linked in a romantic way. One possibility would be Mary Kittera Snyder, the niece of Thomas Kittera, Buchanan's friend in nearby Philadelphia with whom he stayed when he was in town on business. Thomas Kittera lived with a widowed mother and sister named Ann. Kittera also took care of three young orphan girls, one of whom was his niece, Mary. Letters from Buchanan to Kittera often include a comment about Mary. One of the letters, however, does contain a line that suggests that they were more than acquaintances. Buchanan asked his friend to "be particular in giving my love to my intended." The likely explanation was that Buchanan was simply teasing with the young girl, something that he did often and from the safe vantage point of someone who was more an adopted uncle. Not that Buchanan ever seemed serious about the union with Mary, but one of the drawbacks for him would have been that he might have to care for Mary's siblings. It was not in his nature to accept such responsibility. Interestingly, young Mary's sister, Elizabeth, would later marry one of Buchanan's friends named van Dyke.

The other woman was Anna Payne, the nineteen-year-old niece of none other than the legendary First Lady and Washington socialite Dolley Madison, who would have been an important political catch for any ambitious politician. In 1842, Anna became "seriously interested" in Old Buck. Anna lived in Lafayette Square with her famous aunt, and they were fixtures of the city's social and political scene. One of Buchanan's biographers suggested that Buchanan may have considered marrying Anna had it not been for the dramatic age difference. Both Mary Kittera Snyder and Anna Payne were much younger than Buchanan, something he joked about in a poem he composed for Anna:

> In thee my chilled and blighted heart has found
> A green spot in the dreary waster around
> Oh! That my fate in youthful days had been
> T'have lived with such an one, unknown, unseen,
> Loving and lov'd t'have passed away our days
> Sequestered from the world's malignant gaze!
>
> A match of age with youth can only bring
> The farce of "winter dancing with spring."
> Blooming nineteen can never well agree
> With the dull age of half a century.
> Thus reason speaks what rebel passion hates.
> Passion—which would control the very fates.
> Meantime, where e-er you go, what e-er your lot
> By me you'll never, never be forgot.
> May heaven's rich blessings crown your future life!
> And may you be a happy, loving wife!

One of Buchanan's biographers suggests that "whether Buck became attached to [these women] remains an unsolved puzzle." However, it seems rather clear that Buchanan never felt romantically or passionately about any woman. These two rumored romances were likely just political ploys to advance Buchanan's career. He even admitted to the advantage of courting a woman around the time of his Senate and presidential campaigns. Even these rumored romances were dismissed by his contemporaries in part because he always had an "excuse" to avoid courting in general. In typical Buchanan fashion, he was also more concerned with his own money and did not want it being spent on these young women or their families. Moreover, Buchanan was not only worried but also upset about the cost of supporting his own orphaned nieces and nephews. Indeed, the only women Buchanan ever showed any interest in were the older society women with whom he gossiped, and his interest was purely in the gossip. The only women whom Buchanan seemed to appreciate were his housekeeper and his favorite niece, Harriet.

In 1834, Buchanan moved into one of the homes where he used to court Anne Coleman. We do not know if Buchanan thought about her because he did not comment on it, but surely he would have been haunted by memories of her. Buchanan's concern at this time was for a permanent full-time housekeeper. One of the places Buchanan frequented was the old White Swan Hotel in Lancaster's downtown, and while there he inquired about the inn's employees. The owner of the inn recommended that Buchanan hire his niece, Esther Parker, known to Buchanan as "Miss Hetty."

Miss Hetty, twenty-eight at the time, was working at the inn and has been described as "clean, neat, happy in disposition, and a fine cook and housekeeper." Miss Hetty lived at the White Swan and started working for Buchanan, who then asked her to live in the large, quiet home while he was away serving in the U.S. Senate. Old Buck came to depend on his housekeeper, who remained in his employ until his death thirty-four years later.

Harriet

The other woman who knew Buchanan best was his niece, Harriet, who moved to Buchanan's home, Wheatland, in 1849 and remained in her uncle's service through his presidential years. Harriet Rebecca Lane, born on May 9, 1830, in Mercersburg, was the youngest of five children born to Buchanan's sister. After his sister's death in 1839 and their father's death the next year, Buchanan became the guardian of his nieces and nephews. The children decided where they would live and selected various relatives, something that Buchanan encouraged them to do (he did not want them), but Harriet picked her favorite uncle, "Nunc" Buchanan.

Buchanan promoted his niece's education, encouraging her love of reading and introducing her to the classics and British literature. But Harriet's youthful passion was politics, and she grew up talking politics with her uncle and meeting the leading public figures of the day. Her interest in both politics and older politicians simultaneously shocked and flattered many of the powerful men she met who were quite unaccustomed to young women with such interests and opinions. Indeed, Harriet developed a reputation as boisterous, opinionated, confident, and flirtatious. Buchanan sent his niece to Misses Crawford's Boarding School because of its emphasis on discipline, something Harriet needed. Sure enough, she soon wrote to her uncle protesting his choice of schools. As described by Laura Carter Holloway Langford, Harriet complained of "early hours, brown sugar in tea, restrictions in dress, stiff necks and cold hearts." Eventually, Buchanan sent her to another boarding school in Lancaster, then to a school in Charles Town, Virginia.

At age eighteen, Harriet moved to Wheatland with her uncle and became his personal hostess during his long political career. She joined him in the British Court of St. James when he served as U.S. minister during the presidency of Franklin Pierce. Harriet was very popular in London and was a notorious flirt with the political leaders she met. As a result, Harriet attracted many suitors, including the former Lord Chancellor Sir Fitzroy Kelly, who was fully forty years her senior and thoroughly charmed by young Miss Lane. However, Buchanan discouraged the romance because of this age difference. She was also a personal favorite of Queen Victoria, who called her "Dear Miss Lane" and extended every courtesy to her as if she were the wife of the U.S. minister.

A few years later, during Buchanan's presidency, Harriet served as the White House hostess, again endearing herself to the public and proving to be quite capable. A steamboat was named in her honor, and Harriet became one of the most popular names for young girls in the 1850s. However, Harriet was known as much for her scandalously low-cut dresses and for her political savvy as she was for her social graces, earning the nickname "Our Democratic Queen." During a visit by the Prince of Wales, Harriet made news on both sides of the Atlantic when the teenage prince fell hard for his twenty-something hostess. The two were seen dancing the night away at the White House, with the prince's head buried in Harriet's ample, exposed cleavage.

Buchanan seemed to enjoy his niece's skills as a hostess and recognized her influence and popularity, even as his own base of support evaporated and his administration became embroiled in scandals and ineptness. Their relationship was close, and the two exchanged many letters that reveal as much. While Old Buck provided fatherly advice to his niece, these letters also reveal his passion for social gossip and take on an odd tone—one that bordered on being creepy—not expected of an older man and young female relative. For instance, Buchanan often discussed the social scene with his niece and was intrigued by her relationships and experiences, commenting that it would be "quite romantic and interesting to witness your exploits." His interests seem almost voyeuristic—wanting details—rather than paternalistic—looking out for her best interests.

Harriet stayed with her uncle through his presidency and ended up marrying late. In October 1864, as the Civil War wound down, Harriet became engaged to Henry Elliot Johnston, a prominent citizen in her home state of Pennsylvania. The two were married on January 11, 1866, by Buchanan's brother, the Reverend Edward Y. Buchanan, at the Oxford Episcopal Church in Pennsylvania. After a honeymoon in Cuba, the newlyweds moved to Baltimore. The initial years of her marriage were happy for Harriet, as she enjoyed the birth of two children and her husband made a fortune as a banker.

Harriet was named her uncle's beneficiary after his death and inherited his Wheatland estate, but she was hit very hard by Buchanan's death. Tragedy continued, as her fifteen-year-old son, who had been named for Buchanan, died of rheumatic fever on March 25, 1881. This was followed on October 13, 1882, by the death of her son, Henry, of the same illness and at the tender age of thirteen. On May 4, 1884, Harriet's beloved husband died unexpectedly of pneumonia. Somehow Harriet survived these four tragic losses.

Late in life, Harriet sold both Wheatland and her Baltimore home and moved to Washington, D.C., where she devoted herself to philanthropy. While in London during her uncle's ambassadorship, Harriet developed a strong passion for exotic art from the Orient, India, and Africa and began collecting art. With her vast fortune, Harriet amassed one of the finest international art collections in America. When she bequeathed her collection to the Smithsonian Institution, her art helped form the basis of the National Gallery.

Another one of her passions was the plight of the American Indian, and Harriet promoted native cultures and advocated on behalf of education and medicine for reservations. So well recognized as a leader on this topic was she that many Indian families named their children for her, and the Chippewa referred to her as "great Mother of the Indians." Harriet's charity also helped found the Saint Alban's School and Choir in the nation's capital city, and she supported other children's issues in the region. For instance, Harriet established the first children's hospital and the Harriet Lane Home for Invalid Children in Baltimore. Today, her efforts became a part of the Johns Hopkins Hospital. Harriet died on July 3, 1903, in Narragansett Pier, Rhode Island.

"MR. AND MRS. BUCHANAN"

There were a few men who shaped Buchanan's life and for whom he displayed great affection. One of them was his childhood pastor at the Presbyterian

Church in Mercersburg, Dr. John King. The Reverend King was the most influential person in Buchanan's formative years, and he also served as a trustee at Dickinson College in Carlisle, where he was instrumental in both Buchanan's decision to attend the school at age sixteen and the school's decision to readmit Buchanan after he had been expelled.

King was witty and charismatic yet down to earth and was much admired by his congregation. Buchanan, in particular, was entranced by the young minister. Although he would never be an ardent practitioner of religion, Buchanan's lifelong interest in religion and Christianity was inspired by King, stating that he had "never known any human being for whom I felt greater reverence than for Dr. King." King was also perhaps the first older man that set Buchanan's heart aflame.

But it was another King—William Rufus de Vane King—who became Buchanan's friend, roommate, counselor, colleague, life partner, and perhaps lover. Although both were politicians and senators, Buchanan's King should not be confused with Senator Rufus King, one of the signers of the U.S. Constitution.

William Rufus King was five years older than James Buchanan and was elected to Congress in 1819, the same year that Anne Coleman died and just two years before Buchanan won election, so the two men served together for many years. King represented North Carolina in the U.S. House but then moved to Alabama, where he was the new state's first U.S. senator. They first met in 1821 after Buchanan's election to Congress and immediately became very close friends and, later, one another's closest confidante in Congress. At the urging of Buchanan, they lived together in Washington. The couple boarded at Mrs. Ironsides' Boarding House on Tenth and F streets. Some members of Congress—bachelors or those whose wives were unable to join them in Washington during legislative sessions—occasionally shared a room at a boardinghouse. But Buchanan and King lived together for the next sixteen years, even though both were older and quite wealthy and were from different states and opposite parts of the country, making their rooming arrangement unusual among their colleagues. Other than a brief time when they had two politicians from Virginia board with them, the two were inseparable.

King's influence on Buchanan's politics stretched even to the issue of slavery. Despite coming from a part of Pennsylvania known for its support for abolition—an area that welcomed slaves from the famous Underground Railroad—Buchanan became an ardent defender of the South and adopted King's view that slavery helped "civilize" blacks. It was because of King that Buchanan became a moderate but pro-South on such issues. Writing to Buchanan, King stated that the problem was that the North kept "agitating" and, as a result, "then we will separate from them." Buchanan also adopted King's mannerisms and romanticized view of southern culture filled with aristocratic gentlemen farmers, the social class divisions of plantation life, long meals with even longer conversation, and slow, southern manners. Biographer Jean Baker sees King as Buchanan's political mentor, leaving "an indelible impression on him."

So close was their friendship and political alliance that, in 1844, Buchanan planned to run for president and wanted King as his vice president. Both men were intensely ambitious and intertwined their political careers, supporting one another for president and vice president. Buchanan even pushed friends, politicians, and newspapers in Pennsylvania to oppose their interests and support a southerner, King, for vice president. Because of Buchanan, his home county in Lancaster did vote for King, but the rest of the state went for Van Buren and Johnson.

Because of their political ambitions, the two were forced to be apart from one another, such as when King accepted the position of U.S. minister to France. During that time, King wrote back to Buchanan in 1844 that "I am selfish enough to hope you will not be able to procure an associate who will cause you to feel no regret at our separation." His use of the word "associate" is vague but seems obvious. The two were likely in love and suffering from the separation. Buchanan sent a letter to France on May 13, 1844, saying that he feared the mission to France would require King to "stay longer than your friends would tolerate." It was obvious that Buchanan was pining away for both King and his good friend Mrs. Roosevelt, who was also in France, where she visited King. Buchanan wrote to Mrs. Roosevelt, "I envy Colonel King the pleasure of meeting you & would give any thing in reason to be of the party for a single week." Both King and Buchanan were always cautious and cryptic in their exchanges, sometimes writing in an awkward tone as if they did not even know one another, likely to cover up the true nature of their relationship.

King ultimately was picked as Franklin Pierce's vice president in 1852, and this produced in Buchanan mixed feelings in part because of King's declining health. King had to travel to Cuba in an effort to treat his tuberculosis, becoming the only vice president in American history to take the oath of office on foreign soil. Tragically, King would become one of the shortest-serving vice presidents in history, dying only forty-five days into his term.

Buchanan, who never revealed his feelings, nonetheless seems to have been deeply hurt by King's death. He did describe his late partner: "He is among the best, purest, and most consistent public men I have ever known, and is also a sound judging and discreet fellow," adding that King was "a very gay, elegant looking fellow."

With his partner gone, Buchanan never seems to have found another friend, counselor, or lover to replace King. After King's death, Buchanan wrote an uncharacteristically revealing letter to one of his gossip pals, Mrs. James J. Roosevelt, wife of the New York Supreme Court justice who served as U.S. district attorney in New York City during Buchanan's presidency. Cornelia Roosevelt, as the daughter of Cornelius P. van Ness, the former governor of Vermont, was from one of the country's leading families. She was a gossip queen and one of Buchanan's favorite gossipers. The two exchanged many letters, sounding like two old hens clucking, one of them on Buchanan's loneliness after King's death. Says Buchanan,

> I am now "solitary and alone," having no companion in the house with me. I have gone a wooing to several gentlemen, but have not succeeded with any one of them. I feel that it is not good for man to be alone; and should not be astonished to find myself married to some old maid who can nurse me when I am sick, provide good dinners for me when I am well, and not expect from me any very ardent or romantic affection.

The description in Buchanan's letter of pursuing another male companion after King's death seems unmistakable and points to the probability of a gay relationship. Buchanan was very cautious in his letters, never revealing much about his feelings or relationships, but he appears to have let down his guard with Mrs. Roosevelt, someone with whom he was more open and sincere in letters. She was one of his closest friends, as is evident from the warm manner in which he closed the previously mentioned letter: "Believe me that wherever you roam my kindest regards will follow you & no friend on earth will greet your arrival in your native land with more joy than myself. Ever you friend most Sincerely & Respectfully." It is obvious that Buchanan was missing both his gossip partner and his life partner.

The letters that have survived between Buchanan and King do point to a special relationship. But the problem is that both men avoided discussing personal feelings to the extent that many of the letters are written in a cold, formal tone. For instance, Buchanan often avoided any small talk, failed to ask how King was doing, did not inquire into personal matters, and did not share any information on how he was doing. This is very odd indeed. Few people who know one another, much less live and work together, fail to mention a single personal item such as the usual pleasantries about health, weather, family, or friends. Moreover, Buchanan and King were at times writing from different countries and had not seen one another in months. Utterly lacking any social niceties, the only conclusion is that the two were going to great lengths to hide any detail of their relationship. Even when Buchanan wrote to King, who was in France, to congratulate him on his service and provide news from President Polk, Buchanan's letter is devoid of any humanity or social tone and is signed in the format that Buchanan used for professional letters to people he did not know well: "I am, Sir, respectfully, Your obedient servant, James Buchanan."

Unfortunately, history may never know the full answer, as many of the surviving letters exchanged between them appear to have been burned by their nieces, Catherine Ellis and Harriet Lane. We are left with hearsay, Washington gossip, and letters from third parties to piece together the full extent of their relationship.

Washington Gossip

Buchanan and King were described as "inseparable," and professor and author James W. Loewen even dubbed them the "Siamese Twins," echoing the joke that Washingtonians shared about the couple. Buchanan referred to their relationship as a "communion." They even shared temperaments and tastes. Both men were soft, effeminate, and eccentric; had a passion for silk handkerchiefs and stockings; were very meticulous about their tastes in clothing, food, and their appearance; and could be haughty and aloof. Historian Paul Boller described their prevailing traits as "fastidious" and "fussy."

As expected, the "conspicuous intimacy" between Buchanan and King was subject to rumors and countless jokes in official Washington about their sexuality and their relationship. One newspaper described how King's "fastidious habits and conspicuous intimacy with bachelor Buchanan gave rise to some cruel jibes." Washington politicians referred to them as "Buchanan and his wife" or "Mr. and Mrs. Buchanan," and it was common to hear politicians describe them with such slurs as "Aunt Nancy," a slang term for being gay, and "Aunt Fancy." None other than Andrew Jackson called King "Miss Nancy," and during Buchanan's presidency, the wife of one of Old Buck's cabinet members referred to the president as "Old Gurley."

Aaron Brown, a Tennessee Democrat, former law partner of President James K. Polk, and close friend of Polk's wife, Sarah Childress Polk, often called King "Buchanan's better half" and referred to Buchanan as "Mrs. Buchanan." The congressman wrote letters back to the Polks in Tennessee to keep them informed of both the official and the unofficial business of Washington, noting in one letter during 1844 that politicians were mocking Buchanan and King to their faces about their effeminate temperaments. Mrs. Polk always felt that the Buchanan–King relationship was abnormal and suspect, and Congressman Brown described the teasing as occurring "in the presence of Mr. Buchanan and his wife." In another letter marked "confidential" and written to Mrs. Polk, the congressman described in detail a public spat between Buchanan and King and the interest it generated in the city. In the letter, he repeatedly refers to both men as women and in the feminine tense of "she" and "her":

> Mr. Buchanan looks gloomy & dissatisfied & so did his better half until A little private flattery & a certain newspaper puff which you doubtless noticed, excited hopes that by getting a divorce she might set up again in the world to some tolerable advantage. Since with casual events, which she had taken for neat and permanent overtures, Aunt Fancy may now be seen every day, triggered out in her best clothes and smirking about in hopes of securing better terms than with her former companion.

Brown was not the only one to describe Buchanan and King as women. Rather, it was somewhat common and not just among Washington politicians. In January 1861, a letter from a constituent to his congressman in Pennsylvania complains about President Buchanan, saying, "I do not share in the confidence which some entertain in poor Betsy Buchanan. She is very weak, and I fear, very bad." Elsewhere in the letter, the word "his" was written but then crossed out and replaced with "her." The author goes on to complain about Buchanan's handling of the war by saying, "The shame of leaving it to her cabinet whether he should or not recall his troops" and "let her publicly deny (if she dare) her south Carolina rebels, not to increase her force!"

There are a few interesting observations to be made about Buchanan's letters and his sexuality. The first is that Buchanan not only was the brunt of jokes and gossip but also seemed to revel in gossip in a way that is rarely associated with men. As a favored pastime, Buchanan had a circle of gossipy women from high society with whom he dished the dirt. Perhaps the preferred outlet for his gossip, as mentioned earlier, was Mrs. Cornelia Roosevelt, the wife of the New York attorney and judge. Buchanan routinely sent news of what he described as the "gay world of Washington" to Mrs. Roosevelt. After her departure for Europe, Buchanan complained to his gossip partner, "How changed for me the gay world has been since you left." Even though the term "gay" did not in the nineteenth century denote homosexuality, Buchanan was nonetheless keen on such effeminate and colorful descriptions.

This tone is found in numerous letters. For instance, another one of Buchanan's female pen pals was the socialite Miss Eliza Watterston. He writes to Eliza, "I have this moment received your saucy letter of the 13th and although about to leave home, cannot deny myself the pleasure of giving it a brief answer . . . I regret that I must be off; for I feel in good trim to write you a long gossiping letter." Miss Watterston confided in Buchanan about her love life, and he enjoyed hearing of her romances, saying in one letter that her "poetic lover must be in a bad way." He also continues with the same tone, apologizing in that letter for not "sooner answering your charming, sprightly and gossiping letter." On another occasion, Buchanan says to Eliza, "Now about what can I write which would interest you? . . . We have had a little gaiety in our good old town of Lancaster in which I have participated; but nothing has occurred in our provincial fashionable world which could interest you for a single moment." Another one of Buchanan's favored gossipers was the widow Mrs. Jane Slaymaker. The two gossiped constantly, and Buchanan looked forward to her letters while he was serving overseas, as she provided him with the social dirt he so enjoyed. For example, in one letter to Mrs. Slaymaker, Buchanan said that in St. Petersburg one can "scarcely know anything" except for the contents of her letters. He goes on to say of her letters that nothing "could have afforded me more greater solicitude." One of their favorite topics was to gossip about the royals, especially Empress Catharine, whom Old Buck said "lacked religion," something that, he reasoned, was "the surest safeguard of female virtue." As a result, the two agreed that they "cannot with truth defend [her] chastity." Buchanan informed Mrs. Slaymaker that the Russian royals were stark-raving crazy—he found Paul a crazed tyrant and Alexander a libertine, but as to the sitting emperor, Buck was enamored, describing him as "the finest looking man, take him altogether, I have ever beheld."

The second interesting and odd point is that, even though he is fascinated with social gossip, Buchanan often avoids social events, preferring to complain that he does not have the time to attend them, but this was not true. Buchanan, who often opted for a quiet evening alone or the quiet company of William Rufus King, solicited the gossip about others but always made excuses as to why he could not personally attend functions.

A third and final point about Buchanan's correspondence is that, while Buchanan enjoyed writing to older women in order to gossip and enjoyed hearing gossip about women, he does not describe women in any of his letters. For instance, Old Buck wrote often to his trusted housekeeper Miss Hetty and shared gossip with her, but whenever he discussed a woman, he would mention only that the individual was a woman. His letters curiously lack description, as in a letter to Miss Hetty that said only that "the ladies whom I meet treat me with much civility and kindness."

Yet Buchanan often describes men in great physical detail and notes certain features and traits. This is even true for men who were not political leaders. For example, when mentioning that he had hired a butler in London, Buchanan discussed that the African butler, Jackson, "has behaved himself very well. He is very attentive & I think perfectly honest. He is a good looking mulatto." Buchanan does not fail to notice an attractive man but never mentions attractive women.

Nowhere is this more evident than in Buchanan's descriptions of a monk he met on a visit to a monastery during his ministerial duties in St. Petersburg. When not exchanging gossip with older women, Buchanan's letters are often formal and excessively dry. During his time in England in the early 1850s, he missed America, and his tone was often gloomy, even writing that he had thanked God that he "was born in America rather than an Englishman." This was also the case in the 1830s while Buchanan was the American minister to St. Petersburg. Reading Buchanan is like watching paint dry. But his letters about a certain monk are markedly different.

Before Buchanan departed from St. Petersburg in August 1833, he toured Russia. In his diary, he describes in brief the schools, architecture, and people he saw. But then Buchanan met Father Antoine, the abbot of a monastery he toured in June, and devoted more detail, pages, and excitement to this meeting than he did any other topic with the exception of his interest in the royal family. It is clear that Buchanan was impressed and smitten with the friar, saying, "In my life I have never beheld a more heavenly expression of countenance." The father spoke no English or French but did not need to, as Buchanan was breathless in his mere presence and Buchanan also had an interpreter named Mr. Gretsch.

The American minister described the abbot as approximately thirty-five years old, intelligent, modest, and unassuming. Likewise, "his long beard was of a most beautiful chestnut color, and made his appearance venerable not withstanding his comparative youth." Even though the two had barely met and communicated through an interpreter, Buchanan gushed, "I shall never forget the impression which this man made upon me."

Buchanan retells the story, over and over, in letters, and each time he does it, he describes the father and the kiss he received from him in excited and vivid detail. Buchanan even expressed his interest in the history of the fort and adjacent monastery, although he mentions only in passing the other rectors and church leaders he met. In one letter, Buchanan described, "Upon taking leave of Antoine, I submitted to be kissed by him according to the Russian fashion, first on the right cheek, then on the left, and then on the mouth. This was my first regular experiment of this kind." To a close friend in Congress, Old Buck also shares the details of meeting the monk and of the kiss: "From him I submitted to the operation of being kissed, first on the right cheek, then on the left—& finally plump on the mouth. This is the general custom of the Country; but it was my first experiment of the kind." Buchanan then proceeded to sing the father's merits. Even in a letter written from St. Petersburg to his brother, Edward, back in Pennsylvania, Buchanan devotes more detail and attention to his impression of Father Antoine than to the fact that the brothers' mother had just passed away.

THE BUCHANAN LEGACY

Presidency

Historians have rated Buchanan's presidency as one of the worst in American history, and some of the scholarly polls even list Buchanan as dead last among presidents. Indeed, if not for how bad his presidency was, it is doubtful Buchanan's presidency would be remembered at all.

Buchanan's anemic leadership is surprising when one considers how successful he was throughout his professional life. For example, he did well in college despite a lack of effort, his law practice was hugely prosperous, and he amassed a good amount of money. Buchanan seemed blessed by good fortune, such as when mentors helped him get back into college after he was dismissed, and he was lucky enough to be able to apprentice under James Hopkins, perhaps the best attorney in the region when Lancaster was functioning as a temporary capital for Pennsylvania. So too was Buchanan's political career successful. He won numerous elections, including those to the Pennsylvania state legislature in 1814 and 1816, five terms in the U.S. House of Representatives, and a dozen years in the U.S. Senate from 1833 to 1845. He also served as an ambassador, being appointed in 1831 to the post in Russia and two decades later in England, and was President James K. Polk's secretary of state from 1845 to 1849.

Buchanan tried several times to secure his party's presidential nomination but was unsuccessful in doing so, as his popularity was mixed, and while he was long in the résumé, he was short on accomplishments. But Buchanan benefited by the fact that he was a prolific letter writer and had built a base of support and important contacts across the country through his writing. He also benefited by luck. By 1856, the country was so fed up with the disastrous deal made by the Missouri Compromise and the bloodshed in Kansas that they were ready for something else. Buchanan had been out of the country, a fact that he had worried would hurt his chances, but it ended up ironically helping him get elected. Both North and South were ready for anyone but those in Washington.

But, successful as he was in obtaining all these posts, Buchanan's body of work was far less than impressive. For instance, as secretary of state, Buchanan was a very poor diplomat and was the main author—along with John Y. Mason, the U.S. minister to France, and Pierre Soule, the U.S. minister to Spain—of the Ostend Manifesto, named for the city in Belgium where it was presented to the world community in October 1845. All three diplomats were proslavery and pro-South and were thus motivated to promote this embarrassing document calling for the United States to take Cuba by force if Spain did not relinquish control of the island. Spain, it seemed, was both unwilling and unable to suppress its colonial slave populations. Southern slave owners had long worried about slave uprisings in the Caribbean and the ramifications for successful revolts in the American slave population. They also did not want another Haiti—an independent black state that overthrew European colonization and slavery—on their southern doorstep. Ultimately, Spain took Buchanan's measure as an insult, and the United States backed down.

Buchanan did not enjoy his problematic tenure as Polk's secretary of state, but by the same token, Polk had a very low opinion of Buchanan, as he indicated in his diary. As secretary of state, he also ham-fistedly tried to seize additional lands from Mexico in 1848. The relationship with Polk was strained, and Buchanan continued to oppose much of what the president did. Not surprisingly, Polk grew to regret appointing Buchanan. Old Buck handled the stress very poorly, developing a nervous tic and a number of health problems that required multiple hospitalizations and surgeries during his tenure at the State Department. As Buchanan stated to one friend, "I have wished 1000 times that I had never entered this Department as Secretary." Old Buck could not make tough decisions.

Buchanan's presidency seems to have been doomed from the outset. The country was being torn apart by the bitter sectionalism over the slave question, and Buchanan, who was elected president on November 4, 1856, saw his office not as a means to serving the country or way of leading on the issues but simply as the final jewel in his formidable crown. The presidency was the end goal, not the means to a greater end, and Buchanan lacked the energy and temperament to see the office as anything but.

Another part of the problem for Buchanan was that he was weak and indecisive. Timid and conflict avoidant, Buchanan always shrunk from controversy and relied on others to make decisions for him. This is apparent in that he started his political career as a Federalist but moved 180 degrees to wind up as a Jacksonian. Buchanan was unable to manage and motivate those around him and lacked conviction about most issues of the day. He also surrounded himself with the wrong people and was easily coerced into acting. For instance, when Buchanan was president, one of his friends, Congressman Thomas Florence of Philadelphia, talked Buchanan into swapping lucrative government contracts for political support, something that he readily did. Likewise, Buchanan's aides and supporters paid off newspapers and handed out government printing contracts to them in order to suppress negative stories. Buchanan's administration wallowed in public bribes and kickbacks, overpayments for friendly contractors, and awarding governmental and naval contracts for political favors.

The House of Representatives investigated Buchanan and his aides. Led by Committee Chair John Covode, a fellow Pennsylvanian, they found ample evidence of corruption, wrongdoing, patronage, and bribery, making the administration one of the most corrupt and worst in history. There was also the matter of Buchanan's secretary of war, John Floyd, who used his office for personal financial gain and as a platform for advancing his friends. When the War Department's finances did not add up, it became clear that the secretary had to be fired and prosecuted. But Buchanan asked others to take care of the decision for him, and when Floyd still refused to resign, the president backed down.

The corruption that dogged Buchanan was such that, while campaigning for office, reporters and a pamphlet in his home state dubbed Old Buck "Ten Cent Jimmy." Even his Presbyterian church back in Lancaster refused to allow him membership because of his support for slavery. Buchanan had alienated any natural base of support in the North because he blamed the North for agitating southern slave owners and tried to avoid a position on all critical issues, such as the *Dred Scott* Supreme Court case. He was known as a "dough face," which was a northerner who was pro-South and could, like dough, be molded to do the bidding of southern plantation owners.

So prevalent were his abuses and mistakes that, on June 13, 1860, Buchanan was censured by Congress. In fact, Buchanan's corruption and ties to the "good ol' boy" network were so shameful that it helped Abraham Lincoln run as an anti-establishment candidate in 1860. With his cabinet paralyzed by incompetence and a lack of leadership and his administration plagued by scandal and corruption, Buchanan did not seek his party's renomination in 1860. By the end of his presidency, he had utterly given up trying to save the Union or prevent war, and no one on either side of the debate paid him any attention. In his last annual message, delivered on December 3, 1860, the president still blamed the North for southern succession. No one was listening.

Buchanan's party lost the election to an upstart party and an uneducated rail-splitter from Kentucky by way of Illinois. Buchanan was exhausted and disgraced, commenting to Mr. Lincoln on Inauguration Day, "My dear sir, if you are as happy on entering the White House as I am on leaving, you are a very happy man indeed." On April 12, 1861, only weeks after Buchanan slunk out of the capital city, the Rebels fired on Fort Sumter in South Carolina, and the Civil War began.

Buchanan and King

In 1861, Buchanan retired unceremoniously to Wheatland, where he was condemned by the northern press. However, Buchanan faded from public interest, and he died in relative obscurity given the fact that he had been president. He spent his final years quietly at Wheatland and worked on his memoirs, which were published in 1866. In them, he barely tried to defend his failed presidency, insisting that he had done his best and that he was "satisfied" with himself. In more than 300 pages, Buchanan offers little, blames others, and appears not to understand the severity of his mistakes. Shortly before his death, Buchanan confided to a friend, "I have always felt and still feel that I discharged every public duty imposed on me conscientiously. I have no regret for any public act of my life, and history will vindicate my memory."

Historians have been rightly harsh on Old Buck, considering him to be perhaps the worst president in U.S. history. His legacy is utterly tarnished, and he has been all but forgotten—Buchanan is one of the least known and least studied of the American presidents. One of the few scholarly works on Buchanan, by author James W. Loewen, is excessively critical of Buchanan. Even the history preserved by the James Buchanan Foundation and his Wheatland home, a history that Loewen believes ignores Buchanan's sexuality and abysmal record, has difficulty defending the man. There is a biography of Buchanan, written by George Ticknor Curtis, that is overly friendly, but it was authorized by descendants of Buchanan's siblings and has been completely dismissed by many scholars.

Forgotten by his country and forever condemned by history, James Buchanan died on June 1, 1868, quietly of pneumonia. He was seventy-seven and passed away alone in his bed at home. The details surrounding his engagement to and breakup with Anne Coleman remain obscure. Apparently, Buchanan had retained Anne's letters in a packet tied with a silk ribbon. During the Civil War, while he was in his seventies, Buchanan may have placed the sealed documents in New York City for safekeeping with the promise that one day he would finally explain his fallout with Anne. After Buchanan's death, the letters were discovered by the executors of his will. They had been separated from his other papers and documents, most of which survive. However, a note from Buchanan requested that Anne's letters be destroyed without being read. They were burned, unopened.

Neither James Buchanan nor his partner William Rufus King enjoyed the company of women outside the purpose of sharing social gossip, nor did they have any interest in courting, marrying, or even dancing with women. But Buchanan was also able to sidestep some of the suggestions about his sexuality and much criticism over his lifestyle because of the poignant story of Anne Coleman's death. The tragedy became something of an ironic excuse for Buchanan never marrying. During Buchanan's presidential campaign, however, his opponents used the catchy ditty, "Who ever heard in all his life, of a candidate without a wife?" But in 1856, Old Buck handily beat his opponent, John C. Fremont.

But attitudes toward homosexuality were far more naive and innocent at the time than they would be in contemporary politics, even if individuals were uncomfortable with the subject. Few people talked about such things, and the probability that Buchanan and King were gay never seemed to hinder either Buchanan, who was the nation's only unmarried president and possibly the first gay president, or King, who was the nation's only unmarried vice president and possibly the first gay vice president, in their political careers. When King died in 1853, the two men had spent twenty-three years together, living much as a married couple would.

Abraham Lincoln struck a majestic pose in this 1864 photograph by Anthony Berger. Library of Congress Prints and Photographs Division, LC-USP6-2415-A DLC.

⊰ 9 ⊱

"I Can Never Be Satisfied"

The Lord prefers common-looking people. That is why he makes so many of them.

—Abraham Lincoln

THE UGLIEST MAN ALIVE

When history discusses Abraham Lincoln, rarely is it in terms of his romances, marriage, and love life. It is hard to imagine the stoic Lincoln courting women or behaving as so many politicians and a few presidents have done. But there was another side to the tall man from the prairie.

Lincoln was generally considered by his contemporaries to be homely, awkward, and even downright ugly. As a boy, Lincoln was rudely called the homeliest child in town, according to his neighbor Alexander Sympson. One young girl who knew Lincoln during his childhood echoed this sentiment, remarking that he was "so awful homely." Later, as a young man in Indiana and Illinois, he was described as "extremely awkward and homely to a marked degree" by J. Edward Murr and similarly by many others. The daughters of the Camron family, neighbors in New Salem, commented rather vividly that Lincoln was "thin as a beanpole and ugly as a scarecrow." Such slights dogged Lincoln his entire life and likely contributed to his insecurity about courting women. Indeed, Lincoln was often tongue-tied and shy around women.

Lincoln's neighbors and especially his political opponents could be downright unkind in their descriptions. Clark Carr said that "the first time I saw Mr. Lincoln I thought him the homeliest man I had ever seen," and in 1858, the Reverend George C. Noyes agreed: "I thought him about the ugliest man I had ever seen." On October 1, 1862, a Union soldier recorded that the president "not only is the ugliest man I ever saw, but the most uncouth and gawky in his manners and appearance." Poor Lincoln!

The disparaging comments on Lincoln's appearance were also the result of his lack of attention to his appearance. As described by his law partner, William Herndon, Lincoln "was not a pretty man by any means, nor was he an ugly one; he was a homely man, careless of his looks, plain-looking and plain-acting." Lincoln's clothing was often rumpled and unpressed, his signature black bow tie frequently crooked, and his hair untidy. Lincoln had naturally wavy and unruly hair, so much so that when he sat for a portrait, the photographer typically had to try and comb his subject's hair. Yet, more than once, Lincoln afterward ran his fingers through his hair to return it to its natural state, telling the photographer that he wanted people to see and know him as he actually looked.

Even the woman who would marry him agreed with the general assessment, saying in 1847 that her beau was "not pretty," but Mary Todd added, "Mr. Lincoln may not be as handsome a figure, but the people are perhaps not aware that his heart is as large as his arms are long." A woman named Lillian Foster agreed, adding, "His face is certainly ugly, but not repulsive; on the contrary, the good humor, generosity and intellect beaming from it, makes the eye love to linger there until you almost fancy him good-looking." An old friend, Charles Coffin, said in May 1860 while Lincoln was campaigning for president that Lincoln's smile was capable of "lighting up every homely feature" on his face. A month later, the Utica newspaper reported a similar assessment, saying, "After you have been five minutes in his company you cease to think that he is either homely or awkward."

For whatever deficiencies Lincoln was alleged to have in the "looks" department, he more than made up with his wit, personality, and intellect. It also helped that Lincoln enjoyed self-deprecating humor. The brunt of his jokes was frequently his own appearance. For instance, Lincoln was fond of saying, "The Lord prefers common-looking people. That is why he makes so many of them." When introducing himself to audiences, Lincoln joked that now that he was onstage and could see the audience and they could see him, he was certain that "I had the better part of the bargain." And when criticized by political opponents as being two-faced, Lincoln was said to have retorted, "If I were two-faced, would I be wearing this one?"

Lincoln agreed with his critics, often describing himself as homely and ugly and rarely missing an opportunity to weave his poor appearance into a joke. One of his favorite stories to tell was that a man had encountered a woman while traveling on horseback, and she said to him as they passed, "Well, for the land's sake, you are the homeliest man I ever saw!" But the man responded, "Yes ma'am, but I can't help that," to which the woman reminded him, "No, I suppose not, but you might stay at home." Lincoln told variations on this story, including the following:

> I was once accosted . . . by a stranger who said "Excuse me, sir, but I have an article in my possession which belongs to you." "How is that?" I asked, considerably astonished. The stranger took a jackknife from his pocket. "This knife," said he, "was placed in my hands some years ago, with the injunction that I was to keep it until I found a man uglier than myself. Allow me now to say, Sir, that I think you are fairly entitled to the property."

There was yet another Lincoln spin on that yarn. A man came up and pointed a gun at him. "Says Lincoln, 'What do you mean?' The man replied that he had promised to shoot the first man who was uglier than himself." Looking at the man's face, Lincoln said, "If I am uglier than you, then blaze away."

The self-deprecating humor points to Lincoln's even temperament, sense of humor, and ability to diffuse tense situations and win over enemies. He often resorted to humor during uncomfortable and difficult situations. One such example was on December 3, 1863, when Lincoln was ill with smallpox. He joked, "There is one consolation about the matter, Doctor, it cannot in the least disfigure me!" Relatedly, when Lincoln was informed by his staff that Secretary of War Edwin Stanton had, in a fit of frustration, disgraced the president by blurting out, "We've got to get rid of that baboon in the White House," Lincoln responded, with characteristic levity and forgiveness, saying, "Insult? Insult? That is no insult. It is an expression of opinion. And what troubles me most about it is the fact that Stanton said it, [because] Stanton is usually right."

"Lincoln's Little Correspondent"

Arguably the most famous story about Lincoln's appearance and his good-natured view of the criticism he received because of it is the letter he received from Grace Bedell. Grace, nicknamed "Lincoln's Little Correspondent" because of the letter, was eleven years old when she wrote to Lincoln and recommended that he grow a beard in order to improve his appearance.

Grace's father, Normal Bedell, who built stoves for a living, had attended a campaign fair in Westfield, New York, in October 1860. There he obtained a campaign pamphlet featuring the pictures of Lincoln and his vice-presidential nominee, Hannibal Hamlin. After bringing the picture home to his wife and six children, it was his precocious daughter, Grace, who decided that she wanted Lincoln to win and that she would write him a letter. And so, on October 15, she penned a letter to Lincoln that was missing punctuation but would change his image in the eyes of history and perhaps even contribute to his victory that November. Wrote Grace,

> My father has just home from the fair and brought home your picture and Mr. Hamlin's. I am a little girl only 11 years old, but want you should be President of the United States very much so I hope you wont think me very bold to write to such a great man as you are. Have you any little girls about as large as I am if so give them my love and tell her to write to me if you cannot answer this letter. I have got 4 brother's and part of them will vote for you any way and if you let your whiskers grow I will try and get the rest of them to vote for you you would look a great deal better for your face is so thin. All the ladies like whiskers and they would tease their husband's to vote for you and then you would be President. My father is going to vote for you and if I was a man I would vote for you to but I will try to get every one to vote for you that I can I think that rail fence around your picture makes it look very pretty I have got a little baby sister she is nine weeks old and is just as cunning as can be. When you direct your letter direct to Grace Bedell Westfield Chatauque County New York

Lincoln answered Grace on October 19, 1860, addressing her as "My dear little Miss." He seemed to pick up on Grace's spunky personality, which was evident in how she closed her letter: "I must not write any more answer this litter right off Good bye." Lincoln signed his warm letter, "Your very sincere well wisher." In the letter, he playfully dismissed her idea that he should cover his face with a beard:

> Your very agreeable letter of the 15th is received—I regret the necessity of saying I have no daughters—I have three sons—one seventeen, one nine, and one seven years of age—They, with their mother, constitute my whole family—As to the whiskers, having never worn any, do you not think people would call it a piece of silly affection if I were to begin it now?

However, as history now knows, Lincoln thought about Grace's advice and decided to grow his signature beard, which, as his eleven-year-old admirer correctly noted, dramatically improved his physical appearance. As for the little girl who quite literally changed the face of history, Grace wrote again to Lincoln four years later. Still precocious, she asked Lincoln for a job in his administration. Only two years later, at age seventeen, Grace married George Newton Billings, a schoolteacher and veteran of the Civil War, and moved to Kansas. There she had a child of her own and lived a full and adventurous life, surviving everything from Indian raids and tornados to droughts and prairie fires.

The Physical Man

Most anyone today who gazes at the famous photographs of the nation's sixteenth president has heard the stories of his unattractive appearance yet has likely found themselves captivated by his commanding yet comforting gaze as well as his stoic yet sympathetic face. And it was not always his face that critics heckled; part of the widespread ribbing that Lincoln received about his appearance was about his ungainly limbs, large ears, and uncommon height.

Lincoln was six feet four inches at a time when men were slightly shorter than in modern times. The ungainly teen passed the six-foot barrier as a boy and was all feet and ears. As one noted biographer said of Lincoln, it was as if "parts of him did not seem to fit." Scholars in recent years have even pondered whether Lincoln had Marfan's disease, which is a congenital malady characterized by abnormal body proportions and seems to describe Lincoln—who was long limbed with a small head and big hands, feet, and ears. In fact, a panel of leading experts and the National Museum of Health and Medicine examined Lincoln's case and stated that the findings were inconclusive one way or the other. Either way, Lincoln suffered from color blindness and a muscular imbalance in one eye that caused double vision and severe headaches. His health problems may also have stemmed from his childhood when he was once knocked unconscious by a vicious kick in the head from a horse and, another time, nearly drowned in a pond as a boy.

But Lincoln's extraordinary height was complimented by an extraordinary physical prowess. Lincoln might have been rail thin, but he was a powerful and energetic man. When he was a child, his father put him to the task of removing rocks from the fields he intended to plow, and Lincoln did the work of ten men, moving tons of rock. He also wielded an ax like it was a third arm and was no stranger to a hard day's work, all of which packed muscle onto his growing frame. Indeed, there are no shortage of legitimate stories and imagined folktales about Lincoln's strength—so many that he emerges as something of a political John Henry or Paul Bunyan.

As friends noticed, Lincoln "enjoyed the brief distinction his exhibitions of strength gave him" and frequently showed off. His relative Dennis Hanks noted, "My, how he could chop! His ax would flash and bite into a sugar-tree or sycamore, and down it would come. If you heard his fellin' trees in a clearin' you would say there was three men at work by the way the trees fell." Another account claimed of Lincoln that he

> was equal to three men, having on a certain occasion carried a load of six hundred pounds. At another time he walked away with a pair of logs which three robust men were skeptical of their ability to carry. He could strike with a maul a heavier blow—could sink an axe deeper into wood than any men I ever saw.

Lincoln was known to wrestle at county fairs, where he proved such an effective foe that he made money at it and may have been undefeated. Once, while traveling on the Mississippi River with a group of young men, Lincoln was challenged by Daniel Needman, a famous wrestler, known for making quick work of his foes. At Wabash Point, Illinois, Lincoln met the man in a contest of strength, and twice threw Needman "with comparative ease, and thereby demonstrated such marked strength and agility as to render him forever popular with the boys of the neighborhood." Because the outcome of Lincoln's wrestling matches was always the same—he won them all—townsfolk later forced him to serve as the referee for matches in order to give other men a chance.

Lincoln was known for demonstrating his feats of strength not only for financial reward or to impress his friends. In typical Lincoln fashion, he put his strength to more honorable ends as well. In the small town of New Salem, where Lincoln lived as a young adult, there was a group of boys known as the "Clary's Grove Boys," who seem to have terrorized the town and anyone unlucky enough to get in their way. Their leader was Jack Armstrong, who was described as "a hardy, strong, and well-developed specimen of physical manhood" and known for "cleaning out" with brute force the places he visited. In a confrontation, Lincoln made quick work of Armstrong and the Clary's Grove Boys.

MAN FROM THE FRONTIER

The Lincolns were uneducated farmers and laborers who settled in the woods of Kentucky. At the time, Kentucky was the wild frontier; Abe's grandfather was even killed by Indians in a raid on a frontier settlement. Thomas Lincoln, Abe's father, owned three small farms and worked as a carpenter. Simple, hardworking, and illiterate, Thomas believed in fulfilling one's civic duty and served on juries, opposed slavery, and continually moved his family in search of better land and opportunity. It was into this hardscrabble family that Abraham Lincoln was born on February 12, 1809, in a simple cabin near Hodgenville, Kentucky.

In every way, Lincoln was a product of the frontier—he was hardy, humble, and handy with tools. Comfort and prosperity continually eluded the family, and Thomas Lincoln was a man who showed no affection or emotion toward his wife or children. Consequently, Abe seemed to be embarrassed by his father and perhaps even his mother. He rarely ever mentioned his father, visited him only a handful of times as an adult, and appears not to have visited Thomas Lincoln's grave site. It was a cold and strained relationship defined almost singly by brutally hard work—Thomas worked young Abraham to the bone.

In 1816, when Abraham was a boy, Thomas moved his family across the Ohio River into southern Indiana. It is possible that he did so because of his dislike of slavery, but it is more probable that he heard of an abundance of affordable, fertile land. He was also experiencing legal problems. Once again, he and his strapping, young son hacked a dirt farm out of the frontier on a small plot of land near Little Pigeon Creek and the town of Gentryville. This is where Lincoln spent his adolescence.

Two years after the move, when Abraham was only nine years old, his mother, Nancy Hanks Lincoln, passed away. So rural was the region where the Lincolns lived that Abraham's father abandoned his children for six months in order to travel in search of a new wife. When Thomas Lincoln returned with bride in hand, he found Abraham and his sister, Sarah, two years his senior, dirty, starved, and living like wild animals. A cousin, Dennis Hanks, who had no family or job, was living with them briefly, but he was utterly unhelpful to the children.

Abe was closer to his mother, and she was the first of three women in his life to die. Her death was a severe blow to the boy, who rarely ever talked about his mother except to note her wretchedly poor and short existence. But it was the young boy who took it on himself to see that his mother had a proper burial. Young Lincoln wrote a letter to her former preacher asking him to come and eulogize her. Shortly thereafter, when the weather improved, the preacher came to preside over a simple service.

Lincoln never said much about his mother. Whether it was to suppress the pain he felt or because he was embarrassed by his family is uncertain. Although he clearly had deep affection for his mother, he may have visited her grave only once and later described her matter-of-factly as missing teeth, having a weather-beaten appearance, being born illegitimately, being illiterate, and suffering a tough life without warmth or love. Lincoln's mother had been taken from her mother and sent to live with an aunt and uncle when she was just a girl. We do know that she was a very tall woman—possibly five feet ten inches—and Lincoln attributed not only his height but also his ambition to her.

Abe was closest to his sister Sarah, whom he called Sary. As such, when she died during childbirth at age twenty, it was a devastating blow to Lincoln, and the emotion of it appears to have worsened Lincoln's chronic battle with depression, which he referred to as "hypo" and was known at the time as "melancholy." Several years later, Lincoln would have two more severe bouts with depression—once when his first, true love died and again when he broke off his engagement to the woman who would eventually become his wife.

It is often suggested by Lincoln scholars that the loss of his mother and sister may have impaired his relationships with women. The loss of his first love a few years later likely only exacerbated the situation. Lincoln could be downright bumbling around women, often hesitated in courtship, and ultimately married quite late. However, some of Lincoln's male relatives and closest friends also seem to have been hesitant about marrying.

The new wife whom Abe's father brought home was Sarah Bush Johnston, and the young boy developed a warm relationship with his stepmother. One of the reasons was that she could read and write and brought a few books to the Lincoln home. Young Abe had virtually no formal education but had a voracious appetite for reading and learning. It seems likely that Lincoln's later skill as a wordsmith comes from reading the likes of Shakespearean plays and the Old Testament as a boy. Indeed, years later, Lincoln would famously put to use his familiarity with Scripture and his photographic memory to the cause of emancipation and leading the nation.

Despite his interest in morality and knowledge of Scripture, Lincoln never belonged to a church and, according to his law partner, William Herndon, "died an unbeliever." As a young man, Lincoln even wrote a scathing tract against religion and viewed Christian doctrine and biblical teachings, such as the story of the flood and Garden of Eden, with skepticism. The many hardships Lincoln faced in life and the loss of so many women he loved likely hardened his heart to faith.

Lincoln was also greatly offended by hypocrisy, self-righteous people, and "fire-and-brimstone" preachers. In 1846, while running for Congress, this side of Lincoln became apparent. One of Lincoln's opponents, a Methodist preacher named Peter Cartwright, famous for heated and judgmental revivals, was in the middle of a sermon when he asked his audience to stand if they did not want to go to hell. All did but Lincoln. Cartwright, apparently seeing an opportunity to embarrass his opponent and make an example of a nonbeliever, called out, "May I ask of you, Mr. Lincoln, where are you going?" To the taunt, Lincoln replied, "Brother Cartwright asks me directly where I am going. I desire to reply with equal directness. I am going to Congress."

Young Lincoln spent fourteen years in Indiana before the family moved to Illinois, again seeking better opportunities. They settled first along the Sangamon River near Decatur, then in 1831 purchased a farm in Coles County near Charleston. Around this time, Abraham moved away from home and rarely saw his father and stepmother again. Two trips on a flatboat down the Mississippi River to New Orleans, one in 1828 and again in 1831, opened the young man's eyes to the larger world beyond the simple frontier farms of his youth and seem to have fashioned his ambition and restlessness.

Lincoln remained in Illinois, living in New Salem and then Springfield, where he famously pursued careers in the law and politics. Lincoln ran for his first public office—the state legislature—only seven months after arriving in New Salem. He lost but ran again in 1834 and won, ultimately serving four terms in the statehouse and one term in Congress. Politically, Lincoln was a Whig who favored an active, stronger role for government and supported projects like internal improvements (canals and roads), a protective tariff, and an expansion of individual rights. He gained fame as a speaker and champion of the common man. So too was he a vigorous and popular campaigner, employing a variety of tactics to win, including running in footraces; refereeing wrestling matches; visiting farms, fairs, and such popular activities as cornhuskings and barbecues; and sitting for hours talking to anyone who would listen. In addition to his political career, Lincoln served as a postmaster (he said so that he could read the papers before having them delivered) and was licensed to practice law in 1836. Lincoln never attended college, nor did he ever formally study the law or know much about the law. But he was a quick study and a vigorous reader who had a gift for gab. By the 1850s, his law practice was enormously successful. Asked by an early biographer to describe himself, Lincoln summed up his life with a line from Thomas Gray, saying, "The short and simple annals of the poor."

ABE'S GIRLFRIENDS

There are too many jokes made at the expense of Lincoln's appearance to tell them all. And there are as many examples of Lincoln's self-deprecating humor. Yet it appears that the man from the frontier had several girlfriends and may have been engaged to his true love, all before ever meeting Mary Todd, the woman who would become Mrs. Lincoln.

At the same time, Lincoln's awkwardness around women is worth examining. The fact that the man who delivered the Gettysburg Address was prone to being tongue tied around attractive young women is rather ironic. Lincoln's trademark eloquence and knack for light storytelling seem to have failed him in matters of the heart. One possible explanation is that Lincoln was insecure. The constant ribbing he took because of his physical appearance, along with his long struggle to overcome poverty (something that turned many a prospective father-in-law against him), surely affected the young man.

William Herndon, Lincoln's former law partner, discussed the matter of his friend's interest in women, saying,

> Mr. Lincoln had strong, if not terrible passion for women. He could hardly keep his hands off a woman; and yet, much to his credit, he lived a pure and virtuous life. His idea was that a woman has as much right to violate the marriage vow as the man—no more, no less. His sense of right, his sense of justice, his honor, forbade his violating his marriage vow. Judge Davis said to me in 1865, "Mr. Lincoln's honor saved many a woman," and this is true to the spirit. This I know on my own knowledge. I have seen Lincoln tempted, and have seen him reject the approach of women.

One of Lincoln's best friends, Joshua Speed, also provides some insight into Lincoln and women. Speed, as well educated, handsome, and popular as Lincoln was poor and awkward, invited Lincoln to live with him. Speed, who was also from Kentucky and was five years Lincoln's junior, first met Lincoln when the tall stranger came into his store in Illinois. Lincoln wanted to purchase provisions but informed the store owner that he was too poor to do so. But Lincoln claimed that he was an attorney and anticipated doing well. As such, if Speed would provide him credit, Lincoln said that he intended to pay him back by Christmas. Speed described looking up at the most "gloomy and melancholy face in my life." But there was honesty and integrity in Lincoln, and Speed invited the new arrival to town to board with him.

Speed noted with amusement that Lincoln, without thinking about the offer, asked the location of the room, then immediately walked up the stairs carrying his saddlebags. A moment later, he came downstairs and announced, "Well, Speed, I'm moved."

The two roomed together for four years, during which time they organized a literary society in town and became fast friends. So close were they that some irresponsible authors have suggested that the two were lovers. There is no evidence for the claim. At the time, it was customary to extend neighborly courtesies to individuals in need of boarding. Also, most boardinghouses had a room with a very large bed that was shared by several men traveling through the town. Such arrangements were as common as someone today staying at a Holiday Inn for the night. However, the spurious rumors about Lincoln's sexuality are largely because Lincoln frequently boarded in such large beds while serving as an attorney riding the judicial circuit and because Speed and Lincoln shared a bed.

Speed and Lincoln courted or, in Lincoln's case, attempted to court young, beautiful, and wealthy women. Lincoln had quite liberated views on the status of women, even recognizing the double standard that existed against women in almost all aspects of life. So too did he advocate equality for women. Yet at the same time, Lincoln was very much drawn to physical beauty and could be superficial in his interests in women. The two friends also appear to have visited prostitutes. One example is in the fall of 1839. Speed had enjoyed the company of an attractive young woman who was a professional. Lincoln, pining away for physical companionship, asked his experienced friend, "Speed, do you know where I can get [one like her]?" Speed answered, "Yes, I do. I will send you to the place with a note. You cannot see her without a note or by my appearance." Lincoln may have preferred a letter of introduction himself, and after Speed gave him the note, the young attorney visited the prostitute.

Lincoln handed the letter of introduction to the woman and asked her how much she charged. When she informed her customer that the price was five dollars, Lincoln admitted that he was poor and had only three dollars. Lincoln apparently made quite an impression on the hooker, who said that she trusted him and offered him a credit of two dollars. But Lincoln was either very honest or very nervous because he informed the young woman that it had been so difficult to gather what little money he had that he did not know if or when he could muster the remaining balance. He told her that he did not want to dishonor or cheat her, to which she replied, "Mr. Lincoln, you are the most conscientious man I ever saw." Some accounts suggest that she offered services to Lincoln "on the house," and it appears that Lincoln had cold feet and excused himself without completing the task.

Lincoln did not tell his friend what happened, but it appears that when Speed again saw his lady friend, she gave him the details. Cold feet or not, Lincoln likely used the services of prostitutes on other occasions. He was even worried at one point that he had contracted syphilis from a prostitute and contacted a Dr. Daniel Drake in Cincinnati for advice. The physician, however, refused to provide medication or advice without first seeing the patient, and the record suggests that Lincoln never went to see Dr. Drake.

For all his likely insecurities and despite the tales of his homely appearance, many women were intrigued by Lincoln, especially married woman who felt the need to cook for the tall bachelor. Indeed, it has been said of the young man that "all [married] women liked Lincoln and he liked them as well." The wives of the leading men of New Salem—Bowling Green, Jack Kelso, Jack Armstrong, and Dr. John Allen—all committed themselves to helping Lincoln marry. These women would not have felt compelled to "fix Lincoln up" with dates had he not had admirable qualities; but there was also a reason they felt the need to assist him. Lincoln was shy and uncomfortable around women.

As has been noted in political biographies of Lincoln, the man possessed an extraordinary intellect and a mixture of the rarest variety of kindness and humility. Lincoln loved to read, could recite from memory with ease verse from plays and great literature, and had a fondness for animals and children. Such qualities were not lost on women. One can only imagine the impact on some women living on the frontier when they met a man who treated them as equal. Uncharacteristic of men at the time and from the frontier, Lincoln did not use tobacco, was not a drinker, and could not even bring himself to hunt or fish because he disliked killing any animal. In so many ways, Lincoln was not the type of man to which women were accustomed. He never mixed with the rowdy boys in town, and he abhorred violence. After once giving a customer the incorrect change at the general store where he was employed, Lincoln walked six miles after closing in order to give the man the money owed him. For this, he earned the nickname "Honest Abe."

Lincoln's sense of honor extended to women. He was not a womanizer and was known for treating women with respect. For example, when Lincoln worked at Speed's general store, he caught a man named Charlie Reavis cursing in front of female customers. Lincoln told Reavis to mind his manners and his vocabulary. Later, when Reavis repeated another string of profanities in the company of women, Lincoln grabbed a plant called smartweed, known for its irritating, poisonous sting, and marched straight to Reavis. Lincoln told Reavis that he had been fairly warned and threw the man to the ground. Lincoln then stepped on his chest to pin Reavis down and rubbed the stinging smartweed in the man's face until Reavis screamed. Lincoln made Reavis promise never to swear again around women. One girlfriend, Ann Rutledge, said to Lincoln that, if women could vote, he would win every election.

Courting

As one biographer said, "To winnow the few grams of truth about [Lincoln's romances] from the stacks of chaff that have been written, and tell the story as it really occurred, is far from being an easy task." True, but Lincoln did court women, and several young girls did fall for Lincoln's charms. Lincoln had at least four girlfriends we know of, all of whom were from Kentucky. He also tried to court above his social status. Two of his girlfriends—Sarah Rickard and Matilda Edwards—were quite wealthy, much like Mary Todd, and were introduced to Lincoln by their sisters.

Lincoln also experienced more than his fair share of rejections, generally because either the object of his affection or her parents deemed him too poor to be worthy of marriage. Others felt that he was too homely and awkward. Still others, like a Springfield woman named Rosanna Schmink, dumped Lincoln because of his bad manners. Apparently, Lincoln invited Miss Schmink to pick wool, but they had to share a horse. Not only was Lincoln too poor to provide a separate horse for his date, but he showed bad judgment in not walking while she rode.

One of Lincoln's early romances reveals how some women were attracted to his qualities. In the summer of 1830, candidates for public office were campaigning in Decatur, Illinois. Lincoln was among those who gathered to hear the stump speeches, only to discover that some of the candidates were less than overwhelming. As Lincoln's relative, John Hanks, described,

> A man by the name of Posey came into our neighborhood and made a speech. It was a bad one, and I said Abe could beat it. I turned down a box and Abe made his speech. The other man was a candidate—Abe wasn't. Abe beat him to death . . . the man, after Abe's speech was through, took him aside and asked him where he had learned so much and how he could do so well . . . the man encouraged him to persevere."

One of those in the crowd who was impressed with the tall newcomer to town was a young girl named Mary "Polly" Dillard Warnick, daughter of Major Warnick, the sheriff of Macon County. Lincoln found work making rails for Polly's father and visited the family, who lived a few miles outside of town by the Sangamon River. When Lincoln tried to court Polly, who was said to be very smitten with him, Polly's father prohibited the relationship because of the suitor's poverty. Polly ended up marrying Joseph Stevens, a far wealthier man. Other young women in town were equally impressed, but history indicates that all of them were interested in marrying someone with more means. This rejection due to his low standing is a recurring theme in Lincoln's early love life and surely scarred him emotionally. However, on a subsequent visit to Polly's home after she had married and moved out, Lincoln's feet were frostbitten when he crossed a frozen river with old shoes. Among those who cared for his aching feet was Mrs. Warnick, Polly's mother. Late in life, Polly spoke very warmly about her would-be suitor. This is another recurring event in Lincoln's romantic life—though rejected, many married women and the objects of his affection were drawn by his warmth and felt the need to "mother" him and would later reflect on him with kind memories.

Caroline Meeker

Many of the small towns that lined the Ohio River did not have a dock that the large steamboats that plied the waterway could use to load and unload passengers. As such, one of the many jobs that young Lincoln had was rowing passengers from the shoreline out to the boats. Lincoln was a strapping lad, familiar with a hard day's work, and was quite capable in the task. One day, however, when he was nineteen years old and rowing passengers on the river, an older boy on the other side of the river—Lin Dill—yelled for Lincoln to cross the Ohio. Lincoln did as requested, rowing himself to the opposite shore. But when he walked ashore, Lincoln discovered that Dill and his brother, John, were lying in wait for him with a plan to beat Lincoln as punishment for "stealing" their customers on the river.

With a fight pending, Lincoln did not back down; rather, he informed the Dill brothers that they may have bitten off more than they could chew. A standoff ensued as the Dills contemplated their options—be beaten by the tall stranger or take him to court. The Dills wisely chose the safer course of action.

Little ever happened in Kentucky's Hancock County, so a number of bored and curious townsfolk came out to see the case. Presiding was Judge Samuel Pate, only thirty-two at the time and wealthy. Pate was also caring for his seventeen-year-old orphaned niece, Caroline Meeker. Caroline, with big brown eyes and long, curly hair, was one of the onlookers who came to view the trial.

The charge was that, unlike the Dill boys, Lincoln did not have a license from the State of Kentucky to operate a ferry service on the river. The attorney for the Dill brothers made the case: It was simple—the Dills had a license from Kentucky to operate a ferry service. Lincoln did not and had rowed a prospective passenger out to a passing ship, resulting in financial loss to the Dills. Lincoln decided to represent himself and pled "not guilty."

Lincoln stood and admitted that he had ferried passengers out to the passing ships, including some individuals who may have been prospective customers for the Dills. In fact, Lincoln agreed with all the facts presented, including that he lacked a license. However, noted the tall teen, he had one question. Lincoln asked if the Dills' license precluded him from ferrying passengers. Moreover, said Lincoln in his close, he had done so on the opposite shoreline, in another state's (Indiana, not Kentucky) jurisdiction, and because the Dills were negligent in their service, had Lincoln not done so, the customer in question would surely have missed his boat. Said he,

> The question I want to ask is, "Do the rights of John T. Dill, under his license, forbid any other person to operate a ferry from the Indiana bank to the middle of the river?"
>
> It is not the right of the state of Kentucky to the whole width of the river that I question, but the extent to which the license of Mr. Dill applies to forbid traffic from the Indiana shore to vessels in the middle of the stream.
>
> I did what these men say I did. A man came to the bank of the river to catch a passing boat. That boat could not land because of low water, but stopped in the middle of the river. John Dill was not in sight, and his boat was on the other side of the river. Somebody had to take that man from the Indiana shore to the boat, or the man would miss the boat. The steamer would not wait. I was there, and the man offered to pay me to take him out to the boat. Now, it seems to me that it was not fair to expect me to sit there in my boat, and let that man miss his steamer, just because the Dill boys were not attending to their business. And I did not set that man across the river, as Dill claims the exclusive right to do; I only set him half-way across.

Judge Pate dismissed the case, and the Dills walked out of court grumbling. The townsfolk were duly impressed with Lincoln's defense, especially Caroline Meeker. The judge's niece was so smitten with Lincoln that it was said that, noticing the budding puppy love, the judge was inclined to give Lincoln a fair trial. Pate invited Lincoln to join him on his porch and share his life's story. Lincoln accepted, and the judge was so taken by Lincoln that he encouraged him to study law. Caroline, who had been gathering apples in the orchard, returned and joined the tall guest on the porch. Offering Lincoln an apple, she said,

> I'm glad you beat them. It was mighty mean of them to call you over the river in the lying way they did, and then both jump on you, two to one. I think it was right clever the way you showed that setting folks out from the shore on to a boat was not the same as setting them across the river.

The judge permitted Lincoln to have access to his law books, affording the future attorney his first experience with the law. The judge also allowed Lincoln to court Caroline, who told her new beau that "if Uncle Sam had fined you, I would have scolded him." We are not sure whether Lincoln was more interested in Caroline or the law books (likely the former), but they enjoyed a warm but brief romance. Lincoln accompanied her to a corn-husking party. At such events, it was customary that, if a boy discovered a red ear of corn or Indian corn, he could hold it up as a "pass" to kiss any girl in the barn. It has been said that Lincoln husked more corn than anyone had ever seen, but it was Caroline who uncovered a red ear that she hid in her apron and later snuck to Lincoln. He kissed her and escorted her home that evening.

It is possible that Caroline wanted to marry Lincoln, but there is no record to indicate what became of the romance. Caroline seemed a good catch—her uncle was a wealthy judge who liked Lincoln, and she was of marrying age and attractive. It has been suggested that the judge's wife, however, disapproved of the courtship because Lincoln was too poor. Lincoln later embarked on one of his river trips to New Orleans and returned to visit Caroline but then moved away and never saw her again. History records that Caroline waited a long three years before marrying. She ended up marrying Eli Thrasher, a male relative, who was twenty-five years old and wealthy. Sadly, a few years later, after giving birth to a baby daughter named for her, Caroline died. She was only twenty-five and passed away on Christmas Day of 1835. Thrasher never overcame the loss of his beloved Caroline and died heartbroken just a few years later on June 6, 1842.

Mary Owens

Lincoln's awkwardness around women and the effect of the emotional scars he collected by losing the women closest to him were nowhere more apparent than in Lincoln's embarrassing and disastrous courtship of Mary Owens. In 1836, Lincoln was still suffering from the loss of his first true love the year prior. Three years before that event, in October 1833, the sister of Elizabeth Abell arrived in New Salem for a four-week visit. This newcomer from a fairly prosperous Kentucky family made quite an impact on the small village. She was outspoken and very flirtatious, wore fancy clothing and silk gloves, and impressed the town with her cultured ways. One relative of hers described Mary as follows: "She has large, blue eyes, was jovial, social, loved wit and humor, had a liberal English education, and was considered wealthy."

It appears that Mary was not attractive and was a bit overweight, but her clothing and personality seemed to strike those who met her and left the stronger impression. Mary described herself in a letter written in 1866: "Born in the year eight; fair skin, deep blue eyes, with dark curly hair; height, five feet five inches, weighing about one hundred and fifty pounds." This description was from her first visit to New Salem in 1833.

All married women seemed to like Lincoln and felt the need to cook for him and generally look after him. And so it was when Lincoln's friend, Mrs. Bennett Abell of New Salem, informed the bachelor in 1836 that her sister, Mary, who had visited three years prior, was still eligible. Lincoln remembered Mary and had fond recollections of her, so Mrs. Abell agreed to arrange for her sister to visit again if Lincoln would agree to marry her. It is uncertain how serious this "deal" really was, but Lincoln's courtship was described as "prompt and vigorous" and "probably the most regular and industrious courting that New Salem had ever seen, or that Lincoln had ever done." Indeed, it appears that all the involved parties attempted to satisfy the marital arrangement.

During Mary's first visit to town, Lincoln was frequently at her side and went out of his way to visit Mrs. Abell in order to see Mary. Thus, Mary came to New Salem again in the fall of 1836, and she was as her sister described and as Lincoln remembered her. The two also held similar political views, and Mary was an outgoing, outspoken woman. However, one item had changed in the three years since Lincoln had last seen Ms. Owens—her physical appearance. Mary had gained an enormous amount of weight and had aged poorly, something that was evident by the wrinkles in her face and missing teeth.

Mary's cousin, Mrs. Hardin Bale, described her around the time of her second visit to New Salem, and this and other accounts are less charitable than those surrounding the descriptions from her earlier visit to town. Said Mrs. Bale rather repetitiously, "She was blue-eyed, dark-haired, handsome—not pretty—was rather large and tall; handsome, truly handsome, matronly looking, over ordinary size in height and weight. Miss Owens has handsome, that is to say noble-looking, matronly." Another cousin, Thomas G. Green, echoed the praise of Mary's intellect but also the unflattering physical descriptions, adding that she was also "a nervous and intelligent woman, the most intellectual I ever saw, with a forehead massive and angular, square, prominent and broad."

Still single at age twenty-five on her first trip, Mary was a veritable old maid by standards of the time. Lincoln realized, albeit too late, that Mary had been a bit too willing to travel to another state to marry someone whom she had not seen in years. He felt that she was desperate. Indeed, at twenty-eight and missing her teeth, Mary was just that. Lincoln tried to focus on her admirable social and intellectual traits and attempted to convince himself that he had to do the honorable thing and marry her. However, his heart won out over his head in a contested struggle, and he ended up avoiding her as much as possible. At the same time, Mary hesitated on her end, likely recognizing Lincoln's cold feet and the reality of his poor social and financial condition.

Both Lincoln and Mary were hesitant about the arrangement, and Lincoln attempted to weasel out of the engagement but wanted to do so in a way that saved face. In December 1836, he departed for Vandalia, which at the time was the state capital, and attended the legislative session. Lincoln wrote to Mary but avoided the main topic, instead focusing on the weather and complaining that he was not happy. In fact, Lincoln loved politics and wanted to move to either Vandalia or Springfield, which was about to become the capital city that February. While away, Lincoln also met Ninian Edwards, the state attorney general, who was a force behind the relocation of the capital, and his wife Elizabeth Todd Edwards, older sister to Lincoln's future wife.

A misunderstanding between Lincoln and Mary Owens brought the matter of their awkward relationship to a boil. Lincoln was away for three weeks, and when he returned, he was supposed to meet with Mary. Lincoln stopped to visit her at the Abell residence, but Mary was not there. Lincoln appears to have accused her of breaking the date, but it is possible that he was not clear in his communication. It is also possible that Mary was avoiding Lincoln. One account notes that Elizabeth Abell tried to cover for her sister, but the children in the home blurted out the truth that Mary had gone to Mentor Graham's home. Mary responded that Lincoln should have met her at the Graham home. As it was, she walked home alone. The two argued over who was at fault.

During the winter of 1836–1837, Lincoln became a lawyer and received a job in Springfield, departing on April 15, 1837, on a horse borrowed from his friend Bowling Green with a grand total of seven dollars in his pocket. Springfield was only twenty miles from New Salem, close enough to have salvaged the relationship. But Lincoln did little to remedy things. He wrote to Mary that spring and informed her of the town's lovely homes and prominent residents with their fancy carriages. But he also made a point of telling her that she would not have such items because he was too poor. Then Lincoln tried his ploy to back out of the engagement with face—he asked Mary to marry him, knowing that she would decline, which she did. Lincoln asked her for her hand three times, but Mary knew that he was doing so only out of a sense of reluctant obligation, something that was but thinly veiled in his letters.

One letter, in particular, highlights the awkwardness. In April, Lincoln wrote his "friend Mary" a letter, saying,

> Whatever woman may cast her lot with mine, should any ever do so, it is my intention to do all in my power to make her happy and contented; and there is nothing I can imagine, that would make me more unhappy than to fail in the effort. . . . My opinion is that you had better not [marry me].

. . . You have not been accustomed to hardship, and it may be more severe than you can imagine. I know you are capable of thinking correctly on any subject; and if you deliberate maturely upon this, before you decide, then I am willing to abide your decision. . . .

I want in all cases to do right, and most particularly so, in all cases with women. I want, at this particular time, more than any thing else, to do right with you, and if I know it would be doing right, as I rather suspect it would, to let you alone, I would do it. And for the purpose of making the matter as plain as possible, I now say that you can now drop the subject, dismiss your thoughts (if you ever had any) from me forever, and leave this letter unanswered . . . our further acquaintance shall depend upon yourself. If such further acquainteance would contribute nothing to your happiness, I am sure it would not to mine. If you feel yourself in any degree bound to me, I am now willing to release you.

It is clear that Lincoln took the easy road out of the relationship by putting the ball in Mary's court and forcing her to end the engagement. Three months later, Mary visited Springfield, then returned home to Kentucky. Lincoln's pride and embarrassment led him to claim that he was made the fool, even writing to Mary's sister, Elizabeth Abell, "Tell your sister that I think she was a great fool because she did not stay here and marry me." But he correctly noted of his behavior that no one would ever marry him the way he behaved. As for Mary, she responded to Lincoln's emotional outburst that it was "characteristic of the man."

A year later, in April 1838, reflecting on the disastrous romance, Lincoln good-naturedly shares the embarrassing story with the wife of his good friend Orville H. Browning. In it, Lincoln says of Mary that it was impossible for any one person to accumulate so much weight in such a short period of time:

Without apologizing for being egotistical, I shall make the history of so much of my life as has elapsed since I saw you the subject of this letter. And, by the way, I now discover that, in order to give a full and intelligent account of the things I have done and suffered since I saw you, I shall necessarily have to relate some that happened before.

It was, then, in the Autumn of 1836 that a married lady of my acquaintance and who was a great friend of mine, being about to pay a visit to her father and other relatives residing in Kentucky, proposed to me that on her return she would bring a sister of hers with her on condition that I would engage to become her brother-in-law with all convenient dispatch. I, of course, accepted the proposal, for you know I could not have done otherwise, had I really been averse to it; but privately between you and me I was most confoundedly well pleased with the project. I had seen the said sister some three years before, thought her intelligent and agreeable, and I saw no good objection to plodding life through hand in hand with her. Time passed on, the lady took her journey, and in due time returned, sister in company sure enough. This stomached me a little; for it appeared to me that her coming so readily showed that she was a trifle too willing; but, on reflection, it occureed to me that she might have been prevailed on by her married sister to come, without anything concerning me ever having been mentioned to her; and so I concluded that, if no other objection presented itself, I would consent to waive this. All this occurred to me on hearing of her arrival in the neighborhood; for, be it remembered, I had not yet seen her, except about three years previous, as above mentioned. In a few days we had an interview; and, although I had seen her before, she did not look as my imagination had pictured her. I knew she was oversize, but she now appeared a fair match for Falstaff. I knew she was called an "old maid," and I felt no doubt of the truth of at least half of the appellation; but now, when I beheld her, I could not for my life avoid thinking of my mother; and this, not from withered features, for her skin was too full of fat to permit of its contracting into wrinkles, but from her want of teeth, weather-beaten appearance in general, and from a kind of notion that ran in my head that nothing could have commenced at the size of infancy and reached her present bulk in less than thirty-five or forty-years; and, in short, I was not at all pleased with her. But what could I do? I had told her sister I would take her for better or for worse; and I made a point of honor and conscience in all things to stick to my word, especially if others had been induced to act on it, which in this case I had no doubt they had; for I was now fairly convinced that no other man on earth would have her, and hence the conclusion that they were bent on holding me to my bargain. "Well," thought I, "I have said it, and, be the consequences what they may, it shall not be my fault if I fail to do it." At once I determined to consider her my wife; and, this done, all my powers of discovery were put to work in search of perfections in her which might be fairly set off against her defects. I tried to imagine her handsome, which, but for her unfortunate corpulency, was actually true. Exclusive of this, no woman that I have ever seen has a finer face. I also tried to convince myself that the mind was much more to be valued than the person; and in this she was not inferior, as I could discover, to any with whom I had been acquainted.

Lincoln then fessed up that he was able to back out of the relationship in an interesting way—with "no violation of word, honor or conscience." How, he said, was a matter of being able to "muster my resolution" and propose, knowing that Mary would decline the halfhearted offer. But then Lincoln admits that his pride got the best of him and that he was deeply hurt by the rejection, so he impulsively proposed again and again, but still she turned him down. It turned out, he admitted, that "I was really a little in love with her." Lincoln admits to Mrs. Browning that his "vanity was deeply wounded," and he even speculates that he was "mortified" to discover that he had been played the fool by her all along; she wanted out of the relationship as much as he did.

Lincoln concludes that "others have been made fools of by the girls, but this can never with truth be said of me. I most emphatically, in this instance, made a fool of myself." Comically, he stated, "I have now come to the conclusion never again to think of marrying, and for this reason: I can never be satisfied with any one who would be blockhead enough to have me."

Years later, when Lincoln was serving in the presidency, Orville Browning recalled the April Fool's Day letter, saying that he and his wife "were very much amused with it, but both Mrs. Browning and myself supposed it to be a fiction, a creation of his brain; one of his funny stories." Likewise, many years later, while preparing his book on Lincoln's life, William Herndon tracked down Mary Owens in Missouri. She failed to return his requests for a letter, but Lincoln's former law partner was persistent. It turned out that Mary had moved back to Kentucky but eventually married a man from Missouri named Jesse Vineyard and had two sons fighting for the Confederacy during the Civil War. Mary said of that long-ago-doomed romance, "Mr. Lincoln was deficient in those little links which make up the path of a woman's happiness." But she also recalled that "he was a man with a heart full of kindness and a head full of good sense."

ANN RUTLEDGE

For thirty years after her death, Ann Rutledge remained a mystery, her name all but obscured from history. It was not until Lincoln's former law partner William H. Herndon gave a now famous Friday night lecture in the courthouse of Springfield, Illinois, on November 16, 1866, that the world learned of the woman Lincoln loved. In the lecture, with the cumbersome title "A. Lincoln—Miss Ann Rutledge, New Salem Pioneering," Herndon discussed the details of Lincoln's romance with Ann. He also read a poem about the romance called "Immortality—or, Oh! Why should the Spirit of Mortal be Proud," which had been read at Ann's eulogy a few decades earlier.

The lecture was poorly attended, perhaps because a famous humorist named Josh Billings spoke the night prior or perhaps because of Herndon's poor choice in titling his address. Also, at the time of Herndon's lecture, the town of New Salem where Lincoln had courted Ann no longer existed, having long since been abandoned. But Herndon was the first to unearth the touching story of a young couple in love. The affair with Ann Rutledge, claimed Herndon, was the "Rosetta Stone to interpret Lincoln." Why? After Ann, Lincoln was incapable of truly loving another woman. His heart hardened, and he battled melancholy. At the same time, claimed the former law partner, in forever turning away from domestic happiness, Lincoln was driven to greatness. Not surprisingly, word of this unknown love was greeted with great skepticism and a fair amount of criticism of Herndon. Such denials of the love affair continue to the present day.

Lincoln's True Love

One year after Thomas Lincoln moved his family to Macon County, Illinois, the twenty-one-year-old Lincoln departed on a riverboat headed for New Orleans. Aboard the boat were three of Lincoln's friends: Denton Offutt, John Hanks, and John Johnston. In March 1831, the four men began preparing the boat and loading supplies. It took the four men four weeks to build and supply the boat before sailing down the Sangamon River. On April 19, however, the boat became stuck for an evening at the Rutledge Dam, about thirty miles from Springfield. With the boat taking on water, people from the town gathered on the bank to watch the ordeal as the crew worked frantically to save their ship. What they saw was a very tall man take charge by transferring the goods and supplies to a ferryboat. He then waded ashore to introduce himself to the residents of New Salem and invite them to assist him by having them stand on the bow of the boat in order to raise the stern high enough into the air to drain the excess water from the craft.

The plan worked. Afterward, the men repaired the leak, and the tallest of the crew thanked the residents for their assistance. Lincoln made an impression on the people of New Salem not only for his resourcefulness and charisma but also for his appearance. One fellow, Henry Onstot, described him as "grotesque" looking, while others noted that he was disheveled with a chest that was too thin, head that was too small, cheeks that were too gaunt, and a nose and ears that were too big. In addition, his pants legs were shin high. But not everyone in New Salem shared such viewpoints, especially a young girl.

After the voyage to New Orleans, Lincoln and his friends returned in August to New Salem, where Denton Offutt built a general store and invited Abe to be his business partner. The store opened in mid-September but failed not long after. As had been his lot in life, Lincoln worked a variety of jobs from surveyor to farmer, eking out a meager existence. He also helped out his fellow citizens in every way possible, large and small; wrote articles for the town's Debate Society; and was the referee for wrestling matches. He boarded with Rowan Herndon and anyone who would have him for a meal and warm bed in exchange for errands and labor. All the while, however, the newcomer's reputation was growing.

In New Salem, Lincoln entered politics, running for office soon after arriving but losing an election in 1832. He also served as a military officer, commanding a small unit of men from the county in the Black Hawk War during the spring of 1832. Lincoln served for one month, then reenlisted twice more for two additional monthlong tours. Although he served three months, his command never saw combat, leading Lincoln to joke that the only blood he encountered was from the mosquitoes that pestered him.

The young girls of New Salem enjoyed joking about "Old Plain Abe," but many of the married women in town cooked for Lincoln, sewed his torn clothing, and tried to fix him up with a wife. One of the families with whom Lincoln boarded was that of the Reverend John Camron, who had one son and a whopping eleven daughters, all of whom delighted in teasing Abe. But when Lincoln suffered a bad fever, it was an elder Camron daughter who nursed Lincoln to health. When he was recovered, the tall boarder joked that when he became president, he would repay young Ms. Camron by appointing her postmaster of New Salem.

A close friend of the Reverend Camron was his uncle, James Rutledge. The two men had founded New Salem in 1829 and were members of the Whig Party and fond of the tall newcomer to town. As such, Lincoln also boarded at the Rutledge farm and tavern, a home also filled with young children: four boys, aged six to twenty-one, and four girls, aged three to nineteen, with another child on the way. The charge was one dollar per week, plus helping with errands and chores. Lincoln also worked at a mill owned by Rutledge and Camron and operated by his pal Denton Offutt and would enjoy many pleasant evenings dining with the Rutledge and Camron families. Lincoln moved in with the Rutledges for four months, beginning in November 1832, but had previously dined with the family.

The Rutledge family hailed from a reasonably prosperous South Carolina family and were Scotch–Irish but devout Presbyterians. One relative had even signed the Declaration of Independence. They had lived in Kentucky, but after hearing from a visitor who described rich, fertile land in Illinois, the Rutledges joined seven other families in traveling to the plains of Illinois in 1813. It was an arduous journey, and the families suffered long, cold winters and other hardships. Mrs. Rutledge rightly opposed the move.

Among the thirty children who populated the new community of New Salem was Ann Rutledge, who was a newborn infant when the family arrived in Illinois. Ann was born in the frontier village of Henderson, Kentucky, near the Ohio River, the third child and second daughter of

James and Mary Ann Rutledge. She had blossomed into an attractive girl, five feet four inches in height, with large, dark eyes and curly reddish hair with tints of yellow. An avid reader and perhaps the smartest, most popular girl in the county, Ann was described as amiable and gentle. She was a hard worker, a good seamstress and cook, and uncommonly fun to be around. Her cousin, James McGrady Rutledge, described Ann as the most attractive girl in the county, "always cheerful . . . and a good conversationalist." Not surprisingly, Ann captured the attention of the tall young man who boarded at the family's tavern.

Ann's sisters teased the man who occasionally boarded at their home, saying, "He's as thin as a beanpole and as ugly as a scarecrow!" Ann did not share the view of Lincoln held by many others. The feelings for one another were mutual. At eighteen, Ann was already of marrying age and was, in fact, engaged. But it was more complicated than that.

In May 1833, Lincoln became New Salem's postmaster. Through his job, he had discovered that twice a week Ann visited the post office to inquire as to whether her fiancé had written to her. She left depressed and empty-handed. Letters never arrived, and Lincoln's heart ached for Ann's impossible situation. As best as we can tell from surviving letters, Ann's father had fallen on hard times and had to sell the tavern and farm. A strange newcomer to town named John McNeil, who was twelve years older than Ann, was buying up property in the area, and it was he who bought out the Rutledges. Little is known about McNeil except that he was from New York and had money. McNeil proposed to Ann Rutledge soon after arriving in town in the fall of 1831, and she agreed to the union. It is uncertain—but seems possible—that Ann may have felt that she had no choice but to marry. McNeil, after all, was buying her father's business and home, then turned around and leased it back to him. And Ann was a teenager.

That quickly, McNeil announced that his father was gravely ill and that he had to return to New York to care for him. McNeil departed in 1832; passed through Ohio, where he became very ill for one month; and then made his way back to New York. Some sources say that McNeil's father died in April 1831; others list the date as April 10, 1833. Either way, these accounts conflict with the story told by McNeil. Back in New York and severely depressed, McNeil suffered another blow. His two brothers passed away in the spring of 1833.

There are conflicting accounts, but many of New Salem's citizens neither liked nor trusted McNeil, and he comes across as selfish, opportunistic, and callous. McNeil may never have even written Ann during the years they were separated, or, if he did, it was only very infrequently. In fairness to

McNeil, he may have suffered terribly from the loss of so many loved ones in such a short time. But we also know that he made up an alias: while known to the people of New Salem as John McNeil, he admitted that his real name was John McNamar. His father's tombstone spelled the name McNamarah.

An Engagement

Lincoln consoled Ann and even volunteered to write to McNeil or go east to try to find him. Ann wanted to honor her engagement, but McNeil failed to return, and her feelings were turning to Lincoln. The two started taking walks together, and a romance soon blossomed. Lincoln escorted "Annie," as he called her, to parties, fairs, wrestling matches, and the town's Independence Day celebration. They enjoyed horseback rides and picnics, and Ann even inspired Lincoln to do something he disliked—attend church. But mostly, they loved reading together. Ann's father, who was a member of the Debate Society with Lincoln, nurtured his daughter's passion for learning, something that was rare at the time. One account even suggests that the Rutledge home contained thirty books, which, for the region, would have made it a veritable library. Ann and Abe, who read every book in the "library," especially enjoyed reading Shakespeare together and acting out scenes from his famous plays.

Ann was fond of animals and must have been shocked to discover that Lincoln did not like to hunt or fish because of his love of animals and inability to kill an animal. Together, they tended to the pigs, chickens, and other animals on the Rutledge farm. Once, Lincoln found three baby rabbits whose mother had died. He carried them to the Rutledge farm as a surprise present for Ann, and together they raised the baby bunnies. Lincoln was also exceptionally playful with Ann's younger siblings and entertained the whole family with funny, homespun tales. Mrs. Rutledge noted of her houseguest, "He's so good natured everybody loves him."

Lincoln enjoyed some success for the first time in his life. In the summer of 1834, he was elected to the Illinois legislature and was now receiving a small but regular income. By this time, Lincoln was seeing Ann Rutledge every day when he was not away on political business, and his reputation in the area was growing. Ann's father and others all supported his political career.

Lincoln was in session from December 1 through February 1835 and returned by stagecoach. During his absence, the Rutledges had moved but only a few miles away, and Lincoln once again boarded with the Camrons. It appears that not long after returning from the legislative session—perhaps in the spring of 1835—Lincoln proposed marriage to Ann. Ann's sister, Jean, and brother, Robert, claimed that "Annie's whole soul seemed wrapped up in Lincoln." Lincoln assisted Ann in writing to McNeil to obtain from him "an honorable release" of the engagement, but they never heard back from him. Ann wanted to marry Lincoln. She was twenty-two, and he was twenty-six, and it appears that they were waiting for word from McNeil or for his return before marrying. Some sources suggest that they planned a wedding for the fall of 1836 or when Ann heard back from McNeil. Either way, her heart now belonged to Lincoln.

Just when Lincoln's prospects were looking good, a typhoid/malaria epidemic swept through New Salem in the summer of 1835. Bad weather that summer, including floods, a tornado, and a heat spell, led to an outbreak of mosquitoes and horseflies. Crops failed, and the residents of town began falling ill. Many died. Lincoln even helped build coffins for the town. Unfortunately, the Rutledges' well may have been contaminated, and the family fell ill.

One of the casualties was Ann. She came down with the symptoms in August, suffering from a high fever and unable to eat. She was likely treated with laxatives, bloodletting, and the raising of blisters, all in an effort to purge her and bring out the infection. This was the common remedy used for her neighbors who also suffered that summer. As her health deteriorated, Ann wanted to see Lincoln and her brother, David, who was away at school. Bowling Green was sent to summon Lincoln, who was away on a surveying mission. James McGrady Rutledge was sent to find David. On hearing of Ann's illness, Lincoln immediately raced to her home in the middle of a severe lightning storm. The storm delayed Lincoln for the evening as he took cover in the home of the Reverend John Berry, where he most uncharacteristically prayed and, noted Berry, was distraught and overwhelmed by emotion.

At first light, Lincoln set off and arrived to find Ann in bed and dying. Lincoln's former law partner, who later interviewed Ann's siblings, described the scene: "The meeting was quite as much as either could bear and more than Lincoln, with all his coolness and philosophy, could endure. The voice, the face, the features of her; the love, sympathy, and talk fastened themselves on his heart and soul forever." After spending time at Ann's bedside, Lincoln could do no more. Both were crying, and, as Lincoln walked out of the home, Ann's fifteen-year-old sister described the moment: "I can never forget how broken-hearted he looked."

Ann lost consciousness and died on August 25, 1835, at age twenty-two. A simple service was conducted, and she was buried at Concord Cemetery, seven miles from New Salem. The Reverend John Camron offered the eulogy, and Lincoln quoted the poetry of William Knox:

Oh, why should the spirit of
mortal be proud?
Like a swift-fleeting meteor, a
fast flying cloud,
A flash of the lightning, a break of
the wave,
He passes from life to his rest in
the grave

Numerous accounts exist that depict a devastated Lincoln, unable to function after Ann's death. A neighbor, Hannah Armstrong, said that Lincoln would "weep like a baby." Lincoln's friend, Mrs. Abell McHenry, said that he was "wrapped in a profound thought, indifferent to transpiring events, had but little to say, but would . . . wander off in the woods by himself, away from the association of even those most esteemed." But Lincoln's neighbors, while worrying about him, supported him. The Reverend Camron was so concerned that he invited Lincoln to stay at his home. Likewise, Bowling Green and his wife brought Lincoln into their home for a week, concerned about his severe melancholy and mood swings. Some friends worried that Lincoln might be suicidal, but records show that Lincoln managed to attend to his affairs.

The residents of New Salem did note that Lincoln frequently walked to the grave site, including when it rained. In doing so, Lincoln was heard to comment, "I cannot bear the idea of it raining on her grave." Lincoln, always skeptical of religion, questioned God and strongly rejected the teachings of preachers who said that God did not make mistakes so that all that happened was part of a plan. He had lost his mother and his sister; now Lincoln lost the woman he loved and "erected a defensive wall of passivity around himself—a wall that antagonized other women who sought to be close to him." William Herndon echoed these sentiments when he interviewed Lincoln's former New Salem neighbors, discovering from them that Lincoln was "sad and broken" after Ann died. He could not eat or sleep, and "his mind wandered from its throne." Herndon also noted that Lincoln would never truly love again, and after Ann's passing, he stopped writing or talking about love. From that point on, Lincoln did not sign his letters using the word "love." Rather, even to women he was courting and to his eventual wife, he signed his name as "yours affectionately."

Sadly, no likeness of Ann Rutledge has survived history. As for John McNeil (or John McNamar), he returned to New Salem in October 1835, soon after Ann's death. He was surprised to learn of Ann's fate but, according to several accounts, expressed or showed no emotion, even when

Ann's mother gave him a lock of the deceased's hair. Nor did he ever visit her grave.

That December, Ann's father died, possibly of the same ailment. On February 23, McNeil evicted Ann's mother and siblings, giving them only one week's notice. With the Rutledge widow still pleading, the family was removed from the home on March 1 in the middle of a late-winter storm with nowhere to go. They moved in with John Miller Camron, their relative and neighbor.

As for McNamar, he married in 1838 and had four children. His wife died, but he remarried in 1855 and had one additional child. Lincoln knew McNamar. Their time in New Salem overlapped, and both courted Ann at one point or another. Also, when Lincoln was campaigning, he asked John McNeil (McNamar) to proof a newspaper article for the *Sangamon Journal* because McNamar was allegedly well educated. Unfortunately, history has not recorded what Lincoln thought of McNamar, but it is easy to guess that he held him in the lowest of esteem once McNamar abandoned Ann and showed little concern for her or her family when he returned to Illinois. When Lincoln's former law partner, William Herndon, talked to McNamar while tracking down stories about Ann and Abe, McNamar would barely speak to him and even denied that he ever was engaged to Ann. A cheat and swindler, McNamar enjoyed an undeservedly long life, dying at age seventy-three in 1879. His neighbors described him to Herndon as "cold and unusual." Even McNamar's second wife told Herndon that "there was no more poetry or sentiment in him than in the multiplication table."

Lincoln stayed in New Salem a year and a half longer, serving in the state legislature, until moving on March 15, 1837. Soon after, the town failed completely. Ann's widowed mother and siblings moved to Iowa, but her beloved brother, David, remained nearby in Petersburg, Illinois, and practiced law. David, however, passed away at twenty-six and is buried next to his sister. The newspaper baron William Randolph Hearst bought the land that was the town in 1906, then donated it to the Old Salem Chautauqua Association, which built historic cabins on the site.

The romance of Abraham Lincoln and Ann Rutledge is compelling. The late John Y. Simon, a respected Lincoln scholar, noted that for every Lincoln scholar who accepts the relationship as true, there is another who questions the validity of the story. Simon summed up the debate this way, saying, "The romance of Abraham Lincoln and Ann Rutledge inspires both poetry and polemics." The affair has inspired Hollywood, which famously captured Lincoln's love affair with young Ann Rutledge in such classic films as *Young Mr. Lincoln*, starring Henry Fonda in 1939, and *Abe Lincoln in*

Illinois, with Raymond Massey in the title role, in 1940. The story has indeed inspired poetry. Ann's body was exhumed in 1890 and reinterred at Oakland Cemetery in Petersburg, Illinois. Thousands have visited the grave site. In 1921, a new monument was placed at her grave with an inscription from Edgar Lee Masters:

> Out of me unworthy and unknown
> The vibrations of deathless music,
> "With malice toward none, with
> charity for all."
> Out of me the forgiveness of millions toward millions,
> And the beneficent face of a nation
> Shining with justice and truth.
> I am Ann Rutledge who sleep
> Beneath these weeds,
> Beloved in life of Abraham Lincoln,
> Wedded to him, not through union,
> But through separation.
> Bloom forever, O Republic,
> From the dust of my bosom!

Love or Legend?

Ann Rutledge was likely the love of Lincoln's life, but the topic still invites debate and even denial among scholars. Perhaps the first biography of Lincoln (the J. G. Holland biography), published the year after Lincoln's assassination, fails to mention Ms. Rutledge. But the book by Lincoln's friend Ward Lamon Hill, published in 1872, suggests that Ann was Lincoln's true love. Curiously, the biography by Isaac Arnold in 1884 suggests that the two were engaged, yet he barely mentions Ann in the book. Likewise, another scholar, William E. Barton, working in the late nineteenth century, visited Sarah Rutledge, Ann's then ninety-three-year-old sister, who confirmed the love story.

The debate continued through the twentieth century, with some leading Lincoln scholars such as David Herbert Donald and J. G. Randall dismissing the story as a "hoax" or "legend." But both of these leading scholars were nonetheless intrigued by the story. Randall even encouraged Donald, who was then his most promising graduate student, to research what they called the "Rutledge Tradition." Randall also encouraged his wife, the historian Ruth Painter Randall, to research the fuller nature of Lincoln's marriage. He also included a special appendix on Ann in his famous book on Lincoln. The historian Paul M. Angle says that the love affair is folklore and dismisses it as "the great American myth." Yet these positions are countered by the dean of all Lincoln scholars, Carl Sandburg, who wrote that Lincoln and Ann were in love.

Unfortunately, history does not have Lincoln's own words on the subject to settle the matter once and for all. However, there are five sources perhaps nearly as reliable as Lincoln's own word. One of the best sources is the voluminous work by Lincoln's faithful White House secretaries, John Nicolay and John Hay, both of whom Lincoln treated as sons and knew the man as well as anyone. They do mention Ann but devote only eight lines to her. In fairness, it was not customary to write about such private matters at the time, and, as they note, Lincoln was not one to discuss his love life. Moreover, there is evidence that Lincoln was so devastated at the loss of Ann that he could not bring himself to mention her name. Said Nicolay and Hay of the issue,

> Besides his stepmother, who was a plain, God-fearing woman, he had not known many others until he came to live in New Salem. There he had made the acquaintance of the best people the settlement contained, and among them had become much attracted to a young girl named Ann Rutledge, the daughter of one of the proprietors of the place. She died in her girlhood, and though there does not seem to have been any engagement between them, he was profoundly affected by her health.

A second source was Lincoln's former law partner, William H. Herndon, who conducted extensive research, both writing to former acquaintances of Lincoln and visiting them. He also interviewed Ann's relatives and was tireless in tracking down their stories, collecting their letters, and obtaining signed statements of authenticity from them. Douglas L. Wilson, director of the Center for Lincoln Studies at Knox College, looked up the statements collected by Herndon from 1865 and 1866, which included twenty-four individuals who knew both Lincoln and Ann from their New Salem days—Ann's teachers, siblings, friends, and relatives. Of them, fifteen claim that Lincoln and Ann were engaged, twenty-two said that Lincoln courted Ann, and seventeen remembered that Lincoln "grieved excessively" when Ann died.

While such evidence seems overwhelming, some Lincoln scholars still refuse to believe that the great Lincoln could have loved someone other than Mary Todd. Some scholars attempt to blame Herndon, who they claim never liked Mrs. Lincoln and was simply trying to hurt her by telling the story of Ann. It is true that Herndon and Mrs. Lincoln disliked one another, with Herndon once describing her as a "serpent" and her referring to him as a "miserable man."

In truth, Herndon was disorganized and a sloppy speaker who was prone to rambling. Yet he was an attorney who was loyal to Lincoln and dedicated to the truth. One of the sources Herndon relied on was Ann's brother, Robert, who wrote a seven-page statement, saying,

> In 1830 my sister being then but 17 years of age a stranger calling himself John McNeil came to New Salem . . . a friendship grew up between McNeil and Ann which ripened apace and resulted in an engagement to marry—McNeil's real name was McNamar. It seems that his father had failed in business and his son, a very young man had determined to make a fortune, pay off his father's debts and restore him to his former social and financial standing. With this view he left his home clandestinely, and in order to avoid pursuit by his parents changed his name. . . .
>
> He prospered in business and pending his engagement with Ann, he revealed his true name, returned to Ohio to relieve his parents from their embarrassments, and to bring the family with him to Illinois. On his return to Ohio, several years having elapsed, he found his father in declining health or dead . . . he was absent two or three years.
>
> In the mean time Mr. Lincoln paid his addresses to Ann, continued his visits and attentions regularly and those resulted in an engagement to marry, conditional to an honorable release from the contract with McNamar. There is no kind of doubt as to the existence of this engagement. David Rutledge urged Ann to consummate it, but she refused until such time as she could see McNamar—inform him of the change in her feelings, and seek an honorable release.
>
> Mr. Lincoln lived in the village, McNamar did not return and in August 1835 Ann sickened and died. The effect upon Mr. Lincoln's mind was terrible; he became plunged in despair, and many of his friends feared that reason would desert her throne.

They also point out that Ann's brother claimed that McNamar was from Ohio when he was from New York. But this may have been a mistake and does not necessarily discredit the existence of a romance. McNamar did travel to Ohio, and this might be the source of Robert Rutledge's confusion. Also, McNamar was a despicable person, yet Robert does not present him as such, a point used by critics. However, Robert consulted with his mother, who lived to be ninety-one, dying in 1878, in order to confirm his story.

Lincoln's former maid, Mariah Vance, is yet another source for the controversy. Ms. Vance recollected Lincoln and Mrs. Lincoln getting into fights over the memories of Ann. Another source comes from 1944, when an old newspaper article written in 1862 was discovered. The article, which appeared in the *Menard Axis*, a county newspaper, was written by a John Hill, who happened to be Lincoln's rival from in his New Salem days, both in politics and for Ann's affections. In the article, Hill publicly criticizes Lincoln, who was then president of the United States, and recalls Lincoln's romance with Ann, saying of his rival,

> He chanced to meet with a lady, who to him seemed lovely, angelic, and the height of perfection. Forgetful of all things else, he could think or dream of naught but her. His feelings he soon made her acquainted with, and was delighted with a reciprocation. This to him was perfect happiness; and with uneasy anxiety he awaited the arrival of the day when the twain should be made one flesh.—but that day was doomed never to arrive. Disease came upon this lovely beauty, and she sickened and died. The youth had wrapped his heart with her's, and this was more than he could bear. He saw her to her grave, and as the cold clouds fell upon the coffin, he sincerely wished that he too had been enclosed within it. Melancholy came upon him; he was changed and sad. His friends detected strange conduct and a flighty imagination. They placed him under guard for fear of his committing suicide.

The final source is Isaac Cogdale, who offers history Lincoln's own words on the subject. An old friend of Lincoln's who visited the president-elect after the 1860 election, Cogdale said that the two discussed old times and past friends. Cogdale asserts that he asked Lincoln, "Well, Abe, is it true that you fell in love and courted Ann Rutledge?" Lincoln answered, "It is true—true. Indeed I did! I have loved the name of Rutledge to this day. I have kept my mind on their movements ever since, and love them dearly." Cogdale then asks, "Abe, is it true that you ran a little wild about the matter?" To the reference about Lincoln's severe bout of depression after Ann's death, the president said,

> I did really. I ran off the track. It was my first. I loved the woman dearly. She was a handsome girl; would have made a good, loving wife; she was natural and quite intellectual, though not highly educated. I did honestly and truly love the girl, and think often, often of her now.

Critics of this story point to the fact that Lincoln always called himself "Lincoln," as did his friends and associates, including his law partner, William Herndon, and his dear friend Joshua Speed. However, what they fail to note is that, as a young man, Lincoln was called "Abe." Cogdale was a lawyer who lived only twenty miles from Lincoln and knew him as "Abe." The other criticism is that, though the story rings true to what we know, it is still questioned as to whether Lincoln would ever really have talked openly about Ann. He was uncommonly closed when it came to private matters, especially those that caused him pain. John W. Bunn, a friend from Springfield, said of Lincoln,

What was strictly private and personal to himself, he never confided to any man on earth. When men have told of conversations with Lincoln in which they represent him as giving out either political or family affairs of a very sacred and secret character, their tales may be set down as false.

Yet Lincoln did tell Nicolay and Hay (and others) about Ann. Thus, although he was tight lipped on this and related topics, such did not preclude him from ever mentioning the romance. Lincoln's love of Ann might very well be the definitive event in Lincoln's early life, and her passing likely contributed to his famous bouts with melancholy, a point noted by many of his contemporaries. We will likely never know the full story.

Mary Todd Lincoln photographed during her first ladyship. Library of Congress Prints and Photographs Division, LC-USZ62-25789 DLC.

⊰ 10 ⊱

An Unlikely Union

Nearly all men can stand adversity.

—Abraham Lincoln

BEAUTY AND THE BEAST

Their relationship was, in many ways, an unlikely union. While Mary Todd and Abraham Lincoln were attracted to one another from their initial meeting, Lincoln was as tall, thin, poor, introspective, melancholy, and disheveled in appearance as Mary Todd was short, plump, wealthy, talkative, flirtsy, and impeccably dressed. But both were ambitious and shared Kentucky roots and a passion for politics, especially Whig Party politics. Mary Todd was headstrong, but fortunately, unlike most men of the day who did not tolerate such a spirit in a woman, Lincoln was patient and indulgent of his wife's opinions and strengths. Both had also lost their mothers at tender ages, something that bound them together later in their marriage during the many tragedies that befell them.

Mary Todd had more than her fair share of suitors in Springfield, many of them quite successful, yet in Lincoln she picked perhaps the poorest and most unlikely among them. Interestingly, one of Mary Todd's suitors was the famed orator and politician Judge Stephen A. Douglas, Lincoln's eventual rival for the U.S. Senate in 1858, a contest made famous by the "Lincoln–Douglas debates" over the future of the union and institution of slavery. The two men again squared off for a third time when they campaigned for the White House in 1860. As such, the debates and campaigns between the short, round segregationist and his upstart rival who abhorred human slavery but valued nationalism held together with common purpose and a strong hand of the federal government were intensely personal, given their history of vying for the affections of a lady.

Mary Todd's powerful father strongly disapproved of the relationship with Mr. Lincoln, as did her sister, Elizabeth, because of the usual reasons—Lincoln was uneducated, poor, and from a lower social class and showed little or no prospect for success. But Elizabeth also felt that Lincoln was awkward, noting of his courtship of Mary that "Mr. Lincoln would sit at [Mary's] side and listen. He scarcely said a word, but gazed on her as if irresistibly drawn towards her by some superior and unseen power." Mary Todd's other sister living in Springfield, Frances, also advised against dating Lincoln, flatly calling him the ugliest man in town. The uppity Todd clan was united in their opposition to Lincoln, something that would be but one of the many challenges of this unusual and strained union. As for Lincoln, he found the light side of the situation, quipping of the pretentious Todds, "One 'd' is enough for God, but the Todds need two."

Lincoln, like George Washington and so many other political leaders before him, had fixed his sights on marrying up socially yet was uncertain about courting Mary Todd. At the same time, Mary recognized Lincoln's immense potential in politics and, since her childhood, had intended to marry up politically. The two were intrigued by one another and had an almost animal attraction to one another physically, but it was an on-again, off-again courtship, marked by a very difficult and ugly breakup, and remains one of the least understood of all presidential marriages. Lincoln's dear friend Joshua Speed would later claim that Lincoln married Mary only for "honor," while Mary's cousin Elizabeth Brimsley observed that Lincoln lacked "over mastering depth of an early love." Lincoln's friend Orville H. Browning echoed these observations, saying that Lincoln had "anxiety" about the marriage and always felt that it was a "mistake" but felt "honor-bound" to marry Miss Todd.

Although Lincoln was a long shot as a suitor, Mary Todd fell for what she described as "the most congenial mind" not just in Springfield but "ever." It also helped Lincoln that the two had many friends in Springfield, including several of Mary Todd's relatives who were in politics with Lincoln. Still, in the words of one biographer, the marriage was "Lincoln's greatest tragedy."

The Todds of Kentucky

Mary Ann Todd was born on December 13, 1818, to Elizabeth Parker and Robert Smith Todd in Lexington, Kentucky. Both the Todds and the Parkers were prominent, established families. Mary's grandfather Levi Todd was a founder of Lexington, and there were a number of Todd generals, politicians, and attorneys. Mary's father was a wealthy banker and cotton manufacturer who owned ten slaves and was a Whig Party member of the Kentucky state legislature.

Mary was the third daughter of seven children. After the birth of the fourth daughter, who was named Ann, Mary stopped using her middle name. Shortly after the birth of the last child (a son), Mary's mother died of puerperal sepsis, a postbirth bacterial fever that claimed the lives of many women in an earlier time. Mary Todd was six years old at the time, and the ordeal scarred her for life. A few years later, in 1828, Robert Smith Todd remarried, but Mary and her older sisters disliked their new stepmother, Elizabeth Humphreys, to the extent that they wanted nothing to do with her. Mary and her stepmother were constantly at odds, and all the older sisters would eventually move out of the home at the first opportunity.

Very well educated for a woman of the time, Mary attended John Ward's Female Seminary and a boarding school in Lexington. Among the topics she studied were French, literature, writing, arithmetic, and the obligatory home arts—embroidery, sewing, and the like. Smart, sassy, and a good conversationalist, young Mary Todd already exhibited some of the signs that would later earn her both praise and condemnation. She was flirtatious, outgoing, and surprisingly ambitious. Yet the same fun-loving girl was prone to mood swings and could be playful one minute but depressed and emotional the next. The third Todd daughter developed a complex and volatile personality, something that would further strain the Lincoln marriage.

A good student, Mary developed a passion for politics, something that was considered a most unladylike thing to do. In a day when women were discouraged from even listening to political discussions much less taking an interest in them, Mary Todd made politics her avocational passion. She delighted in meeting many of the leading political figures of Kentucky. One of her other interests was horses, and she combined the two by riding her pony to visit her prominent Kentucky neighbor Senator Henry Clay, one of the most powerful politicians in the country and a three-time candidate for the presidency. Clay and little Mary used to tease one another about living in the White House. It seems that both of them planned to do so. During Mary's visits to Ashland, the Clay estate, the senator would tell her that when he was president, she could move with him to Washington, at which point she informed him that she intended to be in the White House as the president's wife.

Even though she enjoyed a privileged upbringing and the Todds were among the leading citizens of Lexington, Mary always wanted to leave the city to discover new social experiences and opportunities. Moreover, she longed to be away from her stepmother. Eventually, Mary's two older sisters,

Elizabeth and Frances, moved to Illinois and did quite well for themselves. In 1832, Elizabeth married Ninian Edwards, a lawyer, politician, and Springfield's wealthiest citizen. Frances followed her older sister, marrying William Wallace, a Springfield physician. Mary planned to follow in their footsteps, visiting Springfield in 1837 when she was nineteen years old. Enjoying the bustling social season, Mary returned in 1839, now twenty-one years of age and ready to make a splash in the new Illinois capital.

"Worst, Indeed!"

Mary moved into her eldest sister's spacious home in Springfield. Her timing was perfect. The political career of Mary's brother-in-law, Ninian Edwards, was on the fast track. The son of the first governor of the Illinois Territory and later the new state's first governor, Ninian was emerging as one of the most powerful and best-known politicians in the city. He was a member of the state legislature and would go on to become the state's attorney general. Ninian and Elizabeth hosted some of the most grand and memorable parties in Springfield. Ninian's personality matched his home and galas. He was aristocratic and debonair but was an egotistical elitist. Edwards made no attempt to hide his contempt for democracy and the masses, boasting his dislike and distrust of democratic government "as the devil is said to hate holy water."

Politics is said to make for strange bedfellows, and there is no better example of this given the vast differences in personality, upbringing, and political temperament than Ninian Edwards and his raw but promising friend Abraham Lincoln. Lincoln, a member of the state legislature, was new to the city. Even though he was shy and did not have "two cents to rub together," Lincoln attended one of the galas at the Edwards home. It was a good start for his political career. Lincoln was thirty and still single and, most of all, met Mary Todd at the party.

Mary was engaging and graceful and had already become well known in Springfield because of her sisters and her visibility during the social season. She attracted a great number of suitors. If her cute blue eyes, thick brown hair, cleavage-revealing dresses, and plump figure did not charm Springfield's political elite, then her bubbly personality was sure to do the trick. As Ninian said of his sister-in-law, "Mary could make a bishop forget his prayers." At the party, Lincoln watched as Mary Todd worked the crowd in a very low-cut pink lace gown that flared at the hips over a skirt hoop. Eventually mustering enough courage, Lincoln joined the line waiting to dance with Miss Todd. Once his turn arrived, Lincoln unceremoniously blurted out, "Miss Todd, I want to dance with you in the worst way." To which she said, observing him attempt to dance, "Worst, indeed!"

"A STORMY COURTSHIP"

Lincoln called his sweetheart "Molly" and, later after marrying her, always addressed her as "Mother." He was "Mr. Lincoln," but after marriage Mrs. Lincoln called her husband "Father." Despite the terms of endearment, the Lincoln courtship was, according to a biographer, "stormy." His preoccupation with ideas and politics were seen by her as competing with her need for affection. His hesitancy about the courtship and disinterest in fashion and social conventions grated on her nerves. When Lincoln arrived late to a dance, Mary Todd was furious. When he spent weeks away from home "riding the circuit" as a young lawyer, she was frustrated. When he cast his eyes on another attractive belle, she went into a fit of hysterics. On many levels, the two did not belong together. Lincoln was absentminded and neglectful, while Mary was high maintenance.

Mary Todd spent much of the summer of 1840 visiting her family in Missouri. At the time, Lincoln and Mary Todd had feelings for one another, and family members were both wondering and worrying about a pending wedding. However, the long separation strained the relationship, and Mary put on a lot of weight over the summer, leading Lincoln to quip, "Verily, I believe the farther West a young lady goes the better her health becomes . . . if she visits Missouri she will soon grow out of our recollection and if she should visit the Rocky Mountains I know not what would become of her." The two continued to write, and when Mary returned, they continued their courtship. Lincoln had reservations about the relationship almost from the beginning, and his doubts about their compatibility came to the fore when she returned. The relationship stalled, and both of them made overtures to dating others at the time. That November, Mary was being courted by Joseph Gillespie and catching the attention of other men. Lincoln was attending the legislative session in the late fall of 1840 and through the winter. One of his colleagues was Cyrus Edwards, a Whig Party leader who brought along his beautiful eighteen-year-old daughter, Matilda.

Matilda, well educated, flirtatious, elegant, tall, and blond, was *the* hit during the winter social season, especially with Lincoln, who described her as "perfect!" But Matilda, as it happened, was distantly related to Mary Todd. The young socialite was also boarding that winter with her relatives, Ninian and Elizabeth Edwards, meaning that she was under the same roof and likely shared the same bedroom as Mary Todd. Because it was the custom of the time, the girls may even have shared a large bed, along with one of the Edwards's daughters. One can only imagine the tension and rivalry between the two divas.

Lincoln fell for Matilda, making him realize that he never felt the same spark for Mary. As was the case when he was younger, he again found himself worrying about how to back out of a relationship while saving face and not hurting the feelings of his girlfriend. Desperate, Lincoln asked his close friend Joshua Speed for advice and even sheepishly asked Speed to deliver to Mary a letter he composed that would end the relationship. But Speed cast the letter into the fireplace, advising, "If you have the courage of manhood, go see Mary yourself; tell her, if you do not love her, the facts, and that you will not marry her. Be careful not to say too much, and then leave at your earliest opportunity." Lincoln took his friend's advice, marching straight to the Edwards's mansion, at which point he informed Mary that he did not love her and wanted to end the relationship. But Mary burst into tears. Even though she had been openly flirting with another man in order to make Lincoln jealous and recapture his attention, she loved Lincoln and was unaccustomed to rejection. When Mary started to cry, it made Lincoln cry as well. Lincoln apologized for hurting her feelings, kissed her, and then departed, feeling conflicted and ashamed of his behavior. When he informed Speed what had transpired, Speed was angry: "You not only acted the fool, but your conduct was tantamount to a renewal of the engagement, and in decency you cannot back down now." Lincoln resigned himself to marrying Mary Todd, saying, "Well, if I am in again, so be it."

"The Fatal First"

Despite the tumultuous courtship, Lincoln asked Mary Todd for her hand in marriage, and she agreed. A date was set for January 1, 1841. But the wedding did not occur. The historical record is mixed on the subject—some friends and family members suggested that Lincoln did not show up, while others remembered that the date had simply been called off. Mary Todd's niece, Katherine Helm, attributed the breakup to Lincoln becoming emotional because of Mary's flirting with Stephen Douglas, but most scholars and several of Lincoln's friends suggest that Lincoln was conflicted in his feelings toward Mary and his hesitancy about losing his freedom. His bouts with depression also likely factored in his last-minute decision to not get married. What we do know is that Lincoln broke down emotionally and later forever called the day that he called off his wedding "the fatal first."

It has also been said that Lincoln "couldn't bear to leave [Matilda]" because "he was deeply in love with her," although it would appear that Lincoln was more in lust with her than anything else. Either way, Lincoln's friends were upset with his behavior toward both Mary and Matilda. Of course, most single men—and a few married men—who attended the winter social events sought Matilda's attention. One of them was Lincoln's best friend, Speed, who made much more progress in gaining Matilda's attention than Lincoln. However, Speed had been courting sixteen-year-old Sarah Rickard, but Sarah broke up with Speed in January 1841, likely because of his obvious affection for Matilda. That same month, Speed proposed to Matilda, but she turned him down. Sulking, Speed closed his store and departed immediately for Kentucky. Speed's timing could not have been worse for Lincoln, who now had no place to work or live and no trusted friend in whom to confide. Consequently, Lincoln's depression, which he called "the hypo" ("hypochondria" was at the time a term to describe an unstable personality), became worse than it had ever been. He became even more depressed, saying,

> I am the most miserable man living. If what I feel were equally distributed to the whole human family, there would not be one cheerful face on the earth. Whether I shall ever be better, I can not tell . . . to remain as I am is impossible; I must die or be better, it appears to me.

Herndon, in his recollections of Lincoln after the breakup with Mary, described his old friend, saying,

> Did you know that Mr. Lincoln was "as crazy as a loon" in this city in 1841? He did not sit, did not attend to the legislature . . . that he was then deranged? Did you know that he was forcibly arrested by his special friends here at that time; that they had to remove all razors, knives, pistols, etc . . . from his room and presence, that he might not commit suicide?

One of Lincoln's rivals for Mary's affections, James Conkling, the grandson of Patrick Henry, noticed the same thing: "Poor Lincoln! How are the mighty fallen! He was confined about a week, but though he now appears again he is reduced and emaciated in appearance and seems scarcely to possess strength enough to speak above a whisper. His case at present is truly deplorable." Conkling thought that Mary Todd would marry him the year prior, but it did not happen, and Conkling ended up betrothed to Mary's best friend, Mercy Levering. Ironically, in the summer of 1840, Mary confided in none other than Mercy regarding the marriage proposal from Conkling, saying, "Yet Merce I love him not, & my hand will never be given, where my heart is not." This is telling in that it suggests that Mary would not have married Lincoln if she did not love him or that the need for true love might have been a factor in the failed engagement to the tall politician.

Matilda left a trail of broken hearts in her wake, turning down not only Lincoln and Speed but also a good part of Springfield, including Judge Douglas. She was just playing the field and enjoying the attention. Satisfied, in the fall of 1841, Matilda headed back home to Alton, Illinois. All along, she had a beau waiting for her named Newton Strong, who had graduated Phi Beta Kappa from Yale and was the son of an old-money family. Ironically, Lincoln and Strong knew one another and were political allies. Their mutual admiration for Matilda and her flirting did not harm the friendship, as Strong was among the men who nominated Lincoln for governor of Illinois. Matilda got what Matilda wanted—after a three-year courtship, she married Strong. She was happy in marriage, she said, because her husband "has lots of horses and gold."

Angry over the treatment of Mary Todd, Elizabeth and Ninian Edwards no longer permitted Lincoln to dine with them. Lincoln moved in January to the home of Mr. and Mrs. William Butler, and he also visited Dr. Anson Henry, who diagnosed him as suffering "hypochondria"—depression and anxiety—at the time. That summer, Lincoln passed a message through Dr. Henry to Mary that he still cared for her. Dr. Henry, who could find no cure for his patient, asked Mary Todd to write to Lincoln in order to cheer him up, which she did. However, on receiving word from Mary, Lincoln felt only worse because of how he treated Mary. Filled with guilt and remorse, Lincoln moped around town but did begin a new law partnership with Stephen T. Logan. In part, the new business venture was undertaken because he felt like he was done with politics and women.

In August of that year, Lincoln also traveled to Lexington, Kentucky, to visit his dear friend Speed, staying there for about five months for rest and recovery. It was the first time Lincoln had ever lived in a comfortable home. Speed's mother and sister, Mary, nursed Lincoln back to health, although his depression did not entirely disappear. Interestingly, a few weeks after, Speed would suffer the same anxiety and hesitancy over a woman named Fanny Henning. In a role reversal, Speed turned to Lincoln, who helped his friend through the ordeal and, in so doing, seems to have helped himself in that he realized that it was possible to get over a woman and also find happiness in a woman.

Speed and Lincoln returned to Springfield together in January 1842, one year after Lincoln ended his engagement with Mary Todd. In the Illinois capital, Speed completed some old business, then returned to Lexington and, on February 15, 1842, married Fanny. He found love in marriage, something he shared with his hesitant friend. Said Lincoln to Speed, "Your last letter gave me more pleasure than the total sum of all I have enjoyed since that fatal first of January, 1841."

At the same time, Mary Todd moved on, making herself the center of the winter social season, dining and dancing with Judge Douglas, who was exactly one foot shorter than Lincoln. She was also courted by Edwin B.

Webb, a wealthy widower and father, twenty years Mary's senior. But Mary Todd and Lincoln shared a strange but powerful attraction that neither one ever truly put behind them. They seemed incapable of living with one another but also of living without one another. At one point, Lincoln confronted Mary about her openly courting the judge, but she gave it right back to him, reminding him that he broke his honor and was smitten by Matilda Edwards.

It would be fully fifteen months since the couple had ended their engagement before they would see one another again. The breakup took a toll on Lincoln, even on his political career. He was uninspiring on the campaign trail and barely won reelection. His carelessness led to a minor scandal when one of Lincoln's rivals, Jesse B. Thomas Jr., accused Lincoln of authoring a scurrilous letter. It turned out that Thomas had written it himself and tried to blame it on Lincoln. The two met in a debate, and Lincoln utterly embarrassed Thomas in public. However, not content simply to win, Lincoln uncharacteristically demeaned and belittled Thomas but did so to the extent that it engendered sympathy for Thomas and anger toward Lincoln. Lincoln, who was usually the vanguard of magnanimity and graciousness, was ashamed of his behavior. All the while, friends worried about Lincoln's mental health and whether he would take his own life. His depression and erratic behavior in fact almost did cost him his life.

Duel

Early in the fall of 1842, Lincoln was contemplating another proposal to Mary Todd. The community took a keen interest in the on-again, off-again courtship between them but also in a series of scandalous and sensational letters published in the local paper known as the "Rebecca" letters. Among the followers of the letters were Lincoln and Mary. The letters lampooned James Shields, a powerful Democratic politician in town who was both handsome and popular with the ladies but who had also made some foolish political decisions. Lincoln decided he would join in on the prank and decided to write his own Rebecca letters, submitting them to the *Sangamon Journal* for publication. The paper's editor, Simeon Francis, was one of Lincoln's friends.

Lincoln drafted a letter dripping with satire, saying that Shields wanted to marry all the women of Springfield, but apologized for being "so handsome and interesting" that he would have to hurt so many of them because he was unable to marry them all. Lincoln signed it "Rebecca." While many appreciated the humor in the letter, some, such as Mary Todd and her good friend Julia Jayne—who would later be a bridesmaid in the Lincoln wedding—took offense to the letter. It happened that the two of them had been on the receiving end of some of Shields's advances. Francis, the editor of the paper, received a lot criticism for the letters and asked Lincoln for advice. Lincoln suggested that Francis simply blame all the letters on him, even though he had written but one or two of them.

But the plan did not work. Rather than accept the apology, Shields challenged Lincoln to a duel of heavy swords or pistols. Duels were, by this time, illegal in Illinois. So the two men traveled 100 miles to Missouri and, on September 27, 1842, met on the "field of honor." Lincoln was neither a hunter nor a good shot, but he felt he could kill Shields in a sword fight because of his advantage in size, reach, and strength. Fortunately for Lincoln and maybe Shields—and certainly for history—Revel English, a Democratic politician, and John J. Hardin, a Whig and Mary Todd's cousin, intervened to stop the duel and settle the matter peaceably. Most agreed that, depending on the weapons selected, the outcome would have been different. Lincoln noted that "I did not intend to hurt Shields unless I did so clearly in self-defense. If it had been necessary, I could have split him from the crown of his head to the end of his backbone." But if pistols had been selected, the outcome might have been much different.

Lincoln took the high road and apologized for his behavior. Years later, when asked about the matter of the duel by a Union general, Lincoln was embarrassed and said, "I do not deny it. But if you desire my friendship, you will never mention it again."

Fate intervened again in October 1842 when Hardin's younger sister, Martinette Hardin, married a man from Kentucky and invited Lincoln to attend the wedding. Both Lincoln and Mary Todd attended the affair, but Lincoln arrived with Sarah Rickard, the seventeen-year-old former girlfriend of his friend Joshua Speed. Sarah was a friend of the bride, and even though Lincoln lusted after her, he was simply escorting her. As Sarah would note of the relationship many years later, "I always liked him as a friend, but . . . his peculiar manner and his general deportment would not be likely to fascinate a young girl just entering the society world." Sarah eventually married Richard F. Barret, who was far more refined, wealthy, and handsome than Lincoln.

Hardin sat both couples—Lincoln and Sarah and Mary Todd and her date—at the same table, a bold move given how volatile the former couple could be. However, the two were said to have chatted cordially, speaking for the first time in many months. Later that fall, Elizabeth Francis, the wife of the editor of the town's newspaper, and John Hardin and his wife, Sarah, invited Lincoln and Mary Todd to a social event in nearby Jacksonville but did so with the intention of getting the couple back together. Neither Mary nor Lincoln knew that the other was attending. The matchmakers gave Lincoln and Mary Todd a later time to meet, informing them that all the guests would be traveling together to the event. But they sent the other guests ahead to the party in their carriages. Thus, when Lincoln and Mary arrived, they were the only two waiting. They ended up traveling together to the party.

Hardin saved Lincoln's hide from the duel over the Rebecca letters and brought him back together with Mary. He was a trusted friend and supporter of Lincoln. Rich, smart, and successful both in law and in politics, Hardin was elected to Congress and appeared destined for even more fame. It is likely that Hardin would have included Lincoln in his future political plans and equally likely that Lincoln would have brought Hardin into his presidential cabinet, but Hardin was killed in the War with Mexico in 1847. However, in late 1842, he did manage to nurture the passions of the town's most controversial couple. By late October, Lincoln and Mary were back together, but the relationship remained an enigma.

THE LINCOLN MARRIAGE

Mary kept the reengagement a secret, so we do not know much today about the details of it. Perhaps she did so in order to save face if it failed to work out for a second time. She is also likely to have been concerned about her sister and brother-in-law, who ardently disapproved of the relationship. Thus, as discreetly as possible, Lincoln and Mary Todd courted at the home of Simeon and Elizabeth Francis for three weeks in October 1842.

It seems to have been a spur-of-the-moment engagement, befitting the unusual but passionate nature of their relationship. Perhaps Lincoln worried that he would again back out. Perhaps they had premarital sex and Mary thought she was pregnant. Mary did, for example, admit that she used "every art given to me" to woo the reluctant Lincoln back to the altar, including the fact that she "trespassed, many times and often, upon his great tenderness and amiability of character." Indeed, Lincoln's friend Orville Browning observed that Mary was very aggressive and physical in courting Lincoln. And so, their first child, Robert, was born just shy of nine months after the wedding day. As Lincoln recalled about his first child and the details of his birth, the boy "has a great deal of that sort of mischief that is the offspring of much animal spirits."

For whatever reason, the first thing on the morning of November 4, 1842, Lincoln visited the Reverend Charles Dresser, saying, "I want to get hitched tonight." Lincoln then headed for Chatterton's Jewelry Store to buy a ring and have it engraved, "A.L. to Mary, Nov. 4, 1842. Love is Eternal." At noon, Lincoln visited James H. Matheny and asked him to be his best man, as there was no time to contact his best friend, Joshua Speed, in Kentucky. Matheny later commented that "Lincoln looked and acted as if he was going to the slaughter." Likewise, the son of Lincoln's landlord saw him all dressed up and walking to the wedding. The boy asked Lincoln where he was headed, to which his tall neighbor replied, "To hell, I suppose."

Meanwhile, Mary visited Julia Jayne, Caroline Lamb, Anna Rodney, and Elizabeth Todd, her seventeen-year-old cousin, and asked all of them to be bridesmaids. Mary did not inform her sister and brother-in-law until just hours before the wedding. According to a shocked Mrs. Edwards, "[Mary] came down one morning and announced she and Mr. Lincoln would be married that night and I can tell you I was angry, I said 'Mary Todd, even a free Negro would give her family time to bake a ginger cake.'" Mary dug her hole a little deeper by then asking Elizabeth if she could use their home for the ceremony. Mary's sister responded, "How could you marry someone who humiliated you? He's white trash, a common person, a plebian."

Against all odds, the wedding occurred. There were thirty guests at the Edwards's mansion for the ceremony. Mary Todd was twenty-three and Abraham Lincoln a decade her senior. Best man James Matheny later recalled an amusing moment at the wedding that made everyone in attendance laugh with nervousness:

> It was one of the funniest things imaginable . . . old Judge Brown was a rough "old-timer" and always said just what he thought without regard to place or surroundings. There was . . . a perfect hush in the room as the ceremony progressed. Old Parson dressed in clerical robes . . . handed Lincoln the ring, and as he put it on the bride's finger . . . [Lincoln said] "With this ring I thee endow with all my goods and chattels, lands and tenements." Brown, who had never witnessed such a proceeding, was struck by the utter absurdity and spoke out so everybody could hear . . . "Lord Jesus Christ, God Almighty, Lincoln, the statute fixes all that."

After the brief ceremony, the guests adjourned to the Globe Tavern, which was a short walk away. Because Lincoln was still in debt, the newly-weds were forced to rent upstairs at the Globe, something that was difficult for the new Mrs. Lincoln, who was accustomed to something far nicer than a cramped room atop a bar. It was not a good start for a marriage.

A House Divided

Emotionally, Lincoln seems not to have been able to move beyond the mess he had made of his initial courtship with Mary Todd. In fact, he seems not to have moved beyond the loss of Ann Rutledge, his first love, and the botched affair with Mary Owens. At the time of his marriage to Mary Todd, he was also still lusting after Sarah and Matilda, both younger and more attractive women than the person he married. For her part, Mary was prone to wildly emotional, compulsive, and nervous behavior even during the best of times. Mrs. Lincoln was melodramatic and suffered terrible headaches and great mood swings, and the marriage was a mystery to most who encountered the couple, who seemed so obviously incompatible. She was also the daughter of a political dynasty, unfamiliar with performing household duties by herself, something that she was now forced to do. Friends remember Mary being constantly exhausted, embarrassed, and infuriated with the endless demands of cooking, sewing, and cleaning, all of which became only more daunting for her once their son, Robert, was born that summer. It was a house divided from the start.

For instance, visitors to the Globe Tavern recall Lincoln purposely sitting on the porch at night telling stories to anyone who would listen as a way of avoiding having to go upstairs to his wife. All the while, Mrs. Lincoln would periodically cough and clear her throat loudly from their apartment on the second floor and frequently call out for her husband to come upstairs. Visitors were also treated to embarrassing "performances" by the couple, such as when Lincoln came running out through the door of their apartment with his wife not far behind throwing potatoes at him or when Mrs. Lincoln threw a large cut of meat at her husband, hitting him in the face.

Once Lincoln could afford it, he hired a maid to help his wife. However, no maid could stand to be around Mrs. Lincoln, who was an impossible taskmaster. Mrs. Lincoln also refused to pay a fair wage, causing at least one of the maids to threaten to quit. Lincoln then asked Mary to pay the maid the going rate, but she again refused. Said Lincoln, "But Mother, I don't want her to leave. Pay the twenty-five cents. We can afford it." But Mrs. Lincoln still refused: "No! I won't do it." Lincoln then told the maid not to worry and not to ask his wife for payment, that he would simply slip her the extra money. Unfortunately, Mary caught on to her husband's scheme, fired the maid, and screamed at Lincoln. The saga continued when Mrs. Lincoln slapped and then fired the replacement maid—and the three after that, including a boy servant who had his belongings thrown out the window by Mrs. Lincoln.

Lincoln's job required him to travel, such as when he rode the judicial circuit. With another attorney and judge, Lincoln traveled from town to town to handle the legal cases awaiting them. He was also a hard worker who put long hours into his job. All this created additional strain on the relationship, but Lincoln grew to enjoy the time away from his wife. Lincoln took to sleeping on the couch or on the couch at his office. He also visited the post office, chatting up the postmaster until it was time to return home. The postmaster recalled Lincoln complaining, "Well, I hate to go home," at which point an invitation would be extended to Lincoln to stay at his home. Lincoln would immediately accept the offer.

Mrs. Lincoln embarrassed her husband by her uncontrollable outbursts and temperamental behavior. This would continue during the presidency. Friends and, later, the press picked up on her tantrums. Unfortunately, the fact that Mary was thin skinned meant that she handled quite poorly the criticism that her behavior attracted. One of the many things that set Mrs. Lincoln off was her jealousy of younger, attractive women. Lincoln appears to have been faithful, but Mary accused the wives of military officers and others in Lincoln's company of being whores.

Children

The turbulent Lincoln marriage was stabilized a bit by the birth of children. The couple's constant arguing subsided a bit more with the birth of each child, and Mary and Lincoln functioned better together as mother and father than they ever did as husband and wife. Children brought them both immense joy and heart-wrenching grief.

The Lincolns had four boys—Robert, Edward, William, and Thomas—the last nicknamed "Tad." Mary, who was already emotional and neurotic, worried incessantly about her boys. For instance, when Robert was a child and she could not momentarily find him in the yard, she would scream, "Bobby will die! Bobby will die!" She then sent for Lincoln, who would rush home only to find the boy playing contentedly in the yard.

Lincoln, on the other hand, had a carefree approach to raising his children that included indulging their every whim and playing with them much as an older brother might do. Indeed, at a time when fathers were stern disciplinarians and largely absent from the nitty-gritty of child rearing, Lincoln carved out as much time as possible for his boys. When elected to Congress, for instance, he moved the whole family to the capital city even though it was common for members of Congress to travel and live by themselves while in Washington, leaving their wives and children "back home." However, with Lincoln working much of the day and Mary both lonely and overwhelmed by the city, she moved back home to Kentucky. Lincoln took the move worse than his wife, writing tender "little letters" to his sons, saying, "I hate to stay in this old room by myself."

When Lincoln was elected president, the idea of having children in the White House was a novel one. It was the first time that a president had young children during his time in office, and the public and press were fascinated by what the children were doing and how the Lincolns raised their sons. And the Lincoln boys did not fail to deliver. The younger two sons, Willie and Tad, drove the presidential staff crazy with their mischievous pranks, such as summoning the staff to phantom meetings in various rooms and at all hours with the building's system of bells. Dressed in full military uniform, they also lined up the staff, ordered them to attention, and made them drill. The boys also placed a toy cannon on the roof of the White House in order to defend it from Confederates. While meeting with members of the press, Lincoln's son Willie rushed into the office begging frantically for a quarter. Lincoln responded, "I can't let you have a quarter. I can only spare five cents." As Willie ran out of the office complaining, Lincoln calmly placed five pennies on his desk. The president then smiled to the reporters while nodding to the money, saying, "He will be back after that in a few minutes." No sooner had Lincoln resumed answering their questions than Willie returned and took the five cents.

Lincoln had a way not only with his children but with all children as well. When his boys were young, children in the neighborhood would hang on Lincoln's legs and arms, follow him like the pied piper, and pull pranks on him, all of which Lincoln knowingly allowed them to do. The most popular one was to pull a string across a walkway at the height of Lincoln's signature stovepipe hat. When the tall man walked by, the string would knock his hat off his head, and Lincoln would laugh as if he had not been expecting it. Although the social mores at the time frowned on grown men being playful with children, Lincoln was routinely seen carrying one of his boys on his shoulders or behind him in a wagon. In fact, the absentminded Lincoln was once so engrossed in a book he was reading while pulling sons Willie and Tad in a wagon that, when little Tad fell out, he did not immediately notice and kept reading and walking. Playmates of Lincoln's sons would hang from his long legs and wrestle with him, and the Lincoln boys and the three Taft siblings loved to tackle the president and sit on him so he could not escape.

The youngest Lincoln son, Tad, who struggled with a learning disability and pronounced lisp, was a handful. The staff found his toy soldiers everywhere; he dug up the White House garden for a pretend burial for one of his toy soldiers; his pet goat, Nanny Goat, trampled through the building, slept in Tad's bed, and ate the flowers in the gardens; and Tad once snuck into the kitchen and ate all the strawberries that had been carefully cleaned and arranged for an upcoming White House dinner. Tad earned the nickname the "Tyrant of the White House." But Lincoln did not mind and, in fact, seemed to take great delight in Tad's antics, which he properly saw as a child simply being a child. For example, Tad once refused to take his medicine and was running and screaming around the White House with a nurse and a panicked Mrs. Lincoln in hot pursuit. Eventually, Mrs. Lincoln ordered the nurse to interrupt the president, who was in a meeting. "Mrs. Lincoln insists I see you," explained the nurse. "Tad won't take his medicine." Lincoln told the nurse, "You stay here and I'll see what I can do." He then excused himself and walked Tad to his bedroom. There was peace and quiet in the room. Tad took his medicine. When Lincoln returned to the meeting, he announced, "It's alright. Tad and I have fixed things up." In Tad's room, the nurse found Tad resting comfortably with a note in his hand that read, "Pay to Tad (when he is well enough to present) Five Dollars. A Lincoln."

On a regular basis, the two boys would burst into a presidential meeting and hound their father with requests or jump on his lap. Lincoln's generals complained continually about the president's sons, and Lincoln's otherwise dutiful secretaries, John Hay and John Nicolay, said that they wanted to "wring the boys' little necks." Lincoln's former law partner William Herndon, whose patience was regularly tested when the boys would overturn the shelves of law books in the office or blot black ink on papers and then "dance" on them, echoed these sentiments, complaining that his friend was

> so blinded to his children's faults . . . that, if they [defecated] in Lincoln's hat and rubbed it on his boots, he would have laughed and thought it smart. . . . He worshipped his children and what they worshipped . . . disliked what they hated, which was everything that did not bend to their . . . whims.

Indeed, Lincoln was affectionate and tolerant with his two young boys. When the boys misbehaved and Mary ordered her husband to fan the boys' backsides, Lincoln would march them to their bedroom and make them scream bloody murder while he pretended to be spanking them. His friends agreed that he was "too kind, too tender and too gentle to his children; he had no domestic government—administration or order." Lincoln's skills as a father were deemed to be as "loving & Tender as a nursing mother." Rather than sweat his boys' misbehavior, Lincoln commented that "it is my pleasure that my children are free and happy, and unrestrained by parental tyranny. Love is the chain whereby to bind a child to its parents."

Lincoln's friends noted his ability to tune out his surroundings, something that helped him deal not only with his emotional wife but with his unruly boys as well. His friend J. P. McEvoy called it Lincoln's "protective deafness," "the mark of every happily married man." While the boys would run wild around the office, driving Mrs. Lincoln and the White House staff to wit's end, Lincoln would sit contentedly, unfazed by the commotion. Or he would simply laugh at it.

Many details of Lincoln's parenting style come courtesy of Julia Taft, a teenage babysitter who looked after Willie and Tad in the White House and lived until 1933. Julia, whose two younger siblings, Bud and Holly, were the Lincoln boys' playmates, wrote a book about her experiences titled *Tad Lincoln's Father*. Young Julia became family to the first couple and was the daughter Lincoln never had. He nicknamed her his "Fibbertigibbet," which he said playfully was "a small, slim thing with curls and a white dress and a blue sash who flies instead of walking."

One of the many stories Julia passed on to history was of the boys' toy Union soldier, Jack. Willie and Tad once marched into the president's meeting over the objections of Julia and the White House staff. But hearing the commotion outside, Lincoln invited his boys into the meeting, at which point they informed him that they were putting Jack to death. When Lincoln asked why, they informed their father that Jack had fallen asleep while on guard duty. Lincoln reasoned with the boys that Jack had been put to death at least a dozen times and that each time a hole was dug in the White House garden, angering Major Watt, the gardener. But the boys remained firm in their support for another death penalty. They had previously had Jack shot but wanted him hanged this time. So Lincoln suggested a trial. During the testimony, Lincoln rose to speak on Jack's behalf, reminding his boys that no man ought to be tried twice for the same crime and that a president can extend a pardon. After imparting the lesson on the boys, Lincoln scribbled a note that he handed to them. It read, "The doll Jack is pardoned by order of the President. A. Lincoln." The boys agreed and quietly exited the office. When they did, Lincoln said to his secretary, "I only wish, Hay, they were all that easy."

Tragedy and Scandal

Tragedy visited the Lincoln household numerous times. Only their firstborn son, Robert, would live to adulthood. The second Lincoln son was Edward Baker Lincoln, named for a local Whig politician and family friend and born on March 10, 1846, at the new Lincoln home on Eighth and Jackson streets in Springfield. Lincoln was characteristically playful with Eddy, often carrying him around on his shoulders and referring to him as "my dear codger" or my "blessed child."

Just prior to Christmas Day of 1849, Eddy became very ill. Mary's father had died of cholera not long before, as had the child of a close friend. As such, Mary was filled with anxiety as Eddy was becoming ill. It remains uncertain as to whether it was diphtheria or pulmonary tuberculosis, but the young boy suffered for fifty-two days before succumbing on February 1, 1850, just shy of his fourth birthday. Less is known about Eddy than any other Lincoln child, but we do know that the parents suffered tremendously. Mrs. Lincoln became even more neurotic and began worrying that every sniffle or cough was the end for those she loved, a condition that would stay with her to the end of her life. Neither of the Lincolns believed that they could endure the loss. Mrs. Lincoln was inconsolable, refusing to eat for weeks or to care for her older son, Robert. She shut herself into her room and cried uncontrollably for much of the remainder of the year. Lincoln was so distraught that the verbose and poetical future president could muster only the words, "We lost our little boy" and "We miss him very much." Lincoln also struggled to save his wife from her grief, saying to her, "Eat, Mary, for we must live." He also became ever more doting on the next two boys to be born.

A little less than eleven months after Eddy's death, a third Lincoln son was born. On December 21, 1850, the Lincolns welcomed son William Wallace, named for a local physician who was married to Mary's sister, Frances. Willie's birth helped Mrs. Lincoln come out of her depression a little, but it transformed Lincoln. Willie would become Lincoln's favorite child. The two would become uncommonly close. Just as Robert was in so many ways a Todd, Willie, who was playful, charmingly gregarious, and cerebral, was all Lincoln. Mary's cousin, Elizabeth Todd Grimsley, said of Willie that he was "a noble, beautiful boy of nine years, of great mental activity, unusual intelligence, wonderful memory, methodical, frank and loving, a counterpart of his father, save that he was handsome." Julia Taft, Willie's babysitter, described him in similar terms, saying that he was "the most lovable boy I ever knew, bright, sensible, sweet-tempered and gentle-mannered." Lincoln took great pleasure in his son's ability to memorize the names of the towns from Springfield to Washington during Lincoln's famous train ride to the inauguration. Later, while in the White House, he served as the unofficial greeter of presidential visitors and as the mansion's tour guide.

During the winter social season of 1862, Willie became violently ill. It was diagnosed as bilious fever and was perhaps typhoid fever. Because of the threat of a Confederate attack on Washington, Union troops were stationed on the White House grounds, meaning that latrines had to be dug among the tents and drilling soldiers. It is believed that Willie, who played on these same grounds, may have contracted his malady from the polluted water on the grounds.

The peak of Willie's illness also coincided with one of Mrs. Lincoln's grandest social events. Where other first ladies had been celebrated for hosting galas and renovating the executive mansion, Mrs. Lincoln was harshly condemned for her events and decorating. Although she was a capable hostess, the appearance of gaiety and dining during times of war struck the wrong chord, and the First Lady's many critics seized the opportunity to use the social affairs against the Lincolns. There were snubs of the hostess and boycotts of the events by the city's political elite.

Congress had appropriated the large sum of $20,000 to redecorate the White House. Mary was excited about the endeavor, believing that she needed to spruce up the building in order to bring some cheer to a president and the nation in the throes of a terrible war. But Mary spent the entire amount almost at once. She purchased cabinets, decorations, fabrics, furnishings, and wallpaper, including fancy and expensive items from France. The most egregious offense occurred when she purchased a 190-piece Limoges china service, the most expensive available in the country. The First Lady decided it was so nice that she needed a second set. Mrs. Lincoln ended up spending far more than the allotted amount. At first she tried to hide the costs. She then contacted Benjamin B. French, the commissioner of public buildings, informing him that she went $6,700 over budget. She begged French to please talk to her husband, who was furious with her, then started to cry, pleading,

> That it is common to overrun appropriations—tell him how much it costs to refurbish, he does not know much about it, he says he will pay it out of his own pocket . . . you know, Major, he cannot afford that, he ought not to do it . . . do go to Mr. Lincoln and try to persuade him to approve the bill . . . but do not let him know you have seen me.

Mary then approached Lincoln's trusted secretary, John Hay, asking him to provide her with the salary of a job that was vacated. Of course, Hay refused and was firm in his reproach. Hay had dealt with the First Lady before, including when she tried to get the president to hire her friends and relatives. A furious Mary lit into Hay, who recorded in his diary, "Madame has mounted me to pay her the Steward's salary." Of the First Lady's erratic behavior, Hay also noted that "the Hell-cat is getting more Hell-cattical day by day." Hay declined Mary's request.

However, unbeknownst to the president, Mrs. Lincoln arranged for the White House gardener to divert funds to cover her expenses. She talked the gardener into overstating the expenses for flowers and plants and then forwarding the surplus to her. Also, at a state dinner for Emperor Napoleon II of France, Mary billed the Department of State $900 even though the cost of the event was roughly $300. Secretary William Seward, however, declined to pay the difference. Unfortunately, the press learned of the arrangements, and the ironic contrast of Lincoln's efforts to rally the nation to sacrifice and frugality with his wife's extravagant shopping and decorating hurt the president politically. Mary feebly said in her defense, "Mr. Lincoln has but little idea of the expense of a woman's wardrobe."

When the scandal broke and Mary asked her husband for more funds, Lincoln exploded, arguing,

> I'll pay it out of my own pocket first. It would stink in the nostrils of the American people to have it said that the President of the United States had approved a bill over-running an appropriation of $20,000 for flub dubs for this damned old house, when the soldiers cannot have blankets!

Congress ultimately did approve extra funds for the First Lady's expenses, but Lincoln declined and paid it from his pocket.

A compulsive shopper, the First Lady was known to visit Philadelphia and New York City for shopping sprees that included countless pairs of gloves. When word of her shopping bonanzas reached the press, Lincoln told his wife in stern terms that the "flub-dubs," as he called them, must stop. He cut her off financially. Mary had become a celebrity but also a scandal. She wore the latest fashions (much as is the case today), dressmakers lent her gowns as advertisements, and the First Lady opened the White House to the public, making it more accessible than it had been in years. But in the midst of a bloody war, her actions were seen as simply too extravagant.

Unfortunately, Mary took the criticisms of her behavior poorly. With each critical comment, the First Lady became more neurotic. William O. Stoddard, Lincoln's secretary, even resorted to going through Mrs. Lincoln's mail before she had a chance to do so in order to destroy the most critical letters. He forwarded to her only the most flattering letters because he understood her fragile state. Said Stoddard, "It was not easy, at first . . . to understand why a lady who could be one day so kindly, so considerate, so generous, so thoughtful and so hopeful, could, upon another day, appear so unreasonable, so irritable, so despondent, so even niggardly." One of Mary's most important galas was held on February 5, 1862. It would be the First Lady's chance at redemption in front of the leading citizens of the capital city. However, Willie, who had earlier bouts with the measles and scarlet fever, became very ill, and young Tad also took to his bed with a fever. Mary was anxious and unable to function at her own social, spending most of the evening upstairs with her boys. The physician Robert K. Stone was summoned, and both Lincolns grew desperate as Willie's condition worsened. On February 18, he slipped into a coma and died two days later.

This loss would the most challenging personal ordeal of Lincoln's difficult life. Both he and his wife were on the verge of complete mental and emotional collapse. Elizabeth Keckley, the First Lady's seamstress and confidante, remembered the president's countenance, saying, "Great sobs choked his utterance. He buried his head in his hands, and his tall frame was convulsed with emotions." Lincoln described the loss simply: "It is hard, hard to have him die." Said the grief-stricken father of his son, "He was too good for this earth, but then we loved him so."

Willie's body was embalmed and placed in a coffin in the Green Room, where Lincoln spent many hours alone and in tears. Later, Lincoln would have many emotional and solitary visits to Willie's grave site. Mrs. Lincoln was too distraught even to attend the funeral services. She took to wearing "shroudlike mourning clothes" that covered her entire body and head like an "immense black veil" such that people had trouble recognizing her. Her husband and friends began worrying about her mental faculties when Mrs. Lincoln started visiting spiritualists such as Mrs. Laury and Mrs. Colchester, who helped her communicate with her deceased children. She became increasingly reliant on the occult and messages that the spiritualists said they were transmitting from Willie.

It can be said that Mrs. Lincoln never fully recovered from the loss of Willie. From then on, she exhibited mood swings and depression-like symptoms. She was a changed person. However, the fact that both Lincolns had lost their mothers when they were young helped them comfort one another during these difficult times, and their marriage improved somewhat, although both continued to suffer the losses. Lincoln also never fully recovered from the loss of his beloved Willie, but he managed better than his wife. However, an incident occurred that would set him back emotionally. A few weeks after Willie's death, there was a terrible fire in the White House stables. Willie's favorite horse was one of the horses trapped. Lincoln tried frantically to run to the stable to save Willie's horse but had to be restrained because of the danger. The horses were not able to be saved, and Lincoln slid back into a deep melancholy.

The fourth Lincoln son, Thomas, named for Abe's father, was born on April 14, 1853. When the boy was born, his head appeared to be too large for his body, and he wiggled like a tadpole, thus earning him the nickname "Tad." The Lincolns were hoping for a girl but were pleased that young Willie had a playmate. Unfortunately, Tad suffered from a learning disability and speech impediment that was so pronounced that most guests to the White House could understand little to nothing of what he said. In those instances, Tad's older brother, Willie, served as his "translator." Tad was slow to read and write and never progressed very far in any subject, especially after Willie's death, as Tad had grown to be totally dependent on his older brother. He was also prone to temper tantrums and inherited his mother's impulsive and uninhibited nature. Lincoln called him "Little Troublesome Sunshine" and would say of Tad's lack of discipline and antics, "Let him run. He has time enough left to learn his letters and get pokey. Bob was just such a little rascal, and now he is a very decent boy." Elizabeth Todd Grimsley, Mary's cousin, said of the boy that he was "a gay, gladsome, merry, spontaneous fellow, bubbling over with innocent fun, whose laugh rang through the house, when not moved to tears. Quick in the mind, and impulse, like his mother, with her naturally sunny temperament, he was the life, and also the worry of the household."

Willie's death was very hard on Tad. After the loss, Lincoln became Tad's playmate, and the two became inseparable. They helped each other through the ordeal. Lincoln allowed Tad to play or slumber on his lap during meetings, took him shopping, and designed clever "errands" and tasks for Tad. Once, Tad came running into the White House crying and asking for his father. When Lincoln asked what was bothering Tad, the boy told him that a woman was out front wanting to see Lincoln. She needed the president's help because her husband was going to prison. Amidst the tears, Tad insisted that his "Pa" help. Lincoln promptly dropped everything he was doing and saw to it that the man was pardoned. Tad rushed to inform the woman of the good news, and both broke down and cried together, hugging one another.

Tad's other trusted companion was his pet goat, Nanny Goat. Poor Lincoln suffered to inform his wife and son, traveling in New York City, that Nanny Goat was lost. Writing on August 18, 1863, Lincoln informed his wife,

> Tell dear Tad, poor "Nanny Goat" is lost, and Mrs. Cuthbert & I are in distress about it. The day you left Nanny was found resting herself, and chewing her little cud, on the middle of Tad's bed. But now she is gone! The gardener kept complaining that she destroyed the flowers till it was concluded to bring her down to the White House. This was done, and the second day she had disappeared and has not been heard since. This is the last we know of poor Nanny.

Tad's friendship with animals continued. Lincoln, who could not bring himself to say no to his sons and who shared his youngest son's passion for animals, pardoned a turkey that was set to be Christmas dinner at the White House. Lincoln did so because Tad wanted the turkey as a pet. Sure enough, the turkey, which Tad named "Jack," lived at the White House. During the 1864 election, Lincoln observed voters milling about the White House. Among them was Jack the turkey, who paraded across the lawn. Quipped Lincoln to Tad, "What business has the turkey stalking about the polls in that way? Does he vote?" Tad answered, "No, he's not of age!" The two enjoyed a hearty laugh together, one of the many light moments between father and son that they managed to find amid the turmoil of Lincoln's presidency.

War

Living in the White House is stressful for any first family, but especially so when there are children involved and the nation is at war. The Lincolns endured the stress of the Civil War and regular threats to their safety and were reminded of this by the presence of troops stationed on the grounds of the mansion. There was also the matter of the eldest Lincoln son, Robert, who was born on August 1, 1843. The son of the president leading the war effort was, himself, not in the fight.

Robert had attended a preparatory school in Illinois, and Lincoln was hoping to send his son to Harvard College. However, in 1859, he failed the entrance exams. Lincoln was able to enroll Robert in the Phillips Exeter Academy, another elite institution in New Hampshire. Eventually, Robert was admitted to Harvard, where he was studying during the Civil War. Unlike the other Lincoln boys, Robert, who could be prickly and standoffish, had a strained relationship with his parents, especially with his father. Robert, according to his father, was "entirely Todd" in his disposition. As one scholar noted, Robert "was an anomaly, a slightly perplexed mystery to both his mother and, especially, his father." The sources of the cool relationship are many, but scholars point to the fact that "there was an estrangement between them reminiscent of the coldness between Lincoln and his father." Robert had also been teased as a child for a "lazy" eye and proved to be as sensitive to criticism as his mother. Of course, poor Robert had the misfortune of being raised in a dysfunctional marriage. Unlike Willie and Tad, who were children when the Lincolns resolved most of their differences and enjoyed a stable, prosperous home, Robert would have felt the tension between his parents during the most strained early years of their marriage. Robert was born less than nine months after his parents' sudden and loveless betrothal, Lincoln offers a clue when he said that his son possessed "a great deal of that sort of mischief that is the offspring of much animal spirits."

Both father and son were unsuccessful in repairing the relationship. Lincoln, for example, did little to hide his preference for the younger boys, even musing about his son that "I sometimes fear he is one of the little rare-ripe sort, that are smarter at about five than ever after." To his trusted friend Joshua Speed, Lincoln commented only that Robert was "smart enough." Perhaps the only time Lincoln lost his temper with his children occurred during his famous train ride from Springfield to his inauguration in 1861. In an effort to make Robert feel a part of the momentous events, Lincoln entrusted his oldest son with his Inaugural Address. Robert was assigned to carry the satchel during the long trip to the capital city. However, Robert misplaced the speech. Although it was eventually found, the incident caused Lincoln much anxiety, and he uncharacteristically vented his anger at his son. During Lincoln's presidency, the Prince of Wales visited the White House but drank too much and was far too flirtatious and reckless in his behavior. Robert also embarrassed himself. These incidents were not lost on the press, who took to calling Robert the "Prince of Rails." Lincoln, after all, had represented the railroads as an attorney, and the nickname was not a compliment.

Thus, when many of Robert's classmates and professors at Harvard withdrew from school in order to join the war effort (and a few of them failed to return alive), Robert's inaction began a minor scandal. It also caused strain in the Lincoln marriage. Mrs. Lincoln, rightly terrified of losing another son, refused to allow Robert to serve. This is understandable. With the constant threat to the first family's safety and constant reports arriving of massive Union losses, the Lincolns felt the pain of the nation with each death. While many spouses of political leaders abandoned the capital city, Mary courageously demanded to stay in the White House. However, Mary's black seamstress and White House confidante, Elizabeth Keckley, recalled the fights between the couple over the issue:

> Mrs. Lincoln: "We have lost one son, and his loss is as much as I can bear, without being called to make another sacrifice."

> The President: "But many a poor mother has given up all her sons. Our son is not more dear to us than the sons of other people are to their mothers."

> Mrs. Lincoln: "That may be; but I cannot bear to have Robert exposed to danger. His services are not required in the field, and the sacrifice would be a needless one."

> The President: "The services of every man who loves his country are required in this war. You should take a liberal instead of selfish view of the question, Mother."

Mary's half-sister, Emilie Todd Helm, remembered a similar conversation between the First Lady and the president over their eldest son's safety, with Mary saying, "I know that Robert's plea to go into the Army is manly and noble and I want him to go, but oh! I am so frightened he may never come back to us!" Lincoln responded, "Many a poor mother, Mary, has had to make this sacrifice and has given up every son she had—and lost them all."

The issue was also problematic because Mrs. Lincoln was from a slave-owning family from a border state. Her relatives, like half-brother, Sam, fought and died for the Confederacy. As such, she was subjected to accusations of disloyalty from both northerners and southerners who saw her as abandoning her roots and embracing the abolitionist cause. It was thus a scandal ripe to be exploited when Mary's half-sister, Emilie, moved to the White House. Mary, who was depressed and needed comforting, wanted the company and also wanted to help her half-sister, whose husband had died in the war and who was destitute. In an effort to help his wife deal with the grief of losing sons, Lincoln agreed to have Mary's relative live with them. The problem was that Emilie's husband, Benjamin Hardin Helm, had been a general of the Confederacy. Amidst protests that Lincoln was allowing a Confederate spy into the White House, Emilie moved in during the month of December 1863. However, Emilie refused to take the loyalty oath to the

Union, tried to sell cotton illegally (against the Union boycotts and prohibitions), and may even have stolen one of Lincoln's speeches. These incidents occasioned a rift between Mary and Emilie and, of course, caused another public embarrassment for Lincoln.

TRAGIC ENDING

Robert Lincoln graduated from Harvard in 1864 and, near the end of the war, finally joined the fight. Lincoln had intervened with General Ulysses Grant, asking the commander to place his son "into your military family with some nominal rank." Robert was placed safely as a member of Grant's staff. The commission quieted the scandal over Robert's lack of service and satisfied Lincoln but unnerved Mrs. Lincoln. Lincoln's gesture also had the effect of thawing the chilly relationship between father and eldest son. As the war concluded, Robert and his father began to patch up their differences. Lincoln even sent his son with General Grant to witness the surrender of General Robert E. Lee.

Assassination

On April 14, 1865, Robert, fresh off his participation in Lee's surrender, had breakfast with his father in the executive mansion. As Mrs. Lincoln's seamstress observed that morning, the relationship between father and son was "more cheerful than I had seen it for a long while, and he seemed to be in a generous, forgiving mood." The two talked about Lee and the end of the war. With the war effectively over, Lincoln looked forward to a change in the demands of his office. He also planned to attend the play *Our American Cousin* that evening at Ford's Theatre in Washington. The Lincolns had invited General Grant and his wife, Julia Dent, to join them, but the general was exhausted and declined. Lincoln inquired as to whether Robert wished to attend the theater in Grant's place, but Robert was also tired from the trip back to Washington.

That afternoon, the Lincolns enjoyed a carriage ride together. Both husband and wife were more relaxed than they had been in years. Mary had inquired as to whether Lincoln preferred company for the ride, but he declined: "No, I prefer to ride by ourselves today." They talked of the future and moving forward together from the tragic losses and terrible war. Lincoln vowed, "We must both, be more cheerful in the future—between the war & the loss of our darling Willie—we have both, been very miserable." It would be the last afternoon of their lives together.

Entering the theater, the first couple was greeted by a standing ovation. Major Henry Rathbone and his young fiancée, Clara Harris, the daughter of Senator Ira Harris of New York, ended up being the Lincolns' guests that night in the state box. About ninety minutes into the play, Mary leaned her head onto Lincoln's shoulder and whispered to him, "What will Mrs. Harris think of us holding hands?" Another account has Mrs. Lincoln asking, "What will Miss Harris think of my hanging on to you so?" The president smiled and said, "She won't think anything about it." As the Lincolns were exchanging tender words, John Parker, the security guard assigned to the state box, decided to take a break and abandoned his post. That very instant, the noted actor and southern sympathizer John Wilkes Booth entered the private box. He was carrying a dagger and a pistol.

Interestingly, Lincoln had watched Booth on the very same stage a few years earlier. From point-blank range, Booth shot Lincoln in the back of the head. While attempting to jump off the ledge and onto the stage, Booth stumbled and landed awkwardly onstage, breaking his left leg above the ankle. As the audience gasped at the scene unfolding onstage, Booth theatrically sang out, "Sic semper tyrannis," meaning "Thus to tyrants," and fled the stage to a waiting horse. From the state box, Major Rathbone yelled that a doctor was needed. In the audience was a military surgeon, Dr. Charles Leale. It was Dr. Leale and Rathbone, joined by others, who carried the mortally wounded president out of the theater. They took Lincoln across the street to William Peterson's Boardinghouse. Unbelievably, it was the exact place—even the same room—where Booth boarded on a visit to the capital city just a few months prior, likely while planning the assassination.

Lincoln had dreamt of his own assassination. In the dream, he awakened to the sound of people sobbing in the White House. Following the sounds, Lincoln walked downstairs and there observed a funeral with a corpse displayed in the East Room of the White House. When he asked a soldier stationed in the room who had died, he was informed, "The President. He was killed by an assassin."

At the boardinghouse, the dying president was so tall that he could not fit in the bed and had to be placed diagonally across the bed, with his feet hanging over the edge. Physicians cared for Lincoln, but all knew it was useless. Robert Lincoln and Mrs. Lincoln were summoned. Seeing her husband dying, Mary screamed hysterically and babbled incoherently that they had to fetch little Tad because Lincoln would want to talk to Tad: "Bring Tad— [Lincoln] will speak to Tad—he loves him so. . . . Oh! That my little Taddy might see his father before he died!" When Secretary of War Edwin Stanton arrived late that evening, he took control of the situation and ordered the

First Lady be taken out of the room. Early the next morning, the sky blackened, and it started to rain. A little over an hour later, at 7:22 in the morning, the president was pronounced dead. It was then that Stanton allegedly offered the immortal words, "Now he belongs to the ages."

Thus ended the greatest presidency in American history and started the largest manhunt in the nation's history. Even though there were several other attempts on Lincoln's life and rumors of plots, the nation was shocked. Only one month prior to the assassination, Lincoln enjoyed his second inauguration, giving one of the greatest addresses in American history. In fact, Lincoln preferred this speech to his immortal Gettysburg Address. Lincoln's wife never recovered from the loss of her husband. Mary was unable to function back at the White House, remaining in bed and refusing food. She did not even accompany the bodies of her husband and son, Willie, on the train ride back to Illinois, an iconic ride in a car draped in black witnessed by tens of thousands of Americans who lined the tracks from Washington to Illinois to pay their respects to the Great Emancipator.

Mrs. Lincoln remained at the White House for forty days after the assassination before she was able to travel. The assassination was part of a larger plot that also included failed attempts on the lives of Vice President Andrew Johnson and Secretary of State William Seward. During the manhunt, Secretary Stanton acted with swift and ruthless vengeance, but the White House itself was in chaos. Many staff members did not come to work or attend the building, and, with the First Lady locked in her room, looters broke in and stole the building's furnishings. The situation was so devastating that Commissioner Benjamin French testified before Congress about the White House, saying, "There was absolutely nothing left." When Mary Lincoln finally moved out of the home, she was accused of stealing the furnishings. But Mrs. Lincoln did herself little good, lashing out hysterically at everyone and suspecting everyone of complicity in her husband's murder. She accused Vice President Johnson of conspiracy because he did not send her a note or pay the proper condolences. She also blamed John Parker, the guard at Ford's Theater, for Lincoln's death because he abandoned his post. Cried Mary to the guilt-ridden official, "I shall always believe you guilty!"

Young Tad Lincoln also suffered his father's loss. Shortly after the assassination, Tad was informed of what had happened. He was twelve and, despite his slight disability, understood the reality of the situation immediately. The poor boy ran screaming, "They've killed him! They've killed him!" Tad had to be taken away by the staff. A few days later, at his father's funeral, Tad sobbed,

Pa is dead. I can hardly believe that I shall never see him again. Yes, Pa is dead, and I am only Tad Lincoln now, little Tad, like other little boys. I am not a president's son now. I won't have many presents any more. Well, I will try and be a good boy, and will hope to go some day to Pa and brother Willie, in heaven.

Tad had been especially close to his father in the three years since Willie's passing. It is also apparent that Tad understood the extraordinary pressures his father faced. For instance, a visitor to the White House tried to comfort the boy in the days after Lincoln's death by telling him that Lincoln was in heaven. Remarked Tad, "I am glad he has gone there, for he never was happy after he came here [the White House]. This was not a good place for him!"

Insanity

Robert Lincoln, the only Lincoln child to survive to adulthood, went on to enjoy successful careers in law, business, and politics. After moving to Chicago and being admitted to the bar in 1867, Robert followed in his famous father's footsteps as a lawyer. He then went on to lead one of the nation's most successful companies and served three presidents—as secretary of war for James A. Garfield and Chester A. Arthur from 1881 to 1885 and as U.S. minister to Great Britain under Benjamin Harrison, himself a grandson of a president, from 1889 to 1892. All the while, Robert was rumored to be a presidential contender. All the more impressively, he succeeded despite the impossibly high expectations of him and the crushing tragedies the family experienced. In a bizarre twist of fate, Garfield had a nightmare that he would be assassinated. Soon thereafter, while awaiting a train, he was shot. Garfield was planning a trip to New Jersey and was planning on meeting Robert at the train station.

In 1868, Robert married Mary Harlan, the daughter of a congressman. They had three children, their eldest named for Robert's mother and their youngest named Jesse. The middle child was named for the late president. Sadly, the boy died at age seventeen. Equally tragic was that Mary Lincoln did not know her grandchildren. Her relationship with her only surviving son, Robert, deteriorated alarmingly after Lincoln's death, as did Mary's mental health.

After her husband's assassination, Mary Todd Lincoln adopted the convention of wearing widow's black. She wore it everywhere and all the time, head to toe. Even though she took to draping herself in black in place of the more stylish clothing for which she was famous, Mrs. Lincoln continued her habit of shopping compulsively. The widow stockpiled chests of new clothing she would never wear. She even ran out of space for the trunks of unworn dresses, gloves, and hats she accumulated. Yet, curiously, Mrs. Lincoln did not purchase new mourning attire, the result of which was that when the extra pounds of advanced years were added to her short frame, the old black dresses became so tight that she could hardly move. A number of sources described the widow as even having trouble moving her neck and head from side to side because of the tightness of her collar.

Mary Todd's many fetishes and tics became noticeably worse after the assassination. Indeed, without her skeptical, rational husband to temper her eccentricities, her quirkiness, phobias, and paranoia began dictating her behavior in destructive ways. The widow became fixated on money and was terrified that she would go broke, yet she did not control her impulsive shopping frenzies and began seeing an oddball array of spiritualists, participating in séances and communions with the deceased. During such interludes, she claimed that she saw faces "on the other side." She also spoke nonstop about the assassination to anyone who would listen and became jumpy around loud noises, as they reminded her of the pistol shot that ended her husband's life.

After the White House, Mary moved to Chicago with Tad, then traveled in 1868 to Europe, where she visited France and Germany and found some relief from the negative publicity she had received in America. She also drew great comfort from her youngest son. Mary and Tad became inseparable, and she came to rely on him as much as he needed her. As she proclaimed, "Only my darling Taddie prevents me taking my life." In 1871, Mary and Tad returned to the United States. But tragedy greeted the former First Lady. Tad contracted pleurisy (pleuritis is inflammation around the lungs). He may also have had severe pneumonia or tuberculosis. After an agonizing illness, Tad died in Chicago that summer. He was only eighteen.

Mary had become emotionally and mentally unstable after Willie's death in 1862, and she would never again be the same. As her friend, Moyes Miner, described, "From the moment her husband was shot down by her side . . . to the day of her death, Mrs. Lincoln never saw a well day nor a happy hour." The assassination of her husband sent her spiraling into depression and uncontrollable mood swings. Already quite mentally ill, the blow of losing Tad was too much for the already impaired and volatile Mrs. Lincoln. Through the decade of the 1870s, Mary's mental and physical health further deteriorated. Mrs. Lincoln had always suffered from severe migraine headaches, for example, but they became increasingly regular and far more painful late in life. She even described them in vivid and imaginative terms as feeling as if Indians were pulling the bones out of her face and her eyes were being yanked out by wires. The widow sought relief through a variety of medicines, including chloral hydrate and laudanum, an opium-based drink, but soon developed addictions, and some of the remedies may have exacerbated her condition. Mary began suffering from hallucinations and was haunted by nightmares.

The only surviving Lincoln child, Robert, became alarmed at what he saw and estimated that his mother was blowing at least $5,000 per year on shopping, so he acted. The widow was living in the Grand Pacific Hotel in Chicago, and she continued the impulsive shopping outings that embarrassed her during the presidential years. Mrs. Lincoln purchased entire inventories of products, including countless pairs of gloves and fancy dresses. So, Robert hired a woman to care for his mother. While he was right to involve himself in his mother's life, Robert's motives and measures were themselves alarming. For instance, in April 1875, he hired detectives from the famed Pinkerton agency to follow Mary and obtain evidence of her quirky behavior. In 1867, to his then fiancée, Robert described the situation as follows:

> My mother is on one subject not mentally responsible . . . it is very hard to deal with one who is sane on all subjects but one. You could hardly believe it possible, but my mother protests to me that she is in actual want and nothing I can do or say will convince her to the contrary.

Mrs. Lincoln began begging for money from not only her son but everyone around her. She ended up selling parts of her extensive wardrobe and did so under an alias so as to not further embarrass herself. Yet, all the while, she continued shopping. Robert believed that his mother was becoming either a danger to herself or an unacceptable embarrassment to his own political career and inheritance—or both—so, in the spring of 1875, he decided to have his mother committed to a mental institution. Mrs. Lincoln's antics had become fodder for the press, but the trial and the institutionalization that followed marked a new low for both surviving Lincolns.

Mary had endured not only the deaths of nearly everyone she loved but also, on the heels of Lincoln's assassination, the public airing of William Herndon's stories of Lincoln's love affair with Ann Rutledge. The speeches of Lincoln's former law partner about the late president's youthful passions were more than Mary could bear. Mary also felt betrayed by Elizabeth Keckley, her former seamstress who became a trusted confidante and friend. Keckley's interviews and writings about the Lincolns were seen by Mary as a breach of their friendship.

Robert hired attorneys in order to bring charges against his mother that she was insane. He also appears to have paid six physicians for favorable testimonials against his mother at the trial that ensued. The rigged trial was held on May 19, 1875, and Mrs. Lincoln was notified of the charges against her only one day in advance of the proceedings. Of the seventeen witnesses called to testify against Mrs. Lincoln—including physicians, neighbors, and merchants in the stores where she shopped—a few had never even met her. Even Mrs. Lincoln's attorney, Isaac N. Arnold, thought that she was insane and was reluctant to defend her. The star witness, however, was Robert Lincoln himself. Mary was never placed on the stand. One juror recalled many years later that "there seemed to be no other course than for the jury to find the lady guilty as charged."

After a three-hour sham trial in which Mrs. Lincoln was not permitted to testify, the wife of the sixteenth president of the United States was pronounced insane by a twelve-to-zero vote by the jury and committed to an asylum for life. Yet another personal blow to Mrs. Lincoln was that the judge and attorney presiding, David Davis and Leonard Swett, respectively, had been friends with her late husband. She thus initially believed that the trial was designed to help her. Mrs. Lincoln wrote to her husband's friends before realizing the real treachery afoot:

> It is a painful gratification to me, that the two friends, whom my dearly beloved husband, most loved—should be the ones, to use their influence in endeavoring to extricate me from this painful and humiliating dilemma. The God of the Widows and orphans, will bless you in all time to come, for your kindness!

That night, Mary managed to elude three guards whom her son had hired to watch over her. She fled to a druggist to get a large dose of laudanum. Ingesting the powerful medicine, the widow would attempt to commit suicide. Fortunately, the druggist recognized her, guessing correctly her intentions, and made a harmless potion that Mary drank. Mary was in shock at the turn of events, even calling her son a "wicked monster." On the morning of June 14, 1875, Mary Lincoln was sent to Bellevue Asylum in nearby Batavia, Illinois.

Bellevue, which was about thirty-five miles from Chicago, was run by Dr. Richard J. Patterson. The asylum was rather progressive in its approach to medicine and mental health, advocating such treatments as rest, proper diet, baths, fresh air, and only a minimal reliance on medicines. It was also an aesthetically pleasing three-and-a-half-story limestone home on sixteen wooded acres. But, despite the scenery and the fact that residents were allowed out for carriage rides under the supervision of the Bellevue staff, it was an involuntary confinement and a major embarrassment for the former First Lady. Each night, the asylum was locked down, and Mary's condition seems to have been made worse with each passing day. There she lived with about twenty other female inmates, Mrs. Lincoln residing at the asylum from June through September 10.

Robert visited his mother each week, but she was not at all happy about seeing him and often refused to speak to him. All the while, Mary planned to escape from the asylum. She tried speaking to Dr. Patterson about leaving, she planned to sneak out of the facility, and she solicited help from friends on the outside. In July, Mary asked permission to mail a letter. Permission was given, but Mary slipped a second letter past the staff, who checked all incoming and outgoing mail. The secret letter was sent to Judge and Mrs. James B. Bradwell, old friends of the Lincolns who lived in Chicago. In fact, after her husband's assassination, Mary briefly lived with the Bradwells. The highly influential judge was a former member of the state legislature and had friends on the staff of the *Chicago Post and Mail*, a legal newspaper. With Mary's letter and urging, they unveiled the facts of Mrs. Lincoln's detainment and promoted her cause. They also raised the profile of the case by arranging for Frank B. Wilkie, a reporter with the *Chicago Tribune*, to see Mrs. Lincoln. The newspaper published details of Mrs. Lincoln's confinement. On August 22, the *New York Times* picked up on the story with front-page coverage. On August 24, the *Chicago Times* followed suit. Even though both Robert Lincoln and Dr. Patterson opposed her release, public pressure was building, and the entire ordeal proved to be a major embarrassment. The former First Lady was released on the morning of September 10. She said, "When all others among them my husband's supposed friends, failed me in the most bitter hours of my life, these loyal hearts, Myra Bradwell and her husband, came to my assistance and rescued me, and under great difficulty secured my release from confinement in an asylum." A free (but not well) woman, Mary moved in with her sister, Elizabeth Edwards. The widow finally stopped shopping and lived off the checks, totaling roughly $4,000 sent by Robert. She lived for nine months at the Edwards's mansion in Springfield. However, in October 1876, she traveled back to France, staying there until the spring of 1878, when she moved to Italy. Mrs. Lincoln continued her travels until a fall off a ladder in December 1879 injured her badly. Her health had already been on the decline when she returned to the United States in October 1880.

POSTSCRIPT

From the most humble origins in the backwoods of Kentucky, Abraham Lincoln emerged as perhaps the most unlikely dark-horse candidate in the history of the American presidency. Indeed, with no administrative experience, virtually no military experience, and no education, Lincoln was arguably the least qualified candidate in history when he ran for the presidency in

1860. Only two years prior, Lincoln had lost a Senate race against the "Little Giant," Judge Stephen A. Douglas. But the two had squared off over the future of the Union and the issue of slavery. Although Lincoln lost the race, the nation won, for it could not forget the humble, honest voice it had heard during the seven famous debates of 1858. Yet polls of presidential historians often rate him as the greatest president in American history.

His widow fared far worse. Mrs. Lincoln was despised by some, distrusted by both sides during the war, and an embarrassment to others. At the end of her life, she lived alone in a dark, dirty boardinghouse room, her eyesight failing and arthritis limiting her mobility. Toward the end of her life, she asked, "Why, why was not I taken when my darling husband was called from my side?" Not long thereafter, the former First Lady suffered a stroke and slipped into a coma. She died on July 15, 1882. In her room were trunks of unworn clothing and unused knickknacks. Robert Lincoln lived until 1926, enjoying enormous wealth but always living in his father's shadow and with guilt over his treatment of his mother.

It was one of the oddest and most strained marriages in the history of the White House. Yet the two shared a passion for politics, and Mrs. Lincoln was a supporter of her husband's career, nurturing his ambition and improving both his manners and his dress.

James Garfield photographed around the time of his presidency. Brady-Handy Collection, Library of Congress Prints and Photographs Division, LC-USZ62-13020 DLC.

❦ 11 ❧

Full House

Ann Landers said that you are addicted to sex if you have sex more than three times a day and that you should seek professional help. I have news for Ann Landers: the only way I am going to get sex three times a day is if I seek professional help.

—Comedian Jay Leno

A REAL HORATIO ALGER STORY

When he was a candidate for public office, it was said that James A. Garfield was the quintessential all-American success story. Indeed, Garfield's life seems to have been torn straight out of one of author Horatio Alger's rags-to-riches stories about success. His story mirrors that of Alger's characters who overcame humble and challenging roots through honesty and hard work. (Alger was even inspired to write one of Garfield's campaign biographies.) Garfield, who was said to be the last American president to be born in a log cabin, was fatherless as an infant, was raised in poverty, and worked difficult jobs, including as a carpenter and a canal worker, in order to put himself through school. In the words of President Rutherford B. Hayes, Garfield "is the ideal candidate because he is the ideal self-made man."

Adding to the Garfield mystique is the fact that he never lost an election and that his dark-horse campaign during the primary election of 1880 was one of the most unlikely victories in campaign history. Garfield did not secure his party's nomination until the thirty-sixth ballot. With the Republican Party split going into its summer convention, Garfield was the long-shot outsider who emerged late in the process as someone to heal the ugly rift and win the White House. The intrigue of that primary was matched by November's general election, which was one of the most exciting and closest elections in history. During the late summer and fall of 1880, Garfield invented what would become known as the "front-porch campaign," when he met the public face-to-face in a folksy manner from his front porch. Thanks to this novel approach to campaigning, Garfield pulled out another upset, defeating the better-known son of a political dynasty, Winfield Scott Hancock, by less than one-tenth of a percent of the total votes cast.

But there was a darker side to Garfield's "American Dream." The new president was insecure, emotionally troubled, and wracked by guilt, in part stemming from the multiple sexual affairs he had during his marriage.

Garfield

Born James Abram Garfield on November 19, 1831, in Orange Township, Ohio, the future president was named for an older brother, James, who died in infancy, and his father, Abram, and was the youngest of five Garfield children. His father was a farmer from Worcester, New York, who had been in love with a young girl named Mehitabel Ballou. But Abram Garfield's belle left him for another man, and he ended up marrying her sister, Eliza, in 1820. Eliza Ballou was born near Richmond, New Hampshire, and raised in both New York and Ohio, and it is, unfortunately, uncertain how she felt about the uncomfortable circumstances surrounding her marriage. The couple relocated to Ohio near the Cuyahoga River, and tragedy struck shortly after the birth of their youngest son.

Abram Garfield was a powerful man, known as the best wrestler anyone had seen and someone who performed feats of strength for his neighbors. Yet, while putting out a forest fire in 1833, he caught a bad cold and died suddenly. His son, James, was only eighteen months of age. In subsequent years, the widow struggled to support her family, and James was raised with few material comforts. Nine years after her first husband passed, Eliza married a man named Alfred Belden. But it was a strained relationship, and she and her children ended up moving away from Belden after a few years of marriage. Belden later divorced her on grounds of abandonment.

The widow raised her children near Cleveland, and despite his modest circumstances, young James proved to be special in many ways. He walked at nine months and read at age three. But he developed an angry and aggressive personality as a child, jealous of children of affluence and comfort. He would later outgrow these traits and develop a warm personality, but the insecurities remained. Young Garfield turned to his books to escape his condition, reading history, religion, and adventure stories. By his teen-age years, James wanted to be a sailor, inspired by both the swashbuckling tales he read and the dream of escaping his dreary life. At sixteen, he even traveled to a dock to enlist as a sailor, but his doting mother intervened and spoiled the plan. Her actions proved to be fortuitous. James never even learned to swim and knew nothing of sailing. He was also a clumsy child, frequently injuring himself by falls, cuts, and absentminded accidents. While working on a canal boat owned by his uncle Amos Letcher, the teen fell overboard on a regular basis.

Eliza seems to have made her young son the center of her life, showering him with affection. As James Garfield later noted of his mother, "At almost every turning point in my life, she has been the molding agent." They were exceptionally close, and Mrs. Garfield lived with her son after his marriage. She would later become the first mother to attend her son's inauguration as president; Eliza then moved into the White House. The hardy widow ended up outliving her own son by almost seven years.

Despite his impoverished upbringing, Garfield believed that he was "marked out for some special purpose." Indeed, he believed that he was destined for greatness from an early age, a point reinforced by his mother. So certain was he in this premonition that, rather than pursue his ambition, Garfield allowed destiny to guide his life and career. This contributed to his popular image as humble and disinterested in power, as did Garfield's motto that "I so much despise a man who blows his own horn."

Those who met Garfield had little trouble sharing in the view that he was destined to accomplish great things—he looked the part. Garfield was six feet tall with piercing blue eyes, had a thick chest and commanding shoulders, and wore a full but regal beard from an early age. So too was he an eloquent speaker. A good scholar and decent poet, Garfield spoke several languages, had a near photographic memory, and was said to be able to write simulta-neously with both hands—Greek with one hand and Latin with the other. Garfield also had the good fortune of being cerebral but unaffected by his intellect and many talents. Indeed, he was unassuming and easily won people over through his amiable, gregarious, and affectionate demeanor. The future president was well liked by almost everyone he encountered. He enjoyed suc-cess in almost every undertaking, excelling in school, graduating at the top of his class from what is now Williams College in Massachusetts, and becoming a professor and college president at a very young age. Garfield rose from lieu-tenant colonel to major general during the Civil War and was also ordained as a preacher in the Disciples of Christ Church.

However, Garfield was a vastly more complex and troubled individual. The future leader happened to struggle with insecurities, was filled with contradictory passions, and wrestled with a number of emotional demons. As a young man, he was zealous in his religious convictions and believed that godliness required him to refrain from any sinful thoughts or actions. Yet Garfield was consumed by lust and sexual temptation and was both awkward around and deeply attracted to young women. In both cases, such traits were a recipe for trouble. He agonized over his thoughts and punished himself emotionally each time he indulged his sexual needs.

Garfield also suffered from depression, which he called his "years of darkness." This condition manifested itself in different ways. For instance, during his political career, he struggled with a dark sense of foreboding doom, and this is interesting given the fate that awaited Garfield. After his election as president, he was haunted by nightmares that included a recurring dream that he was lost and naked.

One example of Garfield's conflicted emotional state occurred during his work on the canal. The bookish and ultrareligious teenager took a job driving mules and horses that pulled flatboats on the canals of Ohio. Garfield was a fish out of water around the salty canal workers who had a fondness for hard liquor and frequent visits to brothels in Cleveland. James joined his coworkers on such outings and appears to have visited the houses of ill repute with them. Afterward, he would repent, loathing his weakness for female companionship. Said the Disciples of Christ preacher about his wild adolescence, "At that time I was ripe for ruin and an active and willing servant of sin." The guilt ate away at Garfield's mental health.

In seminary school, Garfield was obsessed with sex and masturbation, reading Scripture and popular books on the subjects, including Henry Ward Beecher's "seven lectures" for young men on the evils of the flesh and Orson S. Fowler's remedies for sexual perversion, which included excessive interest in or enjoyment of sex. Fowler also deemed masturbation as a most evil sin. Masturbators, according to Garfield's readings, were said to have the telltale "pallid, bloodless countenance . . . hollow, sunken and half-ghastly eyes . . . half-wild, half vacant stare." Such images haunted Garfield's conscience and dreams. Garfield, like the preachers who taught him (and conservative politicians of a latter age), was also fascinated by homosexuality. He studied the Bible looking for passages on it, listened to sermons for Christian teachings on it, and read voraciously on the topic, including the works of Cicero, Plutarch, Seneca, and Virgil. He came to the conclusion that homosexuality was a grave sin and that excessive masturbation led to homosexual tendencies. As such, he was very much a product of his times and the church. Yet with Garfield, it went much deeper, and his dysfunctional and maladjusted views of sexuality would create emotional and physical trouble for him the remainder of his life.

Young James Garfield bought into the fearful old dogma on sex, believing that men of character were able to control their sexual impulses. Because he had trouble suppressing his own urges, Garfield remained conflicted about sex. He tried abstinence, which was taught by his teachers and preachers at seminary. He tried cold showers to deal with temptation. He tried prayer. When all else failed to eradicate his attraction to libertine women and his weakness for primal urges, Garfield married an asexual wallflower.

Crete

Garfield's wife was Lucretia Rudolph. The eldest of four children, Lucretia was born on April 19, 1832, in Garrettsville, Ohio, to a family of prosperous farmers. Her father, Zeb Rudolph, was from Virginia and of German descent; her mother, Arabella Mason, also of German ancestry, was from Vermont. The family was comfortable, hardworking, and very serious—to the point of being dour, judgmental, and socially awkward—in their disposition. As such, they were anything but warm or expressive with their eldest daughter, who grew up lacking proper emotional adjustment. One biographer described her as "emotionally repressed" because of her childhood. She was unable to "let her hair down." Accordingly, James Garfield would later describe his wife matter-of-factly as having a "good, practical, sound common sense . . . a well balanced mind . . . logical and precise." All of Garfield's descriptions of his wife, like his treatment of her, lacked any hint of romantic passion or tenderness.

As a child, "Crete," as she was nicknamed, was sickly, often bedridden, and isolated from friends. Although very close to her brothers John and Joe and her sister Nellie, Crete's only source of comfort and recreational outlet was her books. Crete loved to read and was a bright young woman with a studious disposition. Although she was raised to be prudish and serious, her family was enlightened when it came to education and supported a women's right to a quality education. As such, her family saw to it that Crete was well educated. She attended college at age fifteen at the Geauga Seminary, a small academy in a rural area where she boarded while studying, and she later worked as a teacher.

In 1848, at the age of sixteen, Crete had her first romance. His name was Albert Hall. It occurred while she was away at boarding school and was a serious relationship—the couple dated for two years, enjoying hayrides, attending school functions together, and, of course, discussing the books they read. The relationship was also such that Crete seemed to be coming out of her emotional shell. However, her family disapproved and intervened. They worried not only about her infatuation—which they saw as a "wild tumult of passion"—but also that young Mr. Hall was of a different religion. In addition, he was, for the austere and introverted Rudolphs, too socially outgoing and happy. Poor Crete was disenrolled from Geauga. She took the news hard. Ironically, though socially maladjusted and devoutly religious, Crete had a weakness for "bad boys." Interestingly, her future husband was attracted to "bad girls." It was also while at Geauga in 1848 that Crete met James Garfield, who agreed with Crete's parents that Albert Hall was not a good Christian and was too wild.

THE ODD COUPLE

At the same time that Crete was forced to end her romance with Albert Hall, the leadership of the Disciples of Christ was in the process of building its own school in Hiram, known as the Eclectic Institute. The school's charge was to train preachers and produce graduates imbued with the Disciples' teachings, which included foundational biblical lessons rather than the more ceremonial aspects of Christianity as seen in the Catholic and Episcopalian faiths. Against her will, Crete was enrolled at the new school in 1850. As it happened, James Garfield transferred to the school the same year. At Hiram, both studied music, art, languages such as Greek and Latin, and, of course, religion and were perhaps the school's two best students. Garfield was so popular and so far advanced that, when one of the professors had a mental breakdown, he was asked to take over the class. Soon afterward, the promising student was offered a job on the school's faculty.

Garfield's first romance occurred in 1847. Like Crete, Garfield's love affair occurred at the age of sixteen and while at Geauga Seminary. It was with a girl named Mary Hubbell. Garfield met Mary through his teaching—she was one of his students. Garfield was working while attending Geauga, teaching at a neighboring school in Warrensville, where Mary, also sixteen at the time, happened to be a student. The romance threatened his job at Warrensville and likely placed him in hot water at Geauga, a school with stern religious beliefs and conservative social views. But this was a pattern with Garfield. Passion often clouded his moral judgment and threatened his career. Likewise, he was always attracted to women who were socially flirtatious, uninhibited, and beautiful. "Bad girls" would be his weakness, and Mary fit the bill. She even transferred for a while to study at Geauga, likely in order to be closer to him.

The two young lovers were so close during the 1852 school year that their friends assumed that they were engaged. But Garfield never proposed, stating that he wanted to first complete his studies. Mary was patient, and her parents encouraged the relationship, hoping that Garfield would marry their daughter. They even cared for Garfield when he was ill, fed him, and also let him stay at their home. Well over one year into the romance, Garfield and Mary had the occasion to be home alone without her parents and likely had sexual intercourse when the opportunity presented itself. Garfield wrote cryptically in his diary about their passionate moment together and then demonstrated what would become a trademark trait—he developed "cold feet" and guilt over the affair, then withdrew into depression over his sinful indulgence.

Mary was heartbroken and dropped out of school in the spring of 1853. Friends in town were upset at Garfield for his sudden and inexplicable behavior toward poor Mary. Six years later, Mary married a young man named William Taylor but died during their seventh year of marriage.

A Roller-Coaster Relationship

The relationship between Garfield and Crete was, at best, slow to develop and lukewarm. At times, the union was downright odd and uncomfortable for both of them. The one healthy facet of the relationship—and the main source of their interest in one another—was their mutual academic tastes and pursuits. It was never an affair of the heart. Some of the earliest letters exchanged by the budding couple were on the topic of their study of foreign and "dead languages." Ironically, the couple often got along better when they were living in different towns or when Garfield was traveling, and their letter writing was friendlier and more honest than the face-to-face interactions.

Garfield and Crete had known one another since 1848 and had been classmates at the new college in Hiram since 1850, but they did not start courting until November 1853. Over the winter, when their friendship grew closer, they exchanged a number of letters. By spring, they were dating. As Garfield noted in his diary in 1854, "We love each other, and have declared it."

Garfield was half a year older than Crete, and she was one of his students, enrolled in his Greek-language course. Their fellow students noticed the relationship. The conflict of interest was also likely noticed by the Geauga administration. It appears, however, that Garfield was not reprimanded or discouraged from pursuing Crete. All the while, the relationship remained cerebral, and Garfield's physical passions remained directed at other girls. He once wrote about Crete, "There is no delirium of passion nor overwhelming power of feeling that draws me to her irresistibly." Indeed, their letters were warm but were filled with information and educational matters rather than poetry, promises, or even polemics. In short, there was no spark between them. Crete realized this as well. Garfield could be cold and flat-out uncomfortable when in her presence, almost as if he was "put off" by her. At one point, Crete tried to encourage her beau to spend more time in her presence rather than simply writing her letters, saying, "Is it not true that here to fore all you have known of me was gained not from my life or my actions but from my pen?" Both remained hesitant in their courtship.

When Garfield departed Hiram for Williams College in 1854, he proposed to Crete. His studies in Massachusetts took him away from her for two years. Accordingly, one would think that the two would have had an agreement about the status of the engagement or plans to get together as often as possible across the considerable distance that separated them. But that was not the case. Garfield departed with the nature of their engagement somewhat unclear, and he made little effort to see her while at Williams.

While Garfield was away at Williams, Crete stayed home in Ohio and taught algebra and Latin at the Eclectic Institute. She also continued her studies in the classics, French, and piano. In 1855, she received another teaching job in Ravenna, roughly twenty miles from Hiram, and enjoyed living by herself and being independent financially and otherwise. This period constitutes some of the happiest times of her life, even though she and James were separated from 1854 to 1856 or, perhaps, precisely because of their separation. For all Garfield's hesitancy about their relationship and later philandering, Crete was also someone who disliked abandoning her autonomy—as well as her job and financial independence—to the strictures of a nineteenth-century marriage and the life of a housewife. She was an independent woman, even writing on the subject of the status of women while in college. Moreover, although Garfield admired Crete's intellect, like most men of the times and especially most preachers, he was uncomfortable with her independence. Worried Crete, "My heart is not yet schooled to an entire submission to that destiny which will make me the wife of one who marries me."

A source of Garfield's eternal frustration over their relationship was that Crete was too reserved, controlled, and cautious. Garfield preferred more affectionate, impulsive, and physical women. Crete recognized her lack of passion and discomfort with her own sexuality and was often as upset by it as Garfield was. One of her biographers went as far as to describe her as "rigid, cold and formal, and silent." Garfield complained that his fiancée was distant and unable to relax around him, especially in matters of intimacy, where she seemed to be frigid and embarrassed. Consequently, when in her company, he suffered from mood swings that fluctuated from confusion to disappointment to anger.

When Garfield would return to Hiram while away at Williams or other travels, two things would happen. The couple committed themselves in letters to lighting a spark in their romance when they were reunited, and Garfield would return to Ohio with high hopes. But passion never followed the pen, and the two would be disappointed. It was as if they were willing themselves on paper to fall in love. Garfield described the situation as follows:

> When I returned to Ohio four weeks ago and hurried away all full of the brightest hope and the most joyous anticipations to see her, there came over me, I cannot tell why, the most dark and gloomy cloud, and it has deepened and thickened till the present moment. It seems as though all my former fears were well founded and that she and I are not like each other in enough respects to make us happy together.

Consequently, at times, Garfield wanted nothing to do with Crete when he returned. At one point after he returned from Williams, he managed to avoid her for one month despite the fact that Hiram was a small town. Obviously, such behavior pained Crete greatly and embarrassed her. When they did meet one month later, Crete opened her diary to have her fiancé read the many entries she recorded that stated her love for him. But words in the privacy of one's diary never translated into passions in person, and Garfield departed on September 18, 1855, traveling back to Williams. Nothing had changed, and they would be apart for another year.

It is likely the lack of deep passion may have contributed to Garfield's numerous affairs outside the relationship, although this does not excuse him for indulging his appetite. It is also obvious that the couple never really had deep romantic or passionate feelings for one another, and it became painfully obvious to them. Try as they might, they were never able to rationally talk themselves into true love.

It is also possible that Garfield would not have been happy with any woman, as he was always hesitant and incapable of making a commitment, and the closer he became to someone, the more his own insecurities came to the fore. Garfield was conflicted not only about his feelings for Crete but also about the institution of marriage in general. He was also troubled by his continuing sexual urges and biblical notions of sin and was working through a number of personal emotional issues. Poor Crete attributed her lover's hesitancy and frustration to being "impossibly romantic." If only.

Rebecca

When Garfield was away at Williams in December 1855, he met Rebecca J. "Rancie" Selleck, who was also studying at Williams and hailed from

Lewisburg, New York. Rebecca was the same age as Crete, but that is where the similarities ended. This new flame was attractive, flirtatious, witty, and very outgoing. Garfield was smitten, and while still engaged to Crete back in Ohio, he began courting Rebecca with gusto.

The two young lovers were introduced by a mutual friend, Maria Learned, of Poestenkill, New York. Mrs. Learned, like Garfield and Rebecca, was a member of the Disciples of Christ Church, and despite the church's strict and almost repressive teachings, she enjoyed playing matchmaker with young couples. She knew about Crete but also about Garfield's unhappiness with his fiancée, but mostly Mrs. Learned was a social gossip and butterfly who was utterly bored with her husband. She looked to meddle in the lives of her friends.

As an up-and-coming Disciples preacher, Garfield was frequently invited to deliver sermons in the area. When he went to Poestenkill, Rebecca would travel to meet him there. Curiously, Garfield wrote to Crete back in Ohio informing her of his exciting new female friend. In fact, Garfield gushed about the beautiful young woman in his company, saying, "I have been reading Kingsley's 'Alton Luck' and Tennyson's poems with her and have enjoyed it very much." He also reassured Crete, saying, "She is so much like you that I like her." So much for reassurance. It would seem either that Garfield was his usual conflicted self, callously disrespectful of Crete's feelings, or that his letters about Rebecca were some sort of cowardly attempt to push Crete away and out of the engagement without having to do so himself.

Garfield was in a quandary in the spring of 1856. He had seen Crete only once during his time at Williams, but his fiancée wanted to attend his upcoming graduation ceremony. Of course, Rebecca would be there too. In August, Crete traveled with her friend Lizzie Atwood Pratt and her husband, Albert Pratt, who, like Garfield, was a graduate of Williams. In fact, Garfield graduated with honors and, as expected, was first in his class.

Once again, Crete and Garfield exchanged letters prior to her trip to Massachusetts. In them, they expressed concerns about whether there would be any sparks when they met at graduation. She asked, "Will you not censure me too severely, for not overcoming that strange dread of another meeting?" He responded, "I have no fears. I look back on that terrible experience of last year as perfectly natural under the circumstances. . . . It cannot occur again." But it did. They again fizzled. The two were so fixated on this problem that they may have doomed any chance for spontaneity and passion. At the least, the expectations were set impossibly high, especially given the couple's track record. Both Rebecca and Crete attended the ceremony. During the visit, Garfield was more interested in Rebecca than Crete—or even the commencement ceremony.

Afterward, Garfield moved back to Ohio to take up his teaching and preaching careers. Once again, however, Garfield struggled with depression. Rebecca, it seems, was not the intellectual he thought she was, nor was she as genuinely enthusiastic about literature as she had seemed to be. Rather, Rebecca was simply feigning interest in order to be closer to Garfield and win his love. Garfield did not know which woman to pursue and was wracked with feelings that Rebecca was not intellectual enough for his tastes but that Crete was not passionate enough for his tastes. Moreover, his head would not allow him to propose to Rebecca as long as he was engaged to Crete, but his heart could not abandon Rebecca.

Garfield returned to the Eclectic Institute as a professor and, soon thereafter, was running the school. But his mental condition and age-old insecurities were such that he complained that he was not a good enough teacher, not a good enough preacher, and not a good enough person. He was also upset that he was cold to Crete but that, at the same time, she was frigid toward him. All this he told to Crete, who dutifully listened. And the couple fell back into their usual hesitant limbo, which they described as "not a wild delirious passion" but "a calm strong deep resistless current." All the while, Rebecca remained in the picture. Garfield had little interest in visiting Crete while at Williams, but Rebecca was encouraged to come visit her lover while he was teaching at Hiram.

Marriage

Ultimately, Crete began to abandon any prospect of their marrying. So too was she embarrassed by the way Garfield was ignoring her in Hiram. After she had not heard from him in a month, Crete ended the engagement in the fall of 1856. Writing to her former fiancé, she said that she had shed enough tears and would cry no more. Now it was Crete's turn, saying, "You no longer turned coldly away and chilled my heart to ice. Nothing ever seemed more real, and all day long I have been so unspeakably happy." She moved to Cleveland and obtained a teaching job there in the winter of 1857. Even though they saw one another in Cleveland, Crete wrote to him on May 27, 1857, saying, "I strive to forget the past, and have no thought for the future." The problem was that, while the couple was not happy together, it turned out that they were not happy when apart.

Garfield became depressed in the winter of 1857. He was torn by the guilt over the broken engagement, yet he still had strong feelings for Rebecca. Even though he received the presidency of the Eclectic Institute in Hiram at a young age, he was unhappy with his job and bored and even began questioning his purpose in life. Either he shared these thoughts with Crete or word got back to her about his depression because, in September 1857, she wrote to her former fiancé about his situation. Crete finally let him have it. In the letter, Crete revealed her knowledge of his affair with Rebecca and her anger over it, calling his behavior "the keenest dagger to my heart." She reminded him that they knew each other very well and chastised him for being dishonest about his relationship with Rebecca and then avoiding her. Or, as she put it, it pained her that he would "shrink away from me as though you could not endure my presence." Crete surmised that it was Garfield's "generous and gushing affection of your warm impulsive nature" that led him to the sexual affair. Then she concluded, "Go ahead and marry Rebecca," but she reminded him of Rebecca's disinterest in his intellectual passions by saying that "if she can satisfy the wants of your better nature . . . I could never be your wife unless every feeling of your heart seconded the decisions of reason."

The two continued to write, but Crete tried to move on with her life, taking art courses and attending theater shows with her new roommate, Mary White. Garfield remained depressed and indecisive. He also continued his affair with Rebecca, visiting her in New York. However, word of the affair with Rebecca reached Crete's father, who sat on the board of the Eclectic Institute. He and the other trustees of the school and church paid their young school president a visit in the spring of 1858 to discuss his personal behavior.

It is not certain why Garfield had a change of heart, but whether to save his job and reputation or because of his religious guilt, Garfield again proposed to Crete. This time, however, he needed to convince her to accept the proposal. In doing so, he conceded that they did not love one another or feel a sense of passion, but, he reasoned, they could "try a life of union." He also promised to respect her independence. Crete, who had moved to a village near Toledo to teach drawing classes, knew that he was marrying her only out of a sense of religious responsibility or obligation. But she agreed. They planned to marry later in 1858. Crete was the ripe old age of twenty-six, James was twenty-seven, and the nature of their relationship, they reasoned, would finally improve.

Hardly. That summer, Garfield was traveling to Indiana and stopped to visit her in Bryan, Ohio. However, he stayed only one day. Crete was upset and let it be known, writing, "Really I am beginning to think Man too slippery a fish to build many hopes on. . . . Don't you love to come and stay with me?" And the couple was back to where they had always been, with Garfield responding that he was unsatisfied with her and restless. As he explained in a bizarre letter, "When I am sitting I long to be walking, and when I am walking, I long to be sitting. I either stagnate and rust with inactivity, or am consumed with excessive action."

It is doubtful that the explanation made Crete feel better. Still, she showed concern for him, writing late that summer of their problem and of the forthcoming marriage:

> I expect James you will see sad dark hours. But do not fear to tell me of them; at least do not hide them from me through a fear that they might awaken in my bosom some dark suspicion. Why James, I would not love a man so tame that he had never a wrong feeling to subdue. We cannot hope for a future all unclouded, but with the Right ever before us as it has been this our final decision, and with our trust in God to guide us, I believe we shall find more of joy than sorrow awaiting us.

The couple agreed to a small private wedding. Crete even expressed a preference for it to be in the small town where she was teaching rather than back home in Hiram. Her reasons were that she was embarrassed by the rocky relationship and worried that her betrothed might not show up for his own wedding. Her father, Zeb, even suggested that Crete send an invitation to her fiancé in order to remind him. She actually sent an invitation to James. Strangely, they planned a civil ceremony even though they were devout Disciples and the church was in their hometown. But a civil affair would allow the couple to square their orthodox religious beliefs with their unorthodox sexual lives—the couple likely had sexual relations before marriage. Garfield, who had numerous sexual affairs and likely visited prostitutes, was conflicted about taking vows in his beloved church because of his sinful life. Of course, the many peculiar circumstances surrounding the wedding were not lost on the community.

James Garfield and Lucretia Rudolph married on November 11, 1858, at the home of the bride's parents in Hiram. They exchanged vows without a Disciples preacher presiding. Instead, they opted for a Presbyterian minister, the Reverend Henry L. Hitchcock, who was also the president of Hudson College (which is now Case Western). There was no honeymoon. It was a poor marriage and one of the most unusual in the history of the American presidency. The first few years were terrible, with neither husband nor wife happy. However, at the end of their lives together, the marriage warmed.

Trouble

One of the many tests for the marriage was their choice of where to live. After the wedding, the Garfields moved to the second floor of a Hiram home owned by a Mrs. Northrop. On the same floor and in a room adjoining the Garfields' room happened to live Almeda Booth. Miss Booth was a flirtatious vixen who long had a crush on Garfield. Garfield also had feelings for Almeda. In fact, as early as 1851, Garfield's mother warned her son to avoid Almeda, whom she believed was trouble. Indeed. Fortunately for Mrs. Garfield (and likely other mothers of young men), Almeda moved in 1851. Crete was aware of the situation because she joined Garfield's mother in being relieved that Almeda was gone. But the same year that Garfield married Crete, Miss Booth returned to Hiram.

Garfield and Almeda were not only neighbors; now, their beds were separated by only one wall and a few feet. Of course, the housing arrangement was such that it begs the question of whether it was coincidence or planned by Garfield. In such a small town, it was common to know such matters. Moreover, Almeda Booth's lover had died not long before, and she had returned to work at the Eclectic Institute. Garfield was the president of the school, and Almeda was a teacher. He obviously knew that she was coming back and where she was living. He likely had a hand in hiring her—and more.

THE "GREAT MISTAKE"

Garfield described his marriage as a "great mistake" and busied himself with work and projects in order to take his mind off marriage. He also looked for reasons and excuses to travel in order to be away from his wife. And so it was that he entered politics. Ironically, Garfield's political career was as much a result of his natural restlessness, growing dissatisfaction with his teaching career, and need to distract himself from his poor marriage as it was anything else. He ran for and was elected to the Ohio state senate in 1859.

In 1860, Garfield traveled to Columbus for the state legislative session. Crete was pregnant at the time, and the two had one of their worst arguments. She expressed her frustration that their child would be born into a "failed marriage" and described the family's prospects for happiness as "desolation." She also rightly accused her husband of not caring, not trying to improve the relationship, and not being able to move beyond the past. Throughout their courtship and marriage, Crete was the one who tried to get them to move forward and to try being happy together, but it did not work. Garfield remained, in her words, "heartless" and depressed.

Yet Crete even blamed herself for her husband's unhappiness. In letters, her coded words seem to suggest that their sexual incompatibility was at the root of their other problems. But rather than finger Garfield's extramarital affairs as the culprit, Crete saw it as her own fault. She was frigidly dispassionate and hesitant about sex, admitting that she had only "lain down among the flowers and waited." She even apologized for what she called being "withered leaves." Yet, as she did in all matters of their relationship, she promised to work on improving the marriage, including the sex, even saying that she would try "diving into the honey cups."

Crete also wanted to be a better wife and to support her husband's new political career. Although uninitiated in politics, she was willing to learn. She wrote to him enthusiastically about his election: "I want you to be so great and good. So worthy of the highest respect and love of all. So unimpeachable in every relation that your bitterest enemy can find no just cause for accusation." But when Garfield traveled to legislative sessions, he forgot about his wife and child, Eliza Arabella, who was born in July 1860. Shockingly, even though he had been absent for part of the pregnancy, after Crete gave birth, Garfield took a vacation on a boat with his pal Harry Thodes. On board was Almeda Booth, the vixen who was Garfield's neighbor and likely mistress. Crete, who was having difficulty breast-feeding her baby, remained home and was both ill with a bad cough and lonely.

Garfield was also taken away from his wife and child by the Civil War. In 1861, at the outbreak of the fighting, Garfield volunteered in the Union army. Initially, his interest was in being commissioned as a colonel in charge of volunteers from the Hiram area. However, the command selected someone else, and, as usual, Garfield became depressed and complained to Crete, who stoically tried to boost his spirits. She also counseled him wisely that because he lacked military experience, he should not have expected the rank. Garfield eventually, however, rose to the rank of general.

Garfield received his orders and departed Hiram later that year. He also stopped writing to his wife. Frustrated, Crete continued to ask him for letters. His occasional letter contained complaints that he was too busy to write. Crete complained he said little about their child. Crete wrote back, "How desolate it seems here. . . . Dear little Trot has been calling 'Papa, Papa,' all day. Every time she has heard a step in the hall she would call out 'Papa' and go away with such a disappointed look that it made my heart ache." It seems likely that Crete embellished the details of her infant's actions. However, she can be excused for doing so, as she was lonely, neglected, and having difficulty raising a child on her own. She later was forced to move back home in order to get support from her family.

War and Disease

During the war, Crete had to endure regular reports coming into town of local men dying. In the summer of 1862, a close friend of the Garfields named

Augustus Williams, a teacher, died of typhoid fever. Crete's brother, John, also came down with typhoid and was taken to a military hospital in Lexington, Kentucky. In a panic, Crete placed her infant in the care of John's wife, even though she had newborn twins, and rushed to be by her brother's side. Soon after her arrival in Lexington, however, John succumbed to the illness.

Despite all these hardships, Garfield callously interpreted letters from his wife as "nagging" and incorrectly believed that she was always looking for his faults and that it was she who was bringing him down. In an ironic twist, however, it was their long separation from 1861 to 1863 that may have saved the marriage. The two were always more cordial in correspondence than in person.

Garfield also became very ill during the war, contracting what may have been malaria. So ill was he that he was permitted to travel home in order to recuperate. During the ordeal, Garfield worried that he would die. He thus became dependent on his wife, asking that she never leave his side. During this time, their marriage improved a bit. As Crete nursed her husband back to health, he finally began to appreciate her abilities and strengths. As one biographer noted, "There can be no doubt that as this happened, he was coming to realize qualities of depth and concern in Lucretia he had not seen before." As Garfield improved that fall, he arranged for Crete to move out of her parents' home and to a rented house near the Eclectic Institute. Even though Garfield moved his mother into the home as well, Crete was delighted to be in her own house again. She also returned to teaching.

Well enough to fight, Garfield received orders to return to the battlefield. Once again, he failed to write and may have been seeing Almeda Booth prior to his departure and while away. Angry with his wife's constant urgings to write, Garfield also discovered that Crete had read his infrequent letters to her friends back in Ohio. He accused her of doing so to criticize him. Dejected, she wrote back that "I shall not be forever telling you how much I love you when there is evidently no more desire on your part for it than present manifestations indicate." Garfield asked his wife to stop reading his letters out loud and announced that he would not be coming back to Hiram for his Christmas leave. Instead, he informed her that he was going to New York to see Rebecca. Utterly crushed, Crete wrote one of her most interesting and sad letters to her husband: "I looked at her [a friend's pretty wife] and thought of Rebecca, while my own faults and imperfections trooped before me. And I felt as I had never before that had it not been for me, you too might have been blessed with such a wife." A guilt-ridden Garfield did make it back to Ohio in January 1863 for a monthlong stay. The feuding couple could not have been too angry with one another because a second child was conceived. Born in September 1863, the boy was named Harry

Augustus after the couple's friend and colleague who died in the war. Once again Crete struggled to care for her mother-in-law and two infant children while enduring her husband's inattention. That December, baby "Trot" became very ill with diphtheria. Garfield rushed home to help care for the child, but she died just days later.

The Other Women

Garfield had been elected to Congress during the Civil War and in 1864 traveled to the nation's capital city. While he was there, he had a sexual affair with Lucia Gilbert Calhoun of New York. He had met Lucia earlier during a visit to Washington in October 1862, and the two became lovers. Unfortunately, history knows little of the affair except that it was intimate and that Lucia had been married, was very passionate, and longed to be a writer. During his time in Washington, Garfield again abandoned his obligation to write to his wife. But Crete did make an uncharacteristic effort to travel to the capital city in March 1864 to visit him.

Garfield was not only enjoying Lucia; he was also enjoying politics. In the summer of 1864, he was in Baltimore to see Abraham Lincoln nominated at the Republican convention. Something else happened that summer. Apparently, Garfield was, as usual, reckless and not very secretive about his affair. Gossip spread around Washington. Back in Ohio, a man named Wallace Ford made the mistake of blabbing about his friend's sexual affairs, joking that Garfield could never be content with just one woman. Not only was Garfield having an affair with Lucia Calhoun, but he was still seeing Almeda Booth. The story made it back to Ohio, and Crete heard about it. Even Garfield's own mother complained, "If Miss Booth should tell James the moon was made of green cheese and he had got the first slice, he would believe it." Crete confronted her husband, and he admitted to the affair, later apologizing for what he called "lawless passion." Crete forgave him.

Back in Ohio in the late summer of 1864, Garfield was ill and appears to also have been suffering emotionally from his moral lapses. Crete again nursed Garfield through his illness. He was but one of many in the full house under Crete's charge. Baby Harry and Garfield's high-maintenance mother were in the rented home. Garfield's sister, Mary, moved in with her newborn. As if that was not demanding enough of Crete, shockingly Garfield also moved his mistress, Almeda Booth, into the house. Crete was cooking, cleaning, and taking care of all of them. All the while, Crete was pregnant and suffering emotionally. Perhaps not surprisingly, she suffered a miscarriage. One unintended consequence of the tumultuous house was that Almeda had a chance to observe her lover. What she saw was Garfield selfishly demanding Crete's attention, showing no concern for his wife's suffering, and doing little to help anyone in the home. Almeda cared little for this side of her lover, labeling his behavior as "perfect childishness." She moved out of the home and ended the affair.

Garfield's mother was a difficult woman, and Crete suffered her wrath while trying to live with her. The one trait they shared was that neither one cared for or trusted Almeda Booth. But a year later, in 1865, Almeda moved back to town. Aware that she was back, Garfield returned home to deliver an Independence Day address. Back in Ohio that summer, he once again ignored his wife, who was pregnant, and resumed his affair with Almeda. Miss Booth taught for a time in Hiram and then, around 1865 or 1866, moved away.

Two things happened after this string of affairs. First, after Crete requested him to do so, Garfield used his influence as a general and a member of Congress to have her surviving brother Joe, who was fighting in the war, assigned to a safe desk job in Washington. Second, Garfield admitted to Crete his affairs with Lucia Calhoun, Almeda Booth, Rebecca Selleck, and others. Garfield was emotionally exhausted and depressed. His conscience, he said, would not allow for him to any longer live with the lies. He desired, finally, to come clean and end his womanizing. Crete's response was to tell her husband to go see each mistress and put an end to the affair. She also cleverly suggested that he gather the love letters from each one and destroy all of them. She also told her husband that, had he cleaned up his act earlier, he would not have embarrassed himself in front of his beloved Almeda. Lest her shrewdness suggest otherwise, Crete was deeply embarrassed and hurt by her husband's revelations.

Garfield promised his wife, "I here and now renew with new fervor and completeness of devotion the covenant of my life to you till there shall be no more on earth or in heaven." In the years after the war, Garfield traveled to visit his mistresses to collect love letters and end the affairs. In New York, he saw the widow Lucia Calhoun. It is probable that Garfield would have hesitated in ending the affair, but Lucia was now engaged to an attorney named Cornelius Runkle. The affair was over.

But Garfield's mettle would be tested when he saw Rebecca Selleck. Ever since his college years and even through the Civil War, Garfield had continued to visit Rebecca on vacations in Michigan and visits to New York. He even did so while carrying on affairs with Lucia and Almeda. When confronting Rebecca about the status of their affair, she apparently informed him very emotionally that she had lost her mother and brother, both of whom she cared for and buried. It worked. Garfield remained under her spell. In October 1868, Garfield informed Crete that he was again visiting Rebecca.

Crete pleaded, "I hope you will not go to meet Rebecca. It would hurt me so to have you meet her there among so many friends, who would think, 'James loves her yet better than he does Crete.'" But Garfield ignored his wife's plea, and the affair continued. Rebecca never married and lived until 1909.

After the war, Garfield was on the verge of a nervous breakdown. His physician advised that he rest. Leaving baby Harry with Garfield's sister, Mary, the couple headed to Europe. For over three months in the late summer and early fall of 1865, they toured England, Scotland, France, Germany, Italy, and Switzerland. Traveling was difficult for Crete because she was in her third trimester of pregnancy. When they returned in October, a baby, James, was born.

The Garfield marriage did not really improve until 1869, when they moved to Washington. There, the family was together, and Crete took an active interest in his political career, which had progressed in an impressive manner. Three more children were born in 1867, 1870, and 1872. Garfield also purchased a run-down farm in Mentor, Ohio. While he was in Washington, Crete set about completely refurbishing the home and farm. The transformation was astonishing, and the family finally enjoyed their lovely home, complete with a second-floor library and spacious office. Wrote Crete to her husband about her work on the home, "Everything here now seems to give life and health . . . it is cool, and the cleanliness and freshness surpass either previous year. The old farm bursts into gladness under each caress and grows more beautiful with every touch."

ASSASSINATION

By 1876, Garfield was gaining national recognition. With a crowded but unacceptable field of candidates for the Republican nomination for president in 1880, one that included James G. Blaine, John Sherman, and possibly the former president, Ulysses S. Grant, Garfield emerged as a long-shot but alternative candidate. Crete took the news with mixed emotions, writing to her husband on June 4, 1880, "I begin to be afraid that the convention will give you the nomination." Indeed, during the heated convention in Chicago, delegates found themselves gridlocked on ballot after ballot. After considerable jockeying, Garfield won on the thirty-sixth ballot.

Crete was not with her husband in Chicago when he won the close and surprising nomination. Although she had been supporting her husband's political career, she worried about the challenges of the presidency and loss of privacy that comes with it. During the general election campaign, the

Garfields played host to thousands of well-wishers and prospective voters in his famous "front-porch campaign." Throngs of people stopped to chat with the candidate, who sat on the front porch and shook hands. The downside to this folksy and popular approach to campaigning was that people were trampling the Garfields' yard, expected to be fed or given a refreshing drink, and came to visit at all hours. The amount of food that Crete prepared and drinks she poured was staggering. But she soldiered on. Crete also worried about something else. Garfield's many affairs were ripe to be exploited by his opponents. In fact, an ugly rumor appeared during the campaign that the candidate visited a prostitute in a brothel in New Orleans.

Both the campaign and the task of governing in office were very taxing on the whole family, but what really bothered them were the criticisms. The Garfields were thin skinned. Public life required Crete to meet new people, host visitors, and open her life up to the press, and she was uncomfortable doing all this. She was also clearly no Dolley Madison and was, at best, a reluctant and reserved hostess. The press picked up on this and portrayed her as a wallflower, lacking physical beauty or social grace. Before the inauguration, a reporter from Detroit interviewed her, describing the prospective First Lady rather neutrally as

> a slender, graceful lady, with a transparently clear complexion, with delicate features, and clear, penetrating brown eyes; hair the same shade of brown, worn in a braid at the back, and frizzled quite in the conventional style in front. A dark blue dress, simple lace tie, and little or no jewelry, complete the lady's home appearance.

There were a few bright spots from the campaign and the White House. In her diary, Crete described the corrupt maneuvering of bosses like Roscoe Conkling, demonstrating a degree of political savvy. Indeed, both during the campaign and later in the White House, the couple confided openly with one another about strategy. Crete also studied the history of the presidency and the White House in order to better prepare herself, and as First Lady, she was ahead of her time in trying to obtain public funding to renovate the executive mansion. The full Garfield house also carried over into the presidency. Garfield's mother and the family's children moved into the mansion, and the presidency also marked a slight improvement in the status of the strained Garfield marriage.

As president, Garfield continued his pattern of ignoring his wife and family at times but less so than earlier in the marriage. At the inauguration, he even kissed his mother before kissing his wife, upsetting Crete. However, she later teased him about the minor scandal. Crete's health also became an issue. She was quite ill in the White House, perhaps suffering from typhoid or malaria, and was thus unable to perform many of the duties of the First Lady. From the March inauguration through June, she was ill. It was not until June 8 that she was even able to sit up in bed. Four days later, she was carried downstairs for one of her few dinners at the White House. It was decided that both husband and wife needed a vacation that first summer in office. They decided on Long Branch, New Jersey.

The president departed for New Jersey in advance of his wife, something that reflected the continuing coolness of their marriage despite the slight improvement while in office. Crete was back in the White House packing for the vacation with her daughter, Mollie. Suddenly, a messenger, Major Swaim, burst into the home with a telegram from Colonel Rockwell reading, "The President wishes me to say to you from him that he has been seriously hurt. How seriously he cannot say. He is himself, and hopes you will come to him soon." Garfield had been shot, after only 120 days in office, on July 2, 1881.

A crazed religious fanatic named Charles Guiteau was the assassin. Guitteau felt that he was owed a job in the administration or in government because he supported Garfield and also wanted Vice President Chester A. Arthur to be the president. Interestingly, Guiteau had planned to shoot Garfield earlier, but while waiting for the right opportunity, he happened to see Crete. He later commented after being arrested that she looked so sad that he felt sorry for her. The result was that he delayed the assassination attempt, saying, "Mrs. Garfield looked so thin and clung so tenderly to the President's arm, my heart failed me to part them." But Guiteau was only momentarily moved by Mrs. Garfield's plight because he waited at the railway station in Washington in early July, pistol in hand, for the president to show up.

Crete nearly collapsed when she first saw her husband but regained her composure in order to attend to him. She nursed the president for two months. Letters poured in from around the country and from around the world during the ordeal. Queen Victoria, Alfred Lord Tennyson, the writer Henry James, and others wrote to the First Lady. The *Washington Star* newspaper opined in August 1881, with the president still hanging on to life, "On every side her praises are heard, and whatever the result, Mrs. Garfield will ever occupy a high place in the esteem of not only the people of this country, but the civilized world."

Even the legendary Alexander Graham Bell joined the effort, working frantically to invent a device that would help physicians find the exact location of the bullet. All the while, there was no improvement in the president's condition. In the end, Crete decided that a change was needed, so she took her husband to Elberon, New Jersey, organizing a special railcar fitted as a private hospital. Near the coast, he hung on for another two weeks before losing consciousness and dying on September 19, 1881. In all, Garfield endured eighty days near death after the shooting. Before passing, he told their mutual friend Harriet Blaine, "Whatever happens I want you to promise to look out for Crete." Crete broke down, crying out, "Oh, why am I made to suffer this cruel wrong!"

Widow

Lucretia Garfield organized her husband's funeral service. Afterward, she organized his political papers at their home in Mentor, Ohio, and collected books and newspaper articles about him. The result was a simple predecessor to the modern presidential library at the family farm, Lawnfield. Valuable items were stored in a fireproof vault, and some 1,200 letters she had sent to him were donated to the historian Theodore Clarke Smith of Williams College so that he might prepare an official and friendly biography of Garfield. Although an intensely private and shy person, Crete was determined to promote the legacy of the man she always called "The General" and dedicated the remainder of her life to that task.

It was a tragic ending to a tragic marriage. One of the many sources of strain in the Garfield marriage was that the couple had seven children but endured a miscarriage and the deaths of two in infancy, including their first-born, Trot. Having so many children with an absent father was difficult for Crete, and she also lamented the fact that she had to abandon her career as a teacher and her many avocational interests. The remainder of the Garfield children, however, enjoyed long, successful lives, giving Crete some comfort. Harry grew up to be a lawyer and educator, graduating from his father's alma mater, Williams, and later became the school's president after a stint teaching at Princeton. During World War I, President Woodrow Wilson appointed him to head the nation's food and energy programs. The third child, James, was a terror as a youngster but ended up becoming a lawyer and a successful politician who served as a U.S. commissioner and as secretary of the interior for President Theodore Roosevelt, living until 1950. Daughter Mary, nicknamed "Mollie," was born in 1867 and was very well educated for a woman at the time and married her father's presidential secretary, Joseph Stanley-Brown, who later worked as an investment banker. The fifth Garfield child, Irvin, was also educated at Williams and at Columbia Law School and became an attorney. Their youngest child, a boy named Abram, for Garfield's father, attended Williams and the Massachusetts Institute of Technology and became a successful architect.

Three years after her husband's passing, Crete was paying her respects at his grave site but did so at the exact same time as Rebecca Selleck, one of Garfield's mistresses. The two were cordial to one another at the meeting. Perhaps the years had healed the passion. Although ever loyal to her husband, the widow changed her political views, campaigning for Democrat Woodrow Wilson in 1916. She died in obscurity in March 1918 at the age of eighty-five in Pasadena, California.

The rotund Cleveland captured at the end of his first term as president.
Library of Congress Prints and Photographs Division, LC-USZ62-7618 DLC.

⊰ 12 ⊱

"A Terrible Tale"

Ma, Ma, where's my Pa? Gone to the White House, ha, ha, ha!

—A popular joke about President Cleveland's
illegitimate son

"MA, MA, WHERE'S MY PA?"

Prior to his presidency, Grover Cleveland may have fathered a child out of wedlock. This juicy story was the source of severe criticism from a few preachers, conservative-leaning newspapers, and the candidate's opponents. Yet, unlike the John Edwards paternity scandal, which stayed in the news from 2008 through 2012, it was never a major nationwide controversy. But it was equally interesting. The scandal was also the inspiration for a cute chant used by Cleveland's Republican opponents during the 1884 presidential campaign and at the Republican Party convention. It went like this: "Ma, Ma, where's my Pa?" Despite the controversy—and, curiously, in a way *because* of that very controversy—Cleveland ended up winning the election, allowing his Democratic supporters to add a line to the rhyme: "Gone to the White House, ha, ha, ha!"

The story of Cleveland's love child broke just ten days after he secured the Democratic nomination for president, so it was not an issue during the primary election. Even though the sexual incident in question occurred several years before Cleveland's presidential campaign, it was not an issue during his earlier campaigns for mayor and governor. The reason is that the story was dug up by the Republican Party and, more precisely, those working for Cleveland's opponent in 1884, James G. Blaine. Also, even though Cleveland was single at the time that the child was born (and was still a bachelor when he was campaigning for president) and his mistress was either widowed or divorced, it was the Victorian age, and the details of the story were both intriguing and greatly exaggerated.

It was July 1884 when the candidate's hometown newspaper, the *Buffalo Evening Telegraph*, ran a special exposé on the affair. The headline screamed out, "A Terrible Tale: A Dark Chapter in a Public Man's History." The main claim in the story was that Cleveland had "accomplished the seduction" of a widow who heretofore had been innocent and virtuous. Pregnant, the poor woman bore a son who, at the time of the campaign, was ten years old and named for Cleveland. This much was true, except that the woman in question—Maria Halpin—was anything but virtuous. Cleveland was but one of her sexual partners. From there, the story took a bizarre twist. Cleveland's paternity was likely but not certain, yet the story alleged a long and sordid history of lecherous and lascivious acts by the candidate, and the scandal ended up hurting those who used the exaggerated details against Cleveland.

A few preachers who were being paid by either the Republican Party or its candidate, Blaine, used the controversy to try to destroy Cleveland, fabricating details of the affair and pursuing the story with messianic zeal. Key among them was the Reverend George H. Ball, the pastor at the Hudson Street Church in Buffalo, who was fixated on the sexual affair and thought of Cleveland as Satan himself. Ball, a sanctimonious moralizer and loyal Republican, was a fire-and-brimstone preacher with the ability to stir a flock of the faithful into a frenzy of song, sweat, and visions of heaven and hell. The Reverend Ball and his colleagues fanned the fires of fear and immorality by taking great liberties with the facts and framing the affair as

> not between the two great parties but between the brothel and the family, between indecency and decency, between lust and law, between the essence of barbarism and the first principles of civilization, between the degradation of a woman and due honor, protection and love to our mothers, sisters and daughters.

Using such inspired language, the good reverend vowed to destroy Cleveland. The task was a necessary "mission," he said, against a man whom he described as the worst of the worst and something of a vampire who, under cover of darkness, stalked innocent mothers and young girls. The Reverend Ball insinuated that Cleveland may have killed his victims and characterized the affair as "an epic of moral depravity such as no city in christiandom had ever witnessed"—let alone Buffalo.

Depravity!

Maria Halpin, Cleveland's mistress, was made out to be a virgin and a Christian. Never mind that she had at least two children from an earlier marriage in Pennsylvania, both of whom she abandoned when she moved to Buffalo, and she may even have sold her sexual "services" as a professional. Functioning in public as somewhat of a grand inquisitor, the Reverend Ball described Maria and the "facts" of the relationship as follows:

> The woman, so far as known, had borne an irreproachable character up to that time; that her employers [a popular Buffalo store], with whom she had been about four years, had a high regard for her and considered her a virtuous Christian woman; that Mr. Cleveland had taken her to the Lying-in-Hospital during their confinement; that the woman became depressed and threatened his life; that he became apprehensive that she might attempt some injury to him or herself and appealed to the Chief of Police, Col. John Byrne, to keep her under surveillance; that Mr. Cleveland had her taken by force from her room at Mrs. Baker's [boardinghouse] to the Providence Lunatic Asylum [and she] was seen there by Doctor Ring, who did not think her insane; that after several days she escaped and no efforts were made to retake her; that she put her case into the hands of . . . an attorney, alleging kidnapping and false imprisonment; that she finally gave up the child and received $500 from Mr. Cleveland [and] these are matters of common repute in Buffalo, to substantiate which numerous witnesses can be found.

Ball's prosecutorial tone served as the voice for a committee of preachers who allegedly investigated the affair and offered the public their report. The report "documented" a lifestyle of depravity, including many offenses deemed too disturbing to share with the public. The public would simply have to take the committee's word for it, concluding,

> Investigations disclose still more proof of debaucheries too horrible to relate and too vile to be readily believed. For many years, days devoted to business have been followed by nights of sin. He has lived as a bachelor . . . lodged in rooms on the third floor in a business block, and made those rooms a harem, foraged outside, also, in the city and surrounding villages; champion libertine, an artful seducer, a foe to virtue, an enemy of the family, a snare to youth and hostile to true woman hood. The Halpin case was not solitary. Women now married and anxious to cover the sins of their youth have been his victims, and are now alarmed lest their relations with him shall be exposed, some disgraced and broken-hearted victims of his lust now slumber in the grave. Since he has become governor of this great state, he has not abated his lecheries.

While the Reverend Ball was obsessed with Cleveland, most papers around the country did not pick up on the story. However, a few did. The *Boston Journal* ran the story as front-page news. Suffragettes and suffragist newspapers, such as the *Women's Journal*, also attacked Cleveland, saying that he was "an affront to decent women." Interestingly, despite this affair, Cleveland held more progressive views on the status of women than did his Republican opponent, James Blaine, or most politicians. Conservative papers and Christian publications ran article after article on the scandal, dubbing Cleveland a "moral leper," "the father of a bastard," "a man stained with disgusting infamy," "a gross and licentious man," and other fantastical characterizations. A personal favorite was the description of the Democratic nominee as "worse in moral quality than a pickpocket, a sneak thief or a Cherry Street debauchee, a wretch unworthy of respect or confidence." Soon, cartoons appeared in papers showing Cleveland grimacing as an illegitimate baby cries in the arms of a mother rejecting him.

However, other newspapers, such as Joseph Pulitzer's *The World*, reported that Republican leaders had fed Ball the story and encouraged him to use it against Cleveland. For his part, Cleveland commented that the stories were "so improbable and so filthy that they seem to have been hatched by street walkers and sold to Dr. Ball for a dollar a piece." But the *Buffalo Evening Telegram* kept the story in the fore. It even saw its circulation greatly increase because of the scandal and began embellishing other stories in one of the more obvious forerunners of the "yellow-journalism" scourge to quality journalism that would soon sweep the country.

The Harlot

While most of the sordid details of the affair were made up by Cleveland's Republican opponents and their paid character assassins, Cleveland himself was not entirely innocent in the matter. He did have sexual relations with Maria Halpin and possibly visited brothels with his cadre of male friends. Cleveland could also have been labeled a draft dodger. He avoided serving in the Civil War in a manner used by other prominent men in the North, a manner that was perfectly legal but perhaps less than patriotic. Under the Conscription Act, one could pay another to fight in one's place. Cleveland chose to pay a young Polish immigrant named George Benninsky, who fought in his place. The fee was $150.

Nor did Maria Halpin, Cleveland's mistress, fit the description of the woman portrayed in the Reverend Ball's stories. At the time of the affair, she was thirty-six and Cleveland thirty-seven. Maria was a widow from Pennsylvania who left her two children to move to Buffalo around 1871. She worked in a dry-goods store as a clerk and was even promoted to oversee the cloak department. She was described as a "lithesome beauty" with a "pleasing demeanor," possessing some "fluency in conversational French." Given the latter talent, Maria would have been educated and the daughter of an established family.

On September 14, 1874, a son was born to Maria. She had been sleeping with various men, including Cleveland and his best friend and law partner, Oscar Folsom, most likely since 1873. Uncertain as to the paternity of the child, Maria narrowed it down to the two friends—Cleveland and Folsom—but complicated the affair by naming her son Oscar Folsom Cleveland. Because the other men, including Folsom, were married and fathers, Cleveland agreed to pay for the child's care. This might also be taken as admission to paternity, as this was how it was interpreted in 1874 and later.

Distraught that Cleveland would not marry her, Maria turned to the bottle, and her behavior became increasingly reckless. Cleveland not only did not marry Maria but also wanted nothing to do with her. What he did do was even more alarming. He made arrangements for the baby boy to be sent to an orphanage, and he paid the five-dollar-per-week cost of the institution. To support his actions, he asked his friend Roswell L. Burrows, the county judge, to investigate Maria and have her committed to a mental institution. This hardly would seem to be the action of a father, suggesting that maybe the child was not his. We do know, for example, that many years later, Cleveland was a good father to his children. In fact, Cleveland's youngest child, who would live until 1995 and was interviewed late in life by scholars, always claimed that his father was not the boy's biological father. However, a son would likely be expected to say as much, and in 1874, Cleveland, in order to avoid a scandal and responsibility for the child, went so far as to separate the child from his mother. As far as we know, Cleveland never showed any further interest in the boy.

It is not possible today to assess the extent of Maria's mental health, but it appears that she was against having her child taken from her, and it is unlikely that she was incapacitated mentally. She was, however, terribly lonely and attempted unsuccessfully to regain custody of her son, even abducting him in 1876. But the plan was foiled, and the boy was returned to the orphanage. Some time later, the child was adopted by a prominent family in western New York State. It is likely that the boy never saw his mother or Grover Cleveland again. The evidence is also inconclusive as to what became of Oscar Folsom Cleveland. Some accounts indicate that he did well for himself and enjoyed a career in a profession, perhaps accounting or medicine. The historical record is, sadly, missing. As for Maria, after she was released from the institution, Cleveland arranged a job for her in Niagara Falls, where she continued unsuccessfully to try to regain custody of her son. However, Cleveland eventually paid her the considerable sum of $500, and, realizing that he would never marry her, she moved away.

Maria does not appear to have gone back to Pennsylvania to be reunited with her children from her first marriage, but she did leave Buffalo. A decade later when Cleveland was president, she sent him letters from New Rochelle, New York, writing at least two asking him for money and threatening to release or publish "certain facts" about their relationship and her son. However, Cleveland does not appear to have answered the letters or paid the bribe, and Maria eventually stopped writing.

The scandal was but a minor story at the time. But, after 1876, it vanished from print, letters, and social gossip in Buffalo society. It was not until Cleveland secured the Democratic nomination in 1884 that the story resurfaced.

Shotgun Wedding

Grover Cleveland's opponent, James G. Blaine, was as corrupt as politicians came in the 1880s. For example, he was shameless in routinely accepting bribes from railroad companies and others. Consequently, Blaine saw public office as a means to prosper financially, and he did so. One of his scandals—the Little Rock and Fort Smith Railroad scandal—was so spectacular that it involved bribery, influence peddling, conflicts of interest, and other crimes, but much of the evidence was destroyed by Blaine and his cronies. However, it helped earn for Blaine the nickname "Slippery Jim."

Blaine was the type of person who had no qualms about using the story of Cleveland's illegitimate son to destroy his opponent. Initially, the negative campaigning was working. Blaine was quoted in an opinion editorial asserting, "We do not believe that the American people will knowingly elect to the presidency a coarse debauchee who would bring his harlots with him to Washington, and hire lodging for them convenient to the White House." However, during the campaign, it was revealed that Blaine likely had an affair and that his wife had given birth only about twelve weeks after their wedding. Blaine danced around the issue, offering denials and a variety of explanations, including different dates for his wedding, suggesting that his child was actually born six months later, claiming that it was all a misunderstanding, and so on, all the while lying through his teeth. Blaine, it turned out, also had premarital sex and came across as a moral hypocrite, especially after the way he used the Cleveland affair. Moreover, it was ironic to hear a man of Blaine's ethical reputation criticizing others. It was Blaine, for instance, who labeled his Democratic opponents as the party of "Rum, Romanism, and Rebellion."

Newspapers began picking up on the irony and hypocrisy. The *Indianapolis Sentinel*, for instance, ran the story of Blaine's premarital fling, saying,

> There is hardly an intelligent man in this country who has not heard that James G. Blaine betrayed the girl who he married, and then only married her at the muzzle of a shotgun . . . if, after despoiling her, he was too craven to refuse her legal redress, giving legitimacy to her child, until a loaded shotgun stimulated his conscience—then there is a blot on his character more foul, if possible, than any of the countless stains on his political record.

Two letters helped change the debate. The first was one that emerged incriminating Blaine and his cronies in a different scandal. It even contained instructions to "burn this letter" after reading, but obviously someone failed to follow through. The other letter reflected the far more judicious and honorable way in which Cleveland handled the affair.

Initially, Cleveland admitted to the affair and potential paternity or, in his words, to an "illicit connection with a woman." He also accepted that "a child had been born and given [my] name." Cleveland employed a team of trusted allies to help him deal with the attacks. This included "Shan" Bissell, Charlie Goodyear, John Millburn, and Dan Lockwood, all of whom were instructed to emphasize the fact that Cleveland paid for Maria Halpin's son, thereby assuming responsibility for the child, and to watch for any letters to or from Maria that might emerge. Should any do so, Cleveland instructed his team to expose them as fraudulent. He told his team and Democratic supporters, "Whatever you do, tell the truth." At the least, Cleveland looked honest, something that was helpful given the low standards set during the campaign. He also demonstrated a willingness to release the facts from the start. Cleveland had organized a committee comprised of Democrats and Republicans as well as ministers to investigate the claims by Blaine and the Reverend Ball. The committee issued a report, finding,

> The examination of the general charges which have been made against Governor Cleveland's private character shows that they are wholly untrue. In every instance in which the reports and insinuations have been tangible enough to . . . guide us in our investigations they have been positively proved to be false. The attack upon Governor Cleveland's character is thoroughly discredited when we consider the sources from which it comes.

As such, Cleveland responded to the attack and did so through the help of others outside the scandal in question. But most important, Cleveland held himself above the fray and refused to use Blaine's scandals in the campaign.

Cleveland had a reputation for being a reformer and for being honest, helping him weather the attacks. Likewise, during his tenure as mayor of Buffalo in 1880 and governor of New York in 1882, he was an effective politician and practitioner of "good government." Accordingly, the details of the charges being leveled against Cleveland went against public perception of him. However, the clincher came from the second letter.

Reporters approached the candidate with evidence, in the form of letters, that he could use against Blaine, including details on the Blaine child's birth only three months after the Blaine wedding. One of the individuals in the meeting, according to William Hudson and Dan Lamont (who were there), also offered to sell Cleveland a letter. Cleveland proceeded to purchase all the documents and then asked Hudson, "Are the papers all here?" Satisfied that he had all the evidence, Cleveland, without looking at the papers, tore them into pieces and handed them to a servant. Dismissing the reporters from the room, Cleveland then told the attendant to toss the scraps into the fireplace. To the surprised staffers gathered, Cleveland stated, "The other side can have a monopoly of all the dirt in this campaign."

This story made its way into the newspapers, and the response changed the nature of the campaign. One paper opined that Cleveland's sin should not disqualify him, but it should be asked "if his opponent be free from this stain; and is as good a man in all other ways." Another journalist framed it poignantly:

> We are told that Mr. Blaine has been delinquent in office but blameless in private life, while Mr. Cleveland has been a model of official integrity, but culpable in his personal relationships. I should therefore elect Mr. Cleveland to the public office which he is so well qualified to fill, and remand Mr. Blaine to the private station which he is admirably fitted to adorn.

Senator George Vest, a Democrat from Missouri, cracked of the whole controversy over Cleveland's premarital sex, "What of it? We did not enter our man in this race as a gelding!" Indeed. The influential Henry Ward Beecher dismissed Blaine's campaign as "a-whoring after votes." Even Mark Twain weighed in on the matter, finding the moralizing to be puritanical and silly. Said the great writer of the fuss over Cleveland's scandal as only he could,

> To see grown men, apparently in their right mind, quoted seriously arguing against a bachelor's fitness for the presidency because he had private intercourse with a consenting widow! Those grown men know what the bachelor's other alternative was—and tacitly they seem to prefer that to the widow. Isn't human nature the most consummate sham and lie that was ever invented?

Blaine did more harm by attacking those who criticized him, even saying that if "men who broke the Seventh Commandment" voted for Grover Cleveland, the Democrats would "win in a landslide." The *New York Times* had fun with Blaine's foolhardiness, joking that he had issued "a call to adulterers to vote Democratic." Ultimately, in addition to the famous chant "Ma, Ma, where's my Pa? Gone to the White House, ha, ha, ha," another saying was inspired by the scandal: "Blaine, Blaine, James G. Blaine, the continental liar from the state of Maine!"

Cleveland ended up looking good for not using Blaine's scandal against him, whereas Blaine merely looked like the corrupt hypocrite he was. Cleveland, despite having premarital sex and an illegitimate child, won the 1884 election. It was one of the closest races in history, with Cleveland carrying 48.3 percent to Blaine's 48.1 percent and the winner securing his home state by only 1,200 votes. The scandal likely proved the difference in the outcome of the election. Of course, had the story come out earlier, it is possible that Cleveland may never have been nominated, or, if the attacks broke only days prior to Election Day—thereby without sufficient time for the full story about Blaine's scandal or Cleveland's response to it to come out—history would have been much different.

A WHITE HOUSE WEDDING

A few widowers served as president. However, only Grover Cleveland and James Buchanan, the nation's fifteenth president and only lifelong bachelor to serve in that office, entered the White House as bachelors. But unlike Buchanan, Cleveland married during his presidency. And he did so in the White House, wedding his twenty-one-year-old goddaughter, who was twenty-eight years his junior, in a somewhat secret ceremony. Not surprisingly, it shocked the country.

Frances

Grover Cleveland's law partner and closest friend, Oscar Folsom, was from a wealthy family. His father, Colonel John B. Folsom, owned a mill and lived in a mansion in a town near Buffalo. Oscar Folsom's mother, Emma Harmon, also came from money in Caledonia, Vermont. Folsom and his wife had only one child, a daughter named Frances, who was born on July 21, 1864, in Buffalo, exactly one decade before Grover Cleveland's scandal involving Maria Halpin and two decades before Cleveland would win his party's nomination for president. Because Cleveland and Folsom were friends, the future president knew Frances since the time of her birth.

Frances enjoyed a privileged upbringing. She was extremely well educated for a woman of the times (and even for our time), attending elite finishing schools and academies such as Madam Brecker's French Kindergarten, Miss Bissel's School for Young Ladies, the Medina Academy, and the Central School. Frances was always popular and was the most mature and best student in her classes. Indeed, all accounts suggest that she was a beautiful and intelligent girl, and all those around her recognized that she was "special."

Her charmed upbringing would be shattered in 1873 and 1874. In 1873, Frances's paternal grandmother, uncle, and aunt all died during the winter season. Her father had three surviving siblings, and a sister, now widowed, was struggling to raise her children. Thus, Oscar Folsom moved his family to be near his siblings. Consequently, he started commuting to his law practice in Buffalo by train. The distance from his family caused problems. Folsom started spending more time in Buffalo with his law partner, Grover Cleveland, and the two spent more time going out to dinner, drinking, and possibly visiting professional women. They also started their affairs with Maria Halpin around this time.

In 1874, Frances was celebrating her tenth birthday, so the whole family gathered at her mother's family estate for a party and vacation. While there, her father was driving a carriage too fast. Attempting to pass a slower carriage, his carriage overturned. Folsom was thrown from the seat, landed on his head, and broke his neck. The wreck killed him. It had been a difficult two years. After the death of her husband, Frances's mother seemed unable to cope with the loss and sent her young daughter to live with the maternal grandmother for a time. Curiously, Oscar Folsom had not written a will, requiring Grover Cleveland to function as executor of the will and estate. Cleveland also provided money for the widow and daughter and even became Frances's legal guardian. The ten-year-old girl nicknamed him "Uncle Cleve," and he called her "Frank" or, affectionately, "Frankie." Later, Emma and Frances Folsom would move to Medina, New York, then back to Buffalo.

Throughout her school years, Frances had excelled in everything she undertook. She had a talent for reading, painting, photography, and other subjects and was also very social. As such, it came as a surprise when she decided to discontinue her education in October 1881. It remains uncertain as to why, but an arrangement was made to award her a certificate of completion. Cleveland intervened and encouraged Frances to continue her education, sending her to Wells College in Aurora, New York, one of the first liberal arts schools for women in the country. It was during her time at Wells that the relationship with Uncle Cleve changed.

Grover

The Clevelands could trace their roots to English and Irish laborers and ministers. Perhaps the first to cross the Atlantic was Moses Cleveland of Ipswich, England, who arrived in Plymouth, Massachusetts, in 1635 and worked as an indentured carpenter. Among the line were noted ministers, such as Aaron Cleveland, the future president's great-great-grandfather, who was an Anglican and close friend of Benjamin Franklin. In fact, the Reverend Cleveland passed away while in Franklin's home in 1757. His son, who became a Presbyterian minister, was elected to the Connecticut state legislature during the American Revolution. It was to this line of Clevelands that the future president was born, Stephen Grover Cleveland, on March 18, 1837, in Caldwell, New Jersey, the fifth of nine children. Cleveland's father, Richard, was a Presbyterian preacher who had graduated with honors from Yale. The Reverend Cleveland named his son for his predecessor at the church.

As a teen, Grover began using his middle name, signing "S. Grover Cleveland." It was also while still a teenager that he planned to attend a prestigious college. His older brother, William, followed in their father's footsteps, becoming a Presbyterian minister, and his older sister, Anna, married a missionary, the Reverend Eurotas Hastings. However, the Reverend Richard Cleveland died when Grover was sixteen, and the boy had to work in order to help provide for the family, which struggled financially. As such, his education was limited. He had been educated at home until age eleven, when he enrolled in the Fayetteville Academy and Clinton Liberal Institute in New York. Because Cleveland's father had congregations in Connecticut, New Jersey, and New York, the family moved a lot. It was shortly after assuming the pastorship in Holland Patent, New York, that he died. The family stayed in the new town despite the reverend's death and despite being new to the community.

Cleveland taught for a while at the New York Institute of the Blind but made no money and did not see a career in education. As such, the teenage Cleveland moved to Buffalo in order to seek the support and advice of his wealthy uncle, Lewis P. Allen, a prominent attorney in the city. Allen arranged for his nephew to have access to his law library and to study in his firm. This Cleveland did for four years, and at age twenty-two in 1859, he was admitted to the bar and began practicing law the following year.

Cleveland was an atypical president, sharing little in the way of temperament and passion with other commanders in chief. As was mentioned earlier, Cleveland avoided military service in the Civil War and never regretted his decision. Two of his brothers did join the Union army. Nor was he passionate about the Union cause during the war. Although he believed in preserving the Union, he had no deep feelings about slavery and felt that the practical matter of taking care of his mother outweighed any need to be in the conflict.

Cleveland had few hobbies and interests outside of work, except for fishing. Disinterested in literature or academic pursuits, he was not well read, and this son of a preacher even stopped attending church. He was dull and disinterested in both social activities and physical or outdoor pursuits, except for an occasional afternoon carriage ride. His only interest seemed to be going out for dinner and a game of cards at corner saloons with a small circle of friends. There, he would indulge his enormous appetite for sausages and German cuisine and wash it down with a quart of beer and a cigar. Cleveland, a big man and grossly overweight at 250 pounds and nearly five feet eleven inches, was slow moving and noted for his walrus mustache and double chins. He was anything but flashy, but Grover Cleveland was fair and confident and had integrity. He was also a workaholic, putting in long hours in the office. Where others dismissed the idea of living in Buffalo, Cleveland liked the city, which suited his minimal ambition.

Nor was he overtly political. He did not seem to need adulation or public attention like so many other politicians, and he came to politics later than most elected leaders. Cleveland became interested in public affairs only in 1863 during the war when he was elected ward supervisor. When the war ended, he became the district attorney for Erie County, then, in 1870 at age thirty-two, was elected sheriff of Buffalo County. In 1873, when his term as sheriff ended, Cleveland went back to his law practice, making a good deal of money. However, in 1881, he became the mayor of Buffalo.

Cleveland's return to politics was fortuitous in that the Democratic Party of New York was looking for a no-nonsense outsider and reformer to combat corruption. There was an anti–Tammany Hall, anti–Boss Tweed mood in political circles, and Cleveland was the perfect candidate for governor. He was a reformer willing to combat corruption, he was not tied to any political machine, he was fiscally cautious, and, aside from the Maria Halpin sexual scandal, he was known for being scrupulous and prudent. Cleveland, honest if unimaginative, was one of the first "good-government" politicians, interested more in governing and making government work for the people than in notions of power or praise. He was elected, and after a term as governor, he was considered an ideal candidate for president, once again being an obvious contrast with James G. Blaine, a corrupt establishment politician.

An Unlikely Romance

Cleveland had always spoiled his goddaughter. But while Frances Folsom was attending Wells College, her Uncle Cleve, then in his second year as New

York's governor, began sending her flowers, gifts, and love letters. Frances was no longer his little Frankie. In fact, she grew to dislike the nickname but not her "uncle's" affection. A few years later while pregnant, she even answered a letter inquiring as to whether she would name her child Frankie by saying, "I am never called Frankie, and will you do me the favor not to call her Frankie, but Frances or [if a boy] Frank?" Aside from the nickname, Cleveland wisely asked his goddaughter to keep the matter of his letters and flowers private, saying that he wanted to spare her the publicity. Of course, it was also in his own interest as a presidential candidate to avoid such a salacious story as seducing his ward who was less than half his age. According to the strict social codes of the day, however, Cleveland asked the widow Folsom for permission to court Frances.

During the summer of 1885, Frances and her mother decided to take a European vacation for roughly nine months. Tours such as this were common among leading families and were a way of both introducing and exposing young belles to society. At social events, it was also the practice to have a male escort. In Frances's case, a male cousin served as her chaperone. Cleveland proposed marriage just prior to the departure, and Frances said yes. Even though the engagement was a secret, Cleveland worried about her being away from him and cabled to the ship love letters to his young fiancée. Unfortunately for the couple, the cable operator noticed that the message was from the president and likely informed his superiors and crew members of the love affair. He may also have sold the story for money. Also, while in England, Frances mistakenly entrusted a friend with news of the engagement. When the friend in question received a letter with details of the love affair, she had the poor judgment of reading it openly at a dinner party. As a result, word of the pending marriage spread.

However, many of those in the press wrongly assumed that it was the Folsom widow who was the object of Cleveland's affection and not the daughter. Fortunately, this resulted in the media generally leaving Frances alone during her European tour. But Cleveland complained about it both ways. He complained that the media were infringing on his privacy and on items that he deemed not to be newsworthy. At the same time, when the press reported that the affair was with the widow, Cleveland grumbled, "I don't see why the papers keep marrying me to old ladies. I wonder why they don't say I am engaged to marry her daughter?" This comment reveals the president's vanity. To think that a fat, older man should automatically be linked romantically with a beautiful woman less than half his age was obvious, according to Cleveland, who had just turned forty-nine; Frances was twenty-one. Officially, however, Cleveland did not comment on the matter; nor did he share his wedding plans with his friends or closest aides.

Wedding Bells

As the wedding date approached, Cleveland did inform his sister, writing, "I expect to be married pretty early in June—very soon after Frank returns. I think the quicker it can be done the better and she seems to think so too." Cleveland asked his sister, Mary Hoyt, to organize the details of the wedding, which would be a small and intimate affair. Family members were invited, along with a few friends and politicians. Only days prior to the ceremony did Cleveland notify his close friends and cabinet members, announcing on May 29, 1886, in handwritten letters, "I am to be married on Wednesday evening at seven o'clock at the White House to Miss Folsom. It will be a very quiet affair and I will be extremely grateful at your attendance on the occasion." The president also sent announcements to the five living first ladies (Julia Tyler, Sarah Polk, Julia Grant, Lucy Hayes, and Lucretia Garfield) as a courtesy.

A cable arrived at the White House informing Cleveland that Frances and her mother were sailing back to New York City aboard the *Nordland* and preparing to dock in the late afternoon of May 27. Cleveland, still trying to keep the affair quiet, dispatched his trusted aide, Daniel Lamont, to keep Frances from disembarking in view of the public and press. The media put a tail on Lamont, but he managed to elude them, commandeer a tugboat at night, and eventually board the *Nordland* prior to the ship's docking. Lamont snuck Frances off the ship and took her to the Old Gilsey House on Fifth Avenue in the city. Confident that they arrived undetected, Lamont wired Cleveland, "Arrived safe. All in good hands"

Word spread quickly, though, and the Old Gilsey House was mobbed by the press and the public the next day. Frances Cleveland wisely avoided interviews but did treat onlookers to an occasional appearance while in the city. Cleveland, who had been traveling to Old Gilsey, arrived soon thereafter. He had not seen his bride-to-be since September, fully nine months earlier. During the reunion, the president offered his famous quip, "Poor girl, you never had any courting like other girls." Cleveland also met with the public at Madison Square Garden, where the Twenty-Second Regimental Band played Mendelssohn's wedding march and other wedding tunes, and, to the delight of the crowds, Frances appeared from a balcony for a pleasant wave and smile. Á la Evita, she waved her handkerchief to Cleveland below, who responded with a smile and tip of his bowler hat.

Frances Folsom had been thrust into the limelight, and the response was a mixture of curiosity over the secret affair and fascination with the beautiful young bride. Cleveland remained concerned about the impact of bad publicity on both his presidency and Frances's mental health. "It seems rather hard to subject Frank to such an ordeal at that time," he wrote around the time of the wedding. He also naively hoped that the public and the press would leave his bride alone while worrying how she would hold up:

> I should be pleased not to hear her spoken of as "the First Lady of the Land" or "The mistress of the White House." I want her to be very happy and to possess all she can reasonably desire, but I should feel very much afflicted if she lets many notions in her head. But I think she is pretty level-headed.

Frances would exceed all expectations, proving to be wise and poised beyond her years. The young woman was familiar with politics, having followed and supported her Uncle Cleve's career. In fact, when he won his party's nomination for president, she was with him at the convention. Her presence there even created a bit of a stir, especially among Cleveland's young aides. One of Cleveland's friends commented to the young male staffers eying up the attractive girl, "If one of you young fellows doesn't take an interest in that pretty Miss Folsom the Governor is likely to walk off with her himself." Little did the aide know.

With the public and press still clamoring for access and details, Frances and her mother arrived in the capital city by railcar. A White House wedding had been planned to ensure maximum privacy for the couple. The Folsoms were met by Cleveland, who arranged for their accommodations, but in typical manner, he immediately went back to work, barking to his aide, "Get those documents here as quick as the good Lord will let him!" The workaholic president was eager to finish some last-minute business before the nuptials.

Grover Cleveland married his twenty-one-year-old goddaughter on Wednesday, June 2, 1886, in the Blue Room of the White House. The twenty-nine guests arrived at 6:30 in the evening. At 7:00, church bells rang out in the capital city, and inside the White House, Captain John Philip Souza led the Marine Band in playing the "Wedding March" as the first couple descended the stairs into the Blue Room, which was adorned with flowers and plants. The Reverend Byron Sunderland presided, and the couple exchanged their vows minus the word "obey," which the president had removed. It seems that Cleveland was less the progressive on women's rights than he was simply worried about charges that he had robbed the cradle in a highly inappropriate manner. After the ceremony, the guests moved to the East Room for a reception, then to the State Dining Room for an opulent dinner. Sitting amid the table was a floral ship centerpiece complete with three masts. Although a regal affair, it was very much a private one, with no attendants in the wedding party. No gifts were exchanged, but Cleveland presented Frances with a diamond necklace as a wedding present.

Immediately after the wedding, the first couple disappeared upstairs to change into comfortable clothing. Cleveland planned a honeymoon away from the city, and a carriage stood ready outside the South Portico of the White House. To ensure privacy, Cleveland had his staff erect tents and walkways to the carriages. It helped, as large crowds of well-wishers and the curious gathered in the streets around the White House. The carriage whisked the newlyweds to a train depot, where they boarded a private two-car train headed for Maryland, where they settled into a cottage named Deer Park for a six-day stay as husband and wife.

As one might expect, reporters followed the first couple by train, but the adjoining cottages and nearby hotel would not rent rooms, and police kept the public at bay. With the aid of a spyglass, newspapers reported sightings from afar of the Clevelands breakfasting on their porch, walking in the woods, and enjoying carriage rides. Cleveland was not happy, complaining that the press had a "sniggering desire to make copy out of a sacred personal experience." After the *New York Evening Post* ran extensive coverage of the wedding and honeymoon, the president fumed,

> They have used the enormous power of the modern newspaper to perpetuate and disseminate a colossal impertinence, and have done it, not as professional gossips and tattlers, but as the guides and instructors of the public in conduct and morals. And they have done it, not to a private citizen, but to the President of the United States, thereby lifting their offense into the gaze of the whole world, and doing their utmost to make American journalism contemptible in the estimation of people of good breeding everywhere.

Such comments reflected presidential naïveté, given the salacious details of the relationship and his earlier sexual scandal. Either way, he would need to get used to such coverage, as the public could not get enough of their new First Lady. And the interest never wore off.

THE FIRST COUPLE

Because Cleveland entered the White House as a bachelor, his unmarried sister, Rose, served as his hostess. Rose Cleveland, an English teacher and author, cared very little for social hosting and the requisite mixing with Washington's political elite that came with the territory. Indeed, she was more than happy to abandon her role after the wedding, making way for the woman who would become one of the most beloved first ladies in history.

Rose's brief tenure did raise a few eyebrows, however, as it was whispered that she was a lesbian. Of course, those were far more innocent times, and sexual orientation was simply not something that was discussed in public—a good thing for Cleveland and his sister because it appears that Rose was gay. A lifelong bachelorette, Rose moved to Italy after her brother's wedding and lived in what was likely a loving lesbian relationship with a rich widow for many years. The two were even buried side by side.

Grover Cleveland's relationship with Frances grew in the White House. Probably because of her age and the fact that they did not properly court, Cleveland had little confidence in her skills as a hostess and her ability to deal with the demands of one of the most difficult "jobs" in the world. However, as time passed, Frances blossomed in the role of First Lady. The press and public quickly forgot the scandalous nature of the surprise wedding and were enchanted by the young, charismatic hostess. The tone of the media coverage of Mrs. Cleveland and the letters that poured into the White House about her were overwhelmingly warm and laudatory. Her Saturday receptions were enormously popular, and when she initiated the custom of inviting "any store clerks, or other self-supporting women and girls who wished to come to the White House," she opened the people's house to the people. This earned for her even more applause. She also courageously invited African American women to the executive mansion, marking perhaps the first time in history that such had happened.

Perhaps more than Julia Tyler—the controversial young bride of another much older president—and not since Dolley Madison had such a popular First Lady presided over the capital city. Some papers even compared her to the beloved "Queen Dolley." It would not be until the great Eleanor Roosevelt or the elegant Jacqueline Kennedy before another First Lady so captured the hearts of the country. Also, much like Mrs. Kennedy after her, Frances emerged as a fashion trendsetter. Women wanted to look like her, dress like her, and have their hair done "á la Cleve" at salons. They also named their daughters after her. And when it was wrongly reported that the First Lady did not wear a bustle, women across the country stopped wearing them, and the restrictive female garment went the way of the Edsel, courtesy of Mrs. Cleveland.

Women in New York City attempted to establish a "Frances Cleveland Influence Club," but Mrs. Cleveland discouraged them from doing so. Likewise, knowing that the public followed her every action, wardrobe choice, and purchase, the First Lady received numerous requests to endorse products. Offers poured in from manufacturers of perfumes, soaps, pills, and ashtrays—even women's undergarments. However, she declined all invitations to advertise or affix her name on products. Yet her image and name were used against her will and agreement. As such, Mrs. Cleveland asked Congress for federal trade legislation to prevent such branding practices where an individual is associated with a product or used in an advertisement without written consent. However, while the public found her irresistible, Congress did not, and it would take several more years before Congress was willing to regulate commerce.

Because of Frances's popularity, there was always much interest in the Cleveland children. The couple had five children: three daughters and two sons. The first, Ruth, was born in New York City in 1891 in between Cleveland's two nonconsecutive terms as president. A darling of the press who followed her every move during Cleveland's second term in office, she was nicknamed "Baby Ruth" and had a candy bar named for her. Sadly, Baby Ruth Cleveland died in 1904 from diphtheria. Another daughter, Esther, had the distinction of being the first (and still only) presidential child born in the White House when she was born in 1893. During World War I, Esther was volunteering in England when she met and married a British officer named William Bosanquet. She resided in Yorkshire. Another daughter, Marion, was born near the conclusion of Cleveland's presidency in 1895, and a son, Richard, was born in 1897, the year the Cleveland presidency concluded. Richard distinguished himself as a marine during World War I, graduated from Princeton and Harvard Law School, and was a successful attorney in Baltimore. The couple's last child, Francis, was born in Massachusetts in 1903 and became an actor.

Frances was good for her husband. She smoothed his rough edges, calmed his temper, and made him reduce his heavy work schedule. Progressive, independent minded, and talented, Mrs. Cleveland was fluent in French and German; read Latin; was an accomplished dancer, pianist, and painter; and had a magnetic personality. She was everything Cleveland was not. He once said that "a woman should not bother her head about political parties and public questions." However, Cleveland came to appreciate her political acumen and independence. To him, she was perfect in every way, a point not lost on the press, which delighted in stories about a smitten president and his confident, strong, young wife. Once, when Cleveland planned a fishing trip on a Sunday, his wife announced, "No one goes out of this house on Sunday!" Cleveland threw his coat down in anger, but she soothed his temper. Another time, after the president grew tired of waiting by the carriage for her to get dressed, he impatiently announced that there would be no carriage ride today. But when Frances appeared at the door, saying, "I am ready now," Cleveland sheepishly got into the carriage and went for his planned ride.

An ugly rumor tied to Cleveland's slight temper was fabricated by the same group of preachers who raged against Cleveland's affair with Maria

Halpin. The rumor claimed that the president beat his wife. Mrs. Cleveland even received letters from concerned citizens asking if she was okay. Frances helped her husband refute the claims. For instance, in one letter, she answered a question about the alleged beatings:

> I can only say in answer to your letter that eery statement made by [clergyman] is basely false, and I pity the man of his calling who has been made the tool to give circulation to such wicked and heartless lies. I can wish the women of our country no greater blessing than that their homes and lives may be as happy, and their husbands may be as kind, attentive, considerate, and affectionate as mine.

Frances's popularity had another downside. The president worried constantly about her safety. The White House, at the time, was a completely open building, accessible to the average citizen. This became all the more problematic after Frances had a child. The First Lady was such a celebrity that the Clevelands, in an attempt to gain some privacy, spent less time in the White House than just about any first couple. They resided in the mansion during the winter social seasons from December through March but opted for the home called Oak View, which they nicknamed "Red Top," located near the present-day Washington Cathedral. It was there that Frances, who actually shunned publicity, was happiest. She also surrounded herself with her beloved pets, including foxes, cats, ducks, and lots of dogs—a beagle, a St. Bernard, a dachshund, and her personal favorite, her French poodle, which she taught to respond to commands in its namesake language.

Frances was also very popular among voters. One Republican, Chauncey M. Depew, acknowledging the First Lady's image, said of the Democratic president's reelection bid, "My only regret about [the 1888 election] is that it will be so much harder for us to win against both Mr. and Mrs. Cleveland." Even Republicans liked the First Lady to the extent that a popular joke among Cleveland's political opponents was to say, "I detest him so much that I don't even think his wife is beautiful!"

But Frances's popularity did not prevent a disputed election in 1888. Although Cleveland won the popular vote, his bid for reelection fell short when Republican Benjamin Harrison won the Electoral College in a narrow, controversial election. Both Clevelands were upset by the startling results, but Frances helped her husband deal with the defeat. The White House staff, pulling for Cleveland because of their admiration for the First Lady, were also upset to know that they would soon be working for a new first family. Mrs. Cleveland had always remembered the staff with gifts and cards at Christmas and treated the employees with great affection and as family. At a tearful farewell, Frances informed the staff that they would be back in four years.

When Cleveland won the 1892 race, Frances made good on her promise, and Grover Cleveland, the twenty-second and twenty-fourth president, became the only chief executive in the country to serve two nonconsecutive terms. Her return, however, was bittersweet, as the outgoing First Lady, Caroline Harrison, had died suddenly at the close of her husband's presidential term.

POSTSCRIPT

Perhaps because of his weight and poor health habits, Grover Cleveland suffered an array of minor physical maladies but was a relatively robust and healthy president. One exception was a difficult bout with cancer of the mouth when a malignant tumor was discovered in 1893 during the beginning of his second term. Cleveland wanted to keep the operation a secret, so he boarded a yacht owned by Commodore E. C. Benedict in New York City for an alleged vacation. With the team of surgeons, led by Dr. Joseph Bryant, dressed as crew members, the hourlong surgery was performed on board the yacht in the East River off Manhattan. Cleveland's upper left jaw was removed, and the procedure was done entirely through the president's mouth so as to hide any telltale scar. After the successful operation to remove the cancerous growth, Cleveland spent five days recovering at sea and had to learn to speak using a vulcanized rubber prosthetic jaw.

Unfortunately for the president, the operation coincided with the stock market panic of 1893, and his absence exacerbated the crisis and questions about why he would vacation during an economic emergency. As such, rumors circulated that Cleveland was seriously ill. In fact, it was not until many years later—in 1917—that the public even learned the details of the procedure when one of the surgeons, Dr. W. W. Keen, described it in the *Saturday Evening Post*. Once again, however, Mrs. Cleveland helped her husband through both health and political ordeal.

It was a difficult good-bye for Frances Cleveland when she left the White House for good in early March 1897. She grew to love the home, staff, and public to the extent that she broke down and cried. Likewise, Cleveland had more than his share of political battles, especially in his second term. The partisanship, economic recession, and grind of the job eventually overshadowed the rewards of public life, and Cleveland left office "tired, bitter, and defeated." The couple planned to return to New York or Buffalo, but the academic dean of Princeton extended an invitation to visit the campus. While in New Jersey, the couple expressed their fondness for the town and campus, and another invitation was extended—for the former president to teach at the college. The couple used to vacation in New Jersey, as the president sought relief from minor ailments in the sun and surf, so the offer was accepted.

It was in Princeton that Grover Cleveland passed away on June 24, 1908. Frances Cleveland changed her husband for the better. Intelligent, charming, and popular and an astute judge of people, she became an asset to his administration. In fact, reporters and the public frequently asked more questions about the First Lady than the president. Cleveland recognized his wife's contributions and talents. He once declared to an audience gathered at Frances's former hometown, "I don't want to shock anybody when I thank the good people of this city because they neither married nor spoiled my wife; and when I tell them that I had much rather have her than the presidency." But the feelings were mutual. As Frances wrote to her husband late in their marriage, "You know how dearly I love you. You do not mind me saying it over, any day . . . so I repeat it and repeat it."

Frances Cleveland was still a relatively young woman when she was widowed, and she possessed a small fortune. Consequently, the former First Lady declined the $5,000 pension that Congress established for presidential widows. In 1913, Frances remarried, the only First Lady to ever do so. She wed Thomas Jex Preston, a New York businessman born in 1862 who, after making a good bit of money, retired at age forty and moved to Princeton in order to complete a doctorate in archaeology. After his studies, the campus hired him as a professor of archaeology. Coincidentally, Preston also taught briefly at Wells, Frances's alma mater.

Late in life, the former First Lady was invited to a White House luncheon by President Harry Truman. While she was chatting with the president's daughter, Dwight Eisenhower, the former Supreme Allied Commander during World War II and future president, stopped to extend his compliments to Ms. Truman. During the pleasantries, Margaret Truman introduced Ike to Frances Cleveland Preston and informed him playfully that her guest used to live in Washington. Eisenhower, who had no idea that he was talking to the former First Lady, asked, "And where did you live in Washington, Ma'am?" Frances laughed and said coyly, "In the White House."

Frances lived thirty-nine years after her husband's death. During and after her White House years, she remained active in a number of pursuits, including as a board member with women's organizations and charities, and collected and donated food to the Colored Christmas Club. Mrs. Cleveland also founded the Washington Home for Friendless Colored Girls. Despite the awkward names, these worthy organizations offered services and support to needy young women, children, and orphans. During her retirement in Princeton, she spoke out in favor of women's education.

The Clevelands enjoyed one of the better marriages in the White House. Cleveland biographer Alyn Brodsky called it "one of the happiest presidential marriages, if not the happiest, on record." Irwin Hoover, longtime usher in the executive mansion, reflected on the building's occupants and concluded, "No more brilliant and affable lady than Mrs. Cleveland has ever graced the portals of this old mansion." As First Lady, Mrs. Cleveland was the first to marry a president in the White House, the first to have a child in the White House, the first to return for a second nonconsecutive term, the second to earn a college degree, the youngest in the nation's history, and one of the most popular of all residents of the White House. All the while, she never liked the title "First Lady," preferring instead the "President's Lady."

Frances Cleveland Preston died in her sleep at age eighty-three on October 29, 1947, in Baltimore while visiting her eldest son, Richard. She was survived by children and her second husband, who lived until 1955 in his nineties.

What Happens in
the Lincoln Bedroom . . .

The dashing Alexander Hamilton painted by the noted artist John Trumbull. Library of Congress Prints and Photographs Division, LC-D416-444.

⊰ 13 ⊱

Fatal Attraction

And, believe me, I am a lover in earnest.

—Alexander Hamilton

Arguably the most intriguing and deadly sexual affair in the history of the American presidency involved a man who was one of the most influential of the framers and one of the most powerful presidential aides and cabinet secretaries in history. But he was a man who could never be president. Although never a president, this scandalous framer helped to both invent and then define the office. Yet his sexual scandals affected the man who could have been a king (George Washington), three other presidents (John Adams, Thomas Jefferson, and James Monroe), and a vice president whose presidential ambitions were undone in a duel with him (Aaron Burr). It is a true story that reads like the most salacious soap opera or the pages of a tabloid newspaper.

WASHINGTON'S RIGHT HAND

American history, like every other facet of life, is subject to "urban legends," stories that persist in spite of a lack of firm evidence or even basic plausibility. Indeed, there are enough falsehoods about George Washington alone to fill a book, such as that Washington could not tell a lie, he managed to throw a coin across the Delaware River, he cut down his father's cherry tree as a boy, and so on. Some of these fictional legends came courtesy of the imaginative and patriotic pen of Parson Weems, but they are nothing more than made-up tales that have morphed into founding creeds. Although Washington was one of the most domestically traveled men of his time, crisscrossing the colonies

373

as a surveyor and soldier and then later visiting his fellow countrymen as the first president, it is doubtful that all the claims of many historic homes and small towns throughout the country that "Washington slept here" are true.

Yet another of the urban legends about Washington is sexual in nature and involves his military aide and political right hand. Over many years—at first during the Revolutionary War and later during the inaugural presidency—Alexander Hamilton and George Washington forged a close relationship. Their bond was cemented by the momentous business at hand—that of waging a war for independence and shaping a new nation. During the Revolution, Hamilton served as Washington's aide-de-camp, assisting the general with everything from his correspondence and speeches to matters of strategy, supplies, and financing the war. Washington, as president, again called on Hamilton, this time wisely selecting him as his secretary of the treasury. It was from this post that Hamilton developed the new nation's financial and banking system. Hamilton also wrote Washington's speeches and functioned as the president's all-purpose counselor and personal political philosopher.

In many ways, the deep connection between Washington and Hamilton transcended normal social or business friendships, taking on all the traits of a father–son relationship. After all, the elder Washington would never have children of his own but longed for a loyal, brilliant son and namesake. Likewise, it was Hamilton—born into obscurity and to an unmarried mother—who longed for the guidance of a powerful and appreciative father. As historian Broadus Mitchell stated of the Washington–Hamilton relationship, "It is impossible to portray the one without an appreciation of the other."

What does the closeness of Washington and Hamilton have to do with urban legends? Given the age difference between Washington and Hamilton, which was approximately that of a father and son, and the exceptional closeness of their relationship, urban legend suggests that Washington was secretly Hamilton's father. Hamilton, after all, came from shadowy origins in the Caribbean, born illegitimately in the 1750s to a mother who might have been a practitioner of the world's oldest occupation (the one even older than agriculture).

Coincidentally, in the 1750s, Washington made his one and only trip abroad. His destination: the Caribbean. The teenage Washington, though rugged, adventurous, and a full head taller than those around him, was nonetheless long frustrated by one unsuccessful attempt after another at courtship. Hamilton's mother was, at the supposed time of Washington's visit, separated from her husband, down on her luck, and desperate to leave the island and start a new life. Did Washington enjoy more than the weather, beaches, and fruits of the tropical paradise? Urban legend might suggest this.

The Romantic West Indies

Lawrence Washington, George's older half-brother, suffered from pulmonary disease and possibly tuberculosis. Physician after physician and treatment after treatment proved unsuccessful. This included herbal remedies, visits to a mountain spa in Georgia, and the therapeutic springs of present-day Bath, West Virginia. Lawrence's condition worsened, and by the fall of 1751, he feared that he would not survive the coming winter. Desperate for a cure, Lawrence sought the advice of George Fairfax, the Washington family's trusted friend and neighbor. George Fairfax, by way of a friend, suggested the curative weather of the island of Barbados for Lawrence's condition.

Thus, on September 28, 1751, Lawrence and his nineteen-year-old half-brother, George, boarded the forty-ton merchant ship *Success* bound for the West Indies. The younger Washington's first oceanic experience was not what he expected. Growing up hearing swashbuckling tales of Lawrence's naval escapades, George had dreamed of a career at sea, perhaps as an officer in His Majesty's Navy. But the meager crew of eight crusty sailors aboard a midsize ship laden with lumber, corn, and herring was anything but romantic.

George's romantic ideals were further dampened by rough waters. Traveling south along the coast of North Carolina and then east into deeper waters, the ship was tossed roughly about by the stormy seas of the Atlantic hurricane season. Rogue waves from an untimely earthquake in Santo Domingo only exasperated the situation. George Washington was violently seasick for his first nine days at sea. After recovering, Washington spent much of his days fishing in order to resupply the dwindling food and water stocks for the tedious thirty-seven-day voyage. Yet seasickness and maggot-infested biscuits for breakfast could not sour Washington's irrepressible spirit. He was fascinated by the voyage to the West Indies, and arriving at Bridgetown harbor, the young man discovered his personal paradise. We know much about Washington's voyage and experience in Barbados because he took copious notes, detailing everything from nautical navigation to the ship's crew to the flora and fauna of the island.

In Barbados, the Washington brothers were met by James Carter, chief justice of the island, who welcomed them into his home. They also enjoyed the company of the native Bostonian Major Gedney Clarke, a merchant, slave trader, and good friend of George, Lawrence Washington's powerful friend who had recommended the island (George was thoroughly smitten with Fairfax's lovely wife, Sally). Lawrence had come to Barbados seeking treatment for his illness under the care of Dr. William Hilary. When he was not with Dr. Hilary, he spent much of his time brooding under the roof of their seaside cottage, homesick, tormented by the hot sun, and frustrated by his worsening condition. George, however, enjoyed the small leeward island. He explored it on foot and on horseback, chronicling the local plants he discovered, tasting several delicious tropical fruits for the first time, and taking advantage of the short one-mile distance from their cottage to the downtown, where he often socialized.

Tropical Delights

Washington enjoyed the local flavors that the island had to offer, but the question remains as to whether the nineteen-year-old sampled other tempting tropical delights. Could George Washington have enjoyed the company of young women during his visits to Bridgetown? Washington recorded that he enjoyed dancing in Bridgetown and even attended a play—adapted from the London stage—for the first time in his life. Thus, it is a distinct possibility. But could Washington have met the woman who would soon be Alexander Hamilton's mother during his visit? And, if so, could Washington be the father of Alexander Hamilton?

The answer is a resounding no. Washington spent a few weeks in the fall of 1751 on the island of Barbados. He visited no other island, and history is certain of this fact because of the meticulous logs kept by both of the Washington brothers as well as their hosts and the shipping companies. Alexander Hamilton's mother, Rachel, lived on or visited the Caribbean islands of Nevis, St. Kitts, and St. Croix. Hamilton was not born until January 11, 1755, just over three years after Washington's only journey abroad. There is a remote possibility that Hamilton's mother might have visited Barbados, but there is no evidence to support it, and she never came to America. Thus, the Washington–Hamilton paternity tale remains just that—and can safely be filed in the infamous annals of urban legend.

Although his experience on Barbados was enjoyable, George Washington did contract an almost fatal case of smallpox on November 16 that might have killed the young man and that did confine him to bed for several days. How and where he contracted it is unknown. Indeed, the disease would claim many casualties in the West Indies and the American colonies. Some historians believe that Washington must have been inoculated for smallpox back in Virginia in order to have survived the ordeal. There is one possible consequence, however, of his illness. Although he would later father a nation, Washington never fathered a child of his own, and it is believed that his bout of smallpox or possibly another illness while on Barbados is the possible culprit that caused his infertility.

After George's recovery and the failure of Lawrence's treatment, the brothers set sail in December 1751—Lawrence on a ship bound for Bermuda for additional treatment and George aboard the ship *Industry* for a thirty-eight-day return voyage to Virginia. Washington again became violently seasick but, as he noted in his journal, managed to keep down his Christmas dinner of Irish goose and rum, which he ate alone in his cabin. Before making port in America on January 27, 1752, he was robbed of some personal possessions, including the ten pounds he kept in a chest at the foot of his bed. Lawrence, however, fared even worse. Unsuccessful in finding a cure that he desperately sought in the tropics, he soon returned to Virginia, where he died later that year.

While stories of scandalous sexual behavior and even illegitimate paternity by Washington fail to hold up on closer examination, the same cannot be said of the numerous allegations leveled at Washington's friend and aide Alexander Hamilton.

"WHOREDOM"

Christopher Columbus has been accused of being directionally challenged and appears to have had a habit of confusing his landmasses and then misnaming them. While plying the seas around the inaccurately named "Indies" near present-day St. Kitts, Columbus thought that he discovered a snow-covered mountain. He promptly named the nine-mile-long by five-mile-wide island "Las Nieves," which is Spanish for "snow." Obviously, there is no snowcapped peak in the sunny Caribbean. The great adventurer mistook a large white cloud shrouding the small Caribbean island for a snow-covered mountain. Later, when the island came under British control, the name was Anglicized to "Nevis."

An island of thriving sugar plantations, at its peak in the early to mid-eighteenth century, Nevis was home to some 10,000 white settlers and at least twice as many African slaves. Among the island's inhabitants were French Protestants known as Huguenots who fled the Catholic persecution under King Louis XIV, who had revoked the Edict of Nantes, which had offered some protection of other religions. These religious refugees were welcomed by the British by virtue of their shared faith. In addition, the Brits also delighted in the symbolic slap in the face that they simultaneously delivered to their avowed enemy, France.

One of the Huguenots who made his way to the religiously tolerant West Indies was Jean Faucette. Like his fellow émigrés, Faucette braved the treacherous ocean voyage to Nevis in 1678, most likely in order to escape persecution and reestablish his own checkered reputation. The change of venue afforded Faucette many advantages. He practiced medicine, purchased a small sugar plantation, and prospered financially. Faucette also owned a few slaves. Interestingly, years later, a "black town," Faucette, formed on the same island, possibly named for him or for one of his former slaves.

Faucette appears to have also had a reputation back in France as a philanderer, something that he soon continued on Nevis. Faucette fathered a son with the Anglo-friendly name of John, who, like his father, became a physician and plantation owner. The family also Anglicized the spelling of their last name: "Fawcett." The son, also much like his father, lived with a woman without marrying her. However, John Fawcett's lover, Mary Uppington, hailed from a pedigree family, making the union all the more unusual. It was four years before Fawcett married Ms. Uppington; the wedding occurring on August 21, 1718. Such extramarital relationships were less scandalous in the relaxed tropics than they were back in prudish Europe, where the crime was punishable by banishment from one's village, excommunication by the Catholic Church, and even death. Nevertheless, the Fawcett family, whose apples never fell far from the family tree, suffered the stigma of a series of moral improprieties and a chain of sexual, financial, and medical misfortunes.

The couple had two children prior to the marriage and five children afterward. Tragically, five of the Fawcett children died in infancy, with only an older daughter named Ann and a young girl named Rachel surviving. The Fawcett sexual appetite seems to have been genetic, and Mrs. Fawcett, known to be a headstrong and educated woman, ultimately had enough of her husband's roving eye. After years of a bad marriage, most likely coupled with the painful loss of so many children, she obtained a legal separation from her much older husband. A separation, such as the one that occurred around 1740 or 1741, was rare at the time and speaks further to Mary Uppington Fawcett's independence, ambition, and will.

Mary's older daughter, Ann, had moved to St. Croix and had married a reasonably prosperous planter named James Lytton. After a ruinous hurricane sacked Nevis, Mary followed her daughter to the nearby island, taking her youngest child, Rachel, born around 1729, to the Danish isle. Mary hoped for a new life free from the scandal associated with the family name. Her elder daughter's fortuitous marriage, along with a thriving plantation, offered both sanctuary and a chance to start over.

Her daughter, Rachel, was around eleven when she set sail from the Charlestown harbor in Nevis. The young girl grew up on the Lytton plantation on the south side of the island, and she and her mother made frequent visits to the capital city, Christiansted. Rachel's reputation spread throughout St. Croix. She had received a remarkably thorough education for a woman living in the Caribbean at the time and was uncommonly beautiful, with dark hair and enchanting features. Rachel read French literature, was introduced to Greek classics, showed herself to be highly adept at mathematics, and spoke English, Dutch, and her ancestral French with fluency.

But there was another side to Rachel's reputation. She had suffered from the emotionally tumultuous marriage of her parents and her family's reputation for sexual promiscuity. Also, three of Rachel's siblings—Frances, Elizabeth, and Peter—died in a time span of only a few weeks when Rachel was the tender age of seven. Then, in 1745, Rachel's father passed away. However, she inherited her father's land and wealth. Also, under the law, Rachel's mother was now free to remarry. Mary thus set her sights on marrying into money or marrying her daughter into wealth and seems to have "advertised" both the inheritance and their availability. Years later, Rachel's famous son would remember his mother as "a woman of great beauty, brilliance and accomplishment." But there were few eligible prospects available on the island.

Against Her Wishes

Around this same time, the Fawcett women met a Danish German Jew named Johann Michael Lavien. Lavien was the Sephardic version of the more common Levine, and St. Croix and Nevis islands had thriving Sephardic Jewish populations. Lavien, who was something of a traveling snake-oil salesman, had recently sold a store and moved to the Dutch-controlled island. There he purchased a sugar plantation, resold it, and purchased a cotton plantation, all of which, along with his demeanor, gave the appearance that he possessed great wealth. Something of a dapper peacock, Lavien strutted about the island in brightly colored suits while fixing his attention on the stunning sixteen-year-old Rachel Fawcett.

Lavien, however, failed at a number of businesses and would soon be swimming in debt. Years later, Alexander Hamilton would describe Lavien (he spelled it "Lavine") as a "fortune hunter" and a flashy dresser who wore over-the-top clothing studded with gold buttons. Hamilton also described Mary Uppington Fawcett as being "captivated by the glitter." Indeed, she was fooled by Lavien and, perhaps also concerned about the lack of suitors in general and her family's soiled reputation, pushed her unwilling sixteen-year-old daughter into marrying a man at least a dozen years her senior. As Hamilton's son, John, would later note, Lavien "was attracted by [Rachel's] beauty and, recommended to her mother by his wealth, received her hand against [Rachel's] inclination." A better judge of character, it appears that Rachel never cared for Lavien and probably saw him for what he really was—a charlatan.

The couple was married in 1745, and a year later Rachel gave birth to a boy named Peter. From the outset, Rachel found Lavien to be "coarse, repulsive, crude, and insufferable." Lavien also spent Rachel's inheritance, lost his plantation and home, and was facing debtors' prison. Desperate, he took a job as an overseer of a plantation but also lost that position and was likely emotionally and physically abusive toward Rachel. Much like her mother, Rachel defied social conventions of the time and abandoned Lavien in 1750.

Motivated by saving his own hide from the authorities and angered by the humiliation suffered when Rachel separated from him, Lavien testified that his wife "committed such errors which as between husband and wife were indecent and very suspicious." Lavien accused Rachel of being "shameless, rude, and ungodly" and charged that she "had completely forgotten her duty [sex] and let husband and child alone and instead gave herself up to whoring with everyone." Rachel may not have been a prostitute, but it seems that she was sexually active outside her marriage. Without Rachel in attendance or even being able to defend herself, the court ruled that she had "twice been guilty of adultery." The terms of the separation, rendered without Rachel's presence or her knowledge (she would discover that Lavien divorced her a decade later), included the provision that she could never legally remarry. Any future children would be, according to the law, "born in whoredom."

Because Danish law permitted a husband to jail his wife if she were twice found guilty of adultery, Rachel was sent to Christiansvaern, a fort and prison in Christiansted. Despite the view of the bay below, those imprisoned in Christiansvaern suffered the fate of living in dark, filthy dungeons. St. Croix, like many Caribbean islands of the time, had more than its fair share of murderers, pirates, and criminals, and the prison was filled with the worst of the lot. Prisoners were castrated, whipped, and branded, and many died in jail. It also appears that Rachel was the only woman incarcerated in the fort.

Rachel spent several months there but survived the horrendous ordeal. Although Lavien thought that the time behind bars would break his strong-willed wife, she did not go back to him when she was released. Rather, she visited her mother, who may have helped secure her release through the assistance of Captain Bertram Pieter de Nully, the prison commandant. Rachel's mother was living in one of de Nully's properties, and although the historical record is unclear, Rachel seems to have both stayed at de Nully's residence and received money from de Nully, who appears to have been utterly smitten with the twenty-one-year-old beauty despite or perhaps because of her vulnerability and reputation. The warden may have taken personal charge and responsibility for his beautiful prisoner's well-being—in more ways than one. What is clear is that Rachel abandoned both her husband and her young son (under the law, Lavien gained legal custody of the young boy) and within days fled the island in 1750 for St. Kitts.

Any hope that Rachel would ever see her son again or see her reputation restored was dashed. Although she was still young, Rachel faced a bleak future.

"The Bastard Son of a Scottish Pedlar"

From St. Croix and St. Kitts, Rachel made her way back to the island of her birth, Nevis, to start anew. Rachel had been through a lot: a bad marriage arranged against her will, a scandalous separation, the loss of her son, imprisonment, and a guilty verdict charging her with multiple counts of whoredom. Yet she retained her striking good looks, her intellect and command of languages, and her pride. But Rachel failed to learn an important lesson. Soon after arriving back in Nevis, Rachel met and took up with an attractive but hapless merchant named James Hamilton who sailed from Scotland to St. Kitts in 1741 and then on to Nevis.

Hamilton was eleven years her senior and had been born around 1718 in Stevenson Parish, Ayrshire, Scotland. The fourth of nine sons and eleven children of a wealthy landowner named Alexander Hamilton, he was raised in a castle named The Grange. Although he was a pleasant, engaging man, Rachel's new beau was lazy, drank too much, and possessed virtually no business sense or skill that would ensure financial stability. He apparently had disgraced his family's good name back in Scotland and had been drifting about the Caribbean ever since, trying for a fresh start.

James Hamilton was a failure when he met Rachel, likely in St. Kitts in the early 1750s. He owed creditors money and survived on odd jobs and generous contributions from his eldest brother, John, back in Scotland. Both James and Rachel were failed outcasts. Divorce was not an option for Rachel, and it carried a social stigma, just as did her own past, and the couple never married because of Rachel's earlier marriage to Lavien. Instead, they chose to live together in something approaching a common law union, living together for almost fifteen years and even introducing themselves as Mr. and Mrs. Hamilton. Years later and in an effort to defend his own reputation, Alexander Hamilton would insist that his parents were married.

Rachel and James lived on Main Street in Charlestown next to St. Paul's Anglican Church at a property that Rachel inherited from her father. It was there that two illegitimate children were born. The first, a son, named for his father, was born in 1753. A second son, Alexander, arrived on January 11, 1755 (some historians suggest that Hamilton was born in 1757, and Hamilton gave conflicting accounts of his date of birth). No records of the birth survive. Evidence also suggests that the couple had other children who died in infancy.

Nevis was a beautiful but tough place, featuring rugged mountains in the 2,000- to 3,000-foot range and jungles. Britain emptied its prisons, and every kind of riffraff imaginable resided on the island. The island's Anglican preacher, despairing his subjects, once described them as follows: the slaves were prone to "laziness, stealing, stubbornness, murmuring, treachery, lying, drunkenness and the like," while the white population was worse and little more than "whole shiploads of pickpockets, whores, rogues, vagrants, thieves, sodomites, and other filth and cutthroats of society."

The island also suffered more than its share of epidemics. The capital city, Jamestown, was wholly destroyed by a major earthquake and tidal wave in 1690 and replaced with the new capital of Charlestown. But the sloping, upland fields of Nevis were cultivated with sugarcane, coffee, and cocoa and therefore boasted a large population of slaves. Depending on the year, the slave population outnumbered the free white population by anywhere from two to one to four to one. Sugar was seen as "white gold" and was at the heart of both the island's economy and the slave trade.

Because most illegitimate children born on the islands were the product of white masters and black slaves, the rumor that Hamilton's mother and Hamilton himself were mulattoes arose and followed the young man to Britain's American colonies years later. Not surprisingly, as an adult, Hamilton was less than forthcoming about his dubious start in life and his family's scandalous reputation, all of which further contributed to the rumors about his upbringing. He admitted that "my birth is the subject of the most humiliating criticism."

Years later, Alexander Hamilton would go to great lengths to try to craft a more worthy history for himself. Alexander had been filled with romantic stories of Scottish nobility and castles by his drunken father. Painting himself into the realm of the grandparents whom he never knew, he would eventually name his own home in New York after his family's ancestral castle. Hamilton would also suggest that he was born not in 1755 but in 1757, probably in an effort to improve his "bastard" status because British law on the island recognized couples cohabitating for seven years as a common law union. The year 1757 was the seventh year of the illicit relationship between James Hamilton and Rachel Fawcett Lavien.

Not surprisingly, Hamilton always took delight in being descended from Scottish nobility. It seemed to embolden him when, during his political career, leading public figures made fun of his illicit upbringing, including John Adams, who dismissed his rival as "the bastard son of a Scottish pedlar." Hamilton even noted that "the truth is that, on the question who my parents were, I have better pretensions than most of those who in this country plume themselves on ancestry."

As best as we can tell, Alexander Hamilton was born and raised on Nevis, which was a British colony at the time. He was described as slender, with reddish-brown hair and sparkling blue eyes. Hamilton lacked much in the way of a formal education; however, he attended a Hebrew school at the island's synagogue and was tutored by a Jewish woman who taught him Hebrew, how to recite the Decalogue, and possibly much more about her faith and history. Nevis boasted a sizable Sephardic Jewish population—maybe one-quarter of the white population of Charlestown—of traders and sugar planters who had come to the island to escape religious persecution.

As a result of this upbringing and Hamilton's seeming innate advocacy of the rights of others (he would become of the leading voices for abolition during the revolutionary period), he became a lifelong champion of Jews. Hamilton biographer Ron Chernow goes as far as to characterize Hamilton's appreciation of and support for Jews as "reverence." Hamilton understood the lessons he was taught by his Jewish tutor, once many years later defending Jews during a high-profile trial where he argued that "discredit [the Jews] and you destroy the Christian religion." Hamilton would also write later in life,

> The progress of the Jews . . . from their earliest history to the present time has been and is entirely out of the ordinary course of human affairs. Is it not then a fair conclusion that the cause also is an extraordinary one—in other words that it is the effect of some great providential plan?

As fate would have it, Hamilton's familiarity with Judaism would, later in life, facilitate relationships with New York's small but successful Jewish community. Likewise, at critical moments in the American Revolution, such as when Congress failed to provide adequate funding for the war effort, it was Hamilton who, at the request of General Washington, sought alternative sources of funding. With the Revolution's treasurer, Robert Morris, Hamilton worked with the famed Jewish financier of the Revolution Haym Solomon. Solomon, a Polish Jew, had immigrated to New York around the same time as Hamilton and shared his command of languages and flair for mathematics and finance.

Hamilton was also taught by his mother, who was described by her grandson John as "a woman of superior intellect, elevated sentiment, and unusual grace of person and manner. To her he was indebted for his genius." Given her own education, Rachel prioritized her sons' education and attempted to fill the home with books. While firstborn James inherited his father's uninspired disposition and contentedness, Alexander shared his mother's intelligence, passion, industriousness, and restlessness. From early on, it was clear that the boy had a formidable intellect. Rachel enrolled him in school at age five. However, because of the family's bawdy history and his "bastard" birth, the only school that would accept Alexander seems to have been the small Jewish academy with a tolerant approach to both education and those treated poorly by the church and authorities. Hamilton learned French at home and Hebrew at school, and he picked up other languages on the streets of Charlestown and in his mother's library.

The Hamilton family struggled. Rachel ran a small store, but the enterprise did not succeed. Rachel's scandalous life was fodder for gossip and, by the time of her son's birth, the booming sugar industry on Nevis had collapsed. The island's population was down to roughly 900 white residents and a few thousand slaves.

James Hamilton did little to help his family. After bankruptcy and several failed jobs, he gained employment as a clerk in a trading company. The company sent him to St. Croix in 1765 to collect an outstanding debt owed to them. The trip to St. Croix changed their lives. It was while Rachel was briefly back on the island with James and her two sons, ages twelve and ten, that she finally learned that her former husband, Johann Michael Lavien, had officially divorced her. Debt ridden, having failed at various jobs, and now living with a new woman and children from the union, Lavien wanted a divorce. He also wanted money and to ensure that Rachel or her children would never inherit a cent from him. The matter had been settled six years before when a summons was issued on February 26, 1759, for Rachel. Yet, because she had moved to St. Kitts and back to Nevis after leaving Lavien, Rachel never received any notice of the summons or later court proceedings for the divorce, which, not surprisingly, went completely against her.

At the trial (in which Rachel was absent and not represented), Lavien maintained that his wife had "absented herself from [Lavien] for nine years and gone elsewhere, where she has begotten several illegitimate children, so that such action is believed to be more than sufficient for him to obtain a divorce from her." He also labeled her a sinner and a whore, claiming that she had "completely forgotten her duty and let husband and child alone and instead given herself up to whoring with everyone, which things the plaintiff says are so well known that her own family and friends must hate her for it." A divorce was granted on June 25, 1759, and Rachel and, in the words of Lavien and the court, her "whore children" were disinherited from any of her ex-husband's property or wealth.

Because of James Hamilton's new job, the family lived in the capital city. But around this time, Rachel was growing tired of her beau. Not long after, James Hamilton abandoned his family. It seems likely that the ugliness of the news of the divorce and of the claims of Rachel's loose sexual mores figured into the falling-out and his departure. It is also possible that Rachel may have initiated the separation. Perhaps she was emotionally devastated over the belated news of the ugly terms of the divorce or simply exhausted by James Hamilton's continued inability to make a living. Whatever the motivation, the relationship ended.

James moved to St. Kitts and then drifted throughout the West Indies, all the while plagued by his weakness for the bottle. At one point, he had the misfortune of being in Tobago, where he was nearly killed in an uprising by slaves against their oppressive masters. Alexander Hamilton was scarred by the loss of his biological father, always referring to it in the context of a temporary "separation" rather than the obvious truth. It is probable that the family never saw James Hamilton again. Even years later, as a hero of the American Revolution and successful attorney, Alexander Hamilton never forgot his father. Hamilton would repeatedly write to his father. He also sent him money to help erase his debts and even unsuccessfully tried to get his father to move in with his own family in New York or at least attend his wedding. All attempts were unsuccessful. Alexander once wrote to his older brother James,

> What has become of our dear father? It is an age since I have heard from him. Perhaps, alas! he is no more, and I shall not have the pleasing opportunity of contributing to render the close of his life more happy than the progress of it. My heart bleeds at the recollection of his misfortunes and embarrassments.

Yellow Fever!

Rachel prospered on her own. She purchased a two-story home at 34 Company Street in the capital city and opened a shop that sold supplies, including salted fish and beef, as well as rice, flour, and other necessities to the planters and shippers. She was assisted by her brother-in-law, James Lytton, who bought household furnishings for Rachel and likely helped with the purchase of the home. The family also had five slaves and their children to assist them, and young Alexander displayed a talent for the business. Thanks to her business savvy and that of her young son, Rachel managed to make a living better than that she experienced with either of the two men who had been in her life.

Young Alexander also became friends with one of the young slave boys, Ajax, who assisted him with his errands and responsibilities in support of the family store. The two boys developed a friendship that ignored their disparate social status. Young Hamilton seemed to have developed a remarkably progressive attitude for the time about slavery and racial inequality that would stay with him throughout his life as one of the most passionate voices of the Revolution for abolition.

What is also telling is that Rachel acquired at least thirty-four books, an amount that would have constituted a fairly large library for the time, and continued to tutor her youngest son. The books included the poetry of Alexander Pope and an array of classics from Machiavelli to Plutarch. Young Alexander pored through the books and cultivated a passion for reading and learning much like his mother.

The tranquillity and success was short lived, however. In the early days of 1767, a fever of epidemic proportions struck the island. Through much of January and February, both Rachel and Alexander were ill. Visits from a physician and the care of a kind woman who lived nearby were to no avail. The prescribed treatment of bloodletting, enemas, and purging likely worsened the condition, and at 9:00 on the evening of February 19, 1767, Rachel died. She was thirty-nine.

Alexander, age thirteen, was deathly ill when his mother passed away. Within hours of his mother's death, he witnessed the arrival of the town's judge and bailiff, who had callously come to inventory her remaining possessions. The family's few chairs, tables, dishes, and glasses; Rachel's four dresses and her prized collection of books; and even the family goat were all auctioned off as the boy was still recovering from his near fatal bout with the fever. Young Alexander was entitled to nothing. He was the illegitimate son of an adulterer mother. The extent of his suffering is revealed when the town's judge gave the boys money for shoes and the funeral. Because of her past reputation, Rachel Fawcett Lavien was denied a burial at the Anglican Church and was laid to rest on a hill overlooking the blue waters of the Caribbean near her brother-in-law's plantation. Anything of value was confiscated by authorities to cover her debts. It must have been of little consolation that Rachel's brother-in-law bought back a few of her books for Alexander.

What little money remained was sent to Rachel's son from her earlier marriage. Peter Lavien was then twenty-two and living in South Carolina but came to the island to collect what was his. Alexander probably never met his half-brother, nor would he receive any assistance from him during this time of great need. Rachel's opportunistic former husband, Johann Michael Lavien, also reappeared three years later on August 3, 1771, to try to claim anything else that may have belonged to his late wife or her relatives but received nothing. Alexander's father failed even to visit or attempt to see or care for his sons during this time.

Alexander and his brother, both orphans, were sent to live with their aunt Ann and her husband James Lytton. But the once-prosperous family fell on hard times, and a year after his mother's death, Alexander's aunt and uncle died. With his brother James, Alexander Hamilton, the future hero of the American Revolution and founding father, was orphaned at fourteen, alone and penniless. It had been an indescribably tumultuous few years for young Alexander. His grandmother, an aunt and uncle, and his mother had died. His father abandoned the family, they were uprooted and struggled financially, and now he was orphaned and homeless.

The young boys were then sent to live with a young cousin named Peter Lytton. However, Lytton had a tarnished reputation to rival that of Rachel. He kept a slave mistress and had illegitimate children with her. The arrangement contributed to the rumors that Hamilton himself was biracial. Soon after, Lytton was found dead in a pool of blood in his home. Whether he was shot and stabbed to death or he committed suicide is uncertain, but the boys were again traumatically uprooted and apprenticed out to two different families on the island.

Not showing much promise, James Jr. was apprenticed to a carpenter in Christiansted, a job usually reserved for slaves. Alexander was sent to work for Thomas Stevens, a wealthy merchant. Alexander distinguished himself in Stevens's store, impressing everyone he encountered. It was at this time that the boy met a lifelong friend, Stevens's son, Edward. Their friendship was yet another source of scandal, however. Alexander and Edward were close in age and were the spitting image of one another, passing as brothers and even sharing similar personalities. As such, it was suggested that Stevens was Hamilton's biological father, and the question is one certainly worth considering.

OF RICH PATRONS AND EASY WOMEN

After young Hamilton's tragic losses, the adolescent genius reapplied himself to business endeavors. He held a position as a clerk in one of Stevens's stores and in an import/export firm. When the owner went to sea for an extended trip, the boy was left in charge. In that position, Hamilton ingratiated himself to many of the shippers and traders who visited the island as he had earlier done with the Jewish community on Nevis. Hamilton's bookkeeping skills and work ethic made him useful to the unschooled seaman and the island's planters.

With the support of these same appreciative merchants and his island neighbors, Hamilton was able to sail for Boston in the early fall of 1772. But the adventure nearly ended at the outset when a fire broke out on board the ship. However, Hamilton arrived safely in the Massachusetts Colony and from there made his way to New York. He later settled in Elizabethtown, New Jersey.

Occupying such lowly status in society and coming from a difficult and disrespectable upbringing, Hamilton had to claw his way to respectability, literally outworking and out-thinking his contemporaries. One of the greatest minds of the founding generation was also one of the youngest and, in many ways, perhaps the most unlikely. Hamilton did not share the privileged status of most of his fellow patriots, and he was an outsider, an immigrant who knew little of his adopted homeland.

Thanks to the young man's talents, in 1773, Elias Boudinot, Governor William Livingston, and other impressed patrons helped him enter King's College (now Columbia University), where he studied math, literature, Latin, Greek, and geography. While in New York, the passionate Hamilton quickly found himself caught up in the revolutionary fervor of the city and times. In 1774, at age nineteen, Hamilton was penning some of the most widely read and influential pamphlets attacking the British Crown and Parliament. He joined the war effort, enlisting after the Declaration of Independence was drafted. Hamilton so distinguished himself as an artillery officer in the earliest battles that he caught the attention of the commanding general, George Washington. Indeed, the relationship was not coincidental, as young Hamilton sought to endear himself to powerful men, searching for a father figure and a role model.

Two strokes of good fortune enabled Hamilton's meteoric rise to fame. One was to replicate a formula that worked so well as a youth who was eager for more than his island upbringing offered—young Hamilton sought to endear himself to Washington, who responded by offering him an appointment in 1777 as the general's aide-de-camp, a position he held until the Battle of Yorktown in 1781.

Hamilton emerged from the war a hero and with Washington's full trust and admiration. Washington was the powerful father figure Hamilton never had; Hamilton was the dutiful, brilliant son Washington never had. It is not an accident that Washington later picked Hamilton as the first secretary of the treasury, a position from which he would develop the new nation's economic and financial system, remedy the war debt, strengthen the machinery and power of the government, lead the Federalist faction, and emerge as the founding president's most trusted ally and influential adviser—not bad for the illegitimate son of a "whore" from a small Caribbean island.

The second blessing that Hamilton received was to successfully marry into money, although, truth be told, it was, once again, less a blessing than a calculated strategy. One of the traits Hamilton shared with his patron and ally George Washington was a desire to marry into money, a goal that both men achieved.

The American Casanova

Alexander Hamilton was easily among the most important of the framers. Yet leadership and influence come with a bull's-eye on one's back. Hamilton's closeness to Washington, along with his passionate, zealous approach to his work, engendered for him a host of enemies. His opinionated personality evoked strong feelings from both friend and foe. Moreover, Hamilton possessed two obvious weaknesses that his critics would exploit: he could be rash and emotional when confronted, and, despite his progressive advocacy for the rights of slaves, Jews, and women, he had a reckless sexual appetite for the "fairer sex."

For their part, women were responsive to Hamilton. It helped that Hamilton had strong and attractive facial features with piercing dark blue eyes, a natural charm, and gift for gab. He was fair skinned with rosy cheeks and brown hair tinged with light highlights courtesy of living in the sun-drenched tropics. Hamilton's slight frame—at five feet seven inches, a bit above average in height for the time—carried a confidently erect posture and military bearing. Hamilton seemed to always have a purpose, and there was a sense of excitement and urgency about him. Additionally, Hamilton's ensuing reputation as an American Casanova matched his reputation for courage on the battlefield and brilliance in his patriotic endeavors and governance. Many young women visiting the headquarters of Washington's revolutionary army came hoping to meet the dashing Colonel Hamilton. In fact, his pursuit of so many of the belles who partied at the winter headquarters of the army inspired General Washington's wife Martha to name the camp's carousing tomcat, whose straying nightly deeds kept everyone awake, "Hamilton" in honor of the colonel's coquettish conquests.

One incident exemplifies the human tomcat's amorous approach. At age twenty, Hamilton's good friend, fellow aide, and rival for the dubious distinction of camp Lothario, John Laurens, was on a mission to the southern colonies. Hamilton, who wished to indulge his curiosities about southern tastes and belles, ordered his colleague to solicit lady companions for him. The confident Hamilton even instructed the envoy on what to say about him and did so with thinly veiled sexual innuendos:

> To exact [the ladies], it will be necessary for you to give an account of the lover—his *size*, make, quality of mind and *body*, achievements, expectations, fortunes, &c. In drawing my picture, you will no doubt be civil to your friend. Mind you do justice to the *length of my nose* and don't forget that I [text missing].

Hamilton's choice of words reflected the same innuendos written by Laurence Sterne, one of the most popular authors of the day, who frequently used the nose as a metaphor for another part of the male anatomy. The last words of this passage must have been particularly scandalous because they were, unfortunately, scratched out by Hamilton's censoring descendants. The censor was most likely his son, who might have performed the literary surgery as he prepared his biography of his famous father. Unfortunately, Hamilton's son, James, altered or redacted more than the previously mentioned embarrassing reference to his father's sexual organ. James deprived history of many insights into his illustrious father while preparing to write the elder Hamilton's biography.

In the letter in question, Hamilton boldly went on to describe for his friend Laurens his preference for virgins and exactly what type of woman attracted him:

> Take her description: she must be young, handsome (I lay most stress upon a good shape); sensible (a little learning will do); well bred . . . chaste and tender (I am an enthusiast in my notions of fidelity and fondness); of some good nature; a great deal of generosity (she must neither love money nor scolding for I dislike equally a termagant and an economist).
>
> In politics, I am indifferent what side she may be of: I think I have arguments that will safely convert her to mine. As to religion, a moderate stock will satisfy me. She must believe in god and hate a saint. But as to fortune, the larger stock of that, the better. . . . Yet as money is an essential ingredient of happiness in this world, as I have not much of my own and as I am very little calculated to get more, it must needs be that my wife bring at least a sufficiency to administer to her own extravagances.

One of Hamilton's first loves was Katherine Livingston, daughter of the governor of New Jersey. Similar to his mentor, George Washington, Hamilton's taste in wealthy women revealed his youthful audacity and ambition. The young paramour met "Lady Kitty" at a "drawing room" social at her family home when he was just seventeen. New to America, impressionable, and eager for success, Hamilton fell as much for the older woman herself as he did for the lifestyle to which she introduced him. At the Livingston estate, which included gardens and a 500-book library (possibly the largest Hamilton had ever seen), aristocratic families dined, danced, and socialized. It was Hamilton's initial foray into high society, and he loved it. Lady Kitty had many admirers, including Hamilton's close friend and fellow carouser, John Laurens, but he was deterred by neither the competition nor the cold fact that Lady Kitty was unattainable for a penniless student.

Although Hamilton would always have a well-deserved reputation as a prolific lover, this image was only part of the picture. In truth, for all his dalliances with women and his bravado around his comrades during the war, Hamilton shared with George Washington the desire for family life—provided that it was with a wealthy woman. As expected, Hamilton courted Ms. Livingston with a boldness deemed inappropriate by the mores of high society. His off-and-on attraction to Kitty lasted a few years, during which time they danced, picnicked, and went on sleigh rides. The fact that someone with the standing of Lady Kitty even considered Hamilton as a suitor further speaks to his many admirable qualities.

In his letters and courtship of women, Hamilton frequently employed the term "gallant," a word often used as a metaphor for sexuality in the eighteenth century. In one racy letter to Lady Kitty, Hamilton hinted at the possibilities:

> I challenge you to meet me in whatever path you dare. If you have no objection, for variety and amusement, we will even sometimes make excursions in the flowery walks and roseate bowers of Cupid. You know I am renowned for gallantry and shall always be able to entertain you with a choice collection of the prettiest things imaginable.

Washington's command spent the winter of 1779–1780 in Morristown, New Jersey. Here, the general's staff once again endured the hardships of sparse supplies and inadequate funding from Congress. That spring, a near mutiny by the troops almost destroyed the army. But for the resourcefulness of Colonel Hamilton, who worked with Washington on the many strategic challenges facing his command, relief came in the form of several young women who visited camp, thereby diverting the soldiers' attention from sedition to seduction.

Among the belles catching Hamilton's eye at Morristown was Cornelia Lott. Hamilton apparently fell hard for Cornelia, a point noticed by the other officers in camp. In fact, the colonel's comrades were frequently amused by the fact that Hamilton boasted of not ever falling for one woman, yet he so quickly and so frequently fell in and out of love. Another one of Washington's aides, Samuel Blackley Webb, even composed a poem inspired by Hamilton's brief infatuation with the lovely Miss Lott:

To Colonel Hamilton

What, bend the stubborn knee at last,
Confess the days of wisdom past?
He that could bow to every shrine
And swear the last the most divine;

Like Hudibras, all subjects bend,
Had Ovid at his finger's end;
Could whistle every tune of love,
(You'd think him Ovid's self or Jove)
Now feels the inexorable dart
And yields Cornelia all his heart!

Alas, shortly after these lines were composed, Hamilton broke poor Cornelia's heart and was off pursuing another belle named Polly.

THE SCHUYLER SISTERS

General Philip Schuyler, heir to an old family fortune, owned a number of lucrative enterprises, among them timber and fur trading. A hero of the French and Indian Wars and a delegate from New York to the Continental Congress, Schuyler was one of the most respected and powerful men in the colony. Befitting their status, the four Schuyler daughters were among the most eligible and most sought-after debutantes in New York. Not surprisingly, the young women made quite a splash during the winter social seasons of the American Revolution—one young man who toasted the Schuyler daughters was Alexander Hamilton.

An eighteen-year-old Hamilton first met the Schuylers in 1773 at their family home, one of the most lavish in America, while on a mission to discuss matters of war with the wealthy general. He again met the Schuyler daughters when they came to Washington's headquarters in Morristown in 1780. While in camp, General Schuyler's daughters were said to be interested in dancing with the "most gallant men about Morristown." At the front of the pack of gallant men in camp was Hamilton, who began courting his future wife, Elizabeth "Betsy" Schuyler, that winter. Many men attempted to court Betsy and the other Schuyler daughters, including Hamilton's friend and fellow aide Tench Tilghman. But Hamilton had fixed his sights on the second Schuyler daughter and was determined to win her hand. Indeed, his letters show him to be head over heels about Betsy.

Hamilton also seems perplexed that he was falling in love and contemplating marriage so quickly and seriously. He was also surprised that it was a woman like Betsy who captured his heart. Betsy Schuyler was, after all, not the fawning, flirtsy beauty to whom his affections were usually directed and welcomed. A moderately attractive brunette with a passion for the outdoors and riding horses, Betsy Schuyler was less flirtatious and far more serious and thoughtful than her more attractive sisters, especially Angelica, whose beauty was celebrated across New York. Betsy was unlike most of the other women in attendance at the winter social events at headquarters. Consequently, Hamilton did not quite know what to make of Betsy or his feelings for her. He described his new love to his friend John Laurens as follows:

> She has a most good nature, affability and vivacity unembellished with that charming frivolousness which is justly deemed one of the principal accomplishments of a belle.
>
> In short, she is so strange a creature that she possesses all the beauties, virtues and graces of her sex without any of those amiable defects. . . . Several of my friends, philosophers who railed at love as a weakness, men of the world who laughed at it as a fantasy, [Betsy] has presumptuously and daringly compelled to acknowledge its power. . . . I am myself of the number.

The Arnold–André Affair

Hamilton's feelings for Betsy also drove the usually confident and cocky young man to jealousy. Ironically, his chief rival for Betsy's heart was not a direct competitor per se but a man whom Hamilton could never hope to best.

The British officer John Delancy André was a dashing, worldly spy who also happened to be bisexual. It was common for high-ranking officers like André who were captured to be treated more as guests than prisoners of war. Such were the more gentlemanly customs of the day that, while serving as a prisoner of the colonial army, André had the pleasure of spending part of his "confinement" at the Schuyler home, where he dined and flirted with the Schuyler daughters. Betsy, the most serious of the daughters, in particular, was intrigued by the older spy and captivated by his seemingly limitless sophistication and talent for poetry, painting, music, and conversation. André seems to have touched off the old demons of self-doubt that Hamilton never truly absolved from his common and limited upbringing in the West Indies. Recognizing Betsy's feelings for André, Hamilton worried about whether he could ever truly capture her heart, writing with uncharacteristic introspection and self-doubt, "Why am I not handsome? Why have I not every acquirement that can embellish human nature?"

The otherwise confident young man further compared himself to the British spymaster. Hamilton wished that he "possessed André's accomplishment" and longed to be "the first, the most amiable, the most accomplished of my sex." During the time of the André ordeal, Hamilton even seems to have lost interest in the other girls that frequented headquarters. He was used to being the one in control of relationships and not the one consumed with worry about whether feelings of desire were reciprocated. Panicked because of the time that Betsy spent in the company of the dashing spymaster, Hamilton stepped up his letter writing to his love and took to closing his letters to Betsy, "Impatiently my Dearest." He even shot off a letter to Betsy pleading, "For god's sake my Dear Betsy try to write me oftener and give me the picture of your heart."

As fate would have it, André had been involved in the infamous matter of the war's most notorious traitor, Benedict Arnold. The treasonous Arnold was a brilliant and successful general in the Continental army. History remembers him, however, as the classic traitor for switching sides during the war. His treachery was an attempt to surrender West Point to the English while acting as commandant of the venerable fort.

In a more sympathetic account of Arnold's underlying motivation, the general had become embittered by several dastardly intrigues against him, and his decision to "turn coat" was a result of personal frustration with war politics and policies. The general's plot was revealed when André was captured carrying incriminating papers. Arnold was able to escape to England, where he lived out his life comfortably. André was imprisoned and condemned to death for his complicity in the event.

Neither Hamilton nor Washington seemed to be able to put aside their personal feelings in the Arnold–André case. Washington was still bitter about his former friend's actions and embarrassed by Arnold's conniving deceit. Hamilton was still smarting from having been resoundingly duped by both General and Mrs. Arnold. During the ordeal while Arnold was escaping, his wife was interrogated by Hamilton. Mrs. Arnold played on Hamilton's gullibility around women, duping him sufficiently long enough to cover for her husband and help him escape. Making matters worse was the fact that General Arnold's skills and talents were such that the American command deeply suffered his loss.

On a personal note, Hamilton was also now faced with the predicament that André's death would forever martyr him in Betsy's heart and psyche. Even more to the point, the ambitious and patriotic Hamilton found his career goals and loyalty to Washington pitted against his own heart, as the reality of the matter was that he planned to marry a woman whose heart belonged to one of the most dreaded enemies of American independence.

Most assuredly because of his own scandalous upbringing, Hamilton viewed those facing judgment with far more leniency than did Washington, who tolerated no misbehavior and punished any crime with a firm hand. Because of Hamilton's own connections to André and his friendship with General Washington (who was angry with him over the botched interrogation of Mrs. Arnold), when Betsy asked him to intervene on the spy's behalf to try to obtain a commutation of the sentence from Washington, Hamilton felt obliged to do so. Hamilton not only kept Betsy informed of André's well-being throughout the ordeal but also developed a secret plan to swap prisoners with the British: André for Arnold. He risked Washington's wrath when he approached the unyielding commander about the matter.

In the end, Hamilton kept André company in his final moments and even provided the condemned man paper and pen to draft his final letters. The last letter written before the execution was to General Sir Henry Clinton, André's gay lover. Hamilton offered André and Betsy one final gift when he secured from Washington a pledge to grant André his last wish—to be hanged as a gentleman rather than face the firing squad like a common criminal. The spy was hanged in early fall of 1780, a punishment befitting his rank.

Hamilton remained conflicted throughout the ordeal, and the incident produced one of the famous rifts between Washington and Hamilton. Hamilton, for his part, had trouble moving beyond the matter, as the image of Betsy's fondness for André haunted his dreams. Nor could Betsy. She would always cherish her memories of the dashing spy.

Of Love and Marriage

As two of her sisters had done before her, Betsy proposed that she and Hamilton elope, in part to avoid an elaborate wedding in the same ballroom where she spent so many happy moments with André. Hamilton opposed the idea. An elopement only furthered Hamilton's anxiety over the pending marriage. Regardless of the details, Hamilton was having difficulties securing adequate time for leave from General Washington. Washington was angry with Hamilton, and the colonel was simply too valuable to Washington's command to let him go to his lover. Moreover, with two aides already on leave in Virginia for their own marriages and precious few officers who were fluent in French to assist Washington with the French officers in camp, Hamilton's repeated requests to travel to the Schuyler home went nowhere.

Ultimately, Hamilton was reluctantly given leave, his first in the four and a half years of the war. In November 1780, he rode by horseback to the Schuyler mansion near Albany to marry. Betsy's entire family seemed enamored with Hamilton, and the privileged lifestyle of the Schuylers greatly agreed with Hamilton as well. On December 17, 1780, the couple was married in the second-floor ballroom of the family home, the same room where the recently executed André had dazzled the Schuyler daughters and where the bride had hoped not to be wed.

Despite the turmoil that surrounded their engagement, the newlyweds were happy and content in marriage. Hamilton's life was forever changed and his fortune secured. He summed up his feelings and those of his bride in a letter to Betsy's sister Margarita, encouraging the younger Schuyler daughter to follow her sister's lead into betrothal:

> Because your sister has the talent of growing more amiable every day, or because I am a fanatic in love, or both—or if you prefer another interpretation, because I have address enough to be a good dissembler, she fancies herself the happiest woman in the world, and would persuade all her friends to embark with her in the matrimonial voyage.

Scholars are uncertain as to whether Hamilton truly loved Betsy. That he married for money is certain. It is also certain that, like his parents, grandfather, and great-grandfather before him, Hamilton engaged in a number of reckless extramarital affairs throughout his married life. There is also the matter of an incriminating letter that the colonel sent to one of his best friends and fellow womanizers at headquarters, John Laurens. In the letter, Hamilton for the first time informs his friend that he is engaged. Yet, according to Hamilton biographer Willard Sterne Randall, Hamilton breaks the news as almost an "afterthought" and with a "flippant" demeanor. After a lengthy discussion of military affairs, Hamilton finally brings up the subject of his engagement:

> I confess my sins. I am guilty. Next fall completes my doom. I give up my liberty to Miss Schuyler. She is a good-hearted girl who I am sure will never play the termagant. Though not a genius, she has good sense enough to be agreeable, and though not a beauty, she has fine black eyes—is rather handsome and has every other requisite of the exterior to make a lover happy. And, believe me, I am a lover in earnest, though I do not speak of the perfections of my mistress in the enthusiasm of chivalry.

Although the tone of the letter might very well reveal a callous side to Hamilton and his reluctance to end his days as a womanizing bachelor, there is an explanation for the troubling tone. Laurens had been taken prisoner by the British. At the time the letter was written, Hamilton was working to free his incarcerated friend. Yet Hamilton was unsuccessful in gaining Laurens's release, and this explains why the letter discusses military matters before announcing the engagement. Hamilton could not gloat over the good fortune of marrying the most eligible woman in New York while his friend rotted in a British jail. Thus, perhaps Hamilton reverted back to the adolescent remarks used by buddies carousing with women, a tone that the two camp bachelors shared so frequently in the past before Laurens's capture, as a way to sympathize with Laurens.

Over the next eighteen years, Mrs. Betsy Schuyler Hamilton would have eight children and more than one miscarriage. Tragically, the refined, happy, and thoughtful girl whom Hamilton married became a bedridden, nervous, frequently depressed woman because of the strain of so many pregnancies and perhaps in part because of Hamilton's philandering. As time went by, the couple grew apart. Betsy preferred knitting to socializing and dancing and family time at home to politics and visits to New York City. Because of her delicate mental and physical health and numerous pregnancies, Betsy chose to stay with her children at her parents' spacious mansion near Albany. Hamilton, whose law career enjoyed spectacular success, remained alone at their home in New York City. It was an arrangement doomed for disaster.

Governed by Passion

Betsy Schuyler's older sister, Angelica, was widely considered to have been the most beautiful woman in New York. Outgoing, flirtatious, and famous, Angelica had married a wealthy Englishman named John Church. Believing that he had killed a man in a duel and would be punished for the crime, Church had fled England for America. In America, Church exploited his connections on both sides of the Atlantic by supplying Washington's army. Church's lack of a conscience made it easy for him to make an enormous amount of money off the war. Only later did he discover that his former foe on the dueling grounds back in England had, in fact, not died, as he was led to believe. Now pardoned from any wrongdoing, Church returned to London after the war. Despite his work on behalf of the revolutionaries, Church eventually secured a seat in Parliament and began spending less and less time in America.

Angelica Schuyler Church seemed to see her husband for what he really was—dull, cowardly, and obsessed with nothing more than money. As such and because of her closeness with her large family, Angelica chose to remain in New York City alone rather than go with her husband. Her regal home happened to be near Alexander Hamilton's residence in the city. Their affair probably began in 1784. Hamilton was not bothered by the fact that Angelica was his wife's sister or concerned that Angelica's husband was one of Hamilton's first and most important clients. The passion between the lovers was mutual and unlike the passion that either one felt for their spouses.

Angelica frequently wrote to Hamilton and to her family about Hamilton, saying in one letter to her sister Betsy, "Embrace poor Hamilton for me. I am really so proud of his merit and abilities that even you, Eliza, might envy my feelings." Angelica closed her letter with veiled innocence, informing her sister, "You know how much I love and admire him."

Angelica and her brother-in-law engaged in a sordid public affair for many years. The Schuyler family seemed to worry about the affair, as it had the potential to bring pain to their daughter and shame to their family name. They tried to encourage Angelica to go to London to be with her husband. Divorce was never an option, precluded by the Schuyler's Dutch Reformed Church and the family's lofty social status. It would also damage John Church's career in Parliament and Hamilton's law practice. During the years of the affair, Hamilton had become one of New York's most powerful lawyers and politicians. Betsy was already depressed, and she grew even more so at the cruel twist of fate that, if her cheating but beloved sister moved to London, she might never see her again. The historian Randall describes Betsy as now being "inconsolable." Remarkably, the two sisters remained close despite the probability that Betsy was hearing rumors of an affair. Angelica, for her part, continued the charade with her sister by including in her letters thoughts of Hamilton. One such letter ended with the words, "Tell Colonel Hamilton, if he does not write to me, I shall be very angry."

Hamilton shared his wife's concern about the prospect of losing Angelica. When Angelica finally set sail for England in the fall of 1789, Hamilton cried. Writing to one another from opposite sides of the Atlantic Ocean, the lovers took to having their heartfelt letters delivered by private courier rather than being bundled with the other family correspondence. One letter from Hamilton to Angelica evokes Virgil, comparing himself and his distant lover to the characters Aeneas and Dido, lovers forced apart by a cruel fate. Hamilton hinted at the sexual nature of their relationship while pining away for Angelica by assuring her to "judge the bitterness it gives to those who love you with the love of nature." (Hamilton and others of the time often used the word "nature" to express sexual urges.)

But the affair with his sister-in-law was not the one that ultimately did Hamilton in. It was another, more sordid liaison.

DANGEROUS LIAISONS

After sending his wife and family home to Albany for another extended vacation, Hamilton remained at his office during the summer of 1791. It was then that an attractive woman approached Hamilton requesting a favor. Hamilton fell for the deceitful story that the unlucky young woman had been abandoned by her cruel husband and was lonely and destitute. Accepting Hamilton's offer to help, the woman invited the powerful attorney to her home that same evening, presumably to further discuss the manner in which Hamilton could assist her. Hamilton arrived at her home that evening as planned. He had brought with him a donation of cash for the girl's rescue. However, once inside the door, the two fell into one another's arms.

The seductress was Maria Reynolds, the semiliterate, comely wife of a professional swindler named James Reynolds. Without much difficulty, Maria seduced Hamilton in a simple blackmail scheme. It was all orchestrated by Maria's husband. The sexual liaisons continued until one day, when Hamilton was in the arms of Maria, her husband James Reynolds arranged to "walk in" to "catch" the illicit lovers in the act. The plan worked. Reynolds demanded $1,000 in two payments as the price of his silence. Hamilton paid.

Hamilton's weakness for Maria was such that he continued his romantic trysts with her after being caught and bribed by her husband. Even after completing the payments to James Reynolds, Hamilton continued to see Maria. The Reynoldses' new plan was to agree to keep quiet about the affair but only as long as Hamilton's money kept pouring in—and it did. Hamilton eventually had to borrow money in order to pay James Reynolds, yet he continued to have sex with Maria. Hamilton was doomed either way. If his payments stopped, then Mr. Reynolds would go public with the story; if Hamilton stopped seeing his mistress, Mrs. Reynolds threatened to kill herself. Hamilton was in a predicament. He had many enemies, including several who would be eager to employ such a scandal against him.

Eventually, James Reynolds demanded a job with Hamilton in the Treasury Department. This was too much for what remained of Hamilton's conscience. His private family life was one thing, but Hamilton's honor had always shined brighter when in the service of governing. He refused Reynolds the job and decided to disentangle himself from the clutches of the Reynoldses' affair. Unfortunately for Hamilton, Jacob Clingman, a two-bit hustler and business partner of James Reynolds, provided the tantalizing details of the illicit affair to Hamilton's political opponents, who were only too willing to use it to bring the great man down. Among Hamilton's enemies were two future presidents. One of those who leaked the story to the public and the press was James Monroe, future president. It was none other than Jefferson, Hamilton's chief ideological enemy, who orchestrated from afar Monroe's actions against his longtime foe.

In yet another interesting twist, the journalist covering the story was James Callender, a drunken Scotsman—just as Hamilton's father had been—who made a living wallowing in tabloid scandals. Callender was paid by Jefferson to write the story about Hamilton. But what goes around comes around. Thus, a few years later, it was the same Callender who, angry with

Jefferson, first published the story about Jefferson's affair with a slave mistress. Hamilton, who detested the practice of dueling, nonetheless challenged Monroe, a far better marksman, to a duel. Fortunately for Hamilton and for history, this duel never occurred. But the die had been cast. Ironically, it was Hamilton's ultimate enemy, Aaron Burr, who intervened with a diplomatic solution to avert the duel.

The sensational story in the press claimed that Hamilton was guilty of adultery and of using government money to pay Reynolds. Ever the loyal public servant, Hamilton was far more concerned with the false allegations that he used federal funds inappropriately than the accurate charge that he committed adultery. Thus, in 1797, Hamilton admitted to the affair and even published the details of it in a pamphlet. The effort proved to be a severely misguided attempt to try to save his professional reputation. In his public mea culpa, Hamilton even released Maria Reynolds's love letters as proof of the adultery charge but as evidence against the use of treasury funds. The pamphlet became something of an instant "best-seller," and Hamilton ended up disgraced and guilty of an imprudent response to his critics. The public also judged him harshly.

Hamilton's wife stood by him throughout the ordeal, as painful as it was. Betsy always retained her deep love and affection for her husband, a man she knew to be good hearted and caring. Maria and James Reynolds also suffered from the revelations of the affair and their use of blackmail. The couple was scorned by the press and the public. Soon afterward, Maria asked for a divorce, which was granted to her. But then another scandal erupted. It was discovered that Maria intended to marry Jacob Clingman, her ex-husband's business partner who was complicit in the blackmail. Moreover, Maria tried to remarry too quickly and before her divorce was finalized. This latest story of sexual intrigue ended up having the effect of keeping Hamilton's own problems on the front burner of public opinion even though it had nothing to do with him.

In a final ironic and fateful twist in this perverse scandal, one of the lawyers helping to finalize the Reynoldses' divorce was Aaron Burr, Hamilton's new avowed enemy.

Rivalries

Throughout the 1780s, Alexander Hamilton and Aaron Burr were engaged in a heated rivalry to be New York's most prominent attorney and politician. Hamilton rightly believed Burr to be a dangerous and unprincipled man and therefore took it on himself to oppose Burr's bids for public office. In one such instance, Hamilton backed the successful candidate for mayor of New

York City, James Duane, when he learned that Burr was considering running for the same office.

In 1789 and 1790, Burr wrote Hamilton with a warning to stop intervening in city politics and his own career. The feud between the two men had already reached dangerous levels, and the pair would stay locked in a reckless conflict until it ultimately resulted in the most tragic of outcomes.

Relations between Hamilton and his chief political opponent, Thomas Jefferson, were no better. Their relationship had been frosty since the end of the war, with the two brilliant minds staking out nearly polar opposite positions on a range of important questions from political philosophy to the role and structure of government. At the Constitutional Convention, the blueprint that the framers debated and developed was essentially a brilliant compromise based on the beliefs and rivalries of the nation's two chief political architects. Hamilton favored a strong national treasury and the relief of the states' war debts by the federal government as mechanisms to strengthen the wobbly new government. Jefferson believed that government governed best when it governed least. Not surprisingly, Hamilton encountered opposition from Jefferson and his political allies, who opposed a national treasury, strong government, and federal assumption of the war debt.

Most of the revolutionary debt had been incurred by northern states, and the southern states did not want to assist their northern neighbors in relieving the $25 million burden. What the southerners did care about was states' rights, a very limited role for government, and defeating any proposal to build the new capital city in New York, Philadelphia, Harrisburg, or any locale outside Dixie. Thus, Hamilton devised a clever end-around move on the Jeffersonians. The conniving Hamilton played to Jefferson's southern roots and sympathies in an infamous meeting where he agreed to promote among his fellow northerners and Federalists a site in Virginia for the capital in exchange for southern support for federal debt assumption.

Jefferson caught Hamilton coming out of George Washington's New York City home. The treasury secretary was dejected, so his opponent took advantage of the moment, inviting Hamilton to his home for dinner. In what would be the most important dinner party in history, the two framers met in June 1790 to discuss the issues of national debt assumption and the location of the national capital. Jefferson thought that he had the upper hand because of the temporary rift between Hamilton and Washington, and Hamilton offered what seemed to be terms that favored southerners and Virginia, who was exempted from contributing to the debt. The secretary of state took the bait, and the deal was made. The South, it seemed, would have its cake and eat it too. The new capital would be in Dixie, and although displeased with the financing of the debt, at least the southern states did not have to directly pay it off. But unknown to Jefferson was that Hamilton already knew that Washington preferred building the capital near Alexandria, Virginia—close to his beloved Mount Vernon and other landholdings. Thus, Hamilton was "negotiating away" something that was already decided. With Washington supporting the location of the new capital city, it was a done deal that the capital city would be established at this site. What Washington wanted Washington got. Moreover, what Hamilton truly wanted was to pay off the national debt and a strong treasury. The deal to have the federal government assume the northern states' debt necessitated a strong treasury, which Hamilton ran. Game, set, match.

The Hamilton–Jefferson feud had been spiraling downward ever since both were selected by Washington to serve in his cabinet. Hamilton would be the first secretary of the treasury and Jefferson the first secretary of state. Butting heads on many issues, Jefferson had become exasperated by his many defeats at the hands of Washington's friend and treasury secretary. Jefferson ultimately resigned from the cabinet in frustration.

Hamilton's political maneuvering was about to deepen the hatred of another sworn enemy. The year 1796 marked the young nation's first presidential election without Washington on the ticket. Washington's vice president, John Adams, would be representing the Federalist ticket but would be vulnerable to the right challenger. The Jeffersonian faction was debating between George Clinton and Aaron Burr as their preference for vice president. Hamilton entered the fray and used his political connections to deny Burr the spot.

Although no friend of Clinton's, Hamilton nonetheless preferred just about anyone over Aaron Burr. Three years after Hamilton published his ill-fated mea culpa over the Maria Reynolds affair, Hamilton would once again have reason to nurse his vendetta and engage in an unholy political alliance for the purpose of opposing Burr. This time, it was in the 1800 election, where Hamilton engaged in a letter-writing campaign to oppose Thomas Jefferson and Aaron Burr, who were challenging President Adams. Hamilton even enlisted help from the *New York Post*, which joined him in attacking the anti-Federalist candidates. This time, however, Hamilton was unsuccessful, and Jefferson defeated Adams. However, there was a glitch in the election outcome because of a poorly designed feature in the Electoral College that allowed each elector to cast two votes (but not for the same person and at least one for a candidate not of the elector's state).

At that time, the presidential and vice-presidential candidates ran on separate ballots, not as a team on the same ballot as they do today. The person with the most votes became president and the runner-up vice president. (The system was changed in 1804 by the Twelfth Amendment.) Therefore, in 1800, each anti-Federalist elector had cast one vote for presidential candidate

Thomas Jefferson and a second vote for his party's vice-presidential candidate, Aaron Burr. The result was a tie in the vote count for president between Jefferson and Burr. Jefferson did not believe that the tied vote needed to be challenged. After all, the tie occurred within the anti-Federalist ticket and not between it and the Federalist candidates. Moreover, it was understood that he would be the party's presidential nominee, and Burr was slated to be second in command.

With the prospect of being president rather than vice president before him, Burr made his move and challenged Jefferson for the highest office. The tiebreaker mechanism specified by Article II of the Constitution necessitated that the House of Representatives (rather than the people or the states' electors) vote on a second ballot. The result was another tie. A third ballot was ordered, as was a fourth, and both ended in a tie. Thirty-five ballots produced ties, and it was not until the thirty-sixth ballot that the tie was broken and Jefferson narrowly declared president. The tie was broken, in part, because of Hamilton's reluctant support within his party for his foe, Jefferson, over his other foe, Burr. Although facing a choice between the fire or the frying pan, Hamilton encouraged his allies to back Jefferson.

In doing so, Hamilton offered his country a great service—Jefferson was a leader vastly superior to Burr—but he would pay the ultimate price for it. Politically, Hamilton and his Federalists were dealt a stinging defeat. The presidency passed for the first time out of the hands of their political faction. Personally, the Hamilton–Burr feud digressed into an ugly, complicated political vendetta, with both men trying to destroy his opponent by instigating bad-mouthing campaigns directed at the other.

Not long after, Burr, still bitter over the narrow loss to Jefferson, left the vice presidency to campaign for the governorship of New York. Burr hoped to succeed his old nemesis, George Clinton, as the governor of New York in the 1804 election. Hamilton overlooked twenty-five years of opposition with Clinton in order to join forces with his former enemy in order to defeat Burr. For a third time, Hamilton's alliance with a political enemy resulted in Burr losing an election. Burr had had enough.

After the election, Burr dispatched an associate to charge Hamilton with slander. It was alleged that Hamilton, while at a dinner gathering, had defamed Burr's integrity. In fact, Hamilton routinely denounced Burr's character and was probably right to do so. Aaron Burr was a lazy but charming politician who was motivated more by the notoriety, social invitations, and chance to fill one's wallet with the opportunities that came with elected office than by the civic ideals of service that so motivated Hamilton. Burr was also prone to concocting ridiculous ideas to promote himself. He would later attempt to raise a private army to invade Mexico.

Burr demanded a written apology from the man who had cost him so many political victories. When Hamilton refused to do so, Burr sought satisfaction in a manner deemed suitable for gentlemen of the time: he challenged Hamilton to a duel.

DUEL!

In an earlier day and age, dueling was a peculiar contest accepted by "gentlemen" as a proper way to resolve disputes and matters of honor. At one point in the early eighteenth century, there was even an official congressional dueling ground. (Given the performance and behavior of some members of Congress in recent years, it might not be a stretch to envision public support for reinstating this form of political natural selection.)

During a duel, both participants had a "second" in attendance to vouch for their honor. The contests were judged by a set of rules governing the distance apart that each man stood and who was able to secure first shot in the event it was not a "quick-draw" duel. The unlucky duelist who drew second shot had to look down the barrel of his opponent's pistol from a few feet away and await the impact of the lead ball. If he survived the first shot, it was then his turn to return the volley. Custom dictated that to decline a challenge of a duel was to lose one's honor but that to accept was to risk losing one's life. As such, there was often an arrangement made—sort of a wink of the eye—to aim poorly and miss on purpose. This way, both duelers retained their honor—and their lives.

Hamilton was reluctant to accept Burr's challenge. He was a lover, not a fighter. Moreover, three years prior, Hamilton's firstborn son, Philip, died in a senseless duel. Hamilton had never fully recovered emotionally from the loss and was wracked with guilt for having encouraged Philip to defend his honor or risk destroying a promising political career. Hamilton's daughter, Angelica, named for his sister-in-law and mistress, was inconsolable with grief and blamed her father for her brother's death. However, despite Hamilton's reluctance, Burr had challenged Hamilton's honor on the matters of the Maria Reynolds affair and the alleged misuse of treasury funds to pay off James Reynolds and public slander. Hamilton thus believed that he had no option but to accept the duel or else risk the reputation he had worked to develop over his entire life. To Hamilton's mind, he had always been justified in criticizing Burr and opposing Burr's bids for political office because the man was entirely unfit to govern.

The same expensive pair of pistols owned by Hamilton's father-in-law that were used by Philip Hamilton in his fateful duel was again borrowed for the duel with Aaron Burr. On the cool morning of July 11, 1804, Hamilton crossed the Hudson River with an oarsman, Nathaniel Pendleton, who would serve as his "second," and a physician named David Hosack. Hamilton seemed to sense that the end was at hand. While on his way to the duel, Hamilton wrote one last letter to his wife, offering her the explanation that he needed to duel in order to uphold his honor. As always, he had failed to solicit his wife's advice. Had he done so, it might have saved his life.

Both men arrived at the prearranged location near a small rocky cliff not far from the village of Weehawken, New Jersey. Hamilton and Burr stood a few paces apart. Burr had the first shot. With his shot, Burr fired and struck Hamilton in midbody. The blow knocked Hamilton backward. As a reflex to the impact of the bullet, Hamilton squeezed the hair trigger on his pistol. Hamilton's shot fired into the air above him as he tumbled backward and landed on his back under a shady cedar tree. Hamilton must have known that instant that he was dying. The large lead ball tore into him just above his right hip, breaking a rib, puncturing his liver, and ricocheting into the second lumbar disk. With his vertebrae shattered, Hamilton was paralyzed. Nathaniel Pendleton, Hamilton's second, rushed to his friend's side and cradled the dying man in his arms. Dr. Hosack was summoned from the shoreline. When he arrived, the physician recognized immediately that Hamilton was "irrecoverably gone." Hosack later described his patient as "to all appearance lifeless."

Hamilton slipped in and out of consciousness as Pendleton and Dr. Hosack carried him to the boat, but when in the boat, he revived long enough to speak "at length" to the physician. In a panic, Hamilton blurted out, "Take care of that pistol! It is undischarged, and still cocked. It may go off and do harm." Hamilton believed that he had not fired the weapon, even telling Dr. Hosack, "Pendleton knows I did not intend to fire at [Burr]."

Back on the New York shoreline, Hamilton's old friend William Bayard was waiting worriedly. Bayard, on seeing "his poor friend lying in the bottom of the boat . . . threw up his eyes and burst into a flood of tears." Thirty long years before this tragic moment, Hamilton lodged at Bayard's home during the Revolutionary War. Now, Bayard was instructed to again prepare a room for Hamilton on the second floor of his home. In excruciating pain, Hamilton was given a large dose of the popular painkiller laudanum, a powerful potion of opium and cider. The dying man asked that his wife and children be brought to him "immediately" but instructed his friends to take great care in not worrying them. Hamilton was especially concerned about his sensitive and frail wife, advising Bayard and Pendleton to "let the event be gradually broken to her" and to "give her hopes."

Last Communion

The next day, Betsy and the seven Hamilton children arrived, having been told only that Hamilton was having stomach cramps. Unprepared for the sight before her, Betsy Hamilton fainted. When daughter Angelica entered the room, Hamilton completely broke down, knowing that the girl had never reconciled her brother's death from a duel only a few years earlier.

Although Dr. Hosack had no hopes for Hamilton's recovery, the physician sent for a French doctor aboard a nearby warship who would have had far more experience with gunshot wounds. The French physician concurred with Hosack's pessimistic diagnosis. While Hamilton was rapidly losing his fight for life, a note from Burr was delivered to the home inquiring as to his opponent's status. Burr was also concerned but for the reason that a rumor was spreading that Hamilton had announced before the duel that he did not want the duel and would not fire his pistol. Would this put Burr in the position of being a murderer?

One of Hamilton's last requests was to receive the Holy Communion. Because of his illegitimate birth, he had never been baptized or received Communion. Hamilton requested to have Benjamin Moore, the Episcopal bishop of New York and president of Columbia College, brought to his bedside. Although Moore and Hamilton knew one another and had visited socially at the Hamilton home, when the bishop arrived, he refused to administer Holy Communion because of Hamilton's sinful life, because he had been shot during such a "barbaric custom," and because he had never been baptized an Episcopalian. Instead, Bishop Moore lectured the dying man on sin and the meaning of Communion.

A panicked Hamilton then summoned John Mason, who was a Presbyterian preacher. As a child in the West Indies, Hamilton had a religious conversion to that denomination, and the Reverend Mason's father had thought enough of Hamilton to recommend him for admission to a Presbyterian school over twenty years earlier. In spite of the compelling reasons to grant the dying man his last wish, the reverend also refused Hamilton last rites. Bishop Moore finally returned and belatedly agreed to grant Hamilton's request but on the conditions that the sinner agree never to engage in another duel and that he forgive Burr. The arrangement was academic, and both men knew it. Hamilton was dying. Hamilton quickly agreed to both terms and received Holy Communion.

The former hero of the Revolution, founding father, and first secretary of the treasury lived thirty-one hours beyond the duel. His last words to his wife were, curiously, "Remember, Eliza, you are a Christian." In the final moments of his life, however, it was Hamilton's sister-in-law, Angelica Schuyler

Church, with whom he had shared a long, passionate affair, who was beside him. The two had truly loved one another.

Shortly after the noon hour on July 12, 1804, Alexander Hamilton died quietly. He was forty-nine. The irony of being killed during a duel to save one's honor that was presumably challenged because of a sexual affair a few summers earlier was surely not lost on Hamilton. It was a tragic ending to such a brilliant and influential life.

POSTSCRIPT

The highly publicized duel was the beginning of the end for the "barbaric custom." Within a few years, dueling fell out of favor. Aaron Burr, finally satisfied in defeating his avowed enemy, lived three decades beyond the duel, long enough to see his reputation and career completely destroyed, largely because of the duel.

Late in her life, Hamilton's widow was visited by former president James Monroe, loyal disciple of Hamilton's enemy Thomas Jefferson and one of the first men to spread the story of Hamilton's illicit affair with Maria Reynolds. Betsy Schuyler refused to see the former president.

Betsy lived fifty years beyond her husband, long enough to see most of the scandal surrounding her late husband's sex life forgotten to history but also long enough to see Hamilton's bright star overshadowed by Adams and Jefferson. While attempting to secure Hamilton's legacy, Betsy and the family preserved much of his prolific writings and organized the papers that Hamilton did not have time to organize before his death. His widow and sons also likely uncovered his love letters to other women. Therefore, if she had not known it before, after Hamilton's death, Betsy would have discovered the details of her husband's shocking affairs. In spite of any revelations about her husband, Mrs. Hamilton stood resolutely in his corner, working to enshrine his legacy until her dying day.

The young intern Monica Lewinsky poses with President Clinton in the White House. Courtesy of Getty Images.

⧏ 14 ⧐

Making Sense of Presidential Nonsense

Keep thy foot out of brothels, thy hand out of plackets, thy pen from lenders' books.

—Shakespeare

NOT-SO-HIDDEN HISTORY

Presidents and first ladies are people too. There are many examples of presidents and first ladies falling in love, and there are many examples of presidents succumbing to the primal urges of human nature outside the marriage. They share our fears and hopes, our passions and foibles. From the greatest among them to those who have failed in office, our leaders have loved, lusted, and lived, only they have done so in the limelight of the nation's highest office. This much is clear. However, it is far from clear why politicians and presidents misbehave.

Perhaps the English historian Lord Acton was correct when he suggested in 1887 that "power tends to corrupt, and absolute power corrupts absolutely." Or maybe there is something inherently dangerous in any recipe that involves the attainment of power. Even the dour, professorial, former secretary of state, Henry Kissinger, suggested in his thick German accent that "power is the greatest aphrodisiac." Or could it be that the tension and stress associated with high office simply impairs one's judgment? If that were true, then part of the story of White House sex scandals might be about the office rather than the sex. Even a cursory look at history reveals that, with a higher office, comes only heightened temptation and not necessarily higher standards by the individual occupying it. Might it simply be that, in public life, there are more opportunities available for getting oneself into trouble?

Or, when faced with the abundance and availability of willing sex partners that comes with a campaign, elected office, or the White House, might not the firmest resolve be tested and possibly weakened?

In more recent times, this has been the case with Franklin D. Roosevelt, Dwight Eisenhower, John F. Kennedy, Lyndon B. Johnson, and Bill Clinton, all presidents who succumbed to the most basic of human needs. Some politicians emerged as rock stars, combining great personal charisma with the excitement of a national campaign or the trappings of high office. For example, neither Gary Hart nor Bill Clinton was popular with women during their teen years, but both engaged in risky affairs with willing young women during the peak of their political careers.

This raises another possibility. In the White House as in politics in general, perhaps it has something to do with the type of individual attracted to power. After all, the lesser-known second line of Lord Acton's famous quote is, "Great men are almost always bad men." It is often suggested that there is a particular and peculiar type of political personality. Politicians thrive on attention and affection but also on challenge. Those holding high office are usually intelligent, confident, bold, accomplished in multiple fields, successful, and popular. In short, they are individuals used to getting what they want and the type of men whom many women would consider to be attractive.

In comparing contemporary political sex scandals with those from history, it is worth noting that society has seen divorce rates skyrocket in recent decades. If marriages, in general, are failing, it would stand to reason that some White House marriages would be less than ideal. Indeed, the marriage of Franklin and Eleanor Roosevelt stayed together even though Mrs. Roosevelt was aware of her husband's dalliances, but the two had long ended the physical nature of their union by the time he entered the White House. Indeed, why should presidents be any different from other Americans? The presidency has suffered divorces and the full range and possibilities when it comes to sexual affairs. One president (Ronald Reagan) and three wives of presidents (Rachel Jackson, Florence Harding, and Betty Ford) were divorced. Whether sexual affairs in the White House mirror those in the larger society is hard to say, but the divorce rates in the White House are noticeably lower than elsewhere in American society. We know that presidents (and men who one day would become presidents) have sex, fall in love, and at times are intimate with women other than their wives. If professional athletes do it; if rock stars, actors, and celebrities seem to never stop doing it; and if even Catholic priests are not above it, then perhaps we should not be surprised to learn that presidents do it. This should not be much of a revelation, as such misbehavior has always served as inspiration for some of our greatest literary masters, musicians, playwrights, and poets.

Either way, both the prevalence of such scandals and our fascination with them are undeniable and very Shakespearean. After all, the delicious appeal of the Shakespearean tragedy was its premise that the greatest leaders fall victim to the most ordinary of deficiencies. Both involve human nature at its best and worst. Thus, armed with details of both the stories of true love and the sordid history of sexual affairs in the White House, there are a few observations that can be made about presidential passions (which will be discussed in great detail in the second volume of this book covering the White House from the year 1901 to the present).

What Do We Know?

The first observation is that the more things change, the more things stay the same. Sexual desire has been an undeniable part of the history of the office. Yet it is safe to say that many of the presidential sex scandals received little attention from historians or the media. Thus, what explains the relatively inadequate attention paid by historians to affairs other than, say, Bill Clinton's? Most professional historians were not trained in matters of the heart and hearth. A sex scandal in the White House is outside most scholars' area of expertise and definitely beyond their comfort zone. The probability of a doctoral dissertation committee in the hallowed halls of an Ivy League university approving a research question about sex in the White House is almost unthinkable. Likewise, whether highbrowed academic journals would publish such salacious stories or cautious tenure committees would find merit in a professor's "scholarship" on the topic of sex scandals is doubtful. Thus, scholars have too often overlooked this part of presidential history.

A second observation is that the proof isn't always in the pudding. Where there is smoke, there is usually fire, and with the presidency, there is a lot of smoke and almost as much fire. Nevertheless, it has been a monumental challenge to discern the truth about the love lives and sex lives of presidents, but it is a necessary first step to making sense of presidential nonsense. Obviously, few written documents from the hand of a president would ever have been produced, much less saved for history, discussing the details of a mistress or an affair, but, as the old saying goes, "Absence of evidence is not evidence of absence." Of course, most presidents have denied any wrongdoing, sexually or otherwise. Truman, who frequently admitted to his mistakes and shortcomings (although he was loyal to his wife), was an exception to the rule. He typically told the truth with all its ugly bumps and warts. But history cannot simply take the presidents' word for it, nor can it take the word of a president's opponent either. Thus, for a variety of reasons, it is a herculean challenge to get to the truth behind presidential sex scandals.

A third observation is that presidents of both parties partied. Not surprisingly, both Democrats and Republicans have fallen in love and had scandals. In 2009, *Newsweek* magazine published an essay titled "Sex Scandals through the Years: Both Parties Even." The magazine surveyed fifty-three major sexual scandals in American politics and found that twenty-seven of them involved Democrats and twenty-six of them involved Republicans. There is an old political joke that goes something like this: there is no difference between the two parties except in the nature of their scandals. Huey Long, the "Kingfish" and colorful politician from Louisiana, used to point out that both parties would eventually "skin" their constituents, but the only difference was that the Democrats would skin folks from the top down, whereas the Republicans would skin folks from the bottom up. The moral of the story: even though the Democrats hit the privileged first, they would eventually soak even the poor, despite their claims that they support those living at the bottom of the socioeconomic ladder. And even though Republican policies favor those living at the top of the socioeconomic ladder, after they finished fleecing the poor, they would stick it to the privileged and comfortable in the end.

Those who have suggested that the types of scandals reflect the nature of the political parties also joke that the Republicans tend to have financial scandals, whereas the Democrats tend to have the sex scandals. Democratic presidents in the twentieth century—Wilson, Roosevelt, Kennedy, Johnson, and Clinton—did in fact have some noteworthy sexual flings. But the difference in type of scandal is not entirely or always true. At times in history, it would seem that the Democrats have had the upper hand in the latter department, and Republicans have indeed been identified with a number of financial scandals, but the truth is that both parties suffer sexual scandals. Two Republican presidents in the twentieth century had noteworthy sexual affairs: Harding and Eisenhower. In the 2000s, with several Republican men having high-profile homosexual affairs, it became a cruel joke in Washington that the party was hoping for a sexual affair involving a mistress and not a boy.

A fourth observation is that not all love stories or sex scandals are created equal. There is no single type or variety of love affair or sexual affair. That would be boring. They have come in all shapes and sizes. Some were trivial, while others were sensational. The same has been true in the White House, where scandals have run the gamut from overly healthy appetites to premarital and extramarital affairs to sex with prostitutes. Likewise, some have been covered by the media, while others were largely ignored.

This raises the fifth observation—that media sensationalism matters. As is discussed in the second volume of this book, for two years the Monica

Lewinsky scandal dominated print, television, and radio news coverage, and it was a major story internationally that nearly resulted in the removal from office of a president on charges of perjury and obstruction of justice. These serious charges stemmed not from treason, abuse of power, or a secretive plot that threatened national security but from consensual oral sex and, belatedly, lying about it. The media's preoccupation with the story was such that there was no escaping it. The same was true historically for both love stories and sexual scandals, as some seemed to resonate with the public and press—whether rightly or wrongly, whether accurate or not—while others were nonstories.

Similarly, the sixth observation is that some have been accused, others excused. The fifth observation does not help us answer the question of why some philandering presidents and politicians are skewered for their scandals while others are forgiven and why some scandals become media stories and others do not. Does the response by the press or public depend on the source behind the allegation, the president's party, the popularity of the president, or the amount of details available? At the same time, it is not illegal to have a consensual affair, so while the philandering is within the boundaries of the law, high political office usually comes with a higher ethical expectation. Still, while Gary Hart and others had their political careers ended because of sex scandals, many other politicians weathered such affairs. Barney Frank, a Democrat from Massachusetts, and David Vitter, a Republican from Louisiana, were reelected after very embarrassing affairs with prostitutes. In Congressman Frank's case, it was a same-sex affair, and in Senator Vitter's case, he had been a leading proponent of family values and was a vicious critic of any Democrat who suffered a moral lapse.

LOVE AND SEX IN THE WHITE HOUSE: DOES IT MATTER?

In 1998, Republicans in Congress were in the midst of a relentless effort to impeach Bill Clinton because of lies about a sexual affair with a young woman. At the same time and purely by chance, a group of scientists were conducting DNA tests that appeared to link President Thomas Jefferson to the descendants of his former slave Sally Hemings. Inadvertently, science had weighed in on the most divisive political debate of 1998, linking the Clinton impeachment with an unexpected voice from the distant past. If the country's revered third president—and author of the Declaration of Independence—had fathered children out of wedlock with a young slave, then Clinton's sins were neither new nor all that shocking. Clinton, it appeared, was neither the first nor the worst president when it came to sexual shenanigans.

Clearly, President Clinton had a timely, vested interest in the new scholarship about the Jefferson affair. Why? As the scholarly argument played out over Jefferson's affair and paternity, the emerging picture of a sexually active, all-too-human Jefferson coincided with the modern drama of a sexually active, all-too-human Clinton. Among Clinton's defenders was the Pulitzer Prize–winning historian Joseph Ellis. Ellis and other scholars had long rejected, for a variety of reasons, suggestions that Jefferson had fathered children with his slave. However, in light of the new DNA evidence, Ellis and many other historians were forced to reconsider their position on the existence of the Jefferson–Hemings affair. In so doing, Professor Ellis felt compelled to publicly oppose the impeachment of Clinton. As Clinton faced his accusers in both Congress and the court of public opinion, Ellis pointed out that it was as if Clinton had called to the stand one of the most respected character witnesses in all of American history. Or another way to look at it was that the ghosts of so many former presidents stood next to Clinton. It was as if they themselves were by proxy charged with the crime of sexual misconduct.

A vote against Clinton could be construed as a vote against James Garfield, Grover Cleveland, Woodrow Wilson, Warren Harding, Franklin D. Roosevelt, Dwight Eisenhower, John F. Kennedy, Lyndon B. Johnson, and the beloved Jefferson, whose sexual sins, as profiled earlier in this book, were potentially far worse than those of the embattled Clinton. Indeed, the historical revelation about Jefferson made Clinton's misbehavior seem less aberrant and perhaps even somewhat more palatable.

Ironically, Jefferson had always been Clinton's favorite founding father. The men shared much, including their tall stature and intelligence and the fact that both served as southern governors and went on to be presidents. Most assuredly, during the impeachment proceedings of 1998, Clinton continued to favor his distant predecessor.

But the answer to the question of whether true love or sexual scandal matters in the White House depends on one's view of whether the public and private dimensions of the office should be kept separate. Accordingly, one might ask what aspects of a president's personal life the public has the right to question. For example, most politicians and presidents use their family to craft an idealized image of themselves, frequently that of a father figure. Presidential families are carted out for staged public photo opportunities, and presidents often invite the media into their personal lives in order to further massage a favorable image. John F. Kennedy, after all, was packaged as a family man, and the country fell in love with his glamorous wife and young children. Yet many of the same journalists snapping photos of the Kennedy clan at play on a Massachusetts beach were privy to the president's excessive womanizing.

Thus, if politicians use their families and the press for political gain, they then open themselves up for inquiry into their personal and family lives. It is not a one-way street.

The journalist and commentator Michael Kinsley points out that politicians do not really try to keep their private lives private. Rather, they stage and exploit facets of their private lives, contributing to the blurring of the public–private divide in elected office. When it works for them, politicians are willing to use their families and married life. But when it does not, they hypocritically claim that it is not our business. Moreover, argues Kinsley, in a democracy, the people's business must be open to the people. The public has a right to know, and journalists should, on such sensitive matters, err on the side of providing too much information rather than not enough of it.

But not all questions regarding which facets of a politician's life should remain private and which belong in public are so cut-and-dried as the previously mentioned discussion, especially when it comes to the issues of marriage and scandal. There are basically two ways of looking at love and scandal in the White House: whether they involve *public* facets of the president's job or whether they pertain only to his *private* life. If this is true, then the behavior of leaders should be compartmentalized, depending on the nature of the scandals. Certain misbehaviors occur in public, others occur in private, and two different standards would then exist in terms of the scandal's impact on the public and country. The same goes for the impact on the president of having a loving marriage. The argument would be that what happens between the first couple is their business, not ours. If this statement were true, there would be a real, discernible public–private divide. Yet we allow our presidents virtually no privacy because of the way the press covers the office and because of the public's expectations about their leaders.

The blurring of the public–private divide has exacted a terrible price in politics. Who is without any sin? What sane person would want to subject his or her family to such intense and invasive public scrutiny? Moreover, should not private matters of sex stay private? If questioned in public about intimate or harmful details of private sexual behavior, are we not supposed to lie about it to protect loved ones and the innocent? While it is often suggested that we should never trust someone who would lie about sex, it might reasonably be asked whether we should trust someone who would *not* lie about their private sex lives and those of their loved ones.

There is a component of one's life that is *public*. Public actions impact public policy, and the public has a right to know about such matters. But what about purely private deeds? Is there such a thing, and, if so, should it not be beyond the purview of the public? But certain private behavior affects public perceptions and might reveal everything from a president's temperament to his views of women. The key is to try to define the public–private divide in terms of which facets of a president's private life are beyond public inspection.

Aside from sexual behavior, in the White House it is difficult to establish firm boundaries between the public and private realms. Unlike the funny and successful ad campaign for Las Vegas tourism, presidents have not found it easy to say that what happens in the White House stays in the White House. And does that right to know extend to the bedroom or to sexual conduct that occurred *before* the presidency?

Most would likely agree that it depends on the nature of the prepresidential sexual conduct. Intimate details of a marriage are just that and thus should remain private. But a sexual scandal might be another matter entirely regardless of whether it occurred during or before the White House years.

Even if the public is privy to embarrassing private indiscretions of the president or presidential candidate, that information, in and of itself, might not disqualify someone from serving as the president or prevent him or her from receiving our support or vote or even from becoming a great leader. Many great and irreplaceable leaders have had sexual scandals, and many inept and corrupt leaders have not. It is probable that most Republicans would gladly take a Dwight Eisenhower over Rutherford B. Hayes despite Ike's affair with his British driver Kay Summersby during World War II or that Democrats would gladly take a Franklin Roosevelt over Franklin Pierce despite Roosevelt's affair with Lucy Mercer. This raises the question of just how relevant sexual scandals are in the bigger picture of voting for or evaluating presidents.

Incidents of infidelity reflect but one facet of character and not the entirety of a person's life. Are we willing to judge someone on the basis of a single mistake? But if that person was running for the nation's highest office, perhaps a higher standard is therefore entirely appropriate. The notion of moral absolutism might agree that one blemish is one too many, even though most religions espouse a doctrine of forgiveness and most systems of ethics permit for a second chance. Likewise, if the incidents of philandering represent a pattern and not a single, isolated mistake or if the sexual misbehavior is more accurately described as a sexual perversity, then the public might be less forgiving. Others might suggest a criterion (as to whether it is our business) of whether the sexual affair harmed anyone outside of those involved in the affair.

If the public has the right to know all there is to know, might that not exact a terrible toll on the office by scaring away many potentially good leaders? What sane person would want to run for office knowing that the most intimate details of one's personal life (including a youthful indiscretion) will be featured on the evening news? Would we today elect George Washington, who bristled when criticized; Thomas Jefferson, who may have fathered children out of wedlock and was often too shy to speak out publicly; Abraham Lincoln, who likely visited a prostitute and dressed poorly; or great leaders like Roosevelt or Eisenhower because they were not faithful to their wives?

One of the reasons behind writing this book was to gain potentially important insights into presidential character by examining the presidents' dirty laundry and their love affairs. All campaigns and White Houses go to great lengths to prevent negative stories and traits from becoming public, just as they devote great energy to crafting an idealized and often inaccurate image for the president. Through scandal, sexual and otherwise, the public is given a glimpse of what is perhaps the true character of the president, stripped of all the pomp, pageantry, and parade associated with the White House. It is, after all, possible to learn a lot about a person by studying both the good and bad traits as well as the high and low points of his or her life. Few people would dare to suggest that the muckraking reporting of Bob Woodward and Carl Bernstein that uncovered Richard Nixon's Watergate scandal was a bad thing. The United States has suffered through many bad and corrupt politicians and presidents. Had more complete information about the candidates' character and background been available to voters during the campaign, it is possible that voters may have acted differently and spared the country a lot of mistakes.

JUDGING PRESIDENTS

It is a struggle to make sense of presidential nonsense. The public, media, and the scholarly community have yet to determine the proper place of sex scandals in political discourse and the telling of history. But how much focus on scandal is appropriate for the political process or helpful to voters? It is understandable why Bill and Hillary Clinton complained of what they called the "politics of personal destruction," the bitter, personal attacks that fixate on scandal—imagined or real—in an effort to totally discredit a politician. Such unmitigated and noncontextual attacks exact a terrible price on the body politic. The public becomes apathetic, voting rates decline, the press all but ignores "the real" issues, and the tone and tenor of politics drops to tabloid sensationalism. Everyone loses during such occurrences. The nature of the vicious and relentless personal attacks on Barack Obama, when all is said and done, may very well constitute a new low in presidential politics. At what point do questions about Clinton's sexual preferences or Obama's place of birth become redundancies or simply distractions to governing or, more important, affect their decisions about war and peace?

But scandals deserve to be reported and studied because private peccadilloes offer us a new, unique, and useful lens for studying presidential character. Rarely are sexual scandals simply a consensual, physical act suitable only as a human interest story. On the contrary, they are often politically relevant and might determine how the public votes. A number of questions about the nature and extent of presidential sexual scandals, their impact on both the president's standing and the health of the country, and what they tell us about ourselves are worth pursuing. For example, are we willing to forgive presidents who admit to wrongdoing but not those who attempt to cover up the affair? Polls taken throughout the Clinton impeachment ordeal showed the American public to be upset at the president for his affair, but they also revealed that the public's anger was more the result of Clinton's attempt to obfuscate rather than the oral sex itself. Polls also suggested the public was willing to separate the personal from the public. For instance, people were upset at Clinton's personal behavior but supported his public record and were willing to balance the president's sexual scandal against his generally positive presidency in rendering judgment about the affair. In that respect, the public differed from Clinton's Republican critics in Congress who sought to remove him from office for lying about a personal affair yet defended the actions of Richard Nixon and Ronald Reagan, who lied about burglary, theft, national security "black ops," and other highly public matters.

Part of the Clinton affair and part of any presidential scandal is the role of the media in reporting the matter. Neither the press nor the public has figured out exactly what should be covered and how, raising another question—that of what explains the public's fascination with our leaders' private lives, especially the sordid details of their scandals. Thus, in the post-Clinton/Lewinsky world, most candidates must now pass a litmus test on the state of their marital vows.

Another challenge of getting to know the less-than-admirable side of presidents is that some biographers have been guilty of falling in love with their subject. Lo and behold, great leaders become even greater, courtesy of our admiring accounts of their lives. No one wants to see biographies become pathologies or psychoanalytic hatchet jobs that pick apart every facet—true or otherwise—of an individual's life. But "hero worship" has existed to the extent that we were taught that our great leaders could not possibly have told a lie (such as cutting down a cherry tree), much less have had an affair.

To be sure, a nation needs its heroes and its unifying folktales. The "Washington-never-told-a-lie" stuff fulfills a function beyond storytelling. It is part of the American creed, and it is therefore unpleasant to deconstruct such patriotic and unifying presidential lore. Yes, it is true that Washington's sense of honor and duty drove his actions, but as a lad he never chopped down a cherry tree and then admitted to the deed because of an innate inability to tell a lie. Rather, however disturbing it is for those of us who admire the man, the truth of the matter was that Washington had a volcanic temper and was prone to blaming underlings for his own failures.

More recent scholarship has started to pay some attention to social history and the real lives and intimate details of historical figures. As such, our attention is slowly turning from the lore and legend of George Washington to the details of his personal life that allow us to truly "get to know" the "Father of His Country." Likewise, an unfettered account of the life of Thomas Jefferson is complicated by the duality that he is the author of the words "all men are created equal" yet the owner of slaves (one of whom was his mistress). Yes, Jefferson really was an idealist who struggled for over two weeks in a cramped second-story loft amidst the heat and humidity of Philadelphia during the summer of 1776 to produce that finest, most poetic of documents—the Declaration of Independence. But Jefferson also had a poisonous and deceitful pen, often using his literary prowess to attack opponents. He also frequently wrote with an eye to distant history so as to place himself in the most favorable of light for us today.

But these men, perhaps more than any others, made this nation. There is so much more to the story of the presidents than the one-dimensional image that is passed on to generation after generation of elementary school classrooms. Many textbooks and accounts of history have yet to paint the full picture—to get it right—and that includes the history of sexual intrigue, philandering, scandal, and even love. Even two of the best presidential biographers in the business in recent times let their passions and preconceptions color their analysis.

The late, great Eisenhower biographer Stephen Ambrose, who also wrote famously muscular accounts of history, warfare, and gritty leaders like Lewis and Clark, stated that General Dwight Eisenhower could not possibly have had an affair with his stunningly attractive, young wartime driver, Kay Summersby. Even when presented with evidence of an intimate liaison between the two lovers during World War II, Ambrose seemed unable to accept the likelihood of philandering by his research subject and hero. In response to Kay's claim that Eisenhower was temporarily impotent when they tried to make love, Ambrose lamely postulated that it was Eisenhower's "honor" that prevented him from having intercourse. But because Eisenhower's honor allowed him to get as far as lying naked in bed with a young woman who was not his wife, it would seem that a much more likely explanation for the incident was a failure of his plumbing rather than the success of his honor.

The general certainly tried to be less honorable on a number of occasions with the striking Miss Summersby. This reality should not fundamentally change our understanding of Eisenhower's extraordinary leadership during World War II or appreciation for his sense of duty and honor. But it does help us to understand him as a man as opposed to just a general, as it reveals his character and priorities as more complex, emotion based, and vulnerable than is generally stated.

Robert Ferrell, professor emeritus at Indiana University, is rightfully celebrated as a prolific biographer of presidents such as Harry S. Truman and Warren G. Harding. Yet, even when conceding the prevalence of Harding's personality flaws and penchant for lying, Ferrell nevertheless refuted Nan Britton's claim that she was the mother of the president's illegitimate child. Even though overwhelming evidence exists in the form of personal letters and incriminating documents of Harding's numerous sexual affairs, Ferrell gives Harding, who frequently lied, the benefit of the doubt while assuming that his accuser, Miss Britton, was the one lying. Ferrell holds Harding to one standard but Nan Britton to another. Harding surrounded himself with corrupt cronies who tried to cover up scandal after scandal. History remembers them as the "Ohio Gang." On this matter, all historians are in agreement. But Nan Britton's friendship with one shadowy individual is given by Ferrell as a reason to dismiss her otherwise strong claims of an affair.

CHARACTER MATTERS

George Reedy served as President Lyndon B. Johnson's press secretary. As such, he saw up close both the complexities of presidential character and a president engaging in numerous extramarital affairs. Concluded Reedy,

> What counts with a candidate for president is his character, and nothing shows it like his relationships with women. Here you have a man who is asking you to trust him with your bank account, your children, your life and your country for four years. If his own wife can't trust him, what does that say?

Perhaps sexual affairs matter most in what they say about a president's character (or lack thereof). It remains mystifying as to why Bill Clinton, a man so intelligent and politically gifted, a man who knew that he was vulnerable to charges of infidelity, would risk his presidency and his family's reputation for a dalliance with a young intern. Perhaps the answer rests with the fact that Clinton had misbehaved in the past and had "gotten away with it." Or, perhaps, the answer is that there is no simple answer. Clinton was not the first leader to risk his reputation and office on extramarital sex. Through sexual affairs, we see the presidents not at their zenith but at their worst, their most vulnerable moments.

First families have struggled to carve out a degree of normalcy while living in the public fishbowl that the White House has become. Dealing with marital turmoil amidst the backdrop of war, depression, crisis, and public office is a fate not wished on one's enemies. Some first families faced with such scandal have endured, while others have not. This book has not been an attempt simply to dig up dirt, nor has it been an effort to strip the White House of some of its luster. Rather, minus the political propaganda and heavily manicured image that goes hand in hand with the nation's highest office, sexual affairs reveal the raw emotions, imperfections, and temperaments of the occupants of the White House.

Accordingly, the actions involved in the affair provide us with a new conceptual lens by which to study or understand the people and personalities involved. In an office based foremost on the character of the occupant, such things as love, sexual behavior and misbehavior, and scandal provide useful lessons for probing presidential temperament, judgment, and priorities. Thus, the values, beliefs, and actions surrounding the act of sexual impropriety provide potentially important insights into the person and his or her character. In any belief system, among the most cherished ideals include showing respect for one's spouse and family, bringing honor to oneself and one's endeavors, acting with selflessness and not selfishness, honoring one's marital vows, and telling the truth. All these elements of an individual's belief system are brought to bear by the act of sexual infidelity and are thus potentially important keys to understanding or assessing a president's character defects.

Character is king, but studies of presidential character typically focus on examples of admirable traits and the keys to greatness rather than on presidential foibles and folly. When a president's weaknesses come to the fore, the consequences could be devastating. In studying their low points and failures, we learn about another side of presidential character. But character is more than simply having an affair, and the absence of any sexual peccadilloes, per se, does not imply the possession of character.

Millard B. Fillmore, Calvin Coolidge, Jimmy Carter, and George W. Bush were faithful to their wives. Yet no historian would suggest that these men had the requisite temperament for presidential success, much less the stuff of presidential greatness. By the same token, Woodrow Wilson, Dwight Eisenhower, John F. Kennedy, and Lyndon B. Johnson are all considered by scholars to be some of America's better presidents, yet all of them were involved in sexual affairs. Character is about more than sexual fidelity.

One of the presidents who talked the most about family, morality, and honesty turned out to be one of the nation's most deceitful, inept, and scandal-plagued presidents. But George W. Bush is simply the latest in a long line of leaders to say one thing but do quite another. One of the nation's greatest presidents happened to be one of the least faithful presidents. But Franklin D. Roosevelt is simply one of many great world leaders who were not-so-great husbands.

Does leadership matter? Can one person truly make a difference? The answer is a resounding yes. One needs look no further than George Washington. It is hard to imagine the American Revolution without him, and, as was mentioned in the opening pages of this book, it is doubtful that the American experiment in popular government would have occurred had it not been for the character of Washington. The lesson and example of Washington have nothing to do with being well educated or well traveled or being well read or well spoken. But it has everything to do with being principled and possessing a strength of character.

An obvious comparison is between Herbert Hoover and Franklin D. Roosevelt. Both served back-to-back terms in office, with Hoover leaving in 1933, the year Roosevelt entered the White House. Hoover presided during the collapse of Wall Street and the nation's financial markets, and his minimal response did nothing to ease the crisis and may actually have exacerbated it. Inheriting the same financial, economic, and social conditions as Hoover, Roosevelt set about reinventing government and embarking on a New Deal that would save the country and change history. The difference between the two presidents, both of whom were very well educated, successful, bright, well traveled, and possessed of a wealth of public experience, is summed up in a single word—character. Quite simply, Hoover—though happily married and faithful to his wife—was no Roosevelt.

James Buchanan and Abraham Lincoln offer a similar lesson. They served consecutive terms in office, Buchanan from 1857 to 1861, as the Civil War was looming, and Lincoln from 1861 to 1865, during the Civil War. The economic, political, and sectional conditions were the same for both presidents. Yet Buchanan lost the Union, while Lincoln saved it. Ironically, Buchanan was one of the most qualified men ever to enter the White House. He benefited from a solid formal education and had a lifetime of public service at home and abroad, including in both houses of Congress, in a diplomatic capacity, and in the cabinet. On the other hand, Abraham Lincoln was, arguably, the least qualified president ever to serve. He was self-taught and poor, lacked real military experience, and served a single, unremarkable term in the U.S. House of Representatives. But the difference between the two could not be more stark. Buchanan is considered by many historians to have been the nation's worst president, while Lincoln is widely seen as the best. The difference? Character.

Leadership in the White House matters, and it comes down to character. In the White House, character is about conducting oneself with honesty and integrity. It is about taking responsibility for one's actions and having the courage to do what is right even if it is unpopular and difficult. It is about demonstrating resolve yet being able and willing to admit error. It is about treating others with dignity and the office with the highest respect. It is about making informed decisions, accepting advice, and exploring all options with a sense of perspective and history. And much more.

The sex lives of presidents provide one piece—only one piece but a potentially insightful one—of the complex puzzle of character and leadership. It is worth exploring and considering the love and sex lives of presidents as we judge them and their character, but it is but one facet and not the sum total of character. Few historians would render a verdict on the basis of one incident, even though with so many of our leaders, there has rarely been just an isolated incident.

Sources

CHAPTER 1

Most material in this chapter comes from the following sources: Richard Brookhiser, *Rediscovering George Washington: Founding Father* (New York: Free Press, 1996); Joseph J. Ellis, *His Excellency: George Washington* (New York: Vintage, 2005); James Thomas Flexner, *Washington: The Indispensable Man* (Boston: Back Bay Books, 1994); and Richard Norton Smith, *Patriarch: George Washington and the New American Nation* (Boston: Houghton Mifflin, 1993).

Washington's papers and letters have been edited and published, and many of the quotes about his relationship with the three women discussed in this chapter come from them. See William Abbot and Dorothy Twohig, eds., *The Papers of George Washington* (Charlottesville: University of Virginia Press, 1979), and Jared Sparks, ed., *The Writings of George Washington: Being His Correspondence, Addresses, Messages, and Other Papers, Official and Private*, 8 vol. (Charleston, SC: Nabu Press, 2008; reproduced from 1847, 1923, and other reprintings). The website at the Washington home, Mount Vernon, and the Mount Vernon Ladies' Association also provides information on and easy access to some of Washington's writings and was used in this chapter.

Less attention has been paid by scholars to George Washington's youthful romances and love interests. Accounts remain, however, in Washington's diaries. Most quotes from his early years in this chapter are from Dorothy Twohig, ed., *George Washington's Diaries: An Abridgement*, 6 vols. (Charlottesville: University of Virginia Press, 1999).

The poem Washington penned for Frances Alexander is discussed in Douglas Southall Freeman's *George Washington: A Biography* (New York: Scribner's Sons, 1948–1957). See vol. 1, p. 260, for the poem. The poem and accompanying discussion are also available at http://american-poetry.suite101.com/article.cfm/two-poems-by-george-washington.

The claim that Washington had an affair with "Polly" Morris and the rumors about it are found in Nigel Cawthorne, *Sex Lives of the Presidents: An Irreverent Expose of the Chief Executive from George Washington to the Present Day* (1996; reprint, New York: St. Martin's Press, 1998), p. 10. Cawthorne also discusses Washington's clothing being stolen by two young girls on p. 7 of his book and the rumors of "night walking" at the slave quarters on p. 15. There is no evidence that Washington ever partook of this terrible practice that was common with other slave owners. The account of the French officer describing Washington's interest in young women is found on p. 21 of Cawthorne.

The account of George and Martha Washington first meeting at the Chamberlayne estate is told in George Washington Parke Custis, *Recollections and Private Memoirs of Washington* (New York: Derby and Jackson, 1860), pp. 499–501. G. W. P. Custis was Martha's grandson from her first marriage. He lived from 1781 to 1857, and the book was published posthumously and edited by his daughter, Mary Anna Custis Lee, wife of General Robert E. Lee of Confederate fame.

I used a few sources in describing the nature of the Washington marriage, including Elswythe Thane, *Washington's Lady* (New York: Dodd, Mead, and Co., 1954). George Washington's account ledger for 1758 is another helpful source on Washington's marriage and was used in this chapter. In particular, it has information on his orders for clothing for the wedding. It is available at Mount Vernon. Washington's letter ordering a coat and engagement ring from a London merchant is also reprinted in Abbot and Twohig, *Papers*, vol. 5, p. 112. The Custis Papers also provided me with information on the marriage and are both housed in the Virginia Historical Society in Richmond and reproduced in Freeman's *Washington*; vol. 2, pp. 299–300.

I used Thomas S. Langston and Michael G. Sherman, *George Washington* (Washington, DC: CQ Press, 2003) for additional information on Martha Dandridge Custis Washington's wealth and her marriage to Washington, pp. 22–24.

George Washington's letters to the London merchant and trader Robert Cary are discussed in *Papers* and are also available at the University of Virginia. See http://www.virginia.edu/gwpapers/documents/revolutionary/letters/index.html.

Sally Fairfax's descendant who, based on family letters and lore, commented on her relationship with George Washington is Wilson Miles Cary. His book proved to be a valuable source for this chapter. See Wilson Miles Cary, *Sally Cary: A Long Hidden Romance of Washington's Life* (New York: De Vine Press, 1916). The opening quotes used in the chapter are on p. 9 of Cary's book.

One of the sources used to discuss the early criticisms of scholars who contemplated Washington's relationship with Sally Fairfax is Nathaniel Wright Stevenson's noted article "The Romantics and George Washington." It was published in *American Historical Review* 39, no. 2 (January 1934): 274–283. Stevenson was the scholar who dubbed his colleagues who expressed an interest in Sally Fairfax "the romantics."

CHAPTER 2

Most material in this chapter comes from the following sources: Nigel Cawthorne, *Sex Lives of the Presidents: An Irreverent Expose of the Chief Executive from George Washington to the Present Day* (1996; reprint, New York: St. Martin's Press, 1998); William Dudley, ed., *Political Scandals: Opposing Viewpoints* (Farmington Hills, MI: Greenhaven Press, 2001); Kim Long, ed., *The Almanac of Political Corruption, Scan-*

dals and Dirty Politics (reprint, Delta, 2008); Nancy E. Marion, *The Politics of Disgrace: The Role of Political Scandal in American Politics* (Durham, NC: Carolina Academic Press, 2010); Hope Ridings Miller, *Scandals in the Highest Office* (New York: Random House, 1973); Russell Roberts, *Presidents and Scandals* (San Diego: Lucent Books, 2001); Shelley Ross, *Fall from Grace* (New York: Ballantine Books, 1988); and Paul Slansky, *The Little Quiz Book of Big Political Sex Scandals* (New York: Simon & Schuster, 2009). There is also a book on the topic that provides a good background on the nature and frequency of political scandals, but it is geared toward young adults and school students: Barbara Silberdick Feinberg, *American Political Scandals: Past and Present* (New York: Franklin Watts, 1992).

Information on Grant's Credit Mobilier scandal comes from the Central Pacific Railroad Museum, which has primary source materials on the scandal at http:// CPRR.org/Museum/Credit_mobilier.html. The congressional report on the scandal was published by the U.S. Government Printing Office and is available at http://www .corvalliscommunitypages.com/americas/us/usnotoregon/creditmobilierall.htm.

The main source used on Harding's Teapot Dome scandal is Laton McCartney, *The Teapot Dome Scandal: How Big Oil Bought the Harding White House and Tried to Steal the Country* (New York: Random House, 2009).

President Reagan's quote about not remembering the details of the Iran-Contra scandal comes from a televised address to the nation from the White House on March 4, 1987, and is available at the Presidential Rhetoric Project at http://www.presidential rhetoric.com/historicspeeches/reagan/irancontra.html.

Quotes from Gary Hart and the press coverage of the scandal involving his mistress Donna Rice appear in E. J. Dionne Jr., "The Elusive Frontrunner: Gary Hart," *Time,* May 18, 1987; Mrs. Hart's decision to stay with her husband was told to me in a 2004 interview I conducted with Hart's campaign finance chair, Ambassador Henry Kimmelman, in Palm Beach, Florida.

I used Roger Clinton's book *Growing Up Clinton: The Lives, Times and Tragedies of America's Presidential Family* (Summit Publishing, 1997) for some of the information on his scandals. He is, of course, less than reliable but was somewhat frank in dishing the dirt on his misbehavior. His account squared with multiple newspaper accounts.

I also used two books for information on Billy Carter's misbehavior: Bill Carter (with Ken Estes), *Billy: Billy Carter's Reflections on His Struggle with Fame, Alcoholism and Cancer* (Edgehill Publishers, 1990), and William Carter, *A Journey through the Shadows* (Longstreet Press, 1999). Both are overly friendly to the subject, as would be expected, but do examine Billy's antics.

Some of the information on scandals involving first ladies and first families comes from one of my other books. See Robert P. Watson, *The Presidents' Wives: Reassessing the Office of First Lady* (Boulder, CO: Lynne Rienner Publishers, 2000), pp. 34–40. See also Mary Ormsbee Whitten, *First First Ladies* (1948), for a discussion of scandal involving the early presidential spouses.

Betty Ford's quotes in response to the controversy surrounding her public comments appear in "The Last Word on First Ladies," *U.S. News and World Report,* March 30, 1992; for a discussion of the criticism of Mrs. Ford and her comments on sensitive issues, see Jeffrey Ashley, "The Social and Political Influence of Betty

Ford: Betty Bloomer Blossoms," *White House Studies* 1, no. 1 (2000): 101–8. I also conducted an interview with Mrs. Ford in 2000.

The story of whether Mrs. Taylor smoked a pipe can be found in Hamilton Holman, *Zachary Taylor* (Bobbs-Merrill, 1966), 2 vols.—*Soldier of the Republic* and *Soldier in the White House*; see also Lewis L. Gould, ed., *American First Ladies: Their Lives and Their Legacy* (Routledge, 1996), which has a chapter on Mrs. Taylor and discusses the matter.

Mrs. Carter's quote comes from a phone and follow-up written interview with the author, February 25, 1997.

Allegations that Ronald Reagan had mistresses at the time of his marriage to Nancy Davis and of her sexual behavior appear in Cawthorne, *Sex Lives*, p. 253. See also Patricia S. Lawford and Ted Schwarz, *The Peter Lawford Story: Life with the Kennedys, Monroe and the Rat Pack* (New York: Carroll & Graf Publishers, 1988), pp. 56–57, for the quotes and discussion of Nancy's sexual affairs. The Lawford book was also published with slightly varying titles by Futura Publishers (1990, 1988) and Avalon Publishers (1988). The book is difficult to find in the United States, and the word is that the Reagans and Frank Sinatra used their influence to try to suppress the release of the book in the United States.

Professor Paul Boller's question about writing a book on presidential sexual scandal is found in Paul F. Boller Jr., *Presidential Anecdotes* (Oxford: Oxford University Press, 1981), p. 222.

Harry Truman's anger at a military aide who was going to set Truman up with a female companion is found in David McCullough, *Truman* (New York: Simon & Schuster, 1992), p. 435. See also Robert H. Ferrell, ed., *Dear Bess: The Letters from Harry to Bess Truman, 1910–1959* (Columbia: University of Missouri Press, 1998), for a collection of Truman's love letters and discussion of Truman's views on women and romance.

James Madison's famous quote about men not being angels comes from *The Federalist Papers*; see Federalist #51, which was published on February 6, 1788.

CHAPTER 3

Most material in this chapter comes from the following sources: Richard Brookhiser, *Rediscovering George Washington: Founding Father* (New York: Free Press, 1996); Joseph J. Ellis, *His Excellency: George Washington* (Vintage, 2005); James Thomas Flexner's *Washington: The Indispensable Man* (Boston: Back Bay Books, 1994); and Richard Norton Smith's *Patriarch: George Washington and the New American Nation* (Boston: Houghton Mifflin, 1993). For discussions of Washington's character, I also relied on William D. Pederson and Mark J. Rozell, eds., *George Washington: Foundation of Presidential Leadership and Character* (Praeger Publishers, 2001), and James Rees and Stephen Spignes, *George Washington's Leadership Lessons: What the Father of Our Country Can Teach Us about Effective Leadership* (New York: Wiley, 2007). Note: Rees is the executive director of Mount Vernon, and the staff at Mount Vernon was helpful during the author's visit in answering questions and obtaining documents on both George and Martha Washington.

Many of the quotes are taken from Washington's diary and the edited collection of his writings. See Dorothy Twohig, ed., *George Washington's Diaries: An Abridgement*, 6 vols. (reprint, Charlottesville: University of Virginia Press, 1999); see also Worthington Chauncey Ford, ed., *Writings of Washington* (Kessinger Publishing, 2007; reprint series; Nabu Press, 2010; reproduction), vols. 1–4.

The opening quote on Sally's influence over Washington is found in Wilson Miles Cary, *Sally Cary: A Long Hidden Romance of Washington's Life* (New York: De Vine Press, 1916), p. 8. The second quote on Sally's influence over Washington comes from Shelley Ross, *Fall from Grace* (New York: Ballantine Books, 1988), p. 14; the physical description of Sally comes from Cary, p. 6.

Some scholars have dismissed the possibility of a relationship between Washington and Sally. One of the loudest, early voices for this position was Nathaniel Wright Stevenson in "The Romantics and George Washington," *American Historical Review* 39, no. 2 (January 1934): 274–83.

The auction of unknown letters about Washington was covered in the *New York Herald*, March 30, 1877; the actual 1758 letter in question is found in Ford, *Writings*, vol. 2, p. 101.

Wilson Miles Cary's assessment of Washington's famous letter to Sally appears on p. 39 of his book.

Washington's reference to Cato in his love letters appears in Cary, pp. 29–30. Washington's thoughts on glory and heroism are in a letter he wrote to Sally Cary Fairfax, which is also discussed by Cary, p. 30.

Washington's remark about the sound of bullets in battle is in a letter to his younger brother and is discussed in Brookhiser, *Rediscovering*, p. 23. Washington's reflection later in life about his foolish youthful boast about the sound of bullets is found in Robert P. Watson, ed., *American Presidents*, 3rd ed. (Pasadena, CA: Salem Press, 1996), p. 21.

The Walpole quote on the start of the French and Indian War is found at http://www.nps.gov/fore/jumglen.htm; details of the actual battle and quotes on the battle appear in Thomas S. Langston and Michael G. Sherman, *George Washington* (Washington, DC: CQ Press, 2003).

Washington's insecurities and efforts to try to correct his writing and misspellings from his youth are discussed in Smith, *Patriarch*, p. 8.

Washington's quote about his own preference for actions over words is also found in Smith, p. 8, as is the discussion about Washington's humble but embarrassing silence when receiving praise from the Virginia House of Burgesses for his military exploits. Smith also discusses Washington's stoic response to the challenges and difficulties of health problems and a soldier's life on p. xiv.

The story of a young Washington trying to court Sally Fairfax's sister is found in Cary, p. 21. The quote on Washington trying to court Sally and being susceptible to charming women is also in Cary, p. 27. The stories of Sally's father dismissing the young suitor and the old man's advice to Washington about courting wealthy daughters are in Cary, p. 21.

Professor Stevenson's description of Sally Fairfax is on p. 279 of his article "The Romantics." The description of the Cary family is in Cary, p. ix. Cary also discusses Sally being courted by many suitors, her upbringing, and the story of her name being used as the secret password for sentries. This information is on p. 20.

Information on Sally Cary's hosting skills comes from Cary, p. 4.

Young George Washington's impression of life at Belvoir is found in one of Washington's letters; see Ford, vol. 1, p. 7. Washington's admission of his passion for the Cary girls is quoted in Nigel Cawthorne, *Sex Lives of the Presidents: An Irreverent Expose of the Chief Executive from George Washington to the Present Day* (1996; reprint, New York: St. Martin's Press, 1998), p. 6.

Washington's letter to Sally Fairfax on why General Braddock preferred another woman to her is found in Cary, p. 283. Relatedly, the source for Washington's feelings for Sally and his concern about whether she shared his feelings is the Cary book, pp. 31–32.

A description of the Battle of Monongahela and General Braddock's death can be found at the U.S. National Park Service site for the Fort Necessity Battlefield at http://www.nps.gov/fone/braddock.htm.

The Davies sermon that spoke of Washington as having been saved by divine providence during the battle is in the letter "George Washington to John Augustine Washington," May 31, 1754; further discussion of the event is in the letter "George Washington to Robert Dinwiddie," June 3, 1754. Both letters are in Ford, vol. 1.

The discussion and quotes on Bryan Fairfax's concern with the growing closeness of Washington and Sally is found in Cary, p. 35. Washington's letter to Bryan Fairfax during the Revolutionary War is found in Ford, vol. 6, p. 389. See also Paul Leicester Ford, *The True Washington*, 10th ed. (Indy Publishing, 2004), p. 1.

Washington's relationship with Sally during the Revolutionary War is discussed in Robert Hughes, *Washington* (New York, 1926–1930), vol. 1, pp. 193–98.

Colonel Fairfax's letter to George Washington after the Battle of Monongahela, which included Sally's note in it, is "William Fairfax to George Washington," July 26, 1755.

Eliza Powel's letter to Washington informing him of her discovery of a bundle of love letters in his old desk is "Elizabeth Willing Powel to George Washington," March 11, 1797. His reply is in the letter "George Washington to Elizabeth Willing Powel," March 26, 1797. Both letters are available at the Mount Vernon Ladies' Association. The subsequent quote and discussion of the letter and the Washington–Powel relationship is found in Smith, pp. 268–69 and 296. Smith provides a helpful description of Mrs. Powel on pp. 150–51.

The quotes on the George Washington–Sally Fairfax relationship come from Cary, pp. 29–30; Washington's love letter written to Sally late in life is in Ford, vol. 13, p. 497. The quote about an elderly Sally giving advice to a relative on her daughter's wedding is in Cary, p. 45.

It is suggested that Washington wrote in such a way that he would be covered if his letters were ever discovered. This appears in Ross, p. 14.

The quote about Washington never forgetting Sally is in Cary, p. 29. The quote about her thinking of Washington until the end is also in Cary, p. 44; the final quote on the relationship between Washington and Sally is in Ross, p. 12. The description of surviving letters is found in Cary, p. 31. The last quote of the chapter is also from Cary, p. 27.

CHAPTER 4

Most material in this chapter comes from the following sources: Patricia Brady, "Martha Washington," in *American First Ladies: Their Lives and Their Legacy*, ed. Lewis L. Gould (New York: Garland, 1996), pp. 2–15; John Benson Lossing, *Mary and Martha, the Mother and Wife of Washington* (1863; New York: Harper & Bros., 1886); Elseyth Thane, *Washington's Lady* (New York: Dodd, Mead, 1954); Robert P. Watson, "Remembering Martha," *Magazine of History* 14, no. 2 (2000): 54–57; and Robert P. Watson, "Martha Washington," in *American First Ladies*, ed. Robert P. Watson (Pasadena, CA: Salem Press, 2001), pp. 9–18.

Mrs. Washington's letters have been edited and published. Most quotes in the chapter come from this source. See Joseph Fields, ed., *Worthy Partner: The Papers of Martha Washington* (Westport, CT: Greenwood Press, 1994).

Additional quotes on the Washington marriage come from Donald Jackson and Dorothy Twohig, *The Diaries of George Washington*, 6 vols. (Charlottesville: University of Virginia Press, 1976–1979). Martha's writings are also found in the U.S. Library of Congress, Pennsylvania Historical Society in Harrisburg, the Virginia Historical Society in Richmond, Washington and Lee University in Virginia, and Mount Vernon.

The discovery of the existence of these historic letters is discussed in H. B. Adams, *The Life and Writings of Jared Sparks* (Cambridge, MA: N.p., 1893), vol. 2, p. 47.

Information on the state of scholarship on the first ladies and scholarly interest in Mrs. Washington comes from Robert P. Watson, "Toward the Study of the First Lady: The State of Scholarship," *Presidential Studies Quarterly* 33, no. 2 (June 2003): 423–41.

The quotes on Martha describing her life are found in Fields, pp. xxxiv and 15.

The College of William & Mary Library has a copy of Martha's family Bible, which bears the inscription inside the cover.

Information on Martha's upbringing, first marriage, and courtship by George Washington comes from Douglas Southall Freeman, *George Washington* (New York: Scribner's, 1948), vol. 2.

The John Custis quote comes from Lossing, p. 10. Additional information about John Custis comes from Brady, p. 3.

The Dandridge family line is discussed in George Washington Parke Custis, *Recollections and Private Memories of Washington* (New York, 1860; BiblioBazaar reprint in 2008), see p. 20.

The scholar Mary Ashford believes that it was an interest in power that resulted in the meeting between the teenage Martha and her would-be father-in-law, John Custis. See Ashford, p. 2. Ashford also provides a helpful discussion on John Custis.

The letter to Colonel Daniel Parke Custis about Martha that is discussed in the chapter comes from Lossing, pp. 11–12.

The description of the mulatto slave Jack, owned by Custis, appears in Philip D. Moran, "Interracial Sex in the Chesapeake and the British World, c. 1700–1820," in *Sally Hemings and Thomas Jefferson: History, Memory, and Civic Culture*, ed. Jan Ellen Lewis and Peter S. Onuf (Charlottesville: University of Virginia Press, 1999), pp. 52–86.

Information on George and Martha's home life and marriage comes from Custis, *Recollections*. See also GW's Diary, June 19, 1773.

The letter "George Washington to Tobias Lear," July 31, 1797, is found in Tobias Lear, *Letters and Recollections of George Washington* (New York: Doubleday, Doran & Co., 1932), p. 120.

The slave quote about Washington comes from Mary P. Coulling, *George Washington and the Custis and Lee Families* (Washington and Lee University, 1997), p. 57.

The quotes on Martha finding George Washington filled with anxiety in his winter encampment when she arrived is found in Custis, *Recollections*; Mrs. Westlake's letter that describes Martha Washington in the winter camp is discussed in the Lossing book; additional descriptions of camp life for the Washingtons during the war come from the letter "Martha Washington to Mercy Otis Warren," March 7, 1778, from Valley Forge in the Fields book of Martha's letters; George Washington's letter to Martha as he is leaving to assume command during the Revolutionary War is found in Armistead Peter, *Tudor Place, Georgetown*, 3rd ed. (privately printed, 1969), pp. 44–45; the letter was discovered by Martha's granddaughter.

A good discussion of the fake Washington letters can be found in Fields, p. 477. The subsequent quote on the topic is from Lossing, p. 99; the noted Washington scholar, Douglas Southall Freeman, criticized the letters as being forged. A discussion of the letters appears in Freeman, vol. 2, pp. 405–6.

The information on George Washington writing to Sally Fairfax about his engagement is found in Wilson Miles Cary, *Sally Cary: A Long Hidden Romance of Washington's Life* (New York: De Vine Press, 1916), pp. 36–38.

The source used for the concluding remarks in the chapter is Richard Norton Smith's *Patriarch: George Washington and the New American Nation* (Boston: Houghton Mifflin, 1993).

CHAPTER 5

Most material in this chapter comes from the following sources: Andrew Burstein, *The Inner Jefferson: Portrait of a Grieving Optimist* (Charlottesville: University of Virginia Press, 1995); Joseph J. Ellis, *American Sphinx: The Character of Thomas Jefferson* (Alfred A. Knopf, 1997); E. M. Halliday, *Understanding Thomas Jefferson* (New York: HarperCollins, 2001); Kevin J. Haynes, *The Road to Monticello: The Life and Mind of Thomas Jefferson* (Oxford University Press, 2008); and Willard Sterne Randall, *Thomas Jefferson: A Life* (Harper Perennial, 1994).

The president's papers and letters have been edited and published. Most quotes from the presidential correspondence come from Julian P. Boyd, ed., *The Papers of Thomas Jefferson*, multiple volumes (Princeton NJ: Princeton University Press, 1952).

For information on and quotes from the opening discussion about Jefferson's possible relationship with Sally Hemings, see Fawn M. Brodie, *Thomas Jefferson: An Intimate History* (New York: Norton); Virginius Dabney, *The Jefferson Scandals: A Rebuttal* (New York: Dodd, Mead, 1981); Gordon Langley Hall, *Mr. Jefferson's Ladies* (Boston: Beacon Press, 1966); and Jan Ellen Lewis and Peter Onuf, eds., *Sally Hemings and Thomas Jefferson: History, Memory, and Civic Culture* (Charlottesville: University of Virginia Press, 1999), p. 3; see also a helpful study of Sally Hemings and her possible relationship with Jefferson available through Monticello's website at http://www.monticello.org/plantation/lives/sallyhemings.html.

The study linking the DNA of Jefferson to the son of Sally Hemings is E. A. Foster et al., "Jefferson Fathered Slave's Last Child," *Nature* 196 (November 1998): 27–28; the Thomas Jefferson Foundation study on Jefferson's possible paternity of Sally Hemings's children is at http://www.monticello.org/plantation/hemings contro/appendixj.html and http://www.monticelo.org/plantation/hemingscontro /hemings_report.html. See also http://wwww.himticello.org/plantation/hemings contro/minotiry_report.html for a different opinion. The report of the Thomas Jefferson Heritage Society is at http://www.tjheritage.org/documents/americanheritage_2 .pdf. For another refutation of the paternity, see http://www.opinionjournal.com /extra/?id=95000747; a number of scholars have weighed in on the debate over the 1998 DNA tests and the larger issue of the existence of a Jefferson–Hemings affair. See, for example, Brodie, 1974; Ellis, 1997; Annette Gordon-Reed, *Thomas Jefferson and Sally Hemings: An American Controversy* (Charlottesville: University of Virginia Press, 1997); and Dumas Malone, *Jefferson and His Time*, 6 vols. (Boston, 1948–1981). The quote from Jefferson's overseer, Edmund Bacon, comes from Dabney, pp. 79–80.

The quote from Jefferson about his love for a sculpture and a house is in Andrew Burstein, ed., *Letters from the Head and Heart: Writings of Thomas Jefferson* (Chapel Hill: University of North Carolina Press, 2002), pp. 104–5.

The historian whose defense of Jefferson was blatantly racist is James Parton.

Byron Woodson claims to be a descendant of the Jefferson–Hemings union. See Byron W. Woodson Sr., *A President in the Family: Thomas Jefferson, Sally Hemings, and Thomas Woodson* (Westport, CT: Praeger, 2001), p. 1.

The description of Jefferson as an awkward youth is from Claude G. Bowers, *The Young Jefferson, 1743–1789* (Boston: Houghton Mifflin, 1945), p. 14.

The description of Rebecca Burwell is found in Bowers, p. 25. The quote from Jefferson about Rebecca Burwell after her portrait is ruined is found in Bowers, p. 26. Jefferson's tongue-tied nervousness around Rebecca is discussed in Bowers, pp. 37–38, and Ellis, p. 35; Jefferson's Christmastime letter about his interest in Rebecca and other belles is found in Burstein, *Letters from the Head*, 2002, p. 136.

Jefferson's youthful and boastful comments to his friend, Will Fleming, about not wanting to get married is in John dos Passos, *The Head and Heart of Thomas Jefferson*

(New York: Doubleday, 1954), p. 125; for a discussion of how poorly Jefferson took rejection from the belles of Williamsburg, see Bowers, p. 42.

The quotes about John Wayles come from the Halliday book, p. 30, and Jefferson's *Autobiography*, p. 7.

Regarding the possibility that Jefferson destroyed all his wife's correspondence and portraits, see Burstein, *The Inner Jefferson*, p. 24; see also Bowers, pp. 145 and 228; Bowers also suggests that Mrs. Jefferson may never have sat for a portrait; the argument that Jefferson rarely mentioned his wife after her death on account of the pain it caused him comes from Dumas Malone, in vol. 1 of his six-volume biography. The quote about Jefferson not discussing his wife and the loss to history as a result is from Halliday, p. 37; the argument that less attention has been paid to Jefferson's wife than his other lovers and that less is known about her than other wives of American presidents is found in Robert P. Watson, *The Presidents' Wives: Reassessing the Office of First Lady* (Boulder, CO: Lynne Rienner Publishers, 2000).

The quote from Jefferson to John Page during his courtship of Martha is found in Burwell, p. 25.

Sarah Randolph's description of her great-grandmother Martha is found in Gordon Langley Hall, *Mr. Jefferson's Ladies*, p. xiv; see also Sarah N. Randolph, *The Domestic Life of Thomas Jefferson* (1871; reprint, Charlottesville: University of Virginia Press, 1978), pp. 43–44. Granddaughter Ellen Randolph Coolidge's description of Martha is available in Ellen Randolph Coolidge's *Letter Book*, vol. 4, pp. 66–67 (available at Monticello); the descriptions of Martha's beauty by scholars are found in Bowers, p. 47; Ellis, p. 28; Halliday, p. 30; and Randall, p. 156.

Details on Jefferson's courtship of Martha and the story of other suitors hearing the couple playing music together are found in Bowers, pp. 47–48, and Randall, vol. 1, p. 64.

Jefferson exchanged letters with Robert and Tabitha Skipworths about his pending marriage. See, for instance, "Robert Skipworth to Thomas Jefferson," 1771, in Randall, pp. 158–59, and "Thomas Jefferson to Robert Skipworth," 1771, in Randall, p. 157.

Jefferson's wedding gifts to Martha are quoted in Randall, pp. 158–59; other quotes and a discussion are available in Bowers, p. 33; Burwell, p. 26; and Ellis, p. 28. The quote from Jefferson to his brother-in-law Robert Skipworth about the courtship of Martha appears in Randall, 1994, p. 157.

Jefferson's letter to Martha about the construction of Monticello is quoted in dos Passos, p. 149.

Mrs. Drummond's letter to Jefferson about his engagement to Martha is quoted in Randall, 1994, pp. 157–59.

Discussions and quotes about John Wayles's apprehension about Jefferson marrying his daughter are in Bowers, p. 15; dos Passos, p. 150; and Randall, p. 157. Wayles's complaint about not hearing from his daughter after her marriage is quoted in Randall, p. 160.

Jefferson's description of his wedding and his growing wealth are found in his autobiography, p. 7. See Ellis, p. 28, for a discussion of the marriage in terms of Jefferson's self-image as a "paterfamilias"; the newlyweds' ordeal through the snow to reach Monticello is described in Jefferson's autobiography on p. 34. See also Jefferson's garden and farm books edited by Robert C. Baron (Golden, CO: Fulcrum, 1987), entry for January 26, 1772, p. 26.

The quotes and letters describing Mrs. Jefferson and her hosting are "W. Phillips to Thomas Jefferson," March 31, 1781, vol. 5, pp. 97–98. The Marquis de Chastellux wrote a widely read travel book titled *Voyages dans l'Amerique.* For his comments on life at Monticello, see Halliday, pp. 37 and 48, as well as Bowers, p. 308. Another letter was "George Gilmer to Thomas Jefferson," April 13, 1781, vol. 5, p. 431. Jefferson's unkind words on Mrs. Mazzei are quoted in Philip Mazzei, *Memoirs of the Life and Peregrinations of the Florentine Philip Mazzei, 1730-1816,* New York: Columbia University Press, 1942, pp. 284 and 293. See Bowers, p. 224, for a discussion of this; information on the musical dinner parties hosted by the Jeffersons is found in Bowers, p. 232. Quotes from the Jeffersons' German guests are found in the letter "General Riedesel to Thomas Jefferson," March 19, 1781, vol. 5, pp. 184–85.

I used Halliday, p. 40, for information on slaves' remembrances about Martha's work at Monticello.

The pleas by political leaders such as Nelson, Gates, and Pendleton for Jefferson to remain in public life and/or to bring his wife along to political affairs is found in Randall, p. 257; the letter "Horatio Gates to Thomas Jefferson," August 2, 1781, vol. 6, p. 110; and Halliday, p. 42. The letters and quotes of Jefferson worrying about his wife's health while he was away and the fact that she wrote back to him so infrequently are quoted in Bowers, p. 136, and Randall, p. 251. The letter after the signing of the Declaration of Independence where Jefferson stated his concern about not hearing from his ill wife is "Thomas Jefferson to Francis Eppes," July 15, 1776, vol. 2, p. 62; the letter to a friend describing his unwillingness to leave his ill wife is "Thomas Jefferson to David Jameson," April 16, 1781, Boyd, vol. 5, p. 468; Jefferson's account ledger shows that he bought his wife seven pairs of women's gloves on July 4, 1776. See Halliday, p. 43; see also Jefferson's account ledger.

Jefferson's wartime letters to his wife and those of his friends attempting to calm her concerns are "Thomas Jefferson to John Page," in Worthington Chauncey Ford, *Thomas Jefferson and James Thomson Callender, 1798–1802,* Brooklyn, NY, 1897, vol. 2, p. 187, and "James Madison to Thomas Jefferson," June 18, 1781, vol. 6, p. 95. See also Bowers, p. 277, and Randall, p. 252, for quotes and information on these letters. Jefferson's letter to Monroe about Martha's declining health is "Thomas Jefferson to James Monroe," May 20, 1782, Jefferson Letters, vol. 6, p. 186. The description by their daughter of Jefferson at his dying wife's side is found in Randall, p. 347.

The quote from Jefferson's daughter about her mother's death is in vol. 6, p. 196. Descriptions and quotes about Jefferson in the days after losing his wife are found in Boyd, vol. 6, p. 200; Halliday, pp. 48–49; and Randall, p. 348. Jefferson's letters to family and friends after and about his wife's death are found in "Thomas Jefferson to Chastellux," November 26, 1782, vol. 6, p. 203. One of the first letters Jefferson wrote after his wife's death was to his sister-in-law: "Thomas Jefferson to Elizabeth Wayles Eppes," October 3, 1782, vol. 6, pp. 198–99. For the letters by friends and family worrying about Jefferson's sanity after losing Martha, see "Edmund Randolph to James Madison," September 20, 1782, quoted in Kenkel's Catalogue, 1892, lot 86, p. 696. See also Boyd, vol. 6, p. 199. Mazzei's letter is in Mazzei, *Memoirs,* p. 282.

The story from Monticello's overseer claiming that Jefferson pledged to his dying wife never to remarry is in Halliday, p. 49. The discovery of a lock of Mrs. Jefferson's hair and a previously unknown verse in her handwriting is discussed in Halliday, pp. 50–51. It is also discussed in Jefferson's letters and writings, vol. 6, p. 197. The *Tristram Shandy* verse by Laurence Sterne is discussed in Boyd, vol. 6, pp. 196–97.

The quote about the loss of his wife being traumatic to Jefferson comes from Ellis, p. 66; the quote from Jefferson in reference to his turning down diplomatic offers in Europe is found in Paul M. Zall, *Jefferson on Jefferson* (Lexington: University Press of Kentucky, 2002), p. 57.

Descriptions of Maria Cosway and the details of her relationship with Jefferson are from John P. Kaminski, ed., *Jefferson in Love: The Love Letters between Thomas Jefferson and Maria Cosway* (Madison, WI: Madison House Publishers, 1999); the descriptions of Richard Cosway are found in Burstein, *The Inner Jefferson*, p. 76. Descriptions of Maria Cosway are found in Ellis, p. 93, and from Helen Dupery Bullock, as quoted by Burstein, p. 76.

The letters regarding Jefferson breaking his right wrist, such as "Thomas Jefferson to William Stephens Smith," October 22, 1786, and "Thomas Jefferson to Maria Cosway," October 5, 1786, are discussed and quoted in Hall, p. 86.

Among the historians describing Jefferson's affair with Maria as a real love affair are Ellis, Kaminski, and Randall. Their quotes on the subject are found in Ellis, p. 93, and Kaminski, p. 9.

Various perspectives on Jefferson's "head-and-heart" letter to Maria are found in Burstein, p. 97, and Ellis, pp. 27–29 and 93. See also Hall, p. 85, who also suggests that Jefferson's daughter Martha might have been jealous of Maria.

Jefferson's infatuation with Angelica Schuyler Church and his letters to her are described as "playfully intimate" by Ellis, p. 93. Maria Cosway's letter to Jefferson about Angelica is found in Burstein, p. 108. Angelica's letter to Jefferson from England describing her time with Maria is found in Burstein, p. 109. Jefferson's letter to Angelica about traveling with him to America is also discussed in Burstein, p. 109.

Jefferson's sad letter after his daughter Maria's death was written to his friend John Page, who became Virginia's governor. It is discussed in Ellis, p. 228; see also Hall, p. 171.

Scholars doubt the authenticity of Madison Hemings's claims. See Dumas Malone, *Jefferson and His Time*, vol. 4 (Boston, 1948–1981), pp. 494–98. The quotes and memories of Jefferson's grandchildren on the subject of the paternity of Sally's children is found in Dabney, pp. 785–98.

The newspaper story about Jefferson's mistress was James T. Callender, "The President, Again," *Richmond Recorder* (September 1, 1802). For more information on the poems and stories about the Sally affair, see Paul F. Boller, *Not So! Popular Myths about America from Columbus to Clinton* (New York: Oxford University Press, 1995), p. 46. The Dennie poem in *Port Folio* is discussed in Shelley Ross, p. 41.

The story of the Betsy Walker affair and the letters and newspapers discussing it are found in Boller, p. 47; Burstein; and Shelley Ross, *Fall from Grace*, New York: Ballantine Books, 1988, pp. 33–34.

The interviews with Jefferson's grandchildren about the validity of the affair with Sally Hemings are found in Randolph, p. 1230.

Jefferson's use of sexual innuendo, borrowed from the writer Sterne, is discussed in Burstein, pp. 102–4.

Jefferson's quote expressing his intellectual interest in the similarities and differences between Africans and whites is discussed in Hall, p. 32. Jefferson wrote at length about the races in his *Notes on the State of Virginia* (London, 1787), see query XIV. For the quotes, see also the letter "Thomas Jefferson to Francis Gray," March 4, 1815, in Andrew Lipscomb and Albert Ellery Bergh, eds., *The Writings of Thomas Jefferson*, vol. 14 (1903 and 1904), pp. 267–71. See also Philip D. Morgan, "Interracial Sex in the Chesapeake and the British Atlantic World, c. 1700–1820," in *Sally Hemings and Thomas Jefferson: History, Memory, and Civic Culture*, ed. Jan Ellis Lewis and Peter S. Onuf (Charlottesville: University of Virginia Press, 1999), pp. 52–86.

The idea that Martha Jefferson (and other southern women) were ignorant of the affairs that took place between white masters and African slaves is discussed in Dabney, p. 27, and Winthrop Jordan, *White Over Black: American Attitudes Toward the Negro, 1550–1812*, Chapel Hill: University of North Carolina Press, 1968, p. 467.

Maria and Jefferson teasing one another and flirting with one another in letters is quoted in Burstein, p. 107.

Jefferson's comments that he would not expose his "soul" again to pain is discussed in Ellis, p. 93. The three quotes on Jefferson's good marriage are found, respectively, in Bowers, p. 238; Hugh Brogan and Charles Mosley, *American Presidential Families*, New York: MacMillan, 1993, p. 141; and Ellis, p. 28.

Jefferson's advice to his daughters on marriage and happiness is found in Malone, pp. 2, 4, 160, and 251–52. His quote to daughter Polly is found in Halliday, pp. 36–37. Jefferson's admission that he favored domestic women is found in Randall, p. 142; his description of the tempting Parisian women is found in Ellis, p. 85; and his letter to young John Banister Jr. is found in Burstein, p. 113.

Jefferson's letter to Angelica Church about women not being suited for politics is found in Burstein, p. 268.

Jefferson's letter to Madison about the pain of public life is found in Randall, p. 335. Jefferson's fondness for private life and the quotation about his not wanting to leave his wife is found in the letter "Thomas Jefferson to David Jameson," April 16, 1781, vol. 5, p. 468. Jefferson's quote about being happy at home is found in Bowers, p. 95. Jefferson explaining to politicians that his wife's illness was the reason for his absence is found in a letter to Pendleton and quoted in Ellis, p. 60; the letter begging to be replaced as a delegate in Philadelphia is "Thomas Jefferson to Richard Henry Lee" and discussed in Ellis, p. 60. The letter to Chastellux about retirement is "Thomas Jefferson to Chastellux," November 26, 1782, vol. 6, p. 203; see also Randall for discussion, p. 349. Jefferson's letter to Monroe about balancing public and family life is "Thomas Jefferson to James Monroe," May 20, 1782, vol. 6, pp. 184–86; Monroe's reply is "James Monroe to Thomas Jefferson," June 28, 1782, vol. 6, p. 192.

Jefferson's comparison of the women of Paris and Virginia is found in Ellis, p. 91, and Halliday, pp. 5–6.

The possibility that Jefferson was not really ready to retire but was simply wracked with guilt over the loss of children and his wife's health is suggested by Boyd, p. 187, and Malone, vol. 1, p. 395.

CHAPTER 6

Most material in this chapter comes from the following sources: Jon Meacham, *American Lion: Andrew Jackson in the White House* (Random House, 2009); Robert Vinent Remini, *Andrew Jackson: The Course of American Empire, 1767–1721,* vol. 1 (Baltimore: Johns Hopkins University Press, 1998); Robert Vincent Remini, *Andrew Jackson: The Course of American Freedom, 1822–1832,* vol. 2 (Baltimore: Johns Hopkins University Press, 1998); Robert Vincent Remini, *Andrew Jackson: The Course of American Democracy, 1833–1845,* vol. 3 (Baltimore: Johns Hopkins University Press, 1998); and Sean Wilentz, *Andrew Jackson* (Henry Holt, 2005).

The president's papers and letters have been edited and published. Most quotes from the presidential correspondence comes from John Spencer Bassett, *Correspondence of Andrew Jackson* (1926–1935), and *The Papers of Andrew Jackson,* 8 vols., part of the Andrew Jackson Papers Project, University of Tennessee Press.

Rachel Jackson's widowed mother's plea to Andrew Jackson to defend her daughter's honor is described in Shelley Ross, *Fall from Grace* (New York: Ballantine Books, 1988), p. 56.

The quote on how the marriage benefited Jackson and was a good union is found in Robert P. Watson and Richard Yon, eds., *American Presidents,* rev. 3rd ed. (Pasadena, CA: Salem Press, 2006), p. 137.

The argument between Governor Sevier and Jackson that ran in the *Gazette* in July 1803 is quoted in Michael Farquhar, *A Treasury of Great American Scandals* (New York: Penguin, 2003), p. 63; the charged public exchange between Sevier and Jackson that led to their duel is quoted in Robert V. Remini, *The Life of Andrew Jackson* (New York: Harper & Row, 1988), p. 46; the letter Jackson published in a newspaper calling out Sevier is quoted in Carl S. Driver, *John Sevier: Pioneer of the Old Southwest* (Chapel Hill: University of North Carolina Press, 1932), p. 146; the outcome of the Sevier duel is described in Remini, p. 47.

Dickinson's marksmanship is described in Michael Farquhar, *A Treasury of Great American Scandals.* See Farquhar for details of the string that Dickinson was alleged to have shot in half and the quote about it, pp. 58–59; general information about Jackson's duels is found in Meacham, pp. 25–27.

Quotes between Jackson and the Bentons pertaining to their feud are found in Farquhar, p. 60; Jackson telling Benton that he was going to punish him is quoted in Farquhar, p. 61; Thomas Benton's realization of the threat from Jackson is quoted in the same source but on p. 62.

Quotes from the showdown with the convict Russell Bean are described and quoted in Remini, p. 43; the quote on Bean's surrender to Judge Jackson is found in the letter "James A. McLaughlin to Amos Kendall," January 3, 1843; see also James Parton, *Life of Andrew Jackson,* 1866, vol. 1 (3 vols.), pp. 228–29.

General information on Jackson's many duels can be found in Remini, pp. 42–54.

Descriptions of Jackson needing Rachel and vice versa, along with quotes on them not wanting to be apart, are found in Watson and Yon, p. 137.

Jackson's enemies' warning that he would arrive in Washington with a scalping knife is found in Remini, p. 149.

Jackson's quote to John Coffee about the corrupt process of King Caucus is found in the letter "Andrew Jackson to John Coffee," February 15, 1824, Coffee Papers in the Tennessee Historical Society, Nashville; Jackson's quote about the political battle and Clay's deal making in the wake of the close 1824 vote is found in the letter "Andrew Jackson to Lewis," December 27, 1824, The Jackson Papers, Massachusetts Historical Society, Boston; Jackson's quotes about the corrupt vote in the House after it occurred is found in Remini, p. 155; Jackson's quote about Clay being the Judas of the West is in Farquhar, p. 159.

Mrs. Jackson's quote when she discovered her husband had won the presidency is found in Remini, p. 169.

Jackson's admission that, after Rachel's death, the presidency meant little is found in the letter "Andrew Jackson to John Coffee," January 17, 1829, The Coffee Papers in the Tennessee Historical Society, Nashville.

A general discussion of the 1824 and 1828 elections is found in Remini, pp. 150–56. Comprehensive facts on both elections are found in William G. Shade and Ballard C. Campbell, *American Presidential Campaigns and Elections*, vol. 1 (Armonk, NY: Sharpe Reference, 2003), pp. 214–31 (for the 1824 race) and pp. 232–49 (for the 1828 election); additional information on the election of 1824 and Jackson's reaction to it are found in Meacham, pp. 33, 38, 44–45; for the ugly public attacks against Rachel during the 1828 campaign, see Meacham, pp. 4, 5, 17, 39.

A discussion of Jackson's ordeal when captured during the Revolutionary War and quotes, including the advice given by his mother, are found in Marquis James, *The Life of Andrew Jackson* (Indianapolis: Bobbs-Merrill, 1938), p. 383.

A discussion of Jackson's youthful romances and the quotes from young girls about his "presence" are found in Marquis James, p. 35. The story of Jackson inviting prostitutes to the Christmas Eve party is found in Nigel Cawthorne, *Sex Lives of the Presidents: An Irreverent Expose of the Chief Executive from George Washington to the Present Day* (1996; reprint, New York: St. Martin's Press, 1998), p. 66.

A discussion of the Battle of New Orleans and quotes from the city's leaders about Jackson's fitness for command are found in James Parton, *Life of Andrew Jackson*, vol. 2, p. 31. Information on the Battle of New Orleans also comes from Remini, pp. 88–100. The letter and quote where Jackson discusses the Battle of New Orleans and owing the British payback is "Andrew Jackson to Rachel Donelson Jackson," August 5, 1814, the Jackson Papers, Huntington Library, Huntington, California.

The quote about Jackson not forgiving Rachel's critics and information on Rachel's death is found in Farquhar, p. 161.

The physical descriptions of Margaret "Peg" O'Neale and quotes about her beauty can be found at http://www.foundersofamerica.org/making.html; see "The Story of Peggy Eaton, Andrew Jackson, and the Making of a President." See also http://www.foundersofamerica.org for quotes about Jackson's feud over Peg's affairs and his defense of her in public and with his cabinet.

CHAPTER 7

Most material in this chapter comes from the following sources: Oliver Perry Chitwood, *John Tyler: Champion of the Old South* (1939; reprint, New York: Russell and Russell, 1964; reprint, American Political Biography Press, 1990); Edward P. Crapol,

John Tyler: The Accidental President (Chapel Hill: University of North Carolina Press, 2006); and Gary May, *John Tyler* (reprint, Time Books, 2008).

The Tyler letters, diary, and papers are published. However, most were lost during the Civil War. Tyler's son, Lyon, collected and published those that remained between 1884 and 1896 in three volumes as *The Letters and Times of the Tylers* (reprint, New York: Da Capo Press, 1978). The John Tyler Papers, which include papers, correspondence, and his diary, are in the Library of Congress.

There are two other books that were used to discuss the Tyler White House, marriage, and children: Elizabeth Tyler Coleman, *Priscilla Cooper Tyler and the American Scene, 1816–1889* (Tuscaloosa: University of Alabama Press, 1955), and Gilson Willets, *Inside History of the White House* (New York: Christian Herald, 1908).

The quote from Tyler's mother about her son's stargazing as an infant comes from William A. DeGregoria, *The Complete Book of U.S. Presidents* (reprint, Fort Lee, NJ: Barricade Books, 2001), p. 151.

The information on Tyler's service in Congress and his wife, Letitia, joining him in the capital city comes from Chitwood, p. 144.

The description of Tyler by George Wythe Munford is found in Lyon Tyler, ed., *Letters and Times*, vol. 1, p. 356.

The information on Tyler's prudish ways and opposition to dancing and the waltz, as well as his efforts to discipline his children, is found in Tyler, *Letters and Times*, vol. 1, p. 553. Likewise, Tyler's quote about watching a dance that appears in his letter of advice to his daughter is also in Tyler, vol. 1, p. 390.

Details of Tyler's slow courtship of Letitia and concerns from her family about the marriage are found in Chitwood, p. 23; Tyler's letter to Letitia while courting her discussing his concern about money is found in Robert Seager II, *And Tyler Too: A Biography of John and Julia Gardiner Tyler* (1963; reprint, Easton Press, 1988); Tyler's lone surviving letter to Letitia from the time of their courtship is available in the John Tyler Papers, vol. 1, p. 6224; the general information on Tyler's courtship of Letitia is found in Chitwood, pp. 22–23, and the quote is on p. 23.

Tyler's letter to his brother-in-law regarding the wedding is "John Tyler to Dr. Curtis," March 23, 1813, and is found in *Letters and Times*; the quote on Tyler's lovemaking is in Chitwood, p. 23.

Tyler's advice to his daughter on marriage and the way for a woman to conduct herself is in Tyler, vol. 1, p. 546.

Quotes on William Henry Harrison when he arrived for his inauguration come from Robert P. Watson, ed., *The American Presidents*, 3rd ed. (Pasadena, CA: Salem Press, 2006), pp. 179–80.

The quotes on and descriptions of Letitia Tyler while in the White House are in Chitwood, 1964, pp. 228–29; Priscilla Cooper Tyler's description of Letitia in the White House is found in Seager, p. 183.

The quote from Julia Gardiner remembering her father's handsome appearance is in a letter written by her on August 16, 1845. It is found in the John Tyler Papers, vol. 8, p. 654.

Information on the controversial poem that was written about Julia Gardiner and the scandalous advertisement in which she appeared is available online through the National Archives at http://clinton4.nara.gov/wh/glimpse/firstladies/html/jt10.html.

Julia Gardiner's description of first meeting Tyler is found in a letter in the John Tyler Papers, vol. 3, pp. 196–97.

The letter from Julia to her concerned mother about living in the White House and marrying the president is in the John Tyler Papers, July 1844; the information on the strong marriage between John and Julia comes from Chitwood (1964); Tyler's quotes praising and gushing over his new bride are in the John Tyler Papers, vol. 2, p. 6471; see also a letter from John Tyler to his daughter written on June 28, 1844; the quotes from Julia about her husband and marriage are available online through the National Archives at http://clinton4.nara.gov/wh/glimpse/firstladies/html/jt10.html.

Priscilla Cooper Tyler's letter to Julia offering advice and information on hosting in the White House is quoted in Chitwood, p. 391; the original is "Mrs. Robert Tyler to Ms. Julia and Margaret Gardiner," the John Tyler Papers, undated.

Tyler's joke about his farewell party is found in Lewis L. Gould, ed., *American First Ladies: Their Lives and Their Legacy* (New York: Garland Publishing, 1996), pp. 117–29.

The quotes by James Buchanan and Benton describing John Tyler's new First Lady are found in George Ticknor Curtis, *Life of James Buchanan*, vol. 1 (Harper & Bros., 1883), p. 529; see also Jessie Benton Fremont, *Souveniers of My Time* (1887; reprint, General Books, 2010), pp 99–100.

CHAPTER 8

Note: Sources spell Anne Coleman's name both ways: Anne and Ann. So do historic records. However, in correspondence with the helpful staff at the Buchanan Home in Wheatland, and the James Buchanan Foundation in Lancaster, Pennsylvania, the administrative staff, including Patrick Clarke and Sue Small, spelled her name with the "e" at the end. Therefore, I will spell Ms. Coleman's name "Anne" in this chapter.

Most material in this chapter comes from the following sources: Jean H. Baker, *James Buchanan* (Times Books, 2004); George Ticknor Curtis, *Life of James Buchanan*, 2 vols. (Harper & Bros, 1883); and Philip S. Klein, *President James Buchanan: A Biography* (American Political Biography Press, 1995).

Buchanan's papers and letters have been edited and published, and most quotes come from these letters. See John Bassett Moore, ed., *Works of James Buchanan: Comprising His Speeches, State Papers, and Private Correspondence*, 12 vols. (Philadelphia: Lippincott, 1908–1911; reprint, New York: Antiquarian Press, 1960).

Quotes in the chapter also came from other holders of Buchanan's unpublished letters, including the library at Dickinson College in Carlisle, Pennsylvania; papers and information on Buchanan's youth are in the Pennsylvania Historical Museum

Commission and Historical Society of Pennsylvania on Locust Street in Philadelphia (call no. FC BU); the Lancaster County Historical Society on President Avenue in Lancaster, Pennsylvania; the William Frederick Worner collection of Buchanan letters and correspondence, unpublished; and Sally Smith Cahalan, "James Buchanan and His Family at Wheatland," James Buchanan Foundation, 1988, Lancaster, Pennsylvania, unpublished.

Information on Buchanan's courtship of Anne Coleman and her tragic life comes from Philip Shriver Klein, "James Buchanan and Ann Coleman," *Pennsylvania History* 21 (January 1954): 1–20.

Information on Buchanan's years as Lancaster's most eligible bachelor comes from Klein, *President James Buchanan*, p. 28; see also Philip S. Klein, *A History of Pennsylvania* (University Park: Pennsylvania State University Press, 1976), and William Riddle, *Story of Lancaster, Pennsylvania: Old and New* (Lancaster, 1917), pp. 122–23.

The quote about Anne's mood swings and personality is found in Klein, *President James Buchanan*, p. 28.

The discussion about Anne's parents and their concerns about her engagement to Buchanan are found in Klein, *President James Buchanan*, pp. 27–32; the quote on why the engagement of James and Anne was ended is from Baker, p. 19–20; the quote from Anne's neighbor about Mr. Buchanan's poor treatment of Anne is found in the letter "Hannah Cochran to husband," December 14, 1819, Slaymaker Collection, Lancaster Historical Society.

The long quote about the source of trouble between Anne and Buchanan is the letter from the niece of Mrs. Jenkins, Blanche Nevin, who was also the daughter of the Reverend John W. Nevin and Martha Jenkins Nevin; the letter is in the Ruth Scrapbook, Lancaster County Historical Society, Lancaster, PA, p. 44, and is also quoted in Klein, *President James Buchanan*, p. 31.

The long quote from Thomas Kittera describing Anne's final moments in Philadelphia comes from Klein, *President James Buchanan*, pp. 31–32. The Kittera Diary excerpts on Anne's death are in the George Ticknor Curtis Collection, Buchanan Manuscripts, Historical Society of Pennsylvania, but the original diary was not found.

The gossip in town that Buchanan was guilty and responsible for Anne's death comes from the letter "Hannah Cochran to husband," December 14, 1819, Slaymaker Collection, Lancaster Historical Society.

The historian Paul Boller Jr. feels that Buchanan may have been gay, and Boller discusses the mater of Anne suffering from hysterical convulsions, which might indicate suicide, in Paul F. Boller Jr., *Presidential Anecdotes* (Oxford: Oxford University Press, 1981).

The source used to discuss Buchanan's ego and his lack of empathy for Anne and her family is Klein, *President James Buchanan*, p. 30; quotes on Anne's death and Buchanan's response are found in the same source on p. 32; see also Ruth Scrapbook, pp. 56 and 64; the memorial that Buchanan wrote (with the help from others) to commemorate Anne's death is listed in Curtis, *Buchanan*, vol. 1, p. 16.

The idea that Anne's father, Mr. Coleman, may never have even read Buchanan's letter and likely returned it unopened is maintained by Patrick Clarke, the director of Wheatland, from an interview with the author on July 2, 2006.

Buchanan's recognition that, after Anne's death, he could no longer remain in Lancaster over the Christmas holiday is found in Klein, *President James Buchanan*, p. 33. The quote about Buchanan returning to Lancaster after Anne's death comes from the letter "Hannah Cochran to husband," December 14, 1819, Slaymaker Collection, Lancaster Historical Society.

The quote that Buchanan was fond of saying, which reveals part of his dark personality after Anne's death, is discussed in Klein, *President James Buchanan*, p. 34.

The quotes describing Buchanan's feminine physical and social qualities come from Baker, p. 26, and Boller, p. 75; a number of reputable historians have suggested that Buchanan may have been gay; see Baker, p. 20, Boller, p. 76; and Shelley Ross, *Fall from Grace* (New York: Ballantine Books, 1988), p. 86. Baker, p. 147, also ponders why Buchanan and his sexuality were largely overlooked by history.

The Dickinson College president's quote about the poor state of the school is found in Klein, *President James Buchanan*, p. 8; Buchanan's similarly dismal view of the school is on the same page in Klein, *President James Buchanan*; see also "James Buchanan at Dickinson," John and Mary's College, Carlisle, PA, 1956, pp. 157–79, for a discussion of the school; Buchanan's description of his partying at college is found in Klein, *President James Buchanan*, p. 9; the discussion of Buchanan being kicked out of Dickinson and his participation in the graduation ceremonies are in Klein, *President James Buchanan*, pp. 9–12.

Buchanan was not a believer and struggled halfheartedly with questions of morality, which is discussed in the letter "James Buchanan to Edward Buchanan," January 9, 1833, in *Works*, pp. 311–12.

The quote from Buchanan being fussy with Congressman Miller and other examples of his prissy behavior are from the letter "James Buchanan to Jesse Miller," Washington, D.C., June 24, 1847, *Works*, p. 254; see also *Works*, vol. 7, 1846–1848, pp. 353–54, and *Works*, vol. 6, 1844–1846, pp. 111–12.

Buchanan's relationship with President Jackson and the possibility of serving as Jackson's vice president is discussed in the letter "George W. Buchanan to James Buchanan," April 29, 1831, vol. 2, *Works*, pp. 172–73; the discussions between Jackson and Buchanan about Buck's appointment are in letters "John Eaton to James Buchanan," May 31, 1831, *Works*, vol. 2, p. 173; "John Eaton to James Buchanan," June 7, 1831, *Works*, vol. 2, p. 174; "James Buchanan to John Eaton," June 12, 1831, *Works*, vol. 2, p. 175; and "John Eaton to James Buchanan," June 15, 1831, *Works*, vol. 2, pp. 175–76; Buchanan's letter complaining to Roger Taney is "James Buchanan to Roger Taney," August 2, 1831, *Works*, vol. 2; the letter from Buchanan's mother expressing displeasure and concern about his appointment and absence is "Mrs. Buchanan to James Buchanan," October 21, 1831, *Works*, vol. 2, p. 181; Buchanan's remark that he was "fagged out" is in "James Buchanan to Andrew Jackson" from St. Petersburg, December 20, 1832, *Works*, vol. 2, p. 306.

The rumors of Buchanan enjoying being kissed by and kissing ladies while touring country are listed in Nigel Cawthorne, *Sex Lives of the Presidents: An Irreverent Expose of the Chief Executive from George Washington to the Present Day* (1996; reprint, New York: St. Martin's Press, 1998), p. 94; the idea of Buchanan having an affair with Mrs. Polk is discussed in the same book, p. 92; the various letters where Buchanan talks about women or getting married are found in *Works*, vol. 6, p. 61; see also J. Fred Rippy, *Joel Poinsett* (Durham, NC: Duke University Press, 1935), p. 168; Klein, *President James Buchanan*, p. 101; there are three letters exchanged with Kittera: "James Buchanan to Thomas Kittera," October 9, 1834, September 25, 1837, and April 25, 1843, where Buchanan discusses marriage and Kittera's niece; Buchanan's discussion of Dolley Madison's niece, Anna Payne, is in Klein, *President James Buchanan*, p. 152, and Cawthorne, p. 93; Buchanan's poem to Anna Payne was written on March 18, 1842, and is found in the Buchanan Manuscripts of the Historical Society of Pennsylvania.

The quote by Buchanan's biographer about the remaining questions over his romances is Klein, *President James Buchanan*, p. 101; the discussion of Buchanan admitting to the advantage of courting women in order to get elected is discussed in Klein, *President James Buchanan*, p. 124.

Descriptions and quotes about Miss Hetty, the housekeeper, are found in Klein, *President James Buchanan*, p. 100.

Buchanan's letters with his niece, Harriet Lane, are found in *Works*, vol. 7, 1846–1848, p. 25, and July 3, 1846.

The quote by Buchanan stating his admiration for Dr. King is found in Klein, *President James Buchanan*, p. 7.

The story about King and Buchanan rooming together is in James Sterling, *The Washington Community* (New York: Columbia University Press, 1966).

The quote on King's view of slavery is found in a letter "William King to James Buchanan," December 20, 1837, in the Buchanan Manuscripts, Historical Society of Pennsylvania; the quote about King's political influence on Buchanan comes from Baker, p. 138; the discussion of Buchanan supporting King's bid for vice president is found in Klein, *President James Buchanan*, pp. 13 and 130.

Buchanan's love letter about King to Mrs. Roosevelt was written on May 13, 1844, and is found in James W. Loewen, *Lies across America: What Our Historic Sites Get Wrong* (New York: New Press, 1999), p. 367 (this is the same source for Buchanan's own description of King, p. 367); see also George Ticknor Curtis, *The Works of James Buchanan*, 12 volumes, New York: Harper & Bros., 1883 (reprint 1960), vol. 1, p. 519; *Works*, vol. 6, pp. 1844–46.

The letters exchanged between Buchanan and King are "James Buchanan to William King," March 27, 1846, *Works*, vol. 6; "James Buchanan to William King," March 25, 1845, *Works*, vol. 6, pp. 127–28; and "James Buchanan to William King," November 10, 1845, *Works*, vol. 6, pp. 292–93.

The quote about Buchanan and King being "Siamese Twins" is in Loewen, p. 367; quotes on the gossip about the two men and their relationship are in "James Buchanan to Thomas Elder," November 7, 1836, Buchanan Manuscripts, Historical Society of Pennsylvania, Philadelphia; see also Ross, p. 89, and Boller, p. 75.

Newspaper accounts and letters describing the two men with feminine and homosexual slang are found in Cawthorne, p. 95, and Boller, p. 75; the letters between Congressman Brown and Mrs. Polk are "Aaron Brown to Sarah Polk," January 14, 1844, The Polk Papers, University of Tennessee; see also Ross, pp. 87–89; the quote from Brown's letter about Buchanan and King having a public falling-out is in Klein, *President James Buchanan*, p. 111, and "Aaron Brown to Sarah Polk," January 14,

1844, The Polk Papers; the letters from Buchanan's Pennsylvania constituents referring to him as a woman are found in Carl Sferazza Anthony, *First Ladies: The Saga of the Presidents' Wives and Their Power, 1789–1961* (New York: William Morrow, 1990), p. 167.

Buchanan's love of gossip and "womanly tone" in his letters are found in "James Buchanan to Eliza Watterston," July 16, 1851, *Works*, pp. 418–19; Buchanan's interest in learning of Watterston's romances is in "James Buchanan to Eliza Watterston," November 17, 1851, *Works*, pp. 424–25; see also "James Buchanan to Eliza Watterston," January 20, 1851, from Wheatland, *Works*, pp. 412–13; Buchanan's gossipy letters with Mrs. Slaymaker about the royals in St. Petersburg are found in "James Buchanan to Mrs. Slaymaker," October 31, 1832, from St. Petersburg, *Works*, pp. 263–65.

Buchanan's frequent habit of ignoring women but describing men in physical detail is found in "James Buchanan to Miss Hetty," December 16, 1853, *Works*, pp. 113–14; Buchanan's vivid description of meeting the monk is in his diary, June 18, 1833, pp. 361–63; his description of being kissed by the monk is in a letter written on June 18, 1833, from St. Petersburg, *Works*, vol. 2; "James Buchanan to George Gray Leiper," July 13, 1833, *Works*, vol. 2; "James Buchanan to Edward Buchanan," July 20, 1833, *Works*.

Several leading polls that rate the presidents place Buchanan dead last or near the bottom. See, for example, Schlesinger 1948, Schlesinger 1962, Porter 1981, *Chicago Tribune*, 1982, Murray-Blessing 1982, Schlesinger Jr. 1996, C-SPAN Historian Survey 2000, and so on. See "Special Issues: The Uses and Abuses of Presidential Rankins," *White House Studies* 3, no. 1 (2003); all of the polls are discussed in this issue.

Buchanan's quote stating that he regretted serving as secretary of state is found in "James Buchanan to Plumer," March 19, 1848, Buchanan Manuscripts, Historical Society of Pennsylvania, Philadelphia; Buchanan's thoughts on looking back at his presidency and legacy are in Watson, *The American Presidents*, p. 239; the Curtis biography has been dismissed by scholars as being overly friendly to Buchanan; see, for example, Loewen, p. 367–70.

The two men, King and Buchanan, spent over two decades together and were likely gay, although we may never know the true answer. See Klein, *President James Buchanan*, pp. 28–32; Klein, "James Buchanan and Ann Coleman," pp. 1–20; and Ross, p. 89.

CHAPTER 9

Most material in this chapter comes from the following sources: Michael Burlingame, *At Lincoln's Side: John Hay's Civil War Correspondence and Selected Writing*s (Carbondale: Southern Illinois University Press, 2006); Michael Burlingame, *Inside the White House in War Times: Memoirs and Reports of Lincoln's Secretary* (Bison Books, 2000); Michael Burlingame, *The Inner World of Abraham Lincoln* (Chicago: University of Illinois Press, 1994); David Herbert Donald, *Lincoln* (New York: Simon and Schuster, 1995); Mark E. Neely Jr., *The Abraham Lincoln Encyclopedia* (New York: McGraw-Hill, 1982); Stephen B. Oates, *With Malice toward None: The Life of*

Abraham Lincoln (New York: Harper and Row, 1977); J. G. Randall, *Lincoln the President: Springfield to Gettysburg*, vol. 2 (New York: Dodd, Mead, 1945); Ruth Painter Randall, *Mary Todd Lincoln: Biography of a Marriage* (Boston: Little, Brown, 1953); Carl Sandburg, *Abraham Lincoln: The Prairie Years*, vol. 1 (New York: Harcourt Brace, 1926); and Benjamin P. Thomas, *Abraham Lincoln: A Biography* (New York: Alfred A. Knopf, 1952).

Information on Lincoln's romantic life comes from the following sources: William E. Barton, *The Women Lincoln Loved* (Indianapolis: Bobbs-Merrill, 1927); Olive Carruthers and R. Gerald McMurtry, *Lincoln's Other Mary* (Chicago: Ziff-Davis Publishing, 1946); William H. Herndon, *Lincoln and Ann Rutledge and the Pioneers of New Salem* (reprint, Herrin, IL: Trovillion Private Press, 1945); William H. Herndon and Jesse W. Weik, *Herndon's Life of Lincoln* (1889; reprint, New York: Da Capo Press, 1983); Jay Monaghan, "New Light on the Lincoln-Rutledge Romance," *The Abraham Lincoln Quarterly* 3 (September 1944): 138–45; Thomas Reep, *Lincoln at New Salem* (Petersburg, IL: New Salem Lincoln League, 1918); John Y. Simon, "Abraham Lincoln and Ann Rutledge," *Journal of the Abraham Lincoln Association* 11 (1990): 13–33; Douglas Wilson, "Abraham Lincoln, Ann Rutledge, and the Evidence of Herndon's Informants," *Civil War History*, December 1990; Douglas L. Wilson and Rodney O. Davis, eds., *Herndon's Informants: Letters, Interviews, and Statements about Abraham Lincoln* (Urbana: University of Illinois Press, 1997); and H. Donald Winkler, *Lincoln's Ladies: The Women in the Life of the Sixteenth President* (Nashville: Cumberland House, 2004).

The unflattering physical descriptions of Lincoln at the beginning of the chapter and the jokes Lincoln made at his own expense come from John G. Sotos, *The Physical Lincoln: Finding the Genetic Cause of Abraham Lincoln's Height, Homeliness, Pseudo-Depression, and Imminent Cancer Death* (Mount Vernon Books, 2008); John G. Sotos, *The Physical Lincoln Sourcebook* (Mount Vernon Books, 2008); quotations website at http://www.quotationspage.com; and companion websites for the *Physical Lincoln* books at http://www.lincolnportrait.com/physical_man.asp and http://www.physical-lincoln.com/appearance.html.

The discussion of Grace Bedell's letters to Lincoln and a transcript of the letters are available at the Grace Bedell Foundation website at htttp://gracebedellfoundation.org.

The quote that parts of Lincoln didn't seem to "fit together" comes from Oates, 1977, p. 34 and the discussion of Lincoln's height, ungainly physique, and physical maladies are from John R. Baumgarner, *The Health of Presidents*, Jefferson, NC: McFarland, 1994 (2004).

The quote from Dennis Hanks, Lincoln's cousin, on Abe's ability to swing an ax is found in Browne's biography of Lincoln, Francis Fisher Browne, *The Every-day Life of Abraham Lincoln; A Narrative and Descriptive Biography by Those Who Knew Him*, New York: G.P. Putnam, 1915, p. 53; the quote about Lincoln being equal to three men when it came to strength is Albert Kaplan, *Abraham Lincoln: The Physical Man*; I also used Kaplan for the stories of Lincoln's wrestling matches at http://www.lincolnportrait.com/physical_man.asp.

Lincoln's upbringing and the quote about his early life from Thomas Gray is from Robert P. Watson and Richard Yon, *The American Presidents*, rev. 3rd ed. (Pasadena, CA: Salem Press, 2006), p. 242.

Barton on p. 201 claims that some of Lincoln's male relatives and friends were equally hesitant about marrying. It is possible Lincoln was scarred emotionally from the loss of his mother and sister; see Frank J. Williams's foreword to the Winkler book and Winkler's own discussion on p. xi.

The story of Lincoln meeting and rooming with Joshua Speed is found in Herndon and Weik, p. 149; details on Lincoln's encounter with Speed's prostitute comes from the letter "Joshua F. Speed to William H. Herndon," January 5, 1881; books claiming that Lincoln was gay are C. A. Tripp, *The Intimate World of Abraham Lincoln*, New York: Free Press, 2005; Larry Kramer, *The American People: A History* (unpublished manuscript; rights owned by Farrar, Straus and Giroux for 2012 release); whether Lincoln contracted syphilis from a prostitute and his request of Dr. Drake to treat him are discussed in Winkler, p. 95.

The quote that women liked Lincoln is found in Winkler, p. 53; Winkler, on p. 49, also tells the story about Lincoln punishing Reavis for repeatedly cursing in the presence of women.

Lincoln's misfortunes in courting, including his not providing Rosanna Schmink with a separate horse for their date, are found in Winkler, p. 93.

The details of Lincoln meeting Polly and the quote from John Hanks about Lincoln's budding political oratory impressing the crowd (and Polly) are found in Barton, pp. 157–58; Barton, p. 163, also discusses Polly's fond memories of Lincoln later in life.

The quote about the challenge of discovering the truth about Lincoln's romances is Barton, p. 167; on p. 187, Barton provides a helpful discussion about women's views on Lincoln and married women trying to fix him up with a wife.

I used Barton for details on the story about the Dill brothers suing Lincoln for rowing their passengers across the river and the quotes on Lincoln's romance with Judge Pate's niece, Caroline Meeker, on pp. 145–49.

Similarly, Barton provides information on Lincoln's courtship of Mary Owens on p. 192; the descriptions of and quotes regarding Mary's physique are from Barton, p. 190; Mary's description of herself is in the letter "Mary Owens to William H. Herndon," August 6, 1866.

Details and quotes on the strained engagement between Mary and Lincoln come from the letter "Mary Owens to William H. Herndon," August 6, 1866, and are discussed in Barton, pp. 193–94; information on Lincoln traveling to and enjoying himself in Vandalia and Springfield are found in Wilson and Davis, p. 531, and the letter "Johnson Gaines Greene to William H. Herndon," 1866; Lincoln's awkward "Friend Mary" letter was written to Mary Owens on August 16, 1837, and is described in Wilson and Davis, p. 263, and the letter "Mary Owens to William H. Herndon," July 22, 1866; details of Lincoln's hesitancy about what to do are found in Philip B. Kunhardt Jr., Philip B. Kunhardt III, and Peter W. Kunhardt, *Lincoln: An Illustrated Biography* (New York: Knopf, 1992), p. 54.

The Lincoln letter and comments that he made a fool of himself are discussed in Barton, p. 202; Mary's reply to Lincoln's emotional outburst are discussed in Kunhardt et al., p. 55; the embarrassing letter Lincoln wrote to Mrs. O. H. Browning was written from Springfield on April 1, 1838, and is discussed in Kunhardt et al., p. 55.

William Herndon tracked down Mary Owens in 1866; details are discussed in the letter "Mary S. Owens Vineyard to William H. Herndon," May 1, 1866; these letters are discussed in Carruthers and McMurtry, p. 201. Mary's quotes about Lincoln late in life are discussed in Barton, p. 204.

There is much debate over the Ann Rutledge romance. See Paul M. Angle, "Lincoln's First Love," *Lincoln Centennial Association Bulletin*, December 1927, pp. 1–8; David Donald, *Lincoln's Herndon* (1948), pp. 184–241; David Donald, *Lincoln Reconsidered: Essays on the Civil War Era* (Alfred A. Knopf, 1956), p. 156; and the books by Oates, Randall (pp. 321–42), and Thomas. The quote from the Nicolay and Hay book regarding Ann Rutledge is discussed in Barton, pp. 178–79; Cogdale's recollection of his conversation with Lincoln about Ann is discussed in Angle, p. 6. The quote from John Bunn about Lincoln's reluctance to talk about past loves is in Angle, p. 7. See also Simon, pp. 13 and 26, for thoughts and a quote on the affair with Ann. The story of the 1862 article being found that sheds new light on the romance is in Monaghan, pp. 138–45.

Robert Rutledge's seven-page statement about his sister's romance with Lincoln is "Robert B. Rutledge Statement," October 1866, in the Herndon-Weik Collection, Library of Congress; see also Emanuel Hertz, ed., *The Hidden Lincoln: From the Letters and Papers of William H. Herndon* (New York: Viking Press, 1938), pp. 312–13; Robert Rutledge confirmed his account of the affair with his elderly mother. For a discussion of this see Simon, p. 21.

I used Winkler, p. xii, to describe the fights between Lincoln and his wife over his memories of Ann.

Herndon's claim that the affair with Ann is a "Rosetta Stone" to understanding Lincoln is discussed in Simon, p. 16; there was widespread skepticism after Herndon's initial speech about the romance with Ann. Among the newspapers opining on the matter were the *Chicago Tribune*, November 28, 1866, and the *New York Times*, March 9, 10, and 17, 1867. On the other hand, there are sources that support the love affair. Barton, p. 185, visited Ann Rutledge's sister, Sarah Rutledge Saunders, who was, at the time, ninety-three years old, but she recalled the love affair between Ann and Abe. The great Lincoln biographer Carl Sandburg also supported the existence of an affair on p. 141. Herndon's own books and papers on the topic are invaluable, as they contain letters from Ann's family and friends.

I used Angle, p. 4, and Winkler, p. 87, for details and quotes on the McNeil/McNamar story; descriptions and quotes on McNamar came from Barton, pp. 173–84, and Simon, pp. 22–24.

Mrs. Rutledge's quote about Lincoln being so well liked is found in Winkler, p. 62; a variety of sources were used for quotes and descriptions about Ann's appearance. See Barton, p. 179; Donald's *Lincoln*, p. 56; Herndon and Weik, pp. 106–7; Sandburg, p. 140; and Winkler, p. 43.

Sources used for the engagement of Lincoln and Ann and nature of their relationship include Barton, pp. 82–83; the letter "Robert B. Rutledge to William H. Herndon," November 18, 1866; and Ann's sisters' descriptions, which are discussed in Winkler, p. 48.

I used several sources for the death of Ann Rutledge and her illness, including Donald's *Lincoln*, p. 57; Herndon and Weik, p. 112; Reep, p. 76; and the letter

"A. M. Prewitt to Miss J. E. Hammand," November 7, 1921, which is housed in the Decatur Lincoln Memorial Collection. Descriptions and quotes about Ann's funeral and Lincoln's emotional reaction include the letter "Wilson G. Green to William H. Herndon," May 30, 1865; the letter "Elizabeth Abell to William H. Herndon," February 15, 1867; and the letter "Henry McHenry to William H. Herndon," January 8, 1866; see also Wilson and Davis, p. 21, pp. 155–56, and p. 557, for quotes; the conversations about Lincoln weeping and subsequently hardening his heart are in Winkler, pp. 83 and 85.

CHAPTER 10

Most material in this chapter comes from the following sources: Michael Burlingame, *At Lincoln's Side: John Hay's Civil War Correspondence and Selected Writings* (Carbondale: Southern Illinois University Press, 2006); Michael Burlingame, *Inside the White House in War Times: Memoirs and Reports of Lincoln's Secretary* (Bison Books, 2000); Michael Burlingame, *The Inner World of Abraham Lincoln* (Chicago: University of Illinois Press, 1994); David Herbert Donald, *Lincoln* (New York: Simon and Schuster, 1995); Mark E. Neely Jr., *The Abraham Lincoln Encyclopedia* (New York: McGraw-Hill, 1982); Stephen B. Oates, *With Malice toward None: The Life of Abraham Lincoln* (New York: Harper and Row, 1977); J. G. Randall, *Lincoln the President: Springfield to Gettysburg*, vol. 2 (New York: Dodd, Mead, 1945); Carl Sandburg, *Abraham Lincoln: The Prairie Years*, vol. 1 (New York: Harcourt Brace, 1926); and Benjamin P. Thomas, *Abraham Lincoln: A Biography* (New York: Alfred A. Knopf, 1952).

Information on Lincoln's romantic life comes from the following sources: William E. Barton, *The Women Lincoln Loved* (Indianapolis: Bobbs-Merrill, 1927); Douglas L. Wilson and Rodney O. Davis, eds., *Herndon's Informants: Letters, Interviews, and Statements about Abraham Lincoln* (Urbana: University of Illinois Press, 1997); and H. Donald Winkler, *Lincoln's Ladies: The Women in the Life of the Sixteenth President* (Nashville: Cumberland House, 2004).

The sources used for information on Mary Todd Lincoln were Jean Baker, *Mary Todd Lincoln: A Biography* (New York: Norton, 1989); and Ruth Painter Randall, *Mary Todd Lincoln: Biography of a Marriage* (Boston: Little, Brown, 1953).

The quote from Mary Todd's sister about Mr. Lincoln's awkward courtship is in Philip B. Kunhardt Jr., Philip B. Kunhardt III, and Peter W. Kunhardt, *Lincoln: An Illustrated Biography* (New York: Knopf, 1992).

Information on Ann Rutledge and her grave site is "New Monument over Grave of Ann Rutledge, Lincoln's Early Sweetheart," *Journal of the Illinois State Historical Society* 13 (January 1921): 567–68.

Quotes from Lincoln's friends (Speed and Browning) and Mary Todd's cousin that he married only out of a sense of honor are found in Winkler, p. 112; the quote from Mary Todd about loving Lincoln's mind is also in Winkler, p. 97. The relationship was described as "stormy" by Jean H. Baker, "Mary Todd Lincoln," in Lewis

L. Gould, ed., *The First Ladies: Their Lives and Their Legacy* (New York: Garland Publishing, 1996), p. 177.

Lincoln's quote about Mary gaining weight "in the west" and information on the couple's hesitancy about marriage comes from Wilson and Davis, p. 474. See also the letter "Joshua Speed to William H. Herndon," 1865/1866, which is quoted in Sandburg, p. 172, and the letter "James C. Conkling to Mercy Ann Levering," September 21, 1840, in Paul M. Angle, "Lincoln's First Love," *Lincoln Centennial Association Bulletin*, December 1927, pp. 1–8.

Lincoln's description of Matilda as "perfect" comes from Winkler, p. 100.

Speed's advice to Lincoln on breaking the engagement with Mary Todd is discussed in Winkler, p. 100, as is their frustration over Lincoln not ending the relationship. See also the letters "Joshua Speed to William H. Herndon," 1865/1866, in William H. Herndon and Jesse W. Weik, *Herndon's Life of Lincoln* (1889; reprint, New York: Da Capo Press, 1983), p. 169. Regarding the historical discrepancy about what happened to the Lincoln engagement on January 1, see the letter "Elizabeth Edwards to Jesse Weik," December 20, 1883; see also Wilson and Davis, p. 592, and Douglas L. Wilson, *Lincoln before Washington: New Perspectives on the War Years* (Urbana: University of Illinois Press, 1998), p. 121.

The matter of whether Matilda factored into the broken engagement is suggested in the letter "Mrs. Benjamin Edwards to Ida M. Tarbell," October 8, 1895, in the Ida M. Tarbell Papers in the library at Allegheny College. The Conkling quote about Lincoln's depression around the time of the breakup is in a letter written on January 24, 1841. See Kunhardt et al., p. 59; the quote from Mary's letter to her friend about not wanting to marry if she wasn't in love is also in Kunhardt et al., p. 58, and other quotes about Lincoln's state after breaking up with Mary are on p. 59. Lincoln's depression around the "fatal first" is discussed in the letter "Orville Browning to John G. Nicolay," June 17, 1875, from Springfield.

Matilda's materialistic quote about her marriage is in the letter "Elizabeth Todd Edwards to William H. Herndon," 1865/1866; see Wilson and Davis, p. 444.

Lincoln's letter about finding happiness is "Abraham Lincoln to Joshua Speed," March 27, 1842.

Winkler, on p. 101, discusses the Lincolns confronting one another about other romances. Lincoln's uncharacteristic behavior in politics after the breakup with Mary is discussed in Wilson, p. 110. Likewise, Lincoln's bravado in the near duel with swords is mentioned in the letter "Abraham Lincoln to Major J. M. Lucas," which is available in Michael Burlingame, *An Oral History: Abraham Lincoln: John G. Nicolay's Interviews and Essays* (Carbondale: Southern Illinois University Press, 1996), p. 185. Another source about the duel is Justin G. Turner and Linda Levitt Turner, *Mary Todd Lincoln: Her Life and Letters* (New York: Knopf, 1972), p. 296.

Late in life, Sarah Rickard reflected on her relationship with Lincoln, telling Barton details of it. See Barton, p. 259. See also the letter "Sarah Rickard Barret to William H. Herndon," August 12, 1888, and Wilson and Davis, p. 665.

The story of Lincoln and Mary being set up to travel together to a party is discussed in Winkler, p. 111.

Lincoln's description of the "animal spirits" surrounding Robert's birth is found in Winkler, p. 114. See also the letter "Mary Todd Lincoln to Josiah Holland," December 4, 1865, and the letter "Orville Browning to John G. Nicolay," June 17, 1875.

Details and quotes regarding the morning of the Lincoln wedding are found in Winkler, p. 113, and Wilson and Davis, p. 251; see also the letter "James H. Matheny to William H. Herndon," May 3, 1866. Details and quotes regarding Mary's morning of the wedding are in Kunhardt et al., p. 62. See also the letters "Elizabeth Todd Edwards to William H. Herndon," 1865/1866, which are discussed in Wilson and Davis, p. 444. The funny story about the Lincoln wedding ceremony is in Kunhardt et al., p. 64.

Winkler, on p. 118, describes Mrs. Lincoln firing the family maids. On p. 120, he also describes Lincoln trying to avoid his wife and sleeping on the couch.

Lincoln missed his family when he was alone during his term in Congress. This is discussed in Oates, 1977, p. 81.

Tad's nickname "the Tyrant in the White House" and his antics are described in David Herbert Donald, *Lincoln*, Simon & Schuster, 1996, p. 121. The story about Willie wanting a quarter from his father during a White House meeting is in Thomas, p. 232. The discussion of the many complaints regarding the boys' wild behavior is in the letter "William H. Herndon to Jesse Weik," Springfield, February 18, 1887; see the Herndon-Weik Manuscripts, U.S. Library of Congress.

Quotes and the discussion about Lincoln being a tender and indulgent father and his view on allowing the boys to be boys comes from Paul M. Angle, "Analysis of the Character of Abraham Lincoln," *Abraham Lincoln Quarterly* 1 (December 1941), and Paul M. Angle, *Herndon's Life of Lincoln: The History and Personal Recollections of Abraham Lincoln as Originally Written by William H. Herndon and Jesse W. Weik* (Cleveland: World Publishing, 1942). The examples of Lincoln playing with his children and other children come from John C. Waugh, *One Man Great Enough: Abraham Lincoln's Road to Civil War* (Houghton Mifflin, 1997), p. 159 and Oates, p. 64. Lincoln's "protective deafness" and wanting to ring the necks of the Lincoln boys are discussed in the letter "William H. Herndon to Jesse Weik," January 8, 1866, Herndon-Weik Manuscripts, U.S. Library of Congress. The story of Lincoln pulling his boys in a wagon comes from Ruth Painter Randall, "Mary Lincoln, Judgment Appealed," *Abraham Lincoln Journal* 5, no. 7 (September 1949): 385.

The discussion of little Eddy's brief life and his nickname is in Jerrold M. Packard, *The Lincolns in the White House: Four Years That Shattered a Family* (St. Martin's Griffin, 2006), p. 18. Packard also discusses Lincoln's plea to his wife to eat and live.

Mrs. Lincoln's cousin's description of Willie is in Elizabeth Todd Grimsley (Brown), *Six Months in the White House* (Springfield: Illinois State Historical Society, 1926), p. 48. Julia Taft's description is in Julia Taft Bayne, *Tad Lincoln's Father* (reprint, Bison Books, 2009), p. 8. Oates, on p. 97, describes Willie learning the names of the towns on their 1861 train trip and his popularity and playfulness in the White House.

Criticisms of Mrs. Lincoln's shopping and excesses are discussed in Robert P. Watson, *The Presidents' Wives: Reassessing the Office of First Lady* (Boulder, CO: Lynne Rienner Publishers, 1999), and Robert P. Watson, *Life in the White House: The Social*

History of the First Family and the President's House (Albany: State University of New York Press, 2004).

Lincoln's quotes when Willie died are in Doug Wead, *All the Presidents' Children: Triumph and Tragedy in the Lives of America's First Families* (Atria Books, 2004). See also Donald, 1996, p. 336. The quotes about Mary in mourning, wearing a shroud, and seeing spiritualists are found in Packard, p. 123. The discussion of Abe's depression and Mary's struggles after Willie's death are in Burlingame, 2006, p. 94; Donald, p. 96; Oates, p. 94; and Sandburg, pp. 1926–39.

The quote by Mary's cousin describing Tad is in Grimsley (Brown), pp. 48–49. Lincoln's quote about Tad's lack of an education is in Burlingame, 2006, pp. 111–12.

Lincoln's letter concerning Tad's pet goat is in Thomas, p. 483. The story about Jack the turkey is in Waugh, pp. 347–48. Information on Tad obtaining a pardon for a woman's husband is in Sandburg, vol. 3, p. 527.

Information on Robert at Harvard and the Lincolns arguing about him enlisting is found in Donald, 1996, p. 198. The Lincoln's quotes on the sensitive subject are found in Elizabeth Keckley, *Behind the Scenes in the Lincoln White House: Memoirs of an African-American Seamstress* (1948), pp. 121–22. Mary's half-sister's quote is in Sandburg, vol. 3, 1930, p. 416.

The quote on Robert being a mystery to his folks comes from Packard, 2005, p. 18. Lincoln's quote on Robert's intelligence is also in Donald, p. 109. Oates, pp. 96–97, observed that Lincoln's relationship with Robert mirrored his own strained relationship with his father. The quote about Robert's birth coming from "animal spirits" is found in Packard, p. 67. For information on Lincoln's anger with Robert over the lost inaugural speech, see Donald, p. 275. Lincoln's request to have Robert serve on Grant's staff is found in Burke Davis, *To Appomattox: Nine April Days, 1865*, Eastern Acorn Press, 1959, p. 381.

Mrs. Lincoln's cost overruns on White House furnishings are in the commissioner's letter to his sister-in-law; see the letter "B. B. French to Pamela French," December 24, 1861, French Manuscripts, U.S. Library of Congress. The quotes on the topic are also found in J. G. Randall, p. 394. Lincoln complaining about his wife's shopping is quoted in Hope Ridings Miller, *Scandals in the Highest Office* (New York: Random House, 1973), p. 94. John Jay's unflattering description of Mary as a "Hellcat" is in Tyler Dennett, ed., *Lincoln and the Civil War in the Diaries and Letters of John Hay* (New York, 1939), p. 41. Mary's quote about the cost of a woman's wardrobe is in Miller, p. 95. Information on Mary's mail being screened by staff is in William O. Stoddard, *Inside the White House in War Time* (New York, 1890), p. 62.

The source for Lincoln dreaming of his own assassination is Rudolph, 1960, pp. 177–78. Information on Lincoln and Robert getting along prior to the assassination is found in Keckley, p. 137.

Lincoln's last afternoon with his wife and their final discussions are found in the letter "Mary Lincoln to Francis B. Carpenter," November 15, 1865, and discussed in the book Carl Sandburg and Paul M. Angle, *Mary Lincoln: Wife and Widow* (Harcourt Brace, 1932), p. 242. The Kunhardt et al. book provides quotes on Mrs. Lincoln blaming others for her husband's death and a discussion of her remaining at the White House for several days after the funeral. See p. 394. Tad's reaction to the news of his father's death is in William A. DeGregoria, *The Complete Book of U.S. Presidents* (reprint, Fort Lee, NJ: Barricade Books, 2001), p. 227. Tad's quote about his father at the funeral is in Sandburg, vol. 4, p. 288, and Tad's quote about his father in heaven comes from Francis B. Carpenter, *Six Months at the White House with Abraham Lincoln* (1874; reprint, BiblioBazaar, 2009), p. 293.

Mary's eccentricities as a widow are discussed in Ruth Painter Randall, "Mary Lincoln: Judgment Appealed," *Abraham Lincoln Quarterly* 5 (September 1949): 389. Information of Mary's declining mental health and her son's loss are in Ward H. Lamon, *Recollections of Abraham Lincoln, 1847–1865*, edited by Dorothy Lamon Teillard (Chicago, 1895), p. 164. Mary's quote that only her "darling Taddie" kept her from suicide is in Kunhardt et al., p. 394, as is the description of Mary by her friend Moyes Miner.

Robert Lincoln's description of his mother's illness is in the letter "Robert Todd Lincoln to Mary Harlan," October 16, 1867. See also Katherine Helm, *The True Story of Mary, Wife of Lincoln* (New York, 1928), p. 267.

Quotes and details relating to Mrs. Lincoln's trial are in the letter "Mary Todd Lincoln to Swett," February 1876, David Davis Papers. See also William A. Evans, *Mrs. Abraham Lincoln: A Study of Her Personality and Her Influence on Lincoln* (New York: Alfred Knopf, 1932), and Rodney A. Ross, "Mary Todd Lincoln: Patient at Bellevue Place," *Illinois State Historical Society* 63, no. 1 (Spring 1970): 5–34. Comments from the juror who recalled the trial of Mrs. Lincoln is in the letter "Lyman J. Gage to Rev. William E. Barton," January 20, 1921, Papers of William E. Barton, Barton Collection of Lincolniana, University of Chicago. The source for Mary's comment that her son was a "wicked monster" is Baker, p. 208. Mary's quote on her released from Bellevue is Ross, p. 19. And the final quote from Mary is in the Kunhardt et al. book, p. 394.

CHAPTER 11

Most material in this chapter comes from the following books: Kenneth D. Ackerman, *Dark Horse: The Surprise Election and Political Murder of President James A. Garfield* (Carroll & Graff Publishers, 2003); Allan Peskin, *Garfield: A Biography* (Kent, OH: Kent State University Press, 1978); and Ira Rutkow, *James A. Garfield* (Times Books, 2006). I also read reviews and excerpts of the forthcoming book by Candice Millard, *Destiny of the Republic: A Tale of Madness, Medicine, and the Murder of a President* (Doubleday, 2011).

Many of the quotes about Lucretia Garfield or Garfield's family life are found in John Shaw, *Lucretia* (Hauppauge, NY: Nova History Books/Nova Publishers, 2004). Garfield's papers are also available and quotes are taken from them. See Harry James Brown and Frederick D. Williams, *The Diary of James A. Garfield* (East Lansing: Michigan State University Press, 1967–1981). Most of the material from Garfield's childhood and teenage years discussed in the beginning of the chapter is found in Allan Peskin's book *Garfield: A Biography*.

An interesting discussion of Garfield being filled with lust and guilt and possibly visiting brothels while working on the canal is found in Nigel Cawthorne, *Sex Lives of the Presidents: An Irreverent Expose of the Chief Executive from George Washington to the Present Day* (1996; reprint, New York: St. Martin's Press, 1998).

Quotes about Lucretia's temperament come from Lewis L. Gould, ed., *American First Ladies: Their Lives and Their Legacy* (New York: Garland Publishing, 1996); see the chapter by Allan Peskin and p. 231. Crete's preference for the wrong boys and her relationship with Albert Hall is discussed in Shaw, p. 7.

Cawthorne, p. 120, examines the possibility that Garfield had sex with his teenage girlfriend when they were left unattended at her parents' home.

Garfield's quote about a lack of delirium or passion in his relationship with Crete comes from Gould, p. 232. The quote from Crete that Garfield knew her only from her letters is from Shaw, p. 26. Shaw also discusses Crete's rigidity and coldness on the same page. Likewise, the passage from Garfield to Crete hoping his return will be met with passion is in Shaw, p. 26. On p. 27, Shaw discusses the couple's examination of the status of their relationship and description of it as lacking in passion but as a steady current.

Garfield's thoughtless letter to Crete singing Rebecca Selleck's praises is quoted from Shaw, p. 27. On the same page, Shaw quotes Garfield telling Crete that the discomfort in their relationship cannot occur again.

Crete's reply to Garfield that she is trying to forget the past is in Shaw, p. 30.

The quotes of Crete describing the end of their engagement as her being "unspeakably happy" and Garfield's change of heart as the "keenest dagger" are in Shaw, p. 30 and 31, respectively. Crete's quotes asking Garfield why he visited for only one day and Garfield's complaints of being restless and dissatisfied are in Shaw, p. 33.

Shaw also quotes Crete's long letter to Garfield prior to their wedding, encouraging him to share his concerns with her. See p. 34.

Crete's letters about her lack of passion in the bedroom, including such quotes as "withered leaves" and "honey cups," are from Shaw, pp. 36 and 37.

Crete's quote about their baby missing her father is in Shaw, p. 40. The observation that Garfield finally began to appreciate his wife's qualities during the war when he was ill is from Shaw, p. 39.

Crete's Civil War letter saying that she felt no love from her husband and her letter on learning he was not coming to visit her but rather Rebecca are quoted in Shaw, pp. 42 and 51, respectively. The quote from Garfield's mother about her son's infatuation with Miss Booth is found in Shaw, p. 45.

Garfield's poetically religious vow to his wife to end his affairs and reaffirm his commitment to her is in Shaw, p. 44. Her plea for him not to visit Rebecca in 1868 is in Shaw, p. 51.

Crete's concern about Garfield's election as president and a reporter's description of Crete are found in Laura C. Holloway, *The Ladies of the White House* (Philadelphia, 1881), p. 678. The rumor during the presidential campaign about the candidate visiting a brothel is in Cawthorne, p. 123.

Guiteau's quote about Mrs. Garfield looking sad is found in Shaw, p. 102. Garfield's last words and Crete's painful quote when her husband died are in Shaw, p. 106.

CHAPTER 12

Most material in this chapter comes from two excellent books on Grover Cleveland: Alyn Brodsky, *Grover Cleveland: A Study in Character* (New York: St. Martin's Press and Truman Talley Books, 2000), and the Pulitzer Prize winner Allan Nevins's *Grover Cleveland: A Study in Courage* (Dodd, Mead, 1938). There are also two other books that proved to be helpful in examining Cleveland's marriage and scandals: Henry Graff, *Grover Cleveland* (part of the American presidents series) (Times Books, 2002), and Charles Lachman, *A Secret Life: The Lies and Scandals of Grover Cleveland* (Skyhorse Publishers, 2011).

The quotes from the Buffalo newspaper about Cleveland's affair and Reverend Ball's commentary on it are found in Brodsky, p. 87; quotes from the committee of preachers who issued a report on Cleveland's affair are found in Michael Farquhar, *A Treasury of Great American Scandals* (Penguin, 2003), pp. 165–66; Cleveland's response to the vicious stories about him is found in the letter "Grover Cleveland to Daniel Lockwood," July 31, 1884; see Nevins, p. 165.

Another helpful source on the details of the coverage of the scandal during the 1884 election is Marvin and Dorothy Rosenbert, "The Dirtiest Election," *American Heritage*, August 1962.

The description of Maria Halpin and quotes about her come from Brodsky, p. 90.

The quote by James G. Blaine about Cleveland's affair appeared in an opinion editorial by Charles A. Dana in the *New York Sun*, July 1884.

The report from the committee Cleveland convened to study and refute the charges about the Maria Halpin affair are quoted in Nevins, pp. 164–66. Cleveland told his campaign to be sure to tell the truth when dealing with the scandalous attacks and, in general, all matters. The quotes about this come from the letter by Grover Cleveland's nephew "Cleveland Bacon to Allan Nevins," December 15, 1931, and are discussed in the Nevins book; the quotes and discussion about Cleveland gathering all the evidence of Blaine's affairs and then burning it is found in the article by Marvin and Dorothy Rosenberg in *American Heritage*; see also the book William Hudson, *Random Recollections of an Old Political Reporter* (New York: Cupples and Leon, 1911). Some quotes about this incident come from Farquhar, pp. 166–67.

The funny quote by Sen. George Vest about Cleveland's sexual affair is in Brodsky, p. 89, and Farquhar, p. 89; Mark Twain's amusing quote on the scandal is in Farquhar, p. 166.

A source used for the quotes and stories on the revelation of Blaine's scandals and the criticism of Cleveland is the Miller Center at the University of Virginia. See http://millercenter.org/academic/americanpresident/cleveland/essays/biography/3.

Frances Cleveland's letter about her nickname "Frank" is discussed in Farquhar, p. 161, and the Brodsky book.

Information and quotes on Cleveland's anger with the press coverage of his courtship of Frances (and incorrect assumption that he was courting her mother) come from Robert McNutt McElroy, *Grover Cleveland: The Man and the Statesman*, vol. 1 (New York: Harper, 1923), pp. 139–40. Cleveland's aide commenting on the male staffers' interest in Miss Folsom is in Farquhar, p. 162.

Cleveland's letter to his sister about the wedding is quoted in Brodsky, p. 163. His famous quote when he saw Frances after nine months apart is also in Brodsky, p. 172. For a good discussion of this topic, see Horace Samuel Merrill, *Bourbon Leader: Grover Cleveland and the Democratic Party* (Boston: Little, Brown, 1957), p. 89.

Quotes regarding Cleveland's concern over the publicity surrounding the wedding and Frances are in Brodsky, pp. 103 and 163. Cleveland's orders to his staff on the eve of his wedding are quoted in Brodsky, p. 173. Cleveland's complaints about the media coverage of his wedding are discussed in Brodsky, p. 174.

Frances Cleveland's role as a fashion icon and her impact on the bustle and other women's apparel is discussed in Paul Boller, *Presidential Anecdotes* (Oxford: Oxford University Press, 1981), p. 174. For details on Mrs. Cleveland's first ladyship, including her hosting and projects, see Robert P. Watson, *The Presidents' Wives: Reassessing the Office of First Lady* (Boulder, CO: Lynne Rienner Publishers, 2000), and Robert P. Watson, *First Ladies of the United States* (Boulder, CO: Lynne Rienner Publishers, 2001).

Mrs. Cleveland's letter about the rumors she was beaten by her husband is discussed and quoted in McElroy, vol. 1, p. 286.

Cleveland's speech at his wife's former hometown was covered by the *New York Times*, October 8, 1887.

The description of Cleveland as tired and beaten on leaving office is in Robert P. Watson and Richard Yon, *The American Presidents*, rev. 3rd ed. (Pasadena, CA: Salem Press, 2006), p. 350.

The story of Eisenhower not recognizing Frances in the White House is discussed in Margaret Truman, *Souvenier: Margaret Truman's Own Story* (New York: McGraw-Hill, 1956), p. 172.

Mrs. Cleveland's quote to her husband about how much she loves him is in Carl Sferrazza Anthony, *First Ladies: The Saga of the Presidents' Wives and Their Power, 1789–1961* (New York: Quill, 1990), p. 262. Brodsky claimed that the Cleveland marriage was one of the happiest in the White House, see p. 159. "Ike" Irwin Hoover, the former White House usher, declared Mrs. Cleveland to be one of the best first ladies in history. See Irwin H. Hoover, *Forty-Two Years in the White House* (Houghton Mifflin, 1934).

CHAPTER 13

For information on Hamilton's upbringing and relationships, see Ron Chernow, *Alexander Hamilton* (New York: Penguin, 2004), and Broadus Mitchell, *Alexander*

Hamilton: Youth to Maturity (New York: Macmillan, 1957). For information on the famous duel with Aaron Burr and Hamilton's character and vulnerabilities, see Thomas Fleming, *Duel: Alexander Hamilton, Aaron Burr, and the Future of America* (New York: Basic Books, 2000). Hamilton's papers and letters have been edited and published, and most quotes from him come from them. See Harold C. Syrett, ed., *The Papers of Alexander Hamilton*, 27 vols. (New York: Columbia University Press, 1961–1987), and John C. Hamilton, *Life of Alexander Hamilton*, 7 vols. (Boston: Houghton, 1841–1864).

General information on Hamilton's youth comes from Chernow and vol. 1 of *Papers*, pp. 2–3.

The quote on Hamilton's relationship with George Washington is found in Broadus Mitchell, *Alexander Hamilton*, p. x. Details on the Washington brothers' voyage to Barbados appear in John R. Alden, *George Washington* (Baton Rouge: Louisiana State University Press, 1984), p. 8. See also Willard Sterne Randall, *George Washington: A Life* (New York: Henry Holt & Co., 1997), and Willard Sterne Randall, *Alexander Hamilton: A Life* (New York: HarperCollins, 2003), pp. 57–61, for a discussion. Finally, for information on Washington's visit to the Caribbean, see also Douglas Southall Freeman, *George Washington: A Biography* (New York: Scribner's Sons, 1948–1957), vol. 1, p. 255.

The story of Jean Faucette and his progeny settling and thriving in Nevis, along with the legal separation by Mrs. Mary Uppington Fawcett, appears in Ron Chernow's *Alexander Hamilton*, p. 9.

The discussion of Rachel Fawcett Levien's upbringing in St. Croix and difficult marriage to Lavien as well as the quotes from Hamilton about his mother are found in *Papers*, vol. 25, p. 89, and Hamilton's letter to William Jackson, August 26, 1800. Hamilton's description of his mother's beauty and abilities is also discussed in Lawrence Henry Gibson, *The British Empire before the American Revolution: The Triumphant Empire*, 15 vols. (Alfred A. Knopf, 1967), vol. 2, p. 223.

Information on Hamilton's mother, Rachel, and her unhappy marriage and being pushed into marriage are discussed in Randall, *George Washington*, p. 13. Additional information and quotes on Hamilton's view of his mother's marriage to Levien is found in the letter "Alexander Hamilton to Elizabeth Schuyler Hamilton," 1781, *Papers*, vol. 3, p. 235, as well as Chernow, *Alexander Hamilton*, p. 11, and Holger U. Ramsing, *Alexander Hamilton's Birth and Parenting* (Copenhagen: unpublished, 1939), p. 4; the Ramsing quotes are also discussed in Chernow, p. 11. Quotes about the divorce and court proceedings against Rachel Fawcett Levien appear in Randall, *George Washington*, pp. 9 and 18, as well as in Mitchell, p. 6. Hamilton's view of his mother's separation and divorce and the family struggles at the time is found in the letter "Alexander Hamilton to James Hamilton," June 22, 1785, New York Public Library manuscripts; Hamilton's letter to his brother, James, also discusses their father.

Another good source used for information about Hamilton's youth in the Caribbean is Hamilton's son. Information on Hamilton's youth comes from John Church Hamilton, *Life of Alexander Hamilton*, 2 vols. (New York, 1834). Hamilton's admission that his dubious birth and upbringing were both embarrassing and the source of scandal, comes from Chernow, p. 8.

The description of Hamilton as a "bastard" is by John Adams and is quoted in Alden, p. 241; Hamilton's status as an orphan on Nevis is discussed in the letter "Alexander Hamilton to William Hamilton," May 2, 1797, *Papers*, vol. 21, p. 77. Hamilton's quote about the fact that, unlike other leading public figures during the revolutionary figure, he actually was descended from nobility is found in his letter to William Jackson in August 1800.

The unpleasant description of Nevis in its early days and the quote from the frustrated Anglican preacher is found in Vincent K. Hubbard, *Swords, Ships, and Sugar: History of Nevis to 1900* (Corvallis, OR: Premiere Editions, 1998), p. 40.

The quote about Hamilton's positive relationship with Jews comes from Hamilton, *Life of Alexander Hamilton*, vol. 7, pp. 710–11. The description of Hamilton's "reverence" for Jews is found in Chernow, p. 18.

The description of Hamilton's mother tutoring him and the quote about her intellect is found in Hamilton, *Life of Alexander Hamilton*, vol. 1, p. 42.

Information and quotes on the divorce trial of Hamilton's mother are found in the April 1952 edition of the *William & Mary Quarterly*; Chernow, p. 20; and Ramsing, *Alexander Hamilton's Birth and Parentage*, p. 8.

Information on Hamilton as the child prodigy and his move to America comes from Randall, *Alexander Hamilton*, and Alden.

Hamilton's letter to his friend Laurens discussing women is quoted in Andrew Burstein, *The Inner Jefferson: Portrait of a Grieving Optimist* (Charlottesville: University of Virginia Press, 1995), and the letter "Alexander Hamilton to John Laurens," April 1779, is found in *Papers*, vol. 2, pp. 34–38.

Hamilton's letter to Lady Kitty is "Alexander Hamilton to Katherine Livingstone," April 11, 1777, *Papers*, vol. 1, pp. 225–27. Other personal observations of love and the opposite sex are found in *Papers*, vol. 2, pp. 261–62. The poem about Hamilton's love affair is quoted in Flexner, *Young Hamilton* (New York: Fordham University Press, 1997), p. 271.

Hamilton's courtship of Betsy Schuyler and the descriptions of her are found in Randall, *Alexander Hamilton*, pp. 188–90.

Hamilton's expressions of jealousy regarding General André and his courtship of Betsy are found in several letters, including "Alexander Hamilton to Elizabeth Schuyler," October 5, 1780, *Papers*, vol. 2, pp. 455–56, and "Alexander Hamilton to Elizabeth Schuyler," October 13, 1780, *Papers*, vol. 2, pp. 473–75.

Hamilton's letter on his happiness after marrying is "Alexander Hamilton to Margarita Schuyler," January 21, 1781, *Papers*, vol. 2, pp. 539–40.

The description of Hamilton's controversial and curious letter to John Laurens about his friend's imprisonment and his own engagement with Betsy Schuyler is discussed in Randall, *Alexander Hamilton*, p. 194. The actual letter about the engagement is "Alexander Hamilton to John Laurens," August 1780, *Papers*, vol. 2, pp. 397–98.

Information on the affair between Hamilton and Angelica Schuyler Church comes from Flexner, *Young Hamilton*. The letter "Angelica Schuyler Church to Elizabeth Schuyler" is quoted on p. 329 in Flexner. Angelica's quotes are found in the letter

"Angelica Schuyler Church to Elizabeth Schuyler Hamilton," 1785, *Papers*, vol. 1, pp. 530–34.

Betsy's inconsolable depression is discussed in Randall, *Alexander Hamilton*, p. 383. Hamilton's letter about being apart from Angelica is "Alexander Hamilton to Angelica Schuyler Church," November 8, 1789, and is in the Angelica Schuyler Church Papers, manuscript collection of the University of Virginia. The letter where Hamilton hints at their sexual relationship is quoted in Robert Hendrickson, *Hamilton* (New York, 1976), vol. 1.

Information on the animosity between Hamilton and Burr and details of the duel come from Fleming. Quotes and details of the duel also appear in Randall, *Alexander Hamilton*, pp. 2–4.

Dr. Hosack's recollection of the details of Hamilton's final hours and final words after the duel appear in the letter "David Hosack to William Colemen," August 17, 1804, *Papers*, vol. 26, pp. 344–47. See also Harold Coffin Syrett et al., *Interview in Weehawken* (Wesleyan University Press, 1960).

CHAPTER 14

The John Adams quote on mistresses appears in Robert Williams, *Political Scandals in the USA* (London: Fitzroy Dearborn, 1998), p. 11.

The quote by Lyndon Johnson is from George Reedy, as quoted in Ben Bradley, *A Good Life: Newspapering and Other Adventures* (New York: Simon & Schuster, 1995), p. 483.

The article in *Newsweek* comparing Democratic and Republican scandals was published on June 25, 2009, at "Sex Scandals through the Years" at http://www.newsweek.com/blogs/the-gaggle/2009/06/25/sex-scandals-through-the-years-both-parties-even.html.

Joseph Ellis's opposition to the impeachment of Bill Clinton is discussed in the Warbird Forum at http://www.warbirdforum.com/ellis.htm.

Selected Bibliography

BOOKS

Abbot, William, and Dorothy Twohig, eds. *The Papers of George Washington*. Charlottesville: University of Virginia Press, 1979.

Ackerman, Kenneth D. *Dark Horse: The Surprise Election and Political Murder of President James A. Garfield*. New York: Carroll & Graf, 2003.

Adams, H. B. *The Life and Writings of Jared Sparks*. Vol. 2. Cambridge, MA: Houghton Mifflin, 1893.

Alden, John R. *George Washington*. Baton Rouge: Louisiana State University Press, 1984.

Angle, Paul M. *Herndon's Life of Lincoln: The History and Personal Recollections of Abraham Lincoln as Originally Written by William H. Herndon and Jesse W. Weik*. Cleveland: World Publishing, 1942.

Anthony, Carl Sferazza. *First Ladies: The Saga of the Presidents' Wives and Their Power, 1789–1961*. New York: William Morrow, 1990.

Baker, Jean H. *James Buchanan*. New York: Times Books, 2004.

Baron, Robert C., ed. *Jefferson's Garden and Farm Books*. Golden, CO: Fulcrum, 1987.

Barton, William E. *The Women Lincoln Loved*. Indianapolis: Bobbs-Merrill, 1927.

Bassett, John Spencer. *Correspondence of Andrew Jackson*. Washington, DC: Carnegie Institution of Washington, 1926–1935.

Baumgarner, John R. *The Health of Presidents*. Jefferson, NC: McFarland, 2004.

Bayne, Julia Taft. *Tad Lincoln's Father*. Reprint. Lincoln, NE: Bison Books, 2001.

Boller, Paul F., Jr. *Not So! Popular Myths about America from Columbus to Clinton*. New York: Oxford University Press, 1995.

———. *Presidential Anecdotes*. Oxford: Oxford University Press, 1981.

Bowers, Claude G. *The Young Jefferson, 1743–1789*. Boston: Houghton Mifflin, 1945.

Boyd, Julian P., ed. *The Papers of Thomas Jefferson*. Princeton, NJ: Princeton University Press, 1952.

Bradley, Ben. *A Good Life: Newspapering and Other Adventures*. New York: Simon & Schuster, 1995.

Brodie, Fawn M. *Thomas Jefferson: An Intimate History*. New York: Norton, 2010.

Brodsky, Alyn. *Grover Cleveland: A Study in Character*. New York: St. Martin's Press and Truman Talley Books, 2000.

Brookhiser, Richard. *Rediscovering George Washington: Founding Father.* New York: Free Press, 1996.

Brown, Harry James, and Frederick D. Williams. *The Diary of James A. Garfield.* East Lansing: Michigan State University Press, 1967–1981.

Burlingame, Michael. *The Inner World of Abraham Lincoln.* Chicago: University of Illinois Press, 1994.

———. *Inside the White House in War Times: Memoirs and Reports of Lincoln's Secretary.* Lincoln, NE: Bison Books, 2000.

———. *At Lincoln's Side: John Hay's Civil War Correspondence and Selected Writings.* Carbondale: Southern Illinois University Press, 2006.

———. *An Oral History: Abraham Lincoln: John G. Nicolay's Interviews and Essays.* Carbondale: Southern Illinois University Press, 1996.

Burstein, Andrew. *The Inner Jefferson: Portrait of a Grieving Optimist.* Charlottesville: University of Virginia Press, 1995.

———, ed. *Letters from the Head and Heart: Writings of Thomas Jefferson.* Chapel Hill: University of North Carolina Press, 2002.

Carpenter, Francis B. *Six Months at the White House with Abraham Lincoln.* Reprint. Charleston, SC: BiblioBazaar, 2009.

Carruthers, Olive, and R. Gerald McMurtry. *Lincoln's Other Mary.* Chicago: Ziff-Davis Publishing, 1946.

Carter, Bill, with Ken Estes. *Billy: Billy Carter's Reflections on His Struggle with Fame, Alcoholism and Cancer.* Newport, RI: Edgehill Publishers, 1990.

Carter, William. *A Journey through the Shadows.* Atlanta: Longstreet Press, 1999.

Cary, Wilson Miles. *Sally Cary: A Long Hidden Romance of Washington's Life.* New York: De Vine Press, 1916.

Cawthorne, Nigel. *Sex Lives of the Presidents: An Irreverent Expose of the Chief Executive from George Washington to the Present Day.* New York: St. Martin's Press, 1998.

Chernow, Ron. *Alexander Hamilton.* New York: Penguin, 2004.

Chitwood, Oliver Perry. *John Tyler: Champion of the Old South.* New York: Russell and Russell, 1964; reprint, Newton, CT: American Political Biography Press, 1990.

Clinton, Roger. *Growing Up Clinton: The Lives, Times and Tragedies of America's Presidential Family.* Artlinton, TX: Summit Publishing, 1997.

Coleman, Elizabeth Tyler. *Priscilla Cooper Tyler and the American Scene, 1816–1889.* Tuscaloosa: University of Alabama Press, 1955.

Coolidge, Ellen Randolph. *Letter Book.* Vol. 4. Unpublished (available at Monticello).

Coulling, Mary P. *George Washington and the Custis and Lee Families.* Lexington, VA: Washington and Lee University, 1997.

Crapol, Edward P. *John Tyler: The Accidental President.* Chapel Hill: University of North Carolina Press, 2006.

Curtis, George Ticknor. *Life of James Buchanan.* 2 vols. Harper & Bros., 1883.

Custis, George Washington Parke. *Recollections and Private Memoirs of Washington.* New York: Derby and Jackson, 1860.

Dabney, Virginius. *The Jefferson Scandals: A Rebuttal.* New York: Dodd, Mead, 1981.

DeGregoria, William A. *The Complete Book of U.S. Presidents.* Reprint. Fort Lee, NJ: Barricade Books, 2001.

Dennett, Tyler, ed. *Lincoln and the Civil War in the Diaries and Letters of John Hay.* New York: Dodd, Mead, 1939.

Donald, David Herbert. *Lincoln.* New York: Simon and Schuster, 1995.

———. *Lincoln Reconsidered: Essays on the Civil War Era.* New York: Alfred A. Knopf, 1956.

———. *Lincoln's Herndon.* New York: A. A. Knopf, 1948.

dos Passos, John. *The Head and Heart of Thomas Jefferson.* New York: Doubleday, 1954.

Driver, Carl S. *John Sevier: Pioneer of the Old Southwest.* Chapel Hill: University of North Carolina Press, 1932.

Dudley, William, ed. *Political Scandals: Opposing Viewpoints.* San Diego, CA: Greenhaven Press, 2001.

Ellis, Joseph J. *American Sphinx: The Character of Thomas Jefferson.* New York: Alfred A. Knopf, 1997.

———. *His Excellency: George Washington.* New York: Vintage, 2005.

Evans, William A. *Mrs. Abraham Lincoln: A Study of Her Personality and Her Influence on Lincoln.* New York: Alfred Knopf, 1932.

Farquhar, Michael. *A Treasury of Great American Scandals.* New York: Penguin, 2003.

Feinberg, Barbara Silberdick. *American Political Scandals: Past and Present.* New York: Franklin Watts, 1992.

Ferrell, Robert H., ed. *Dear Bess: The Letters from Harry to Bess Truman, 1910–1959.* Columbia: University of Missouri Press, 1998.

Fields, Joseph, ed. *Worthy Partner: The Papers of Martha Washington.* Westport, CT: Greenwood Press, 1994.

Fishman, Ethan M., William D. Pederson, and Mark J. Rozell, eds. *George Washington: Foundation of Presidential Leadership and Character.* New York: Praeger Publishers, 2001.

Fleming, Thomas. *Duel: Alexander Hamilton, Aaron Burr, and the Future of America.* New York: Basic Books, 2000.

Flexner, James Thomas. *Washington: The Indispensable Man.* Boston: Back Bay Books, 1994.

Ford, Paul Leicester. *The True Washington.* 10th ed. Indy Publishing, 2004.

Ford, Worthington Chauncey, ed. *Writings of Washington.* Vols. 1–6. Whitefish, MT: Kessinger Publishing, 2007, reprint series; Charleston, SC: Nabu Press, 2010, reproduction.

Freeman, Douglas Southall. *George Washington: A Biography.* New York: Scribner's Sons, 1948–1957.

Fremont, Jessie Benton. *Souveniers of My Time.* 1887; reprint, General Books, 2010.

Gardiner, Lyon, ed. *The Letters and Times of the Tylers.* 3 vols. 1884–1896; reprint, New York: Da Capo Press, 1978.

Gibson, Lawrence Henry. *The British Empire before the American Revolution: The Triumphant Empire.* 15 vols. New York: Alfred A. Knopf, 1967.

Gordon-Reed, Annette. *Thomas Jefferson and Sally Hemings: An American Controversy.* Charlottesville: University of Virginia Press, 1997.

Gould, Lewis L., ed. *American First Ladies: Their Lives and Their Legacy.* New York: Garland, 1996.

Graff, Henry. *Grover Cleveland.* New York: Times Books, 2002.

Grimsley (Brown), Elizabeth Todd. *Six Months in the White House.* Springfield: Illinois State Historical Society, 1926.

Hall, Gordon Langley. *Mr. Jefferson's Ladies.* Boston: Beacon Press, 1966.

Halliday, E. M. *Understanding Thomas Jefferson.* New York: HarperCollins, 2001.

Hamilton, John C. *Life of Alexander Hamilton.* 7 vols. Boston: Houghton, 1841–1864.

Haynes, Kevin J. *The Road to Monticello: The Life and Mind of Thomas Jefferson.* Oxford: Oxford University Press, 2008.

Helm, Katherine. *The True Story of Mary, Wife of Lincoln.* New York: Harper, 1928.

Hendrickson, Robert. *Hamilton.* New York: Mason/Carter, 1976.

Herndon, William H. *Lincoln and Ann Rutledge and the Pioneers of New Salem.* Reprint. Herrin, IL: Trovillion Private Press, 1945.

Herndon, William H., and Jesse W. Weik. *Herndon's Life of Lincoln.* 1889; reprint, New York: Da Capo Press, 1983.

Hertz, Emanuel, ed. *The Hidden Lincoln: From the Letters and Papers of William H. Herndon.* New York: Viking Press, 1938.

Holloway, Laura C. *The Ladies of the White House.* Philadelphia, 1881.

Holman, Hamilton. *Zachary Taylor.* 2 vols. Indianapolis: Bobbs-Merrill, 1966.

Hoover, Irwin H. *Forty-Two Years in the White House.* Boston: Houghton Mifflin, 1934.

Hubbard, Vincent K. Hubbard. *Swords, Ships, and Sugar: History of Nevis to 1900.* Corvallis, OR: Premiere Editions, 1998.

Hudson, William. *Random Recollections of an Old Political Reporter.* New York: Cupples and Leon, 1911.

Hughes, Robert. *Washington.* Vol. 1. New York, 1926–1930.

Jackson, Andrew. *The Papers of Andrew Jackson.* 8 vols. Part of the Andrew Jackson Papers Project. Knoxville: University of Tennessee Press, c1980.

James, Marquis. *The Life of Andrew Jackson.* Indianapolis: Bobbs-Merrill, 1938.

Jefferson, Thomas. *Notes on the State of Virginia.* London, 1787.

Kaminski, John P., ed. *Jefferson in Love: The Love Letters between Thomas Jefferson and Maria Cosway.* Madison, WI: Madison House Publishers, 1999.

Kaplan, Albert. *Abraham Lincoln: The Physical Man,* http://www.lincolnportrait.com.

Klein, Philip S. *A History of Pennsylvania.* University Park: Pennsylvania State University Press, 1976.

———. *President James Buchanan: A Biography.* American Political Biography Press, 1995.

Kunhardt, Philip B., Jr., Philip B. Kunhardt III, and Peter W. Kunhardt. *Lincoln: An Illustrated Biography.* New York: Knopf, 1992.

Lachman, Charles. *A Secret Life: The Lies and Scandals of Grover Cleveland.* New York: Skyhorse Publishers, 2011.

Lamon, Ward H. *Recollections of Abraham Lincoln, 1847–1865.* Edited by Dorothy Lamon Teillard. Chicago, 1895.

Langston, Thomas S., and Michael G. Sherman. *George Washington*. Washington, DC: CQ Press, 2003.

Lawford, Patricia S., and Ted Schwarz. *The Peter Lawford Story: Life with the Kennedys, Monroe and the Rat Pack*. New York: Carroll & Graf Publishers, 1988.

Lear, Tobias. *Letters and Recollections of George Washington*. New York: Doubleday, Doran & Co., 1932.

Lewis, Ellen, and Peter S. Onuf, eds. *Sally Hemings and Thomas Jefferson: History, Memory, and Civic Culture*. Charlottesville: University of Virginia Press, 1999.

Lipscomb, Andrew, and Albert Ellery Bergh, eds. *The Writings of Thomas Jefferson*. Vol. 14. Washington, DC: The Thomas Jefferson Memorial Association, 1903 and 1904.

Loewen, James W. *Lies across America: What Our Historic Sites Get Wrong*. New York: New Press, 1999.

Long, Kim, ed. *The Almanac of Political Corruption, Scandals and Dirty Politics*. Reprint. New York: Delta, 2008.

Lossing, John Benson. *Mary and Martha, the Mother and Wife of Washington*. 1863; reprint, New York: Harper & Bros., 1886.

Malone, Dumas. *Jefferson and His Time*. 6 vols. Boston: Little, Brown, 1948–1981.

Marion, Nancy E. *The Politics of Disgrace: The Role of Political Scandal in American Politics* Durham, NC: Carolina Academic Press, 2010.

May, Gary. *John Tyler*. Reprint. New York: Times Books, 2008.

McCartney, Laton. *The Teapot Dome Scandal: How Big Oil Bought the Harding White House and Tried to Steal the Country*. New York: Random House, 2009.

McCullough, David. *Truman*. New York: Simon & Schuster, 1992.

McElroy, Robert McNutt. *Grover Cleveland: The Man and the Statesman*. Vol. 1. New York: Harper, 1923.

Meacham, Jon. *American Lion: Andrew Jackson in the White House*. New York: Random House, 2009.

Merrill, Horace Samuel. *Bourbon Leader: Grover Cleveland and the Democratic Party*. Boston: Little, Brown, 1957.

Millard, Candice. *Destiny of the Republic: A Tale of Madness, Medicine, and the Murder of a President*. New York: Doubleday, 2011.

Miller, Hope Ridings Miller. *Scandals in the Highest Office*. New York: Random House, 1973.

Mitchell, Broadus. *Alexander Hamilton: Youth to Maturity*. New York: Macmillan, 1957.

Moore, John Bassett, ed. *Works of James Buchanan: Comprising His Speeches, State Papers, and Private Correspondence*. 12 vols. Philadelphia: Lippincott, 1908–1911; reprint, New York: Antiquarian Press, 1960.

Neely, Mark E., Jr. *The Abraham Lincoln Encyclopedia*. New York: McGraw-Hill, 1982.

Nevins, Allan. *Grover Cleveland: A Study in Courage*. Dodd, Mead, 1938.

Oates, Stephen B. *With Malice toward None: The Life of Abraham Lincoln*. New York: Harper and Row, 1977.

Packard, Jerrold M. *The Lincolns in the White House: Four Years That Shattered a Family*. St. Martin's Griffin, 2006.

Parton, James. *Life of Andrew Jackson*. 3 Vols. New York: Mason Bros., 1860–1866.

Peter, Armistead. *Tudor Place, Georgetown*. 3rd ed. Privately printed, 1969.

Peskin, Allan. *Garfield: A Biography*. Kent, OH: Kent State University Press, 1978.

Ramsing, Holger U. *Alexander Hamilton's Birth and Parenting*. Copenhagen: N.p., 1939.

Randall, J. G. *Lincoln the President: Springfield to Gettysburg*. Vol. 2. New York: Dodd, Mead, 1945.

Randall, Ruth Painter. *Mary Todd Lincoln: Biography of a Marriage*. Boston: Little, Brown, 1953.

Randall, Willard Sterne. *Alexander Hamilton: A Life*. New York: HarperCollins, 2003.

———. *George Washington: A Life*. New York: Henry Holt & Co., 1997.

———. *Thomas Jefferson: A Life*. New York: Harper Perennial, 1994.

Randolph, Sarah N. *The Domestic Life of Thomas Jefferson*. 1871; reprint, Charlottesville: University of Virginia Press, 1978.

Reep, Thomas. *Lincoln at New Salem*. Petersburg, IL: New Salem Lincoln League, 1918.

Rees, James Rees, and Stephen Spignes. *George Washington's Leadership Lessons: What the Father of Our Country Can Teach Us about Effective Leadership*. New York: Wiley, 2007.

Remini, Robert Vinent. *Andrew Jackson: The Course of American Empire, 1767–1721*. Vol. 1. Baltimore: Johns Hopkins University Press, 1998.

———. *Andrew Jackson: The Course of American Freedom, 1822–1832*. Vol. 2. Baltimore: Johns Hopkins University Press, 1998.

———. *Andrew Jackson: The Course of American Democracy, 1833–1845*. Vol. 3. Baltimore: Johns Hopkins University Press, 1998.

———. *The Life of Andrew Jackson*. New York: Harper & Row, 1988.

Riddle, William. *Story of Lancaster, Pennsylvania: Old and New*. Lancaster, 1917.

Rippy, J. Fred. *Joel R. Poinsett*. Durham, NC: Duke University Press, 1935.

Roberts, Russell. *Presidents and Scandals*. San Diego: Lucent Books, 2001.

Ross, Shelley. *Fall from Grace*. New York: Ballantine Books, 1988.

Rutkow, Ira. *James A. Garfield*. New York: Times Books, 2006.

Sandburg, Carl. *Abraham Lincoln: The Prairie Years*. Vol. 1. New York: Harcourt Brace, 1926.

Sandburg, Carl, and Paul M. Angle. *Mary Lincoln: Wife and Widow*. New York: Harcourt Brace, 1932.

Seager, Robert, II. *And Tyler Too: A Biography of John and Julia Gardiner Tyler*. Reprint. Norwalk, CT: Easton Press, 1988.

Shade, William G., and Ballard C. Campbell. *American Presidential Campaigns and Elections*. Vol. 1. Armonk, NY: Sharpe Reference, 2003.

Shaw, John. *Lucretia*. Hauppauge, NY: Nova History Books/Nova Publishers, 2004.

Slansky, Paul. *The Little Quiz Book of Big Political Sex Scandals*. New York: Simon & Schuster, 2009.

Smith, Richard Norton. *Patriarch: George Washington and the New American Nation.* Boston: Houghton Mifflin, 1993.

Sotos, John G. *The Physical Lincoln: Finding the Genetic Cause of Abraham Lincoln's Height, Homeliness, Pseudo-Depression, and Imminent Cancer Death.* Mount Vernon, VA: Mount Vernon Books, 2008.

———. *The Physical Lincoln Sourcebook.* Mount Vernon, VA: Mount Vernon Books, 2008.

Sparks, Jared, ed. *The Writings of George Washington: Being His Correspondence, Addresses, Messages, and Other Papers, Official and Private.* 8 vols. Charleston, SC: Nabu Press, 2008; reproduced from 1847, 1923, and other reprintings.

Sterling, James. *The Washington Community.* New York: Columbia University Press, 1966.

Stoddard, William O. *Inside the White House in War Time.* New York, 1890.

Syrett, Harold C., ed. *The Papers of Alexander Hamilton.* 27 vols. New York: Columbia University Press, 1961–1987.

Syrett, Harold Coffin, et al. *Interview in Weehawken.* Middletown, CT: Wesleyan University Press, 1960.

Thane, Elswythe. *Washington's Lady.* New York: Dodd, Mead, 1954.

Thomas, Benjamin P. *Abraham Lincoln: A Biography.* New York: Alfred A. Knopf, 1952.

Truman, Margaret. *Souvenier: Margaret Truman's Own Story.* New York: McGraw-Hill, 1956.

Turner, Justin G., and Linda Levitt Turner. *Mary Todd Lincoln: Her Life and Letters.* New York: Knopf, 1972.

Twohig, Dorothy, ed. *George Washington's Diaries: An Abridgement.* 6 vols. Charlottesville: University of Virginia Press, 1999.

Watson, Robert P. *First Ladies of the United States.* Boulder, CO: Lynne Rienner, 2001.

———. *Life in the White House: The Social History of the First Family and the President's House.* Albany: State University of New York Press, 2004.

———. *The Presidents' Wives: Reassessing the Office of First Lady.* Boulder, CO: Lynne Rienner, 1999.

Watson, Robert P., and Richard Yon, eds. *American Presidents.* 3rd ed. Pasadena, CA: Salem Press, 2006.

Waugh, John C. *One Man Great Enough: Abraham Lincoln's Road to Civil War.* Boston: Houghton Mifflin, 1997.

Wead, Doug. *All the Presidents' Children: Triumph and Tragedy in the Lives of America's First Families.* New York: Atria Books, 2004.

Wilentz, Sean. *Andrew Jackson.* New York: Henry Holt, 2005.

Willets, Gilson. *Inside History of the White House.* New York: Christian Herald, 1908.

Williams, Robert. *Political Scandals in the USA.* London: Fitzroy Dearborn, 1998.

Wilson, Douglas L. *Lincoln before Washington: New Perspectives on the War Years.* Urbana: University of Illinois Press, 1998.

Wilson, Douglas L., and Rodney O. Davis, eds. *Herndon's Informants: Letters, Interviews, and Statements about Abraham Lincoln.* Urbana: University of Illinois Press, 1997.

Winkler, H. Donald. *Lincoln's Ladies: The Women in the Life of the Sixteenth President.* Nashville: Cumberland House, 2004.

Woodson, Byron W., Sr. *A President in the Family: Thomas Jefferson, Sally Hemings, and Thomas Woodson.* Westport, CT: Praeger, 2001.

Zall, Paul M. *Jefferson on Jefferson.* Lexington: University Press of Kentucky, 2002.

ARTICLES AND CHAPTERS

Angle, Paul M. "Analysis of the Character of Abraham Lincoln." *Abraham Lincoln Quarterly* 1 (December 1941).

———. "Lincoln's First Love." *Lincoln Centennial Association Bulletin*, December 1927, 1–8.

Ashley, Jeffrey. "The Social and Political Influence of Betty Ford: Betty Bloomer Blossoms." *White House Studies* 1, no. 1 (2000): 101–8.

Brady, Patricia. "Martha Washington." In *American First Ladies: Their Lives and Their Legacy*, edited by Lewis L. Gould. New York: Garland, 1996, 2–15.

Callender, James T. "The President, Again." *Richmond Recorder*, September 1, 1802.

Dionne, E. J. "The Elusive Frontrunner: Gary Hart." *Time*, May 18, 1987.

Foster, E. A., et al. "Jefferson Fathered Slave's Last Child." *Nature* 196 (November 1998): 27–28.

Klein, Philip Shriver. "James Buchanan and Ann Coleman." *Pennsylvania History* 21 (January 1954): 1–20.

"The Last Word on First Ladies." *U.S. News & World Report*, March 30, 1992.

Monaghan, Jay. "New Light on the Lincoln-Rutledge Romance." *The Abraham Lincoln Quarterly* 3 (September 1944): 138–45.

Morgan, Philip D. "Interracial Sex in the Chesapeake and the British Atlantic World, c. 1700–1820." In *Sally Hemings and Thomas Jefferson: History, Memory, and Civic Culture*, edited by Jan Ellis Lewis and Peter S. Onuf. Charlottesville: University of Virginia Press, 1999, 52–86.

"New Monument over Grave of Ann Rutledge, Lincoln's Early Sweetheart." *Journal of the Illinois State Historical Society* 13 (January 1921): 567–68.

Randall, Ruth Painter. "Mary Lincoln, Judgment Appealed." *Abraham Lincoln Journal* 5, no. 7 (September 1949): 385.

Rosenbert, Marvin, and Dorothy Rosenbert. "The Dirtiest Election." *American Heritage*, August 1962.

Ross, Rodney A. "Mary Todd Lincoln: Patient at Bellevue Place." *Illinois State Historical Society* 63, no. 1 (Spring 1970): 5–34.

"Sex Scandals through the Years." *Newsweek*, June 25, 2009.

Simon, John Y. "Abraham Lincoln and Ann Rutledge." *Journal of the Abraham Lincoln Association* 11 (1990): 13–33.

Stevenson, Nathaniel Wright. "The Romantics and George Washington." *American Historical Review* 39, no. 2 (January 1934): 274–83.

Watson, Robert P. "Lincoln's Boys: The Legacy of an American Father and an American Family." *Americana* 6, no. 1 (2010).

———. "Martha Washington." In *American First Ladies*, edited by Robert P. Watson. Pasadena, CA: Salem Press, 2001, 9–18.

———. "The Real Mrs. Lincoln? The Nature and Extent of Scholarship on Mary Todd." *Lincoln Herald* 110, no. 1 (Spring 2008): 658–60.

———. "Remembering Martha." *Magazine of History* 14, no. 2 (2000): 54–57.

———. "Toward the Study of the First Lady: The State of Scholarship." *Presidential Studies Quarterly* 33, no. 2 (June 2003): 423–41.

Wilson, Douglas. "Abraham Lincoln, Ann Rutledge, and the Evidence of Herndon's Informants." *Civil War History*, December 1990.

Index

About the Author

Robert P. Watson, PhD, has published three dozen books and roughly 150 scholarly articles, book chapters, and essays on topics in American politics and history. He has been interviewed by hundreds of news outlets in the United States and internationally; writes a Sunday column for the *Sun-Sentinel* newspaper; serves as the political analyst for WPTV 5 (NBC) in West Palm Beach, Florida; and blogs for media outlets. Watson has also served on the boards of many scholarly journals, academic associations, community organizations, and presidential foundations; coconvened seven national conferences on the American presidency; and received numerous awards for his service to the community and teaching excellence including Professor of the Year at both Florida Atlantic University and Lynn University. Robert resides in Boca Raton, Florida, with his wife Claudia and children Alessandro and Isabella, where he is professor and director of American studies at Lynn University.